Seeking solitude on mountain peaks in Idaho, circa late 1980s.
Photo courtesy of Stanisław Skrowaczewski.

Seeking the Infinite

THE MUSICAL LIFE OF STANISŁAW SKROWACZEWSKI

FREDERICK E. HARRIS, JR.

Foreword by Gunther Schuller

ISBN: 1439257744
ISBN-13: 9781439257746
Library of Congress Control Number: 2009909305

Front and back cover photos courtesy of Stanisław Skrowaczewski.

Dedicated to Krystyna Skrowaczewski

CONTENTS

FOREWORD

The first time I read the name "Stanisław Skrowaczewski" was in 1958 in a glowing review of his Cleveland Orchestra debut, his first guest-conducting appearance in the United States. Because the writer of the review was someone I respected very much, I took special notice of this (to me) fascinating Polish name. By the time the then Minneapolis Symphony Orchestra appointed Stanisław two years later as its new music director, I had heard quite a bit more about his talents as a conductor-composer, while Stanisław had begun to hear of me as an "up-and-coming" composer. He soon began to invite me regularly to Minneapolis, both as a composer and a conductor.

We quickly discovered that we had a lot in common philosophically in regard to our goals as artists/musicians, our work ethics, and the composers—both traditional and modern—we most admired. Beyond that we were surprised to learn how many parallel experiences we shared in our childhoods and formative years—crucial influences, mentors, and special artistic encounters—that illuminated and directed our lives.

The world knows Skrowaczewski primarily as a conductor, although in recent decades—since his return (after a nearly fifteen-year hiatus) to composing—it has become quite clear that Stanisław is also one of the outstanding composers of our time. His musical talents were many and showed very early, first at the piano—at age four—and soon thereafter on violin, then composing (his true first love), and eventually, almost reluctantly, sliding into conducting. It all came naturally and relatively easily.

If one of those four pursuits were ultimately to predominate, it might easily have been as a composer. But fate and circumstances took over, and by the early 1950s Skrowaczewski had embarked on a full-time conducting career and had given up composing almost entirely.

That was our loss, but the music world gained one of the finest conductors of our era. His conducting career comprises not only several extensive major music director-ships—Kraków and Katowice Philharmonics, Minnesota Orchestra, Hallé Orchestra, and Yomiuri Nippon Symphony Orchestra—but also many decades of guest conducting most of the world's other greatest orchestras.

Stanisław brings to his music making a deep knowledge of an astonishingly wide-ranging repertoire—including the moderns, which so many famous maestros reject and ignore—and an artistic/professional integrity that springs from two primary sources: an innate respect for the composer and his works, and a humility and unpretentious-ness vis-à-vis the art of music and the conductor's profession.

The list of conductors who began their lives in music as composers is substantial, and so is the list of those who *gave up* composing, or kept at it as a more or less hidden sideline once they became established as major conductors. Most of the latter, as it turns out, were not as creatively gifted as they may have thought, or else discovered that creating music (composing) and re-creating music (performing) were somehow in serious conflict with each other. Skrowaczewski is a rare dually gifted musician whose early work as a composer—in the late 1940s through the 1950s in Europe—was immediately and consistently recognized as of the highest order, garnering broad public acclaim.

It was near the end of his Minnesota Orchestra tenure in the late 1970s that Skrowaczewski returned to composing, subsequently producing over the last three decades a most exceptional catalog of distinctive orchestral works.

By any reasonable assessment, Stanisław's life and career must be considered remarkably successful: major international musical directorships, combined with an amazingly diverse career as a guest conductor, and highly honored for his numerous award-winning recordings (complete orchestral works of Ravel, complete symphonies of Beethoven, Schumann, Brahms, and Bruckner, etc.). It has been, and continues to be, as full and artistically rich a life in music as is imaginable.

And yet there remains the nagging question: how is it that Stanisław Skrowaczewski remains so relatively unrecognized? The answer—not unheard of in the annals of musical history—lies in the reality that sometimes very great artists who approach their life's work with total selfless devotion, great humility, and modesty remain underappreciated and their legacy undervalued.

There isn't an ounce of self-promotion in Stanisław's genes. His deeply probing artistic nature does not mesh well with the dictates of the marketing and business of music. The title (*Seeking the Infinite*) of Harris' richly informative biography encapsulates these very thoughts. This profound identification of a creator's art with nature, the search for eternal truths through one's art—these are not themes that win you many points in the rough-and-tumble of the marketplace. As Stanisław himself once put it:

> To me, art is a dialogue with the unknown. This dialogue encompasses all fundamental human concerns—such as the meaning of life and death, love and cruelty, sacrifice and redemption—in the constant hope of knowing that which cannot be known.

Stanisław is now in the twilight of his career. It is well that we have a wonderfully researched, deeply insightful account of this outstanding musician and his contributions to our lives and to our culture.

Gunther Schuller
Newton Centre, Massachusetts
October 4, 2009

INTRODUCTION

Although I had heard of Stanisław Skrowaczewski, it wasn't until I read about him in Gunther Schuller's *The Compleat Conductor* that my curiosity was piqued. Soon after, I attended a Saint Paul Chamber Orchestra concert that he guest conducted, and I experienced firsthand the qualities of his musicianship that Schuller describes.

A year and a half later, in 1999, I interviewed Maestro Skrowaczewski about the ways in which a conductor conveys musical feeling, the subject of my dissertation. I was fascinated by his responses to my questions. He was resolute in his views, but some answers were ambiguous, even slightly mysterious. I sensed that his life experiences colored his responses, and that discussion left me wanting more.

It also left me wondering why so little had been written about this captivating conductor-composer who survived World War II (with three occupations of his home city) and fled communist Poland at age thirty-six to become the head of a major American orchestra. With an international classical music career reaching from the 1940s to the present, he has crossed paths with many of the greatest artists of the 20th century. The longevity of his creative life is not unprecedented in the world of classical music, but the consistently high quality of his achievements as a conductor and composer—and his intense dedication to both arts—is rare. His life merits research, understanding, and documentation.

Through tracing the journey of Stanisław Skrowaczewski's life, I have attempted to capture his character, artistic spirit, and complexity. His ultrasensitivity to music, nature, language, and life in general defines who he is as a man and an artist. Many musicians are sensitive human beings, but in Maestro Skrowaczewski's case, his level of sensitivity is heightened by an unrelenting drive to uncover the meaning in art and to analyze it. It is one of his greatest artistic assets and, at times, a limitation.

Life, too, has inflected his artistry. Life has brought him triumph, joy, wonder, suffering, pain, and loss—and through the conduit of music he transforms these experiences into burnished gold.

In today's technology-driven society, Stanisław Skrowaczewski's extraordinary model of sensitivity is important and necessary. His life story provides a compelling perspective for the generations born after World War II. It is my hope that this biography not only chronicles the life of this distinctive Polish-American conductor-composer but also reminds us of an artist who never compromised his integrity and stayed true to his personal values.

ONE

METAPHYSICAL SHIVERS

Art thrives on metaphysical ideas, which I believe are as old as human consciousness. A great work of art, reflecting the powerful intellect and compelling imagination of its creator, elicits from us a metaphysical shiver as it confronts us with a vision of ultimate reality.

—Stanisław Skrowaczewski, "The Resurrection of the Invisible"

Christmas was coming, and three-year-old Staś Skrowaczewski had noticed that something strange was going on in his home. The waiting room for his father's patients had been locked for over a week, and the usual coming and going of patients had ceased. Finally, December 24th arrived, and after a grand meal his parents, Paweł and Zofia, told their toddler that the windows had been opened in the locked room so that angels could bring them their Christmas tree. He was filled with excitement as his father slowly opened the massive door, revealing a gorgeous Christmas tree that touched the ceiling. Little Staś marveled at the dozens of white candles flickering on nearly every branch of the perfect tree, illuminating the sweets and decorations on it and the gifts beneath. "You see," Paweł said as he gestured toward an open window, "the angels just left." Entranced, Staś continued to believe in the Christmas angels until he was five years old.

Although he later was disappointed to learn the truth, Staś retained that feeling of being in a different world, where angels could fly and he could touch their wings. Decades later, at age eighty-five, Skrowaczewski said, "It has nothing to do with religion, this entire atmosphere of enchantment, something that is not water and earth, only something surreal. I believed in it. And I still feel it today."

The renowned conductor and composer Stanisław Skrowaczewski's sense of reality was influenced by surreal occurrences during his childhood in Lwów, Poland, where he was born on October 3, 1923. As a very young child, he had a dream about outer space in which he saw stars and a huge flying god wearing a white dress; the dream was so intense that he woke up screaming. About the same time he also had dreams of exotic, steep green mountains standing like columns. These dreams recurred a few more times and then suddenly stopped. He was amazed ten years later to see this dream landscape in photographs of China's Sichuan province. In 2007 he learned through a DNA test that his ancestry was four percent Chinese. These revelations and similar experiences throughout his life led Skrowaczewski to believe in the possibility of reincarnation.

Staś (his childhood nickname, the Polish equivalent of "Stan") was fascinated by fables about dreamlike worlds, the forces of good and evil, and ghosts that his French governess, Madame Francille, read to him. She spent considerable time with Staś, speaking French exclusively, and by age six he was fluent in that language, surpassing his skill in Polish. His fascination with German music soon led to his learning enough German to read stories by E.T.A. Hoffmann, whose tales of fantasy and horror enthralled him.

At age seven, while walking with his best friend, Jan, outside Lwów's city center, Staś heard sounds coming from an open first-floor window. He stood transfixed by music he had never heard before. "It was the same shock that someone who believes would have from seeing God in front of him," he later recalled.[1] Staś' trancelike state confused and frightened Jan, who immediately took his friend back home. Staś had a fever of 104 degrees and remained bedridden for the next two days, raving and talking nonsense. A gifted physician, Paweł nevertheless could not understand what had happened to his son, so he brought colleagues to his house to assess the situation. "I was in a trance, I was in heaven—the world didn't exist for me," Skrowaczewski remembered.

Staś discovered that the music he'd heard through the window was the Adagio movement from Bruckner's Seventh Symphony. "Very quickly I obtained the score," said Skrowaczewski. "Since that moment I was fascinated with Bruckner."[2] Fifty-five years later, in 1985, Skrowaczewski paid homage to this experience by referencing this Bruckner Adagio in the second movement of his Concerto for Orchestra. The movement is entitled *Anton Bruckner's Himmelfahrt* (Bruckner's Heavenly Journey).

The aural and visual "metaphysical shivers" Skrowaczewski experienced as a young child shaped his innate sensitivity. Lwów's distinctive environment, his parents, and his home life were all major influences.

During Skrowaczewski's childhood, Lwów had a special ambience and cultured atmosphere. It was a beautiful metropolis with clean streets bearing historic Polish names, Italian Renaissance and gothic architecture, ornate baroque churches, lush parks, and an historic walled city within the city. It had several superb musical venues, such as the Lwów Opera (Teatr Wielki) and the Lwów Conservatory, and it also was a hub for important Polish visual artists, poets, writers, and theater groups. An erudite community, Lwów (today L'viv, Ukraine) remains a major academic center with outstanding schools and several universities. L'viv University is among the oldest such institutions in Central Europe, home to world-renowned philosophy and mathematics scholars for over two centuries.

Many of Skrowaczewski's compositions begin and end with dark, mysterious colors and hues: distant bells, chimes, string bass pedal notes, gongs, and tam-tams. This "fascination with nocturnal imagery," as musicologist Mary Ann Feldman calls it, stems in part from Skrowaczewski's earliest memories of exploring the streets of Lwów as a small boy.[3] In the evenings his governess took him on walks in the city. The streets were eerie during autumn: dead leaves underfoot, flooded streams, the fog and mist in the air dimly illuminated by gas lamps. Winter's storms, blizzards, and distant snowy peaks gave Lwów a different aura. The images remain fresh in Skrowaczewski's mind:

They were very mysterious, vague, and impressive to me. All of these images, though realistic, were unrealistic to me, creating a surreal vision of the world. The atmosphere of Lwów, supported by the fables I knew, created a special openness in me. They produced sensitivity to music, pictures, paintings, and books, building my sensitivity to art in general. Later these images connected music with its mystery, like I felt with Mozart's *Don Giovanni*, for example: one world that is alive, another dead.

The city has a dramatic history of intellectual activity, ethnic diversity, political occupations, and unrest. For six centuries it had been a thoroughly Polish, extremely patriotic city. Founded in the 13th century, Lwów came under Polish rule in the middle of the 14th century and remained so until the late 18th century. Under the Austrian Habsburg Empire from 1772 until 1918—the longest of three partitions of Poland—Lwów was known as Lemberg, capital of the province of Galicia.

"It was the biggest city in southeast Poland and the most original," Skrowaczewski noted, "more original even than Kraków and Warsaw. Its character was formed from being on the crossroads between east and west and north and south for several centuries, which shaped the culture, architecture, cuisine, everything."

The end of World War I set the stage for Poland's independence in 1918.[4] Lwów was returned to Poland in 1919 after a few weeks of battles between Lwów's largely Polish population—especially high school and college students known as the *Orlęta Lwowskie* (Lwów Eaglets)—and the Austrian-created Ukrainian Legion, whose original objective was to create a new Austrian-Ukrainian monarchy under the Habsburgs.

But Poland's independence was fraught with territorial conflicts; within the span of three years, six border wars occurred. A war with the Soviets from 1919 to 1920 was the largest conflict. This struggle, in which Paweł Skrowaczewski served as a medical colonel, delayed the establishment of Polish borders. It was not until 1921, two years before Skrowaczewski's birth, that the eastern border of Poland (formerly Little Poland or Eastern Malopolska or Galicia) was finally confirmed by the Treaty of Riga and by the League of Nations.

As a result of these turbulent years, Poles frequently possessed only a sketchy knowledge of their family histories. Many records were lost or destroyed during 150 years of Austrian rule, two world wars, and the chaotic interwar period. Little is known about Skrowaczewski's lineage, although the meaning of his surname dates back to the mid-19th century. It may be connected to land possessions called *skrowaczewo*, whose owners were likely called *skrowaczewski*.

Skrowaczewski's paternal grandfather, Józef, was a lawyer and supervisor who oversaw large properties owned by Polish princes and counts, including small cities and villages. He also participated in the Austrian and German revolt against the Russians in 1915 and 1916. Little is known of his wife, Michalina Poraj-Podgórska. The couple had four sons: Karol, Paweł, Józef, and Jan.

Paweł, a highly regarded laryngologist, often practiced medicine outside his specialty. Skrowaczewski explained, "Many people after the war would say to me, 'Your father saved my life. He took a tumor from my brain.' Back then doctors had a broader scope. Sometimes in the winter he traveled far away for one or two days to be with a sick patient, even if the illness involved the heart or lungs. Doctors during and after the war had to be generalists helping people."

Fortunately, Paweł had been a "partial" prisoner (internee) of the Russians in Kiev during 1916 and 1917. This situation allowed him to practice medicine and to learn from other physicians without being involved in battle.

Although he never played an instrument, Paweł was an ardent music lover. Before the war he studied medicine in Vienna, where he often attended opera performances at the famed Wiener Staatsoper. As a student he had little money, so for a few pennies he purchased standing-room- only space in the house's highest balconies. Staś loved hearing his father's stories about the opera performances he attended in Lwów. Pre-World War II Lwowian audiences customarily brought scores to follow during concerts, and the sound of hundreds of people quietly turning pages simultaneously was part of a concert's ambience. Years later, audience members brought scores to Skrowaczewski's concerts in Lwów.

While in Vienna, Paweł met his future wife, Zofia Karszniewicz, a concert pianist—very likely at one of her performances. They married before World War I and lived in Kiev for a couple of years. The couple had two children: Krystyna, born in 1918, and Stanisław, born five years later.

At age four Staś had a brush with death that fixed in him a loving memory of his father. The family was on summer vacation at the Baltic Sea when the little boy contracted a serious case of typhoid. The closest well-equipped hospital was located in Warsaw, 250 miles away. Paweł took Staś there alone by train, and during the entire journey the father was very protective, forbidding anyone to approach the compartment where his son lay. In Warsaw a team of doctors helped Staś through a slow recovery, during which father and son stayed with a cousin from Zofia's side of the family, Professor Merunowicz, president of Warsaw University and a renowned scholar of literature. Eventually Staś felt well enough to explore nearby Łazienki Palace and its gorgeous surrounding parks and gardens.

Paweł instilled in his son a lifelong love of the natural world and outdoor activities. During summer vacations with Staś' friends, they climbed mountains, sometimes taking up to six or seven hours to reach summits in the Carpathian (Karpaty) Mountains, located about sixty miles south of Lwów. They also climbed the Tatra Mountains, the highest range in the Carpathians. Staś loved to go there in late August to eat blackberries, raspberries, and blueberries the size of cherries and to gather the hazelnuts that flourished in the mountains. He also enjoyed occasional sightings of brown bears, wolves, lynx, and other wild animals on the range. Throughout Skrowaczewski's life, mountain climbing and skiing have provided a respite and rejuvenation.

Staś loved Lwów's continental climate with its four seasons, particularly the hot summers and snowy winters. He enjoyed snowstorms and the sight of streetcars completely blanketed by snow and temporarily unable to move. The hills surrounding

Lwów were particularly picturesque during the harsh but beautiful winter season. He began skiing there at age four with his father. Staś was already brave enough to ski on makeshift jumps on the natural slopes in Stryjski (Kilińskiego) and Żelazna Woda parks in Lwów, and on the real wooden ski jump in Pohulanka Park. (Even in his eighties, Skrowaczewski continues to ski on the long slope in the back of his Minnesota home, often going up and down the hill twenty times without taking off his downhill skis for extra exercise.)

On Sundays, Paweł took Staś and Krystyna on long walks around the parks of Lwów. The highlight for Staś was waiting for the express trains that came through Lwów on the main line leading to Bucharest and Vienna. The boy eagerly awaited the noon arrival, listening for the locomotive before it emerged between two hills. As a treat, Paweł allowed his son to place fake coins on the tracks and to retrieve the flattened discs after the train had passed.

Skrowaczewski's earliest musical experiences are connected with his mother. A pianist who began performing as a young girl in her hometown of Kołomyja, Zofia toured Poland before World War I. She continued to perform after Krystyna's birth but ended her career after Staś arrived. Zofia's grandmother, Papagesko, was a Greek who had inherited certain Mediterranean physical characteristics visible in Skrowaczewski's chiseled features. Zofia may have been a descendent of Napoleon's first wife, Josephine de Beauharnais, the Empress of France (1763–1814).

Zofia played the piano daily. Two-year-old Staś would escape his crib and crawl underneath the instrument, his chosen spot for listening. "Underneath, the piano loses the sort of metallic, dry quality. It sounds like a rich, big organ," Skrowaczewski noted. "Why I went there, I don't know, but my love of the sonority of the organ and the orchestra was born." Zofia was fond of playing music by minor romantic composers from the early 19th century, such as John Field, the Irish-born creator of the nocturne. Staś, however, developed an aversion to such music, preferring works of Haydn, Mozart, and Beethoven, which he learned while listening to the radio. Scarcely able to stand, he discovered how to spin the radio dial until he found the stations that broadcast his preferences exclusively.

The boy began spending long periods of time at the piano. Because Zofia did not have teaching experience, she found an instructor for her son. His lessons began formally at age five with Florentyna (Flora) Listowska, a highly respected piano teacher in Lwów. After teaching him Czerny's *Erster Einfang*, she focused Staś on Bach, Haydn, and Mozart. "She cared very much about all the parameters connected with playing: tone, rhythm, technique, dynamics, etc. I remember she was severe about these fundamentals. She was very warm but also efficient and didn't spoil me by overly praising my playing," Skrowaczewski recalled. Progress was rapid, and Flora graded his performance by marking his music with pluses or a star as the top grade. He did not have to be goaded into regular practice and had an innate desire to perform exactly what was on the page.

"I remember that Flora told me I will have a 'competitor' because Staś was joining her 'school,' and that he is excellent because he has perfect pitch," remembered Wacław (Wacek) Szybalski, a distinguished professor of oncology and one of the founders of gene therapy and synthetic biology. He befriended Skrowaczewski for a time during the Nazi occupation of Lwów, and their friendship ultimately saved both their lives.

The Skrowaczewski home was rich in listening opportunities. In addition to his mother's daily practice, Staś heard chamber music on the weekends when his father's colleagues visited and joined Zofia in presenting concerts for neighbors and friends. These experiences, along with listening to the radio, gave the young piano student a natural feel for the music he was learning. "My teacher didn't have to tell me when to slow down, when to speed up—I felt it. The music showed me what to do," he remembered.[5]

Staś initially used the piano as a creative tool for composition. "When I was listening to music in my childhood—almost since the beginning—I always wanted to create my own music, as good as the music I listened to, but my own. I started to play what I wanted to write," Skrowaczewski said.[6] Soon after beginning piano lessons, he composed short pieces in the style of Haydn or Mozart, written without his teacher's help. Clearly modeled after the classical piano pieces he studied, they nevertheless were sophisticated creations for a child of four or five years. In *Thank You Maestro*, a 1979 program aired on Twin Cities Public Television (KTCA), Skrowaczewski played impromptu examples of these works.

Although the piano served Staś' early creative desires, he did not use it to compose by improvising. "I had the composition already in my head," he explained. "I just wanted to make it sound somehow, especially from a harmonic point of view." Staś kept these compositional efforts a secret from his teacher and his family. He was shy about his music, which was too personal to share with anyone, with one exception.

Throughout his early childhood, Staś told no one about his secret life as a composer except his close friend Jan Łopuszański, whom he met when they were six years old. An artistically gifted child, Jan drew portraits, created sculptures, played piano, composed, and spoke perfect German. The boys discussed and critiqued each other's compositions and wrote letters about them to one another in German. Skrowaczewski still remembers one humorous but brutal critique peppered with foul language, which Jan wrote about a work he composed in Mozartian style.

More than seventy years later, Łopuszański described Staś' pieces as "fantastic" and said that he felt discouraged because he knew he was not as talented as his friend. The two boys were obsessed with Beethoven's music, and according to Jan, they detested the works of Rachmaninoff, which Staś parents' loved but which they considered overly romantic, café-style music.

At age five Staś obtained his first score, Beethoven's Fifth Symphony, a work he had heard during a German radio broadcast. That experience led him to explore Beethoven's piano sonatas. The great composer became "the summit" for him, and eventually Staś heard the symphonies at concerts. He obtained scores for the nine

Beethoven symphonies and Mozart's major symphonies; by age six Staś added scores by Schumann, Wagner, and Brahms to his collection. He learned orchestration primarily by following the scores while listening to the radio and by slowly playing passages on the piano. He also read books on instrumentation and orchestration.

Staś also decided to play an instrument from the orchestra in addition to piano and chose the piccolo, which he loved. "When I listened to symphonies on the radio with the scores, I played along with the flute part on the piccolo," Skrowaczewski remembered. "My parents were terrified!"

By age six he made a preliminary sketch of his own symphony (part of one movement and ideas for a scherzo) and composed six piano sonatas. In 1930, at age seven, Staś composed his first orchestral work, an eight-minute overture. Written for a full orchestra of strings, double woodwinds, two horns, two trumpets, and timpani, it was unabashedly modeled after Mozart. From the beginning he composed the overture in a full-score format, not as a piano reduction. By now he was familiar with at least ten Mozart and ten Haydn symphonies, and all the Beethoven symphonies, so this instrumentation was not difficult for him. He considered the overture "perfect in terms of form, with an exposition with two themes, a development section, recapitulation, and a coda."

The work so closely resembled Mozart's style that Skrowaczewski later made it the basis of a joke. After the war he told people that Mozart's son composed the score and that he had discovered it in the Lwów Conservatory library. (This notion was not unreasonable because Mozart's son, Franz Xaver Wolfgang, taught in Lwów for several years after his father died.) Despite the quasi-romantic, Brahmsian modulations in the overture's second theme, Skrowaczewski's joke was taken seriously; however, in 1940 he had to come clean when the Lwów Philharmonic expressed interest in performing some of his music. He promptly titled the piece *Overture in the Classical Style*. The program was Skrowaczewski's first public concert as a composer, and also included songs for alto voice and orchestra that he set in German to poems by Heinrich Heine.

About the same time that Staś composed his orchestral overture, he began playing the violin. His father's colleague Dr. Heisig, a fine violinist who regularly visited the Skrowaczewski home, often played duets with Zofia. He began teaching the instrument to Staś, who found the violin fascinating but very tiring physically due to the necessary body position.[7] This initial training proved fruitful during the war years, when the teenage Skrowaczewski played with a "quartet in hiding."

Although music was Staś' primary childhood interest, he also developed a passion for mathematics and chemistry. Between ages five and seven, he had the phenomenal ability to rapidly solve complex multiplication and division problems in his head. "The word 'computer' didn't exist back then, but people described my mind at that time as if it had a little machine in it," Skrowaczewski said. "Once I entered school, though, I lost this ability."

TWO

ENTERING THE TEMPLE

Music is the most mysterious of the arts, veiled by something solemn, far from the realities of life. Its soul is revealed only to those who desire and are willing to go through certain stages of ceremony and mystery to reach it. A concert hall should be the temple where music leads us gradually from the secular life into the realm of the extraordinary, to the life that is innermost.

—Stanisław Skrowaczewski, "The Light in Our Eye"

During Skrowaczewski's early childhood, Poland still suffered growing pains associated with its newfound independence. Its economy had been destroyed by over one hundred years of foreign occupation, and Polish society was fragmented culturally and politically.[1] At the time, sixty-four percent of Poland's population consisted of rural peasants, whereas the intelligentsia, to which the Skrowaczewski family belonged, totaled only five percent.[2]

Skrowaczewski was fortunate to have a privileged and cultivated home life. A woman who worked as cook and maid lived with the family, but Zofia loved cooking and did so often. The family valued languages: Paweł and Zofia spoke Polish, French, and German. Occasionally at dinner they conversed with the children in French in order to maintain their fluency. Because Germany was a Polish adversary, the German language was not "popular with cultivated people," Skrowaczewski said. "France, however, was the center of the cultural world for Poland. But in terms of music, German music was predominant."

Despite Staś' upper-class background, his parents impressed upon him an appreciation of life's small joys. He recalled:

> I was not spoiled by having everything. When I was a baby, Poland was barely recovering from war and many years of occupation. Numerous things could not be obtained previously because commerce outside of Poland was not allowed. I remember the first time we had imported oranges from Spain. At that time we didn't get any children's toys. You could hardly buy things you needed for life. When I was around three, I was sick in bed for a week with a temperature. My parents brought me a toy wooden streetcar. Later I had electric trains with rails. But this streetcar was just simple and wooden. And today I still remember the joy!

By their example his parents instilled in him a strong sense of character, morality, and discipline. After Paweł finished work at the hospital, he saw patients at home. Part of the Skrowaczewski domicile was designated as waiting and examining rooms where he treated patients with general medical issues. Zofia, a devout Catholic, spent much of her time looking after Krystyna.

Staś' formal education began at the renowned school of Dr. Jan Niemiec. After a year or two of being accompanied by his governess on the mile-long walk to school, Staś was allowed to go alone. He loved the small school, which stood on a hill next to a citadel surrounded by a huge garden of fruit trees. Elementary school studies came quite easily to Staś, who had a "strong mathematic predilection" and who was "always the first to answer a math question."

Staś was popular with his fourteen classmates, who came from similar backgrounds.[3] He often sat in front of the blackboard at the head of the class. Sometimes when bored by a lesson, he wiggled his ears, much to the amusement of his friends and the consternation of his teacher.

The star of all musical events, he also was quite fond of acting in plays. His dramatic roles ranged from a penguin to a coal miner to an old 16th-century Polish nobleman. He was so proud of the latter role that he paraded around the streets of Lwów in an authentic costume complete with a little saber, prepared to "fight the Tartars."

"I loved these experiences because they brought me back to the surreal feelings of my very early childhood," Skrowaczewski said. "I really believed I *was* a penguin." Later, if the plays required it, he composed music for the piano or any available instruments. These experiences influenced his film composing decades later.

His parents took him to concerts by the Lwów Philharmonic, to the opera, and to programs at the Lwów Conservatory, which was near his home. Each performance he attended as a child affected him. Chamber music concerts influenced his piano playing, and orchestral programs piqued his desire to compose because of the "physical power of big sound and the beauty of the compositions."

By age eight he was allowed to attend concerts without adult supervision. At a performance of Mussorgsky's *Night on Bald Mountain,* Staś and his friend Jurek Baczyński couldn't stop laughing when a percussionist lifted a huge chime and struck it at the work's finale. Another such incident occurred when the boys noticed the odd mannerisms of a violin player. "It was a little scandal for boys to be bursting into laughter at such an event," Skrowaczewski said.

Jurek, later nicknamed "Yoga" by his classmates because he was "spiritually bonded with strange ideas," was a violinist. He performed Staś' first violin sonatas, and the two boys were frequent concert companions. They attended a chamber music concert together that left an indelible mark on Skrowaczewski. While they were listening to the Adagio movement of Beethoven's Violin Sonata in C minor, a man seated in front of them died of a heart attack. The performance was stopped, the man's body was removed, and after a long pause the concert resumed. The experience shocked the two young musicians. Skrowaczewski later remarked, "It's not a surprise that from that moment on I connected Beethoven's adagios with death; at first, only sonatas but then Beethoven's quartets. Now I know I also transferred this death-adagio connection to Bruckner's music."[4]

Several of Skrowaczewski's relatives were accomplished in their chosen professions. His three paternal uncles greatly influenced his childhood. Staś felt closest to Karol, an attorney general for Lwów, who was married but childless. Karol lived in Lwów, so he and his wife often dined with Paweł's family. He took a great interest in Staś' musical development. "He was perhaps the most intellectual of all the brothers in a general sense, in his knowledge of life, literature, theater, philosophy. He even tried to teach me English," Skrowaczewski recalled.

Józef, whose son Roman was about the same age as Staś, was a technical engineer and director of a sugar factory located in Wożuczyn, a village near the city of Zamość, 120 miles northwest of Lwów. He lived on the west side of Wożuczyn, and Staś' youngest uncle, Jan, lived just a few miles away on the east side, an area of wheat fields and beautiful flowers. An agricultural engineer, Jan oversaw management of twenty-five miles of land belonging to former Polish princes. He had an enormous country home where Staś enjoyed spending part of his summer vacations.

In 1934, when Staś' sister became ill with scarlet fever, Paweł and Zofia sent their son to stay with Józef's family for the entire summer. He spent many hours playing with his cousin Roman. A narrow-gauge railway transported sugar beets—which are widely grown in Poland—from the fields to the factory. The two boys played on the rail, riding at high speeds in a little cart they maneuvered by hand. The production of sugar from beets fascinated Staś; it fed his interest in science, machinery, and chemistry. He had long discussions with Józef about technical matters.

Wożuczyn and Lublin are located in gorgeous countryside with fertile soils, "one of the reasons why Stalin wanted to snatch eastern Poland so much," according to Skrowaczewski. A sixteen-acre garden of vegetables and fruit trees was near the Wożuczyn residence, where Staś and Roman climbed trees and played volleyball and ping-pong. They also rode around town on a pony that pulled a small cart. Staś became skittish about riding after he fell off the pony, and later on, when he fell off a horse and sprained his arm, he decided he was permanently finished with riding.

Another summer vacation site provided more vivid memories. When Staś was about three or four, his parents rented a cottage near the village of Niemirów, famous for its hot springs and a spa where Zofia treated her arthritis. One night, during a fierce storm that hit the village, a lightning bolt struck their cottage and threw Zofia from her bed. Another bolt split a small tree nearby in half. The next morning, ever-inquisitive Staś went to the tree to "look for the bolt." The budding scientist was curious to see if copper or other metal were associated with this phenomenon.

Staś' cousin Zofia influenced his deep fascination with chemistry, the only field that ever came close to rivaling his life in music. She began her career as a chemist in Warsaw before joining the faculty of Lwów Polytechnica (an impressive feat for a woman during this era). At the time of her death in 1993 she was professor emeritus at the University of Wrocław. "She became famous because she discovered a special glue substance that was used on planes," Skrowaczewski noted.

Each day when school was not in session, Staś visited his cousin's laboratory, where he enjoyed her lectures and mingled with her students. He created his first chemistry experiments in Zofia's laboratory. "The awful smell of the sulfur gas intrigued me," explained Skrowaczewski. "I was inspired by the creativity involved in mixing substances and producing different results. It involved my fantasy and imagination and engaged both the mathematical and the musical parts of my mind. Ultimately, it all influenced my composing."

During Staś' preteen years, his parents hoped that he would become a professor of chemistry or a mechanical engineer like his uncle Józef. For a year or two Staś also believed that science might be his calling, but when he caused an accidental but dangerous explosion in Zofia's lab and then another at home, he had second thoughts:

> My parents were very concerned because after the explosion at the university, I built a primitive little laboratory at home, conducting experiments that produced more explosions and fire. They forbad me to do any more experiments in the house after that. At that point, chemistry for me was like instrumentation. I mixed certain substances without any idea exactly what the result would be. It was the idea of creating something that intrigued me so much.

> I remember that around this time I built a little electric machine with a turbine and four magnets that turned it. An uncle from my mother's side who was a professor of physics at Lwów University came to visit. He was skeptical and quite critical of what I made. He was a rather dour man. He shouldn't have acted that way toward a child, but I wasn't angry, just a bit sad. I stopped building such things but kept up my chemistry for a while. Zofia was my inspiration. Chemistry at that age was part of my search for what we are, how we fit into the universe. I realized later that music is in the genes. It's one of the elements of the cosmos.

Cousin Zofia's influence on Staś extended beyond chemistry. "She was a sort of rebel regarding religion, as far as whether to believe or not," Skrowaczewski said. "She sometimes quarreled with my mother on this topic." Paweł basically followed his wife's views on religion but with "a grain of salt, just looking through your fingers at it." As a young child Staś was fascinated by the pageantry of the Catholic Church: children in procession, candles, incense, the priests' vestments, and organ music. To him the liturgy resembled a big opera, and the holiday services particularly enthralled him. By age ten or eleven, however, he questioned the institution of religion: "I liked the concept of religion, but I didn't like how it was institutionalized, and I felt that a lot of priests were dishonest people. I had religious feelings through music from the very beginning, sensing it represented something 'beyond me.'"

For a brief period he and Jan Łopuszański were altar boys, enjoying the "theater" of the church. Occasionally they became caught up in the spectacle of the Mass and forgot to perform their tasks. In later years, playing the organ kept Staś active in the church because it created a "mystical atmosphere." On one occasion he became so involved in his performance that he forgot to stop playing when the priest was supposed to present his sermon. "They fired me," he said.

Staś' religious doubts coincided with the loss of his sister, Krystyna, who was only sixteen when she died of scarlet fever and heart complications in fall 1934, just before Staś' eleventh birthday. Tall and attractive, Krystyna possessed a beautiful voice. She had been taking lessons and just discovering the power of her voice when she became ill. Her teacher considered her talented, and there was hope she might have a singing career. Aside from a few opportunities at school, she never had the chance to perform. Krystyna also had studied piano, but it wasn't her passion. Although she had no musical interactions with her precocious younger sibling, she was aware of his musical talent. Roman recalled that when Krystyna practiced, Staś often chastised her for playing "false notes."

Her death devastated Paweł and Zofia, but Staś accepted the tragedy philosophically. The experience provoked deep discussions with Jan about God, existence, and a possible afterlife. He read metaphysical essays and discussed them with friends. "It certainly deepened my curiosity about the world and the universe," he commented. "Today, eleven-year-old boys probably talk about baseball, not about God. Times have changed."[5]

Krystyna had been particularly close to her father, and her death took a great toll on Paweł, who generally kept his pain to himself. Zofia turned towards the church for consolation but never quite recovered from losing her daughter. Tragedy marked Zofia's family history. Her only sibling, Adam, a handsome, creative young man who wanted to become a poet, died in his early twenties of pneumonia. Several years before Krystyna's death, Zofia's mother died in a bus accident while en route to visit the Pauline monastery of Jasna Góra in the city of Częstochowa, midway between Katowice and Warsaw. (The monastery is home to one of Poland's most important religious relics, the Black Madonna painting, also known as Our Lady of Częstochowa.)

For many years after Krystyna's death, Zofia dressed only in black and never played piano. After World War II ended, Roman's mother eventually persuaded her to play again and to abandon her morbid dress.

Zofia adored Staś, and after the loss of her daughter she became obsessively devoted to her son. He appreciated his mother's love, and they shared a special bond, but he sometimes found it difficult to be the constant object of her attention.

Zofia fretted that Staś didn't eat enough. At dinner, after he took the modest portion he wished to eat, she added more. Annoyed, he would take the extra cutlets and stuff them into drawers underneath the big dinner table. During his high school years she insisted on giving Staś a "second breakfast" (the Polish equivalent of lunch). "My mother would always give me enormous sandwiches with butter—which I hated—so I always gave them to poor boys in my class. One boy especially ate my 'second breakfasts.' I didn't eat because I wasn't hungry. I would arrive home from school around two or three in the afternoon and have dinner and then a light supper in the evening," Skrowaczewski recalled. He loved physical exercise, both as a discipline and as a means of counteracting the extra calories his mother foisted on him.

During a brief period in high school Staś was slightly overweight, and his muscular gymnastics teacher mocked his student's lack of fitness. The words hurt Staś but motivated him to perfect his body. He increased his participation in sports and began intensive exercise regimens that he maintains to this day. Years later, when Skrowaczewski lived in Katowice and worked as a conductor, he impressed his musicians with his physical prowess. During their summer practice retreats in the mountains, they observed that their young maestro's physical routine included headstands and handstands.

Zofia, who endorsed her son's penchant for healthy foods, brought him homemade beet or pomegranate juice, walnuts, fresh fruits, and vegetables when she visited him in Katowice. Even after Skrowaczewski was married, his mother continued to look after him attentively and sent his wife long letters prescribing in detail her son's diet and wardrobe.

Realizing that Staś was headed toward a musical career, Zofia sought opportunities for him. He loved the sound of the organ, and she eventually arranged for him to play at various churches in Lwów, including the Bernardine church and monastery, which date to 1630. "The sound of the pipes was stunning, and of course, someone had to be there to pump the air. It was still a non-electric instrument," Skrowaczewski remembered.

By the time Staś reached his preteen years, Zofia knew about his efforts at composing. When Roman visited the Skrowaczewski home to see his cousin, Zofia told him to be quiet and not bother Staś because he was busy composing. But Staś interrupted his work and joyously burst out of his room to greet his cousin.

Staś' piano lessons with Flora Listowska progressed well. Music of Haydn, Mozart, and Beethoven continued to be his staples, but he expanded his listening to include Szymanowski, Tchaikovsky, and Mussorgsky. "I enjoyed Russian music to some degree," Skrowaczewski said. "It was powerful, very close to my aesthetics, but it was not on the same musical level as Beethoven, Haydn, or Mozart."[6] Stravinsky, however, held a special fascination for him.

Staś made his public debut as a pianist in 1934 at age eleven on Polish Radio Lwów. Someone had heard Staś play at one of Flora's private recitals and recommended that he perform on the radio. Then only four years old, Polish Radio Lwów was becoming extremely popular in Poland, second only to Warsaw Radio.[7] It programmed classical music, news, lectures, and church services. By 1939 Lwów had more homes with radios than any other city in Poland.[8] His debut was broadcast throughout Poland. Skrowaczewski remembers that it lasted about thirty minutes and included a Haydn sonata and a piece by Bach.

Two years later, in 1936, Staś played and conducted Beethoven's Third Piano Concerto. The Lwów Musical Association sponsored the concert by an orchestra of freelance professional musicians, some of whom were members of the Lwów Philharmonic. Skrowaczewski vividly remembers the concert setting:

> It was in a large room at Kasyno i Koło Literacko-Naukowe on Akademicka Street, in a building where scores of writers and other intellectuals met.

> It had golden baroque décor, similar to what one might find in Vienna. The walls were yellow-white, and the windows were ornate. The orchestra was small, [with] perhaps twenty strings including one bass, woodwinds in pairs, timpani—altogether about thirty-five musicians. I conducted from the piano.

This concert marked his debut as a conductor, a milestone event that felt completely natural to the boy, who was accustomed to "conducting" in a variety of chamber music settings. In those rehearsals he always led and critiqued, so taking charge of a large group of musicians in a piece he knew extremely well was not difficult.

> I didn't feel like a conductor. I just felt that I was one of them. When I didn't play piano, I moved my hands automatically to show the pulse and dynamics and to cue instruments. I do remember that I was a bit of an "enfant terrible," always asking something from the musicians, making corrections, changing tempos, etc., from my own ideas, and not always to their acceptance!

An unusual choice for a thirteen-year-old pianist-conductor, the Third Piano Concerto is Beethoven's only piano concerto in a minor key (C minor), and a considerable number of the solo gestures require musical introspection rather than virtuosity. The dark opening orchestral statement of its first movement is the longest Beethoven ever wrote for any concerto.[9] The pensive Largo, the second movement, entails tricky negotiation between orchestra and soloist. No matter how well the musicians may listen to one another, the concerto demands strong leadership from the podium. Skrowaczewski remembers being told that he played very well. To generate positive results with this piece as both pianist and conductor, he must have exhibited an impressive level of maturity for his age.

The teenage Skrowaczewski thrived in his educational pursuits. In high school he was enamored with Greek and Latin. An engaging professor gave lectures on Greek mythology, the *Odyssey*, the *Iliad*, and Italian culture. Fascinated by southern European society, Staś particularly enjoyed stories about Italy. When he finally traveled to Rome and later to the south of France, he understood firsthand his former professor's love of this culture:

> After being in southern France for the first time, Ravel and Debussy came almost automatically to me. It was as if this music had been a part of my culture, and to such a degree that when I was conducting Ravel pieces in Paris [in the late 1940s], a concertmaster of a French orchestra told me, "It's interesting—you feel this music better than many Frenchmen." And indeed, I feel these pieces. Conducting them comes naturally to me.[10]

The study of French held special interest for Staś, who had acquired skills in that language and an affinity for French culture during childhood. The best schools in Poland had strong curricula in the subject, and Staś participated in the French-language section of his class. As a teenager he also took private German lessons to advance his knowledge of that language.

The study of history did not interest the young Staś; he was too busy with music, languages, and mathematics to give it much attention.[11] In his adult years he compensated for this gap in his education by reading widely on a variety of historical topics, notably the two world wars. The writings of Winston Churchill especially intrigued him, and to this day there are various books about Churchill in his home library.

While attending Dr. Niemiec's elementary school, Staś had his "first big sympathies with girls." During high school, he and his classmates had girlfriends whom they often accompanied on walks home. Most of Staś' girlfriends were "summer girlfriends" from Warsaw or other cities, so he didn't have the opportunity to connect with them again. An exception was Anna Lenkiewicz, who was a bit older than he. Intellectual, musical, artistic, and an avid mountain climber, she became a doctor; her brother, Władysław, also a good friend of Staś, became a renowned professor of mechanical engineering and robotics. Their father was a professor of literature at Lwów University.

"Władysław was at the center of our youth in Lwów," noted Skrowaczewski. "He was interested in several fields: science, philosophy, literature, music, etc. He was also a good poet. I still see him occasionally when I conduct in Poland, and he still writes beautiful poetry, this on top of his work as an engineer."

Staś dated Anna until just before the start of the war and maintained a close friendship with her and Władysław throughout his time in Lwów. Surviving the German and Soviet occupations of their city forged a strong bond between them.

For five summers, 1935 through 1939, the Skrowaczewski family spent vacations in Mizun, a remote village in the Carpathian mountain range in southeast Poland, near the border with Romania. The small village comprised about thirty-five cottages; most residents were Germans who had settled there during Bismarck's time and who spoke a strange mixture of Polish and German. The Skrowaczewskis rented a cottage from a Herr Schmeltzer and usually vacationed together with six to eight other families, including several of Staś' friends.[12]

This bucolic section of the Carpathian range was lush with flora and fauna. "It was like a virgin jungle, with fruits, vegetables, and fields completely red with strawberries," Skrowaczewski remembered. Some of his friends hunted, and despite the nearsightedness he inherited from his parents, Staś was a good shot. Once he shot an osprey but so regretted it that he never hunted again. Hiking was a popular activity in Mizun, and Staś often took visiting friends on long, steep hikes up the mountains, sometimes for an entire day. Often he hiked alone. "I would slip out of the house before sunrise, at 4:00 a.m., and climb to the highest peaks," Skrowaczewski recalled. "My mother was scared to wake up and not find me. I loved being alone in the mountains. Even from an early age it was a part of my special relationship with nature."

Dozens of young people brought their instruments to Mizun and played chamber music together on rainy days. Roman recalled the day that a local person ran to Zofia and reported that someone was playing beautifully on the church organ. Staś had found an organ in a tiny chapel located in the woods. "It was all wood and had the smell of fresh wood," he remembered, "and there was a small and primitive organ there that I had to pump myself, but it was the only keyboard for miles around." He became friendly with the local organist, who gave him the key to the chapel so he could play there on rainy days.

Intellectual activity also engaged Staś and his friends in Mizun. They discussed the latest literature as well as writings from the 19th century. They read Polish, French, and German poetry, listened to music, and discussed philosophy (Kant, Schopenhauer, and Ingarden were of particular interest). "I think I developed more during my vacations than in the winter at my high school," Skrowaczewski once remarked.[13]

At Mizun, Staś had one frightening brush with the metaphysical world. Since his earliest years he had heard fables about ghosts and supernatural phenomena. Some of these tales were set in the Carpathian Mountains, which are steeped in mysterious legends. Novels such as Jules Verne's *Le Château des Carpathes* (The Carpathian Castle) and Bram Stoker's *Dracula* are two familiar examples. Ukrainian folklore abounds in witches and various strange creatures whose origins some believe are based on actual occurrences. After one summer experience Staś considered believing as well:

> Over one mountain I discovered a tiny village, really just a few houses together. The inhabitants were strange mountain people from the east who had farms and performed rituals late in the summer. I got scared when I saw things there that I couldn't explain. People standing next to me suddenly disappeared like ghosts. Incredible! And this was under a full August moon, which is known for animals acting strangely and other bizarre happenings. This experience was in the 1930s, so I could only imagine what things might have been like in the 16th and 17th centuries in these parts. Knowing fables that dealt with such occurrences, and then having this experience in the mountains, all these things colored my childhood in a very special way. Later I learned that professors and scientists from universities in Warsaw and Lwów who went to these villages to study these people and their rituals supported what I had observed. Like me, they couldn't understand what was happening. It was so mysterious and secretive that you really couldn't get close to it. In fact, these people were so clannish that it was thought that if they discovered someone was trying to watch them, you could be in danger.

The prewar years were indeed idyllic for Staś, whose musical, social, and intellectual development laid a strong foundation for his future life as an artist. At the end of summer 1939, Staś had much to anticipate, including advanced studies with a new piano teacher, Helena Ottawowa, a renowned pedagogue whom Flora had recommended for him. But his entire life was about to change. A week after the Skrowaczewski family took the last train out of Mizun, Hitler's forces attacked Poland from the west, and soon Stalin's Soviet Union, allied with Hitler, treacherously attacked Poland from the east.

THREE

STATE OF OCCUPATION

We are fighting to save the world from the pestilence of Nazi tyranny and in defense of all that is most sacred to man.

—Winston Churchill, address to the House of Commons, Sept. 3, 1939

After achieving independence at the end of World War I, enduring the Russo-Polish War (1919–20), and finally achieving nearly two decades of stability, prosperity, and growth, Poland was suddenly attacked by two neighboring countries within the span of seventeen days.

The German-Soviet Nonaggression Pact, signed Aug. 23, 1939, gave Germany carte blanche to invade Poland without fear of Soviet intervention. In a secret clause of this pact, Germany and Russia agreed to split Poland evenly and then progressively annihilate it. At dawn on September 1, 1939, Germany's armed forces attacked Poland from the west, north, and south. Forty-one bombers raided Warsaw on the first day of the attack.[1] The air assault was particularly shocking: bombs were dropped on civilian centers as well as on military targets. Two days later, on September 3, Britain and France declared war on Germany. World War II was underway.

On September 12, Polish soldiers in Lwów held off approaching German troops and thwarted repeated attempts to capture the city. Staś heard artillery fire at night as he tried to sleep. He seized an old, rudimentary gun used for target practice and left his house to meet a high school friend. Together they ran to the front line located near a woodland area not far from the city limits. "We were terribly excited," Skrowaczewski remembered, "full of young, stupid, crazy exhilaration." Initially the Polish soldiers there did not welcome help from the two teenagers—Staś was less than three weeks shy of his sixteenth birthday—but within minutes the boys received real weapons and joined the men in a foxhole. They spent a day and a night on the front line. Staś' friend was hit by shrapnel and died right next to him.

At 4:00 a.m., September 17, the Soviet Union, in accord with the secret protocol, sent troops to occupy eastern Poland, which included Lwów. Stalin's treachery broke five recent treaties or nonaggression agreements between Poland and the Soviet Union—most notably the Treaty of Warsaw (1920), the Treaty of Riga (1921), and the 1932 nonaggression pact (renewed in 1934). Upon learning that Soviet tanks were in Lwów, Staś and his military companions ceased fighting and returned home. It was impossible to fight two of the world's most powerful armies attacking from both sides. "I gladly fled and headed back home," Skrowaczewski said later.

The Polish military could not compete with the magnitude of German and Russian troops and equipment, but it valiantly attempted to defend Poland during the entire month of September. Even after Warsaw fell on September 27, pockets of Polish troops continued fighting. The final Polish unit surrendered on October 6.[2] By the end of September the Nazis and Soviets had executed twenty-five thousand Polish civilians and sixty thousand Polish soldiers.[3]

Although Britain and France had declared war on Germany on September 3, Poland fought the German and Soviet forces singlehandedly for thirty-five days. President Franklin D. Roosevelt declared the United States a "neutral nation" at the start of Germany's campaign in Poland.

When Staś returned home on September 17, he told his anxious parents that he had been visiting a friend. Soon the family received news that Paweł's nephew Zygmunt had been killed on the front line and that Tadeusz, Zygmunt's brother, had been deported by the Soviets to a gulag in Siberia. Although Tadeusz survived the war, he never returned to Poland, and the family never saw him again.

On September 28 the two invading powers signed the Soviet-German Boundary and Friendship Treaty, which stipulated the division of Poland. Germany assumed control over western Poland, which had a population of more than twenty-two million as well as most of the nation's industry and raw materials. The Soviets controlled eastern Poland, an area with a population of thirteen million, including the cities of Lwów, Bialystok, and Wilno (today's Vilnius, Lithuania). Poland as a state ceased to exist.[4]

Daily life in Lwów was grim. Loudspeakers blared communist propaganda and revolutionary songs throughout the day, and people lived in constant fear of arrest, with good reason. During the next few years hundreds of thousands of Polish prisoners of war and civilians were arrested, deported, or murdered. Laborers and peasants generally were left alone, provided they were politically inactive and did not resist the confiscation of their property, but the Soviets frequently targeted members of the intelligentsia for arrest. To prevent members of similar ethnic groups and nationalities from uniting in rebellion, Stalin's plan grouped deportees with dissimilar backgrounds and scattered them among areas such as Siberia, Kazakhstan, Kyrgyzstan, and Turkmenistan.

Paweł was devastated to witness Soviet tanks rolling along the streets near his home. Soon after the Soviet occupation began, Staś heard his father remark, "And now another hundred years without independence." Paweł hated the Soviet brand of communism as much as he despised the Nazis' goals of eliminating minorities, particularly Jews. He was proud of Poland's long history as an open society that accepted minority populations.

Paweł's medical skills, valuable to the Soviets, protected his family for nearly two years. On June 22, 1941, Germany launched a surprise attack on the Soviet Union, whose military forces dispersed to battle its former ally. A few weeks later a deportation list was discovered in a nearby Soviet militia station. Had it not been for Germany's surprise attack, the Skrowaczewskis would have been among a group of Poles deported to Siberia in late June.

During the Soviet occupation Staś focused his energies on schoolwork. Before the war started he had finished four years of high school ("gymnasium," as it was called) but had two higher grades left to complete. His former school had been transformed into a technical institute, so his parents enrolled him in a prestigious girls' school that suddenly had become co-ed. He was one of three boys in a class of thirty girls. "We had a wonderful life at the school," Skrowaczewski recalled. "The two other boys were very bright, and we were well respected by the girls in the class and by the teachers." The curriculum was rigorous, and Staś studied hard. He remembered teachers who tried to present "both sides" of Polish history in an attempt to refute Soviet-manufactured revisionist versions.

Sports provided another diversion for the young Skrowaczewski. Lwów has an impressive history of organized and professional sports teams, but the Soviets used these athletics programs as a propaganda tool throughout World War II and later during the Cold War. Staś served as captain of his school's soccer team and also was a skilled volleyball player. He belonged to a sports club with excellent facilities, where he played volleyball and swam during the winter.

Food was scarce during the first winter of the Soviet occupation, and Skrowaczewski's parents struggled at times to maintain an income and find enough for the family to eat. Occasionally he took advantage of the free lunch with the "bad soup" that his sports club provided after some games. Lunch ("dinner" in Lwów) was served between 2:00 and 4:00 p.m.—the main meal of the day—and a light supper usually was served in the evening. "From day to day we didn't know what we would eat," Skrowaczewski remembered. "Sometimes it wasn't even a question of money. You just couldn't get food."

Staś' formal piano lessons were put on hold during the Soviet occupation. He had one or two lessons with Helena Ottawowa, but the constant disruptions of daily life made structured activity difficult. A general feeling of instability permeated everyday life. Each week brought new Soviet edicts, church closings, and name changes for buildings and streets. Staś' favorite activity, playing chamber music with his friends, essentially ended, but he continued to practice piano and to compose. On one occasion he had a reading of one of his chamber pieces, but the experience was memorable for reasons other than the music itself. Skrowaczewski recalled:

> When I attended some rehearsals of the Lwów Opera Orchestra, I got to know some of the musicians, especially one of the clarinet players. I had written a piece for string quartet and clarinet, and he organized a reading for me in one of the rooms at the opera house. I remember this only because after the rehearsal there was a gas leak in the room we were in, and it caused a big explosion in this room and some others in the house. They were destroyed, but the main structure of the house was undamaged. Afterwards the musicians joked that my music, which they couldn't stand, was so horrible it provoked this explosion sent by God! It was a cruel but funny joke.

A bright artistic light during this time was the influx of thousands of Jewish artists, musicians, and intellectuals to Lwów from Nazi-occupied western Poland. Before the war Lwów had nearly 110,000 Jewish residents, the third-largest population in Poland. After the Nazis invaded western Poland in 1939, many Polish Jews fled to the Soviet-occupied east, where they had equal or privileged status with other nationalities, depending on their cooperation with the Soviets. After 1939 Lwów's Jewish population increased by 160,000.[5] The city was "pulsating with music," according to Skrowaczewski: "There were four orchestras plus the opera and the conservatory student orchestras. There were plenty of wonderful concerts and famous musicologists, musicians, and conductors coming from the east of Russia and the west of Poland." He attended as many rehearsals and concerts as possible.

Named after the communist emblem, the "Star Orchestra" consisted of refugees from the west, and Staś attended its rehearsals, which were held in a large barn. He was friendly with the young Polish conductor, although he wasn't impressed by the man's large movements and beat patterns. When the orchestra needed the triangle and tambourine parts covered, Staś volunteered but quickly discovered the challenges of playing percussion. "Some conductors at that time were primitive, but most were excellent. They didn't critique my playing because they knew I was a composer and interested in music, so they were nice to me," he said, "but I realized that what I was doing wasn't very good." Skrowaczewski particularly remembered one outstanding Ukrainian conductor, Natan Rakhlin, who guest conducted the Star Orchestra and the Lwów Opera.

Although Staś enjoyed Lwów's flourishing musical scene, he failed to comprehend its underlying motivation—propaganda. In 1936 the Soviet government unleashed its venom on Shostakovich's opera *Lady Macbeth of the Mtsensk District*, in an infamous *Pravda* editorial entitled "Chaos Instead of Music."[6] Music that was even remotely abstract in subject matter or in idiom was banned. Musicians in Lwów quickly realized that artistic censorship was the price they paid for the city's abundant musical activity during the Soviet occupation.

The Soviets staged a huge festival on May 1, 1940. During the unusually frigid afternoon, everyone was forced to attend the grand parade extolling the benefits of communist rule. Staś shivered in the cold as he watched the Soviet militia roll through Lwów and distribute candy to people on the street. "This was the first taste of sugar we had in a long time," he recalled, "and they said, 'You see how wonderful our father Stalin is to provide us with gifts.'" The irony of the event was not lost on Staś as he stood in the cold, sucking on his candies.

By the end of June 1940, Germany had conquered Austria, Czechoslovakia, Poland, Denmark, Norway, Belgium, Luxembourg, the Netherlands, and France. Stalin had attacked Finland the previous November, eventually assuming partial control over it, and Mussolini declared war on France and Great Britain.

In August, Hitler unleashed the massive air offensive known as the Battle of Britain. A few days later he began "The Day of the Eagle" attack.[7] The Blitz, a prolonged series of full-scale air attacks on several British cities, followed in early September. German forces continued to bomb the United Kingdom (U.K.) during the next nine months. Staś began learning English and followed the war's progress by listening secretly to the BBC (British Broadcasting Corporation). He heard about the courageous Kościuszko Polish Fighter Squadron and its role in the Battle of Britain. He felt proud of the squadron's significant contribution to the defense of the U.K., Poland's key ally in the war.

That fall, as Skrowaczewski began his last year of high school, the war intensified. In Warsaw, 150,000 Jews were ordered by the Nazis to be walled up in a Jewish district of the city, creating a ghetto of over four hundred thousand people in a space that previously accommodated only 250,000.[8] Within six months deaths from starvation in this ghetto and another in Łódź totaled more than 15,000.[9] Reports of the horrors at Auschwitz and other concentration camps spread throughout Poland.

Nearing his final exams, Skrowaczewski pondered his future. Pursuing a higher education in chemistry seemed probable. Music also was on his mind, but uncertainty was attached to that profession. "It was not possible to dream about any life beyond the war because no one knew what would happen day to day," he recalled. "To have something to eat was already a good life."

On June 21, 1941, Skrowaczewski received his high school diploma, and that evening he was at his school enjoying food with his friends at a celebration party. It was a beautiful summer night with a light breeze in the air. The full moon shone down on the young adults as they took a respite from their uncertain futures and reveled in their accomplishments until midnight.

Four hours later Skrowaczewski awoke to the sound of bombs falling on the Lwów airport. Germany had launched a surprise attack on the Soviet Union. "I'll never forget the contrast of these events," Skrowaczewski said, "our party and wonderful weather, and then suddenly a new war."

FOUR

THE UNDERGROUND

When the Nazis came, it was all over. It was impossible; even gatherings for trios or quartets were not allowed. You risked being killed on the spot if they discovered any local culture.

—Stanisław Skrowaczewski

Artillery fire and exploding bombs were heard on both sides of Lwów for a week before the Nazis entered the city on June 29, 1941.[1] Most of the fighting took place about thirty-five miles outside the city; inside, the Soviet army and 300,000 "imported" Soviet administrative and party officials were in a panic. With the Nazis fast approaching, the Soviets focused on their own safety and not on their prisoners.

Eight months earlier the Soviets had arrested and imprisoned Staś' friend Jan Łopuszański for reasons then unknown. After the war Jan learned that a classmate had denounced him, "probably because of some old vengeance," according to Skrowaczewski. "Just by saying that he had belonged to the [Boy] Scouts, or something like that before the war, was enough for them to arrest him." Deeply affected by the news, Staś wondered if he would be next.

"When Germany launched its surprise attack on the Soviet Union in 1941, they took Lwów in a week," Skrowaczewski said. "There was such a panic in the Soviet administration that in a few prisons they forgot to kill all their inmates. A Soviet militia was headed for Jan's prison, but he escaped just minutes before they arrived. He was very lucky." In three other prisons Soviet security forces brutally murdered an estimated six thousand to eight thousand Polish and Ukrainian prisoners in their Lwów prison cells during the last two days of the occupation.[2]

Within weeks after Nazi occupation forces entered Lwów, universities and other schools were closed. Nazi *Einsatzkommandos* murdered twenty-five professors and members of their families and friends within hours of their arrest.[3] "They had a list prepared at the beginning of World War II," Skrowaczewski said. "The SS Nazi *Einsatzkommandos* came with some collaborating Ukrainian nationalist groups and arrested those professors and their families. This cast fear and terror over what might happen next."

The city remained eerily calm. The emotional devastation and anxiety that had tormented Paweł two years earlier returned. He doubted that his family, particularly his almost eighteen-year-old son, could stay alive under the Nazi regime. Staś' first survival test came the week before the Nazis entered Lwów.

The Germans bombed Soviet positions in areas north and south of Lwów, but the city itself remained relatively safe during this campaign. The young Skrowaczewski decided to visit friends who lived in Nowy Lwów, a small residential area developed during the 1920s as an alternative to the crowded city center. The main railroad line leading to Bucharest and Vienna, a potential bombing target, was located half a mile from Nowy Lwów.

Staś was socializing with friends when they heard an explosion. Fearing they could be hit next, they tried to escape the villa. His friends made it out safely, but Staś hesitated, unsure about the best course of action. Just then a bomb exploded nearby, causing one of the villa's brick walls to collapse on his hands. (Had the mass of bricks struck his head, he would have been killed.) Shaken, Staś rose to his feet and walked home alone.

The full extent of the injuries to Staś' hands was not readily apparent. Paweł took his son to medical colleagues who put casts on both hands. Although most of the fingers were only badly sprained, some bones were broken, and his hands suffered permanent nerve damage. Only after six months of therapy did Staś recover functional use of his hands. Everyday tasks posed no problem, but when he played the piano, his hand muscles cramped within fifteen or twenty seconds. Eventually he could play the piano for short periods of time, and he resumed violin playing, although the hand positions caused even greater pain. Today Skrowaczewski can play Bach's Prelude in C minor for only a minute before his hands shut down. Occasionally the cramps recur when he's driving a car or simply holding a fork and knife, but he rarely experiences pain while conducting. In 2008 an accidental fall at home triggered terrible pain in one of his fingers. Doctors discovered that the finger probably had been broken in the bombing incident sixty-seven years earlier and had never properly healed.

A career as a pianist was no longer an option, but even before the accident Skrowaczewski had begun to doubt his commitment to that path. "This was the solution from heaven!" he declared years later. "I was not afraid of the struggle to obtain the freedom of technique," he said. "The question in my mind was the direction. I had severe doubts."[4] In a sense, the piano was too limiting for his musical appetite—the orchestra was always what had most interested him. Composing and studying the great musical literature fully engaged his mind and spirit. Soon it became clear to him that composition—and later, conducting—were his true callings.

Within the first months of the German occupation, life in Lwów became extremely restricted. Each day brought new orders and rules. Anticipating battles with the Soviets during the winter, the Nazis confiscated every item that might help them, including skis. It was difficult to find and purchase food. The Soviets had banned Polish currency (without any exchange), and now the Germans outlawed Soviet rubles. A special German currency was introduced that was also in use in Nazi-occupied central Poland.

To supplement his father's income and to give himself a margin of safety, Staś undertook odd jobs. Initially he had hoped his chemistry talent might earn him a wage, and when the Nazis opened several labor schools, including one for chemistry, Staś took some courses there. The school was soon dissolved, however, forcing him to work as a construction laborer repairing bombed or dilapidated buildings. This physical work often involved transporting wood and cement. Later he worked in the suburbs of Lwów polishing and stacking fine imported woods. Surprisingly, Staś managed this hard manual labor despite his injured hands; the nerve damage affected only his fine-motor skills.

He occasionally worked as an organist at the Bernardine church. On one occasion the job put Skrowaczewski in a precarious situation:

> As usual, during the Mass at the Bernardine church I was playing music from *Tannhäuser* and *Parsifal* on the organ, and the priests had to stop me so they could go on with ritual. After the service I heard the sound of boots coming up the stairs to the organ loft, so menacing: "boom, boom, boom." I stopped playing, and two German soldiers stood before me. One was a high officer with many stars on his chest, and the other was his assistant. I was sure they were going to take me. But suddenly the officer saluted and said, "How superbly you play! We enjoy so much this Wagner." And then they left. Thank God I wasn't playing Mendelssohn!

He found solace in composing. By the time he left Lwów with his parents in December 1945, he had written six piano sonatas, three violin sonatas, four string quartets, two sets of songs for soprano and piano, *Overture in a Classical Style*, two symphonies, and a few *a cappella* choral pieces. The choral pieces were rehearsed and conducted by the organist at a local church attended by the Skrowaczewskis. One work was a setting of "Salve Regina" (Hail, Holy Queen), in honor of the Blessed Virgin Mary—which no doubt pleased Staś' mother—and another was based on a poem by Alexander Pushkin. The songs for soprano and piano, some of which Skrowaczewski later set for soprano and orchestra, were inspired by literature from the neoromantic school of "Young Poland" of the late 19th century. Leading Polish writers of this period, such as Stanisław Wyspiański, Stefan Żeromski, Maria Konopnicka, and Nobel laureate Władysław Stanisław Reymont, were influenced by French poetry and by the work of Nietzsche. "These poets represented a new wave in Poland during the last decade of the 19th century," Skrowaczewski explained. "They were romantic but also more modern."

Skrowaczewski performed his violin sonatas with a gifted young violinist named Baczyński. An older professional German violinist who was a member of one of the orchestras in Lwów also played the young composer's sonatas. Ever inquisitive, Skrowaczewski visited the violinist at his home to seek advice on writing for the instrument.

Musical life ceased for Poles under the Nazi regime. The occupiers took over the Lwów Philharmonic and the Opera, added some of their own musicians, and installed German conductors. Performances were *Nur für Deutsche* (only for Germans). A gathering of Lwów citizenry of any size was suspect, and the penalty for such action could be death. In response to this artistic oppression a "musical underground" developed, consisting of a network of musicians who gathered secretly to play with one another and to present informal concerts occasionally.

Residents of the Skrowaczewskis' apartment building met outside Lwów to play string quartets in isolated homes, performing for families and small groups while sentries kept watch. Paweł's colleague Dr. Budzanowski, an ophthalmologist and professional violist, organized the quartet. Staś had a crush on the first violinist, and he remembered that the cellist was outstanding. When he couldn't secure his regular players, Budzanowski asked Skrowaczewski to play second violin:

> My playing was terrible. I know it was bothering them, but they didn't have any choice. They valued me as a composer and played my first quartets; however, they were not impressed with my violin playing. This was not a surprise to me, as my learning how to play violin was not deep (it was not my principal interest). However, it gave me a lot, for I grasped musical nuances that were helpful in later years. Our quartet repertoire was rich, from Haydn and Mozart to Beethoven and Schumann. Schumann was especially interesting to me: very deep and different from other composers.[5]

Staś also explored other music-making opportunities with his friends. To the extent that his injured hands allowed, he gave private piano concerts for five or six people at a doctor's apartment near his home. The programs consisted of traditional repertoire and occasionally his piano sonatas. He also played violin, viola, and piano with small ensembles of underground musicians. Although he had no idea then that conducting would become his dominant profession, Skrowaczewski's experiences as a chamber musician during the war years profoundly affected his future career. He explained the connection years later:

> Any of the chamber works of composers such as Mozart, Brahms, Dvořák, or Schumann are quite different from their symphonic compositions; they are sometimes much richer and, in a sense, they explain the symphonic works. To know only four Brahms symphonies and nothing else of Brahms, no piano literature or chamber music, is unsatisfactory. It is not enough for a conductor.

Playing chamber music gave Skrowaczewski a sense of co-creation. During rehearsals he had heated discussions with his fellow musicians about artistic interpretation. This collaborative process exposed him to a variety of performing possibilities and gave him confidence in his own feeling for musical style. "In such discussions a conductor woke up within myself," he recalled. "It was the best conducting school for me. I absorbed such basic knowledge that conducting would come automatically, quite naturally."[6]

Through the musical underground Skrowaczewski developed his budding conducting instincts with a chamber orchestra of twenty players. He and colleagues biked ten miles outside Lwów to a village where the father of one of the cellists had a farm. The youthful musicians rehearsed and presented informal concerts in a large barn. One by one, audience members entered the barn surreptitiously, for this enterprise was dangerous for everyone. Skrowaczewski led the orchestra in standard repertoire, his own compositions, and works by other young Lwów composers. He conducted the premiere of a chamber opera scored for three voices, single woodwinds, and strings by Aleksander Frączkiewicz (1910–94), an acquaintance who later became an important teacher of music theory. Waldemar Voise, a brilliant young man fluent in several languages, participated in these underground gatherings and after the war became a professor at the Université Paris Sorbonne.

During the Soviet occupation Skrowaczewski had attended rehearsals of the Lwów Philharmonic, but now that the Nazis controlled the orchestra, he could no longer do so. Having spent many hours in the Lwów Conservatory, he knew the building's layout extremely well. He climbed into the conservatory's attic and secretly watched the Philharmonic's rehearsals through a tiny window. The venture was worth the risk because Fritz Weidlich, a well-known conductor at that time, led the orchestra. For the first time, Skrowaczewski heard a skilled German conductor prepare the standard German repertoire of Beethoven, Brahms, and Bruckner.

Meanwhile, the war's rampant destruction continued. Hitler had misjudged Germany's ability to defeat the Soviets in a mere few weeks.[7] By early December, less than six months after Germany launched its attack, 171,000 German soldiers had been killed.[8] Nazi retribution was brutal. One horrific example was the mass murder of one hundred thousand Soviet prisoners of war. In mid-winter the Nazis corralled them into an exposed field enclosed by barbed wire, with no protection and no food.[9]

Mass deaths became a daily occurrence in Russia, Poland, and Ukraine. During the harsh winter of 1941 more than four thousand people a day died from starvation in the Warsaw ghetto. In Leningrad the rate was four hundred starvation deaths per day.[10] In December 1941 the Germans forcibly segregated the Jewish population of Lwów, which numbered well over one hundred thousand, into a ghetto. Nearly five thousand of the elderly or ill were shot to create more space there.[11] More than half of Skrowaczewski's forty former classmates were Jewish, and many of his friends were killed within the first year of the Nazi occupation. After the war he stayed in contact with a few Jewish friends who had avoided the ghetto by hiding, with the help of Christian Poles. In the late 1970s and early 1980s, when Skrowaczewski was conducting in Australia, he reunited with three survivors who had moved there following the Soviet's ethnic cleansing of Lwów.

The Nazis' persecution of Lwów Jews included the murder of Dr. Juliusz Schauder, Skrowaczewski's secondary school mathematics professor and an ardent Polish patriot. Schauder posthumously became one of the important names in the history of mathematics: the formulation of his fixed-point theorem made lasting contributions to solving differential equations. Skrowaczewski had been one of Schauder's favorite pupils because he usually was the first student to raise his hand when the professor asked a question.

By the second year of the German occupation, Skrowaczewski—nineteen years old and in excellent health—was a prime candidate for deportation. After a routine medical checkup, the Nazis considered him fit and ready for a labor camp. Fortunately, through a connection his father had with a colleague, he secured a job at the Weigl Institute of Typhus Research, a situation that ultimately saved his life.

A brilliant scientist and notable Polish patriot, Rudolf Stefan Weigl (1883–1957) protected many members of the Lwów intelligentsia as well as minorities. He employed them at his institute as lice feeders and general or scientific workers during the first Soviet occupation and the subsequent German occupation.

In 1909, Nobel laureate Charles Nicolle of the Pasteur Institute in Paris discovered that a particular species of louse was the vector of typhus. Weigl, a professor of biology at the University of Jan Kazimierz in Lwów, developed the first successful typhus vaccine during the early 1920s. After a failed effort to produce the vaccine on a large scale using pigs as lice feeders, human feeders were used. During World War II the vaccine was mass-produced in Weigl's laboratory until spring 1944. Thanks to Weigl, typhus is not of major significance today, but up until the mid-20th century it caused millions of deaths, including the demise of Napoleon's Grand Army in 1812.[12]

Wacław Szybalski, professor emeritus of oncology at McArdle Laboratory for Cancer Research at the University of Wisconsin, supervised a breeding unit of lice feeders comprised of world-renowned mathematicians, including Stefan Banach from the Lwów School of Mathematics, and important scientists. Szybalski and Skrowaczewski had been friends since their early years as students in Flora Listowska's piano class. Szybalski described the benefits of employment:

> During the Nazi occupation of Lwów (1941–44), employment in Weigl's Institute provided some degree of protection from the random arrests and deportation to the Nazi concentration camps; [the] Gestapo seemed to prefer to avoid "dealings" with persons from whom they might accidentally acquire typhus-infected lice (it was well known that carrying lice was our occupational hazard). Moreover, all employees carried an impressive-looking identification card (*Ausweiss*) from the *Oberkommando des Heeres* (Office of the Commander-in-Chief of the Germany Army); this *Ausweiss* was another of Weigl's life-saving "inventions".... [Employees of Weigl were] entitled to special food rations and [were] at least partially immune from arrests, deportations, and/or death during the Nazi occupation. Aspects of employment in Weigl's Institute had some elements in common with Spielberg's Hollywood movie *Schindler's List*.[13]

To produce the vaccine, lice were infected with typhus, and human feeders, although vaccinated, put themselves at risk in offering a blood meal. Seven to eleven cages, each housing hundreds of lice, were placed on feeders' legs for forty-five minutes once a day for twelve days. Each cage had one wall constructed of fine-screen mesh through which the lice could access human skin and blood.

Skrowaczewski remembers feeling a slight burning and itching sensation, especially as the lice matured, but the overall experience was not entirely negative. "Nice girls" working at the institute taught him how to place the cages on his legs, and the general atmosphere in the laboratory was pleasant. However, he suspects that the occasional recurrence of an itchy rash may be a residual effect of his lice-feeding more than sixty years ago. Before and after lice application, feeders' legs were washed with alcohol containing a mercury chloride solution ("sublimat"), a commonly used disinfectant at that time, despite being known to be very toxic when swallowed. Possibly this chemical might have had a lasting impact.[14]

While working at the Weigl Institute, Skrowaczewski began "underground university classes." The Nazis closed all Lwów universities, but dozens of professors held well-organized secret sessions for interested students. It was important for Skrowaczewski to "mentally survive and to develop somehow and not completely lose time because of the war," he later explained.

Roman Ingarden (1893–1970), the eminent Polish phenomenologist, philosopher, ontologist, and aesthetician, invited Skrowaczewski and a few other young people to study with him. Ingarden, who played and hosted chamber music in his home and attended concerts regularly, was well aware of Skrowaczewski's talents as a pianist and composer. The opportunity to meet with Ingarden, particularly for a young man at an impressionable age, profoundly influenced the development of Skrowaczewski's aesthetic principles.

Born in Kraków, Ingarden studied math and philosophy in Lwów before attending Göttingen University, where he was the prized pupil of Edmund Husserl from 1912 to 1915. A realist phenomenologist, Ingarden opposed his teacher's turn to transcendental idealism during his Göttingen period. His best-known work, *The Literary Work of Art* (1931), presents an ontological approach to various types of works of art and a means of mentally processing them. From Ingarden's perspective, ontology of art is a form of conceptual analysis that explores the meaning of experiences that could be presented as a work of art.[15]

Ingarden's explorations of aesthetic objects and values were the primary areas that influenced Skrowaczewski. Ingarden made clear distinctions between what constituted a physical object, a work of art, and an aesthetic entity. Skrowaczewski explained how studying with Ingarden affected him:

> My musical tastes were organic in me because of all the music I was exposed to and studied in my childhood. And then came this man who, although he never told me "this is good, this is bad," liked the music that I liked. It somehow deepened in me my preferences, even though I already felt them innately. The whole metaphysical atmosphere in his house contrasted with the danger that every day there was the possibility you could be killed on the street. This contrast really formed my feeling for what to compose and how and what to conduct. It was not just the notes but also the meaning beyond the notes, which from the beginning I kept as more important.

Sometimes Skrowaczewski had individual sessions with Ingarden; at other times he was joined by Jan Łopuszański and one or two more students. They arrived and departed at different times so as not to cause any suspicion of a group gathering. Because it was impossible to meet with any regularity, they chose certain weeks when they could meet every other day. During the winter, when the Nazis imposed curfews, they sometimes spent the night at the professor's home.

The young men and their teacher analyzed and discussed works of art from several philosophical viewpoints, including their meaning within the historical contexts of their creation. Schopenhauer, Thomas Mann, Nietzsche, and the phenomenological ideas of Husserl were among the class topics. Ingarden took a Socratic approach in these sessions, and Skrowaczewski prepared many questions for his esteemed professor. The open-ended sessions sometimes lasted for hours. They listened to music and explored Ingarden's library long into the night.

Skrowaczewski later commented, "Nietzsche held my interest because of his connection to Wagner and Strauss, but the philosopher who interested and affected me most was Schopenhauer, who wrote so beautifully about music."

Proud of his association with Ingarden, Skrowaczewski asked him for a letter confirming that he was his student. His early professional biographies even note that he earned a diploma in philosophy—a benign misnomer when one considers the intimate nature of Skrowaczewski's study with Ingarden, which undoubtedly would have earned him a formal degree if held under the auspices of a university.

Skrowaczewski also attended underground classes of Dr. Chyliński, a recognized musicologist in Poland. He gave Skrowaczewski various music history books and his own articles to study and discuss. These sessions were informative for Skrowaczewski but did not compare to his Ingarden sessions "in the way that the study of philosophy would completely open your mind," he said.

In January 1943, Britain's prime minister, Winston Churchill, and U.S. president Franklin D. Roosevelt met at Casablanca, Morocco, to discuss a joint strategy for ending the war. Their plans included a persistent massive bombing campaign on Germany and a secret plan to liberate part of German-occupied Europe, beginning in June 1944 with the D-Day landings in Normandy. Desperate for the end of the Nazi regime, Poles nevertheless feared the prospect of a Soviet "liberation."[16] Memories of Soviet tyranny during the recent occupation—including the murder and deportation of tens of thousands of Poles—remained fresh in their minds.

Germany suffered military setbacks and defeats throughout 1943, but the deportation of Jews to concentration camps continued unabated. Jews in the Warsaw ghetto valiantly resisted German deportation squads, but by the spring they succumbed to the onslaught of Nazi forces. In April, Stalin broke relations with the London-based Polish government-in-exile, whose prime minister, Władysław Sikorski, died in a mysterious plane crash. This break in diplomatic relations was in response to the Polish government's call for an International Red Cross investigation into one of the most grisly events of the war.[17] In March the German army discovered mass graves in the Katyń Forest near Smolensk, Russia. The Germans formed an international commission and found the Soviets guilty of the murders, though Western media at the time held Nazi Germany responsible.[18]

The horrific situation began in late spring 1940, when at least 21,857 Polish prisoners of war—military officers, doctors, civil servants, teachers, and other professionals—suddenly disappeared from three prison camps in the Soviet Union. Forty-four hundred prisoners were taken to the Katyń Forest and shot in the back of the head. The Soviets, who had been at war with the Germans for two years by this time, perfidiously blamed the deaths on the Nazis. Mass graves of the remaining 10,600 victims were not discovered until 1990, when Soviet authorities unearthed them. Not until 1992, a year after the fall of the Soviet Union, did the Russian government publicly acknowledge its remorse over the Katyń massacre and other mass killings, and provide some documents to Poland detailing additional mass graves.[19]

Stalin demanded huge territorial concessions from Poland as the price of reestablishing diplomatic relations. He wanted to reassume control of eastern Poland (the area specified by the German-Soviet Nonaggression Pact of 1939), with the Baltic coast of East Prussia thrown in for good measure. Furthermore, he supported the Soviet-established Polish Communist Committee rather than the Polish government-in-exile in London and the Polish underground.[20] Although the United States and Britain suspected that Stalin's demands were part of an overall plan for communist expansion, the two Western powers declined to confront the Soviet leader for fear that that they could not defeat Germany without Soviet support. When the "Big Three" (Roosevelt, Churchill, and Stalin) met for the first time in person at the Tehran Conference in late 1943, they secretly agreed on a division of postwar Europe that would leave Poland largely under Soviet control.[21]

The "liberation" of Poland began on January 4, 1944, when the Soviets crossed the 1939 Polish border; however, six months elapsed before the Red Army entered "official" Polish territory by crossing the River Bug on July 19. A week before the Soviets crossed the Bug, they had delivered a massive blow to the Germans during a battle in Brody, a fortress town thirty-five miles from Lwów. Thirty thousand Nazi soldiers died during the weeklong battle.[22]

After the invasion Stalin installed a pro-Soviet government, the Polish Committee of National Liberation, which had no connection to the Polish government-in-exile. Entering eastern Poland, the Soviets systematically dismantled the Polish underground resistance army, the Armia Krajowa (AK), by arresting, deporting, or killing AK soldiers.[23]

When the Soviets advanced to Lwów, Skrowaczewski faced the greatest threat to his survival. For several days before the battle inside the city began, Skrowaczewski hid in a secret space, accessible only by a ladder, under the floor of his parents' apartment. The concierge of the five-story apartment building, an unfriendly Ukrainian, knew of this hiding place, and Skrowaczewski's parents feared that he would report them and turn in their son.

Members of the Ukrainian nationalistic group in Lwów believed that the city, which they had battled the Poles to possess immediately after World War I, had been ceded to them first by Austria. However, the Poles took back Lwów from the Ukrainians, and it remained under Polish rule until World War II. The Ukrainians' resentment of the Poles spurred their cooperation with the Nazis during the German occupation of Poland. As the Soviets fell upon Lwów, the Germans were fortified around the city, and some radical Ukrainian nationalists murdered Poles.

Fearing that their son might be discovered and killed by the Ukrainian police, Paweł and Zofia decided he should change his hiding place to the cloister at the Bernardine church. The beautiful 16th-century baroque structure was a ten-minute walk from the Skrowaczewskis' apartment, but it was a dangerous trip to make alone. As a cover, Skrowaczewski marched alongside columns of Soviet troops, by then already in the city's streets, advancing block by block. He felt relieved when he reached the church's fortress-like wooden doors. The Bernardine monks knew Skrowaczewski from his organ-playing days and willingly harbored him. The monastery, adjacent to the church, had a huge garden surrounded by a thick twenty-foot-high wall. The church, monastery, and cloister felt like a safe enclave to Skrowaczewski. Fortunately neither the Soviets nor the Nazis were interested in the buildings. Skrowaczewski spent two nights at the monastery lying awake listening to the eerie, distant sounds of a lone plane dropping bombs. He worried constantly about his parents.

After the Soviets further infiltrated the city, he decided to return home. He ran in a panic amid the chaos and commotion in the streets, where citizens ran helter-skelter, carrying food and seeking safety. He maneuvered around corpses that lay on the streets and sidewalks, and he never forgot the sight of the charred body of a German soldier still manning a tank.

Gun battles flared in Lwów during the next two days. Skrowaczewski watched from his parents' window as Soviet and German soldiers darted in and out from street corners, shooting at each other. Soviet tanks suddenly approached a large ornate government building used as a German command center, located one street over from the family's apartment. The tanks blew up the bunkers surrounding the building and then the building itself. Pressure from the huge explosion blew out the windows of the Skrowaczewskis' first-floor apartment. No one was injured, but furniture and paintings were destroyed. Stray bullets were imbedded in a wall of their home, and corpses littered the street outside. The battles ended when unexpected support from the doomed Polish AK army helped the Soviets fend off the majority of the German troops.

Although the Soviets had driven most of the Germans out of Lwów, remaining Nazi troops moved battalions around the city, and pockets of Ukrainian police continued to murder Poles. Skrowaczewski decided to flee. His parents suggested that he stay with the Zakrzewski family, close friends who lived near a cemetery located high on a hill overlooking the city.

Again using a small battalion of Soviet troops for cover, Skrowaczewski began making his way to the Zakrzewski home. When the troops asked him where he was going, Skrowaczewski, speaking half in Polish and half in broken Ukrainian, explained that he was escaping because he feared the Germans would be back. The Soviet troops scoffed at this notion, gruffly telling him that all the Germans had fled. That evening the Germans surprised the Soviets at the cemetery near the Zakrzewski residence. Skrowaczewski spent all night with the Zakrzewskis in their cellar while German and Soviet machine-gun fire lit up the cemetery. When the battle ended, the remaining German troops moved on, and the Soviets began their second occupation of Lwów undeterred. The Germans did not depart quietly, however; they dropped bombs over the entire city. From Skrowaczewski's vantage point on the hill he could see Lwów for several miles in all directions:

> The Zakrzewskis' home was set a good four hundred feet high on a hill. There were rows of hills forming a valley with the city below. You could see almost the entire downtown of Lwów from this view. I witnessed the most incredible scene standing there. The city was completely dark, so in order to see their bombing targets, the Nazis released burning phosphorus lamps attached to parachutes to illuminate the sky. The sight of these lampions patiently falling, producing blinding white light and huge clouds of black and white smoke, was unreal. This image coinciding with exploding bombs was absolutely incredible. It was like a slowly falling rain of bright light, almost as if night had turned to day. Combined with smoke and light coming over the vapors from these illuminating bombs, I felt like I was in hell. I'll never forget this searing image. If I were a painter, I could paint it.

He went home the next day, relieved to find that his parents had survived. "It was extremely quiet," he remembered. "You didn't know what to expect. You could be killed on the street, yet I wanted to go home, so I took this risk. It was a very hot period; everything was risky."

FIVE

FORMAL EDUCATION

I received diplomas from the conservatory, but I never studied there. They closed me in a room for one hour and asked me to write a theme and variations.

—Stanisław Skrowaczewski

As the Soviets began their second occupation of Lwów in late July 1944, Warsaw braced for a battle that was destined to be one of the most devastating Polish defeats of World War II. The German occupation of Warsaw had weakened, and the AK resistance forces saw an opportunity to reclaim their capital city. They believed that the Soviets could not disregard a successful uprising against the Germans, and they hoped to thwart the installation of Stalin's puppet government in Poland. Expectations were high, and the commander of the AK forces told the Polish government-in-exile in London to be prepared to assist them with bombardments.[1]

But military support for the AK never came. Beginning on August 1, the AK battled German forces singlehandedly for sixty-three days. Unbeknown to the AK, the Germans were planning a counterattack against the Soviets and had enhanced their forces in Warsaw. The AK's resistance gave Hitler the excuse to unleash the full wrath of the Nazis on the city. Heinrich Himmler, Germany's Reichsfürer-SS, ordered his troops to kill every inhabitant and to destroy every home.[2] Though Soviet-controlled radio earlier had appealed to the people of Warsaw to rise up against the Germans, Stalin privately denounced the AK's efforts and stopped the Soviet militia from approaching Warsaw. The Soviet Army remained a mile from the city, where it watched and listened to Warsaw's ongoing destruction.[3] Stalin simply allowed the Germans to do his dirty work for him.

Without Soviet help the Warsaw uprising was doomed. Churchill, who had relied heavily upon AK intelligence reports to wage war, urged Stalin to assist the Poles, but the Russian leader refused. Stalin also denied the Allies access to Soviet bases for refueling planes that could carry much-needed supplies to the city. Roosevelt could not pressure the Soviets, due to his secret quid pro quo agreement with Stalin that allowed American bombers to use Soviet airfields in Siberia en route to Japan.[4] Determined to help Warsaw, Churchill acted independently, sending twenty-eight bombers with thirty-five tons of arms and ammunition to be dropped by parachute on the city. Less than half of the bombers completed the dangerous mission, and less than five tons of supplies actually made it to the beleaguered Polish soldiers.[5]

The insurgents' heroic efforts ended in surrender to the Nazis on October 2, 1944. Polish casualties included an estimated 200,000 to 250,000 civilians (many of whom had been savagely murdered) and more than fifteen thousand AK and civilian soldiers. Warsaw lay in ruins.[6]

To restore a semblance of normalcy to his life in Soviet-occupied Lwów, Skrowaczewski returned to his music studies, having decided to obtain degrees in composition and conducting. Because of his experience in both areas, the leadership of the Lwów Conservatory waived formal courses required for the degrees; his reputation as an outstanding young musician was known to most of the conservatory's professors. During the German occupation Skrowaczewski showed some of his compositions to Adam Sołtys, the composer, conductor, and musicologist who led the conservatory before the war. The musically conservative Sołtys, a professor of composition, had little advice to offer Skrowaczewski on his modern music. He later served on Skrowaczewski's exam committee for his composition degree, but his predilection for a conventional style did not hamper the outcome.

Skrowaczewski met occasionally with renowned Ukrainian composer, conductor, and educator Mykola Kolessa (1903–2006), who was on the conservatory faculty. Kolessa briefly mentored Skrowaczewski while he prepared for his conducting-exam performance, which included his *Overture in the Classical Style*, Mendelssohn's Violin Concerto (featuring a talented student as soloist), and Weber's Overture to *Euryanthe*.

Kolessa influenced several generations of Ukrainian musicians. He championed Ukrainian composers and gave distinguished performances of the standard repertoire. His book, *Foundations of Conducting Technique*, was published in the Ukraine in 1967. He also composed orchestral, chamber, and choral works, including numerous songs.[7]

Wasyly Barwiński (1888–1963), the Ukrainian composer who directed the conservatory during the second Soviet occupation, was lead examiner for Skrowaczewski's composition test. Skrowaczewski recalled the event:

> They closed me in a room for one hour and asked me to write a theme and variations. My theme used very classical harmonies, but there was a chord that had a B-flat with a B-natural in the bass. Barwiński, who was quite conservative musically, took exception to what I wrote. For me, this was just everyday bread. I explained to him that in any Mozart composition one can find this type of harmony, such as in his Requiem. Barwiński was taken aback with this explanation. But they gave me the diploma anyway.

Barwiński oversaw an expansion of music education opportunities in L'viv, as the city of Lwów was known under the Soviet occupation. The suppression of the arts under the German occupation was lifted under the Soviets, who funded the opera house and the L'viv Philharmonic Society, which included a full symphony orchestra and a chamber orchestra. But this artistic support did not come without prohibitions. A chapter of the Union of Soviet Composers was established in L'viv, and Barwiński, Sołtys, the Kolessas (Mykola and his ethnomusicologist father, Filaret), and several other prominent local musicians were forced to become members. Established in 1932, the Union consisted of Soviet-approved composers charged with "supervising" all musical works created in the U.S.S.R. Stalin wanted music to promote Communist Party values, and musicians had to abide by this oppressive edict or suffer the consequences. During the first Soviet occupation, Lwów's musical community had just become aware of this policy; now the artists had to live by it.

With composition and conducting degrees in his pocket by 1945, Skrowaczewski gave new thought to his musical career. He was inspired by the rehearsals and concerts he attended, most of them led by Russian conductors who drew heavily on the Tchaikovsky repertoire. Natan Rakhlin was one such conductor who impressed him. Largely forgotten today, Rakhlin (1906–79) was an extraordinary musician who could play most of the instruments of the orchestra—an ability he believed all conductors should possess. A gifted orchestra builder and teacher, he served as music director of the National Symphony Orchestra of Ukraine, the Kiev Philharmonic, and the State Orchestra of the U.S.S.R., which he conducted in the premiere of Shostakovich's Symphony no. 11 in 1957.[8]

The events leading to the war's conclusion unfolded rapidly. The Soviets entered a devastated Warsaw on January 17, 1945, just three days after beginning their major offensive and three months after the AK surrendered to the Germans following the uprising.[9]

In February 1945, Churchill, Roosevelt, and Stalin met at Yalta, the resort city on the Black Sea in Crimea (now an autonomous republic in Ukraine). With Germany's defeat on the horizon, the three leaders had to agree on postwar issues, and Poland came out the loser, just as it had at the Tehran meeting two years earlier. Essentially all of eastern Poland was approved for Soviet acquisition, and the trio agreed that the leadership of the Polish government-in-exile had to join the Soviet-installed administration, newly established in Warsaw, and form a new "united" provisional government.[10]

Like millions of Poles, Skrowaczewski was outraged and saddened by the results of the meetings at Tehran and Yalta:

> Tehran and Yalta especially, in my opinion, were the most depressing political aspects of the war. Roosevelt, of course, was very sick and dying around the time of Yalta, but at least his advisors could have been aware of what was happening. Roosevelt gave everything to Stalin, and poor Churchill was completely shut out. He couldn't do anything. The agreement at Yalta was one of the most tragic mistakes of the end of the war. Unfortunately, Roosevelt is the guilty one, to give in so easily to Stalin. From the very beginning he never understood or had an interest in the history of Poland and the stupid Curzon Line. The English—who also didn't know anything about Poland's history—back in 1919 did this demarcation between Poland and Russia.

Unfortunately, Stalin used this Curzon Line history, and Roosevelt took it as a true, safe, and wise division, which is nonsense. Roosevelt gave Stalin Poland on a silver plate!

On May 8, 1945, Germany surrendered, ending the war in Europe. "In proportion to its size Poland incurred far more damage and casualties than any other country on earth," notes Norman Davies.[11] Six million Polish lives were lost out of the country's total prewar population of thirty-five million.[12]

In an effort to avoid future wars, representatives of fifty countries signed the United Nations Charter on June 26 in San Francisco. In late July 1945, as the war in the Pacific neared its end, U.S. president Harry S Truman met with Churchill and Stalin in Potsdam, Germany, for the final "Big Three" conference. (During the conference Clement Atlee replaced Churchill after the Labour Party defeated the Conservatives in Britain). Among other issues, the Potsdam Agreement delineated, albeit vaguely, how the Americans, British, French, and Soviets would administer Germany in four zones of occupation.[13] Poland's hope for a free and democratic society ended when it was decided that the Soviet-controlled Provisional Government of National Unity would be the recognized leadership rather than the Polish government-in-exile in London.[14] Ironically, the newly recognized government agreed "to the holding of free and unfettered elections on the basis of universal suffrage and secret ballot."[15]

The end of World War II brought peace to many areas, but fighting in Poland continued. The Soviets, armed with the authority granted them at Potsdam, progressed toward their goal of imposing a one-party communist government on Poland. Three distinct underground armed forces emerged to combat the recognized Polish government: members of the recently disbanded AK army (now known as the Freedom and Independence Movement), the right-wing National Armed Forces, and the Ukrainian Insurrectionary Army.[16] A civil war of ambushes and raids continued for the next two years.[17]

In Lwów the Soviets had to defeat the Ukrainian Insurrectionary Army to end the fighting between Poles and Ukrainians that had wreaked havoc upon many villages. Thousands of Poles—Skrowaczewski and his parents among them—fled the city to avoid the violence and to seek refuge from the second Soviet occupation. They headed west to the territory that had been awarded to Poland at the Yalta conference as a concession for the Soviet's taking the eastern region of the country.

"We would have left earlier," Skrowaczewski said, "but we always hoped something would change, especially with the new president, Truman. We thought he might turn back what had been established in Tehran and Yalta. But by Potsdam, it was too late. What Roosevelt had done at Yalta was firm. We left because we could no longer live in a Soviet city, as Lwów became."

It was devastating for Paweł and Zofia to uproot and leave behind their home, belongings, and Krystyna's grave. Skrowaczewski shared his parents' grief, but his eye was on the future. Lwów as he knew it was lost to him forever.

Two weeks before Christmas 1945, amid snow, bitter winds, and a temperature of minus twenty degrees Fahrenheit, the Skrowaczewskis left their home with one suitcase. Crammed into a cattle car with twenty-five people and dozens of suitcases lining the sides, they traveled for six days on a train carrying emigrants to the west. There was very little food for the arduous journey, and space inside the car was standing room only, although some people eventually sat on the floor. A little stove in the center of the car helped everyone stay warm, but throughout the trip men took turns securing the stove with sticks to prevent it from toppling over each time the train stopped. At some stops, people melted snow for making tea, which provided marginal comfort for the weary travelers.

When they reached the outskirts of Kraków, Skrowaczewski leaped from the train and ran to a friend's house in the city. Paweł and Zofia didn't want to be separated from their son, but they knew Kraków was already overcrowded. They continued southwest to Opole, which borders Wrocław, and Paweł found work at the hospital there. He and Zofia spent the rest of their lives in Opole.

When Skrowaczewski rang the bell of his friend's flat on Lobzowska Street, the door opened but was immediately slammed shut in his face. His terrified friend assumed that a bandit had come to his door. Unshaven, weary, and buried in layers of clothes and furs, Skrowaczewski resembled a dirty bear. He rang again, but this time he was recognized. He had found a temporary home.

Twenty-two years old and without an income, Skrowaczewski needed to connect with the musical scene in his new city. The timing for his arrival couldn't have been better. While Warsaw was just beginning to recover from its destruction, Kraków became the beacon of musical life in Poland.[18] The Soviets had prevented the Nazis from destroying the city, so it was only minimally damaged.

Prominent composers such as Witold Lutosławski (1913–94) and Andrzej Panufnik (1914–91) shifted their artistic lives from Warsaw to Kraków. During the war the pair earned their living performing as a piano duo, playing in cafés and giving underground concerts in Warsaw. In summer 1945 Lutosławski became the secretary-treasurer of the new Polish Composers' Union (ZKP), founded in Warsaw and now active in Kraków. Panufnik began working as a guest conductor with the Kraków State Philharmonic, founded the previous February.[19] The Philharmonic was the first music institution created in liberated Poland.[20] Also in 1945 Kraków became home to Polskie Wydawnictwo Muzyczne (Polish Music Publications, or PWM). Founded in 1928 to publish authentic editions of Polish music, it was the only music-publishing house in Poland until 1988.[21]

As with the rest of Poland, the liberation brought an overhaul to the music education system in Kraków. The nationalization of schools created three educational levels, and in 1946 the State Conservatory of Music became the "State Higher School of Music" (renamed the Academy of Music in 1979).[22] "I have a strong memory of rejecting this strange name, 'State Higher School,'" said Skrowaczewski. "It was yet another action by the Soviets to make anything with an air of elitism or specialness seem populist."

A number of Poland's distinguished composers and conductors studied at the Academy of Music, including Stanisław Wiechowicz (1893–1963); Artur Malawski (1904–57); and Witold Rowicki (1914–89). Wiechowicz and Malawski taught at the Academy, a work continued today by their most famous pupil, Krzysztof Penderecki (b. 1933).

Soon after arriving in Kraków, Skrowaczewski headed to the Academy with his compositions in hand. He met Walerian Bierdiajew (1885–1956), a member of the conducting faculty who had been a student of Arthur Nikisch and Max Reger in Leipzig.[23] The sixty-year-old maestro recognized Skrowaczewski's talents and immediately made him his assistant. "He was older and didn't seem to care much," Skrowaczewski remarked. "I was suddenly leading the class of young conductors as a professor. It wasn't difficult for me with my background. Bierdiajew was seldom there; it was funny." Bierdiajew was no doubt happy to pass on his responsibilities and concentrate instead on his appointment as conductor of the newly formed Kraków State Philharmonic and the Kraków Opera, which had been reactivated after the war.

Skrowaczewski also earned money teaching private lessons to young pianists and score reading to musicians interested in conducting. Within three months, by spring 1946, he earned his degrees in composition and conducting by taking the necessary exams, as he did at the Lwów Conservatory. After obtaining his degrees Skrowaczewski studied privately but sporadically with Roman Palester (1907–89), the outstanding Polish composer and musical citizen who was considered one of the finest artists of his generation. Skrowaczewski was an advocate of his music throughout much of his career.

In May, thanks to his reputation at the Academy of Music, Skrowaczewski had the opportunity to conduct the Kraków State Philharmonic in a performance of Panufnik's *Five Polish Peasant Songs* for voices and wind instruments. It was his first real engagement as a professional conductor performing the music of an established contemporary composer. By this time Skrowaczewski had made trips to Warsaw to see new colleagues and to visit the office of the Polish Composers' Union, of which he was an active member. He was becoming a part of Poland's artistic milieu; Lutosławski, Panufnik, Palester, and others recognized him as a rising young star. When the position of associate conductor with the Breslau Opera became vacant, Skrowaczewski's composer friends recommended him for the job. He accepted the offer of the appointment, which began in fall 1946.

Breslau (the German name for Wrocław) is the birthplace of numerous well-known Jewish musicians, including conductors Otto Klemperer, Georg Henschel, and Julius Stern. Opera resumed in the city after the war, and Stefan Syryllo became the music director of the Breslau Opera. Like several German opera orchestras, Breslau's orchestra gave concerts in addition to its opera performances. In its wartime destruction Breslau resembled Berlin and Warsaw, but its opera house, located in the center of the city, miraculously was left unscathed. On his way to the opera house Skrowaczewski always traveled by train or car to avoid contact with the Soviet soldiers in the city, who might attack anyone on a whim.

A friendly atmosphere greeted Skrowaczewski when he began his first professional appointment. Half the orchestra members were German, and the other half consisted of Russians, Lithuanians, Slavs, and Jews and Christians from eastern Poland, many of whom were old friends of Skrowaczewski's from Lwów. "When I started rehearsals," Skrowaczewski remembered, "I was speaking half Polish and half German to them. It was a bit humorous, but from a conducting point of view, I knew the music so well I didn't need to use a score." His first concert, which included Beethoven's *Pastoral* Symphony, was held in the opera-house pit because the stage was being used for a production.

Now Skrowaczewski could develop fully the craft of a conductor—using gestures and brief remarks to transmit clearly his knowledge of the score. He studied constantly. His knowledge of the standard literature dated back to his childhood, and he already knew most repertory works by heart but had never conducted them. For the first time he conducted symphonies of Tchaikovsky, Brahms, Beethoven, Shostakovich, and Prokofiev, and works by Ravel, Debussy, and Strauss. He also led a concert performance of excerpts from Mozart's *The Marriage of Figaro* and programmed two of his own works: *Overture in the Classical Style* and the premiere of Symphony no. 1, a piece he later discarded.

Skrowaczewski was invited to guest conduct again in Kraków and in Poznań, north of Breslau, where a new orchestra had been formed. He also continued his association with the Polish Composers' Union in Warsaw. Somehow he managed to find time to compose *Overture 1947*, which remains in his present body of work, and he began composing his Symphony for Strings.

In his scant free time Skrowaczewski visited his parents in nearby Opole and his cousin Zofia, now a professor of chemistry, at the newly organized University of Wrocław. He had friends who were also at the university, so there were fine opportunities for intellectual stimulation. This period of slightly more than a year in Wrocław offered a prophetic snapshot of Skrowaczewski's future segmented life of conducting, composing, travel, and time dedicated to family and friends.

As 1947 neared its end, two events opened the door for Skrowaczewski's artistic opportunities over the next decade. *Overture 1947* earned second prize at the Karol Szymanowski Competition in Warsaw, the first major recognition he received as a composer. Panufnik, nine years older than Skrowaczewski and already established as an important composer, won first prize for his Nocturne. Panufnik, then conductor of the Warsaw Philharmonic, invited Skrowaczewski to guest conduct the orchestra.

In fall 1947 the Warsaw Philharmonic was still recovering after enduring the wartime destruction of its concert hall and the deaths of thirty-nine of its seventy-one players. The Philharmonic resumed its concerts immediately after the war ended, but two years later it was still relegated to performing in theaters and sporting arenas while the hall was under construction.[24] Skrowaczewski's concert took place in the

Warsaw Roma, the only movie theater that hadn't been destroyed. He conducted a matinee performance that ended with Beethoven's Seventh Symphony, and after enthusiastic applause he received many visitors in his dressing room. A tiny older man approached him and asked if he spoke French, to which Skrowaczewski responded in the affirmative. The man, who said that he was very impressed by Skrowaczewski's conducting, introduced himself as Monsieur Francastel, the *attaché culturel* at the French Embassy. He asked Skrowaczewski if he would like a scholarship for three weeks of study at the Sorbonne in Paris.

The young maestro was stunned; he couldn't have imagined such an opportunity. Travel at that time was difficult without sufficient funds, and obtaining a passport and a short-term visa was nearly impossible. By December 1947, however, he was on a train to Paris, bound for a three-week visit that would become a two-year residency.

SIX

PARIS

Two Poles particularly interested Nadia during those days [of the late 1940s]. One was Stanisław Skrowaczewski, an aspiring conductor; the other was Andrzej Panufnik.

—Léonie Rosenstiel, *Nadia Boulanger: A Life in Music*

Skrowaczewski immersed himself in German music, which he loved, but musical life in Paris always held a great fascination for him. "Growing up I heard many radio broadcasts of German concerts, but in Lwów my radio couldn't receive transmissions from France," Skrowaczewski explained. "Paris seemed so distant, and consequently my curiosity about its music and life intensified over many years."

By 1935, fourteen years after the first radio transmission from the Eiffel Tower, music was broadcast nearly twenty-four hours a day. It changed musical life in Paris: a state-funded radio orchestra was formed, and live broadcasts became popular. By 1939, radio audiences could hear seventy-five classical concerts and fifty-two variety programs weekly.[1]

Composer Henry Barraud, a student of composer and teacher Paul Dukas during the late 1920s, helped organize resistance broadcasting during the German occupation. After the war he was appointed the head of France's newly formed and most important radio station, Radiodiffusion Française (RDF). He was instrumental in establishing French radio's reputation as a vehicle for new music, including that of non-French composers.[2] There were several orchestras under the auspices of the RDF, including L'Orchestre National de la Radiodiffusion, headed by composer-conductor Manuel Rosenthal.

Skrowaczewski's journey to Paris in December 1947 was memorable. The French embassy's consul arranged for a short-term visa and passport, but Skrowaczewski had to obtain train tickets himself. He managed to get to the Czechoslovakian border, but from that point on Polish currency was not accepted, and exchanging money was impossible. Skrowaczewski knew it was typical to barter with authorities at border crossings, so he came prepared. Two pairs of women's stockings got him through Czechoslovakia's border, although he still had to wait many hours while Czech police thoroughly inspected every vehicle entering the checkpoint. Cigarettes smoothed his passage through the rest of Germany, and after a three-day journey he finally arrived in Paris.

Liberated from Nazi occupation three years earlier, Paris was still celebrating its freedom. Orchestras and leading musicians from England, Germany, Italy, Switzerland, and America came to Paris to perform and study. It was an ideal environment for Skrowaczewski:

It was a unique time. Paris after the war was really the center of musical life in Europe. Various cities in Europe had been destroyed or badly damaged, and they also suffered from economic problems. Once the Nazi occupation of Paris ended, its artistic luster was revived, and it grew. I arrived during a marvelous period. Food, life, communications, and art were all thriving. The London Symphony and Royal Philharmonic came regularly, as did several German orchestras and Ernest Ansermet with his L'Orchestre de la Suisse Romande. Paris itself had two big orchestras on the radio: Nationale and Philharmonique, and a third—the Girard Chamber Orchestra. There was also the main opera, Opéra-Comique, four big music societies with orchestras, and the Paris Conservatoire. Nearly every day there were two or three concerts, and on Sundays there were four concerts at the same time, so you had to choose. Sometimes I wanted to attend multiple concerts, so I was running from the first half of one to the second half of another. Musical life was incredible.

Roman Palester, the composer with whom Skrowaczewski studied at the Kraków Conservatory, was the only person he knew in Paris. Palester spent the war years in Warsaw, where he was imprisoned for six weeks, and relocated to Kraków after the war.[3] He moved to Paris in early 1947 following the success of his Violin Concerto, which had been performed at the International Contemporary Music Society Festival the previous year. By this time he had won numerous awards for his compositions, both in Poland and abroad.

Palester found Skrowaczewski a room at a cheap hotel in the Latin Quarter. The next day, after receiving his paltry scholarship in francs at the foreign-student center, Skrowaczewski realized he couldn't afford his room for even three weeks. The center found him housing with a French family, but that arrangement didn't work out:

It was bothersome to me because I had to cross several rooms in order to leave my room. Also, they served a horrible breakfast of oat flakes in chocolate; this I remember very well! I couldn't eat it at all. I didn't want to offend them, so I poured it down the rain pipe outside of my window. Every morning there was a little rain of chocolate flakes coming down. The young daughter of the family became quite interested in me, but I had no interest in or time for a relationship, as I knew I would be leaving quickly.

Within days of his arrival Skrowaczewski called Nadia Boulanger, one of the 20th century's most influential and sought-after composition teachers, and asked to meet with her. "Of course, come to me and bring any of your scores that you want to show me," she told him.

By the time Skrowaczewski met the sixty-year-old Boulanger, she was a firmly established international figure. In 1921 she began teaching at the newly formed Conservatoire Américain at Fontainebleau, southeast of Paris, where Aaron Copland was among her first American students.[4] Boulanger soon introduced Copland to Serge Koussevitzky, conductor of the Boston Symphony, and to Walter Damrosch, conductor of the New York Symphony, both of whom championed his music.[5] During the 1920s and

1930s, many other Americans came to Paris to study with her, including Walter Piston, Virgil Thomson, Roy Harris, Roger Sessions, Elliott Carter, and George Gershwin.[6]

It was also during 1921 that Boulanger inaugurated her famed weekly class in analysis and sight-singing, held on Wednesday afternoons at her apartment, 36 Rue Ballu. For the next fifty-eight years—excluding the war years and periods of ill health—she offered the class until her death in 1979 at age ninety-three.[7]

In addition to her world-renowned reputation as a composition teacher, she developed a substantial career as a conductor. Before World War II began, Boulanger made her conducting debuts in Paris, London, and the United States. She became the first woman to conduct the London Philharmonic and Royal Philharmonic orchestras, the Boston Symphony, New York Philharmonic, and Philadelphia Orchestra.[8]

During World War II, Boulanger moved to the U.S. but returned to her beloved Paris in January 1946. She was pleased to finally receive the overdue recognition from the Conservatoire National, which named her a full professor, an honor twenty-three years in the making. She taught again at the reopened Conservatoire Américain at Fontainebleau, wrote music criticism for the *Spectateur des arts,* and guest conducted all over Europe.[9] Her dear friend and colleague Igor Stravinsky composed *Petit Canon pour la fête de Nadia Boulanger,* for two tenor voices, in honor of her sixtieth birthday.[10] She also met a brilliant young American musician named Leonard Bernstein.[11]

Boulanger's ties to Polish composers predated World War II, so her willingness to see Skrowaczewski did not surprise him. Two of Poland's most promising composers of the prewar era, Michał Spisak (1914–65) and Antoni Szałowski (1907–73), both disciples of neoclassicism, studied with Boulanger during the 1930s. She sympathized with the plight of Polish musicians during and following the war, helping as many of them as she could.

Skrowaczewski's first meeting with Boulanger was one of the most memorable events of his life:

> I had no recommendations letters in hand. I was essentially coming to her as a relatively unknown musician. I brought her my newly written and unperformed work, Prelude, Fugue and Postlude. It's about seventeen minutes long, composed for a big Straussian orchestra, with triple woodwinds, brass, timpani, percussion, harp, and strings. The Prelude is more harmonic than polyphonic, with two themes and an exposition—similar to the beginning of a symphony. Then there is an elaborate and large quadruple fugue, with a third and fourth theme and a development section. Finally comes the Postlude, which brings all these themes together more harmonically, but they are also all there polyphonically. It is a complex, nearly one-hundred-page composition that is not easy to perceive upon first perusal.
>
> Nadia sat at one part of the table; I sat across from her. She realized immediately that it was impossible to play the piece because of all the polyphonic aspects, so she didn't asked me to play it. Then she started to turn pages in silence. She stayed on some pages for about fifteen seconds

or less, turning them quickly, but when she came to the Fugue section, she turned the pages more slowly. This went on for about twenty minutes, while I sat in silence thinking, "Oh my God, what will happen?" I became very nervous! I was afraid she might throw me out. Suddenly, when she reached page forty, she burst out, "No, no, you cannot do it! You cannot use this sound in this spot. Why? Because on page twenty of the score, if you use this particular sound, the other is not logical."

I was immediately shocked. She had found the weakest spot in my composition. For several weeks I had struggled with this fragment, and I had put something there just for the sake of finishing it. And this lady, upon one look, without any aural hearing, heard *everything*, and found the problem. It wasn't that it was completely wrong; it was just weak. She asked me why I made various choices, etc., and she finished reading through the work. Then she said, "It is very impressive. I cannot teach you because you know everything already that you want to write. But I can correct you from your own point of view, from your own music. I will tell the radio about you, and you have to show them this piece. Get your scores to Monsieur Barraud, and please, if you stay here, show me other works."

This initial meeting with Boulanger earned him a coveted open invitation to her weekly informal gatherings of composers:

I was always invited to Thursday afternoon teas. These were modest, informal gatherings for any composers or pupils she respected. There were usually thirty to forty people, all talking about music and exchanging ideas; many became my friends—Karel Husa, Mario Zafred, and Julius Katchen. We would often leave and go to an intimate place to have some wine together and discuss music.

Not only composers attended. Once I met Marc Chagall there. He was a short, rather thick, nice man, almost like a big old child. Somehow he had heard of my conducting. He took me off to the corner and complained about Bruno Walter. Chagall was supposed to create one scene for a production of *The Magic Flute* that Walter was conducting, and Walter objected to it. Chagall was very unhappy and offended about this, and he was telling me because he somehow thought *I* could do something about it because I was a conductor! I thought this was quite funny.

Katchen, an American pianist three years younger than Skrowaczewski, had moved to Paris in 1946. Noted for his Brahms performances, he became an international figure in his twenties. A brilliant career was cut short when he succumbed to cancer in 1969 at age forty-two.[12] In 1964, during his tenure as music director of the Minneapolis Symphony Orchestra, Skrowaczewski collaborated with Katchen, performing Gershwin's Concerto in F for Piano and Orchestra. Italian composer and music critic Zafred also benefited from the young maestro's conducting talent. Skrowaczewski performed Zafred's Sixth Symphony in Warsaw in the late 1950s.

Composer and conductor Husa found a kindred spirit in Skrowaczewski. The Czech composer also came to Paris on a French government scholarship. Beginning in 1946, he studied composition with Arthur Honegger and conducting with Jean Fournet at the École Normale de Musique. Boulanger advised the experienced young composer, just as she had helped Skrowaczewski. Composition was Husa's main interest, but he knew that earning degrees in conducting would increase his chance of obtaining an academic position in the West. He was studying at the Paris Conservatoire when he met Skrowaczewski, who came to observe a class.

"We are both Slavs, so we could understand each other even though he spoke Polish and I spoke Czech; they are languages of the same root," Husa said. "He also spoke French very well. He had class. Stanisław dressed impeccably, and he had incredibly fine manners."

Husa and Skrowaczewski lived in different sections of Paris, so they didn't often encounter one another. But Husa has a vivid memory of going with Skrowaczewski to Wilhelm Furtwängler's first Paris concert after the war:

> Furtwängler could not work in Germany at the time, and this was one of the first opportunities he had to conduct. We went to his rehearsal with the French Radio Orchestra, which was forbidden, but I knew how to get to the balcony by a door that a friend of mine who played in the orchestra showed me, so we hid there. The atmosphere was tense with anti-Nazi feelings, and somehow Furtwängler, whether it was right or wrong, was connected. The orchestra visibly showed resentment. They couldn't follow his gesture to start the opening of Beethoven's Fifth. Then we went to the concert, and still it was not clear. As he went on, slowly, it became a very romantic Beethoven. The performance of the Schumann Fourth was magnificent; I will never forget it.

Skrowaczewski also remembered the experience:

> He was quite unclear. But he was a great personality, unique. The Berlin Philharmonic would follow his sometimes-crazy musical ideas: *accelerando*s, for example, that were unplayable. Today such a conductor would be ousted! However, Furtwängler was such a personality that they allowed him to do it, and they knew how to play for him. This French orchestra didn't, so the rehearsals were dramatic. He was a wonderful person who was very much against the Nazis, and he tried to help Jews in German orchestras as much as he could. I met him briefly after the rehearsal. He was very subdued and unsure of himself because of the past and what had happened.

Furtwängler has long been regarded as one of the 20th century's great conductors, but for some his relationship with the Nazis colored his reputation. Unlike various prominent musicians during the war, Furtwängler remained working in Nazi Germany, sometimes performing for Nazi Party officials. A liberal by nature, he was never an official party member. In fact, he was often outwardly opposed to Hitler's regime, and he used his position to help scores of Jewish musicians survive the Nazis. Arnold Schoenberg, among others, felt it was important that Furtwängler stay in his homeland to uphold German music.

When Skrowaczewski's preordained three-week scholarship expired, Boulanger intervened. "She wrote me a beautiful short statement about who I was and what I wanted to do in Paris," he recalled. "And she also helped me with some formalities with the French government. Then I went to the Sorbonne for assistance and dealt with a lot of red tape. Later I managed to obtain a kind of green card that enabled me to stay in Paris for two years and to travel freely."

Skrowaczewski moved to the 14th arrondissement, then an inexpensive working-class neighborhood, and rented a small room in the Hotel Époque, at 40 Rue St. Charles. At the beginning of the 20th century, the Quarter's Boulevard Montparnasse was the center of intellectual and artistic life in Paris. People from around the world flocked there to experience the bohemian lifestyle and catch a glimpse of such personalities as Picasso, Hemingway, and Cocteau, who inhabited its famous cafés.[13]

Soon after moving, Skrowaczewski contacted the Polish Embassy, where he met some helpful officials:

> Ambassador Putrament, who was a writer, was particularly nice to me. He and other people at the embassy invited me to big concerts and receptions they hosted for the promotion of Polish culture. This was great, as I didn't have any money. Their events had some of the most well-known buffets in Paris at the time, filled with caviar, lobster, everything! For a hungry student this was amazing. I didn't eat for three days before these events or three days after!

Food was scarce in Paris, and Skrowaczewski appreciated occasional dining opportunities at various embassy events. In winter 1948 he used food tickets to eat because black-market food was too expensive. By late spring the economy began to revive, and farmers returned to the city to sell their goods. Skrowaczewski's apartment was near a main métro station that boasted a permanent farmers' market nearby. He customarily waited until the late afternoon, when the market was closing, to buy cheese, bread, and fruits for mere pennies. "They saw a poor student," he said, "and rather than carry back their leftovers, they sold them to me for practically nothing."

The locals in Skrowaczewski's neighborhood may have regarded him as a poor student, but his reputation as a rising musician was spreading. At Boulanger's suggestion Skrowaczewski sent his scores—Prelude, Fugue and Postlude and his prize-winning Overture 1947—to Henry Barraud at the RDF. The radio chief was duly impressed and invited Skrowaczewski to make his Paris conducting debut in February 1948 with L'Orchestre Philharmonique de Radio France. The program opened with the premiere of Overture 1947, which gave listeners a taste of Skrowaczewski's neoclassical compositional language, and continued with the Paris premiere of Shostakovich's Fifth Symphony. (Later in 1948 the first performance of Prelude, Fugue and Postlude was heard on the RDF.)

Skrowaczewski's Paris debut was an achievement on all fronts: the orchestra's acceptance of him, the public's response, and the positive reviews. Clearly he had demonstrated his promise both as a conductor and a composer. After the inspiring concert, three musicians visited Skrowaczewski in the green room and invited him to join their new organization, Groupe Zodiaque.

Maurice Ohana (1913–92), a French composer of Spanish origin whose reputation was on the rise, formed Zodiaque in 1947 with Pierre de La Forest-Divonne (an exceptional student of Olivier Messiaen) and Alain Bermat. Zodiaque declared itself independent of any specific school of composition. The group formed partly in reaction to the prevailing serialism and dodecaphonic music (twelve-tone serialism) embraced by its contemporaries, including Pierre Boulez. Skrowaczewski especially admired La Forest-Divonne: "I felt that Pierre was extremely gifted with a vast imagination. If he had not died so young from a heart attack, I think he would have become one of the finest French composers of his generation. It was sad because he had so much promise."

Ohana may have been inspired to form Zodiaque by the example of La Jeune France ("Young France"), a legendary composers' group. In 1936 composer Jean Yves Daniel-Lesur, along with Messiaen and others, created La Jeune France in reaction to neoclassicism and the aesthetics of Le Six, which dominated Paris in the 1920s and 1930s. Ohana, La Forest-Divonne, and Bermat were former students of Yves Baudrier and Daniel-Lesur.[14] Both Daniel-Lesur and fellow composer Henri Dutilleux held programming positions with RDF after World War II. They gave the members of Zodiaque important opportunities for their music to be heard.[15]

Skrowaczewski accepted their invitation on the spot:

> They offered to have me join this group that could have works dually performed at orchestral and chamber concerts. I agreed. Zodiaque turned out to be a great idea; all of us gained a lot from it. We were each different and at different moments of our lives. Maurice Ohana was already a mature and sophisticated composer, with Eastern idiomatic aspects to his compositions. His works had been performed and recorded; it was an incentive for my own composing. Pierre de La Forest-Divonne was interested in more progressive, avant-garde music at the time. Alain Bermat, the youngest member, didn't have a lot of experience, but he had keen observation skills. We had fascinating discussions with him after concerts.[16]

> The music we were writing was relatively new. We wanted to go beyond what Honegger and Messiaen were doing. Messiaen's *Turangalîla* premiered in Paris in 1948; it was tonal, not like what he wrote much later. We came from diverse backgrounds, and we had dissimilar compositional styles, but we were connected by common aesthetic values. We wanted music with a certain depth, with a reason to exist in the sense of form and composition. But what was most important to us was finding beauty in our fresh ideas.

> We all had a feeling for vertical harmonies. That was a key factor of this beauty. It was not that the music had to be tonal or atonal, but there were always certain roots of tonality. The beauty was created through dissonances that were connected to these roots, so you could still hear the reason for the

dissonances. It was not twelve-tone. I tried using the twelve-tone method, but I did it very freely and personally. I felt the rules of the method limiting, but I found the idea of twelve-tone chord building useful. I considered the twelve-tone method most helpful to me as a melodic extension of tonal music. But my use of these methods had to be emotional, not mathematical.

During its first year, Zodiaque collaborated on a work in honor of a new railway between Paris and Strasbourg. A gala event with speeches and music was held to celebrate the line, whose train traveled at the speed of eighty-five miles per hour. "The great speed of the train produced a lot of noise, so they created railway cars with sort of rubber wheels, or at least something quieter than normal," Skrowaczewski remembered. "I wrote a simple piece. It was not Honegger's *Pacific 231*, but at least it was train-related."[17] The 1923 Honegger work, with its references to the sounds of a locomotive, was inspired by the composer's love of trains. ("Pacific" is a class of locomotives, and 231 refers to axle arrangement 2-3-1, a French classification of trains.)

Every few months a work by a Zodiaque composer was performed in Paris, either on RDF or at the Salle Gaveau. The group's collegial relationship extended to informal dinner meetings where members discussed and listened to music, and critiqued each other's scores. Skrowaczewski's conducting skills also were helpful to Zodiaque: he coached his colleagues when they needed help leading their own pieces.

By this time he derived much-needed income from teaching conducting. Ohana was a close friend of the French ambassador to Vienna, who left the composer his posh seven-room, sixth-floor apartment near Saint Germain Church when he was out of town. Skrowaczewski often taught conducting in a room in the apartment. Later the ambassador helped him with papers that allowed him to travel to Vienna. Skrowaczewski also was befriended by a cultural attaché from the Polish embassy:

> He was a writer, a literary man. He and his wife knew me from Poland, so when I saw him at concerts or receptions we would talk about poetry, new books, etc. They were communist but friendly, and they tried to assist me as much as they could. They helped me get a French "green card," so I could travel back and forth from France. I was never questioned. This was a great plus.

The Polish embassy viewed Skrowaczewski's teaching and guest conducting favorably and helped him obtain a travel visa. Now he could accept invitations to conduct in Warsaw, Kraków, Katowice, and Germany, where he had engagements with the Frankfurt Radio Orchestra.

Skrowaczewski's first trip from Paris included one of the most bizarre incidents of his life:

> After my Paris debut with the Shostakovich Fifth, one of the favorable reviews was from Christina Thorsby, an English lady who served as a correspondent for a U.K. paper. Later she came to a Zodiaque concert, and we met. She was very serious about music, stern and reserved, and she always did things by proper English customs. We met several times, and we would occasionally eat

together. She had specific tastes in music, and sometimes I would not agree with her. She really liked my music, though, and she even tried to get me some engagements in England. (I got one invitation from the Hallé Orchestra, but at that time it was very hard to get an English visa). We became friends, and when she returned to London we continued to correspond. She was a strange person; I found that she prided herself on her psychic abilities.

I went to Italy to see Mario Zafred, who was back home in Rome. I went first to Clarens, near Montreux, where I stayed one night with Paul Kletzki. (Dear Mrs. Kletzki had no idea how poorly I lived in Paris. She left me a bunch of chocolates in my room in the attic. They were lovely, but I would have preferred something more concrete, like a steak!) Then the train went via the Alps to Milan. The train to Rome was greatly delayed, so the crowd grew. I remember nearly 2,000 people waiting to board, and they jumped all over the train and even through the windows to get a seat. I was just standing like a sardine in the toilet all night. It was the only place I could fit with the huge crowd. And smoke was coming in the train; it wasn't a pleasant trip! But I got to Rome and spent a few days with Zafred.

Then I continued slowly by train to Assisi, on to Florence, and then to Bologna. From Bologna we went to Venice via Ferrara. As we approached Ferrara, I suddenly felt very strange, and I was compelled to get off the train. I felt like a lunatic. But I got off the train and left my little valise in a locker. I went through the streets—somehow I knew where I was going—and straightaway to Ferrara's ancient castle. I started to feel worse and worse. I quickly went from room to room. It felt like I had been there before; I knew the layout of the rooms. I said to myself, "If I don't get out, I will die." Then by a wall near the dungeon, I experienced a terrible panic. Feeling ill, I fled from the castle and caught the next train to Venice, still in this strange state and disturbed by the mysterious feelings that had overcome me.

Unknown to me at the time, the castle was the site of the horrible murders of Ugo, the son of Prince Azo of Ferrara, and Parisina, his beautiful stepmother and the Prince's second wife. They were rumored to be lovers, so the prince entombed them—both still alive—inside a wall in the castle. They died together slowly, without food, a very cruel death.

Finally in Venice, after a few days, I started to feel better. There was a memorable flood in the Piazza San Marco when I was there; the water was up to my knees. I went to the top of the Campanile, with a fantastic view of the city, when the bells began to toll—so loudly that I had to plug my ears in order to stand there as they rang out. Their power lay in the overtones of B-flat. It was this combination of tones that I discovered in Venice that I later used at the beginning of *Music at Night*. I did not use bells, however, to achieve the chord—just a combination of three horns and one low note on the piano.

Back in Paris, a letter from Christina Thorsby awaited me. It read: "I just found a marvelous subject for a ballet for you, an ancient true tale from Ferrara—the calamitous story of Ugo and Parisina, handed down by Matteo Bandello in his *Novelle* from the 16th century, retold in a poem by Lord Byron." She said that I seemed to be the embodiment of Azo's court musician and poet, who apparently had begged the Prince not to murder his wife and son. She remembered seeing a sculpture of this figure during a sojourn in Italy. The resemblance between us was striking, she thought. When I read this letter I was stunned, and I became awfully sick again. Reflecting on what had happened to me on that brief visit to Ferrara, I felt shattered by the experience. Unless I believed in reincarnation, I cannot come to an understanding of this event. It all could have been coincidental. But the situation was so astonishing. The lack of explanation continues to haunt me.

Miss Thorsby reported in her letter that a scenario for the tragedy was already prepared, and plans were under way for a production in Monte Carlo by the company founded by the Marquis de Cuevas, who had run a ballet school for Paris refugees in New York during the war. I was selected to compose the music.

A year earlier, back in Wrocław, Skrowaczewski had begun sketching a new work that found its way into his ballet *Ugo et Parisina*. The ballet was premiered in 1949, and it was soon adapted to become Skrowaczewski's first major orchestral work, *Music at Night*, his most popular and frequently performed composition.

In fall 1948 Skrowaczewski and his colleagues attended the Paris premiere of Stravinsky's ballet *Orpheus*, a work that received its world premiere by New York Ballet Society the previous spring. Choreographer George Balanchine, Ballet Society's cofounder, had suggested to Stravinsky the idea of using the Orpheus myth as a subject. "Restraint," notes Stravinsky scholar Eric Walter White, "is [*Orpheus'*] distinguishing characteristic."[18] The piece was a favorite example of Boulanger's, and Skrowaczewski remembered her advice to young composers about the value of being "economic" in their approach to writing music:

> At one of our meetings Nadia was criticizing the "abundance" of my use of the orchestra in Prelude, Fugue and Postlude. "Listen," she said, "you know what you want to write, but why do you need so many sets of woodwinds, trumpets, and French horns? You should be more economical and try to avoid using this number of instruments." I explained to her that I came from a tradition of the end of the 19th century when Mahler was increasing the sound of the orchestra by adding more musicians on stage. It was impressive to me. Nadia agreed that a large orchestra could be exciting but that it should be used economically.
>
> She loved Stravinsky, and she felt that a number of his works exemplified an economic use of instruments. His *Orpheus* was one of her favorite examples. He uses an almost Mozartian orchestra with harp, double winds, horns, and strings. "Look at *Orpheus*," she said. "It starts with one viola, playing a lone E, and the harp plays the theme in the background, then the second violins are added. These few instruments fill the entire Theatre Champs-Elysées! So why do you use so many clarinets and brass, etc.?" She always came back to *Orpheus* as an example, also the *Symphony of Psalms*. Even in *The Rite of Spring*—a

piece certainly not known for a judicious use of instruments—Stravinsky creates brilliant *fortissimos* at times without using the entire orchestra.

And she was deadly right about this point! This was advice I utilized throughout my life. It was a great influence on me because I became more judicious in my instrumentation. She taught me composers' logic. All the time in my compositions since then I ask myself, if I am doubling or tripling parts, does the music need it? If a composer does not have this restraint, pieces are not perfect. They can be unnecessarily overloaded, where sound can cover a possible lack of imagination.[19]

Numbers of contemporary composers after World War II were writing without consideration for economy in their works. It was a mistake. Hans Werner Henze, for example, wrote a beautiful dodecaphonic composition in 1953 (which I have recorded) entitled *Ode to the Western Wind*. It was composed for a small orchestra and solo cello, but he used eleven percussionists! The piece last twenty-two minutes, and all of the percussionists only play together in two places in the whole work (thirty seconds in the second movement and about ten seconds in the last movement). Five players could do it, and no one would probably hear a difference because of all the polyphonic elements that are already simultaneously happening. And then when you consider the extra cost to hire the musicians, this is a disaster. And yet this is a beautiful piece that does not receive many performances due to this lack of economy.

During his two years in Paris, Skrowaczewski met privately with Boulanger every two or three weeks. She advised him on his pieces without ever projecting her own compositional tendencies:

Her style preference in new music was the neoclassicism of Stravinsky, but she didn't force me to accept this aesthetic. My style was completely different at the time; it was romantic in some sense. But Nadia was always criticizing me from within my aesthetic—she accepted my style as a fact. When she looked for errors, they were within my own style. Whether she was criticizing or praising, it was without excess; she rarely paid compliments. She was a strict woman, very serious and dignified. She walked beautifully, with a lot of charm, like a dignitary, a king, or a minister. Nadia was simply phenomenal. She had a perfect musical memory; her mind was like a computer. She heard everything. This fact was evident from my first meeting with her when she discovered the major flaw in my Prelude, Fugue and Postlude. And her ability to play complicated scores at the piano was simply astounding.

Through Boulanger, Skrowaczewski broadened his acquaintance with major American composers such as Copland, Piston, Carter, Peter Mennin, Samuel Barber, and the provocative Messiaen, whose renowned organ recitals at La Trinité in Paris he sometimes attended. In the coming decades Skrowaczewski would conduct works by all of these composers in Minneapolis, New York, and other major cities, and they attended his performances. He also met Stravinsky a few times at Nadia's apartment: "There were sometimes thirty people at one time there, so it was difficult to become friendly with him in this environment."

Skrowaczewski also spent time in Paris with major conductors. His relationship with Paul Kletzki was perhaps the closest he ever came to having a conducting mentor. Kletzki embodied several of the musical traits that Skrowaczewski possesses today, and to some degree they share similar personal characteristics.

Born Paweł Klecki in 1900 in Lódz, Poland, he altered the Polish spelling of his last name in an attempt to avoid a lifetime of mispronunciations. A gifted violinist, Kletzki at age fifteen became the youngest member of the Lódz Philharmonic. He later studied composition and conducting with Furtwängler, who was so impressed with his twenty-five-year-old protégé that he allowed him to conduct the Berlin Philharmonic. Kletzki was, in fact, the youngest person at the time ever to conduct Germany's most exalted orchestra.[20]

By 1933 the Nazis were in control, so Kletzki, a Jew, left Berlin for Italy, where he took a teaching post. Within three years anti-Semitism in Italy became intolerable, and he fled to the Soviet Union. There he conducted for a period before moving to Switzerland, where he secured Swiss nationality in 1947. During the next twenty-five years he briefly held several conducting posts, most notably with the Dallas Symphony Orchestra (1960–63) and L'Orchestre de la Suisse Romande (1967–70). His repertoire was vast, and he made a number of highly regarded recordings that remain in print. Kletzki died in 1973 while conducting a rehearsal of Beethoven's *Eroica* Symphony with the Liverpool Philharmonic.[21] His compositions include four symphonies, violin and piano concertos, four string quartets, and other chamber music and songs. But the modest maestro rarely used his conducting positions to perform or promote his music, and many works were destroyed during the war. In 2004, because of the efforts of Timothy Jackson's *Lost Composers* project, Kletzki's Third Symphony *In Memoriam* (1939) and his Flute Concertino (1940) were recorded for the first time and released on a BIS compact disc.

Skrowaczewski described Kletzki's considerable influence on him:

> I went to all his rehearsals and concerts in Paris at the time. I learned everything from him. He sometimes took me for a little lunch after rehearsals, and he would talk about why he did certain things, such as tempo issues, etc. But the greatest lesson was just listening to his rehearsals and concerts. The rehearsals were magnificent, particularly because the repertoire he conducted was often completely unknown to the Parisian orchestras. As a matter of fact, I knew some musicians who played Brahms' Fourth Symphony for the first time in their lives with Kletzki. So he really had to teach what was important in the music—all the inner voices and balances.

> As an interpreter he was precise like Toscanini—perhaps more so—but I think he was closer to Furtwängler in this area. He connected the two antipodes, and this was wonderful; you could learn both approaches. Furtwängler had a vivid musical imagination, which I adore and find very interesting. But in big works, such as Bruckner symphonies, his interpretations were often distorted in the sense of tempos, *rallantandos*, and *accelerandos*. In Brahms and Beethoven, not so much; they were more classical. Kletzki didn't distort like this, but like Furtwängler he intensified the emotional content of the music.

The orchestras loved him and learned a lot. He really had an enormous repertoire and vision for different styles. He was a particular expert with German music, but I also recall great performances of Debussy, Ravel, and Honegger. And his conducting of Russian music was also outstanding. People should listen to his recordings. He was very neglected. He didn't want to travel much, and he had such distaste for administrative issues connected with leading an orchestra. This is why he left both L'Orchestre de la Suisse Romande and the Dallas Symphony.

Husa concurred with Skrowaczewski's assessment of Kletzki and remembered hearing some "absolutely first-class concerts" as well as a Beethoven Fourth Symphony that was "perfect." However, Kletzki's emotional conducting did not always earn Boulanger's approval. The Polish maestro found her, as others did, to be an intimidating force. When a colleague told Kletzki after one of his concerts that she had been in the hall, he responded, "Boy, I'm glad you told me *afterwards!*"[22]

Charles Münch was another conductor whom Skrowaczewski greatly admired and observed during his Paris years. A violinist and concertmaster of Leipzig Gewandhaus Orchestra, Münch began conducting at the late age of forty-one.[23] He became best known as music director of the Boston Symphony Orchestra from 1949 to 1962, following Koussevitzky's historic tenure. His command of the French repertoire was unmatched, and he was known for his spontaneity and ability to bring out orchestral colors during concerts.

Skrowaczewski got to know Münch well in Paris:

> I would go to his rehearsals and concerts, and years later I heard him conduct the Boston Symphony. He did Schumann's Second Symphony very well. He also did a lot of German music well, such as Mozart and Beethoven, but he didn't go much into Bruckner or Strauss. *If* he wanted to work in rehearsals, he was magnificent. I remember a rehearsal of Mozart's *Prague* Symphony when he was really stopping at every bar. But it all depended on how he was feeling. He often would just play through a piece and go. For me, Kletzki was better because he always worked hard with an orchestra; he asked for a lot of rehearsals.

When Skrowaczewski wasn't observing great conductors or conducting, he composed. Along with his ballet *Ugo et Parisina* and its adaptation, he finished Symphony for Strings, which he had begun back in Wrocław. The twenty-two-minute symphony—his longest work at that time—was premiered in Paris on French Radio by a chamber orchestra conducted by André Girard, whose ensemble was an important vehicle for performances by Zodiaque. Symphony for Strings became Skrowaczewski's compositional calling card during the 1950s. Kletzki conducted it at the 1953 Frankfurt International Festival of Music (IGNM), and in 1959 it became the first Skrowaczewski composition heard in the United States when Skrowaczewski conducted it with the Cleveland Orchestra. Along with *Overture 1947* and *Music at Night*, Symphony for Strings is the only piece from his early years that remains in his oeuvre. Skrowaczewski also composed *Cantique de Cantiques* for Soprano and Orchestra while in Paris. The work won him a French Radio Award, but it wasn't premiered until 1951, at IGNM; once again, Kletzki was at the podium for his young colleague.

Skrowaczewski's conducting engagements in Paris and abroad continued in 1949. He took L'Orchestre National de la Radiodiffusion on tour to Germany, and he gave the premiere of Husa's Divertimento for String Orchestra at the Club d'Essai in Paris. "Being a composer," Husa said, "he really understood the piece."

During his time in Paris, Skrowaczewski achieved a comparative balance between conducting and composing; neither activity completely dominated his work. It was a period to savor, for conducting would soon become the focus of his talent and opportunities.

By 1948 Poland had been completely transformed into a one-party communist state. In 1949 the Polish National Convention of Composers and Music Critics issued a proclamation espousing social realism. All works of art had to be vetted as acceptable by committees appointed by the Polish Ministry of Art. Lutosławski's First Symphony became the first major Polish work branded as "formalistic" and thereby banned from performance.[24]

Stalinism had reached a level in Poland whereby any contact with the outside world could brand someone as a spy. During summer 1949 a friendly man at the Polish embassy took Skrowaczewski aside and advised him that if he stayed in France, his parents would be at risk. "He said that Poland was a police state," Skrowaczewski recalled, "and that my being abroad for such a long period of time would appear very suspicious to the Polish government. By this time I had been back to Poland a few times for concerts, but I continued to live in Paris. So he warned me that I might be considered a spy for the West, and as a result my parents would be arrested, deported, or worse."

Soon after receiving this warning, Skrowaczewski received an offer to become music director of the Silesian State Philharmonic of Katowice. The timing couldn't have been better. He accepted, and in July he left Paris. Husa helped him move his suitcases from his apartment to the train station. "We didn't know if we would ever see each other again or what the future would bring," Husa said. All of Zodiaque's members joined Husa at the train station to bid their friend and colleague farewell.

Skrowaczewski boarded the train and settled into his seat. His heart warmed to see his friends waving goodbye and shouting good wishes to him as the train departed. He pressed his hand to the glass and smiled at them, reflecting on the richness of his time in Paris. The twenty-five-year-old conductor and composer never suspected that this journey would be one of his last trips for several years. Issuance of passports for travel outside Poland soon ceased, isolating him from the rest of the world.

SEVEN

MATURATION

Everything I conducted for the first time, the orchestra also played for the first time. It was a positive situation for a young conductor.

—Stanisław Skrowaczewski

Skrowaczewski's summons to lead the Silesian State Philharmonic of Katowice was a key factor in his rise as Poland's leading young conductor. Despite being only twenty-five years old, he brought to the position a great command and knowledge of orchestral literature, although he had no experience as a music director. However, his one-year stint as associate conductor of the Breslau Opera had prepared him well.

The youthful maestro found an idyllic situation in Katowice. The Silesian Philharmonic (named after the Silesian region of Poland and the Czech Republic) was less than four years old when Skrowaczewski became its music director. Among the first artistic organizations established in postwar Poland, the Philharmonic presented its first concert on May 26, 1945.[1] As in other major cities in Poland after the war, the government sponsored cultural performances and educational institutions in Katowice. Excellent young musicians in their twenties and thirties filled the void left by their elders who either perished or left during the war. In their respective roles, conductor and orchestra were learning a new repertoire together. Fortunately Skrowaczewski did not face the challenge of directing musicians who were set in their ways or accustomed to working with a different conductor.

He had to select and conduct approximately twenty-four weeks of programs. During a season that lasted from September through May and included few guest conductors, the music director was expected to carry the brunt of the workload. In summer the Philharmonic retreated to the hills of western Silesia to prepare for the upcoming season, so Skrowaczewski conducted nearly year-round. Rehearsals lasted from four to four-and-a-half hours daily, Monday through Friday, and the Philharmonic presented one weekly concert. An additional concert was added later. "I was preparing myself as best I could, really studying and digging into the music," Skrowaczewski recalled. "I was using all my rehearsal time very specifically, insisting on numerous aspects that I had to correct." He guided the young orchestra, but he also benefited from the experience of several older musicians from the Warsaw Philharmonic, including his concertmaster. To this day he considers himself quite fortunate to have had the chance to create a repertoire from the beginning.

For the first time, he tackled some of the Beethoven, Brahms, Schumann, Shostakovich, Mozart, and Haydn symphonies that had been impossible to program during his previous guest-conducting engagements. As he and the Philharmonic developed, they began to compete with the city's other orchestra, the National Polish Radio Symphony Orchestra (NPRSO), which today is considered the nation's premiere orchestra.

Conductor and composer Grzegorz Fitelberg founded that orchestra in 1935, leading it until the outbreak of World War II. Witold Rowicki revived the NPRSO just after the war in 1945 (three months before the Silesian Philharmonic was organized), and in 1947 Fitelberg again became its music director.[2] (Since the 1990s Skrowaczewski has made annual conducting appearances with the NPRSO, which named him its first principal guest conductor in 2003.)

Fitelberg was seventy years old when Skrowaczewski assumed his post with the Silesian Philharmonic. The elder maestro was friendly to his younger counterpart, who observed him frequently. "He was a decent, pleasant man and a wonderful musician but *very* strange," Skrowaczewski remembered. He enjoyed pretending he was a special person who came from the moon to visit us." Fitelberg's eccentricities also extended to his conducting, as Skrowaczewski explained:

> He did not have any beat, so he couldn't conduct clearly. It was worse than Furtwängler's. So he could only play with his own orchestra, which became used to his lack of technique. I remember when he returned from guest conducting the Czech Philharmonic in Prague—one of the best orchestras in Europe at the time—Jan Krenz and I visited him at his home for tea. "It was a strange orchestra," Fitelberg said. "They don't understand a conductor's gestures." He proceeded to show us an example of one of his "precise gestures"—which was totally unreadable—and explained how surprised he was when the orchestra responded in silence.

In spite of his odd behavior and conducting inadequacies, Fitelberg advanced the cause of contemporary Polish music in the early 20th century. He championed Szymanowski, with whom he and others helped found the Young Polish Composers' Publishing Company. He also conducted for Sergei Diaghilev in the early 1920s, leading the premiere of Stravinsky's *Mavra*.[3] Skrowaczewski remembered a rather famous joke Fitelberg made a few months before his death:

> Stalin and Prokofiev both died on the same day, March 5, 1953. There was silence when Fitelberg came to his rehearsal as the musicians sat tensely before him. Before he started he said, almost tearfully, "Ladies and gentlemen, a great man died." He paused. "A wonderful man." Then he said, "Sergei Prokofiev has died." A grave silence fell over the orchestra, which had expected him to say, "Joseph Stalin." And then Fitelberg turned to the concertmaster and whispered, but in a manner that everyone could hear, almost as an afterthought, "And apparently Stalin died also." The orchestra was afraid to burst into laughter, but the joke had the weight of a bomb going off in the rehearsal. It was terrific!

Forced adulation for the deceased Stalin spread throughout Poland. Katowice was rechristened "Stalinogród," a name it bore until 1955. Like other Poles, Skrowaczewski coped with this indignity to his homeland partially through humor. Instead of using Stalinogród for his return address on letters, he substituted the name of a Polish patriot.

The rival orchestras shared a modest concert hall. The NPRSO usually performed in its small studio, giving public performances only monthly, whereas Skrowaczewski's Philharmonic performed weekly. Aurally the Philharmonic couldn't compete with the larger string section of the well-funded NPRSO, which also had more rehearsal time in which to prepare its public programs. But Skrowaczewski and his young orchestra relished the challenge of having a stronger ensemble next door. "From an interpretation standpoint," Skrowaczewski recalled, "our performances were equal or at least competitive. I developed the orchestra little by little, and the public received us enthusiastically. It was exciting to compete with the Radio Orchestra to see who would present the most interesting programs. Katowice was a lively musical city at that time."

Located in southern Poland, Katowice has a long history of "music for the people" and a variety of folk groups, workers' ensembles, and music societies dating from the late 1800s. Professional musical institutions were established in 1918 when Poland regained its independence. Henryk Górecki, perhaps the most notable composer to emerge from the city, was a student at the Katowice State Academy of Music from 1955 to 1960.[4]

Shortly after World War I, Katowice became Poland's largest economic center, driven by the growth of the steel and coal industries during the war. Seized by the Germans at the start of World War II, Katowice was spared major damage because its coal mines and steel mills were useful to the Nazis. Continued postwar growth shaped Katowice into a scientific and cultural capital, but its reputation as an industrial mecca came at a price.[5]

"Katowice was a gloomy industrial city with factories all around," Skrowaczewski said. "They created terrible pollution; the air was scandalous all the time, all year. People had respiratory problems, but no one paid attention to air pollution back then. I had to go twenty miles outside the city just to breathe fresh air." For a person whose well-being depends in part on a connection to nature, Katowice's environment was difficult to endure. Skrowaczewski coveted any chance to get away and used his three-week vacation each season to ski in the Tatra Mountains. During his third season with the orchestra, a wonderful opportunity to commune with nature almost cost him his freedom.

During the fall, when it was not in use, a summer home near Poland's border with Czechoslovakia was available to writers, painters, composers, and other creative artists working in Warsaw. Skrowaczewski had the opportunity to join the informal union of artists in this beautiful setting and was granted a week in the mountain dwelling to relax and compose. He went alone, savoring the time away from the pressure of giving concerts. He enjoyed tending the garden at the house, digging for potatoes and picking brussels sprouts. In the middle of the week he decided to hike to the mountain's summit. He had progressed a short distance on the trail when two Polish border soldiers suddenly emerged from behind some bushes and confronted him. Skrowaczewski was unaware that he had entered a border checkpoint. Despite his efforts to convince the soldiers of his identity, the soldiers assumed he was a spy attempting to cross the border and brought him to a makeshift prison. A Polish officer came by and greeted the soldiers, who asked him if their detainee was a spy. Fortunately he had seen Skrowaczewski earlier in the week and corroborated the young maestro's story. "If the Polish officer hadn't come by and recognized me," Skrowaczewski reflected, "I would have been interrogated and thrown in prison. I was lucky."

He found a living situation in Katowice conveniently located near the concert hall. The city government arranged for him to have a large room in the flat of the Sieradzkas, a cultured family with whom he eventually became friends. The Sieradzkas socialized with musicians such as Jan Krenz, a conductor and composer who was one of Skrowaczewski's close friends and a "benign" competitor in his role as assistant conductor with the NPRSO. He led the NPRSO after Fitelberg's death and became one of Poland's major conductors.

Baritone Andrzej Hiolski, a friend of Skrowaczewski's from Lwów, was a frequent soloist with both orchestras in Katowice. Skrowaczewski so admired his "cultivated, soft, round, and mellow sound" that he brought the singer to Minneapolis to perform in the premiere of Penderecki's *Passion According to Saint Luke* in 1967. Two years later Hiolski sang in the premiere of Penderecki's *Devils of Loudun* in Hamburg. Born a year before Skrowaczewski, Hiolski attended the Lwów Conservatory and became a major opera, concert, and oratorio singer. He died in 2000.

"In my entire life I never heard a better baritone singer," maintained Skrowaczewski. "It was not only the wonderful timbre of his voice—so dark, so profound, and very centered with wonderful intonation—but also his unbelievable musicianship. He was a musician like the finest violinists or pianists, a unique singer."

The Sieradzkas' teenage daughter, Zofia, became a lifelong friend. She observed the activities of the up-and-coming young musician on her weekends home from the University of Kraków:

> He shared the kitchen, bathroom, and phone with us in our large apartment, so it was easy to get to know him. Staś was very careful about what he ate— only healthy food. He was original in what he chose to eat. I remember he once brought some special fruit teas to a hotel restaurant. He was quite particular. Staś was always doing gymnastic exercises in sport dress, even while he talked on the phone, which he did often. He had diverse interests and was particularly fascinated with French culture and language. Staś had relationships with older professors at the university and often invited them for dinners. He had and has a great openness for music, art, philosophy (especially Nietzsche). He was not a visual artist, but I remember he kept working at a drawing of an orchestra of cats! He was a very charming, contemporary Don Juan. There were many girlfriends. Sometimes he needed to hide from some,

and we would have to say, "I'm sorry, he went out of town. He's not here." He would not intentionally seduce everybody; it was just his way of being—a lot of charm. Composition was always his first priority. This was his fascination, not conducting—even though he was an excellent conductor. He wrote a lot of music for theaters and films at that time.

From 1949 until he left Poland, Skrowaczewski composed few symphonic works, none of which are in his present oeuvre.

> Over this period of a decade while I was still in Poland, I became disgusted with my own music. I was repeating myself all the time; I knew that to develop my own language I would have to concentrate on composition and nothing else. It wasn't possible for me to do that, so eventually I stopped. And when I began in Minneapolis, there was absolutely no time available.

His fallow period lasted until 1969, when he turned a corner with his breakthrough composition, the Concerto for English Horn and Orchestra.

During the Katowice years Lutosławski encouraged Skrowaczewski by describing his own struggles to find his compositional voice. Simply incorporating various compositional techniques into one's works wasn't enough, he advised: one must make a method of those techniques before they become a part of a composer's individual voice. Lutosławski explained that he studied intensively before he could shift from a style influenced by Hindemith, Stravinsky, and Bartók to twelve-tone techniques.

Although he produced no enduring symphonic works during these years, Skrowaczewski nonetheless consistently honed his craft with various projects. In the early 1950s, at the invitation of the Soviet-controlled Polish Union of Composers, he undertook his first and only opera. He despised the libretto, which reflected communist themes, although it was not formally propagandist. The libretto offered a naïve version of Poland's history in the 14th and 15th centuries, idealizing the lives of simple, everyday people.

Skrowaczewski begrudgingly produced a 400-page full score by spring 1953. Soon after it was finished, he left the open score out on his desk. A crow flew into the room through an open window and in its struggle to escape left its "business card," as Skrowaczewski puts it, on the score's last page. Skrowaczewski's friends considered it a good omen for the success of his opera, but he interpreted it literally, as a sign of the opera's quality. He cleaned off the page and flew to Warsaw to show the work to officials at the composers' union. They were indifferent to it, so Skrowaczewski had free rein to discard it. He recycled some of the material into a short Overture for Orchestra but cannot remember if the work was ever performed.

Despite his frustration with composing, Skrowaczewski continued to be honored for his music. In 1953 he received a Polish National Award, third prize, in general recognition of his work as a composer. He commented on the award:

> It was musically not important because the government just wanted to show that it appreciated the arts. It was part of communist propaganda. But the positive results of such propaganda were that they promoted music schools,

orchestras, and musical life. If they didn't care about music, I wouldn't have gotten the directorship of an orchestra. The negative result was the restrictions on programming, but at least orchestras *existed*.

A second award in 1953 meant considerably more to him. His String Quartet earned second prize at the International Competition for String Quartets, held in Belgium. Begun in Paris, the score evolved into the Symphony for Strings. Skrowaczewski then drew from material in that work to create a string quartet for the competition in Belgium. Some of the finest composers from around the world participated in the competition; Elliott Carter won first prize. However, when it was discovered that Carter's quartet had been performed in the United States by the time the competition results were announced, he was disqualified. "They didn't decide on the prize for nearly a year and a half after I had submitted the manuscript," recalled the ninety-five-year-old Carter in 2004. "By that time I had already had a performance of it. I thought Skrowaczewski would be rather angry with me, but he wasn't. Later he played a lot of my works."

In effect Skrowaczewski won by default, although he was never officially recognized as the winner. Three years passed before he found out that he had won second prize; communications to Poland from noncommunist countries rarely occurred. By 1956, travel restrictions had thawed, making it possible for him to make a side trip to Belgium to pick up his prize.

During this seemingly unproductive stage, Skrowaczewski launched his career as a film composer in Katowice, producing about a dozen scores between 1949 and 1960. Classical concert composers frequently wrote for film, with European directors being more adventuresome than their American counterparts in this regard. Among others, Erik Satie, Darius Milhaud, and Paul Hindemith composed scores for silent films during the 1920s, while Georges Auric and Arthur Honegger joined Milhaud in composing scores for important French sound films in the 1930s-40s. Benjamin Britten wrote music for a number of innovative government-sponsored documentaries during the same period, and Ralph Vaughn Williams composed for two wartime documentaries. Kabalevsky, Prokofiev, and Shostakovich made important contributions to prewar Soviet Union films (Shostakovich's *New Babylon* and Prokofiev's *Alexander Nevsky* are notable examples of film scores with strong ideological content.)

In Poland, Roman Palester—Skrowaczewski's short-term composition teacher in Kraków—composed a number of film scores during the 1930s. Lutosławski contributed two scores to the genre in 1946. Film work gave Skrowaczewski a creative outlet, but it also had a practical consideration: "The salaries for conductors in Poland during those years were extremely poor, so income from film work—small as it was—was something extra. But I was not really concerned with getting profits. I was young, and I was attracted to new experiences."

Skrowaczewski did not consider his film work to be "serious composing," but it nonetheless influenced him. He experimented with sound, using a piano in his apartment and recording various effects he created. He played under the piano or on top of the lid, striking the strings and humming into them, trying to invent sounds that would reflect cinematic images. He developed his own version of *musique concrète*, a style created in 1948 by Pierre Schaeffer in Paris. This musical form involved manipulating recordings of instruments or environmental sounds, or the making of such recordings.[6] Skrowaczewski had met Schaeffer in 1948 at the French radio premiere of Symphony for Strings and also visited him at his celebrated studio in Paris.

For historical or more serious films, Skrowaczewski scored for a chamber orchestra, sometimes using source material related to the film's setting, such as French folk songs for a film connected to France. Occasionally excerpts from Skrowaczewski's concert music found their way into his film scores. Films were state sponsored and well financed, so Skrowaczewski had the option to score for full orchestra; however, he often didn't want to take the extra time necessary to do so.

Łódź, a major city located between Katowice and Warsaw, was the center of Polish filmmaking, and its university had a renowned film studies program. Skrowaczewski often traveled to the city to conduct his film scores and consult with directors. "And it was artistically interesting," he said, "because I worked with intellectually gifted directors. There was a wave of excellent films in the early 1950s, especially from France and Italy." At a screening in Minneapolis in 2004, Skrowaczewski's younger son, Nicholas, met Krzysztof Zanussi, who was among the young Polish filmmakers of the Łódź School in the late 1950s. "Your father was an admirable and inspiring artistic figure to me and several others during this period," Zanussi told Nicholas.

This period launched the careers of many innovative Polish directors. *Pod Gwiazda Frygijska* (Under the Phrygian Star), the first major film directed by Jerzy Kawalerowicz, was one of four film scores that Skrowaczewski completed in 1954. Kawalerowicz (1922–2007) was a major figure in Polish cinema, noted for his deft ability to create films with historical, political, religious, and psychological themes, often adapting Polish literature for his scripts. Along with Andrzej Munk and Tadeusz Konwicki—both of whom worked with Skrowaczewski—Kawalerowicz was a leading figure of the Polish Spring movement, which revolutionized filmmaking by shedding the dogma of Marxist-Leninist ideology.[7] Kawalerowicz was so taken by Skrowaczewski's work that he offered to create stories around his original music; he had the composer's programmatic *Music at Night* in mind. But Skrowaczewski didn't have time even for that enticing project.

Other directors with whom Skrowaczewski worked in 1954 included Jan Rybkowski, Jan Koecher, and Wanda Jakubowska. Rybkowski (1912–87) produced twenty-five films during his career. *Autobus Odjezdza 6.20* (The Bus Leaves at 6:20), his film scored by Skrowaczewski, is about a woman who overcomes marital difficulties through her "ideological maturity"—an example from a period when some directors acquiesced to Stalin's procommunist edict.[8] Skrowaczewski remembered the experience because the film was partially assembled in East Berlin:

I had to go to conduct a radio orchestra to create the soundtrack. It was an extremely depressing trip. We went in a plane that seemed ready to fall apart at any time, and we landed in an obscure spot. The terminal was a tiny building that looked like a hut in a field. All the lights in shops were off in the city, and the streets were barren. It was another reminder of how communist oppression suffocated an otherwise vibrant city. This was before the Berlin Wall, so on the first free evening I went with some musicians to West Berlin, which you could get to just by crossing a street. Suddenly we saw neon lights, active shops. It was an amazing contrast.

Koecher's film with Skrowaczewski, *Kariera* (Career), a propaganda story about a spy from the West who tries to recruit collaborators in Poland, was cowritten by Konwicki before he became involved in the Polish Spring movement. A year after the film was released, the script was published as a book entitled *The Iron Curtain*.[9]

Skrowaczewski's fourth film score of 1954 was composed for *Opowiesc Atlantycka* (The Atlantic Tale), a film directed by Jakubowska (1907–98), the first Polish female film director to receive national and international recognition. Her fifty-year career made her the longest-working director in the history of Polish cinema. Social and political issues permeated her work.

In 1929 Jakubowska was a founding member of START, an organization dedicated to producing artistic and socially conscious films. *Ostatni Etap* (The Last Stage), her 1947 breakthrough film about Auschwitz (where she had been a prisoner), was the first Polish postwar film to have international distribution. A prototype for future Holocaust films, *Ostatni Etap* was the second film produced by Film Polski, the state film board of Poland. After World War II Jakubowska became the first high-profile director to join the Polish communist party, often toeing the ideological line in her films and lobbying the party on behalf of the film industry.[10] Skrowaczewski composed scores for three more of her films from 1956 until 1960.

Skrowaczewski, who strongly opposed communism, was never pressured to join the party. Despite his conducting position in Katowice, his film work and his guest-conducting engagements throughout communist countries, he was left alone. "The officials would have loved for me to join," he reflected, "but they suspected I was a 'Western boy' because of my two years in Paris." The Polish ministry secretly denied him guest-conducting opportunities outside the Soviet bloc, but he engaged in his own machinations against them in the name of art.

In 1949, when Skrowaczewski began his appointment in Katowice, he had carte blanche to program any music he wished. This situation changed dramatically by the end of his first season. "From about 1950 on, the Polish communist regime's screw tightened its control of the arts," he said. "Music, films, literature, and visual art had to reflect social realism. It had to be positive for people, depicting the wonderful communist life and order—all tonal harmonies, radiant, joyous music for the masses, with as much nationalistic folklore as possible."

By 1950 the edict announced at the Polish National Convention of Composers and Music Critics in August 1949 was fully implemented. Panufnik's Nocturne was performed at the conference and deemed "unsuitable for the broad masses" because it had failed to express the "joyful life under socialism."[11] The judgment marked the beginning of the end of Panufnik's relationship with his homeland and ultimately led to his defection to the U.K. in 1954. His defection in turn made it impossible for Polish musicians to travel to the West. Skrowaczewski had an invitation to guest conduct the Hallé Orchestra at this time but was denied permission to leave the country. "It was very *doloroso* to me," he recalled. "It was my second missed opportunity to go there."

Palester, whom dozens considered the successor to Szymanowski, already had left Poland to live in Paris. From 1951 to 1972 he lived in Munich, where he hosted a radio program entitled *Muzyka Obala Granice* (Music Breaks Down Borders), playing compositions that were banned in Poland. Music by Palester and Panufnik was outlawed in Poland after their defections, and all records of their musical activities were stricken from Polish documents and history books. Their music was not heard in Poland again until the late 1970s.[12]

Some Polish composers took a different approach. Jan Krenz, along with composers Tadeusz Baird and Kazimierz Serocki, formed Group 49, which was dedicated to upholding principles of social realism without abandoning contemporary compositional techniques.[13] Although their acquiescence to communism no doubt angered many Polish composers, it perhaps aided Baird's and Serocki's ability to found the Warsaw Autumn Festival of Contemporary Music in 1956.

Although Skrowaczewski could not sidestep the restrictions against performing banned works, he took risks in order to play the music of Alban Berg and Arthur Honegger. Berg, a twelve-tone composer like Schoenberg and Webern, was considered a "formalist" and therefore banned. But Skrowaczewski and his violinist friend Tadeusz Wroński were eager to perform Berg's Violin Concerto. The now-classic composition was only about fifteen years old at the time, but both musicians had yet to perform it. Skrowaczewski tells the story with gleeful satisfaction:

> The great violinist and pedagogue Tadeusz Wroński came up with the idea. The Berg Violin Concerto is inscribed *Dem Andenken Eines Engels* (To the Memory of an Angel) [to Manon Gropius, the daughter of Alma Mahler Gropius, who died at age eighteen]. So as a joke Tadeusz suggested that we tell the authorities that it was dedicated to the four "angels" of communism: Marx, Engels, Lenin, and Stalin! He was kidding, but I took this suggestion seriously. So I went to the communist ministry in Katowice with this lie, and they bought it. We played the piece, and it was well received. It may have been the first performance of the work in Poland. It's possible that the Warsaw Philharmonic may have played it, but I doubt it, as the premiere performance only happened in 1936. This was one of my greatest achievements, thanks to Tadeusz's idea. But it was a really big risk because if they had discovered this lie, we both could have been imprisoned and sent to Siberia for twenty years!

At the time it was one of the biggest examples of outsmarting musical censorship. Fortunately the party people were uneducated and completely stupid, so they didn't bother to check my assertion. And we were taciturn about our deed; we didn't spread it around to others. I just had contact with this one official. Others didn't object because they didn't know the parameters of what could be played and what could not.

A gifted performer, Wroński (1915–2000) gained fame as one of the world's great violin teachers. He was a duet partner of Władysław Szpilman, whose life was the subject of Roman Polanski's film *The Pianist* (2002) and a member of the Warsaw Quartet. Beginning in 1949 Wroński was a professor at the Warsaw State Higher School of Music (now the Fryderyk Chopin Academy of Music), and in the 1970s he served as the school's rector. He taught more than 500 violin students, many of whom held major positions in orchestras throughout the world. From 1966 to 1984, he served on the music faculty at Indiana University Bloomington. Since 1990 the Tadeusz Wroński International Solo Violin Competition has been held annually in Warsaw.[14] Wroński's primary colleague at Indiana University was Josef Gingold (1909–1995), eminent violin pedagogue and former concertmaster of the Cleveland Orchestra, who would become an important friend to Skrowaczewski.

Skrowaczewski took sole responsibility for a deception involving Honegger's music, which he loved, particularly after hearing so much of it in Paris. He was eager to perform what he deemed the composer's best orchestral work, Symphony no. 3, the *Symphonie Liturgique*. Completed in 1946, the symphony was, in part, the composer's reaction to the futility of war and its aftermath. Although largely tonal, Honegger's music was dissonant enough to earn the formalist stigma. Playing upon the composer's Swiss heritage, Skrowaczewski told his orchestra's manager to explain to the local communist secretary that the piece was dedicated to Pro Helvetia, the Swiss communist party. Permission granted, the Philharmonic played *Symphonie Liturgique* to great acclaim. "The public went wild for it," Skrowaczewski recalled.

Had officials bothered to check, they would have discovered that Pro Helvetia had no ties to the communist party. Founded in 1939, Pro Helvetia is a foundation under public law "dedicated to promoting cultural endeavors of nationwide interest."[15] Honegger's program note for Symphony no. 3 added another ironic touch:

> In this work I wanted to symbolize the reaction of modern man against the tide of barbarity, stupidity, suffering, mechanization, and bureaucracy, which have been with us for several years. I have musically represented the inner conflict between a surrender to blind forces and the instinct of happiness, the love of peace, and feelings of a divine refuge…a drama which takes place… between three characters who are real or symbolic: misfortune, happiness, and man. These are eternal themes, which I have tried to renew.[16]

Skrowaczewski was busy guest conducting throughout the Soviet bloc. He was a regular guest with most of Poland's main orchestras, including the NPRSO, Kraków Philharmonic, Warsaw Philharmonic, and the orchestras of Poznań and Gdańsk.

Skrowaczewski's official debut with the Warsaw Philharmonic occurred on January 23, 1949, eight months before he assumed his post in Katowice. (However, he had conducted the Philharmonic in fall 1947 at the Warsaw Roma, where he met his benefactor Monsieur Francastel.) He led the Warsaw Philharmonic five more times during his Katowice years, in programs of stylistic diversity. Of note was an all-Beethoven concert in 1953 with Hungarian pianist Annie Fischer playing the *Emperor* Concerto. A world-class pianist at the apex of her long career, Fischer made her American debut with George Szell and the Cleveland Orchestra in 1961. The opportunity for Skrowaczewski to accompany such artists as Fischer and Wroński at a young age was an important factor in his development.

He conducted in Bulgaria, Hungary, Czechoslovakia, and Russia. He observed that the quality of Russian orchestras was consistently high, particularly the Leningrad Philharmonic. "Budapest also had two very good orchestras, the Budapest Radio Symphony and the Budapest Philharmonic," Skrowaczewski remarked. "The Prague Philharmonic was one of the best orchestras in Europe at that time. And the major orchestras in Poland all were becoming better and better every year. They had quick recoveries after the war."

Conducting his own Silesian Philharmonic, Skrowaczewski did not repeat any works during the first three seasons. In addition to repertoire of the 18th through the 20th centuries, he conducted Vivaldi, Geminiani, Handel, and Bach. He also included at least one Bruckner symphony each season. Skrowaczewski's tuba player helped him secure Wagner *tuben* from East Germany so the orchestra could play Bruckner's monumental Seventh Symphony. Other concert highlights from Skrowaczewski's Katowice years were his first performances of Ravel's *Daphnis et Chloé* suites and Beethoven's Ninth Symphony. "The Ninth was a big triumph for everyone because it was the first time it was played in Katowice since the war," Skrowaczewski said.

Given the vast repertoire that Skrowaczewski performed for the first time, it was impressive that he conducted so often without a score. In part this ability resulted from years of deep and thorough study since childhood; nevertheless, interpreting masterworks for the first time is a formidable challenge for a young conductor. Skrowaczewski explained his process of development:

> After my long study of the scores of these composers, playing their chamber music, going to lots of concerts, and listening to the radio and recordings, I formed interpretations. I also knew very well the interpretations of German conductors such as Furtwängler and Erich Kleiber from recordings. I had some records of Toscanini and maybe Bruno Walter, but they were not as interesting to me. And Kletzki's rehearsals and concerts in Paris—especially of Brahms— were so memorable. They were examples for me for whatever I conducted.

Skrowaczewski used his conducting position in Katowice to promote Polish music. He conducted several of Szymanowski's orchestral works for the first time and music by many contemporary Polish composers, including Lutosławski and several from his generation: Piotr Perkowski, Malawski, Serocki, and Panufnik (until he defected and his music was outlawed), among others. Most of these composers attended Skrowaczewski's rehearsals and performances of their works.

Skrowaczewski's parents were fixtures at his Friday concerts in Katowice. Weekly they traveled by train from Opole to see him. Zofia was visibly proud of her son, and Paweł, although more emotionally reserved than his wife, shared her joy in his achievements. Zofia continued to worry about her son and always brought food to Katowice, including her special chocolate torte, which rarely interested him, but he loved the fresh-squeezed beet and carrot juices that she included in her edible gifts. "It was so wonderful," he said, "because at that time we didn't have any vitamins."

Stores in Poland always had shortages, particularly the shops in smaller cities like Opole. In turn, Skrowaczewski purchased items for his parents on his travels, especially hair coloring for his mother: "I was all the time bringing small items for my parents from my trips abroad. It was impossible for them to obtain a lot of products they wanted."

After his fifth season in Katowice, Skrowaczewski received an interesting proposition from the Kraków Philharmonic, which wanted him as its conductor. He always had been received there as an important, rising musical figure, and "as a city," he said, "it was much more pleasant than industrialized Katowice, so I considered it." A minister of culture in Warsaw—who perhaps had hoped that Skrowaczewski might eventually join the communist party—encouraged him to accept the invitation:

> "Why don't you go to Kraków now? They don't have a music director." And I said, "Fine." It was as simple as that. It was friendly, quiet, and with no bad feelings in Katowice. I especially liked the idea of changing cities. The orchestra was not necessarily better than Katowice, but it was different. It was a new challenge.

Significant career and personal developments were on the horizon for Skrowaczewski. Ultimately they would set the stage for a new life, one that he could never have imagined.

EIGHT

OPEN DOORS

We met going up the mountain in a gondola, so we skied together. She was falling all the time—maybe on purpose—so I helped her. Immediately I sensed that she was "the one." This wonderful feeling of "knowing" happened for the first time in my life.

—Stanisław Skrowaczewski

Skrowaczewski's appointment to the Kraków Philharmonic did not free him from Katowice's polluted air. His responsibilities in Kraków were minimal, and he couldn't justify leaving the apartment in Katowice where he had lived since 1949. He had only six to eight concerts a year and basically no administrative duties, so he traveled by train or car to Kraków for his engagements and stayed at a hotel for a week at a time.

"I wasn't there much," Skrowaczewski remembered. "They had guest conductors all season long, which was my preference after having five years in Katowice conducting practically all the concerts. But at that time I preferred my orchestra in Katowice; I felt it was better. The musicians in Kraków were good but less disciplined without one conductor working consistently with them."

However, his trips to Kraków were literally and figuratively a breath of fresh air. Only forty miles east of Katowice, the city was an environmental and cultural upgrade for the young maestro. Largely undamaged by World War II, Kraków became the epicenter of cultural life in Poland during the postwar years. Until Warsaw was rebuilt in the 1950s, Kraków was the first stop in Poland for all major artists.

According to legend, Kraków was named in honor of King Krak, a seventh-century warlord who slew a dragon. (An alternative legend attributes the creature's demise to a shoemaker who tricked the dragon into eating a sheepskin filled with sulfur and salt).[1] The city was the capital of Poland from the 11th century until 1596. It was occupied by Austria for 123 years (1795–1918). During the early 20th century, Kraków was a republic for more than thirty years before once again falling under Austrian control. After World War I it was returned to Poland.[2] The Nazis used Kraków as their Polish administrative headquarters during their occupation, and they ruthlessly ghettoized, deported, and murdered tens of thousands of the city's Jewish residents.[3]

Founded in 1909, the Kraków Philharmonic ceased during the Nazi occupation. Early in 1945 it was reestablished as the first professional orchestra in postwar Poland.[4] Having spent a year in Kraków as a student, Skrowaczewski knew the cultural and physical landscape of Poland's third-largest city. He had appeared regularly as a guest conductor with the Kraków Philharmonic since 1946. His appointment as music director didn't start formally until fall 1955, so he spent the 1954–55 season guest conducting throughout Poland and the communist bloc.

Barely eleven years old, the Kraków Philharmonic already had had several conductors before Skrowaczewski took over. They included Walerian Bierdiajew, Zygmunt Latoszewski, and Bohdan Wodiczko. In 1962 the orchestra was renamed the Karol Szymanowski Philharmonic to reflect its advocacy of the renowned composer's music as well as patronage from his estate.

Having a full choir at its disposal—the vocal ensemble was created soon after the orchestra's rebirth in 1945—the Kraków Philharmonic developed a specialization in oratorio. This forte opened opportunities for the orchestra to tour internationally, particularly at festivals of nonsecular music. Skrowaczewski made good use of the excellent choir—the best in Poland at that time, he recalled—and programmed major works from the choral repertoire, such as Brahms' *A German Requiem*, Beethoven's *Missa Solemnis,* and Mozart's Requiem. A performance of the latter remains in Skrowaczewski's memory as a test of his conducting abilities under distress:

> After the dress rehearsal on the day of the concert, I came down with pneumonia and a fever of 104. I thought I would have to postpone the performance. I had become friendly with the French consul. He looked like a spy from the West (and probably was), and it was risky, politically speaking, for me to have contact with him. But I didn't care. I had given him tickets to the concert, and when he found out I was ill, he immediately sent a bottle of cognac to my room. At the time, food and drink were so scarce in Poland that it was impossible to get something as extravagant as French cognac. He advised me to drink a glass or two before the concert. I took his advice, but I drank a bit more and went to bed. When I got up, I felt much better—very clear, not tipsy at all, so I decided to go forth with the concert. Everything was fine until the end of the Requiem. Suddenly I became dizzy. I grabbed the balustrade of the conductor's podium with one hand so I wouldn't fall, and I conducted with the other hand. Somehow the orchestra finished the piece, and no one knew. Apparently I did well; people told me after it was an excellent concert.

During the spring of Skrowaczewski's first season, the Kraków Philharmonic traveled sixty miles south to give a concert at Zakopane, a resort city in the Tatra Mountains. Skrowaczewski, who had enjoyed countless ski trips in the region, took the opportunity to hike one of the nearby mountains. On the way back he met the Philharmonic's first-horn player, who had the same idea but didn't know the terrain. Skrowaczewski warned the man that he would miss the concert that evening unless he turned back. Checking the time, the musician replied that his maestro was taking a similar risk. The horn player left, but Skrowaczewski proceeded to the summit of the mountain and still made his concert on time.

The region was a favorite hiking and skiing destination for Skrowaczewski during his years in Katowice and Kraków. Skiing there in February 1956, he met Krystyna Jarosz, who was on break from her university studies. "We met going up the mountain in a gondola, so we skied together. She was falling all the time—maybe on purpose—so I helped her. Immediately I sensed that she was *the one*. This wonderful feeling of *knowing* happened for the first time in my life," said Skrowaczewski.

Stanisław and Krystyna had first met in 1952, when she went backstage to greet him after one of his guest-conducting performances with the Kraków Philharmonic. She recalled her first encounter with the dashing maestro:

> My parents always took me to concerts. There was a musical life in Kraków at the time. We went to the Philharmonic, and here was this man—I had never seen anyone who was quite so energetic on the podium. There was this incredible physical strength and personality; it was like a fire, totally amazing. I thought he was terribly interesting and very good-looking. After the concert I went backstage with my parents, and we shook hands, but he was so surrounded by beautiful women that I thought, "Not a chance." It seemed so distant. I was really young and had had a very sheltered life because of the war. I went to a convent school, and I didn't know much about the "big life." He had traveled abroad. It seemed like an ocean between us. I didn't automatically think that something might come out of our first meeting. When we were skiing it was different; we had a lot more in common at the time. I had never been abroad, but I had read so much. We talked about my studies, and he told me about his travels and life in Paris. I don't know if he was impressed with my skiing, but we skied *a lot* after that.

Krystyna's erudite background impressed Skrowaczewski. She spoke perfect French, so he gave her some books in that language on various subjects that interested her.

Born in Kraków a decade after Skrowaczewski, Krystyna grew up on her family's country estate in southeastern Poland, right outside of Lwów. Her mother, Jadwiga, lost her first child at birth. Fearing complications with the birth of her second child, she traveled to a Kraków hospital to ensure that she received the best possible care and also to be with her mother, who lived in the city.

Krystyna's paternal grandfather, Rajmund, married Emma Schoenbec von Zoellner, an Austrian aristocrat. He owned and developed a large resort comprising several properties. Located near natural spring-fed salt lakes, this type of resort—where people often vacationed or sought natural cures—was very popular in Europe in the 1930s. When Krystyna's grandfather died in 1935, responsibility for the resort passed to his son, Roman, who had no interest in managing the family business. Roman, Krystyna's father, wanted to be a diplomat. He graduated from the École des Sciences Politiques in Paris and later earned a doctorate in law from the University of Vienna. Roman hoped to enter the Polish diplomatic service and work in France, but World War II shattered that dream.

Jadwiga spent most of her time taking care of the estate. Hers was a demanding life of overseeing the staff and constantly hosting receptions for the many government officials who came to stay at the resort. Roman, focused on building his diplomatic career, enjoyed socializing with the officials. Hunting on the property was a big draw for these Polish aristocrats. The surrounding woods were filled with boar, hare, pheasants, and wolves, and there were hunting lodges all over the grounds. Krystyna, a lifelong animal lover, detested these "massacres."

Life in this environment was like a fairy tale for the young Krystyna. Under her nannies' supervision she roamed the stunning gardens, admired the regal horses, and played with her younger brother, Rajmund, in the resort's pristine houses. Her parents wanted the best education for her, so she was tutored at home, and at their insistence she learned languages, becoming fluent in French by age six.

Krystyna's idyllic childhood ended abruptly when the Germans invaded Poland in 1939. Within two weeks the Russians occupied most of eastern Poland. The Jarosz family fled its estate a day before the Russians seized it. The horrid events remain embedded in Krystyna's memory:

> The retreating troops, fires, and killings were close by. The Russians were screaming, "Kill the landowners! It is time that you die!" We ran for our lives and hid in a convent in Lwów. It probably wasn't far from where Stan was living. The next day our beautiful horses were shot. Then they filled in all the ponds just to totally erase the memory of the landowners.

Immediately Roman was called into the army to fight on the German-occupied side of Poland. "I remember him leaving us," Krystyna said. "He was on a beautiful white horse in his uniform. It was all so pathetic. Some Poles fought with sabres against these Russian and German tanks. They didn't have a chance. It was very sad." Roman's brother, a captain in the Polish army, perished in the Katyń Forest massacre in spring 1940. Roman waited in agony for two years, not knowing the fate of his wife and children, before they were finally reunited.

Krystyna and her brother, who had led a sheltered life on the family estate, had never been vaccinated. Now living in a dirty convent in Lwów, Krystyna came down with scarlet fever, and Rajmund contracted diphtheria, illnesses that brought them both close to death. Desperate to get her children out of Lwów, Jadwiga headed to Kraków, where her mother lived. Krystyna described what happened next:

> The Germans caught us crossing the border [the Ribbentrop-Molotov Line had partitioned Poland], and they sealed our train so we couldn't escape. They sent us to a kind of concentration camp for women and children in German-occupied Czechoslovakia. It was awful. We only had straw in our pitiful room. All the children had whooping cough, and the dust from the straw made it worse. I remember choking on this dust. The Germans were constantly running inspections to find sick children. They sent them to a hospital where they would just let them die. My mother was frantic all the time.
>
> Fortunately my grandmother was a brilliant woman. She owned a lot of real estate in Berlin, and she spoke excellent German, like all of her generation. She somehow managed to get money from her real-estate holdings and then wired it to this camp. And we were released. We crossed the border and lived with my grandmother in Kraków. There we were finally reunited with my father in 1942.

Krystyna's grandmother owned an enormous apartment and several nearby houses in Kraków. Living conditions improved for the Jarosz family; however, Roman did not get along with his mother-in-law, and the situation led to constant tension in the home. Krystyna, now a preteen, began to sleepwalk as a result of the stress, and when she was sent to a convent boarding school for high school, her anxiety increased. Draconian practices at Lady of Our Sacred Heart—mandatory prayers five times a day, ice-cold water for bathing, and a required black veil—were too much for strong-willed Krystyna. She ran away and returned home. Her mother had also attended the school, so the convent "allowed" her to come back.

Krystyna dreamed of becoming a doctor, but by the time she started her academic career, the communist system was at its zenith in Poland. Social background determined one's academic path. Being the daughter of former landowners—especially wealthy landowners—was a strike against her. Her gender presented another obstacle: at the time, female doctors were rare. Under the communist system she could take any courses she wished, but if the party deemed them unacceptable for her, she received no official credit for completing them. She ultimately decided to major in Romance languages at Jagiellonian University (Uniwersytet Jagielloński) in Kraków. Krystyna was a student and acquaintance of a young professor named Karol Wojtyła. Born in Wadowice, thirty miles outside of Kraków, Wojtyła became the bishop of Kraków and in 1978 was elected pope, taking the name John Paul II.

Krystyna's brother, Rajmund, two years her junior, became a well-known actor and director in Poland, touring the world as a member of the Kantor Theater. Founded by Tadeusz Kantor in 1955, the troupe became one of the most important avant-garde theater groups of the 20th century. Kantor began creating underground experimental theater in Kraków during the German occupation, and at the time of his death in 1990 he was celebrated as one of Poland's greatest artists. Rajmund Jarosz's many film credits include a role in the 1965 counterculture classic *The Saragossa Manuscript*. This bizarre, mind-bending epic, based on a novel by 19th-century Polish writer Count Jan Potocki, was restored and rereleased in 2000 through the financing of two of its biggest fans, film director Martin Scorsese and the late Grateful Dead guitarist Jerry Garcia.

Eight months after their first skiing adventure, Krystyna and Stanisław were married on September 6, 1956, in a simple civil ceremony in Katowice, with only their parents and a few friends attending.

Skrowaczewski's proposal had not been traditional. "He simply said, 'Well, we should get married,'" Krystyna explained. At Krystyna's suggestion, however, he asked her father for her hand in marriage. The two men immediately connected, joking about their shared political views.

Because they both had grown up in eastern Poland and lived through similar experiences, the young couple forged a special bond even before they settled into marriage. Although Krystyna's formal musical training was limited—she studied piano "like every nice little girl is supposed to"—she possessed innate artistic sensibilities. Her parents played the piano, and she was exposed to music during her childhood. She preferred to listen to and read about music rather than play it. Her love of languages extended to visual art. "She's gifted as an artist," Skrowaczewski has said. "If she applied herself, she could go into this field."

From the beginning their marriage was a true partnership in every sense of the word. In a 2004 booklet published in honor of Skrowaczewski's receipt of the McKnight Foundation's Distinguished Artist Award, Mary Ann Feldman pays tribute to Krystyna Skrowaczewski:

> How was [Skrowaczewski's] international career possible from a distant point in the northern heartland of America? Because of a remarkable wife. [Since 1960] Krystyna Skrowaczewski has maintained an elegant household that functions as a kind of command central for her husband's career. Outside, she cultivates her garden of organically grown vegetables that have kept her husband trim and fit. They share a love for mountains, trekking and skiing in high places of the American West and the Canadian Rockies. Inside, Krystyna runs a virtually one-woman office. She might have been a concert agent. A woman of keen intelligence and graciousness, she is also a linguist, communicating in several languages. Nothing flusters her. Concert presenters everywhere rely on her.[5]

May 1956 brought the first in a series of significant professional opportunities for Skrowaczewski during the next two years. The Polish minister of culture chose Skrowaczewski, Jan Krenz (his colleague from Katowice), and Józef Wiłkomirski to participate in an international conducting competition at the Accademia di Santa Cecilia in Rome. Although Skrowaczewski considered foregoing the invitation after his father became ill, he knew he could not afford to pass up his first chance to visit the West since leaving Paris in 1949. More importantly, he would be participating in the first major postwar international competition for conductors.

Skrowaczewski, Krenz, and Wiłkomirski traveled to Rome in the same train compartment. They hardly slept during the nearly two-day trip from Warsaw, focusing instead on their memorized knowledge of scores. They quizzed one another on details of instrumentation and orchestration from a number of standard repertory works. Skrowaczewski soon discovered he was in good company. He was impressed with the astuteness of his colleagues, particularly with Krenz, who like Skrowaczewski already had a permanent position with an orchestra (director of the National Polish Radio Symphony Orchestra of Katowice since 1953).

The challenging Rome competition had an age limit of thirty-five and involved a diverse repertoire. With no warning or time for preparation, Skrowaczewski had to rehearse three works: two Respighi-influenced large orchestra pieces by Ennio Porrino and Ildebrando Pizzetti (two 20th-century Italian composers who attended the competition and later became his friends) and a thirty-minute segment focused on the first movement of Schumann's Fourth Symphony. The international jury consisted of about eight conductors and academics, including Artur Rodziński, a Polish conductor who had started his career in Lwów.

After leading three major orchestras in the United States (Cleveland Orchestra, New York Philharmonic, and the Chicago Symphony) with great success and controversy, Rodziński settled in Italy. Skrowaczewski previously had not met the volatile conductor, who died a year and half later, in 1958.

Rodziński's wife, Halina, wrote about her husband's participation in the Rome competition in her book *Our Two Lives*:

> Ill health kept him from attending most of the preliminaries, but when he was informed that three Poles were among the finalists, Artur forced himself to go. He even invited the young conductors to our apartment on Viale di Villa Massimo and listened raptly to their views of Poland and its musical life.
>
> In the days following, Artur attended the finalists' performances. He was in dreadful condition, having developed a badly ulcerated heel as a result of the edema, which accompanies certain kinds of heart malfunctions. Nonetheless, he took part in the jury's deliberations, which, like most such affairs, were terribly partisan and political. The Italian members wished to award the prize to a Santa Cecilia student. The non-Italians wanted one of the three Poles. Artur cast the deciding vote, less for partisan reasons than [for] the fellow's indisputable gifts. The winner was Stanisław Skrowaczewski.[6]

"I just worked and worked as best I could. I changed some bowings and explained why it created improvements, etc., and corrected them," Skrowaczewski recalled. "Somehow I had the attitude of 'I don't care' [that it was a competition]." He never considered that he might win the contest, and despite Krystyna's urging, he refused to pack his tails (a public concert was part of the reward). Fortunately Krenz, more confident of his odds, had brought concert attire, which Skrowaczewski borrowed. The competition also had a monetary award of one million lire (about $1,200 at the time), but the most important honors were the guest-conducting engagements that resulted from the prize. France, England, and almost all the major Italian cities now opened their doors to him. Praise poured in for Skrowaczewski from the press, particularly in France, but so did animosity from some of his colleagues back in Poland, whose jealousy became apparent after he returned home.

Following the Rome competition Skrowaczewski's high spirits were deflated after he arrived in Paris. He learned from Boulanger, his friends from Zodiaque, and people at Radio France that he had received numerous guest-conducting invitations since leaving there in 1949. They could not write Skrowaczewski directly about these invitations, only to the minister of culture in Poland. The news was regrettable:

> I never received any of them. The Warsaw minister of culture answered the invitations, saying that I was busy or sick. I lost seven years of conducting opportunities. Outside of Poland I had to start all anew. I felt bad. There were invitations from Italy, both radio orchestras in France, and Strasbourg, where they had started a big international May festival, among others. But there was

nothing I could do. Poland was communist, and they wouldn't let me out at the time, so I just had to accept it.

With no time to wallow in lost opportunities, Skrowaczewski had a full season of conducting ahead of him. He soon was off to Italy for two months of concerts, this time with Krystyna.

Back in Poland, Skrowaczewski continued his work with the Kraków and Warsaw Philharmonic orchestras. With the exception of Panufnik's music, he essentially could program whatever he wished. As he did in Katowice, he collaborated with major soloists, including Arturo Benedetti Michelangeli, Emil Gilels, and Sviatoslav Richter. David Oistrakh (1908–74), the Ukrainian-born violinist, was another notable artist with whom Skrowaczewski performed in Warsaw. A giant in the history of violin performance, Oistrakh is largely forgotten today. He spent the majority of his career in Russia and taught at the Moscow Conservatory for a number of years. He toured throughout Russia and in the mid-1950s, when he was allowed to perform in the West, throughout the world. Oistrakh also made important recordings with Eugene Ormandy and Dimitri Mitropoulos.

Although Skrowaczewski had almost no time for composing during his short tenure with the Kraków Philharmonic, he wrote scores for two films in 1956: *Pozegnanie z Diablem* (Farewell to the Devil), directed by Wanda Jakubowska, and *Tajemnica Dzikiego Szybu* (Mystery of a Mining Shaft, or Secret of the Old Pit), codirected by Wadim Berestowski and Krystyna Cekalska. Krystyna Skrowaczewski assisted her husband in the creation of various noises and *musique concrète* he used as sound effects for these films and others over the next few years. The young couple enjoyed working together.

Despite the dearth of concert music written by Skrowaczewski during this period, he won formal recognition for a composition. Without his knowledge, the minister of culture submitted his *Suite Symphonique* to an international competition in Moscow. Based on a popular Polish folk tale, it was a work for chamber orchestra that Skrowaczewski composed while he was conducting in Katowice. *Suite Symphonique* earned the 1956 Golden Prize in Composition. "I have no idea why it won or who was on the panel," he recalled. "I just wrote it for popular reasons. It was a simple piece, written almost for children but with a little contemporary pepper. It was a fine work, but I didn't revive it later; it was just put to sleep. I didn't receive any 'gold' or money for this prize, only a certificate!" Nevertheless, it was another honor to add to his growing résumé.

The latter part of 1956 brought good fortune to the thirty-three-year-old Skrowaczewski. He married, won an international conducting competition, and one of his compositions would be performed at a major music festival (praised by Boulanger, no less). The West was finally opening to him for guest conducting, and he would be offered a new position as a permanent conductor of the Warsaw Philharmonic. Within six months he would meet the man who gave him his American debut, which changed his life and career forever.

NINE

ELECTRIFYING THE STATES

The conducting of Stanisław Skrowaczewski, guest with the Cleveland Orchestra at Severance Hall last night, left one spellbound, transfixed, and electrified. This young Polish conductor is one of the greatest we have heard.

—Herbert Elwell, *The Plain Dealer*

Newly married and appointed to a conducting position with the Warsaw Philharmonic, Skrowaczewski headed to Warsaw with his young bride. During the late 1950s the "Paris of the East" was still recovering from its wartime destruction, particularly the aftermath of the 1944 uprising. The city's musical culture slowly emerged from the shadows. Philharmonic Hall was rebuilt by 1955, the first Warsaw Autumn Festival was held in 1956, and by the late 1950s international artists and ensembles from the West began performing again in Warsaw. The Polish Experimental Studio for Electroacoustics was founded in 1957, and musical societies, opera, and operetta began to flourish. The city's artistic life was reclaiming its prewar self.[1]

As with Skrowaczewski's other postings, the minister of culture in Warsaw simply moved him around like a chess piece. No doubt his rising fame following the Rome competition led to his new position. Long considered the country's premier artistic organization, the Warsaw Philharmonic was the best orchestra with which Skrowaczewski held a position thus far in his career.

Launched in 1901 with a concert that featured pianist Ignacy Jan Paderewski, future president of Poland, the Warsaw Philharmonic Orchestra has an impressive history. Prokofiev, Rachmaninoff, Ravel, Saint-Saëns, Horowitz, Strauss, and Stravinsky were among guest conductors or pianists with the Philharmonic before World War II. The Philharmonic reorganized under national sponsorship in 1947, as did all arts institutions during this period. In 1955, coinciding with the opening of its new hall, the orchestra's name was changed to the Warsaw National Philharmonic Orchestra, its current official title. Many of the world's major musical artists have performed with the ensemble, which has toured and recorded extensively.[2]

Skrowaczewski's appointment in 1956 was as a permanent conductor of the Warsaw Philharmonic, not as its music director. This number-two post, comparable to that of associate conductor, freed him from administrative duties and accommodated his burgeoning international guest-conducting schedule. Bohdan Wodiczko, who was music director during Skrowaczewski's first two seasons, was his predecessor at the Kraków Philharmonic and later became music director of the NPRSO of Katowice.

Wodiczko was an ardent performer of contemporary music, a commitment that contributed to the founding of the Warsaw Autumn Festival. His appointment as music director in Warsaw precipitated a bitter battle with Witold Rowicki, who had reorganized the Warsaw Philharmonic (and before that the NPRSO of Katowice) after the war and began serving as its music director in 1950. He also was a force behind the reconstruction of Warsaw's Philharmonic Hall. Before the Philharmonic was nationalized in 1955, Wodiczko and Rowicki competed for the post of music director. It is unclear exactly what transpired, but Rowicki left in 1955, resumed the position in 1958, and then stayed until 1977. Skrowaczewski recalled his knowledge of the situation:

> The Warsaw Philharmonic at that time was rife with political machinations. I didn't know much about Rowicki other than he was a fine conductor. He was well supported by the minister of culture. Then something happened, and he left. Wodiczko, also a fine conductor, was a very strange, dreamy sort of man. He was always unhappy with something. So it didn't work with him, and Rowicki came back. I had plenty to do, and I was well liked by the orchestra. I never got involved in these machinations, but later I became a subject of them.

Two years after his last engagement with the Philharmonic, Skrowaczewski returned for a concert in February 1956. The program included his Prelude, Fugue and Postlude; the Second Symphony of Honegger; and the Mozart Requiem—this time sans cognac. His next engagement, now as permanent conductor, was at an historic musical event: the inaugural Warsaw Autumn Festival.

Taking advantage of the post-Stalin era "thaw," composers Tadeusz Baird, Jan Krenz, Kazimierz Serocki, and others under the auspices of the Union of Polish Composers held the first Warsaw Autumn Festival of Contemporary Music in October 1956. Although the festival was politically infused for years—its performers and their repertoire were subject to communist authorities' approval—it nevertheless achieved a major cultural breakthrough. It brought performers from East and West together for the first time in order to promote contemporary music from Poland and abroad. With only two exceptions, the annual Warsaw Autumn Festival has continued to the present day, the longest-running festival of its kind in the world.[3]

Skrowaczewski participated in the groundbreaking festival as a conductor and composer. He led the Warsaw Philharmonic in a program featuring the Fourth Symphony of his friend Mario Zafred; *Uwertura Warszawska* (Warsaw Overture) by Perkowski (then a composer on the faculty of the Warsaw Conservatory); and music of Stravinsky. The performance of Skrowaczewski's *Music at Night*, conducted by a fellow Pole, generated an unforgettable encounter with Boulanger:

> It was a magnificent festival. The government was eager to have a meeting of East and West. Even though it was imbued with political overtones, it still was quite important musically. For two weeks there was an amazing number of concerts. All the major Russian, Polish, French, Swiss, Czech, and German orchestras performed. Nadia came, and I greeted her briefly when she first arrived in Poland. It had been seven years since I had last seen her.

My *Music at Night* was performed on Saturday night, after at least a week of concerts. I sat in the balcony for what was the premiere of this adaptation of my ballet, and I noticed Nadia sitting just a few rows away. With the exception of the midnight concerts, she had attended all the performances of the festival up to this point. She had never heard *Music at Night,* and she had never seen the score.

During intermission she came to me very seriously (she was always quite stern and serious, without a smile, but yet with a friendly demeanor) and said, "I wanted to tell you that for me, your piece is so far the best work of the festival." I was stunned. I started to tremble; she had never paid me such a compliment. This was perhaps the tenth concert she had heard at this festival.

"But," she went on to say, "at the very end there is a chord," and from top to bottom she named every tone perfectly—and it was an atonal chord (with some tonal intervals inside it) with nine pitches! "This chord is not good," she said. "It does not belong to this piece." Remarkably, I had struggled with this chord for months, and I had changed it several times. Finally the conductor said I had to make up my mind so that he could have the finished score. I wrote something just to finish, but I wasn't happy with it. And this lady—on one hearing—not only knew that the chord didn't belong but also could name all nine tones from top to bottom! It was unbelievable. It is something that does not exist. Up to this day I have never met anyone who was able to hear so perfectly and analyze music like Nadia. Afterwards I told her that I knew that the chord was wrong, but that I didn't know how to fix it. She simply said, "You must find out."

Skrowaczewski's appointment in Warsaw overlapped with the conclusion of his position in Kraków. He and Krystyna chose to live in his apartment in Katowice after they were married. "It was not my idea of heaven," she said. "We occupied two rooms in Stan's large apartment, and we were sharing the kitchen and bathroom with three or four families. The pollution from all the factories was really awful. When you opened a window you had to shut it immediately to avoid breathing in all the fumes." After moving to Warsaw the newlyweds lived in a hotel that also was far less than ideal, as Krystyna remembered:

> Because Warsaw was completely destroyed during the war, the rebuilding was slow. It was impossible to get an apartment. So we had to live in a hotel in a tiny six-by twelve-foot room. We felt claustrophobic. There was no kitchen, so we ate in the hotel restaurant that served ghastly greasy food. We eventually both became sick from it, so I decided I would cook in our tiny bathroom. Stan had such a particular diet. He wanted a lot of vegetables and fish, and they were not readily available at that time. I remember washing large lettuce leaves—the kind he loved having in Lwów—in the tub. It was horrible. And I had to cook covertly to avoid hotel guests who would tattle on me to the hotel management.

Finally, after a year of this we went to the minister of culture to try to get an apartment. They were dispensed to artists at his will via the Communist Party who "kept all the keys." I was very timid, but I decided to gather up my courage and say, "My husband cannot be a productive musician under these conditions. It is impossible for us to live like this." I was almost in tears. It must have made an impression, because we got an apartment. This also was tiny, with a kitchen the size of a sofa, but at least it was ours.

When Skrowaczewski was not busy conducting or creating film scores, he and Krystyna took advantage of Warsaw's blossoming cultural life. Aside from instrumental music and opera, the city had nearly two-dozen repertory theaters by the late 1950s. Numerous directors, writers, and visual artists made Warsaw their home, and the Skrowaczewskis socialized with several of them, including Antoni Marianowicz, Eryk Lipiński, and Jan Lenica (1928–2001). The latter, a gifted animator, graphic artist, and set designer, was a favorite of Roman Polanski, who used the artist to create posters for his films.

During his first season as Warsaw Philharmonic's permanent conductor, Skrowaczewski led an all-Szymanowski program. The first of two concerts was held on what would have been Szymanowski's seventy-fifth birthday. The country's best-known orchestra celebrated the country's most prominent composer, and this prestigious concert was entrusted to Skrowaczewski. The program opened with excerpts from *Harnasie* (a large ballet inspired by folk music from the Tatra highlands), followed by Violin Concerto no. 1 and one of Szymanowski's last works, *Litania do Parii Panny* (Litany to the Virgin Mary), composed for soprano soloist, female chorus, and orchestra.

Less than two months after his Szymanowski concert, Skrowaczewski met George Szell, who gave him the most important career opportunity of his life.

In fall 1957 the Cleveland Orchestra and Szell, its eminent conductor, rolled into Katowice by train from Vienna. Standing at the train station along with a delegation from his former orchestra—and looking a bit like a younger version of the bespectacled Szell—Skrowaczewski waited to greet the nearly sixty-year-old maestro.

After the Cleveland Orchestra's performance of the first work on the program, a Rossini overture, the audience called Szell back to the stage eleven times. Hearing Szell's orchestra for the first time deeply impressed Skrowaczewski:

> We were almost shocked. It was such beauty, perfection. You couldn't imagine—it surpassed anything that anyone at that time in Poland and throughout Europe could hear: technical perfection, wonderful intonation, and magnificent string sound in all the sections. This orchestra was an absolute gem. But this was not just my opinion. They received such praise wherever they went: Berlin, Paris, and London.

At a dinner after the concert in Katowice, Skrowaczewski chatted with Szell, who knew that the younger maestro had won the Rome competition. A week later the

Cleveland Orchestra was in Warsaw, and Skrowaczewski was the first person Szell wanted to see when he arrived.

The orchestra's program included Mozart's *Jupiter* Symphony, and Skrowaczewski was stunned by the quality of the performance. At a dinner following the concert Skrowaczewski encountered Szell again. The elder maestro had seen a score of Skrowaczewski's Symphony for Strings and was impressed. "You have to come and conduct your Symphony for Strings with the Cleveland Orchestra," he told Skrowaczewski.

Szell's remark was no meaningless pleasantry. He was discerning in his choice of the Cleveland Orchestra's infrequent guest conductors, and he was not a champion of new music. The invitation clearly showed his respect for Skrowaczewski's talents. A year later, in 1958, Skrowaczewski made his U.S. debut with the Cleveland Orchestra, which in turn opened the door for a life-altering engagement in 1959.

Throughout Skrowaczewski's early career, critics cited Szell as the major conductor with whom he shared an artistic sensibility, despite their contrasting temperaments and repertoire preferences. They shared an Eastern European background, worked hard and meticulously, and possessed great musical integrity. Until Szell's death in 1970, Skrowaczewski was a regular guest conductor with the Cleveland Orchestra, both at Severance Hall and at Blossom Music Center, the orchestra's summer home in Cuyahoga Falls, Ohio. The two conductors developed a special collegial friendship over the thirteen years of their acquaintance. It is quite possible that Szell, "by and large accepted as the greatest conductor after Toscanini," as Harold Schonberg of *The New York Times* wrote, saw a younger version of himself in Skrowaczewski.[4]

Born in Budapest in 1897, the year of Brahms' death, Szell was one of the great conductors from Hungary who dominated major American orchestras in the 20th century: Fritz Reiner (Cincinnati, Pittsburgh, Chicago); Eugene Ormandy (Minneapolis, Philadelphia); Antal Doráti (Dallas, Minneapolis, National Symphony Orchestra, Detroit); and Sir Georg Solti (Chicago).

A musical prodigy trained in Vienna, Szell debuted as a pianist at age eleven, performing a Mozart piano concerto in that city's famed Musikverein. The concert also included Rondo for Piano and Orchestra and an overture, both composed by Szell. A European tour following his debut included a performance with the London Symphony. By age fourteen he had an exclusive contract with Universal Edition in Vienna to publish his music. But by this time he had dismissed his efforts at composing and turned to conducting. Two years after Szell's conducting debut at age sixteen, Richard Strauss became his mentor. In his twenties Szell held several positions in German opera houses before Strauss recommended him to Otto Klemperer, who was looking for someone to succeed him at the Municipal Opera in Strasbourg. By 1929 Szell was leading both the German Opera and the Prague Philharmonic. In 1930 he made his American debut with the St. Louis Symphony.[5]

That same year he heard a performance by Toscanini and the New York Philharmonic that permanently changed his standards of orchestral performance. In the late 1930s, as conductor of the Scottish Orchestra, Szell established important ties to the Residentie-Orkest of The Hague, the London Symphony, and the Concertgebouw Orchestra. After World War II began, he settled in the United States, where he took a teaching post at Mannes School of Music in New York, played chamber music (he maintained his piano-playing facility throughout his life), and planned his future. By the early 1940s he had guest conducted Toscanini's NBC Symphony, the New York Philharmonic, and the Boston Symphony, and he was a frequent guest at the Metropolitan Opera. When Artur Rodziński left the Cleveland Orchestra to become conductor of the New York Philharmonic, Szell was a candidate for the post. Erich Leinsdorf ended up with the position in 1943. He missed half of his first season because he was drafted into the army, but after two more seasons his contract was not renewed. Although Leinsdorf had successes in Cleveland, Szell's guest-conducting appearances began to overshadow them. His legendary tenure as the fourth music director of the Cleveland Orchestra began in fall 1946.[6]

The incarnation of the Cleveland Orchestra that Skrowaczewski heard in 1957—the orchestra was on its first-ever European tour—was a high point in the Szell-Cleveland collaboration. Szell was one of his generation's last true orchestra builders. When he assumed command, the orchestra ranked among the finest in the United States, but after a decade of his obsessive work ethic and uncompromising artistry, the Cleveland Orchestra was widely considered to be among the elite orchestras of the world.

Szell's approach to rehearsing and his often less-than-tactful interactions with musicians were legendary. "We begin to rehearse when most orchestras leave off," was one of his famous quotes, and he was probably right. He brought a truly unbelievable level of personal preparation to every rehearsal, each of which he considered a concert unto itself. "The Cleveland Orchestra plays seven concerts a week and admits the public to the final two," was another of his well-known quips. His almost-maniacal penchant for rehearsing obtained astonishing results, but it also brought criticism. "He even rehearsed the inspiration," said Klaus George Roy, a longtime program annotator for the Cleveland Orchestra.[7] John Mack, one of the great American oboists, began playing in the orchestra during Szell's final five years. He cited a rehearsal quote from the maestro that, as he put it, could have served as Szell's epitaph: "I want this phrase to sound completely spontaneous—however, as a result of meticulous planning."[8]

Skrowaczewski again conducted a wide body of literature during his second season in Warsaw. His first concert, held the day after his thirty-fourth birthday, featured a huge program: Toccata by Michał Spisak (an outstanding Polish composer ten years Skrowaczewski's senior); Bartók's *Music for Strings, Percussion and Celesta*; and Beethoven's Ninth Symphony. Over his next series of nine programs Skrowaczewski conducted symphonies of Brahms, Tchaikovsky, Mozart, and Beethoven, and works by Bartók, Strauss, Ravel, Berlioz, Weber, Rachmaninoff, Stravinsky, Prokofiev, and Gershwin. He also led several works by his Polish contemporaries Perkowski, Szabelski, and Turski, and a newly composed Flute Concerto by Kazimierz Sikorski, president of the Union of Polish Composers from 1954 to 1959.

Skrowaczewski's performances of contemporary music during this period were not limited to Polish composers. He conducted the *Warsaw Concerto* by British film and television composer David Aspinall. This widely popular Rachmaninoff-esque piano concerto was featured in the 1941 war film *Dangerous Moonlight*, and Skrowaczewski's performances of the work were perhaps among the first in postwar Warsaw. He also performed *Coro di Morti*, a respected work by Goffredo Petrassi, a major 20th-century Italian composer. Another foremost Italian composer whose music Skrowaczewski conducted was Virgilio Mortari. In the late 1950s Mortari supervised the Teatro La Fenice in Venice, and he often invited Skrowaczewski to conduct the opera house's orchestra. During a Venice engagement in 1957, Skrowaczewski heard a unique vocal duet:

> Mortari was a charming and sweet man and a well-known composer at that time. He invited Krystyna and me to his apartment in Venice. He wanted to share a new choral work with me. The text dealt with some tragic historical events. He sat down on the piano and began to play and sing the important lines, which he did well. It was spring, so the windows were open, and there were hundreds of cats on all the nearby rooftops. As he sang, all the cats began meowing. They produced a wonderful concert together. Poor Krystyna was doing everything she could to contain her laughter while he just kept singing away, but she just couldn't.

Between October 1957 and March 1958, Skrowaczewski conducted an impressive array of repertoire in Warsaw and also maintained a busy guest-conducting schedule. His intense preparation and stamina served him well during the coming years, when he conducted so much music in high-profile situations. Further challenges and rewards occurred when he collaborated with three major 20th-century pianists: Emil Gilels, Sviatoslav Richter, and Arturo Benedetti Michelangeli.

"I didn't realize at the time how important it was for me to work with these great artists," Skrowaczewski reflected. "The soloists in Warsaw, as with the Radio Orchestra of Katowice, were world-class. I was able to compare their artistry with that of other soloists, and I learned from what they would ask me to do with the orchestra for their accompaniments."

Gilels, the Russian whom Skrowaczewski described as "really one of the greatest but *very* strange," had a wide repertoire of over four hundred works ranging from Scarlatti to Shostakovich. A master of sonority and of combining virtuosic technique with passionate poetry, Gilels performed mostly in Russia and the Soviet bloc until his American debut in 1955 and British debut four years later. His recordings include the complete Beethoven concertos with the Cleveland Orchestra under Szell.

Russian-born Richter also had an extensive repertoire and late exposure to the West. By the time Richter made his U.S. debut in 1960 with the Chicago Symphony, he was well known throughout his homeland and the Eastern bloc. His Western debut, however, led to recordings and tours that solidified his worldwide fame. He was notorious for being a challenging artist with whom to collaborate. Russian conductor Gennady Rozhdestvensky explained that Richter was "too powerful for him to collaborate with—he had an energy that tended to crush you."[9] An intense personality, Richter often would "experiment in concerts" through his interpretations. In *The Art of Piano*, pianist Zoltán Kocsis acknowledges the challenges some performers had with Richter but says that "when he reached full concentration, I've never heard more demanding performances by another pianist."[10] Prokofiev dedicated his Ninth Sonata to Richter, with whom he had a close relationship.

Skrowaczewski, who performed Schumann's Piano Concerto in A minor with Richter and the Warsaw Philharmonic, provided a snapshot of his personality in the late 1950s:

> I had no difficulties at all working with him. He was quite subdued in Warsaw. He was very strong emotionally, but he was quite introverted and introspective, almost sad. What was unbelievable was that after our first concert with the Schumann, Richter apparently stayed in the hall until 4:00 a.m., practicing. The following day, before the next concert, the watchman told me Richter had been playing there all night.

Italian pianist Michelangeli was in some respects the antithesis of Gilels and Richter. His repertoire was small, he performed infrequently, and he was obsessed by his physical appearance at the piano. A recluse much like Glenn Gould, the eccentric Michelangeli claimed, among other things, that he was descended from Saint Francis of Assisi. His flawless technique and rare performances created an aura of mystique, while his recordings, a number of which are live performances, are distinctive for their clarity, personality, and control (adjectives that also befit Gould).

A tour to Belgium and England highlighted the close of Skrowaczewski's second season with the Philharmonic. He shared the podium with music director Wodiczko for performances in London and Bristol and at the 1958 Brussels World's Fair, which turned out to be a musically historic event. The fair's theme—"faith in mankind's ability to mold the atomic age to the ultimate advantage of all nations and peoples"— was hopeful and in hindsight, hopelessly naïve.[11] The atomic-age analog in music, with a far more innocuous connotation, was perhaps the advent of electronic music.

Edgard Varèse, the French-born maverick American composer, premiered the first major electronic composition in Paris in 1954. *Déserts* was a forty-year dream of the man who resembled a mad scientist (an observation made by a young Frank Zappa upon seeing the composer's image). *Déserts* combined tape-recorded sounds with instrumental parts, but in Brussels the composer unveiled a solo work for taped sounds, *Poème Électronique*. The first of its kind, the composition was played at the World's Fair over 425 loudspeakers in the Le Corbusier Pavilion, built especially for its performance. Le Corbusier, the Swiss architect who conceived the pavilion, was a maverick in his own right and a major influence on 20th-century architecture. Composer, architect, and civil engineer Iannis Xenakis, who then worked for Le Corbusier, created the shape of the unique structure built for *Poème Électronique.* Varèse's aesthetic of experiencing the spatial qualities of music was fully realized through the fusion of his piece and its performing arena. The achievement was fleeting, however; when the fair ended, the pavilion was demolished, as was the manifestation of his lifelong vision.[12]

Skrowaczewski led the Warsaw Philharmonic in a tour de force all-Polish program at the World's Fair. After opening with the *Bajka* (Fairy Tale) Overture by Stanisław Moniuszko, the leading 19th-century Polish opera composer, Skrowaczewski conducted both Chopin piano concertos (with two different Polish pianists) before ending the concert with Lutosławski's Concerto for Orchestra, a work only four years old.

From Brussels the Philharmonic headed to London, where Skrowaczewski collaborated with Roman Totenberg in a performance of Szymanowski's Violin Concerto no. 1. Born in Łódź, Poland, in 1911, Totenberg debuted with the Warsaw Philharmonic at age eleven. In 1938 he settled in America, where he gave the U.S. premiere of Szymanowski's First Violin Concerto with the Boston Symphony in 1956. A great advocate of contemporary composers, Totenberg premiered the Hindemith Sonata in E, William Schuman's Concerto for Violin, and Darius Milhaud's *Music for Boston.*[13] He was a gifted teacher and administrator who held numerous positions at summer music festivals and music schools, including Boston University, where he is professor emeritus. In honor of his ninetieth birthday in 2001, Totenberg performed Szymanowski's First Violin Concerto with the Boston University Symphony Orchestra. His daughter, Nina Totenberg, legal-affairs correspondent for National Public Radio (NPR), is a familiar name to the network's listeners.

After concluding the Philharmonic's tour with a performance in Bristol, Skrowaczewski conducted his final performance of the season back in Warsaw. The break following the tour was not long enough to afford him time to compose. However, his one effort from 1958 was a score to *Król Macius I* (King Matthew I), an eighty-minute film directed by Wanda Jukubowska and based on a 1919 classic Polish children's novel of the same title. Written by Janusz Korczak, the book tells the story of a boy king who tries to bring reform to his subjects and his kingdom. Korczak was a well-known writer, children's-rights advocate, and progressive school administrator. In 1942, during the Nazis' first round of liquidation of the Warsaw ghetto, Korczak and the two hundred children under his care at a Warsaw orphanage were sent to the death camp in Treblinka in eastern Poland, where they were murdered.[14]

Skrowaczewski's film score for full orchestra is notable for its masterful use of orchestration to create dramatic effects. Deft combinations of woodwinds, strings, and percussion, often in a chamber music setting, and inventive harmonic gestures give the music a voice beyond its intended purpose. The use of thematic development and dissonant textures is also distinctive. This music holds up remarkably well in comparison to other major film scores, past and present. Skrowaczewski dismisses all of his film scores as insignificant, but *Król Macius I* is but one example that could have been crafted into a symphonic suite suitable for the concert hall. Pianist, educator, and film-noir authority Ran Blake commented on *Król Macius I* in 2006:

> There is only one thing wrong with Stan Skrowaczewski's score for the 1958 Polish film *Król Macius I*: there is not enough of it. The score is terrific. We hear brass, chimes, and low strings. There's music for the ceremonial court and the town square, and we have a combination of barbaric Alban Berg [and] the early raw Shostakovich, with a seasoning of horseradish Byzantine.[15]

Film director Jerzy Kawalerowicz was so enamored of Skrowaczewski's music that he wanted to create a film based on one of his existing pieces. "[He envisioned] a visual tone poem on an original, quite abstract composition," Skrowaczewski said. "It never happened, but it was an intriguing proposal."

Skrowaczewski entered his third season as conductor in Warsaw with great anticipation. Szell had followed through on his invitation: Skrowaczewski would make his American debut with the Cleveland Orchestra in early December 1958. Two series of concerts with the Warsaw Philharmonic, both of which featured Skrowaczewski's usual ambitious programming, preceded his trip. He conducted four works by Polish composers, including Palester's Fourth Symphony and a work by Borys Latoszyński. Works by Ravel, Rachmaninoff, and Frank Martin rounded off the programs.

A few days before Thanksgiving, Skrowaczewski and his wife made their first trip to North America. Their route was, as Skrowaczewski recalled, circuitous:

> It was before the jet era, so we flew in a small plane via Copenhagen. From there to New York took seventeen hours because due to bad weather we were diverted to Goose Bay, Newfoundland. It was twenty degrees below zero Fahrenheit at Goose Bay, so they put us in a hangar that was one hundred degrees! From the combination of experiencing this extreme cold and extreme heat, and from the long trip, we were both exhausted. After we finally got to New York, someone from the Polish consulate met us at the airport. We had three hours before boarding for Cleveland, so he took us downtown to see Carnegie Hall from the street. With all the traffic, stopping and going—it was quite demanding—we got motion sickness. It was my first impression of New York, being in this car feeling miserable. Everything was so big in comparison to Europe: streets, skyscrapers, and especially the cars, those huge 1950s American cars. Then we headed to Cleveland, and again we had a small plane. There was a snowstorm, so the flight was rough, and we became sick again. At the airport, the manager and chairman of the Cleveland Orchestra, whom I had met during the orchestra's 1957 European tour, greeted us. They were all dressed formally in black coats and hats, very distinguished. Their hospitality was magnificent.

The Cleveland Orchestra's administration and its musicians received Skrowaczewski graciously. Nevertheless, Skrowaczewski had to earn the musicians' respect, but by the end of the first rehearsal he had won them over:

The first rehearsal was wonderful. As with the Rome competition, I was up to the task; I wasn't nervous at all. I was just correcting their playing, and they apparently liked it. Josef Gingold, the concertmaster, came to me after and said, "Listen, it's wonderful. We are so happy. Your remarks were so new to us." And some of the other principal players said similar comments. They said they were surprised that a young person would have such expertise and depth of musical feeling. I remember a nice bass player who invited Krystyna and me for a chamber music concert at his house. The orchestra was extremely friendly and supportive. That was a great, great week for me.

Skrowaczewski's programming undoubtedly led to his triumphant week with the Cleveland Orchestra: Beethoven's *Leonore* Overture no. 3, Lutosławski's Concerto for Orchestra, and the Fifth Symphony of Shostakovich. The Lutosławski work was completely unfamiliar to the orchestra: Skrowaczewski's performance was its U.S. premiere, and he gained instant credibility in rehearsing it. The Shostakovich, although not unfamiliar to the orchestra, was seldom performed in Cleveland. (Szell never conducted a Shostakovich symphony in his twenty-four years with the orchestra.) At this point in his career Skrowaczewski had probably conducted this symphony more often than any other, and he led the entire concert in Cleveland without scores. The *Leonore* Overture, part of the orchestra's canon, allowed the musicians to compare Skrowaczewski's interpretation with that of Szell, their resident Beethovenite. His artistry in both classical and contemporary realms won their approbation.

A significant event affecting Skrowaczewski's U.S. debut was the death of Artur Rodziński. "Conductor From Poland Brings Cheer," announced the headline of a concert review in Cleveland's *The Plain Dealer*:

> With phenomenal timing, a dynamic goodwill ambassador from Poland, Stanisław Skrowaczewski, stepped onto the Severance Hall podium just one week after ailing Polish conductor Artur Rodziński had died in Boston. The young, lean, thirty-five-year-old director of the Warsaw Philharmonic led the Cleveland Orchestra in electric performances of two Slavic works and Beethoven's *Leonore* Overture no. 3, telling the audience that Poland's musical tradition is as much alive as ever. If Cleveland is mourning the passing of Rodziński, its former conductor, it is also cheering the arrival of Skrowaczewski.[16]

It is doubtful that Skrowaczewski ever thought that he was picking up the torch from Rodziński. As always, he focused on making music, and he reveled in the rare opportunity to work with the exalted Cleveland Orchestra:

> Szell was not in town during my first engagement; he was off guest conducting somewhere. At that time the Cleveland Orchestra and others had very few guest conductors. Szell, Reiner, Ormandy, and others like them practically did their entire seasons themselves. So being a guest back then was something special, and I felt this very much. Today that's gone. Now a music director conducts half or less than half of a season. You are treated well as a guest, but it's nothing special.

The Cleveland Orchestra was magnificent to rehearse and conduct. It was at its peak in the late 1950s and early 1960s. The principal string players were legends like Josef Gingold (concertmaster), Bernhard Goldschmidt (principal second violin), Abraham Skernick (viola), and others. There was such unbelievable precision, intonation, and beauty of tone. A number of the players in the *second* stands later became concertmasters in other great American orchestras. So the second violins were what you'd wish you'd have as first violins these days in some places! And of course the woodwinds: precision, intonation, approach, release, phrasing, togetherness, without saying anything. The brasses were equally fantastic. Myron Bloom, the principal horn, was magnificent. After these players left, they were replaced with excellent musicians, but there was something unique about these particular players in this period of the orchestra's history.

Szell handpicked many of his musicians. The seemingly effortless execution and sense of ensemble that Skrowaczewski experienced while conducting the Cleveland Orchestra resulted in large part from twelve long, hard years of Szell's relentless rehearsing. Late in his career the fastidious maestro explained his approach to molding the orchestra:

> I personally like complete homogeneity of sound, phrasing, and articulation within each section, and then—when the ensemble is perfect—the proper balance between sections plus complete flexibility—so that in each movement one or two principal voices can be accompanied by the others. To put it simply: the most sensitive ensemble playing.[17]

Skrowaczewski's debut won a special reception from the public. His admirers in the conductor's room after the concert included a contingent of Cleveland Poles who beamed with pride over his success. One fan secretly stuck a twenty-dollar bill in the conductor's pocket. "It paid for a good dinner for two at the time," remarked the maestro.

The next morning, two hours after Skrowaczewski read the *Plain Dealer*'s concert review, the phone in his hotel room rang. "This is Arthur Judson," a booming voice declared. "I heard that your concert was wonderful. Would you like to be my artist?" Without hesitation Skrowaczewski replied, "Yes, of course!"

"Good," Judson said, knowing the answer in advance. "You have to come to New York. I'll have a big party for you."

In the world of classical music this brief phone call was the equivalent of a king knighting a subject and handing him the keys to the kingdom. Although Skrowaczewski was far removed from the world of music management, he recognized Judson's name. For a European conductor like Skrowaczewski, a Judson contract was a ticket to engagements with the finest orchestras in the United States. Within hours, he received calls from orchestra managers in New York, Philadelphia, Cincinnati, Pittsburgh, and Cleveland.

Today only a few arts professionals and some older concertgoers recognize Judson's name, which survives as a footnote in biographies of various famous musicians and also through the Arthur Judson Foundation, which dispenses arts grants, various prizes, and an annual award to an outstanding young conductor. But regardless of how Judson is remembered today, he was the most powerful and influential manager in American classical music for over fifty years, towering over the field for much of the twentieth century. He was seventy-seven years old when he added Skrowaczewski to his list of artists in December 1958. Although Judson would soon sever his connections to the empire he had built, Columbia Artists Management Inc. (CAMI), he continued working—albeit in a much-diminished capacity—until his death in 1975, just eleven days shy of his ninety-fourth birthday.

Judson was a discreet, secretive man who preferred to wield his power behind the scenes, and as he wished, there is little written about him. Born in Dayton, Ohio, he studied violin in New York, performed in orchestras, and gained conducting experience with a community orchestra in New Jersey. He moved into music administration, becoming a dean of the Conservatory of Music at Denison University in Granville, Ohio, at age nineteen. By 1907 he moved to New York, where he taught violin and conducted, and later became a critic for *Musical America*. On a trip to review a concert by the Cincinnati Symphony Orchestra in 1910, he was bowled over by its twenty-eight-year-old conductor, the phenomenally gifted Leopold Stokowski, who was a year younger than Judson. Shared ambitions brought the pair together in 1915, when Judson became manager of the Philadelphia Orchestra, which Stokowski had taken over in 1912. Together in 1916 they mounted the American premiere of Mahler's Eighth Symphony and set the Philadelphia Orchestra on a course for world fame. By then Judson had founded his own company on the side, Arthur Judson Concert Management, and Stokowski was his first client.[18]

By 1922 Judson had expanded his influence on American orchestral life by becoming manager of the New York Philharmonic while retaining his position with the Philadelphia Orchestra. Unbelievably, he also became advisory manager of the Cincinnati Symphony Orchestra. This triadic responsibility—coupled with the management of his private company—lasted five years. Then he left the post at Cincinnati but managed the Philadelphia Orchestra until 1935. He didn't leave the New York Philharmonic until 1956. (His departure was due, in part, to a scathing article in *The New York Times* about a possible conflict of interest involving the Philharmonic's management and Judson's company, CAMI).[19]

Judson worked with, and in some cases, managed nearly all of the 20th century's major conductors, including Willem Mengelberg, Arturo Toscanini, Furtwängler, Koussevitzky, Reiner, and Ormandy. He maneuvered maestros and scores of concert artists through the American orchestral landscape. But his greatest accomplishment (or monopoly, as others called it) took root in 1926, when he launched the Judson Radio Program Corporation.[20]

The use of radio as a marketing tool for symphony orchestras was still in its infancy in the 1920s, but Judson foresaw its potential. He established his radio corporation with the intention of supplying music to the National Broadcasting Company (NBC) network. When NBC refused to use Judson's corporation, he obtained seed money from a New York Philharmonic board member to create United Independent Broadcasters, a conglomerate of sixteen radio stations. Columbia Phonograph Company bought significant airtime on the new network, creating the opportunity for a merger. By 1928 Judson was part of a joint venture, the Columbia Broadcasting System (CBS), which had forty-seven affiliate stations. Two years later Judson merged seven of his concert-management competitors under one roof. In 1930 he became the first president of Columbia Concerts Corporation, which managed artists involved with the network and its associate organizations. It quickly became the largest organization of its kind in the world. Following monopoly accusations by the federal government in 1942, CBS sold the company to Judson, and thus CAMI was born. NBC also sold its management company to avoid monopoly investigations. National Concert Artists Corporation (NCAC), headed by the gregarious Sol Hurok, offered CAMI modest competition.[21]

By 1958 Judson's domination of music management was fading, but he still wielded considerable power. After his Cleveland Orchestra debut, Skrowaczewski experienced the magnitude of Judson's reach into America's musical elite at his "welcome to CAMI" party in New York City:

> There were at least forty people gathered in the Oak Room at the Plaza Hotel in New York. It was incredible. Practically all the important musical figures in New York were there: conductors, composers, critics, and impresarios. I knew some of their names, but I didn't realize the magnitude of their artistic weight at the time. I met William Schuman [president of The Juilliard School] and Peter Mennin [Juilliard composition faculty and newly appointed director of The Peabody Institute]. Even Stokowski was there! "Where is the young conductor?" he bellowed after his presence was established in the room. We were introduced, and he took me almost by force into a corner away from everyone. He started firing off lots of questions: what were my impressions of the Cleveland Orchestra, the United States, etc. He, of course, had conducted a lot in Europe but not so much in Poland. He kept his origins mysterious, but supposedly he had some Polish heritage. I told him that if he'd like to come to guest conduct the Warsaw Philharmonic, it would be like a national holiday for everyone in Poland. And he said, "I will."

> I started to tremble a bit because I was not the manager. It wasn't my right—especially as only the second conductor in Warsaw—to make invitations. And it was still the communist era; having guests from the West was still not that easy. I thought maybe Stokowski would say he would come in a few years or something like that. No. He said, "Next May I'm in Vienna. I will come from there." So after the party I ran to the telephone and called the Polish Embassy, "Stokowski will come!" There was a big fuss.

Judson extended Skrowaczewski's visit by inviting him and Krystyna to dinner at his home in Rye, New York. "Both Arthur and his wife had a good sense of humor,"

Krystyna recalled. "She was a petite woman, and he was this tall, imposing figure. He reminded me of my grandfather. I remember he looked at me and said, 'She'll do; she'll do *very* well.' I guess I won his approval as a proper conductor's wife."

After his triumphant American debut, Skrowaczewski increasingly felt the jealousy and animosity emanating from some of his colleagues in the Warsaw Philharmonic. Reprints of his Cleveland reviews appeared in Polish newspapers, and his growing fame did not sit well with other Polish conductors. "Some people did a lot of digging under me at that time," Skrowaczewski revealed. "They were jealous of my achievements and my opportunities to go to the West. These people had connections with the ministry of culture, which had its own brand of strange politics. It created an air of tension around me. Finally, I decided to leave the Philharmonic at the end of the season rather than endure this atmosphere."

He had only a few concerts left with the Warsaw Philharmonic after his trip to America, but the season ended on a high note. True to his word, Stokowski arrived in Warsaw in May 1959 for a week of rehearsals and two concerts. Skrowaczewski was the grand maestro's host.

Like Toscanini—but perhaps without as much reverence—Stokowski's popularity and mass appeal transcended the world of classical music. His was a household name, much as Leonard Bernstein's would become in the second half of the 20th century. But neither Toscanini nor Bernstein matched Stokowski's professional longevity. He held major conducting posts for sixty-three consecutive years, including twenty-four years with the Philadelphia Orchestra and shorter stints with the Cincinnati Symphony, NBC Symphony (one season), and Houston Symphony. His last directorship was with an ensemble of his own creation, the American Symphony Orchestra, with which he presented the world premiere of Charles Ives' Fourth Symphony in 1965. At age ninety-four, he signed a five-year contract with Columbia Records. He was scheduled to record Rachmaninoff's Second Symphony on the day he died, one year later.[22]

In addition to an extensive discography dating from 1920 to 1977, Stokowski created nearly 160 orchestral transcriptions, including nearly forty works by Bach.[23] Many people were troubled by his eccentric personal life (three high-profile marriages, a publicized affair with Greta Garbo, and a proclivity to manufacture an aura around his origins). He also had a penchant for musical spectacle: promotion of the "Stokowski Sound," manipulation of scores, and stylistically controversial transcriptions and interpretations. In the final analysis, however, there is no denying Stokowski's musicianship, splendid conducting talent, and his astonishing record of performing new music. He gave hundreds of world premieres and dozens of American premieres of works by such composers as Rachmaninoff, Stravinsky, Schoenberg, Berg, and Varèse.

As Skrowaczewski remembered, the seventy-seven-year-old Stokowski's conducting prowess and eccentric nature were on full display during his visit to Warsaw:

Krystyna and I and Lutosławski and his wife, Danuta, were waiting for him at 6:00 a.m. at the train station. It was a beautiful, crisp May morning. The train pulled in, and we waited a bit. It wasn't Stokowski who first exited the sleeping train, it was his twenty suitcases! It took two or three porters to load them on carts. Finally, behind this mountain of suitcases, emerges Stokowski. We greeted [him] and then brought him to the best hotel in Warsaw.

He began rehearsals the next day. It was a strange program: Ravel's *Rapsodie espagnole*, Lutosławski's Concerto for Orchestra, and Brahms' First Symphony. Of course, with my position with the Philharmonic, I was at all of his rehearsals. As his host, I was always with him anyway, transporting him, etc. At all the rehearsals from Monday to Friday, he didn't say one word to the orchestra, not one remark. Absolutely nothing! They played through, sometimes repeating some sections, but he never said why he was repeating. The orchestra knew the Brahms and Lutosławski by heart. Only at the dress rehearsal did he speak, telling the first violins during the Ravel how a particular *glissando* had to be played. It was his only remark during the entire cycle of rehearsals! But the orchestra was excellent, they knew the music, and Stokowski really had some magic in his presence and in his fingers. He captured the attention of the musicians, producing excellent results and concerts.

Throughout the week he was extremely social and pleasant. He never played the role of a prima donna. He was like a friendly grandfather to everyone. There were a few meetings and press conferences throughout the week. A violinist in the Philharmonic, Nina Stokowski, showed him a photo of a Polish general in uniform and asked if the person in it was his grandfather. He answered, "Yes," but said nothing more. Nina claimed that she came from the same family that he did. Her great-grandfather was General Stokowski, a historic figure who was a general with Napoleon. Stokowski didn't deny her claim, but he wouldn't say anything more about it.

After his dress rehearsal he surprised me by saying, "After the concert I would like to come to your house for a small supper party. And I would like to have crawfish." It was a kind of specialty and delicacy exported to France and other countries. Stokowski said he remembered having them in Nice, and when he asked where one finds them, they told him Poland. He also wanted white asparagus! Poland is known for crawfish, and May is the main month they are popular to eat, but this is not necessarily common knowledge. Even some Polish people are not aware of it, but Stokowski knew it.

Krystyna was terrified when I told her Stokowski had invited himself for a dinner party. Our apartment was so small. We were on the fifth floor, and there was no elevator. And cooking on a large scale was nearly impossible. Krystyna drove all over Warsaw, hunting down crawfish and white asparagus. Certain foods were still challenging to find in Poland at that time. Fortunately, crawfish were in season in May, and she found some at a local farmer's market. She bought hundreds, storing them on ice in our bathtub. Lutosławski and his wife joined us for the party. Stokowski was very gracious. We didn't have enough chairs for everyone, so he happily just sat on our bed. He didn't talk much about music; he spoke more about life, pleasures, and travels. He drank a lot of wine and later talked about how he loved his sons and how much he detested his wife. After his second concert was over and he had left, I remember feeling a little pride in the fact that I was the conduit for getting him to Poland. He probably wouldn't have come otherwise.

By the time Stokowski left Warsaw, Skrowaczewski had received his itinerary from Judson for his second trip to the United States. During the intervening five months since Skrowaczewski had met the czar of CAMI, Judson had secured for him a return engagement with the Cleveland Orchestra and debuts with the Cincinnati and Pittsburgh orchestras and the New York Philharmonic. The six-week tour began with a triumph in Cleveland on December 17, 1959.

"Polish Conductor Electrifies Severance Hall," trumpeted the headline of *The Plain Dealer* review from an atypical placement on the newspaper's front page.[24] "Not for a year, if ever, have we heard Berlioz' *Symphonie fantastique* transmitted with such vividness and force, such suppleness and grace, such insight into its magnificence, a kind of greatness comparable only to Beethoven, at least so it seemed on this occasion," wrote Herbert Elwell in his review.[25]

Unknown to Skrowaczewski, members of a search committee from the Minneapolis Symphony Orchestra had been in the Cleveland audience that evening. Elwell's assessment of Skrowaczewski as a conductor—"one of the greatest we have heard"—no doubt confirmed what the visitors from Minnesota had experienced. They were seeking a successor to Antal Doráti, who was leaving his Minneapolis post at the conclusion of the 1959–60 season.

"We had been looking at several conductors, and when we heard [Skrowaczewski] we immediately recognized that he was a totally unique and marvelous conductor and interpreter," recalled Kenneth (Ken) Dayton, then a board member. "A group on the committee went on to Pittsburgh to hear him. After that, we decided he was the person we wanted."

Unaware that the Minneapolis Symphony Orchestra was scouting him, Skrowaczewski focused completely on his concerts in America. During his second series of concerts with the Cleveland Orchestra, Skrowaczewski's Symphony for Strings received its U.S. premiere on Christmas 1959—the fruition of the invitation from Szell during his visit to Katowice in fall 1957.

"If this work by the then twenty-four-year-old composer is not a masterpiece," wrote Klaus George Roy in *The Christian Science Monitor*, "it is without question a masterly piece. Superbly scored for the instruments, the music has vitality and design, intense expressiveness, and soaring lyricism."[26] *The Plain Dealer* reported that Symphony for Strings "had an immediate success, not because of sensational novelty, but because of the same kind of vitality and integrity that is observable in his conducting."[27] Later during his tour Skrowaczewski performed the work with the New York Philharmonic. The concert was part of a special event held at the United Nations, so it was an unofficial debut and therefore not noted by the press.

Although Skrowaczewski also made critically acclaimed debuts in Pittsburgh and Cincinnati, his concerts in Cleveland stood out for their quality across a broad repertoire. With one of the great orchestras of the world—arguably the finest in the United States at that time—he had conducted Mozart, Rossini, Berlioz, Debussy, Ravel, Prokofiev, Lutosławski (*Musique funèbre*), and his own work. *The Christian Science Monitor* offered an assessment of Skrowaczewski's second visit to the Cleveland Orchestra:

> At thirty-six, Mr. Skrowaczewski is a master of his craft, a full-blooded artist, an experienced leader who can inspire veteran orchestral players as well as sophisticated and demanding audiences. He impressed all with the sensitivity and individuality of his concepts, his youthful fervor, his genuine romantic feeling tempered by a keen intelligence. There is a warmth to his music-making which established immediate response from performers and listeners alike. If one may disagree with him on some points of interpretation, there is never any doubt that he believes passionately in what he asks for and has the skill to make his approach convincing.[28]

Judson met with Skrowaczewski as he was preparing to return to Warsaw at the conclusion of his U.S. tour in mid-January 1960. "The Minneapolis Symphony would like you to become their next music director," Judson told Skrowaczewski. "I said that you're the right person for them. They're an excellent orchestra. I suggest you take it."

The difficulty for Skrowaczewski was not the decision to take the position but rather the challenge of leaving Poland under difficult circumstances. It was impossible for him to stay in the United States until the fall, when the appointment would begin. Krystyna was still back in Warsaw tending to Skrowaczewski's father, who was critically ill, and Polish authorities were already suspicious of Skrowaczewski's trips abroad. However, he had a three-week engagement in Amsterdam with the Concertgebouw Orchestra in February that could serve as his escape from communist Poland. The Minneapolis orchestra's management agreed to keep Skrowaczewski's appointment a secret until he and Krystyna were safely in the West.

The young maestro boarded the plane to Warsaw, his feelings in turmoil. His recent accomplishments and the rich possibilities for his future were tempered by prescient tensions. Leaving Poland forever was fraught with potential danger and difficult emotions. The promise of a new life, however, gave Skrowaczewski hope against the challenges that lay ahead of him.

A biting winter wind greeted Skrowaczewski upon his return to Warsaw. As he stepped off the plane in mid-January 1960, anxiety over the means of his escape from Poland surfaced, and his excitement over his secret appointment as music director of the Minneapolis Symphony Orchestra waned.

Grief swept these feelings aside when Skrowaczewski learned that his father had died in December during his absence. Paweł, who suffered from kidney disease, was seriously ill when Skrowaczewski saw him before his trip, but his death nevertheless was unexpected. Krystyna waited until her husband returned home before breaking the news of his father's death. There was nothing Skrowaczewski could have done so far from home, and the news would have disrupted his important American engagements.

Skrowaczewski had little time for mourning. After the funeral he had two concerts with the Bucharest Symphony Orchestra in chilly Romania during the last week of January. The engagement was memorable because he conducted all rehearsals and two concerts while seriously ill with pneumonia.

Skrowaczewski kept a diary of the concerts he conducted, numbering each one, and the Bucharest concerts brought his total to 430. The diversity and breadth of repertoire he had conducted by his thirty-sixth year was impressive. Most of his concerts had been with Poland's major orchestras. In a week he would begin a long series of engagements in Amsterdam and South America that would serve as his exodus from Poland.

Although Skrowaczewski had guest conducted in the West several times and had completed a second American tour, he nevertheless faced problems getting out of Poland in winter 1960. "After relatively a little more artistic freedom in 1956 through 1957, the communist screw started to tighten much more, and I had big problems even leaving for my European concerts," he explained.

After he told Krystyna about the wonderful position that awaited him in the States, they devised a secret plan whereby they would leave together for his upcoming engagement in Amsterdam in February and not return to Poland. It was the only way they could make a clean break to live and work in the United States, but their departure would not be easy. Secrecy was essential—they told their families what was happening only at the last moment. "It was very hard. Not to be able to say goodbye to friends, to say goodbye to our parents only, begging them not to say a word," Krystyna recalled. To maintain the ruse of a short trip, they packed only two little suitcases. Their prized possession was a Fiat, one of only a handful in Warsaw at that time, and they hated to lose that modest luxury. Their families sold the car and removed possessions from their apartment before the Polish authorities could seize them.

Skrowaczewski left behind most of his compositions as well as most of his orchestra scores. Some of his conducting scores were later shipped to the United States, but his compositions were lost. "I was so frustrated with my compositions at that point that I really didn't care," he later remembered. "The overall loss we felt in leaving in 1960 was strong, but the bigger loss was when I first left Lwów in 1945 with my parents. We took very little with us. I was young and didn't care about it, but for my parents, they lost everything they had earned during their whole lives."

Oppression was growing in Poland, and the communist government was a formidable force. Skrowaczewski would be allowed to go to Amsterdam, but Krystyna was denied a passport. He insisted he would not go without his wife and that the concerts would have to be canceled. He feared that a scandal would ensue: the stakes were high, and the opportunity in Minneapolis could be lost.

By sheer coincidence, the Skrowaczewskis' trip was saved at the last moment. Near the time of their scheduled departure, members of the Polish Union of Composers were meeting with Józef Cyrankiewicz, premier of the People's Republic of Poland, to discuss plans for an upcoming international music festival. Union member Zbigniew Turski mentioned in passing how unfortunate it was that Skrowaczewski couldn't fulfill his artistic engagements because his wife could not get a passport to Amsterdam. The premier, who had been friendly with Skrowaczewski, immediately made a phone call, and Krystyna received her passport just three hours before their train's scheduled departure.

Stanisław and Krystyna left their homeland carrying one little suitcase each. As their train crossed the East German border to the West in Hanover, they breathed a sigh of relief. It would be twenty-one years before Skrowaczewski returned to his homeland to conduct again.

He would soon begin his relationship with an entity he knew only by name and reputation—the Minneapolis Symphony Orchestra.

TEN

WE BUILD INSTEAD OF MERELY DWELL

From the start, the orchestra embodied the spirit of enterprise that soared in this nation with the new century. Across its first hundred years, Minnesota leadership made bold decisions, breaking paths in touring, broadcasting, and recording. The symbiotic relationship of these undertakings built the fame of an orchestra identified with a state celebrated not only for its support of the arts, but for a pristine wilderness where wolf packs roam and eagles soar above 15,000 lakes.

—Mary Ann Feldman, "The Spirit of Enterprise"

It all began with a bandmaster and his son, a Bavarian violinist-conductor, and a lumberman.

Franz "Frank" Danz, a German native and longtime music director at Manhattan College, New York, began his career in Minnesota in 1877 as leader of the Twentieth Regiment Band at Fort Snelling in St. Paul. With the help of his father-in-law, he began leading his own small orchestra in Minneapolis in 1880, soon to be called "Professor Danz's Orchestra." Three years later Danz enticed his son, Frank Jr., an outstanding violinist performing in New York's top orchestras, to return to the Twin Cities and join his ensemble.[1] The gift of a Stradivarius, worth $20,000 at the time, did the trick.[2] Soon afterwards, Frank Jr. took over his father's orchestra, expanding its size and repertoire. It became a versatile ensemble that could perform as a military band for outdoor fare or as an orchestra of varied size equally suited to a formal concert series or to choral and operatic performances.[3]

Danz's orchestra had its ups and downs over the next two decades. The younger Danz broadened his audiences' musical horizons, but it wasn't easy. The first "hall" in which his orchestra performed was a beer garden; the second, Harmonia Hall, prohibited smoking and drinking, and the orchestra's performances, held on Sunday afternoons, usually were billed as "sacred concerts," although most programs were of secular music.[4]

"Public prejudice against such worldly phenomena as orchestral music on churchgoing days was widespread in the United States," wrote critic John K. Sherman, "but particularly strong in a community where Yankee-Puritan influence and cultural interest often went together."[5] He noted that "Minneapolitans in the 1880s and 1890s were by no means committed to orchestral fare, which in fact was considered rather intellectual; the popular taste leaned toward opera—grand, yes, but particularly light and comic."[6] Given this public sentiment, it was all the more remarkable that Danz managed to hold a concert in 1890 comprised solely of works by Minneapolis composers, a measure of the growing pride and support for classical music in the city.[7]

Danz received a boost of support from a summer concert series performed at Minneapolis' Lake Harriet Pavilion in 1891. The series, which usually featured Danz's military-band configuration, was so popular that he also added summer performances at St. Paul's Como Park.[8]

At orchestra performances a violinist named Emil Oberhoffer occasionally sat in to play viola. Born in 1867, Oberhoffer was a former violin prodigy who also studied piano and became a gifted organist. He went to New York at age eighteen, taught at Manhattan College (as did the elder Danz), and performed both as a violinist and organist in the city. He was traveling with a Gilbert and Sullivan theater company when it ran out of money in the Twin Cities, where Oberhoffer quickly learned that the path to musical employment led to Frank Danz, Jr. After borrowing ten dollars from the maestro to keep himself afloat, Oberhoffer began playing viola for him.[9]

Before long, Oberhoffer created and conducted a choir and orchestra for St. Paul's familiar Schubert Club. A few years later he was appointed director of Minneapolis' top chorus, the Apollo Club, and his success with this organization led to his appointment in 1900 as leader of another choral organization, the Philharmonic Club. After three flourishing seasons of presenting such works as Haydn's *The Creation*, Saint-Saëns' *Samson and Delilah,* and Verdi's Requiem, Oberhoffer tired of creating ad-hoc orchestras to accompany the Philharmonic's singers.[10] By spring 1903 he finally convinced the Philharmonic Club's officers that Minneapolis needed its own permanent orchestra.[11]

Plans advanced rapidly. The Philharmonic's board was expanded, and the goal of a $10,000 guaranty fund was achieved. With the security of a guaranty fund, an orchestra did not have to rely solely on ticket sales and could continue operations even if it lost money. Other major U.S. cities had established such funds, but the concept originated primarily in Boston when Henry Lee Higginson donated a million dollars to the Boston Symphony in 1881 and covered annual deficits of $50,000. Minneapolis did not have a single donor of this magnitude, and therefore its first fund drive "involved an unprecedented marshaling of civic forces and moneyed men and interests, all on behalf of a cultural enterprise of hoped-for community value."[12]

The board dubbed the new enterprise the "Minneapolis Symphony Orchestra" (MSO) and appointed Oberhoffer its leader. The next issue would not be resolved as easily. Qualified musicians were not plentiful in the Twin Cities, and the MSO needed Danz's orchestra members. For twenty years Danz and his father had exposed Twin Citians to orchestral music, but he recognized that it was time to move on. Above all, he wanted to return to his first love, playing the violin. The 1902–03 season was the last for his orchestra. His musicians preferred to have their own maestro lead the new venture, but the younger Danz graciously convinced them that going with Oberhoffer was the right decision, and he led by example. Formerly Oberhoffer's employer, Danz now became his employee, serving as the MSO's first concertmaster. He even donated his music library to the fledgling orchestra.[13]

In fall 1903 the orchestra rehearsed three times weekly for its first season of six concerts and additional performances with the former Philharmonic Club's chorus.[14]

The MSO became the eighth major orchestra to be established in the United States (sixty-one years after the New York Philharmonic, the oldest in the United States; three years after the Philadelphia Orchestra; and fifteen years before the Cleveland Orchestra).

Oberhoffer reigned for the next nineteen seasons, building the orchestra's strong foundation. Chief among his accomplishments were the establishment of Young People's Concerts in 1911 and an extensive touring schedule that made the orchestra the most traveled of any in the country, earning it the reputation as the "Orchestra-on-Wheels." Mary Ann Feldman elaborated on Oberhoffer's feat:

> Here is why Emil Oberhoffer was the most charismatic and visionary figure the orchestra has ever had: he saw that Theodore Thomas had stopped touring with his orchestra because he had settled by 1893 with the Chicago Symphony Orchestra, so there was a void. The eastern orchestras were not covering the country. They were touring from time to time and certainly in their own regions. Frank Danz had set a precedent for Minneapolis because his orchestra had toured throughout the country. Here was Oberhoffer, with a brand-new Minneapolis Symphony in the middle of the country. He saw the potential for touring, and he carried it out with a vengeance. By our 100th-anniversary season, we had played in 660 different cities of the world. Nearly half of them were during the Oberhoffer years.

Extensive touring established the orchestra nationally and, to a certain extent, internationally. It was an expensive undertaking, but Oberhoffer believed that ultimately the organization would profit from it. He funded the first three tours himself before he could convince the board of directors that he was right. The Minneapolis Symphony Orchestra debuted in Chicago in 1911, at Carnegie Hall in 1912, in Boston in 1916, and in California a year later.[15]

Elbert L. Carpenter, a lumberman and amateur musician, supported Oberhoffer's dreams of touring. A founding member of the orchestra's board in 1903, Carpenter became chair of the new committee of management by 1905 and held the position for the next forty years. Born with a good ear and a passion for music, Carpenter wanted to be an operatic baritone but relinquished that dream when his father needed him to take over the family's lumber business. Instead he became an astute, driven businessman. On one of his frequent business trips to Minneapolis, he struck up a friendship with Thomas Shevlin, and the two formed the Shevlin-Carpenter Company, which became one of the nation's major lumber companies.[16]

Carpenter galvanized community support for the orchestra and on several occasion bailed it out financially; however, he was careful not to have all his efforts translate into ownership of the orchestra. "With a calm aggressiveness that lacked all conceit," wrote Sherman, "[Carpenter] placed himself, for three decades, in the front line of the money raisers…."[17] Still, he was as obstinate as Oberhoffer, and after many years the latter felt that Carpenter's role with the orchestra infringed on his. Their symbiotic relationship ended in spring 1922, when Oberhoffer resigned the day before the season's last concert. He never conducted the MSO again.

Oberhoffer's one-day notice of resignation left the orchestra's committee with the problem of finding his replacement by fall. Carpenter invited five guest conductors to cover the season, hoping that one would become the orchestra's next leader. On a trip to New York to search for maestros, he met Belgian conductor Henri Verbrugghen, whose background and personality impressed Carpenter.[18]

Like Oberhoffer, Verbrugghen had been a violin prodigy. He was a student of Eugène Ysaÿe at the Brussels Conservatory and followed his teacher on a tour to England and Scotland. He stayed in the British Isles for ten years, performing in orchestras, conducting a chorus in Scotland, and leading a string quartet that bore his name. Verbrugghen played the British premiere of the Sibelius Violin Concerto in 1907 and performed a complete cycle of Beethoven violin sonatas in London.[19] He honed his orchestra-conducting skills in Australia, where in 1915 he formed a conservatory to train young musicians for an orchestra he would lead. Indefatigable in building what would become the Sydney Conservatorium of Music, Verbrugghen created a large orchestra within a few years.[20]

Of the five conductors invited to lead the orchestra's 1922–23 season, two emerged as finalists for the position: Verbrugghen and Bruno Walter, a native of Germany who at age forty-seven was already a major international conductor. Before he even raised his baton for a Minneapolis downbeat, he would have been the clear choice, automatically enhancing the orchestra's artistic status. It was not to be. During World War I, anti-German sentiment was widespread in the United States, and it lingered after the war. "Carpenter was apparently plagued by some members of the community for having Oberhoffer and so many Germans in the orchestra," said Feldman. "When he met the elegant Belgian Verbrugghen, who had a fine and substantial career in Australia, he knew he had his next conductor for Minneapolis."

As a guest conductor, however, Walter is linked forever to the orchestra's history. On March 2, 1923, his first concert in a series of six with the orchestra was broadcast live on radio stations throughout the United States and Canada, giving the MSO the distinction of being the second American orchestra to hit the airwaves.[21] (The Detroit Symphony was the first to broadcast, about a year earlier; the first commercial radio station in the nation had been launched in 1920.)[22] Verbrugghen's broadcasts with the Minneapolis Symphony Orchestra began in 1927. By the 1928–29 season, the orchestra had broadcast twenty concerts.[23]

About a year after its first radio broadcasts with Walter, the orchestra, now officially under Verbrugghen's leadership, made four recordings in Brunswick-Balke-Collender Company's studio in New York City. Again the ensemble was at the forefront of a new technology. The MSO was the second U.S. orchestra that Brunswick ever recorded, preceded only by the New York Philharmonic. It joined the select company of Boston and Philadelphia, the other major orchestras being recorded then.[24] Newspaper ads for the MSO's first record appeared throughout the country.

Verbrugghen's eight years with the orchestra brought advances on all fronts. Despite his flamboyant podium manner, he left the legacy of a fine craftsman: his great attention to detail in all aspects of rehearsals and performances. His discerning musicianship advanced the orchestra's repertoire by introducing works, many of which were Minneapolis premieres. Just four years after its New York premiere in 1924, Verbrugghen gave the first local performance of Gershwin's *Rhapsody in Blue*.

The other notable firsts of his tenure included two tours to Havana, Cuba, and the hiring of the MSO's first professional manager. Violinist Jenny Cullen, a former student of Verbrugghen's, became the first woman to join the orchestra. Verbrugghen also ushered in the orchestra's inaugural season at Northrop Memorial Auditorium (1930–31), the venue that would be its home for forty-four years.[25]

Sadly, Verbrugghen's first season in Northrop was also his last as the orchestra's conductor. During a brass sectional rehearsal for Strauss' *Ein Heldenleben* held during the second week of the 1931–32 season, the fifty-eight-year-old maestro suffered a cerebral hemorrhage. His doctors advised him to end his conducting career. Verbrugghen never fully recovered from the hemorrhage, but he was able to teach and to return briefly to playing string quartets. He died three years later.[26]

"Who the hell is Ormandy?" bellowed MSO board members at a meeting held the week after Verbrugghen fell ill.[27] Carpenter had just announced that thirty-two-year-old Eugene Ormandy would take over the orchestra's concerts for the next two weeks. The timing was fortuitous. The young conductor had just completed six concerts with the Philadelphia Orchestra, substituting for his idol Arturo Toscanini, who had fallen ill. Mrs. Carlyle Scott, the MSO's new manager, had read of Ormandy's heroics in Philadelphia. She asked a friend in Philadelphia to attend one of Ormandy's concerts and to report back that night. After Mrs. Scott's friend confirmed her high expectations of Ormandy's performance, she called Arthur Judson the next morning.[28] Ormandy had been under Judson's managerial wing for only two years, but his stock as a new star conductor was already high. The Philadelphia victory solidified Ormandy's future.

Ormandy was unknown in the Midwest, but after his first concert with the Minneapolis Symphony Orchestra—which CBS cofounder Judson made sure was broadcast—it was clear to everyone that he was a major talent. Even before his second concert he was offered a one-year contract to become the orchestra's conductor with a beginning salary of $20,000.[29] Another contract followed, and Ormandy would spend a total of five seasons as the MSO's conductor. His departure—as abrupt as his arrival—again involved the Philadelphia Orchestra.

As quickly as Judson gave Ormandy to Mrs. Scott, he took him away from her. When Stokowski made it clear that he was leaving the Philadelphia Orchestra by the end of the 1935–36 season, Judson—also the Philadelphia Orchestra's manager—appointed Ormandy as a co-conductor for the coming season. Mrs. Scott was informed of Ormandy's new job after the fact.[30] Ormandy never looked back, and two years later Judson installed him as music director of Philadelphia's acclaimed orchestra.

Musically, Ormandy's tenure in Minneapolis generally was regarded as the finest in the orchestra's history up to that point. He was an explosive, dynamic, and highly dramatic conductor, the optimal personality to lead the orchestra through the challenging years of the Great Depression. He did not necessarily push the envelope in terms of contemporary music, in part due to pressure from Mrs. Scott and to his desire to keep the masses happy. However, performances of particular note included the year-old *Rhapsody on a Theme of Paganini* by Rachmaninoff, with the composer at the piano, and the orchestra's first commission by a major composer—*Statements* by Aaron Copland.[31] Ormandy also triumphed with large-scale works such as the Verdi Requiem (performed in memory of Oberhoffer) and Mahler's Symphony no. 2.

Recordings put Ormandy and the Minneapolis Symphony Orchestra on the map internationally. The Depression brought the recording industry almost to a standstill. Notes music critic Richard Freed, "By 1931, when Ormandy arrived in Minneapolis, only Stokowski and his Philadelphians were still actively recording."[32] In an essay for *Minnesota Orchestra at One Hundred*, Freed details Ormandy's brief yet substantial recording history. He explains that as record sales gradually increased, "the ever-watchful Judson discovered a clause in the MSO's contract with its musicians that gave management the right to use them for recording and broadcasting without additional payment."[33] The door was open for the orchestra to make relatively inexpensive recordings, and soon the head of Victor's Red Seal classical line was on his way to Northrop Auditorium.

Ormandy's experience working for Judson's CBS radio network had prepared him for such an opportunity; even so, his achievements with the orchestra in just two sessions were extraordinary. A nine-day stint in 1934 and eleven days in 1935 produced recordings of fifty-four diverse works on 169 sides.[34] Premiere recordings included Schoenberg's *Transfigured Night* and Kodály's suite from *Háry János*. Most significant were the first recordings by an American orchestra of Mahler's Second Symphony and Bruckner's Seventh. The 78-rpm recordings were profitable, earning both Victor and the orchestra strong returns worldwide and, as Freed observes, "thanks largely to their being heard on the radio throughout Europe, gave Ormandy and the orchestra international celebrity status."[35] The recordings' popularity reassured the Philadelphia Orchestra that Ormandy could use this relatively new medium to enhance the legacy that Stokowski had created. The recordings effectively won him the coveted position at Philadelphia.

Like Ormandy, his successor at the Minneapolis Symphony Orchestra would move on to an ensemble with greater fame after leaving Minnesota. When Dimitri Mitropoulos, the iconic Greek "priest of music," departed Minneapolis after eleven years to become the music director of the New York Philharmonic, he, too, left a rich legacy for all future MSO maestros.

Born in Athens in 1896 to a deeply religious family, Mitropoulos initially wanted to be an Orthodox monk. Although music became his calling, he embodied an extremely devout and almost sacrificial dedication to the practice of his art. He was the first Minneapolis maestro who was not a violin prodigy (he was a piano virtuoso) and the first who also was a composer. By age twenty-three he had composed an opera that was lauded by Saint-Saëns, and he had studied in Berlin with Italian composer-pianist Ferruccio Busoni.[36] He later returned to Greece to lead the Athens Conservatory Orchestra for more than a decade. Mitropoulos' major break came during a 1930 guest-conducting engagement with the Berlin Philharmonic. He had invited pianist Egon Petri to play Prokofiev's Third Concerto, but shortly before rehearsals began Petri told him that he was too ill and tired to play the work. (In truth, he simply detested the piece.) After failed attempts to find a substitute, Mitropoulos informed the Philharmonic's management that he could easily play and conduct the concerto simultaneously, for the work was one of his specialties.[37]

This sensational feat opened the door to similar engagements all over Europe.[38] Koussevitzky owned the publishing house that held performance rights to the Prokofiev concerto, and consequently the Boston Symphony maestro received notices about Mitropoulos' achievement. In a rare gesture for Koussevitzky—he generally kept the symphony for himself—he invited Mitropoulos to make his American debut with the symphony in 1936.[39] Mitropoulos' Boston conquest received national coverage, and before he left the city to head back to Europe, his dates for a return visit in 1937 were already settled, as were arrangements for an added engagement with the MSO.[40]

Just ten days after Mitropoulos concluded his Minneapolis debut engagement in 1937, cheers rang out in Northrop Auditorium when E.L. Carpenter announced that the Greek maestro would be the orchestra's new conductor.

John Sherman's description of "experiencing" Mitropoulos at his Minneapolis debut conveys the maestro's unique approach to conducting:

> To the audience that night Mitropoulos appeared to be a fanatic who had sold his soul to music and conducted the orchestra like a man possessed. Bald, lithe, and rawboned, he exploded from the wings, walked to the rostrum with the loose-limbed lope of a professional hiker, spread his long arms and tapering pianist's fingers in a mesmeric gesture. With the first downbeat he started punching the air barehanded, unleashing a weird repertoire of frenzied gestures and scowls and grimaces that registered every emotion from terror to ecstasy. His quivering frame and flailing fists gave the picture of a man quaking with a peculiarly vital and rhythmic form of palsy. It was as if the music were an electric current that passed through his body to make it jerk and vibrate.[41]

Mitropoulos' dramatic conducting style manifested his missionary approach to the art. "One does not go to a concert to be entertained," he once said, "but to witness the depths of human emotions, as expressed through the great art form of Music."[42]

This approach to conducting mirrored the conductor's greatest artistic achievement in Minneapolis: making the city an important center for contemporary music. He gave world premieres of works by Hindemith, Ernst Krenek, and David Diamond, and presented dozens of Minneapolis premieres of works by such composers as Berg,

Schoenberg, Shostakovich, Dvořák, and Bartók. (Surprisingly, Bartók's music wasn't performed by the MSO until 1943.)[43] Mitropoulos also championed American music.

Whether a composition was brand-new or a standard repertory work—and regardless of its complexity—Mitropoulos conducted from memory in performance and often did not use a score in rehearsals. Given the diversity of his repertoire, it is possible that his achievements in this area are unique in the history of conducting.

Highly influenced by his religious upbringing, Mitropoulos acquired a reputation as a humanitarian that extended beyond his pious bent toward making music. He thought nothing of using his personal funds to help a musician in the orchestra or others in need. For three months during World War II, he was a "blood custodian" for the Red Cross, going to mobile blood units throughout Minnesota and giving up a summer of lucrative guest-conducting work. He cleaned for the units and sometimes played piano for donors. He also bought a truckload of powdered milk that the Red Cross distributed to needy children in Athens.[44]

Touring waned during the Depression but began to pick up again during Mitropoulos' tenure, in part due to the business skills of the orchestra's new manager, Arthur Gaines. To save money the grueling tour schedule included as many performances as possible.[45] The orchestra gave six tours between 1941 and 1945. "By the end of its 1945 tour," reports William Trotter, "the MSO had given a total of 2,647 out-of-town concerts in 379 American and 18 Canadian cities, and one concert in Havana, Cuba."[46]

The most historic tour performances during Mitropoulos' tenure occurred in summer 1949:

> After logging more than 12,000 miles on the road to seventy-nine cities that season, the MSO was the featured orchestra at the international Goethe Bicentennial Festival held that July in [Aspen], the historic silver-mining town in the Colorado Rockies. Not yet the glamorous ski-celebrity-music festival scene of the 1950s and after, this was where the best minds of the world were going in 1949. Across the three-week celebration, the Minneapolis Symphony, collaborating with guest artists like Artur Rubinstein, Nathan Milstein, and Gregor Piatigorsky, performed for an international press and public. Reports were transmitted everywhere, even to cities like London and Cologne, where the orchestra would appear in person nearly fifty years later.[47]

No other period in the orchestra's history equaled the magnitude of its guest conductors at the Aspen festival. The list includes Stravinsky, Walter, Reiner, Sir Thomas Beecham, Erich Leinsdorf, Münch, Ormandy, and Bernstein.

Like Ormandy, Mitropoulos recorded a wide repertoire. Although not as prolific as Ormandy, he furthered the orchestra's place in classical-music recording history, according to Freed:

> Dimitri Mitropoulos had not made recordings before coming to Minneapolis, but one of those he made early in his tenure, the world premiere recording of Mahler's First Symphony, is perhaps the single most significant entry in

the orchestra's vast discography. It was the recording through which an entire generation of listeners first became acquainted—and fascinated—with the composer's music. It is still in circulation, on CD, and still unmatched in respect to intensity, drive, and sheer excitement.[48]

The Mitropoulos years were not without their challenges. Musicians were lost to wartime military service, and the orchestra struggled financially. It faced new competition from radio broadcasts and recordings of symphonic music. During this period increasing numbers of city dwellers migrated to the suburbs.[49] The addition of "pops" concerts to the regular season was in part a response to the orchestra's financial concerns. However, the format reached its nadir and ultimate demise when the orchestra accompanied baton twirlers and played the "Beer Barrel Polka."[50] In its place, manager Gaines created Sunday "twilight concerts" that lasted slightly more than an hour and offered more suitable light musical fare.[51]

Although Mitropoulos was not without his critics—primarily over his contemporary-music programming and sometimes-overwrought interpretations—those individuals who witnessed his tenure generally consider him the most beloved and perhaps the greatest conductor in the orchestra's history. There was much sadness in the community when he left Minneapolis to "climb the mountain" of the New York Philharmonic, but there was also a great sense of pride that one of their own had, like Ormandy, gone on to greater heights.

Unlike his two predecessors, Hungarian conductor Antal Doráti was not totally unfamiliar to Minneapolis audiences when he joined the orchestra in 1949 as its fifth conductor. He had been a guest conductor in 1944, and during the late 1930s and early 1940s he led the orchestra when it was contracted to accompany the Ballet Russe de Monte Carlo in its Minneapolis performances. Doráti had toured internationally with the ballet troupe for eight years.[52]

In part the management chose Doráti as an antidote to the charismatic Mitropoulos, the spiritual maestro who had without a doubt led his musicians to new emotional levels. Yet it was generally felt that these peaks sometimes were achieved at the expense of nuanced orchestral playing. Issues like balance, ensemble cohesion, and intonation were not always priorities for Mitropoulos, and consequently the orchestra's technique eroded. Doráti had earned a reputation as an orchestra builder during his blazing four-year tenure as music director of the Dallas Symphony Orchestra.

"Doráti had the knack of putting his fingers on excellent musicians, and one of the things he did was to rebuild the orchestra," said Leonard Carpenter, son of the orchestra's founding father, Elbert L. Carpenter.[53] A well-traveled ballet conductor, Doráti knew of many leading freelance musicians throughout the U.S. and abroad. Ballet troupes often employed musicians in various cities to augment their orchestras. When positions became open during Doráti's eleven-year tenure, he had an impressive pool of musicians from which to draw.[54]

Doráti's career had advanced quickly. At age eighteen he became one of the youngest graduates in the history of the National Hungarian Royal Academy of Music. He studied composition, conducting, and piano with Bartók, Kodály, and Leo Weiner.[55] In 1924, the year of his graduation, he began working as a vocal coach and piano accompanist for the Budapest Royal Opera, making his conducting debut there the same year. His first symphonic conducting work began in 1930, but it was his position as conductor of the Ballet Russe de Monte Carlo, starting in 1933, that guaranteed his international reputation. Two other ballet company appointments followed, including one with American Ballet Theatre, Doráti's last post before joining the Dallas Symphony in 1945.[56]

Compared with Mitropoulos, Doráti was a volatile presence on the podium. "Mitropoulos drove himself," remarked MSO violinist Henry Kramer. "Doráti drove others. The wild Hungarian appeared on the scene in the late fall of 1949 like a furious hurricane, sweeping away the past in a cloud of dust. The peaceful coexistence which had endured for the last twelve years was forever shattered."[57]

"I had a short temper, a fault since my childhood," Doráti admitted. "I was to battle this for many years. Finally, in my middle sixties I was able to master this shortcoming. [During my time] with the orchestra, however, my behavior was counterproductive."[58] Although his personality and iron hand weren't popular with some musicians, under his leadership the orchestra made essential artistic progress.

Besides honing the orchestra's technique, Doráti increased and solidified its world fame, building significantly upon the accomplishments and name recognition achieved by his two predecessors. Taking full advantage of the new technology of LP vinyl records in 1949, Doráti recorded more pieces—nearly one hundred—than any other conductor in the orchestra's history. Beginning in 1950 he recorded just four works under the RCA label—one of which was the first American recording of Dvořák's Violin Concerto—before embarking on what audio producer and writer Dennis Rooney calls the "most successful series ever made by the orchestra."[59]

By 1951 the new Mercury label had made its name with a stellar recording of *Pictures at an Exhibition* with the Chicago Symphony under Rafael Kubelik. After a reviewer for *The New York Times* described the sound quality as "living presence," Mercury appropriated the term as the perfect catchphrase for the innovative recording technique of C. Robert Fine. To capture the natural sound of an orchestra as heard by conductor and audience in the concert hall, Fine used a single omnidirectional microphone in his sessions.[60]

From 1952 to 1960, the Mercury engineers made nearly two-dozen trips to Northrop Auditorium to record the MSO under Doráti's baton. Mercury's new recording techniques, Doráti's experience as a recording artist, and a diverse, appealing repertoire made the orchestra and its maestro the brightest stars in the Mercury firmament.

Doráti made classical-music history with his 1958 stereophonic LP of Tchaikovsky's *1812 Overture*, paired with his *Capriccio Italien*. He augmented the orchestra's brass section with the power of the University of Minnesota Brass Band and a dubbed recording of the bells of Yale's Harkness Memorial Tower. On top of those effects he layered spoken commentary by composer and radio personality Deems Taylor (perhaps best known as the voice of Disney's *Fantasia*) and the firing of a 1761 French cannon recorded at West Point. The LP was a popular phenomenon: by 1962 it had sold over a million copies. It garnered a Gold Record for sales and still ranks among the best-selling classical records of all time.[61]

Under Doráti the orchestra's other recording landmarks included the complete versions of Tchaikovsky's three ballets, the first recording of Copland's Third Symphony, and works by the maestro's teacher, Bartók (whose compositions were rarely recorded at the time).

Audio recording was not the only electronic medium in which Doráti excelled. Television, still in its infancy at the start of his tenure in 1949, was largely uncharted territory for symphony orchestras. Toscanini's celebrated six-year run of televised concerts with his NBC Symphony began in 1948. Ten years later, with the New York Philharmonic's Young People's Concerts, the medium found its made-for-TV star in Leonard Bernstein.

From 1949 to 1952, seven MSO concerts were broadcast locally on WTCN-TV, with viewer ratings almost equal to those of football games.[62] For the orchestra's fiftieth-anniversary season (1952–53), the station televised nine consecutive hour-long Sunday programs from January to April on WCCO-TV, complete with intermission segments featuring interviews and special topics related to the orchestra's history.[63] According to broadcaster and writer Burton Paulu, project supervisor for the series, the scale of the broadcasts using a full orchestra was probably unprecedented.[64]

Another first for the orchestra was a four-week, 45,000-mile journey across the Middle East in 1957. The massive tour, which also included stops at the Athens Festival and in two cities of Yugoslavia, marked the first time the orchestra had performed on European soil before 1998.[65]

Writes Feldman, "At a time of Cold War cultural exchanges, geared to promoting good will [*sic*], the State Department offered invitations to several orchestras, [and the MSO was the first orchestra sent abroad]. To the MSO came the most challenging of all: the already troubled Middle East."[66] The tour took the orchestra to Baghdad, Tehran, Karachi, Bombay, Pakistan, Beirut, Lahore, and Turkey, where, as with other stops on the tour, a major symphony orchestra had never been heard before. No other Western orchestra had ever performed in these areas of the Middle East.[67]

It was a rough yet exotic trip full of precarious flights, unusual food, sublime music making, and for many of the musicians, the first and only exposure to many disparate cultures. The tour overall was a triumph in the annals of the orchestra's history, creating new admirers and furthering its already solid international fame.[68]

Doráti made programming a top priority. Mitropoulos laid the groundwork for the orchestra's association with new music, but Doráti's record in this area was equally impressive. Unlike Mitropoulos, whose zeal for uncharted musical waters was so fervent that he sometimes paid scant attention to how such works fit within a program, Doráti took a more calculated approach to programming. He often balanced a diet of new works with familiar standard-repertory pieces in a manner that made musical sense.[69]

Both Doráti and his heir, Skrowaczewski, shared a talent for bringing a diverse repertoire to the orchestra. They also were the only music directors to have created original compositions composed for and performed by the orchestra. Unlike Skrowaczewski, who felt a strong conflict of interest in performing his own works with the orchestra while he was its leader, Doráti had no qualms about programming and obtaining commissions for his own music. But the Hungarian conductor was not as widely recognized a composer as was Skrowaczewski; the totality of Doráti's output was approximately twenty original works and dozens of orchestral arrangements.

However, their conductor-composer commonality reflected their shared Old World musical heritage. The Minneapolis Symphony Orchestra had been established, in part, by the Old World values and innovative approaches of the five conductors who led it from 1903 to 1960. Yet it would be Stanisław Skrowaczewski, possessing both traditional values and a modern sensibility, who would bring the orchestra into a new era, guiding it through critical transitions and developments.

In fall 1960, when Skrowaczewski arrived in Minneapolis, he inherited an illustrious orchestra that was in the best shape of its entire existence.

ELEVEN

OASIS OF THE NORTH

Minnesota exercised a certain fascination upon us musicians. It had a mystery, a lure. It was thought of as an "oasis of the North."

—Antal Doráti

"We are in the free world," Skrowaczewski happily declared on February 8, 1960, in a phone call from Amsterdam to Richard Cisek, then assistant manager of the Minneapolis Symphony Orchestra. On February 9—after nearly two months of secrecy—the orchestra issued the official press release announcing that Stanisław Skrowaczewski had been appointed its sixth music director. He was the first musician from behind the Iron Curtain to take the helm of a major American orchestra.[1] It was also the first time that the term "music director" had been used to designate the person at the helm of the Minneapolis Symphony; previous maestros held the title of "conductor." The modern title reflected the expanded role that conductors fulfilled in the mid-20th century.

Skrowaczewski had seven months of concerts before giving his first downbeat in Minneapolis. His three-week engagement in Amsterdam marked his debut with the famed Royal Concertgebouw Orchestra. Programs included the complete *Romeo and Juliet* by Prokofiev; Ravel's *Daphnis et Chloé* Suite no. 2; Beethoven Symphony no. 4; Mozart Symphony no. 29; Shostakovich Symphonies nos. 1 and 5; and the Lutosławski Concerto for Orchestra, still a relatively new work at that time and a calling card for Skrowaczewski. The orchestra's quality was "very fine, but it was not a revelation" to Skrowaczewski, who had been "spoiled" by working with Szell's Cleveland Orchestra as well as with the Pittsburgh Symphony.

From Amsterdam the Skrowaczewskis traveled to New York, where the maestro conducted sixty members of the New York Philharmonic in a private concert for an invited audience at the United Nations. Held under the auspices of the Polish delegation, the program commemorated the 150th anniversary of Chopin's birth and featured both Chopin piano concertos (Adam Harasiewicz as soloist) and Skrowaczewski's Symphony for Strings.

He then conducted several orchestras in Rome, Bologna, and Venice. The Skrowaczewskis applied for American visas in Rome at the U.S. Embassy, where the kind consul asked Skrowaczewski if the young woman accompanying him was his daughter, which pleased the maestro's vivacious young wife. The next eight weeks were spent in South America on Skrowaczewski's third visit to the continent, where the quality of the orchestras was then quite high. Many top-level European players who fled Europe had joined these ensembles; Buenos Aires had a particularly vibrant artistic environment. The summer season in Europe was relatively quiet (with the exception of the Salzburg and Bayreuth festivals), so South American ensembles were able to engage world-class musicians. Skrowaczewski conducted the National Symphony Orchestra of Argentina and led three programs with the Friends of Music Orchestra, "a private orchestra made up of the best musicians in the city, specializing in baroque and modern music," he recalled.[2] For most of the tour Krystyna remained at a villa in Lima with the Ruszkowskis, professors whom Skrowaczewski had met on previous trips.

During the last leg of the South American tour, two weeks in Peru with the Lima Orchestra, the Skrowaczewskis had an experience that could have been fatal:

> We had one weekend free in Peru between orchestra rehearsals, so the first violist, who was Dutch, invited us to a wedding party of his friends up in the Andes. We drove on a nice highway, and within two hours we became very tired. We were already at twelve or thirteen thousand feet. It was the main road to Brazil that ran through a valley between two phenomenal glaciers. Even wearing sunglasses, we were almost blinded by the glare from these glaciers. Then we went on a dirt road leading to a hacienda on the other side of the ridge, and it kept going up and up. We shared an oxygen bottle, and we had to change drivers as we continued, because after two or three minutes you became black in the eyes, feeling faint. It was terrible.
>
> By the time we reached the hacienda we were all awfully sick. They had us lie in the warm grass to rest, right next to huge long buffet tables with entire pigs on roasters, lamb, and fruits. And all of the young guests were playing soccer nearby. We could hardly move or breathe. Because it was dangerous, they immediately sent us down the mountain to Lima. They said if we stayed the night we would die. The change of altitude by car was too sudden; we had no time to adjust. Back in Lima we went to the hospital and spent part of the next day there. The next week I had rehearsals, and by then we felt better. I'll never forget the contrast of people playing soccer, eating, and drinking while we felt like we were dying from this altitude sickness. We couldn't bear to see any food.

Before leaving Peru they planned to visit Machu Picchu, and while they were en route their plane stopped in Cuzco. Krystyna had developed pneumonia in both lungs and felt horribly ill. When she insisted that her husband see Machu Picchu, Skrowaczewski took a day trip there by train while Krystyna rested in a hotel. By the time he returned, her condition had worsened. He immediately called for a doctor, who gave Krystyna a painful injection. "At the time it was very scary," Skrowaczewski said. "We didn't know what was happening. We thought this was it. I was worried about her life." Slowly she recovered, but they had to wait a few days before it was safe for her to travel again.

Skrowaczewski wanted to take Krystyna to the Caribbean for a much-needed rest. They were told erroneously that they could visit without visas, and they were swiftly put on a plane to Miami when they attempted to enter Jamaica. Krystyna was still recovering when they arrived in the intense Florida heat.

The couple finally headed to Minneapolis in early September 1960, expecting cooler weather. They arrived on Labor Day with their winter wardrobe, ill prepared for a late summer day with temperatures approaching ninety degrees. A crowd of well-wishers greeted them—orchestra officials, the press, and Charles S. Bellows, then president of the Minnesota Orchestral Association (MOA), the orchestra's governing body. "I am utterly moved to see you," Skrowaczewski told Bellows. "We have waited for this moment."[3] They spent their first night in the Curtis Hotel, where a faulty air conditioner made a terrific cacophony.

The next day Minnesotans received their first introduction to Stanisław and Krystyna at a press conference. They fielded questions that reflected the times: Did Skrowaczewski have any political interests? Would he be upset by a bad review? What did he and Krystyna think about jazz? Did they plan to have a family? On this topic Skrowaczewski deferred to Krystyna, who replied, "Of course. We hope to have one."[4] Privately she was surprised by such a bold question but soon realized that for a woman in her twenties to be childless, particularly in the Midwest, was somewhat rare. Skrowaczewski dismissed questions about his political interests and explained that bad reviews can be "helpful—when they are right."[5] Regarding jazz, the Skrowaczewskis said they were familiar with Louis Armstrong, Dave Brubeck, and the Modern Jazz Quartet, and considered it "serious folk music of definite value."[6] Skrowaczewski addressed the public's problem of pronouncing his name by a quick elocution lesson, noting that even in Poland it was mispronounced.

The Skrowaczewskis quickly adjusted to everyday American life. They literally were starting over with nothing, just as their families had done in postwar Poland. But now they were in a foreign country with an entirely different culture. With logistical help from Cisek and MSO general manager Boris Sokoloff, they opened a bank account, purchased a car, found housing, and began to acquire amenities. They rented an unfurnished duplex apartment in Minneapolis on Lake of the Isles. "For the first two days we bought two knives, two forks, one big table, two chairs, a bed. Everything was new! Absolutely from zero, we were buying everything," Skrowaczewski recalled.

For Krystyna, the transition was particularly challenging. Previously she had visited the United States only briefly, when she accompanied Stanisław on his 1958 tour. Fluent in English, French, and Italian, she preferred French and found it difficult to relate culturally to her new surroundings. At the time Warsaw had twenty-two repertory theaters, but Minneapolis' renowned Guthrie Theater did not open its doors until 1963. Ethnic restaurants and markets were scarce, and many Minnesotans were relatively unsophisticated about life outside the United States. In the early 1960s the Twin Cities did not have the rich, diverse cultural milieu that exists there today.

Only twenty-six, Krystyna was somewhat naïve, having made a dramatic exit from communist Poland, leaving her family and friends behind. Suddenly she was cast in the high-profile role as the wife of the new conductor of a major symphony orchestra. She was expected not only to attend official functions but also to entertain in her home, a challenging task in and of itself but difficult to undertake with limited furnishings. She also found it slightly intimidating to interact with the many older, established women in the Minnesota Orchestral Association. But Krystyna immediately impressed everyone with her composure and grace. "She was very brave," said Skrowaczewski. "She was always praised by everyone involved with the orchestra."

Krystyna occasionally endured strange questions from a few Minnesotans, such as "Are there bears in the streets of Poland?" or "Do your cities have movie theaters?" On a few occasions she felt as if some people regarded her and her husband with suspicion because they had fled communist Poland. Although McCarthyism had subsided, negativity and fear in America were still attached to anything or anyone connected with a communist country. During this occasionally stressful transition, Judy Dayton was the shining light who helped Krystyna with the many details of creating a new home and adjusting to life in Minnesota.

Judy and Ken Dayton (of Dayton's department stores and later, Target Corporation), the orchestra's largest benefactors in its history, became close friends and strong supporters of the Skrowaczewskis. At the time of Skrowaczewski's appointment, Ken Dayton served on the MSO's executive board of directors. His dedicated service to the orchestra began as a board member in 1947 and continued as vice president (1952–53), and president (1953–55). He also led the first endowment-fund campaign and was an important force in the creation of Orchestra Hall. Dayton was named life director in 1983 and capped fifty years of formal service in 1997, when he resigned from the board. In the orchestra's 2002–03 centennial season, the title of emeritus director was bestowed on Dayton.

Skrowaczewski's first rehearsal with the Minneapolis Symphony was filled with anticipation. "Practically no one had heard of Skrowaczewski," recalled former concertmaster Norman Carol. "All we knew was that he was involved with George Szell and had success with the Cleveland Orchestra." Henry Kramer, then principal second violinist, noted, "We knew nothing about our new conductor except that he had a Polish name, difficult to write and not easy to pronounce."[7]

For Skrowaczewski, the excitement quickened before he even set foot on the podium: "I was backstage when they were tuning, and I heard an 'A' from the oboe like I'd never heard in my life before. He was blowing a *piano* dynamic, increasing the volume to a big fortissimo, but with such a beautiful sound, it was like ten trombones. You cannot imagine the impression." In fact this indelible moment marked the first time he heard the orchestra live. He had been familiar with his predecessor Doráti's recordings, but in person he was struck by the exquisite tones of several of the principal players. The oboist possessing the beautiful *fortissimo* of "ten trombones" was Rhadames Angelucci, one of four virtuosi wind-playing brothers (the others held posts in Philadelphia and Cleveland). Among the star musicians in the orchestra at that time were concertmaster Carol, first trumpet Stephen Chenette, and first horn Robert Elworthy, all newly hired before Doráti's departure. Other notable members were principals in the woodwind section: Emil Opava, flute; Cloyde Williams, clarinet; and William Santucci, bassoon. Another standout was Robert Tweedy, a former cellist turned percussionist. He was "a phenomenal timpanist," Skrowaczewski said, "one of the finest I can remember in the world."

After a few rehearsals the musicians and press observers offered their assessment of the young director. "He is a purist. He is not a commercial conductor," noted one violinist. "You get the feeling that he really cares about little other than music."[8] Musicians praised Skrowaczewski for having a strong knowledge of their instruments and for adhering to the printed score. One reporter described the characteristics that became the hallmarks of Skrowaczewski's style:

> Clarity in general seems to be a major concern of his. He spent a great deal of time, quite successfully, working on transparency and orchestral balance. Perhaps his most admirable quality is an unusual equilibrium between personal involvement and self-control. Skrowaczewski is quite active physically and stimulates the orchestra enthusiastically, but at the same time remains aware of each detail and keeps the ensemble well in hand.[9]

In his memoir *Following the Beat*, Henry Kramer provides a candid comparison between Skrowaczewski and other conductors with whom he had worked:

> The man who stood on the podium had a very elegant and aristocratic appearance. His face, as he conducted us, showed none of the emotional fervor of a Mitropoulos or the grim visage of a Doráti. It was the face of a man who eschewed emotion in front of an orchestra, not only when he was rehearsing but also during a concert performance. After the wild gyrations of Mitropoulos' hands and the hoop-like circling of Doráti's baton, it was a great relief for the orchestra as a whole to be following a precise beat. Skrowie was not an autocrat like Reiner nor a conductor with the warmth of a Bruno Walter. He was similar to those European guest conductors who had appeared with our orchestra in the past.[10]

"I had the pleasure of building my interpretations with these people," Skrowaczewski reflected. "The only bad thing was the acoustics. So with that started my struggle." A month of touring delayed Skrowaczewski's first experience with the infamous acoustics of the orchestra's home, Northrop Memorial Auditorium, located on the University of Minnesota campus. After only four rehearsals he began a four-week tour of the western United States that had been planned since 1958.

The tour's first concert—Skrowaczewski's inaugural performance with the orchestra—took place in the less-than-perfect acoustics of the Washington High School gym in Brainerd, Minnesota, on October 1, 1960. There was standing room only in the newly refurbished gymnasium in this northern resort town. Five rows of classroom folding chairs covered the parquet floor from end to end, just a few yards from the conductor's podium. The MSO filled the entire basketball court, with the double basses under one basket and the percussion section under the other. The remainder of the two thousand audience members crammed themselves into the bleachers. Before the dress rehearsal Skrowaczewski had lunch in a café in Brainerd. He was amused when a young woman at the cash register asked him if he was "with the orchestra" performing that night. "Yes, yes indeed, I am with them," he grinned.[11]

Brainerd was hardly a typical setting for the conducting debut of an international musician with a major American orchestra, but it didn't matter. Intrigue was building around the thirty-six-year-old conductor with the hard-to-pronounce name, and this event gave Minnesotans the first chance to see and hear him in concert. When the strong-framed, handsome, and elegantly garbed Skrowaczewski appeared, the audience rose in tribute to its new maestro.

"He came swooping into the room with his hands out, open, reaching out to people," Judy Dayton said. "Instead of some conductors we knew who would come shuffling in, Stan always came out with his hands welcoming. The way he appeared made you take a breath and say, 'This is going to be fantastic.'"

His sharp downbeat started "The Star-Spangled Banner," and minutes later, two startling chords reverberated in the gym. "Forgotten were the two basketball hoops left down at either side of the orchestra. The large [crowd] stopped looking at the huge instrument cases piled to the orchestra's left as the first thunderous chords of Beethoven's *Eroica,* Symphony no. 3, filled the air," the *Brainerd Daily Dispatch* reported.[12] It was the official start of a musical relationship that would last more than fifty years.

After intermission the program continued with Elliott Carter's audience-friendly *Holiday Overture* (a work previously unperformed by the orchestra), Debussy's *Nocturnes,* and Ravel's *Daphnis et Chloé* Suite no. 2. After a standing ovation and repeated curtain calls, Skrowaczewski and the orchestra played the *Emperor Waltz* of Johann Strauss for an encore.

At the postconcert party at Brainerd Country Club, Skrowaczewski received a special cake in honor of his thirty-seventh birthday two days later. Reviews for the inaugural concert noted that Skrowaczewski used a score only for the Carter overture and that he had great command of the music and the orchestra. The *Little Falls Daily Transcript* observed: "His direction was accompanied by gestures sometimes as stiffly militant as those of a marionette, and again sweepingly graceful when the music quieted to lyric tones."[13] The *St. Paul Pioneer Press* noted: "The heart is evidently quite important to him. No matter how we admire his no-nonsense, continental tempos on the deliberate side, there is no doubting his personal involvement in all that he does so seriously, so devotedly."[14]

The orchestra proceeded to Moorhead, Minnesota; Fargo, North Dakota; Billings, Montana; Vancouver, Canada; and then south to California. Skrowaczewski remembered:

> It was an appealing tour to us because it went from Vancouver down to San Diego for four weeks. Night after night we gave concerts. The cities were a short trip away by bus or train: Seattle, Portland, L.A., San Francisco, and

others. We'd never seen this part of the United States, and the West is such a beautiful part of the country, particularly Oregon and Washington State. Musically it went well. We received wonderful reviews. The collaboration with the orchestra was on a high level. They were very friendly, and they seemed to know me immediately and know what I wanted. They responded so well!

Sleeping in a Pullman car throughout the tour, Skrowaczewski reveled in his love of trains. The trip evoked nostalgia for his boyhood visits with his father to watch the trains in Lwów. He delighted in collecting Morgan Silver Dollars, which were still circulating around the western United States in 1960. The heavy, oversized rare coins were first minted in 1878 and briefly re-minted in 1921. When Skrowaczewski's pockets became weighted down by his collection, he traded them in for cash—a decision he later regretted when the value of the rare coins increased.

The whirlwind tour offered twenty-six concerts in thirty days. Along with the Carter, Debussy, Ravel, and *Eroica* Symphony, the concert repertoire included Brahms' Third Symphony, Beethoven's Seventh, Mussorgsky's *Pictures at an Exhibition*, Stravinsky's *Firebird* Suite, the Mendelssohn Violin Concerto, Berlioz's *Symphonie fantastique*, Weber's *Euryanthe* Overture, Mozart's *Marriage of Figaro* Overture, and light encore pieces—a total of twenty-two works by seventeen composers.

Skrowaczewski's formal debut in Minneapolis took place on November 4, four days after the tour ended. A full-page advertisement in the *Minneapolis Tribune* placed by Dayton's Department Stores demonstrated Ken Dayton's confidence in the board's appointment: "His debut is tonight, his future limitless in this city of great musical achievement."[15] It was a powerhouse program comprised of the *Eroica* and *Symphonie fantastique*. In a *Minneapolis Tribune* article subtitled "Stanisław Skrowaczewski— Man of Modest Confidence," Skrowaczewski explained that he wanted to perform works known to the public so that they "can judge me just from my performance of something they have heard before."[16]

That evening marked the beginning of a new era for the orchestra. Just two days earlier Dimitri Mitropoulos had died on the podium during a rehearsal of Mahler's Third Symphony with the La Scala Orchestra. His eleven-year tenure with the MSO set the stage for his stardom and the orchestra's prominence. Although Mitropoulos had left Minneapolis in 1949 to become conductor of the New York Philharmonic, he remained a most beloved figure in Minnesota.

A reportedly sold-out house of 4,800 Minnesotans greeted the new maestro with a standing ovation in Northrop Auditorium. "It was a wonderful, moving event for me," Skrowaczewski said. "When I came to the stage, the whole public rose, and they greeted me beautifully. Even the governor was there. It was so festive." Cisek observed Skrowaczewski's reaction to the ovation: "It seemed to take him by surprise. He looked at the group, took a quick bow, turned around, and out came the sounds of 'The Star Spangled Banner.' He seemed very taken aback and wanted to get on with what he came there to do. It was a way of staving off the surprise that was trying to engulf him."

Perhaps the unusually warm greeting acknowledged the long journey that had brought Skrowaczewski to this point, as much as it acknowledged the man himself.

The critics were discerning in their assessments of Skrowaczewski's program. His performance of the *Eroica* was noted for its "drive without harshness, pathos without bathos, and movement without haste."[17] The Berlioz was praised for the "conductor's attention to the inner voices, the polish and restraint he demanded and got from the players produced some of the best music making in recent years in Northrop Auditorium."[18] Another reviewer was equally impressed but observed, "Mr. S. and the *Eroica* still have room to grow and the time in which to do it," and that "at thirty-seven [he] is not Olympian—yet."[19] It was "electrifying," Ken Dayton remembered. "I've never been so turned on in my life as we were that evening." "Vast curiosity and anticipation had been stirred by the slim, intense maestro with the almost unpronounceable name," reported the *Minneapolis Tribune*. "Skrowaczewski and the orchestra received five curtain calls."[20]

The orchestra's board members knew they had achieved something special with Skrowaczewski's appointment. Four days after his Minneapolis debut, they extended his original one-year contract to three years. Orchestra members reacted to the news with a standing ovation at their first rehearsal after the Northrop concert.

Overwhelmed by the public's reaction to the debut concert at Northrop, Skrowaczewski nevertheless realized that the venue's acoustics presented a formidable barrier to achieving his artistic goals:

> I was extremely unhappy about the hall. It was terrible. From the very beginning I said, "This orchestra must have a good hall. You have a great orchestra, wonderful musical life, supportive public, exceptional university, but you don't have any hall of quality to play in." I started to hammer this point and to explain why the hall was inadequate. A substantial documentation was started at that time about the need for a superior hall. I felt it was my duty, and they said: "Well, Doráti before you said the same thing, and Mitropoulos before him, and nothing happened." When they asked Ormandy about how to improve the hall, he said, "A bit of dynamite under it will improve it well." So this was his known answer about the situation. I had a chance as a newcomer to retake action.

Northrop Memorial Auditorium was inaugurated on October 22, 1929, with three concerts: the Minneapolis Symphony under Henri Verbrugghen, the Boston Symphony under Serge Koussevitzky, and an orchestra of university alumni and representatives from throughout the state. The imposing pillared structure—named in honor of Cyrus Northrop, the university's second president—dominates the campus mall near the east bank of the Mississippi River.[21]

The force behind its creation was Verna Golden Scott, manager of the Minneapolis Symphony during the 1930s, who wanted an appropriate venue for her prestigious University Artists Course performance series. (Her husband, Carlyle M. Scott, headed the university's music department, serving from 1905 until 1942.) A massive campaign for donations from students, faculty, alumni, and others raised $1.35 million, and her dream became a reality.[22]

Mrs. Scott's performance series flourished in the new auditorium, dubbed "the Carnegie Hall of the Midwest" at the time of its opening. Throughout the Depression the size of the Friday night symphony audience averaged 3,850. Northrop Auditorium remained the official home of the Minneapolis Symphony Orchestra from 1930 through spring 1974. From 1945 to 1986 the auditorium hosted forty-two annual visits by the Metropolitan Opera on its springtime tour from New York.[23]

Northrop Auditorium became Minnesota's primary large performance venue. It was built as a multipurpose facility with a seating capacity of 4,800, large enough to accommodate the university's entire student body in 1929. Over the years it has been the site of convocations, commencements, performances, lectures, and civic gatherings. Ornate and luxurious in scope and design, the cavernous interior created a distance between the audience and the performers onstage that precluded aural intimacy. Orchestral sounds went up but not out. A stage shell constructed to help the acoustical problem was ineffective. During Doráti's tenure another shell was conceived, but it produced a "thin tone that didn't project," Skrowaczewski remarked. "It was made from plywood, and it shivered from the vibrations caused by the orchestra."

After enduring these acoustics for a season, Skrowaczewski persuaded the management that something in the hall had to be altered. Seeking a solution, the board contacted George Izenour, a Yale University professor of electro-mechanical techniques, who designed a collapsible steel shell weighing thirty-two tons and costing $93,500. The board wanted to have the structure ready for the start of Skrowaczewski's second season, and the affable Yale engineer completed the design within three weeks.[24]

Set on rollers, the steel shell was easily moved out of the way for lectures or opera performances. Visually it was a modernistic hit and suited Skrowaczewski's more adventuresome programs. Stage lighting and sound reflectors placed outside and above the proscenium created the effect of funhouse mirrors. Crazily distorted reflections of brass, string, and percussion instruments—reminiscent of Salvador Dali's art— hovered high above the orchestra. Unfortunately, the shell created a huge sound on stage, making it difficult for the musicians to hear one another. Although it slightly improved the sound for the audience, it still failed to project adequately into the hall.

After this failed experiment, the management consulted Paul Vanaclousen, a West Coast acoustician who had worked on the Los Angeles Pavilion. He recommended that the shell's ceiling be tilted up. This alteration substantially improved sound projection, but the hall itself could not be improved. Even when quality sound came off the stage, the auditorium's size and its thousands of upholstered seats produced a dry, nonresonant acoustic.

In September 1962, Skrowaczewski—along with many other conductors, composers, and critics—was invited to New York City for much-publicized concerts at the new Philharmonic Hall at Lincoln Center (today known as Avery Fisher Hall). The New York Philharmonic, Boston Symphony, Philadelphia Orchestra, Cleveland

SEEKING THE INFINITE

Orchestra, and other ensembles performed a weeklong series of concerts. Although the venue's acoustics disappointed nearly everyone, including Skrowaczewski, the experience boosted his hope that the Minneapolis Symphony Orchestra could have a new hall of its own someday.

Although Skrowaczewski's primary concern as music director was the lack of a suitable concert hall, he also had to form relationships with his principal players and to handle other artistic matters.

Concertmaster Norman Carol proved to be an outstanding colleague. He and Skrowaczewski often spent hours at a time discussing various bowings and approaches to compositions. Carol noted that Skrowaczewski was "constantly searching" for ideas to improve performances, and he "is still doing this today, which is why his performances stay fresh." Carol also observed Skrowaczewski's intense nature and his desire to be alone before a concert, in complete contrast to Ormandy, who enjoyed "the more chaos the better" before going onstage. Carol left the orchestra after six seasons to become concertmaster of the Philadelphia Orchestra, but he remained Skrowaczewski's lifelong friend and advocate. The pair gave the Minneapolis premiere of Samuel Barber's Violin Concerto two weeks after the first formal concert of the 1960–61 season.

Skrowaczewski also wanted to improve the orchestra's quality and to increase its size. He requested more string players and got them. Over time he expanded the woodwinds from three to four musicians per section. The board and executive committee were keenly aware of the improvements Skrowaczewski was making, and, as is typical of the honeymoon stage of a new relationship, they supported him.

In a particularly innovative step, Skrowaczewski created positions of associate principals in the orchestra. Commonplace today, it was relatively rare in the 1960s to have associate principal positions, whereby multiple musicians could play principal and solo parts. Skrowaczewski often split the principal parts between the principal and the associate principal on a concert program. "I introduced this policy that was perhaps dangerous for the principal player because he started to be compared with his assistant," he explained. "Probably not everyone liked this idea of being exposed to competition, often with a younger player. But I found it to be very healthy for the orchestra and the players." Although this practice improved the orchestra's overall quality, it also created friction with older players who felt that they were slowly being pushed out, and it later caused uncomfortable dealings with the musicians' union.

According to Herman Straka, a violinist with the orchestra from 1952 until 2001, the orchestra at that time desired most of all to have conductor with a humane personality, and in Skrowaczewski the musicians got their wish:

> Skrowaczewski was everything Doráti wasn't. He was a gentleman, very soft-spoken, no tantrums. He never did have one in all those nineteen years. He had a very gentleman-like approach at all times. I never saw him in any extreme position, and he never mistreated anybody. Josef Gingold (former concertmaster of the Cleveland Orchestra) said it all: "He's a gentleman. You are going to enjoy him." Those were the first impressions.

116

Skrowaczewski also brought an exacting approach and great discipline to his personal preparations and to rehearsals. His insistence on adhering to dynamics as marked in scores, in relation to orchestral balance, was an early hallmark of his conducting and remains so to this day. Sometimes this approach frustrated the musicians, who were accustomed to being asked to play out continually—a few players even feigned playing to achieve the "ultimate *pianissimo*" their conductor demanded. His meticulous focus on the nuances of orchestral playing often required string players to use a variety of bowing techniques. This sort of attention differed considerably from Doráti's approach, as Straka explained: "[Doráti wanted] more of a brusque approach, percussive, with the idea of the sound as very, very heavy. It was the opposite of the aristocratic sound that Skrowaczewski wanted."

The repertory for Skrowaczewski's first season is notable for its quantity, breadth, and diversity. The inclusion of new music, much of it by American composers, is impressive: Eric Salzman (*Night Dance*); a premiere by Wayne Peterson, a native Minnesotan (*Exaltation, Dithyramb and Caprice*); Henry Brant (*Antiphony One*); and Gunther Schuller (Concertino for Jazz Quartet and Orchestra, featuring the Modern Jazz Quartet, or MJQ). The more established American composers were represented by Carter's *Holiday Overture*, Samuel Barber's Concerto for Violin and Adagio for Strings, *Night Piece* for Flute and Strings by Arthur Foote, and *The Unanswered Question* by Charles Ives. The European representation of 20th-century music included Szymanowski's Symphony no. 4 (Symphonie Concertante) for piano and orchestra, with Artur Rubinstein as soloist, and Honegger's Symphony no. 2.

The Brant and Schuller works were on the same program with the landmark Concerted Piece for Tape Recorder and Orchestra by Otto Luening and Vladimir Ussachevsky. Honegger's Symphony no. 2 for String Orchestra completed that program. Just over a year earlier Bernstein included both the Brant and Luening-Ussachevsky works on a series of programs with the New York Philharmonic. Such "experimental music" was part of the artistic milieu for young maestros of the day.

Along with Varèse, Luening (1900–96) was another pioneering figure of electronic-tape music and an important opera conductor. Russian-American composer Ussachevsky was a former student of Luening. In 1959 they served as directors of the Columbia-Princeton Electronic Music Center in New York City, along with Milton Babbitt and Roger Sessions.[25]

A subscription concert in February 1961 triggered the first major public criticism of Skrowaczewski's programming. Unaware that a program featuring the MJQ might startle his Minneapolis audience, Skrowaczewski included the ensemble as a means of exposing his audience to Third Stream, a new facet of modern music. The term, coined by Gunther Schuller at a 1957 Brandeis University lecture, succinctly describes the conjoining of classical music and jazz style to create a form that is equally respectful of both genres. The MJQ's appearance with the Minneapolis Symphony received good press coverage prior to the concert. Northrop Auditorium had presented jazz groups and orchestras performing together before, but only on the Sunday Twilight series. This program was the first "invasion of jazz into the traditional Friday night [subscription] series."[26] Even Bernstein's New York Philharmonic had not yet presented the MJQ.

Having four nationally recognized black jazz musicians performing with the Minneapolis Symphony was perhaps more newsworthy than the music they played. The burgeoning civil rights movement employed high-profile tactics like sit-ins, nonviolent demonstrations, and Freedom Rides. The Civil Rights Act of 1964 was still three years away from being signed into law. "I was not trying to break down barriers by inviting these musicians. I did it innocently," Skrowaczewski said. "As a Pole, I never experienced any problems with racism. In Poland (before the war) there was absolute tolerance for skin color and religion. I had not yet been brought into the American reality of that time."

However, it was not the MJQ's participation on the February 17 concert that bothered some concertgoers. They objected instead to a program comprised solely of 20th-century music. Although Honegger's Second Symphony and even Schuller's Concertino for Jazz Quartet and Orchestra offered many "user-friendly" moments for untrained ears, the incessant tartness of the Brant and Luening-Ussachevsky works was too much for some concertgoers and musicians. Henry Kramer set a public debate in motion with a letter published in the *Minneapolis Tribune* a week after the concert. Entitled "Violinist Takes a Dim View of Complex Modern Music," the letter's opening read as follows:

> When a musician feels like stuffing paper into his ears in order to shut out cacophonous sounds, then I think the limits of endurance have been reached. Last week's symphony concert in Minneapolis has, it seems to me, brought about the need for reappraisal of the musician's role in our contemporary music culture.... Contemporary composers are rapidly approaching the state where their music could be more accurately performed by machines.[27]

Kramer bemoaned the lack of emotional involvement he and some colleagues experienced while performing modern music, and he declared that musicians should be able to exert "some form of discrimination" in their musical tastes.[28] Today such sentiments are considered somewhat passé, but they were at the forefront of contemporary culture in the 1960s. Other members of the Minneapolis Symphony wrote to the *Tribune's* forum, as did music professors, composers, and symphony patrons. The letters were divided equally between opposing views on programming contemporary music. *Tribune* critic John Sherman expressed his frustration over the notion that the point was worthy of debate:

> People who castigate contemporary expression with words like "ugly" and "cacophonous" are using purely subjective terms. Many of them seem to think that their personal judgments are absolute judgments and that what is ugly to them is ugly to all.... An elementary sense of curiosity should impel any reasonably alert concertgoer to give ear to what is being done.... In fact, what we hear may not be pleasant at all; it may be painful or stimulating or baffling, or it may seem to be futile or inept.

What of it? Do we limit musical experience only to the edifying? …Should the concert hall be exclusively a home of pleasure? Isn't it part of the challenge of concert-going to hear something on which you can render the judgment that it was horrible? Or luckily, that it was different and great? This is all part of the variety of life, and why the concert hall should be roped off as exempt from the gambles we take on the good, bad, and indifferent, I don't know…. Many listeners want to be soothed, uplifted, or "pleasured." So do I, but hang it all, I want to be irritated, challenged, and surprised too.[29]

Skrowaczewski enjoyed the controversy. For him, the whole point of art was being played out in these discussions. Nearly forty years later Kramer wrote, "Despite the fact that I had criticized the programming of an entire Friday night concert by Skrowaczewski, …he never took affront with what I had written to the newspaper nor did he give me any rebuttal to what I had said."[30] Although championing contemporary music became a hallmark of his tenure in Minneapolis, Skrowaczewski included works from all epochs in his well-balanced performance record. Yet the charge that he programmed too much contemporary music originated with this concert, and it lingered throughout his years leading the orchestra.

The performances of standard literature that Skrowaczewski conducted during his first season included music of Palestrina, Bach, Handel, and Wagner, and symphonies by Haydn, Mozart, Schubert, Beethoven, Brahms, Tchaikovsky, and Shostakovich. Mussorgsky's *Pictures at an Exhibition*, Stravinsky's *Firebird* Suite, Ravel's *Daphnis et Chloé* Suite no. 2, Prokofiev's *Romeo and Juliet*, Beethoven's *Missa Solemnis*, Schoenberg's *Verklärte Nacht*, and the Mozart Requiem rounded off the season. Surprisingly, the Minneapolis Symphony had never performed the Requiem, which was paired with *Verklärte Nacht* for the closing programs of the season. They were dedicated to the memory of Mitropoulos.

For many Minnesotans, the first step in knowing their new maestro was learning the correct pronunciation of his name. In a 1960 Young People's Concert program booklet, the phonetic pronunciation of "Sta-nis-lau Skro-vah-chev-skee" was included along with the following "Minnesotan-friendly" sentences: "Aside from music, Mr. Skrowaczewski and his young wife are avid skiers, and he likes swimming, mountain climbing, and handball. If we should have a good snowstorm around Minneapolis, we just may find him racing down one of our ski slides."[31]

Music directors of major orchestras generally don't make conducting concerts for a school-age audience part of their primary mission. The most notable exception was Bernstein, who took the concept into the television age and singlehandedly defined the genre. Skrowaczewski, as is typical today, eventually gave his assistant conductors most of the responsibility for leading these concerts. During his first few seasons, however, he led most of the Young People's Concerts himself. "It was difficult for me," he revealed. "The energy in the air with nearly five thousand children in the huge hall of Northrop Auditorium was like an atom bomb explosion. Even when they were completely quiet, you felt this energy. It was terrifying to face them with this mission of teaching."

From his handwritten scripts for a series of these concerts during his second season, it is clear that Skrowaczewski, like Bernstein, did not talk down to his audience, and his attempts to reference American popular culture were clever. One script begins by taking on the question of "What is good music?" and offering the "short but modest answer" that it's "any music that the Minneapolis Symphony plays." He continues by quantifying quality through a discussion of the stylistic considerations of the great composers and how they put music together. When describing Strauss' programmatic *Don Juan*, he offers the aside that "Don Juan was a kind of Elvis Presley, but I think, more handsome and interesting. We have motifs representing his girlfriends and what you might call his dates with them."[32]

To help his young listeners appreciate Stravinsky's use of Russian folk melodies, Skrowaczewski referenced Gershwin's similar use of American folk rhythms and melodies, asking the audience to "sing along with us instead of just singing along with Mitch on the TV."[33] The young maestro's humorous reference to NBC's *Sing Along With Mitch* show, featuring bandleader Mitch Miller, was his attempt to connect with popular culture of the day.

During his early years in Minneapolis the subtleties of American parlance often puzzled Skrowaczewski, such as the humorous banter that typically occurs within an orchestra. Far from aloof, the maestro had his own brand of subtle humor that the orchestra often failed to grasp. James Clute, bassist with the orchestra for forty-five consecutive seasons, recalled an anecdote from early in Skrowaczewski's tenure: "Back in the days of Standard Oil there was the advertising slogan 'Put a tiger in your tank.' One day Skrowaczewski was trying to get more sound out of the trombones, and finally he said, 'Gentlemen, put tiger in your bell,' but nobody laughed because they weren't expecting it."

Violinist Kramer also commented on Skrowaczewski's struggles with idiomatic language:

> It must have been difficult for such an articulate and thoughtful conductor to speak to us fluently during rehearsals in what was for him a foreign language. He was in no way illiterate in speaking English—quite the contrary—but idiomatic English grammar is sometimes very confusing to Europeans. [For example], Skrowie once told a bass player, "I have to play faster when the hall is full." This comment went the rounds of the bass section [disrespectfully] as a typical "dumb Polish" expression. If Skrowaczewski had said, "I can play [tempos] faster when the hall is full [because all the bodies absorb the extra reverberation]," it would have clearly been understood that this was a wise and logical remark of his. The reverberations of sound in an empty hall last much longer, and the tempos of the music must be a bit slower to avoid the "muddy" sound that results from one note following another too quickly.[34]

Skrowaczewski's conducting workload during his first season in Minneapolis set the pace for his future musical life. It was a grueling repertory: nine overtures, thirteen concertos, and a substantial number of small incidental or vocal-excerpted pieces in addition to the aforementioned large symphonic works. Along with the tour that launched Skrowaczewski's first season, he also conducted twelve "runout" concerts, six Young People's Concerts, and a two-week U.S. tour, all within six months (October 1, 1960, to March 31, 1961). He also had a full spring and summer season of guest-conducting assignments ahead.

By the end of March, Skrowaczewski and the orchestra had recorded Shostakovich's Symphony no. 5, Schubert's Symphony no. 8 (*Unfinished*), and incidental music from *Rosamunde* for the Mercury Living Presence label. The Shostakovich and the two Schubert pieces were recorded in one day. The Schubert works, released prior to the start of Skrowaczewski's second season, marked his first recording on a major label. The Shostakovich Symphony was released soon afterward. One of the most popular symphonies of the 20th century, the Shostakovich Fifth was twenty-four years old in 1961, and only a few recordings of it existed. Both recordings were rereleased on CD in 1992, with Schubert's Symphony no. 5, recorded in 1962, added to the other Schubert pieces.

This schedule left Skrowaczewski practically no time for composing. Always reluctant to program and perform his own music, Skrowaczewski nevertheless included his transcription of the Air from Bach's Orchestral Suite no. 3 during the first season. The first inclusion of one of his compositions did not occur until his fourth season, when Symphony for Strings appeared on a subscription concert in December 1963. Skrowaczewski was steadfastly against using his position to promote his music:

> I considered it unethical to play my own works with Minneapolis while I was music director. There was surprise about this because my predecessor, Doráti, received many commissions from the women's association of the orchestra, and he conducted his works himself. I didn't think that was proper. I didn't even allow guests to conduct my works. The orchestra leadership said, "People will think that you are too shy or that you are not confident that your music can be interesting." So I finally played Symphony for Strings during my fourth season, and it was well received. Additionally, I think it is very difficult for a composer to conduct his own works. There is a conflict of interest. Conducting works by other artists, I can demand a lot from the musicians. But when I am conducting my own compositions, it's like I'm standing naked in front of the orchestra. I feel like I can't push them much.

After Skrowaczewski's few first weeks of subscription concerts, the orchestra's program book included an announcement of an article he wrote for the November/December 1960 issue of *Music Journal* entitled "Should Composers Conduct?" His answer was clear:

> The art of conducting should ideally be widely separated from the art of musical composition. For the active composer, teaching is possible, but conducting will work against the art of composition. It may not prevent him from composing, but it raises barriers, which he must surmount. To interpret and conduct orchestral works of the classical, romantic, or modern periods while trying

to create in the original, progressive school tends to constrict the free artistic atmosphere and untrammeled mind necessary for serious composition.

The composer should not lose himself in the study of other works because the concentration must be on his own mind, not on the mind and genius of another. It would be preferable for a composer to paint, to write, or to be a sportsman rather than to conduct regularly while trying to compose. Also, the composer is not necessarily qualified to be a conductor. These are isolated fields. Regardless of time and money available, the arts of creative composition and creative conducting require the highest order of specialization. A large, brilliant fire is of more value than several small ineffectual ones. Consistent with this opinion, I find it difficult to conduct my own compositions and would rather see my "other self" oriented through the interpretation of a conscientious conductor.[35]

In 1960 Skrowaczewski wasn't the only major conductor leading an American orchestra who struggled to balance conducting with composing. Both he and Bernstein had serious, proven compositional credentials and were recognized interpreters of the music of their homelands. Both men thought of themselves as composers first and conductors second. Skrowaczewski did not have much contact with Bernstein other than brief greetings after a concert or two, but he liked him personally and admired his conducting prowess:

I heard him conduct a performance of Berlioz's *Roméo et Juliette* Suite with the Societé de Conservatoire in Paris in the university hall in the 1960s. I liked so much what he did that I immediately added excerpts from the suite to my repertoire. Sometimes you are presented with a performance that is so committed that it impacts you greatly. Bernstein had lived with this piece. His performance also inspired me to create my own order of excerpts from the suite to perform as a symphony or in place of a major symphony on a program. Of course, Berlioz subtitled his excerpts "*Symphonie Dramatique*." I put the last scene in the middle and ended with the *Roméo Alone* scene and the *Festivities at the Capulets*. I enjoyed the dramatic effect of this reordering. I have always had a special affection for the *Love Scene*.

Skrowaczewski appreciated Bernstein's musicianship, but their personalities could not have been more different. Bernstein, the gregarious extrovert who thrived on making personal connections with musicians and the public, often sought publicity opportunities and seemed quite savvy and "hip" to his peers and young people. More introverted and somewhat guarded, Skrowaczewski welcomed and enjoyed public recognition but did not seek it. He always has had a healthy disdain for the public-relations aspect of being a conductor.

Like most major orchestras of the 1950s and 1960s, the MSO had few guest conductors per season. Of the eighteen subscription concerts of Skrowaczewski's inaugural season, he conducted fourteen. The idea of a music director leading only half of a season began to become more common in the late 1960s and 1970s, when orchestra seasons expanded and conductors began to lead multiple orchestras, jetting back and forth between cities or countries. Skrowaczewski always had one foot in the old era—when being a music director meant really being a part of the community and substantially shaping an orchestra—and one foot in the modern era. He enjoyed the freedom to guest conduct, and he also was adamant that Minneapolis should have the best guest conductors.

Despite his full-time commitment as music director, Skrowaczewski maintained an active guest-conducting career from the beginning of his Minneapolis tenure. When Mitropoulos' death in November 1960 left open two series of programs with the New York Philharmonic, Skrowaczewski was asked to fill the vacancy at the podium. He subsequently gave his official New York Philharmonic debut on January 1, 1961. The program for the first series of concerts included Mozart's Symphony no. 29, Lutosławski's Concerto for Orchestra (the New York premiere), and the Third Symphony of Brahms. Skrowaczewski led the Khachaturian Concerto for Piano and Orchestra and *Symphonie fantastique* of Berlioz for his second series. Making a debut with the New York Philharmonic had a certain luster during the 1950s and 1960s. Skrowaczewski received thirteen telegrams backstage at Carnegie Hall, with Judson and Szell among his well-wishers.

The two-week engagement with a diverse repertoire gave New York critics ample opportunity to assess Skrowaczewski's abilities. They acknowledged his musical integrity as well as his possible interpretive shortcomings, not atypical for a thirty-seven-year-old conductor.

Harold Schonberg of *The New York Times* favored Skrowaczewski's rendering of the Brahms with its "remarkably few idiosyncrasies."[36] However, he thought that the Mozart, with the use of the full orchestra, had "tempos on the deliberate side, the texture sounded thick, and the essential quality of this light-hearted little charmer of a symphony was missing."[37] The *Herald Tribune* recognized Skrowaczewski's efforts to properly balance individual lines in the Mozart and the "translucency of texture" he achieved in the Brahms.[38] The *New York Post* offered this summation:

> In leading his compatriot's [Lutosławski] complex score, Skrowaczewski was dynamic. The music was alive with color and pulsation. It surged. In the Mozart and Brahms music he never left any doubt of his dedication or sound musicianship. His baton technique was efficient and unmannered. He conducted the program from memory. But missing from the Mozart was sparkle and buoyancy. From the Brahms, imagination and sweep.[39]

All in all, Skrowaczewski came away from his New York debut unscathed. During this period the Philharmonic and the New York press were notoriously difficult. (An infamous 1956 *New York Times* article by Howard Taubman,"The Philharmonic— What's Wrong With It And Why," which skewered Mitropoulos and others, is one prominent example.) "It was a good experience," Skrowaczewski remembered, "even though the Philharmonic was very disorganized at that time, and there was no discipline. There was no feeling of love, but they behaved properly." Richard Rodziński, son of conductor Artur Rodziński, sent Skrowaczewski a tape of the radio broadcast of his debut. Careful listening confirms Skrowaczewski's achievement.

Robert Sabin of *Musical America* observed the physical traits that Skrowaczewski displayed on the podium, characteristics that others remarked upon throughout the years:

> He is a conductor of tremendous nervous drive and acumen, always indicating to the orchestra (New York Philharmonic) precisely what he wants and shaping the music with unrelenting tension…. I must confess that I felt worn out, but I retained a healthy respect for his musicianship and authority while wishing heartily that he would relax a bit.[40]

Soon after Skrowaczewski signed the three-year contract with the Minneapolis Symphony, he and Krystyna applied for U.S. citizenship. Judson and Szell wrote letters of support. Szell's letter explained that when he had met Skrowaczewski in Warsaw in 1957, he had been so "impressed with [the younger man's] musical and intellectual stature" that he was "determined to invite him to America."[41] He added that Skrowaczewski's recent invitation from the New York Philharmonic to replace the late Mitropoulos was an honor. "For the first time in more than 100 years of that orchestra," Szell wrote, "a relatively young and hitherto unknown European conductor has been given this responsibility, and after only a few months' stay in this country."[42] Szell concluded the letter by making the case for Skrowaczewski's citizenship. His last sentence emphasizes the difficult challenge of replacing America's aging maestros, including Reiner, Münch, and himself:

> Knowing the orchestral situation in America and Europe as well as I do, I would not hesitate to say that the services of so gifted a man as Skrowaczewski are needed in this country. Anyone familiar with this situation will confirm the fact that we do not have enough men of this caliber to fill all the posts where such services are needed, and this scarcity is likely to become even greater within the next few years.[43]

After being granted status as U.S. nonresident aliens in March 1961—a precursor to their eventual citizenship—the Skrowaczewskis felt secure enough to become first-time homeowners. In early April they moved into a white Dutch colonial home at 2822 Sunset Boulevard in Minneapolis. Coincident with this happy event was an unfortunate car accident that left Skrowaczewski with two broken ribs. Despite the pain, he left for a ten-concert engagement with the Israel Philharmonic Orchestra, performing symphonies of Brahms, Shostakovich, Bruckner, and Beethoven, with Henryk Szeryng as his soloist. "It was miserable. I couldn't laugh or cough with these ribs," Skrowaczewski said.

The Jerusalem Post praised Skrowaczewski's "musical integrity devoid of artificiality" and "beautiful control in respect to dynamics and sound."[44] The concert hall in Tel

Aviv at that time was small, so it was necessary to repeat programs six or seven times. "I hate routine performances," said Skrowaczewski, "so after doing Bruckner's Fourth Symphony a few times, I began to change tempos a bit to keep everyone alert and to not become bored myself." After Israel, Skrowaczewski made his debut with the San Francisco Symphony, which hailed him as "one of the most remarkable guest conductors to lead the San Francisco Symphony in recent seasons."[45]

Skrowaczewski's future was extremely bright. He could mature as the conductor of an excellent orchestra while expanding its artistry. His international guest conducting continued, and he had begun his career as a recording artist. Composition clearly had taken a back seat, but he had accepted the fact that his current obligations required it. An insightful assessment of Skrowaczewski's first season in Minneapolis appeared in the May 1961 *Musical Courier*. It outlines the enduring characteristics of his conducting and personality:

> Skrowaczewski established himself as one to move an orchestra, and an audience, without exaggerated effects, drawing upon inner resources of the scores and pinning his faith in the composers. There was little ego in his season's work. Businesslike and politely insistent in rehearsals, energetic and intense in performance, he drew from the ranks fine unity and precision, blessed with refined lyricism and clarity of solo voices. Some of his work had the character of chamber music. Repeatedly, he demonstrated a remarkable sense of line in keeping quiet or slow movements alive and meaningful. Some of us wished occasionally for a dash more power or passion—a fling to the winds or a super-explosion. But these moments were far outnumbered by those in which we were grateful for honesty, cleanliness, and shining detail.[46]

Ironically, some of the traits cited above were to cause challenges in Skrowaczewski's professional life. His tenacious artistic and personal integrity eventually clashed with the world of management and its commercial aims. These battles began as the 1960s unfolded.

TWELVE

SETTLING IN

Of course, we can never have completely ideal conditions for our work, so we have a continuing struggle with human imperfections. Such imperfections will always exist and—within limits—this is good. Our nature is imperfect. This represents real life in art.

—Stanisław Skrowaczewski

In summer 1961 Skrowaczewski's guest-conducting schedule was full. In early June he recorded Chopin's Piano Concerto no. 1 with Artur Rubinstein and the New Symphony Orchestra of London, a pick-up orchestra of the city's best freelancers. (BMG Classics/RCA Red Seal handsomely reissued the recording in 1999 under the auspices of the Rubinstein Collection.) The London session was part of a project whose goal was to record the complete Chopin piano and orchestral works. Rubinstein had already performed Piano Concerto no. 2 the previous December in Minneapolis.

After completing the recording of the Concerto no. 1, the fellow Poles began work on Chopin's Variations on *Là ci darem la mano* from Mozart's *Don Giovanni*. Abruptly, Rubinstein declared that he could no longer play the pieces well enough to record them. During this period his performances had become less frequent and his repertoire narrower. Though Skrowaczewski regrettably lost the opportunity to document the complete Chopin piano and orchestra pieces with Rubinstein, six years later he recorded the works with Alexis Weissenberg in Paris. They would prove to be among the most important of Skrowaczewski's early recordings.

In 1967, the year of the Weissenberg recordings, another project involving Rubinstein did not materialize. RCA planned a two-record set of Szymanowski compositions: the Fourth Symphony with Rubinstein, Violin Concerto no. 2 with Henryk Szeryng, Violin Concerto no. 1 with Isaac Stern, and the Second Symphony with Skrowaczewski's own reorchestration. It would have been a major artistic accomplishment for the young conductor-composer, as he explained:

> It was a great project. Szymanowski was not recorded anywhere at that time, and with those artists it would have had weight and sold. Unfortunately Rubinstein wouldn't play the Fourth Symphony any longer. "I don't feel like it," he said, and without him the whole project fell through. Even though they had Stern and Szeryng, Rubinstein was the key. Also, Stern was not an RCA artist at the time, so that was another complication. I really regretted the loss of this project.

I love Szymanowski's Second Symphony. Musically it is a great work, but there are weaknesses in the form in the first and second movements, and the instrumentation is not very good. I created a new score in 1967 at my own expense for the materials and performed it, perhaps illegally. We were completely cut off by the Iron Curtain, so I didn't try to contact the Polish publishers to pay them. For two or three seasons I performed the symphony all over the world with great success: Stockholm, London, other major cities in Europe, including performances with the Berlin Philharmonic and major orchestras in America. Then I stopped. I felt there was something improper about it because it was no longer a Szymanowski original. I didn't change the music, of course, but I cut, edited, and repeated many things. So it was performed only over a short period of time.

After other engagements in summer 1961—in France, Spain, Italy, the Netherlands, and Portugal, where he conducted the Lisbon Philharmonic at the Gulbenkian Festival—Skrowaczewski canceled a Scandinavian concert tour in order to get back to Minneapolis and plan for an extra preseason concert. He was eager to try the new Izenour acoustical shell that had just been installed in Northrop Auditorium. A special performance intended to test the new shell preceded the first scheduled subscription concert. Skrowaczewski chose a program from three periods of music history: Bach's Brandenburg Concerto no. 1, Lutosławski's Concerto for Orchestra, and Brahms' First Symphony. It was a programming format he repeated throughout his second and third seasons to "illustrate the patterns of musical development in the last 250 years."[1]

Mary Ann Feldman, then a student at the University of Minnesota, wrote a review of the concert critiquing the Bach performance for its lack of balance between strings and winds and for intonation problems. The shell improved the sound to a degree, but the musicians still had trouble hearing each other, and projection difficulties continued unabated. The subtlety and uniformity necessary for Bach—accentuated by Skrowaczewski's use of a full string section— could not be realized in Northrop Auditorium.

During his second season in Minneapolis, Skrowaczewski continued building his and the orchestra's repertoire. Among the works performed for the first time by the Minneapolis Symphony were Bach's B minor Mass; Szymanowski's *Stabat Mater*; Mikis Theodorakis' Second Symphony and Palester's Fourth Symphony (both U.S. premieres); and Shostakovich's First Symphony. Skrowaczewski continued to work with soloists from previous collaborations, such as Totenberg, Szeryng, and Witold Małcużyński, but he also formed new collaborative relationships with such artists as Leon Fleisher, Philippe Entremont, Yehudi Menuhin, Gary Graffman (a soloist during his first season), and Glenn Gould.

Gould's predilection for unusual tempos was well known. In November 1961, before Gould's arrival for rehearsals of Beethoven's *Emperor* Concerto, Skrowaczewski warned his orchestra not to be surprised if the pianist took slow tempos. Skrowaczewski recalled, "He began the first movement, and it was incredibly slow, but somehow he played with such conviction and strong musical will that it felt completely natural.

I was with him fully." The performance was a triumph, and Gould reportedly told colleagues in Canada how fond he was of Skrowaczewski.

Skrowaczewski remembered an incident at the postconcert party in Minneapolis that revealed a facet of Gould's eccentric behavior:

> Before he came to the party everyone was warned not to shake his hand. He was incredibly protective of his hands, and when he arrived he was wearing gloves. Everyone was hesitant to approach him, so he basically kept to himself. The hosts of the party had a particularly large and somewhat aggressive dog. Suddenly no one could find Glenn. We looked around, and we found him lying on the floor with the dog, gloves off, his hands completely in the dog's mouth. He seemed so happy and comfortable. He connected with animals much more easily than with people.

Five months after Gould's Minneapolis concert, he played Brahms' Piano Concerto no. 1 with Bernstein and the New York Philharmonic. Unlike his experience in Minneapolis, Gould encountered resistance to his musical ideas. Bernstein could not accept Gould's unorthodox interpretation of the Brahms concerto, but rather than delegate conducting duties to one of his assistants (and subsequently pass up a CBS television broadcast scheduled for one of the performances), he transformed his disapproval into a quasi-educational discussion of artistic differences. Before conducting the work, he disassociated himself and the Philharmonic from what Gould was about to do. Some writers believe that this act, in effect a public denouncement of Gould's interpretation, contributed to the reclusive pianist's decision to abandon public performances. But Gould himself felt Bernstein's speech was "completely charming" and "done with great generosity."[2] The pianist blamed the media for creating the adverse publicity surrounding the incident.

Gould canceled his second engagement with the Minneapolis Symphony Orchestra scheduled for spring 1964. Soon afterward he retired from concert performance.

Skrowaczewski's first Minneapolis performance of Beethoven's Ninth Symphony, which occurred during his second season, elicited diverse criticism. Some reviewers praised his ability to make the overall structure of the Ninth discernable, while others criticized the hurried nature of some tempos and his austere approach to the Adagio third movement. All critics agreed, however, that the performance of Bach's Brandenburg Concerto no. 6, which preceded the Beethoven, was weak.

In an effort to fulfill his survey of great masterworks throughout the season, Skrowaczewski bravely programmed three of Bach's well-known concertos on separate concerts. But the cavernous acoustics of Northrop—"the great barn," as composer Eric Stokes called it—worked against the transparency of these pieces. However, this Brandenburg performance was still notable for something other than its deficiencies. It marked the first time that Skrowaczewski conducted from a keyboard in Minneapolis, playing the harpsichord part. Not since the days of Mitropoulos had Minneapolis audiences seen their maestro in this dual role.

Mitropoulos was beloved in Minnesota for his openness off the podium. Skrowaczewski, particularly during his early years in Minneapolis, was more reserved with the public. He was extremely cordial to people when they approached him, but he would not necessarily initiate contact. He is a person whose true personality blossoms upon further acquaintance. Still, Minnesotans could not help but recognize that both Skrowaczewski and Mitropoulos brought emotional depth to their art.

Early in Skrowaczewski's second season he wrote an "Open Letter to WAMSO" (Women's Association of the Minneapolis Symphony Orchestra) that was published in the *Minneapolis Tribune*. (WAMSO, an important fund-raising arm of the Minneapolis Symphony, was founded at the end of Mitropoulos' tenure.) Skrowaczewski's letter is a remarkably concise and effective arts-advocacy piece as well as an expression of gratitude:

> I know now that without your enthusiasm and devotion there would be no symphonic music in the U.S. I will explain why your contributions are so important. These good conditions can develop a conductor's imagination, his thinking, and his performance.
>
> We are all familiar with the picture of a fierce flash of lightning illuminating the dark night. For one instant it reveals, to the last detail, a vast landscape to us, and though we can never describe every single element of this picture, we are sure that nothing has escaped us. We absorb all these impressions, which, compressed as they are, we could never have experienced under normal conditions.
>
> Under very similar circumstances of vision, a whole symphonic work begins to take form in a conductor's mind before he lifts his baton. Thus the re-creative profession of artists reproducing the music of composers becomes creative when the vision they have received as a lightning flash starts to become materialized in time. In this sense, the ideal existence of each piece of written music (of Bach, Brahms, or Debussy) has to struggle against all human imperfections. But exactly in this way the metaphysical existence changes into flesh and blood, which can totally be digested by listeners. According to this, sometimes the recordings, which have been done with the greatest care for precision and perfection, seem to have this touch of "ideal existence." Yet this often does not move us as much as the more imperfect bit of "flesh and blood" performed in the concert hall.
>
> Of course, we can never have completely ideal conditions for our work, so we have a continuing struggle with human imperfections. Such imperfections will always exist and—within limits—this is good. Our nature is imperfect. This represents real life in art. But certain external imperfections such as very bad acoustics or squeaking chairs should be done away with, and I am grateful that you have taken away these annoyances. The improvements you have made possible mean much to the musicians and to me. On our part, we hope to work hard constantly to arrive one day at the moment when every thread we spin will be a golden one.[3]

Skrowaczewski's schedule for his second season was even busier than the first. Subscription concerts were extended by almost three weeks, and the orchestra embarked on a monthlong winter tour to Midwestern and New England states—including Skrowaczewski's Carnegie Hall debut with his orchestra—and a three-week spring tour in Minnesota and surrounding states.

The Carnegie Hall concert was typical of Skrowaczewski's fondness for programming across musical epochs: Mozart's Symphony no. 39, Webern's Six Pieces for Orchestra, and Brahms' Symphony no. 4. A reviewer for *Musical America*, whose native city was Minneapolis, noted that he had heard the Minneapolis Symphony under four of Skrowaczewski's predecessors, and that it "never sounded better…. [Skrowaczewski] puts music making above everything, tricks, 'effects,' and podium antics…. The orchestra plays with remarkable discipline and accuracy, but above all with musicality."[4]

Recordings for the Mercury label continued at a steady pace. Skrowaczewski and the Minneapolis Symphony recorded Schubert's Ninth and Fifth symphonies, Mendelssohn's Fourth, Prokofiev's *Romeo and Juliet* Suites, and Schumann's Piano Concerto, all during the regular concert season. The Schumann concerto with American pianist Byron Janis was recorded in the gymnasium of Edison High School in Minneapolis. Surprisingly, the sound quality is the best among Skrowaczewski's Minneapolis recordings for Mercury. He made his recording debut with the London Symphony Orchestra (LSO) in July 1962 with pianist Gina Bachauer and cellist János Starker as his soloists. Another recording with Bachauer and the LSO followed during the next summer. He would not record again with that orchestra until 1989. Mercury wanted more recordings from Skrowaczewski and the LSO, but the uncompromising maestro refused. "They wanted me to record works with little or no rehearsals. It would have been impossible for me to give any real interpretive imprint, so why bother?"

As Skrowaczewski's workload with the orchestra increased during the 1961–62 season, so did his guest-conducting engagements. Three of the so-called "Big Five" American orchestras—Boston, Chicago, and Philadelphia—had not come knocking; the remaining two, Cleveland and New York, had not yet extended further invitations. The Pittsburgh and Cincinnati orchestras did, however. Skrowaczewski had developed a strong relationship with Szell and the Cleveland Orchestra's manager, but scheduling conflicts delayed his next appearance in Cleveland for two more years. In Europe he had concerts in London with the BBC Symphony Orchestra and in Paris with L'Orchestre National de la Radiodiffusion Française. He also gave a series of three programs with the Israel Philharmonic that included Weber's *Konzertstück* for Piano and Orchestra with Claudio Arrau.

During his conducting debut with the Cologne Radio Orchestra in June 1962, an opportunity arose that might have changed the course of Skrowaczewski's career:

> The Cologne Radio Orchestra (Kölner Rundfunk-Sinfonie-Orchester) was one of the finest orchestras in Europe at the time. After the Berlin Philharmonic, there was this one and Munich, but Cologne was in better shape than Munich

during that period. Before my first concert with them, after my rehearsals, the general director of the entire Cologne Radio, Hans Bismarck, a descendent of the great Bismarck, took me for a long lunch. He had a great personality, and he'd been a politician; at one point he was a candidate for a high position in Germany. His family had lost land possessions in East Prussia, which was given to Poland by Stalin during World War II. He said, "You see, you lost everything in Lwów (during World War II), and my family lost everything, too, so we are close to each other." This was how he began.

Then he said, "Listen, the orchestra likes you very much. They voted, and I would like to invite you to become music director." I was immediately surprised and grateful, but then I thought it would be impossible. At that time, what Minneapolis was asking of me and what this orchestra would want would be in conflict. They needed a music director to be there, not like today when orchestras just need eight weeks or so from a music director. My presence was needed for meetings, union matters, etc. No one at that time had two positions. The jet era was still in its infancy then, and traveling from Minneapolis would have been demanding and long. I seriously considered it, though. I never even asked Minneapolis about it. Perhaps I should have, as it might have improved my situation there. I'm not a politician, from this point of view. Had I done it, both places may have suffered, and certain aspects may have been more superficial. So I don't regret it. But always [afterward] I thought, "Did I do well with this decision? Would my career have been better if I had taken that post?" No one knows what could have been.

The Cologne orchestra was indeed among the elite European orchestras in the 1960s. During the 1962–63 season, when Skrowaczewski had a return engagement, the other guest conductors included Szell, Kubelik, Karl Böhm, and the young Christoph von Dohnányi.

Skrowaczewski enjoyed a positive relationship with his personal management during the early 1960s. Beginning in 1956, in conjunction with winning the Rome competition, Skrowaczewski's European management was handled by Madame Camus, a lovely older Italian woman. In September 1960 Johanna Beek of the Dutch company Nederlandsche Concertdirectie became Skrowaczewski's principal agent for most of Europe; Madame Camus retained Italy, France, and Austria; and CAMI handled North America. Beek had ties with most of the major orchestras in Europe, and she worked hard to secure prestigious engagements for Skrowaczewski.

Arthur Judson, who turned eighty in early 1961, was still the czar of the Division for Conductors at CAMI. He was remarkably attentive to Skrowaczewski, considering that he continued to oversee other major conductors and to groom a successor to his empire. He secured recording exclusivity for Skrowaczewski with Mercury, Columbia, Victor, London, and Capitol, and he made efforts to get the young maestro engagements with only the finest American orchestras. "At this time of your career," Judson wrote Skrowaczewski in spring 1961, "I do not want you to conduct orchestras of the rank of San Diego. It is a respectable organization, but I wish to have you with Philadelphia, New York, Boston, Chicago, San Francisco, and Los Angeles first."[5]

Ironically, CAMI's practice of limiting some of its conductors only to selected U.S. orchestras later prevented Skrowaczewski from engaging certain guest conductors in Minneapolis. After his Minneapolis Symphony debut in 1962, Seiji Ozawa never returned, despite Skrowaczewski's repeated invitations to him throughout the 1970s. By that time Minneapolis became less attractive to some conductors' managers.

Judson went to Minneapolis in winter 1962 to hear one of Skrowaczewski's concerts and to get acquainted with his situation. "We had a small party after the concert at our new home," Skrowaczewski remembered, "and here comes Arthur Judson and a small person carrying his bag. Krystyna said, 'Who is that?' I assumed it was his secretary. It was Ronald Wilford."

By the time of Judson's visit to Skrowaczewski, the octogenarian impresario had already made two coast-to-coast farewell tours of American orchestras. The first took place early in 1961. On that trip he brought Bill Judd, his newly named heir to take over the conductors' division at CAMI, to meet the various managers and conductors of orchestras around the country. But by the time of Judson's second farewell tour, just a few months after his first, Judd was out of the picture. Wilford had become Judson's "chosen son" to take over CAMI's conductors.[6]

Wilford began working for Columbia Artists in 1958 in its small theatrical division. His claim to fame before joining CAMI was bringing French mime Marcel Marceau to the United States in the mid-1950s. Their professional relationship continued for thirty-five years. Prior to scoring his major coup with the iconic mime, Wilford ignited his passion for aiding the careers of powerful conductors; during a single season he produced with the Oregon Symphony, he secured Stravinsky, Otto Klemperer, Arthur Fiedler, and Mitropoulos.[7]

In his 1997 book *Who Killed Classical Music? Maestros, Managers, and Corporate Politics*, Norman Lebrecht describes in detail Wilford's actions to position himself at CAMI. If the account is accurate, it points to a "do what it takes" ambition that would place Wilford as head of the conductors' division by 1963 and as president of CAMI by 1970.

As Skrowaczewski settled into his Minneapolis position, he tackled one of a music director's most difficult tasks, that of hiring and firing musicians. During the early 1960s the omnipotent music director was still a reality in most American orchestras, but the balance of power was shifting. New York Philharmonic musicians went on strike in fall 1961, seeking the security of forty-two weeks of work. They won their objective, and by 1964 they had a year-round contract with four weeks' paid vacation.[8] (Several years later the Minneapolis Symphony secured a similar agreement.) These triumphs paved the way for musicians to reexamine the hiring and retention practices of their orchestras.

Clearly, autocratic podium tyrants and orchestra managements abused musicians, particularly during the first half of the 20th century, and the advent of powerful musicians' unions in the 1960s and 1970s was a needed development. As with any organized operation or business, however, when the quality of productivity is in question, change becomes necessary.

From a managerial standpoint, Skrowaczewski had limited experience as an autocratic conductor before he came to Minneapolis. His positions in Poland dealt largely with musical issues. It was also not in his nature to make steely decisions without weighing their implications. By his second season he knew that the violin sections needed improvement. Efforts to reposition or fire players were met with clear resistance from the orchestra's committee and the musicians' union. "Skrowaczewski did not at first understand that our orchestra committee was the go-between for orchestra personnel and management," Henry Kramer explained. "'Committee' must have had an ominous ring to his ears.'" To Skrowaczewski, the phrase must have seemed analogous to a Soviet-style "music committee" that specialized in censorship.[9]

Decades later Skrowaczewski reflected on a problematic aspect of his approach:

> I relied heavily upon the opinions of Boris Sokoloff, the general manager of the orchestra at the time. My actions were based on his advice, and when I got in trouble by trying to dismiss musicians without the proper procedures, I felt horrible about it. Boris never informed me about the procedures or about how to carry out the process in a careful and intelligent manner.

Whatever confusion Skrowaczewski initially may have experienced regarding personnel matters, he handled this responsibility directly and compassionately. He wrote to one violinist explaining why he was displeased with his work but also assured the musician that nothing would be decided until they met in person. "If you have anything in your heart you wish to say to me before I return to the States," Skrowaczewski wrote from Tel-Aviv, "please do not hesitate to write to me."[10]

In June 1962, Orchestral Association president John Myers told Skrowaczewski—who had been away on tour—that his conflicts with musicians had subsided. Orchestra members had signed a three-year contract providing them with a new level of financial security in line with other leading orchestras, a pension plan for retirement benefits, and confirmation of season extensions (up to thirty-one weeks for the 1964–65 season).

Skrowaczewski's desire to bring in new musicians had been approved. Myers assured him that the board of directors backed his right to reconfigure sections—as stated in the agreement with the orchestra committee—and that everything he had done previously was in complete agreement with the union. Noting that the situation caused the maestro worry and stress, Myers encouraged Skrowaczewski to work with him more closely in the future on such matters. Myers' letter also mentioned several items related to the upcoming season, none of which included an issue of great concern to Skrowaczewski—the hiring of Frederick Fennell as second conductor and associate music director.

For several years Skrowaczewski had not been involved in the process of hiring assistant and associate conductors. Frank Miller, former principal cellist of the Chicago

Symphony Orchestra under Fritz Reiner, was associate conductor of the Minneapolis Symphony Orchestra when Skrowaczewski arrived. After the 1960–61 season Miller returned to his former post in Chicago.

James Dixon, a young American conductor and protégé of Mitropoulos, replaced Miller. "Skrowaczewski and I met in New York. We had a coffee or something, and he hired me on the spot," Dixon recalled. He and Skrowaczewski connected immediately; they had similar aesthetic sensibilities and wonderful musical rapport, and remained lifelong friends. Skrowaczewski described Dixon as a "very thorough, honest musician with a great ear, great taste." Dixon came to Minneapolis from a conducting position at the New England Conservatory, where he was director of the orchestra and symphonic wind ensemble. Previously he was conductor of the University of Iowa Symphony Orchestra.

Dixon observed Skrowaczewski at work developing the orchestra:

> He was very interested in building the orchestra from a musical point of view, and I learned a great deal about how to make an orchestra play well. It is principally taking care of the lengths of notes. It sounds very simple, but it's not so simple. It is what creates an orchestra's sound. In our pedagogy we pay a great deal of attention to the attack of notes and tone quality, but we don't pay nearly enough attention to the length of notes. That is the aspect that's most vivid in my memory. There were certain pieces that we played that year that had been taken on tour by Mitropoulos, and, I presume, also [by] Doráti. They were played every year on tour but never on subscription concerts. They were the sort of pieces that you could put together quickly, like *Till Eulenspiegel* and *Daphnis and Chloé*. My particular year there, he spent a great deal of time cleaning them up. They had been played for so many years without [substantive] rehearsal that everyone had fallen into some bad habits. So he was a disciplinarian in the best sense of the word. He also knew that to build an orchestra's technique one needed to rehearse and perform the Beethoven and Haydn symphonies and the Brandenburg concertos.

Despite a year of musical growth and his artistic kinship with Skrowaczewski, Dixon was pushed out of his position after one season, when Frederick Fennell was hired for the newly created position of associate music director. Although Dixon was compensated financially for the year remaining on his current contract, he was shocked and frustrated by the situation, and Skrowaczewski lost a colleague with whom he was aligned philosophically and artistically.

The Fennell debacle was an unfortunate episode for everyone involved. As Richard Cisek noted, it "is illustrative of the difference between the way the institution was managed then and the state to which it has currently evolved." Cisek, assistant manager of the orchestra during Skrowaczewski's first three seasons, later served as president of the orchestra from 1978 until 1991. He assisted Skrowaczewski with the administrative details and nuances of running an American orchestra, and he was keenly aware of the genesis of Fennell's appointment.

By 1962 Fennell had gained a reputation as a recording artist with the Mercury Record Company. He had twenty-two popular records to his credit, principally with the Eastman Wind Ensemble and also with the Eastman Rochester Pops Orchestra and the London Symphony Pops Orchestra. In 1952 he founded the Eastman Wind Ensemble, which greatly influenced the evolution and growth of the wind ensemble and its literature. Previously, most large ensembles in music schools consisted of orchestras, choirs, and symphonic bands (generally, large bands with multiple doublings).

Fennell's innovative idea paved the way not only for more performances of classic wind-ensemble literature, such as Mozart's Serenade in B-flat (*Grand Partita*) and Stravinsky's *Symphonies of Wind Instruments*, but it also inspired important composers to create original music for this relatively young, vibrant medium. The Eastman Wind Ensemble predated by almost ten years the Netherlands Wind Ensemble, the professional group first conducted by one of its founding members, Edo de Waart.

Fennell's education included studies at the Salzburg Mozarteum, Berkshire Music Center (later Tanglewood Music Center), and Eastman School of Music. He studied the orchestral literature in his youth and early adulthood, but he also had a passion for bands and their histories. Near the end of 1960 he recorded two volumes of authentic Civil War music for Mercury.

Boris Sokoloff was a Civil War buff. His knowledge of Fennell's Civil War recordings with the Eastman Wind Ensemble most likely led him to invite Fennell to conduct the orchestra for a Twilight Concert marking the 1862 Dakota Uprising in Minnesota. The Twilight Concert series, held Sunday afternoons at 4:00 p.m., generally offered lighter, family-oriented musical fare that required minimal rehearsal time. With only one rehearsal Fennell put together his Civil War extravaganza involving collaborative efforts with Minnesota's Macalester College Mens' Choir in March 1962. Curious and unfamiliar with the genre, Skrowaczewski attended the rehearsal.

Symphony president Myers, an amateur pianist and head of the famed Waldorf Box Company, attended the concert and was "bowled over by it," as Cisek recalled. Fennell connected well with the audience, making comments between compositions, much like the format of Bernstein's Young People's Concerts. Fennell possessed "a dynamism, a vitality," as Cisek remembered, and it was "a stellar event."

Without Skrowaczewski's knowledge, Sokoloff and Myers immediately assessed prospects for bringing Fennell to Minneapolis and perhaps creating an arrangement similar to one the Boston Pops had with Arthur Fiedler. A few weeks passed, and Myers called Fennell. Thirty-nine years later, Fennell remembered Myers' words verbatim:

> I have just returned from a conference with the nine other presidents of the ten principal symphony orchestras of the United States, who were gathered together for three days, and all that we discussed was how can we diversify what we do, so that we'll be able to survive. I think what we have to do in Minneapolis to survive is to bring you here as a second conductor of the orchestra.

Both Fennell and the Minneapolis Symphony recorded for the Mercury label, and Myers told Fennell that he could use the winds of the orchestra to continue the type of recording he had done in Rochester, New York. He assured Fennell that he would have his own Sunday concert series during the season and that he also would assume the customary duties of associate music director, although the position was new and its responsibilities not clearly defined. Fennell accepted Myers' invitation to go to Minneapolis to discuss the details, but he thought it odd that his meetings only included Myers and Sokoloff. He never met Skrowaczewski during this time.

With a two-year contract from the Minneapolis Symphony Orchestra in hand, Fennell returned to Rochester to meet with his boss of the past twenty-five years, Dr. Howard Hanson. An American composer widely known for his brand of neoromantic music, Hanson was the longtime director of the Eastman School of Music. He agreed that Fennell could not pass up the offer, and by May 1962, two months after conducting his Civil War concert in Minneapolis, Fennell purchased a home in Minnetonka, Minnesota.

When Skrowaczewski learned of the offer, he became quite concerned about its effect on Dixon's status. Opinions on the nature and scope of Fennell's position varied. Myers and Sokoloff envisioned Fennell's role as a kind of second music director, one with his own concert series of lighter music. Skrowaczewski, who regarded Fennell simply as a more experienced assistant conductor, wrote Myers and asked him to define the precise nature of Fennell's position. Myers responded with a point-by-point description of Fennell's duties (essentially those of an assistant conductor), but he noted that the position of associate music director was offered to Fennell "because of his experience and prominence in the music world and because of his position at Eastman."[11] But he also made it clear that Skrowaczewski was still the music director. He regretted Skrowaczewski's misunderstanding of the situation, and he took full responsibility for the manner in which the hiring took place.

"Stan was taken aback and bewildered by it all," Cisek explained. "I think he somewhat felt that something was being pulled on him that he didn't like. But he wasn't quite sure what his authority was vis-à-vis the president and the manager; therefore, he was trying to be polite and responsive but at the same time holding to his music-director prerogatives." Cisek cited an example of a similar situation within the Los Angeles Philharmonic:

> To me it was rather reminiscent of what happened about the same time, when Georg Solti was appointed music director of the Los Angeles Philharmonic. Shortly after his appointment, before he took the job, when he was still in Europe, Buffy Chandler, then the president of the Los Angeles Philharmonic Association, named Zubin Mehta assistant conductor, which perplexed and, I suppose, infuriated Solti (although he kept good control of his fury). He simply said, "Look, I don't know Mr. Mehta; I have nothing against him. I hear very good things about him, but naming an assistant conductor is the music director's role and not the president's role," and he just terminated his

contract. Whereby Zubin was elevated very quickly, not having conducted a note as assistant conductor. He moved up from that to music director. The rest we all know!

Skrowaczewski couldn't conceive of leaving over such a situation, although he did consult Wilford about that option, and there was confusion and "some jockeying for position," as Cisek explained. Skrowaczewski had just completed his second season as music director, and the board worried that the Fennell situation might disaffect him. Board members wanted him to be comfortable in his position, and they tried to find a solution to mitigate the deed done by Myers and Sokoloff.

During summer 1962, when Fennell was in Michigan conducting at National Music Camp (now Interlochen Center for the Arts), he received a call from Myers asking him to meet with members of the Minnesota Orchestral Association board in Minneapolis. At the meeting, which Myers and Sokoloff attended, Stanley Hawks, a past president of the board in the 1950s, began by saying, "We'd like to know what it would take for us to buy out your contract." No explanation was offered. Stunned, Fennell replied that no amount of money could buy out his contract, which he intended to fulfill. The matter was never discussed again. Towards the end of Fennell's second season, Myers told him that his contract would not be renewed.

During the next two seasons (Skrowaczewski's third and fourth) there existed, as Cisek recalled, "a state of tension that never erupted in any unpleasant sense on the surface," but an-oil-and-water relationship between the two conductors was evident to all. Fennell, who at age fifty was nine years Skrowaczewski's senior, understood that his role was secondary, but he made it clear that he was "nobody's assistant" and a conductor in his own right. An interview with Fennell that appeared in the *Minneapolis Tribune* in September 1962, before he had even formally begun his position, did not ingratiate him with his new boss. He revealed that his nickname for Skrowaczewski was "Slavo" and explained in detail that he derived the name from Skrowaczewski's first and last names. Although the gesture likely was a somewhat innocent effort to force a friendship, Skrowaczewski and others regarded it as disrespectful, particularly because the two men hardly knew one another. Fennell promptly sent a letter of apology to Skrowaczewski stating that the article did not reflect his words properly and that he was sad to have started off on the wrong foot.

Although Fennell had little experience in conducting major orchestras regularly, the orchestra members received him well, and his concerts were popular. In addition to his Sunday series, he conducted many Young People's Concerts. On tours, the extroverted Fennell enjoyed playing poker and blackjack with orchestra members. He frequently dined with the musicians, unlike Skrowaczewski, who often ate alone and studied his scores. The two conductors had little contact, and Fennell regarded Skrowaczewski as a gifted musician who "was always correct" and "very deeply dedicated to contemporary music" but who was sometimes emotionally reserved.

In an effort to further Myers' goal of diversifying the orchestra, Fennell discussed with Skrowaczewski the possibility of conducting the woodwinds, brass, and percussion in the literature with which he was associated at Eastman. He believed that this step would expand the orchestra's programming and afford Skrowaczewski the time to conduct more string orchestra literature. In his opinion, dividing up the orchestra would reach more people, especially on tours, and expose them to repertoire that had proven to be popular. Skrowaczewski disagreed, and the idea was dismissed. Skrowaczewski's mission was to elevate the orchestra's artistic reputation, and consequently he believed it was important to develop the orchestra as one entity. Both conductors had valid viewpoints, but they found it impossible to connect musically or personally. Skrowaczewski was not impressed with Fennell's work musically, a factor that probably amplified his reluctance to try his colleague's interesting idea.

After Fennell completed his two-year contract in Minneapolis, he took a position as a resident conductor at the University of Miami, where he led the orchestra and wind ensemble. He later held posts as principal guest conductor of the Tokyo Kosei Wind Orchestra and Dallas Wind Symphony, and also worked with the Cleveland, New Orleans, St. Louis, London, and Boston Pops orchestras. Fennell's conducting career continued until shortly before his death in 2004 at age ninety. He is most celebrated for his vigorous advocacy of the wind ensemble through recording, conducting, teaching, editing, and arranging of wind literature as well as his scholarly writings.

Despite his disappointment over the loss of Dixon and the issues surrounding Fennell's appointment, Skrowaczewski looked forward to 1962–63, the orchestra's sixtieth-anniversary season. In a flyer that announced "newly revised programs," a "Message from the Maestro" presented an artfully composed rationale for the performance of new and old music:

> Of all the arts, music fulfills a special function that cannot be fulfilled either by the bankrupt idealistic philosophies of the 18th and 19th centuries or even by the all-powerful science of the 20th century.
>
> People have always striven to encompass the infinite, and music has frequently been able to satisfy their metaphysical hunger. But where is the art of music at present? I should answer: in an exceedingly difficult and controversial position. The composer's rebellion against traditional conventions goes in hand with a nervous experimentation—a search for a synthesis, an attempt to create a new musical language.
>
> We often fail to see music in its historical perspective. Let us remember, however, that the magnificent edifice of traditional music, which was based upon tonal harmony, elaborate form, and logic of expression (and which reached its apogee at about 1800), had been built little by little over many hundreds of years. And let us also remember that modern music entails hardships and sufferings not only for the listeners but also for the composers. These hardships and sufferings are nonetheless the price of art, whose supreme law is eternal renewal.

Thus, instead of closing our ears to modern music, let us manfully face the facts of history and life. Such courageous confrontation brings its own rewards: we shall certainly find it exciting to witness the latest developments in music—to put our fingers on the pulse of musical expression. And, by developing a taste for modern art, we shall all the more savor the delicacies of the past. This is what our symphony season offers you: the opportunity to commune with the musical masterpieces, old and new, of the last three centuries.

Perhaps now you see more clearly why, a few months ago, I borrowed the term "New Frontiers" to describe our expanding horizons. I hope that by now you have abandoned your fear of the term "modern music." But even if you haven't, you will find that our programs contain a comparatively small number of modern works and that they do acknowledge our heavy indebtedness to the great artistic periods of the past. I am personally opposed to the tyranny either of elevating the present over the past or of elevating the past over the present.

There are, by the way, in our programs many works that are popularly dubbed "warhorses." But I object, violently, to this figure of speech: there are no "warhorses" for me. When we play, for example, Beethoven's Fifth and *Pastoral* or Tchaikovsky's Fifth and *Pathétique* or Liszt's Préludes, it is not because we want to offer cheap fare to our public, but because we consider these works masterpieces.

We shall strive continually to re-create them—to rescue them from traditional abusage by re-evaluating the original scores and the composers' intentions. Therefore, come to Northrop Auditorium, and take your share of our musical heritage.[12]

Skrowaczewski could secure funding for only one commissioned work for the orchestra's sixtieth-anniversary season, but the chosen composer, Gunther Schuller, had a proven record of accomplishment with the Minneapolis Symphony. After Mitropoulos put Schuller on the map as a composer during the New York Philharmonic's 1956–57 season with performances of two of his works—one of which was commissioned by the New York Philharmonic—Doráti commissioned Schuller to write a piece for Minneapolis. The result was *Seven Studies on Themes of Paul Klee*, which Doráti premiered in 1959 and later recorded with the Minneapolis Symphony. It remains among the most significant works commissioned by the orchestra, and it is Schuller's most-performed orchestral composition. Skrowaczewski conducted the work on two tours with the Minneapolis Symphony during the 1964–65 season and again on subscription concerts in 1975.

A titan of classical and jazz music history for more than a half century, Schuller is the recipient of a Pulitzer Prize, a MacArthur Fellowship, two Grammy awards, and the *Down Beat* Lifetime Achievement Award. He also is an inaugural inductee of the American Classical Music Hall of Fame, composer of nearly two hundred works, and author of six influential books.

There is no American musical figure with whom Skrowaczewski is more philosophically aligned in terms of conducting, composing, and aesthetic values than

Schuller. In the early 1960s they formed a deep personal and collegial relationship that continues to the present. Skrowaczewski had been aware of Schuller's music before he assumed his Minneapolis post, but it was surprising, given his background, that the first piece by Schuller that he programmed was the Concertino for Jazz Quartet and Orchestra. Schuller recognized Skrowaczewski's gifts as a conductor, but his respect and admiration for him grew when Skrowaczewski invited the thirty-seven-year-old Schuller to attend rehearsals for the premiere of his *Composition in Three Parts*:

> I remember getting reports about what a great debut he had in Cleveland. Judson grabbed him immediately and put him in Minneapolis. I recall that much of our friendship and closeness was based on the fact that I was so taken with him as a conductor. He was so good, and we didn't have many people like that, particularly of his kind of integrity and modesty, Mitropoulos having died by that time. So he was very special, and I certainly saw that immediately, and lots of people did. He ranked quite high, and he was top of the line at that point.

> *Composition in Three Parts* brings up an interesting anecdote because it shows what a wonderful, modest, unostentatious, un-arrogant [sic] person Stanisław is. I wrote this piece on commission, and by that time we were already very close somehow, even though he was in Minneapolis and I was in New York. But whenever we'd meet, we'd hit it off immediately because we were just on the same personal and artistic wavelength. And we still are. We are more alike in many respects as conductors and professional musicians than almost anybody I can think of. And therefore we occasionally commiserate about the state of the music business.

> Anyway, he rehearsed the piece, and somewhere along the line (he kept asking me things as I was listening to the rehearsals, and I would respond and tell him things), and it might have been in the penultimate rehearsal—I don't know how it happened—I think he said to me, "You know, maybe it's better if you conduct this." When conductors say that, it's usually with extreme sarcasm. It wasn't that at all. It was with great humility, and he didn't say, "I don't get this piece" because he had done very well, but it was difficult for the orchestra. They hadn't played much of that kind of atonal, twelve-tone, virtuosic music. I remember there was a rather difficult, long bass-section *soli* passage with some gigantic leaps in it. I knew all kinds of players in New York that were capable of playing it, but it was a difficult piece for them. Maybe Stanisław wasn't quite in tune with it stylistically; he might have just felt a bit uncomfortable with this rather difficult and modern piece. In any case, at some point he invited me to conduct, and I kind of jumped at it. I did indeed conduct the premiere. Stanisław did take the piece on tour, but now I recall that it was also sort of a sense of "Once I see you do it, Gunther, then I'll know better how to do it." So that's amazing. That almost never happens with any conductor.

Skrowaczewski's willingness to share the conducting limelight during the season's penultimate concert was a generous act. Held on March 29, 1963, the concert featured Andrés Segovia as a soloist, and it concluded with Bruckner's Seventh Symphony.

The last and only other time that Skrowaczewski had conducted this work, so dear to his heart, was in fall 1952 in Katowice with the National Polish Radio Symphony Orchestra. Works by Bruckner, like those of Mahler, still suffered then from the general criticism that his music is too long and not well constructed. The Minneapolis and St. Paul critics expressed the same thoughts in their reviews.

These jabs at Bruckner caused one audience member, Professor Herbert Feigl, director of the Minnesota Center for Philosophy of Science, to write to Skrowaczewski expressing his admiration of Bruckner and of Skrowaczewski's performance of the Seventh Symphony. A major figure in his field, Feigl helped to establish the philosophy of science as an academic specialty. "Ever since my days as a philosophy student and lecturer at the University of Vienna (1922–30), I have been enthusiastic about Bruckner's symphonies," Feigl wrote, adding that he had heard many performances of the works by the Vienna Philharmonic under such conductors as Bruno Walter and Wilhelm Furtwängler.[13] "You really understand Bruckner!"[14] The professor confided that the only other time he had written a "fan letter" was to Walter regarding the elder maestro's 1959 Carnegie Hall performance of Bruckner's Ninth Symphony.

Skrowaczewski wrote back to Feigl immediately:

> You cannot imagine what a great pleasure you have given me in expressing your admiration of Bruckner's works. I am well aware that Bruckner's music is rather unknown in many countries, with the exception perhaps of Germany and Austria; and this is a pity, generally speaking and also for me personally, because this is one of the greatest composers that I love to perform.
>
> I am glad that you liked our performance. It was still far from our best possibilities, if only because of two reasons: first, our orchestra is not too familiar with this music and would need much more rehearsal time for any Bruckner symphony than for any other symphony of the 19th century; and secondly, we have constant trouble with finding the right extra musicians for the Wagner *tuben*, and until we do have a special quartet for the Wagner *tuben* in this country we will be always risking, with the best of our orchestras, having an inadequacy in Bruckner performances.[15]

A few months before the Schuller/Bruckner concert, the maestro welcomed another leading avant-garde composer to Minneapolis. Thanks to a recommendation from Skrowaczewski, Witold Lutosławski had spent summer 1963 at the Berkshire Music Center—his first trip to America—where he met Copland (who was in his last season as chairman of the faculty), Milton Babbitt, and Edgard Varèse. Before Lutosławski returned to Warsaw in September, he stopped in Minneapolis to see his old friend and colleague. He brought a new score, *Jeux vénitiens* (Venetian Games), which had its U.S. premiere by Skrowaczewski and the Minneapolis Symphony that December.

The thirteen-minute chamber orchestra work, about a year old, represented a major turning point in Lutosławski's development as a composer and conductor of his works. Responding to the "chance music" of John Cage that he had heard on Polish radio in 1958, Lutosławski developed a concept he called "controlled aleatorism," in which musicians are given free will to play certain notated figures within a set time frame. "This is not improvisation because all the notes are written down," Lutosławski explained in a *Minneapolis Tribune* article. "What it allows is a greater freedom, with the chance element in blending of parts permitting an exuberant release from the old rules of every note rigidly pinned down in place and time."[16] It was an attractive technique that Skrowaczewski eventually adopted in his own compositions.

Lutosławski was asked about his new work-in-progress, which required two conductors (including himself). His response underscored Skrowaczewski's conflict with the issue: "Conducting is risky for a composer, and I've not had enough practice in it. It's impossible to combine the two and do justice to either." He shot an amused but chiding look at Skrowaczewski, who had conducted so much in the last five years that he scarcely had time to write a note.[17]

Skrowaczewski virtually had stopped composing. Lutosławski's benign reminder of his friend's first calling might have encouraged Skrowaczewski to share his other talent with the Minneapolis community. During his fourth season he finally included one of his works on a subscription concert. The prospectus for that season listed an "untitled new work," which was perhaps wishful thinking on Skrowaczewski's part when it was printed. But it was an old piece, Symphony for Strings, which made its way into a program that included Claudio Arrau as a soloist in Beethoven's *Emperor* Concerto. "[Skrowaczewski] needn't have been so modest," wrote John Harvey of the *St. Paul Pioneer Press*. "Symphony for Strings is a fine piece that creates the impression the maestro has been holding out on us."[18] Harvey, while noting that the piece was conservative by current standards of contemporary music, concluded that "It's the sort of writing one gets when the composer has something to say and the will to communicate, and has full command of his material and technique."[19]

Several more years would pass before Skrowaczewski the composer emerged again, but a convergence of circumstances, combined with his growing maturity as an artist, would make the wait worthwhile.

THIRTEEN

MINNEAPOLIS MAESTRO

I see little of more importance to the future of our country and our civilization than full recognition of the place of the artist. If art is to nourish the roots of our culture, society must set the artist free to follow his vision wherever it takes him.

—John F. Kennedy, 1963

Although Skrowaczewski wasn't necessarily an accessible public figure, newspaper articles revealed selected aspects of his personality and domestic life. In 1962 a Minneapolis art exhibit featuring Polish painters prompted comments from Skrowaczewski about his native land. Referring to Polish modern art and its long underground history in his homeland, he observed, "We are all a part of the 'cultural explosion' that has taken place in Poland since the war. During the [German] occupation and its deprivations, the one thing worth doing, the one necessity you seized when all others were lacking, was the art you could produce in hiding. It all had to be done in hiding; otherwise, you would be finished."[1]

Stanisław and Krystyna were proud of their heritage. Although they adapted to living in Minnesota, they retained their culture, way of life, perspectives, and tastes. "We represented what we are, to the point that many other people tried to adjust to us," said Skrowaczewski. "Some people were very cultured and developed, which was good for us, but we represented something else, and they were curious, and sometimes they adopted our cultural milieu."

In a *Minneapolis Tribune* article about the Skrowaczewskis' home life, the maestro described his penchant for having many colors in his workplace and for "total tranquility and peace, no other sounds, no other noises."[2] Television was out of the question. He explained that he used his piano only about twenty percent of the time because he usually heard the whole orchestra in his head. He spent half the day preparing his scores, he said, and complained that many of the scores he received were almost illegible because of previous conductors' markings. "Sometimes it's a crime. They change poor Brahms, poor Mozart, so that only God knows who [wrote] the music."[3] When the Skrowaczewskis left Poland in 1960, he had been forced to abandon his collection of scores, and he now was rebuilding his library.

He lamented that snow shoveling was the first exercise he could undertake since his accident in spring 1961. When the interviewer questioned what the chore might do to his precious hands, Skrowaczewski responded, "Whatever it does to the hands, it certainly improves the health of the rest of the body."[4]

He enjoyed being a part of the Minneapolis community, but some Minnesotans' interests occasionally perplexed him. When the Minneapolis Symphony engaged the leading Wagnerian soprano of the day, Birgit Nilsson, it scheduled a special all-Wagner Sunday Twilight concert in November 1962. It was a huge artistic event:

> When Nilsson came it was a weekend concert, and they were always well attended in Minneapolis. We had nearly five thousand seats, and we were sure it was going to be overcrowded. But it wasn't. Why? Because it was the opening of the deer-hunting season! I'll never forget this because I was so angry at this fact. What does deer hunting (and people who kill beautiful animals) have to do with great art? But somehow it worked against me.

Summer 1963 brought European engagements for Skrowaczewski in Austria, France, and Italy as well as a ten-day Swiss tour with L'Orchestre National de France. His debut with the Vienna Symphony in May was the clear, though atypical, highlight:

> I had a rather strange experience in Vienna—my first contact with one of the Viennese orchestras during the May Vienna Festival, conducting an all-Stravinsky concert. The rehearsals were hard because the orchestra just didn't know how to play Stravinsky, or [else] it was new to them at the time. They had technical and intonation difficulties, and they didn't seem to like the music. I was very displeased with the rehearsals. But somehow the concert was apparently fascinating. I could not understand why, but the public loved it. The reviews were great, and they invited me back immediately. Yet I was rather "not in the mood" during the concert. Sometimes I'm happy about a performance, but the result is not what I thought, even on the recording that I listen to a few years later. I think we cannot always judge very well what makes the "happening" greater or lesser at the time.

The judgment of the audience and critics, however, was clear. The program, comprised of *Symphony of Psalms*, dances from *Petrushka*, and the *Firebird* Suite, elicited roars of enthusiasm for the bewildered maestro. "At the end of the standing ovation, the audience moved *en masse* toward the stage instead of filtering out of the exits to go home," one report recounted.[5] Close to the end of a thirty-minute ovation, the Vienna Symphony finally left the stage, forcing Skrowaczewski to take his eighth curtain call alone. Later he was told that Herbert von Karajan was the only other conductor to receive a similar response in the ten-year history of the Vienna Festival. Usually reserved in their praise, Viennese critics in seven newspapers lauded the concert. "The most eloquent testimony to Skrowaczewski," wrote one, "was the attitude of the orchestra…. The evening was by far their best in a long time. Catch him! Invite him!"[6]

A short break in his European schedule allowed him to stop back home and accept an honorary doctorate from Hamline University in St. Paul, Minnesota. In his acceptance speech Skrowaczewski discussed the contrasts and correlations between art and science. Excerpts from the speech convey his more philosophical attitudes toward his profession:

> The aim of science is knowledge; the aim of art somehow escapes verbal definition. In confronting art we feel as if we are standing in front of a veiled mystery: the more we try to unveil it—the more ineffable it remains. The very gist of art, its value, its raison d'être, seems to lie in this mystery.
>
> The achievement of both science and art is an understanding of the self as well as the nonself in the context of reality. This understanding coming from genuine science and genuine art, in any society and any age, is intellectually and emotionally satisfying and spiritually uplifting. I believe that this understanding distinguishes us from all other animate creatures and gives our lives meaning, purpose, and dignity.[7]

Skrowaczewski allowed himself some breathing space amid his summer conducting assignments. He rented a flat in Paris for himself and Krystyna for six weeks. Before their stay in Paris, Krystyna joined her husband for his engagement in Italy with the Santa Cecilia Orchestra of Rome. It was a homecoming of sorts for Skrowaczewski, who had guest conducted the orchestra every season but one since 1956, when he won the international conducting prize leading the ensemble. Krystyna's warm memory of listening to her husband's outdoor concert at Rome's Terme di Caracalla under a full moon contrasted with a frightening experience a few days later in Sanremo, the capital town of the Italian Riviera of Flowers. She and Stanisław woke up to find their hotel room swaying during a brief earthquake.

In Paris Skrowaczewski spent much of the time composing a new work for an upcoming competition in Milan. He submitted it, but neither he nor the committee felt it worthy of consideration. However, this much-needed extended break—his first since 1959—gave the Skrowaczewskis an idyllic interlude. Skrowaczewski had a piano, solitude, and a view of the Eiffel Tower from their apartment. Krystyna enjoyed being a tourist in the city with her mother, who not been to Paris since 1938 and who visited for a month. When her husband left Paris for his Swiss tour, Krystyna headed to a palatial log cabin in Lake Placid, New York—the home of Halina Rodziński, widow of Artur. She asked Krystyna to help organize her late husband's letters, pictures, and concert programs for a biography she planned to write (*Our Two Lives* was eventually published in 1976).

By Skrowaczewski's third season in Minneapolis he was becoming more comfortable in his professional and home environments. He presented concerts that mixed Haydn with Nono, Weber with Carter, and Messiaen (*Ascension*) with Brahms (*A German Requiem*), the latter two pieces comprising the season's last subscription performance. This concert marked Skrowaczewski's 750th performance as a conductor, as the *Minneapolis Tribune* reported, citing his first in 1936 at age thirteen. He enjoyed mostly critical acclaim for the quality of his programming and performances, and many concertgoers went along for the musical ride.

Composer Eric Stokes, then completing a Ph.D. at the University of Minnesota, wrote reviews for *The Minnesota Daily*, the student newspaper. In his criticism Stokes expressed a desire for more diversity in concert programming, specifically for works performed by small ensembles of strings, winds, brass, or percussion. Stokes wrote: "Mr. Skrowaczewski is to be congratulated for his efforts to broaden the scope of his programs by presenting such truly refreshing music as Lutosławski's *Jeux vénitiens*. Certainly there must be other creatively imaginative minds in both management and the profession who can help him revitalize the subscription concerts. Will they?"[8]

Stokes' suggestion that the Minneapolis Symphony look at programming with a broader scope was prescient. In May 1963 the Guthrie Theater, founded by Sir Tyrone Guthrie, opened in Minneapolis and became an example of a successful theater presenting serious works without the commercial pressures of a Broadway atmosphere. Its existence immediately elevated the cultural standing of the Twin Cities. Although not designed with music performance in mind, the 1,400-seat theater was a welcome alternative to Northrop Auditorium. The Minneapolis Symphony began the Adventures in Music series in fall 1963, undertaking ten performances of Weill's *The Three Penny Opera* at the Guthrie. Skrowaczewski and Fennell split conducting duties.

Skrowaczewski turned forty in October 1963. In honor of the occasion Krystyna decorated the doorway of their home with evergreens, red ribbons, and a sign that read *Sto Lat* ("100 years"), wishing her husband a hundred more birthdays. Two weeks later he began rehearsals with the Minneapolis Symphony for his fourth season. Programming highlights included Mahler's Tenth Symphony (the complete five-movement version by Deryck Cooke) and Mozart's Mass in C minor, both of which were first performances for Skrowaczewski and the Minneapolis Symphony.

Early in November 1963 Skrowaczewski and the orchestra had a rare opportunity to collaborate with one of the greatest showmen ever, Jack Benny. Skrowaczewski's reputation as a serious musician working in his "temple of music" was briefly eclipsed when he became a straight man for Benny. "Not so fast," the violinist yelled at his conductor. "No, not yet," the conductor yelled back, admonishing his soloist, and so the routine went. When Benny settled into his own comedic banter, he told his conductor, "Stan, you're so young. You're so young you make me sick!"[9]

Many of the most prominent soloists of the 1960s appeared throughout the season, including Isaac Stern, Claudio Arrau, János Starker, Gina Bachauer, and Yehudi Menuhin.

Menuhin enjoyed a long performing history with the Minneapolis Symphony, beginning with his debut with the orchestra as a twelve-year-old in 1928. During the second movement of the Brahms Violin Concerto the young prodigy experienced a rare memory lapse. He reportedly turned to conductor Henri Verbrugghen and said, "We must not bluff Brahms!" Verbrugghen stopped the orchestra, explaining that the boy's memory faltered, and then they both calmly resumed the performance.[10] Menuhin was back with the orchestra at age sixteen, and he remained a regular guest in Minneapolis for much of his performing life. On the occasion of the orchestra's seventy-fifth anniversary in 1978, he called Skrowaczewski "the most approachable, humane, and generous of all conductors. For him, I have a feeling of real collegial warmth, loyalty, and trust. Not only is he a wonderful musician, but he is a fine human being."[11]

Menuhin's first collaboration with Skrowaczewski occurred on one of the most tragic days in American history—November 22, 1963.

"When I came home that afternoon from rehearsal, I hadn't heard the news that President Kennedy had been shot," recalled concertmaster Norman Carol. "We all came to the concert that night, and they still hadn't decided if we would actually play. Stan was in contact with the management about it, and as soon as I got to the hall we began to discuss it. It was a difficult decision for everyone to make." With Menuhin's cooperation, it was finally decided to change the program to include only the scheduled Elgar Violin Concerto, preceded by the funeral march from Beethoven's *Eroica* Symphony. When news got out that the concert was on, there were reports of possible stink bombs being thrown in protest, but no such incidents occurred. Carol remembered the concert:

> It was dead silent backstage before the concert; nobody was playing or tuning instruments. After Menuhin finished the Elgar, the very sparse audience didn't know how to react, whether to applaud or not. Finally they did, and Menuhin came back on stage and played the Bach Chaconne for solo violin. I don't know whether it was just the night or the meaning of what had happened, but I never remember Menuhin playing as beautifully as he did that night. I remember Stan being on the podium, and everyone in complete silence listening to Menuhin.

When Menuhin finished, silence hung in the air. Skrowaczewski slowly raised his arms, and the orchestra played "The Star-Spangled Banner." Menuhin, who was still standing in front of the orchestra, joined his colleagues. By the end, most audience members were weeping. In his review published the next day, critic John Sherman wrote that the concert had paid tribute to "a president who has done more for music and general cultural values in this country than any predecessor within memory."[12]

Three weeks before he was assassinated, John F. Kennedy gave a speech at Amherst College at a ceremony honoring poet Robert Frost. In his remarks the president affirmed his support for the arts:

> I see little of more importance to the future of our country and our civilization than full recognition of the place of the artist. If art is to nourish the roots of our culture, society must set the artist free to follow his vision wherever it takes him. Art is not a form of propaganda; it is a form of truth and establishes the basic human truths which must serve as the touchstones of our judgment.

> I look forward to an America which will not be afraid of grace and beauty, which will protect the beauty of our natural environment, which will preserve the great old American houses and squares and parks of our national past,

and which will build handsome and balanced cities for our future. I look forward to an America which will reward achievement in the arts as we reward achievement in business or statecraft.[13]

The decision to go forth with the concert could not have been a more fitting tribute to the late president and to Mrs. Kennedy.

A week after Skrowaczewski's concert with Menuhin, he was guest conductor with the Cleveland Orchestra for the first time since 1959. The doors to some of the Big Five orchestras had finally opened to him during the 1963–64 season. Along with his Cleveland Orchestra engagement, Skrowaczewski made his debuts with the Philadelphia Orchestra and the Chicago Symphony. Major orchestras during this period had few guest conductors, and Skrowaczewski's engagements caused speculation in the Minneapolis press. When asked directly whether he had his eye on something bigger than the Minneapolis Symphony Orchestra, he gave the following answer:

> I am looking forward to something bigger with the Minneapolis Symphony: a better orchestra. If you get something like the big Eastern orchestras, like the Philadelphia, you don't have the satisfaction of contributing, do you? I am much more interested, for the moment, to stay here and try to bring the orchestra to a higher level. This can't be done in a day.[14]

The engagement with the Cleveland Orchestra presented Skrowaczewski with the challenge of rehearsing *The Rite of Spring*, a work that was surprisingly unfamiliar to the venerable orchestra. By the 1960s, Stravinsky's masterpiece was considered part of the standard repertoire, although it was not included in the repertoire of Szell and his predecessor Rodziński; probably only a few guest conductors in Cleveland had performed it over the years. The performances were remarkable nonetheless, although one Cleveland critic, while recognizing Skrowaczewski's "mastery and discerning mind," also stated that he had "not set the orchestra on fire as he had in 1959."[15] According to Lynn Harrell, soon-to-be principal cellist of the orchestra, the musicians greatly respected Skrowaczewski. "He was someone very much in the Szell mode," Harrell said, "a serious, thoughtful, probing musician with only the music at heart: no show, no faking, just really great musicianship. We were profoundly impressed with that."

Skrowaczewski enjoyed a strong relationship with Szell and the Cleveland Orchestra throughout the 1960s, but the elder maestro was protective of the "jewel" he had created. With the exception of the Blossom Festival (Cleveland's summer music festival), he preferred to do most of the conducting.

On the other hand, Ormandy was more generous with his orchestra—and could afford to be. Thanks in large part to Arthur Judson, Ormandy's career was set for the remainder of his life. In 1963 he was sixty-four years old and in his twenty-fifth season as music director of the Philadelphia Orchestra (he would continue for another seventeen years—a record forty-four years). Until 1968, his recordings for CBS generated the highest sales of the label's classical artists, even exceeding Bernstein's.[16]

When Ormandy and Skrowaczewski first met in 1958, during the older conductor's engagement in Warsaw, the two men discovered that they had much in common.

They shared an Eastern European background, and Arthur Judson had "discovered" them both. Judson had given Ormandy the opportunity to conduct the Philadelphia Orchestra in 1931 as a substitute for Toscanini. The occasion ultimately led to Ormandy's five seasons as conductor of the Minneapolis Symphony (1931–36) before he replaced Stokowski in Philadelphia.

Skrowaczewski's relationship with Ormandy was the closest and longest he had with another major conductor. He became a favorite of the Philadelphia Orchestra, which he guest conducted regularly well into the 1980s. His first engagement with the ensemble in spring 1964 was indeed generous. After two subscriptions concerts in Philadelphia, Skrowaczewski had a short tour that included his Carnegie Hall debut with the orchestra. He was well received by Philadelphia musicians and critics, and Judson did his part to make the most of Skrowaczewski's special opportunity. A flyer that reprinted most of the concert reviews touted "A New Philadelphia Story" and proclaimed that Skrowaczewski's "recent success as guest conductor of the Philadelphia Orchestra has created great excitement in the music world."[17]

Skrowaczewski's program with the Philadelphia Orchestra was virtually a test for a guest conductor, with four distinct styles represented (music of Mozart, Prokofiev, Schumann, and Stravinsky). Based on the positive reviews of the orchestra's New York concerts, the conductor must have passed the test. Winthrop Sargeant, writing for *The New Yorker*, went from covering a Rubinstein recital to catching the second half of Skrowaczewski's concert, which included Schumann's Fourth Symphony: "It is a compliment to Mr. Skrowaczewski," he wrote, "to say that after leaving a performance by a highly skilled Romantic like Mr. Rubinstein I found his approach to Schumann quite eloquent.... [The performance] was distinctly on the electrifying side...and impetuous. However, he showed a refined sense of phrasing and *rubato*, as well as considerable genuine musical temperament."[18]

During Skrowaczewski's New York visit he lunched with Judson, who at age eighty-eight had left Columbia the previous November to form a new management company. Wilford had assumed control of the conductors' division at Columbia. "Are you going to stay with me, or are you going with Columbia?" Judson asked. Wilford was not yet as recognized or as powerful as Judson had been, and Skrowaczewski asked Judson for his opinion. The octogenarian pointed out that his new company would be a short-term venture and that Columbia was permanent. He advised Skrowaczewski to go to Columbia. "At the time he was still very bright and sharp, but he knew the limitations of his age," Skrowaczewski said, "so I went with Wilford, with Columbia. Later, Wilford became absorbed by machinations and power."

Summer 1964 brought two more important American debuts for Skrowaczewski: with the Chicago Symphony Orchestra at the Ravinia Festival and the Los Angeles Philharmonic at the Hollywood Bowl. The offer to conduct the Chicago Symphony at Ravinia originated in 1962, but both Judson and Wilford had advised Skrowaczewski to forego it in favor of a proper debut on a subscription concert in Chicago. But when that offer didn't materialize, Skrowaczewski accepted the Ravinia engagement and took the podium on a rainy late-July evening. Despite the favorable response to the concert, he has conducted the Chicago Symphony only one additional time. "They relied upon the management to engage conductors, as opposed to some input from the music director," said Skrowaczewski. "John Edwards, the manager at that time, saw me as someone from Minneapolis who was not worthy of the Chicago Symphony. It was sad, but it happens this way. I couldn't care less about it, but it is a pity."

A week before his Ravinia debut, Skrowaczewski was apparently "just what the doctor ordered to pull the Los Angeles Philharmonic's wavering ensemble back into some semblance of order again," according to the *Los Angeles Times* review of the maestro's Hollywood Bowl debut. "He is not a showman, praise heaven, and his concentration is on the music," the critic said, noting that Skrowaczewski "produced far and away the best orchestral response of the season."[19]

While the maestro completed his summer engagements and prepared for the 1964–65 season with the Minneapolis Symphony, the orchestra's administrative leadership was preparing a report for its board of directors that was due in the fall. The document was the result of a special "seminar" held in June by the executive committee. Significant changes had occurred within the Minneapolis Symphony leadership that spring. Sokoloff left his position as general manager to assume the same post with the Philadelphia Orchestra, and Myers stepped down as president. Cisek assumed Sokoloff's position, and board member Judson Bemis became the orchestra's new president.

The June meeting addressed every aspect of the Minneapolis Symphony's future. Two of the objectives set forth would ultimately change the orchestra permanently: setting a target date for annual employment and seeking "a 'new image' for the Minneapolis Symphony Orchestra, including an [emphasis] on identification as a State of Minnesota institution."[20] The latter objective prompted the most controversial move ever made by the orchestra, and Skrowaczewski would find himself in the center of it.

FOURTEEN

BIG FIVE PLUS ONE?

In the devotion of a life to the arts, it seems that the striving after undefined goals is an integral part of such a life, and that the preaching of [an] artistic credo is rather the death of art.

—Stanisław Skrowaczewski, letter to Dr. Muhammed H. Siddiqui, 1964

In an article for *The Wilson Quarterly* entitled "The Other Sixties," Bruce Bawer writes about the early 1960s in America as a period of newness, possibility, and openness. It was a grace period of sorts before the political and social upheaval of the mid- and late sixties, its end marked by the assassination of President John F. Kennedy. "It was a time," Bawer states, "when American mass taste may well have been more sophisticated than it has ever been."[1]

The Twin Cities' cultural leaders embraced the nation's creative energy in the early 1960s. In a 1966 article entitled "The New Twin Cities," Burton Hersh describes the cultural shift as "inspiration over institution."[2] By the 1930s the public had adopted rituals of patronizing arts institutions in Minneapolis, such as attending the symphony on Friday nights and making occasional visits to an art museum. In the early 1960s, however, new artistic ideas flourished, and local arts patrons were ready for fresh, nontraditional experiences.

"We can't do the same things as the major metropolitan cities and do them not quite as well. What the hell has this city got but culture?" said an unnamed Minneapolis business leader in Hersh's article.[3] The early 1960s ushered in the cultural renewal of the Twin Cities, and by the decade's end the community had embraced it fully. Arts patrons in Minneapolis and St. Paul represented a wider demographic than the Boston Brahmins or the New York elite. They were willing to take a chance on new ideas in the arts, particularly in music, as Hersh describes:

> The concertgoers' taste has grown more democratic…. "Even as recently as the middle 1950s," remembers Kenneth Dayton, who was president of the orchestra in 1953, at thirty-one, "whenever Doráti played a concerto by Bartók, people would get up and walk out. Now it's an old warhorse that always brings the house down." Dayton himself—conscientious, Presbyterian, [Yale-graduated], deep in the family department-store business—shares the attitudes of his generation of unself-conscious [*sic*] cultural commissars: "It's the inclination of this community to take a young man and gamble on him and get the best years of his productive life rather than tie itself down with some has-been."

"This community" still means the several dozen well-established local families knowledgeable enough to take such chances but not quite rich enough wholly to underwrite them. The cash itself, as ever, comes from the bourgeois troops, solicited often by a kind of chain letter the officers send down among the rank and file. Each year the symphony automatically loses half a million dollars; each year the guaranteed fund-raisers automatically make it up. Thousands of individuals contribute.[4]

"Culture Outdraws Big Leagues" proclaimed the headline of a 1965 *Minneapolis Tribune* article reporting that concert, theater, and museum attendance surpassed the turnout at Minnesota Twins, Minnesota Vikings, and university athletics events by nearly 250,000.[5]

How did the Minneapolis Symphony Orchestra respond to the Twin Cities' "cultural upsurge" of the mid-1960s? "The Musical Voice of Modern Minnesota"—the orchestra's slogan beginning in 1964—offered three distinct areas of performance by 1965. Along with the steadfast Friday night subscription series, now increased to twenty concerts, Cisek (newly appointed as the orchestra's managing director) revamped the orchestra's Sunday series to feature more popular music and artists. At the other end of the spectrum were innovative concerts of works for chamber orchestra and mixed ensembles, a new series at the Guthrie Theater in collaboration with Walker Art Center.

Daring Minnesotans ventured to the Guthrie for Sinfonia, billed as Skrowaczewski's "bold new dimension in concerts." Sinfonia featured fifteen members of the Minneapolis Symphony, mostly principal players, and a repertoire that ranged from 14th-century composer Machaut to Vivaldi (Skrowaczewski conducted and played the harpsichord) to Varèse. A performance of Stravinsky's *L'Histoire du Soldat* was staged and narrated with the maestro conducting from a stepladder for part of the production. Despite the enthusiasm for Sinfonia from the players, Skrowaczewski, and patrons, the venture lasted only five seasons. "It was an extra job for me but something we could only do with one or two rehearsals because the musicians had to be paid extra. I loved it, but eventually I lost heart for it because of the lack of support from the orchestra management," Skrowaczewski explained. Although artistically engaging, Sinfonia could not generate enough income to justify its costs.

An even more intimate performing entity was the Minneapolis Symphony String Quartet, consisting of Norman Carol and Henry Kramer (violin), Gaetano Molieri (viola), and Robert Jamieson (cello). Formed in 1960, it was then the only string quartet in the U.S. consisting exclusively of principal players of a major orchestra. "Stan was always extremely supportive of the quartet," said Carol. "He came to some of our concerts, and he even conducted on a few that involved an expanded chamber ensemble."

Skrowaczewski made his Vienna State Opera debut in September 1964 conducting *Fidelio*, Beethoven's lone opera. Wrote one Viennese critic, "No other opera is connected here so much with the memory of great conductors such as Mahler, Furtwängler, and Karajan, and newcomers often do not measure up to these men, in the opinion of the audience. It was characteristic of the artistic rank of Skrowaczewski that he won over the audience from the first beat.... His conducting was the sensation of the evening."[6]

What the reviewer did not mention—and probably did not know—was that Skrowaczewski had conducted the opera without benefit of a full orchestra or cast rehearsal. Skrowaczewski recalled the circumstances:

> Karajan had unexpectedly left the Vienna Opera, and they had *Fidelio* without a conductor. All of Karajan's stagings and casts for the season were already in place. It had an amazing cast that included Birgit Nilsson, and they proposed that I conduct it, but with no complete rehearsal! None! I had only half an hour with the choir. I knew *Fidelio* well, and it was close to my heart. The problem was Karajan's staging; everything was dark and far away. Nilsson was quite public with her anger with Karajan over this. The choir of prisoners came from far away, and when they started their first entrance they could not be seen, and I couldn't hear them. Of course the orchestra couldn't hear them, either. They proceeded slowly from backstage looking at television screens to see my beat. It was very risky for about sixty measures. It was quite a challenge not to completely fall apart. Finally, when they were closer, they heard the orchestra. Somehow the entire opera went fantastically.
>
> The next day the director of the opera offered me Karajan's production of *Don Giovanni* in January and also *Die Meistersinger* and *Der Fliegende Holländer* later in the season. I said yes, but with some rehearsals. He said, "No, sorry, we cannot rehearse. We could only have the singers do a run with you at the piano." I said, "Thank you very much, I cannot take it." And I was right. *Don Giovanni* is wonderful, but without rehearsals it is a very dangerous opera. Several scenes vary in levels of richness. Strangely enough, with some exceptions, I don't care musically for *Meistersinger*. For me it is the least interesting of Wagner operas. I prefer *Rienzi* and *Tannhäuser* to it. This one crazy challenge with *Fidelio* went well, but I would not repeat a similar situation with these other operas. So my contact with them broke completely when I refused their proposal. The company changed direction every year, and I was never invited back. When other directors came, they had no knowledge of the *Fidelio* success.

Conductors a generation prior to Skrowaczewski (Szell, Reiner, Karajan, etc.) began their careers in opera. Skrowaczewski is one of the few major conductors of his generation (along with Bernstein, Sir Neville Marriner, and Mstislav Rostropovich) who did not make opera a career priority. Opera-conducting opportunities in Poland did not exist throughout World War II, and Skrowaczewski was reluctant to commit to the weeks that most productions required. More importantly, Skrowaczewski was interested only in a relatively narrow opera repertoire—primarily the major German operas by Mozart, Wagner, and Strauss. Of the latter's operas, he would conduct only *Elektra* and *Salome*. ("I would never do *Rosenkavalier*," he said. "I could, because I feel the music, but I hate it.") Operas by Stravinsky, Britten, Berg, and a few other composers also appealed to him, but Skrowaczewski has little interest in Italian operas, particularly those by Puccini. "I accept Puccini as a great opera composer. His works are a model of how to write an opera," Skrowaczewski said, "but I sometimes find his music to be maudlin."

Ever the purist, he regards all the trappings of an opera production (set designs, costumes, acting, etc.) as detrimental to the music. The few opera experiences Skrowaczewski had in 1969 and 1970 underscored his attitude toward the genre that many hold as the highest musical form in Western music. He explains his preference for performing operas in concert format:

> I love opera, especially when the focus is on the *music*. I don't need an opera house, scenes, and decorations. If you commit to the full preparation of an opera production, you probably will have enough rehearsal time, but you have to stay on site for at least four weeks. There may be a director whom you don't know who was engaged two years ahead of time, and he may have crazy ideas about the production. Opera went to absurdity during my lifetime. It went from realistic representations, with Wagner performed in the epoch for which it was intended, to very abstract realizations by directors who tried to update operas to our times. Mozart would be set in a Los Angeles ghetto, for example, which bothers me because it has nothing to do with Mozart's epoch. And often singers are changed at the last minute, causing great complications. So why should I risk these things? A concert performance is pure music. Then you can have singers that you know—the same ones that you rehearse with—and a fine performance.

Skrowaczewski's 1965 American operatic debut was in fact a concert presentation at Carnegie Hall. The American Opera Society engaged him to conduct Gluck's *Iphigénia en Aulide*, which had yet to be performed by the Metropolitan Opera. The production was the exact version used three years previously in Salzburg with the same star husband-and-wife team of bass Walter Berry and soprano Christa Ludwig. Tenor Richard Cassilly rounded out the cast's major talents. The opera, based on the Greek tragedy of Agamemnon, who sacrifices his daughter Iphigénia to Artemis, was Gluck's last major work. Between 1775 and 1824 it received 500 performances at the Paris Opera.[7] Critics gave it mixed reviews, just as they did for Skrowaczewski's Carnegie Hall performance. He conducted a German version of Gluck's opera (the composer's original language) translated by Paul Freidrich and Günther Rennert. It was unusual for people to hear the work in German; most of Gluck's operas are presented in French or Italian. Skrowaczewski received praise for his conducting from reviewers, with the exception of one who felt he was too rigid in his approach.[8]

During the 1964–65 season, his other operatic experience—again in concert format—was Alban Berg's expressionistic masterpiece *Wozzeck*, with the Minneapolis Symphony. Throughout the rest of the 1960s and 1970s, Skrowaczewski turned to his own orchestra and the concert format for opera performance. Honegger's "stage oratorio" *Jeanne d'Arc au Bûcher* and Benjamin Britten's *War Requiem* were the other large-scale choral and solo works that Skrowaczewski performed during the season. In

1964 he conducted *War Requiem* in the Upper Midwest premiere of Britten's choral and orchestral masterpiece, which also marked its first performance by the Minneapolis Symphony Orchestra. The *War Requiem* had intrigued Skrowaczewski ever since its world premiere in 1962. Cisek reminded his maestro about the new piece:

> I remember reading about *War Requiem* in *Time* magazine. It was commissioned for the reconsecration of England's Coventry Cathedral. The original cathedral was destroyed during World War II. The war was still fresh enough in our memories in the 1960s so that this was big news. I wrote to Stan about the piece, and I heard from him immediately, asking about getting a score, and we started to exchange ideas about how we could mount it in Minneapolis.

Phyllis Curtin, the intelligent and imaginative singer with whom Skrowaczewski worked several times in the 1960s and 1970s, was the soprano soloist in that performance. In 1966 she joined Skrowaczewski and the Minneapolis Symphony in a complete concert performance of Strauss' *Salome*. The *War Requiem* is a favorite of Skrowaczewski's, although his opportunities to conduct it have been rare. His most recent performance of the work was with the Hallé Orchestra in 1996.

The Minneapolis Symphony Orchestra made national news when it announced a five-year contract between its musicians and the Minnesota Orchestral Association (MOA), its administrative organization. At the time, the contract was the longest such agreement of its kind for a major symphony orchestra in the United States. Eight months in negotiation, this contract incrementally expanded the season from thirty-one weeks in 1964–65 to forty-five weeks by the 1969–70 season.

The contract took a major step toward a year-round, fifty-two-week season that would significantly increase income for the musicians and the orchestra, making the ensemble more competitive with similar organizations in obtaining the best musicians. In 1964 the New York Philharmonic became the first major orchestra to have a fifty-two-week season, and the Philadelphia Orchestra followed suit the next season. At the time of the contract the Minneapolis season resembled that of the Cincinnati Orchestra (approximately thirty weeks a year).[9]

Another key contract provision stipulated the segmentation of the orchestra into smaller units of thirty or more for purposes of presenting additional educational concerts in Minnesota communities beyond the Twin Cities area. "If Minnesota is to continue to enjoy and benefit from its own live major orchestra," said Judson Bemis, MOA president, "we must meet and beat our competition."[10]

Cisek led the charge. He made it known that the Minneapolis Symphony was the only major orchestra in the United States that did not receive any government support and that it must do so if it were to expand its reach. The hope was that by establishing more visibility throughout the state and the Upper Midwest, the orchestra would gain this crucial support. The idea led to the notion of the Minneapolis Symphony becoming a regional orchestra.

By summer 1965 the MOA had positioned the orchestra to enter the "financial big leagues" of U.S. orchestras, and Skrowaczewski had completed his fifth season of raising its artistic profile. A monthlong East Coast tour that earned wide praise for the ensemble and its conductor included a performance at Carnegie Hall under the auspices of the International Festival of Visiting Orchestras. A sign of the Twin Cities' rising status as a major cultural center in America was the invitation Skrowaczewski received from NBC's *Today Show*, which he fulfilled during the orchestra's New York visit. The event marked one of the few times he appeared on network television. "I hated it because I had to be there at five in the morning," he remembered.

The soloist for the New York performance and for the first leg of the tour was Skrowaczewski's favorite violinist, Henryk Szeryng. During Skrowaczewski's tenure, no other violinist was a guest with the Minneapolis Symphony as often as Szeryng, who performed seven seasons and on two extended tours with the orchestra. He and Skrowaczewski also were frequent concert partners in Europe and with other American orchestras. "It would be hard to over-praise Mr. Szeryng's playing," wrote Harold Schonberg in his review of the 1965 Carnegie Hall concert. "No matter how difficult and awkward the music, he bowed and fingered with extraordinary ease.… [He] had the kind of technique that he could forget about the difficulties and concentrate on the music."[11]

Skrowaczewski first worked with Szeryng at the 1957 Prague Festival:

> I was flabbergasted. He was one of the finest violinists I had ever heard. We were in the same hotel in Prague, and in the evening we went for walks in the beautiful early June air. I discovered his depth in our conversations about philosophy, music, religion, and life. We became really warm friends, and every time we played together, it was better and better. Usually a soloist and conductor look at each other here and there in a performance. We didn't need to communicate visually because spiritually it was always absolutely perfect. Henryk was the only soloist with whom I had such a relationship.

When Skrowaczewski first met Szeryng, the thirty-nine-year-old violinist was new to the international concert circuit. World War II significantly delayed his career. At age ten he studied in Berlin with legendary pedagogue Carl Flesch, and by 1933 he made his formal debut with the Warsaw Philharmonic under Bruno Walter. Concerts quickly followed in Bucharest, Vienna, and Paris, where he settled for six years. He was drawn to the refined French school of violin playing and to the notion of composing (he studied with Boulanger during his entire stay in the city). When the war began in 1939, Szeryng, who was Jewish, left Paris and joined the Polish army. His elite education and fluency in seven languages soon earned him a position as official translator for Prime Minister Władysław Sikorski's government-in-exile in London. The position saved his life; his parents died in Hitler's gas chambers.

In 1941 Szeryng accompanied Sikorski to Central and Latin America to find homes for more than four thousand Polish refugees. When Mexico accepted them, Szeryng gratefully settled there, too. The country was his base during the war, and he gave hundreds of concerts for the Allies. He became a naturalized citizen of Mexico in 1946 and soon headed the string department at the University of Mexico. His international performing career seemingly over, Szeryng met Artur Rubinstein in 1964, when the pianist was giving a recital in Mexico City. Rubinstein asked the violinist to play for him and was so impressed by what he heard that he contacted his manager, Sol Hurok, and urged him to represent Szeryng. By 1956 Szeryng had made his New York debut and soon became one of the leading violinists of the 1960s. In 1970 he was appointed Mexico's special advisor to UNESCO in Paris, a United Nations post that enabled him to fulfill his passion for humanitarian work.[12]

Despite these achievements, Szeryng resented the lack of recognition he received in comparison to the young violinists of the 1970s, such as Pinchas Zukerman and Itzhak Perlman. Among managers and orchestras, the frustrated Szeryng developed a reputation for being "difficult." Skrowaczewski never experienced this aspect of Szeryng's personality directly, but he recalled aspects of his peculiar behavior:

> He changed his age. It was easy for him to do because he had a Mexican diplomatic passport. He told people in interviews that he was born in 1922 instead of 1918. He thought it would help him compete with the younger violinists. We always had a big party at our house for him when he played in Minneapolis. Once he began handing out large autographed photographs of himself without anyone asking for them. Krystyna pulled him aside and told him that this behavior wasn't proper. She wanted to help because she knew he was suffering from this obsession of not being praised enough. He was so bitter because the war destroyed his prime time for making a big career.

Still, as far as Skrowaczewski was concerned, Szeryng's outstanding musicianship trumped his idiosyncrasies:

> To me and to some people who really knew violin playing, he was the greatest since Heifetz. His tone was so pure and unexaggerated. It was a rare sound for a violinist, a kind of pure classical conception. David Oistrakh had this as well, but Szeryng's tone was warmer. In fact, to me his tone was like mahogany. It was concise, round, warm, and beautiful, without any superficiality. It was a *very* special tone. And, of course, his choice of *tempi* was so musical. His *tempi* struck the music in the heart. His entire musicianship was so natural, and his interpretation of every style was higher than all other violinists I know of, including Heifetz. His identification with the music as written in the score was incredible. I use these strong words because having worked with him so often I have never been as pleased with anyone else since he died.

Like Skrowaczewski, Szeryng was a musical purist and a musician's musician, qualities that did not always win at the box office during the 1970s and 1980s, when flair and youth reigned supreme. Szeryng continued performing and doing humanitarian work until his death in 1988. Skrowaczewski learned of his death while he was in the middle of a recording session with the Hallé Orchestra:

During the afternoon break, in the middle of our recording session, the manager of the orchestra, Clive Smart, told me that Szeryng had died suddenly in Germany while on tour with the Saarbrücken Radio Symphony Orchestra. I could hardly resume conducting the Brahms First Symphony that we were recording at the time. It was terrible to have to conduct after this news. I had been inside of the music and then had to learn of Henryk's death. I don't think Clive realized how this news would affect me. It was such a blow. It was one of the most poignant shocks that I remember in my life. Szeryng was due to perform with the Hallé and me in London in two weeks. The morning after I heard this news, a postcard from Szeryng came to me in the mail saying how much he was looking forward to performing together again. It was as though the card had come from heaven. I realized how much I needed him in my life. His musicianship had given me so much. It was quite sad, because he had married a wonderful French woman, Waltraud, who had really helped him turn around his life. He wasn't exhibiting any of his strange behavior from the past. And he was playing better than ever.

"Poland Tribute Via Minneapolis" read the headline of a New York review of Skrowaczewski's winter 1965 concert with Szeryng, describing the trifecta of Polish conductor, soloist, and composer in the performance of Szymanowski's Violin Concerto no. 2.[13] Two weeks after the Carnegie Hall performance, Skrowaczewski conducted "The Polish Millennium Concert," sponsored by the Polina Civic Center and Polish Arts Group of New York as part of the Minneapolis Symphony's East Coast tour.

Skrowaczewski's fifth season in Minneapolis was, to a certain extent, a tribute to Polish artists. Rubinstein was back, Paul Kletzki (Skrowaczewski's former mentor) was a guest conductor, and Skrowaczewski conducted the world premiere of Palester's *Death of Don Juan: Three Symphonic Fragments.*

Skrowaczewski's Polish pride ran deep, but he also was proud of the life he had established in America. In May 1965 he and Krystyna officially became U.S. citizens. "The government officials approached *us* about formalizing our life in America," Skrowaczewski said. "We still only had green papers at the time. Of course, we were happy to do it. And it was somehow quicker than normal. We took a short test, and that was it."

Having signed a three-year extension to his Minneapolis contract early in 1964, Skrowaczewski felt confident about the longevity of his position. Concert attendance for the 1964–65 season was reported at ninety percent capacity.[14] The next season it rose to ninety-seven percent.[15] Although there were occasional grumblings from some musicians who thought his rehearsal style was pedantic and his performances uninspired, he was lauded locally and nationally for having improved the orchestra significantly within a relatively short period of time.

John Sherman, *Minneapolis Tribune* critic and a longtime follower and scholar of the Minneapolis Symphony, summarized Skrowaczewski's contributions to the orchestra after five seasons: "Skrowaczewski has improved the orchestra's tone, sharpened its expression, given it nuance and refinement. He appreciates the subtleties of the slow and quiet. His restudies of the classics have provided them freshness along with an exacting presentiment of their thought and feeling. 'Light' rather than 'beat' may be a keyword for his interpretations, for lucidity is a major factor in his expression."[16]

Two weeks before the start of the orchestra's 1965–66 season, the *Minneapolis Tribune* published an article by a music critic for *The Philadelphia Inquirer* that caused a mild tremor throughout the Twin Cities' music community. The piece suggested that the Philadelphia Orchestra was looking seriously at Skrowaczewski as a possible successor to sixty-five-year-old Eugene Ormandy. The article was spurred by Ormandy's thirtieth anniversary as a conductor in Philadelphia.[17] Additionally, in 1964 the Philadelphia Orchestra successfully wooed the Minneapolis Symphony's manager, Boris Sokoloff, and a year after hiring Sokoloff as its manager, Philadelphia secured Norman Carol as concertmaster. The Twin Cities worried that Skrowaczewski might be the next artist to leave.

Ormandy stayed with Philadelphia until 1980, but the idea of Skrowaczewski being courted by that orchestra was not unreasonable. He had earned prominent engagements with the Philadelphia Orchestra, and it had been announced that he would share a major tour of South America with Ormandy in spring 1966. Skrowaczewski was also scheduled to conduct the first three concerts of Philadelphia's summer 1966 season at The Robin Hood Dell, the well-known amphitheater.

But three days after the *Minneapolis Tribune* article appeared, Cisek firmly dispelled the notion that the Minneapolis Symphony was a "farm team" for the Philadelphia Orchestra. At a press conference in Rochester, Minnesota, during which the MOA announced a new concert series to be held there, Cisek was quoted in the *Rochester Bulletin*: "We're not Philadelphia's answering service or spring training ground." He noted that Skrowaczewski "figures centrally in our new five-year program, and we will make it as challenging and creative an atmosphere as possible to keep him here."[18]

The main point of the Rochester article was that the city was helping the Minneapolis Symphony become a regional orchestra through a new series of five concerts during the regular 1965–66 season, the first of its kind for the organization outside of the Twin Cities. This article offered the first public hint of a possible name change. "Richard Cisek declared," the article noted, "that the time is coming when [the Minneapolis Symphony] will be known not so much as the Minneapolis as the Minnesota Symphony. We've taken a lesson from the Minnesota Twins and the Vikings, too—it's been an ethical and practical decision to broaden our scope, and Rochester has spearheaded the move first...."[19]

Cisek's responsibility for making the atmosphere of the Minneapolis Symphony "as challenging and creative" as possible in order to keep Skrowaczewski happy was not simply press puffery. Along with presenting a concert version of *Salome* during the 1965–66 season, Skrowaczewski mounted Haydn's *Lord Nelson Mass*, featuring a chorus of 252 voices (the first time the work was presented by the orchestra), and major orchestral works such as the fourth symphonies of Mahler and Ives. The completed version of Ives' Fourth Symphony received its world premiere only a year before Skrowaczewski conducted it in Minneapolis. Stokowski led the American Symphony Orchestra at Carnegie Hall in the first performance of this highly complex work, aided by two additional conductors. In Minneapolis, Skrowaczewski was the sole conductor for the performances of the symphony.

The other major contemporary offering during this season was Elliott Carter's *Variations for Orchestra*. Carter began composing the work in 1954 but prepared a corrected edition in 1966. "Carter is one of the best, most interesting American composers living today," Skrowaczewski said several months before he conducted *Variations*.[20] "You cannot describe anyone's musical language accurately. He uses twelve-tone technique in some of the variations, but he uses the system with freedom. The work is a fine expression of his very delicate nature."[21] Skrowaczewski became a strong supporter and performer of Carter's music, and he and the composer became good friends. At the Minneapolis Symphony's annual Carnegie Hall appearance, Skrowaczewski conducted an all-20th-century program that included Carter's *Variations for Orchestra*. Carter remembered the performance:

> I was sitting in the same box as Artur Rubinstein, who was very enthusiastic about the performance. Skrowaczewski was a very meticulous and careful conductor. He didn't get the excitement that somebody like Leonard Bernstein got from an orchestra. He had much more of a classical point of view about how to conduct rather than such a romantic one as Lenny had. It was a little bit more like Boulez, very accurate and careful. And I thought that was wonderful.

"Mr. Skrowaczewski has achieved quite a reputation as the coming conductor," reported the fastidious Harold Schonberg of *The New York Times*, "and he drew a good audience. Among his hearers were a good number of avant-garde composers."[22] Schonberg had just finished writing *The Great Conductors*, a book that carefully chronicles the art of conducting through examples of the finest maestros in music history, so his analysis of Skrowaczewski in his review carried weight:

> Stanisław Skrowaczewski is in many respects the archetype of what has come to be known as the "modern conductor." Efficiency personified, clear, precise, intelligent, a superior musician, and a fine workman, he knows exactly what he wants and how to go about getting it…. In complicated music, in music that demands logic, layout, rhythmic definition, Mr. Skrowaczewski is as good as any, and better than most. He conducted the Carter and Hindemith [*Symphonic Metamorphosis after Themes by Carl Maria von Weber*], works with unusual resilience and authority. It was not only a matter of knowing the score. Rather it was identification with the spirit of the music, the kind of

orientation where the interpreter has a sheer alliance with the materials that went into the composition…. It should be said that Mr. Skrowaczewski has kept the Minneapolis Symphony at a very high peak. It remains one of the country's best orchestras.[23]

The number of "best orchestras" in the United States increased during the 1960s. *Time* magazine dubbed the top orchestras that were awarded an $85 million Ford Foundation grant in 1966 as "The Elite Eleven." Along with the perennial Big Five the group included Pittsburgh, Detroit, Houston, Los Angeles, Minneapolis, and San Francisco.[24] Increasing numbers of outstanding orchestras meant increased competition and marketing for mass appeal. The Minneapolis Symphony had always played concerts of so-called light classical music, but the Adventures in Music series added programs with popular artists. By the mid-1970s such concerts had found their way alongside the regular subscription series schedule.

The Minneapolis Symphony closed the 1965–66 season with a simple marketing strategy, an all-request program whose results Skrowaczewski cleverly utilized. Said critic Allan Holbert, "Who else but Skrowaczewski, who insists he's not a 'champion of contemporary music,' could put together an all-request program with Schoenberg on it twice?"[25]

Like his previous responses to a vocal faction of contemporary-music opponents, Skrowaczewski displayed his subtle wit in the following comments at the all-request concert:

> Tonight it is your all-request program, for which we have received hundreds of your letters. You might be interested in knowing how the program was selected for tonight's performance. I surely have no intention of detracting anything from Abraham Lincoln's famous comment of not being able to please all of the people all of the time. However, for this particular concert the decision was not too difficult because the decision was not mine, but yours.
>
> Johann Sebastian Bach was your number-one choice. As these requests for Bach mostly did not specify a particular work, I have chosen a work of his using the large, full orchestra [Prelude and Fugue in E-flat for organ, transcribed by Schoenberg] to get along better with the Northrop Auditorium acoustics—if this is possible at all. Number two was Mussorgsky's *Pictures at an Exhibition.* Finally, a surprising result regarding the eternal conflict between new and old. Eighty-seven percent were for playing contemporary music, from which fifty-five percent were accepting of what we have been playing in recent years and thirty-two percent requesting more contemporary music and more avant-garde. Thirteen percent said we play too much contemporary music.
>
> By the way, some of the music reviewers presented me recently with the title "champion of contemporary music." I do object strongly because, first of all, I don't like "title-mania." It distracts people from real facts. Secondly, I do not deserve it more than any of my colleagues in Chicago, Detroit, or Philadelphia. Thirdly, contemporary or past, I couldn't care less if the music is bad; contemporary or past, I could not care more if the music is good. But

if any title is needed, the results of your letters call for passing my crown of championship in this field to our dear concertgoers in the Twin Cities.

As Arnold Schoenberg was often quoted [in your letters], to honor these requests for more advanced music I have chosen some of the most glorious pages of 20th-century music—Schoenberg's *Summer Morning by a Lake* [a movement from Five Orchestral Pieces]. It is a short work, but in its forty-four measures conceives almost every vibration of the human soul since Bach, across *Tristan* of Wagner, *Pelléas* of Debussy, up to Schoenberg's pupil, Anton Webern. Because of the concentration needed to follow each chord, each tone, I would like to ask your permission to play it twice. I hope you will enjoy the rest of the program, and I hope you will miss us during our summer absence.[26]

This concert also introduced the Twin Cites' audience to twenty-year-old Israeli violinist Itzhak Perlman, who would become one of the world's most popular concert soloists during the next forty years.

The Minneapolis Symphony's artistic status received a special boost in January 1966 from the presence of guest conductor Igor Stravinsky, who had last conducted the orchestra in 1940. The eighty-three-year-old composer now was in the twilight of his creative life. He shared the Minneapolis podium with the ever-present Robert Craft, who conducted *The Rite of Spring* while Stravinsky led his brief *Fireworks*, a "fantasy for large orchestra," and music from his 1928 ballet, *The Fairy's Kiss*. (Conductor and writer Craft had been Stravinsky's close assistant, friend, and colleague since 1948. The pair shared more than 150 concerts during a twenty-three-year period.)[27] Skrowaczewski, who had invited Stravinsky to Minneapolis, was conducting in Europe at the time of his visit.

An incident at the concert became part of the orchestra's lore, as reported by Julie Ayer in *More Than Meets the Ear*. The orchestra never had performed *The Fairy's Kiss*, and when Stravinsky lost his place in the Divertimento movement, the performance broke down: "The musicians sat, horrified, as Stravinsky scrambled through the score, peered through his glasses, and screamed, 'Goddammit, number 205!' He gave the downbeat, and the concert concluded without further incident."[28] Despite the fact that musicians who played the concert vividly confirmed Ayers' account, Craft maintains that Stravinsky "*never* cursed—the story is totally out of character."[29] He relates his version of the event:

> Stravinsky did not lose his place but forgot to give the downbeat at bar [166]. The first two beats at the beginning of that bar are silent, and the third beat became the downbeat. The clarinet, which enters in the next bar, did not understand him and did not enter. Since nothing else is played except a harp accompaniment, the music just stopped. Stravinsky was befuddled and went back to bar [166], beating four clear beats and continued—the clarinetist entered, and everything went very smoothly to the end. Exactly the same accident had happened in a previous concert.[30]

Whether the composer swore or was "befuddled"—or both—two reviews of the concert make no mention of the incident. Stravinsky received a roaring standing ovation at the beginning of the concert, before he even conducted a note, and another before leaving the stage, his overcoat casually slung over his shoulders, with a small wave goodbye.[31]

Hermann Scherchen, Robert Shaw, and André Previn were among the other notable guest conductors during the season. Scherchen, the "best-known unknown," as he was called in the title of a 1997 five-CD retrospective set, did not make his American debut until 1964, with the Philadelphia Orchestra. Largely a self-taught musician who temporarily played viola in the Berlin Philharmonic, Scherchen made his conducting debut in 1912 leading Schoenberg's *Pierrot Lunaire*. A maven of 20th-century repertoire, he conducted important premieres by Berg, Webern, and Varèse, among others, but he was equally skilled in conducting traditional repertoire. A noted pedagogue, he wrote *A Textbook of Conducting* in 1929, a classic that is still in print. Scherchen died six months after his Minneapolis debut.[32]

Previn, born Andreas Ludwig Priwin in Germany in 1929, was a year away from obtaining his first major post (with the Houston Symphony Orchestra) when he made his Minneapolis debut in 1966. He made his professional conducting debut four years earlier, but by 1966 Previn's reputation as a conductor competed with his role as a jazz and classical pianist and as an arranger-composer with strong ties to Hollywood and television. In the future Previn would hold important conducting positions in the United States and Europe, and also would join the ranks of Boulez, Bernstein, and Skrowaczewski—major conductors who also are recognized as composers.

Previn's only other Minneapolis Symphony engagement, in 1969, caused a vitriolic response from a patron who was outraged by a *Minneapolis Tribune* front-page photo of Previn and his "pregnant mistress," actress Mia Farrow. "Is the [orchestra] so in need of guest conductors that it must go out and get professed fornicators?" wrote the patron to the orchestra's management. "In this age of permissiveness and increasing immorality… has your organization lost its proper perspective in the realm of decency?"[33]

The conclusion of Skrowaczewski's sixth season with the Minneapolis Symphony was bittersweet. His close friend and concertmaster Norman Carol left to take the same position with the Philadelphia Orchestra. The thirty-seven-year-old Carol could not resist going to "the greatest orchestra in the world," as he called it, and returning to his hometown; nevertheless, it was not an easy decision. He loved Minneapolis, the orchestra, and the friends he had made, but the Philadelphia position was a major career opportunity and a natural progression for Carol. At age eighteen he had won a position in the Boston Symphony and became concertmaster with the New Orleans Philharmonic. Three years later Doráti appointed him concertmaster in Minneapolis.

Carol had formed a close professional and personal bond with Skrowaczewski, and their wives also became wonderful friends. "I always teased Krystyna and my wife, Eleanor," recalled Carol, "because one of the items that the orchestra's public relations department enjoyed mentioning was that Krystyna knew how to tinker with the motor of an automobile. Eleanor and she took their driving tests together, and both failed the first time out! I said to Krystyna, 'All this automotive talent, and you didn't pass?'"

Baseball tested the bonds of friendship in 1965, when the Minnesota Twins played in the World Series against the Los Angeles Dodgers, as Carol remembered:

> Stan learned a lot about me. I happen to be a sports nut, depending on the season. In 1965 I was lucky enough to get World Series tickets, and the Minnesota Twins were involved. My first violin teacher passed his passion for baseball on to me, and I was an ardent Twins fan. The game started at 1:00 in the afternoon. Our rehearsal didn't end until 1:00, and I knew it would take me a couple of hours to get to the game. I went up to Stan a few days before and said, "I have a problem. I have to be at the start of this World Series game at 1:00." I even remember the starting pitcher was a fellow by the name of Sandy Koufax. I said, "Stan, I need your help. I am going to have to leave the rehearsal at intermission." He said, "I don't quite understand all of this, but you leave and just don't tell anyone where you're going." Of course, everyone knew when I left the stage and didn't come back for the second half of the rehearsal where I was. Stan was very caring about silly things like this. It wasn't silly to me; it was very important!

Before the close of the 1965–66 season, Carol's successor had been chosen: Isidor Saslav, an Israeli-born violinist who grew up in Detroit and studied at Indiana University Bloomington with Josef Gingold. Throughout his tenure in Minneapolis, Skrowaczewski frequently turned to his friend Gingold for recommendations for outstanding violinists. Saslav was the concertmaster of the Buffalo Philharmonic Orchestra when he won the Minneapolis audition. Despite the high hopes that Skrowaczewski and the management had for Saslav, he stayed in Minneapolis for only three seasons. "It was not the right fit for the position," reflected Skrowaczewski. "His approach was a less classical and disciplined manner of playing, more suited to his passion for chamber music." By fall 1969 Lea Foli, who had joined the first-violin section of the Minneapolis Symphony in spring 1966, replaced Saslav. Foli remained in the position until 1988, and like Carol, he developed a close relationship with Skrowaczewski.

In mid-May 1966 Skrowaczewski completed an Upper Midwest spring tour with his orchestra before embarking on a five-week Latin American tour as co-conductor of the Philadelphia Orchestra with Ormandy. With his bags barely unpacked from the annual Minneapolis Symphony excursion, Skrowaczewski flew to Miami for a Philadelphia Orchestra concert en route to its first tour destination: Kingston,

Jamaica. Kingston's unbearable heat was tempered by a special tribute the orchestra received at the airport: a 100-piece steel-drum band playing the popular Air from Bach's Orchestral Suite no. 3. "This was funny," said Skrowaczewski, "but they played well, with a proper style and tempo." At customs, instead of checking everyone's passports, officials passed out rum drinks. "And with this heat and without eating, everyone was immediately tipsy, so we had quite a humorous time," Skrowaczewski remembered.

After Jamaica the Philadelphia Orchestra gave a concert in Trinidad and then headed to Caracas, Venezuela, where Skrowaczewski conducted the first of his eleven tour concerts; Ormandy conducted the other fourteen. Along with American compositions by Barber and Mennin and standard repertoire by Beethoven and Berlioz, Skrowaczewski's tour repertoire included works by Argentinean Alberto Ginastera, Brazilian Edino Krieger, and Mexican Silvestre Revueltas.

The Philadelphia Orchestra's three-concert series was part of the Third Music Festival of Caracas, one of several events commemorating the 400th anniversary of the city's founding. The orchestra presented five premieres by Latin composers for the festival.[34] Along with the Krieger work that Skrowaczewski conducted, Ormandy conducted premieres by Ginastera, Villa Lobos, Panamanian Roque Cordero, and Uruguayan Héctor Tosar, who had been mentored by Mitropoulos and Krenek while attending the University of Minnesota in the 1940s.

Ormandy had been warned about nature's undesirable accompaniment that often plagued concerts in the Concha Acustica during late spring. Skrowaczewski experienced it the next day:

> We had a morning rehearsal at the gorgeous Concha Acustica, a huge outdoor amphitheater that could hold 5,000 people. It reminded me of the Hollywood Bowl. The setting was stunning: massive mountains with gray rocks in the background, and the acoustics were supposed to be superior. We started playing *Sensemaya*, an exciting work by Revueltas, when we heard a siren. This unbelievable humming became louder and higher, to the point that we couldn't play at all. What was this? Cicadas on the side of the mountain! When they heard music, they started to sing! So we stopped, and they stopped. I told the orchestra to forget playing *fortissimo* and just play softly so we could get the ensemble together. We began again, and so did the cicadas! The people at the theater said that somehow in the evening it's not a problem, and the cicadas wouldn't sing. Because we didn't want to risk it, we changed the location of the concert.

When he wasn't battling cicadas in Caracas, Skrowaczewski met with Krzysztof Penderecki to finalize plans for the Minneapolis Symphony's U.S. premiere of his new work, the *St. Luke Passion*. After Skrowaczewski learned of its popularity in Europe, Cisek worked hard to obtain the piece for Minneapolis from New York publishers. "It was quite difficult to get at the time. It was restricted somehow," Cisek recalled, "but we made enough overtures so that when it finally became available, we were the ones that were called. I was very proud of that—that I could go to Stan and say, 'We've got it!'" Skrowaczewski's performances of the work would be among the great artistic achievements of his career.

Skrowaczewski's concerts in Buenos Aires two weeks later proved to be his tour's highlight:

> Ormandy had the first two concerts in the Teatro Colón, and I had the last two. It was long because it included *Eroica*. It started at 9:30 p.m., and we finished after midnight with encores and big ovations [the press reported a twelve-minute standing ovation]. There was a huge postconcert party in the ballroom of the theatre, and the president of Argentina—whom I knew very well from my previous tours to South America—Arturo Illia, was there. The party ended around 2:30 a.m., and when I came out of the building I couldn't believe my eyes: about one hundred people were waiting in line for my autograph. It was amazing.
>
> The next morning, as we rode buses to the airport to fly to Santiago, Chile, we were shocked at the front-page headline. While the president was at our party, a coup began by a military junta. They took his palace, and in a month's time he was out of power. This incident was the start of a military regime ruling with horrible conditions. People were arrested, persecuted, and some disappeared. A few days later we arrived in Chile. At the postconcert party, we had the president with us, Eduardo Frei, a wonderful man. And we said to him, "President Frei, aren't you afraid that a junta will take your place while you are with us?" He responded, "Oh no, I have my guards there." We all laughed.

After the tour Ormandy wrote to Skrowaczewski acknowledging his great work at all the concerts: "I am well aware of the emotional strain under which you were throughout the tour, and for this alone you have my grateful thanks."[35]

What had begun as emotional strain for Skrowaczewski—being out of the country while his pregnant wife was due to have their first child—quickly turned to deep grief and disappointment. Krystyna, who had previously suffered two miscarriages, had given birth to a girl just a few days before Skrowaczewski had a break near the end of his tour. What should have been a joyful event turned tragic. Little Anna was born with Incontinentia pigmenti (IP), a rare genetic disease of the skin, hair, teeth, and central nervous system. She was afflicted with a severe form of the disease that included blindness, scoliosis, minimal motor skills, and mental retardation. Judy Dayton described the heartbreaking situation:

> Stan was out of town. I went to the hospital with Krystyna before the baby was born. I was sitting in the fathers' waiting room with all these men waiting for their wives, when the doctor came out with Anna in her arms. She had told Krystyna she was concerned about the baby's health. Meanwhile, our mutual friends in the city and from all over were waiting to hear the news of the birth of the baby. I remember the agony of that afternoon, with people calling me and asking about the baby, and I had to pretend that everything was fine. I didn't think it was my place to say anything before Stan got back.

The next day Ken Dayton picked up Skrowaczewski at the airport and told his friend that his newborn daughter had serious health problems. Charles Fullmer, then assistant manager of the Minneapolis Symphony, brought Stan to Krystyna. Fullmer was often Skrowaczewski's dining partner on orchestra tours, but despite having a close relationship with the maestro, he did not know what to say at this difficult moment. "Stan just put his arms around me and said nothing," Fullmer remembered. "It seemed like we stood in the parking lot like that for hours, but it was probably two minutes."

The Skrowaczewskis were devastated. Stanisław barely had two days at home to comfort Krystyna before leaving for Mexico to complete the Philadelphia Orchestra's concert tour. Fortunately his summer commitments were limited to about a month. He spent the rest of the summer at home with Krystyna, and together they pondered the fate of their newborn.

Anna was kept in isolation at the hospital for two weeks before she could come home. The medical staff needed time to assess the full extent of her mental retardation. Her motor and mental skills were extremely limited, and as she developed, she could not communicate vocally. At home Krystyna worked extremely hard to provide as much normalcy as possible for Anna, including nursing her. A long, trying road lay ahead.

In the first of several efforts to connect with the University of Minnesota School of Music, the orchestra became involved formally with the university's summer session in 1966. Symphony officials hailed the arrangement as the first such collaboration between a major orchestra and a university. At a time when the University of Minnesota was the only American university with a major symphony orchestra on its campus, it only made sense that the two entities would foster a stronger relationship. The initiative came not from the music school but rather from the university's president, O. Meredith Wilson, and Skrowaczewski. (Three years earlier Skrowaczewski had written to the school's director proposing a similar program, and he met with members of the faculty, including composer Dominick Argento.) Wilson believed that the university should take full advantage of the Minneapolis Symphony's presence on campus and go beyond occasional collaborations with the university choirs and a student-ticket discount program. "He was wonderful," said Skrowaczewski. "We talked about starting a new collaboration between the university and the orchestra, and he said he would try to improve the music department. At that time it was not in good shape."

Along with private lessons and master classes taught by orchestra members, the summer session's main event was the weeklong Contemporary Music Workshop led by Skrowaczewski in collaboration with Milton Babbitt. The workshop culminated in a concert by the Minneapolis Symphony of music by Wagner, Schoenberg, Webern, and Babbitt. From the stage Babbitt offered analytical commentary on all the pieces. Due to a lack of rehearsal time the orchestra played only excerpts from the Babbitt composition. The composer explained that a performance of his complete piece—with "no two measures [of its total 500 measures] alike"—needed forty hours rather than the three it received.[36]

Rehearsal time also was limited at Tanglewood. Skrowaczewski's early-August debut with the Boston Symphony Orchestra was scheduled during what was known then as the Berkshire Music Festival. Guest conductors at Tanglewood usually are allotted only one or two rehearsals in which to prepare their programs. Each week the orchestra churns out three separate concerts as well as prelude concerts that generally feature the principal symphony members playing chamber music. Such a schedule is not unusual at major orchestral summer music festivals, but at eight weeks in length, Tanglewood's calendar of events is more intense and extended than most.

Sandwiched between Skrowaczewski's Friday and Sunday programs was a complete concert performance of *The Magic Flute* by Erich Leinsdorf, music director of the Boston Symphony Orchestra. Skrowaczewski's program showcased standard symphonic repertoire, with the exception of *Medea's Meditation and Dance of Vengeance*, a short overture-type work from Barber's 1946 ballet that became a signature opening-piece for Skrowaczewski. His debut generated descriptions typical of the time, noting that he displayed "a businesslike podium style that had a touch of pedantic professor in it" and praising his preference for transparent balances and clarity.[37] *The Boston Globe* reviewer, however, expressed his frustration with the apparent effects of an overworked orchestra as well as Skrowaczewski's contribution to less-than-tidy performances:

> It is difficult to judge a guest conductor who may have insufficient time to work with a strange orchestra or who may be ill-understood by it. Yet the paramount impression conveyed in both programs was that the Boston Symphony is a sloppy group. Skrowaczewski has a wide beat [that] becomes increasingly nervous as the music accelerates or grows louder. Partly due to this agitation, numerous entrances were awkward and inaccurate, especially in the woodwinds. But even when the music was delicate and where the conductor could be easily followed, the orchestra sounded amateurish in its ensemble or lack thereof. In the Prokofiev and the Schumann the violins had serious intonation problems. This was not the conductor's fault. The players ought to take their business a little more conscientiously. Skrowaczewski was able to get across some of his interpretive ideas [in the *Eroica*], a number of which [involved] quiet sound....[38]

Still, Skrowaczewski impressed the Boston Symphony enough to be invited back to conduct subscription concerts in December 1967 and to appear again at Tanglewood in 1968. He remained an occasional guest conductor with the symphony throughout the early 1970s, mostly at Tanglewood.

Before Skrowaczewski began the new season with the Minneapolis Symphony, he and Krystyna took a much-needed vacation to Caneel Bay, at St. John in the U.S. Virgin Islands. Along with the Grand Tetons, this locale became a favorite destination for their rare respites together. Upon their return they attended a concert and reception at the

White House honoring the American winners of the 1966 International Tchaikovsky Competition. Ever since Van Cliburn won the first competition in 1958, such gestures by the White House were common during the ongoing Cold War. Skrowaczewski's only memory of the event was that of meeting President Lyndon Johnson and noticing his "bloodshot, tired eyes, looking completely beaten down." The Vietnam War obviously was taking its toll on the beleaguered president.

In its annual fall coverage of the orchestra's new season, the *Minneapolis Tribune* published a guest column written by Skrowaczewski that was entitled "U.S. May Now Lead Europe in Culture: As I See the Arts." Instead of proclaiming that "the arts are a necessity, and here's how you should support them," he expressed pointed observations about the state of the arts in 1966. A classic example of Skrowaczewski's strong convictions, the article evokes philosophers and writers, condemns artistic conformity and commercialism, and observes societal ills with pithy candor. His uncompromising opinions are both optimistic and fatalistic—a bold piece of writing for a forty-three-year-old new American citizen. (Among his suggestions is a call for a constitutional amendment banning Muzak.)

Excerpts from the article provide a remarkable example of a music director who views himself as an artistic leader in a community, not merely a conductor of its orchestra:

> The title of this column asks for my "ideas" on art, on music. Nothing could be more difficult and perplexing for me. I can easily have ideas and definite opinions on all kinds of things that are outside of myself. But on art? I don't observe art—I live with it, breathe it, and feel it within my very instinctive ego. It should not sound presumptuous—it is no merit of mine—it happens sometimes to be born like that, which represents no greater wonder of nature than the construction of a flower or the variety in color and shape of tropical fish.
>
> Art is like love; it doesn't live because of ideas, it dies from them. It is impossible for an artist to find a prescription for the creation of a masterpiece. (A lady asked Victor Hugo if it is difficult to write a poem; "If it isn't easy, Madame, it is impossible," was the answer.) "*Chi sa piu—meno sa*," says an Italian sage ("Who knows more, knows less"); "Is your music then merely a tinkle?" asks Confucius. No, "It represents the very essence of being," says Schopenhauer. By all means, this mystery is one of the main attributes of art. Like Eurydice, it would die instantly the moment our Orpheian eyes were opened. And maybe art will be the last of all mysteries to die in our research-wise epoch.
>
> We live in a real cultural explosion in many parts of the world, especially in the United States, which is in a leading position. This is said by a former European without any "neophyte" zeal but rather objectively, after crossing the Atlantic Ocean a half-dozen times every year. Some European musical centers seem to me nowadays a bit, let me say, "fatigued" or "blasé"; both conservatives and avant-gardists are most intolerant. Unfortunately, the new European bourgeois

seems to be too busy making money and trying to catch up with the American living standard of thirty years ago. A materialistic Europe and an idealistic United States—however skeptical you may feel, this is it right now.

I think our Twin Cities do quite beautifully in the arts. The devotion and contribution of so many people to the symphony, theater, or museum is stupendous and makes me feel humble. I feel a continuous excitement and ebullience regarding the arts: almost an atmosphere of a religious crusade.

For me, the great danger to the arts lies in its commercialization for the sake of business. Here, the enormous task for the artist is to be able to control, to review, and to change if something is artistically doubtful. One of the greatest psychological, educational, and, finally, artistic errors of nowadays is to confuse terms and their meanings, such as "music" (as an art), "entertainment music" and "entertainment" itself. The latter, besides the popular sense of the word, may also represent a spiritual action, a mind's efforts, even hardships. (Thus, life itself may be the best entertainment. However, as Oscar Wilde says, "Life is a beautiful theatre, only the repertoire is so poor.")

Let us try to clear this jungle-like state. Any music ceases to be an art when used for an extra-musical purpose. Therefore, a waltz of Strauss, for instance, may be perceived in two ways: one—as pure musical art, listened to as a sheer musical composition: two—as a background for business and sociable relations. There is no major social problem (still, there is always an aesthetic!) if a person uses both "musics" at his own will.

But there is a social crime if we all are surrounded in a pseudo-musical envelope in all public places, hotels, lobbies, elevators, banks, restaurants, planes, waiting rooms, etc., etc., not to mention all the radio and television commercials. First of all, it represents an intrusion of our privacy, and I loudly call for a serious action on the highest level. I sincerely hope this will be the next amendment to the Constitution.

Secondly, it is a psychological error, this lulling and stupefying of our thoughts and imagination (almost becoming a slogan: "Don't think— we think for you.") Thirdly, it dulls our senses, making them insensitive to any musical sound. Fourthly, it injects into our blood only a certain convention of musical language, corresponding more or less to some trite formulas of early 19th-century harmony, thereby forming an obvious block in our artistic capacity. Worst of all, our children sip it simultaneously with mother's milk.

Apropos "relax": To all who write me to play pleasant melodies on our symphony series in order to "enjoy" and "relax," may I answer here: Change Northrop for another locale with a Hammond organ.

Excuse, dear reader, this small dipping of my pen in gall. But I have written it really for you. Maybe you do not necessarily like it. As composers always write, conductors always plan for an audience. But not necessarily always what an audience wants![39]

The number of orchestras in the United States (not including youth orchestras, which totaled 300 in 1966) had increased from 600 in 1939 to 1,401 by 1966—an impressive figure, considering that the number of orchestras worldwide totaled 2,000 at the time.[40] Amateur musical activity also had increased substantially, and music programs flourished in the public schools. The issue for Skrowaczewski was how America's "cultural boom" would develop. His concern over the commercialization of this "artistic goodwill" became a recurring theme throughout his life.

On the day of Skrowaczewski's first concert of the 1966–67 season, *Time* magazine reported that the Minneapolis Symphony would give the U.S. premiere of Penderecki's *St. Luke Passion* in fall 1967. The news was significant. Ever since the work's 1966 world premiere it had been hailed as one of the most celebrated contemporary pieces in Europe. Penderecki's rise in the world of contemporary composition was swift, beginning with a performance of his *Strophes* at the 1959 Warsaw Autumn Festival and followed by three major Polish awards. His evocatively titled *Threnody for the Victims of Hiroshima* brought him international fame. The short work—under nine minutes—was emblematic of the 1960s' avant-garde. Scored for fifty-two string instruments and employing graphic notation and a variety of expressionistic effects, it caused a visceral listening experience, instigated in part by its emotional title. Originally called *8'37*, the title was changed in 1960 in observance of the fifteenth anniversary of the Hiroshima bombing. Skrowaczewski harbored some doubts about the piece. After a rehearsal he asked Mary Ann Feldman for her opinion of it, eliciting the following note: "You asked for one word, yes or no, but I give you wow! The impact of *Threnody* is shattering. It seems ironic that I should encounter it on the very day I read that an ex-president of the United States, in his senility perhaps, stated that he would not preclude the use of nuclear weapons in Vietnam."[41]

Although Penderecki had abandoned this style of composition by the time he wrote the *St. Luke Passion*, his ability to create intense atmospheric music led to its use in such films as *The Exorcist* and *The Shining*. In 1991 *Threnody* was featured in the horror/comedy film *The People Under the Stairs*, and the Manic Street Preachers, a Welsh rock band, extracted part of the piece for a song.[42]

Threnody was one of twenty-three works the Minneapolis Symphony presented for the first time during the 1966–67 season. The pieces ranged from Lutosławski's *Musique funèbre* to Mahler's Fifth Symphony. Beethoven's *Choral Fantasy* for Piano, Chorus, and Orchestra—surprisingly another "first" for the Minneapolis Symphony—closed the season and also marked Skrowaczewski's first collaboration with Rudolf Serkin.

Artur Rubinstein returned to Minneapolis, whereupon the MOA solicited the pianist's endorsement of its newly launched $10 million endowment fund campaign for the orchestra. "Under Stanisław Skrowaczewski's direction," the pianist wrote, "your orchestra can become one of the great symphony orchestras of the world. The results of his work are already in impressive evidence."[43] Twenty-four-year-old Daniel

Barenboim, then known primarily as a pianist, not a conductor, made his Minneapolis debut with Bartók's Second Piano Concerto, another work new to the orchestra. Mstislav Rostropovich, who made his Minneapolis debut in 1965, returned in spring 1967. Over the course of his career Skrowaczewski performed with Rostropovich at least fifty times, including engagements in Philadelphia and Europe and at the Casals Festival in Puerto Rico. "He played in such a convincing way musically for certain pieces," Skrowaczewski said. "For example, Tchaikovsky's *Rococo Variations,* for which he had unorthodox approaches that were completely his own. They were lovely and spiritual. His first movement of the Dvořák concerto was extremely slow, so it would seem to take an eternity, but it was so convincing that I didn't mind it."

In preparation for a second Contemporary Music Workshop and as a show of goodwill toward the University of Minnesota, after the orchestra's spring tour Skrowaczewski added an all-contemporary music concert showcasing pieces by four university composers. The highlight was Eric Stokes' *A Center Harbor Holiday,* an Ives-influenced, one-movement concerto for tuba and orchestra depicting a summer day in New England. It featured an array of effects: a fire siren, bicycle bell, radio, firecrackers, and even flag-waving by some players. At a concert concluding the summer workshop Skrowaczewski included the piece in a program that also featured Minnesotan Paul Fetler's *Contrasts for Orchestra* and Elliott Carter's Piano Concerto. Carter co-led a session with Skrowaczewski at the workshop.

In late spring 1967 the exodus of fifteen musicians from the Minneapolis Symphony prompted several articles in Twin Cities newspapers that raised concerns about the orchestra's morale. Only three players actually resigned; the rest left to pursue solo careers, positions with other orchestras, or new forms of employment. Although the number of musicians leaving at once was three times higher than the normal rate, Cisek and Skrowaczewski described it as "sheer coincidence."[44] In fact, as Cisek explained, many orchestras experienced significant turnover, in part because Ford Foundation grants expanded the availability of well-paying, competitive positions across the country.[45] Skrowaczewski added, "Payment for musicians was not at all in proportion to what other major orchestras were offering at the time. I was always fighting to change this situation. This was one of the principal reasons why people left. Even orchestras such as the St. Louis Symphony and Pittsburgh Symphony were paying more than Minneapolis." Skrowaczewski's new challenge was to fill all the positions: "The number of outstanding musicians available at that time was small—not at all like today—and we were not highly competitive for these players."

MOA president Judson Bemis acknowledged that some musicians had "basic disagreement and incompatibility" with Skrowaczewski and Cisek.[46] The issue generated enough concern that the symphony members' committee met with Skrowaczewski, the management, and MOA representatives in an effort to prevent "further deterioration of the orchestra's morale."[47]

"One doesn't achieve excellence without problems," Bemis maintained.[48] Criticisms aimed at Skrowaczewski focused primarily on his unending pursuit of excellence: repetitious rehearsals of small passages, constant attention to rhythmic precision and intonation, and requests that musicians play alone or in pairs (by stand in the case of string players) to assess their contributions to the whole orchestra. Unpopular with certain players, these methods clearly produced results. Primarily, though, communication issues bothered some musicians. "The orchestra is bored to death," said one anonymous player. "[Skrowaczewski] works and studies hard, but he doesn't know how to handle people."[49] This perception is a foreign notion to anyone who has interacted with Skrowaczewski one on one, when his charm and courtly nature are fully evident; however, to some musicians he remained a distant and sometimes stern presence.

A precarious balance characterizes the conductor-player relationship. The conductor must know when to press for certain details and when to trust that the musicians will correct any problems themselves. Not prone to leaving anything to chance, particularly during his tenure as music director, Skrowaczewski often micromanaged rehearsals, and consequently some musicians felt restrained artistically. Although never cold or rude to musicians, Skrowaczewski did not constantly praise them for achieving certain objectives in rehearsals that to him seemed basic.

"Stan was very detail oriented, very meticulous," recalled David Hyslop, a management intern with the orchestra in the late sixties who became its president in 1991. He continued:

> Stan did not suffer fools easily when standards were not up to his level; he would stop and tell them. And because of this, there was sheen and polish. When you're a conductor who's been there a while, there are also people who don't like you. That's just the reality of it, and Stan went through that. The fifteen players left, some of them went on to other jobs, some did not. Fifteen other players came, and Stan was here for nineteen years. Life went on.

Along with his first Boston Symphony Orchestra subscription concert, Skrowaczewski had other major engagements during the 1966–67 season: debuts with the Detroit Symphony, Royal Philharmonic Orchestra (his first public concert in London), Tonhalle Orchester Zürich, Munich Philharmonic, and Berlin West Deutscher Rundfunk Orchestra. However, a recording project in Paris, held two weeks before Skrowaczewski started the new Minneapolis season, proved to be the most important for the advancement of his European career.

French impresario and recording producer Michel Glotz, head of the recording division of Angel Records (later EMI), was looking for a conductor to collaborate with pianist Alexis Weissenberg and record the complete Chopin works for piano and orchestra. Glotz knew of Skrowaczewski's reputation as a "great Polish conductor," and after he and Weissenberg heard Skrowaczewski in concert, they immediately knew he was the right choice. "There is a young phenomenal pianist whom I recommend to you," Glotz told Skrowaczewski. "You don't know him; no one knows him in America, but I guarantee he's a wonderful musician and incredibly gifted technically." Months later, in early September 1967, Skrowaczewski visited Weissenberg's Paris apartment for preliminary rehearsals for the project. "They synthesized immediately," said Glotz. With the possible exception of Szeryng, Weissenberg became Skrowaczewski's most frequent concert collaborator. From the late 1960s through the early 1980s, the pair performed together more than one hundred times.

A French pianist of Bulgarian birth, Weissenberg began lessons at age three with Pancho Vladigerov, one of the few 20th-century Bulgarian composers to win international recognition.[50] Fleeing the Nazis' grip on Bulgaria during World War II, the Jewish Weissenberg spent a year as a refugee in Israel before becoming a student of Olga Samaroff at The Juilliard School. A year later his New York debut with George Szell and the Philadelphia Orchestra launched an international career. Suddenly in 1956, at age twenty-seven, Weissenberg took a sabbatical from the concert stage to study and teach. In 1966, about a year before he met Skrowaczewski, Weissenberg reemerged on stage with a recital in Paris. He soon became a favorite of Herbert von Karajan, with whom he recorded much standard repertoire, including the complete Beethoven piano concertos. The Chopin recordings with Skrowaczewski were the first he made after his decade-long "retirement." Skrowaczewski recounted his first experience with the gifted pianist:

> Can you imagine? We did the entire Chopin repertoire for piano and orchestra (two concertos, *Fantaisie sur des airs nationaux polonais, Andante spianato et grande polonaise,* Variations on *Là ci darem la mano* from *Don Giovanni,* and Grand Rondeau de Concert *Rondo á la Krakowiak*) in five days. These works are not easy for an orchestra or a conductor. L'Orchestre de la Société des Concerts du Conservatoire, which was used for the sessions, had its inconsistencies. It was then in the process of becoming L'Orchestre de Paris. Charles Münch was coming to take it over soon after these recordings. It is truly taxing for a pianist to record all these works in five days, with a long session each day. And yet Alexis was phenomenal, absolutely without any mistakes. Even with the best pianists you repeat takes. If we repeated anything, however, it was because of me or the orchestra or extraneous noises. And each time he was perfect. Those four pieces (not to mention the concertos) are deadly difficult technically. However, what I was taken with was that musically his performances represented the most beautiful Chopin I had ever heard. I don't recall any pianist who was as wonderful and impressive to me at that time. Perhaps Rubinstein, but I was even more impressed with Alexis. His beautiful sensitivity and feeling were similar to that of Szeryng. He was very much a classical player, so there was no hysteria in the music, which is easy to do in Chopin. It was like Mozartian Chopin.

Glotz, artistic director and producer of the recordings, offered his insights:

> Stan is a very difficult man in a studio or with an orchestra because he is— and I admire this, one hundred percent—an absolute perfectionist. He was

in full admiration of Alexis because he's also a perfectionist. Both Slavic, they have this incredible discipline in music and in life, and they want to get as close as possible to perfection in the sound, the rhythm, the phrasing, and the beauty. During the sessions there were moments when Alexis was not satisfied with himself and Stan was not satisfied with what he was getting from the orchestra. I don't know any artist who is constantly satisfied. A great artist never is. Stan was accustomed to the very best orchestras in America. I remember that he was continuously complaining about the quality of the bassoons, not the players necessarily, but their instruments and the tone they produced. The other problem was the sound of the French horns. They played with too much vibrato, so they sounded like saxophones. Fortunately, we were able to bring horn players in from Strasbourg who had German-style instruments that produced the proper sound.

So from time to time Stan was a little bit like a schoolmaster, making speeches to the orchestra that they lacked discipline for this style of music, etc. It wasn't quite what he was used to, coming from the Slavic and American order. But as the sessions went on, the orchestra became more and more interested in Stan and in Alexis, who was already a star, having had great success playing the Tchaikovsky concerto with Karajan. They changed their attitude and did everything they could to please them both. It went extremely well, as evident from the recording that is still in print today. And of course we recorded in Salle Wagram, the best recording hall in Paris, perhaps in Europe.

Glotz, who began his musical career as a pianist, got his start as a recording producer in the late 1950s with Sir Thomas Beecham. Glotz was closely associated with Karajan, serving as his recording producer for nearly every audio and video recording made during the last twenty years of Karajan's life. In 1966 he opened his first artists' management firm, and he became the most powerful and respected impresario in Europe throughout the 1970s and 1980s. Soon after the Chopin sessions, he became Skrowaczewski's European impresario, a fruitful relationship that lasted until 1985.

The Minneapolis Symphony's 1967–68 season—Skrowaczewski's seventh and the orchestra's sixty-fifth anniversary—was among the most artistically significant in the organization's history. The U.S. premiere of Penderecki's *St. Luke Passion* and Skrowaczewski's rising stock as an internationally recognized conductor elevated the orchestra's stature.

The *Minneapolis Tribune* focused its annual fall season preview on the orchestra's cyclic programming. Although thematic programming during a season was not new to major orchestras, Bernstein's penchant for it with the New York Philharmonic made the concept popular with audiences during the early 1960s. In Minneapolis much was made of this transition from "sandwich-based" programming, in which a contemporary piece typically is inserted between an opening overture or concerto featuring a famous soloist and a large-scale, popular romantic symphony. Due to the consistently high ticket sales of previous seasons, Skrowaczewski and the management wanted to move "into cycles and more monographic programming."[51] He also hoped to shift the public's interest in concerts from performer to repertoire. "The ideal is to build programs so that you attract the public, not because of stars and artists, but because of the music you play. And good programs, of course, will also attract better artists," Skrowaczewski said.[52] "I am always hurt as a musician when I see a star making a cheap program because he thinks the public will come anyway."[53]

Skrowaczewski assembled a Beethoven cycle that included a complete concert performance of *Fidelio,* another first for the Minneapolis Symphony, fulfilling what had become an annual inclusion of an opera during the subscription season. Aside from Penderecki's *Passion,* the season's other major vocal offering was Mahler's song cycle *Das Lied von der Erde,* with Dame Janet Baker, one of the finest Mahlerian singers, then at the peak of her powers in the late 1960s and 1970s.

The Passion and Death of Our Lord Jesus Christ According to St. Luke, the complete title of Penderecki's eighty-minute opus (commonly called the *St. Luke Passion*), already had received nearly twenty performances in Poland, Italy, West Germany, and London, and two commercial recordings (on Philips and RCA) had been released by the time Skrowaczewski and the Minneapolis Symphony gave the U.S. premiere on November 2, 1967. The work was commissioned for the 700th anniversary of Münster Cathedral in West Germany, the site of its premiere. When first performed in Kraków, an additional performance was immediately scheduled to accommodate the ten thousand Poles who wished to hear it.[54] Over the first year and half of its existence, the *St. Luke Passion* was presented twelve times in Poland, with fifteen thousand people attending one of the performances.[55]

Penderecki, who believed that the work's phenomenal popularity throughout Europe was "partially by accident," observed that "in the last thirty years most music has been written on a small scale…. People were just ready for a work like this. Possibly the *Passion* was needed less as a form in past years. Perhaps it is more needed now."[56] The scale of the piece was a rarity for contemporary music at the time: full orchestra, three separate choirs, three vocal soloists (soprano, baritone, and bass), and narrator. Penderecki's perception of the need for a work concerned with suffering and death was on the mark: worldwide turmoil during the late 1960s warranted music with such universal themes. He described the *Passion* as "depicting Jesus as typical of all those who have been persecuted. Christ is an archetypal victim, not a figure considered in an orthodox religious context. The problems of man—injustice, persecution—have always been the same. Only the methods of tyranny have become more efficient."[57]

More significantly, the work's acceptance stems largely from the composer's use of basically traditional musical language within an ancient form, peppered modestly with various avant-garde techniques and effects. Medieval chant is mixed with tonal harmony, twelve-tone technique, and instrumental and vocal effects. The *Passion* prefigured the concept of "synthesis" that has become a popular form of contemporary composition in the United States during the last twenty years.

Mounting the *St. Luke Passion* was a collaborative tour de force by the orchestra, the University of Minnesota Choir, Macalester College Choir, St. Paul Cathedral Boys Choir, three vocalists, and narrator Douglas Campbell, then artistic director of the Guthrie Theater. Northrop Auditorium's acoustics further complicated the production. Penderecki had conceived the work for the acoustical setting of a cathedral, and most of its previous performances had been in churches. The challenge was to re-create the effect of such a setting with Northrop's "stiff" acoustics—as Penderecki described them.[58] Skrowaczewski divided one of the choirs in two, giving himself four large vocal entities to manage in an effort to simulate a three-dimensional effect.[59]

In addition to reviewers from local newspapers, critics from Chicago, Cleveland, and San Francisco covered the premiere. Critical and popular response was nearly unanimously positive. The work's overt emotional content, theatrical proportions, and largely accessible musical language resonated with Minnesotans as it had with Europeans (although only half of the average-size Northrop audience attended the concert). Skrowaczewski was lauded for bringing the work and the thirty-four-year-old Penderecki to America for the first time and for leading "a high-tension performance."[60]

Until the day after the performance no one had any idea how high-tension it really was, as Skrowaczewski related:

> A few hours before the premiere, at twilight, I went jogging in the beautiful late fall air. I went around my house to the lake several times. Suddenly my right eye went completely black. I came home immediately, looked in the mirror (with the left eye), and it looked fine. I knew the retina had just burst. I didn't tell anyone. I wanted to get through the premiere. So I did the entire concert using one eye, with the three choirs, soloists, narrator, and big orchestra. It was a stressful situation, but I knew the piece well and just did it. The premiere was a huge triumph. There was a large reception at Northrop after the concert, then an enormous after-concert party at John Myer's house for Penderecki. I had to go to everything. Such parties were deadly, taking so much time away from important rest, but this one was very pleasant and necessary after such a big performance. People gathered to speak about the music. When we finally came home at 2:00 a.m., I told Krystyna what had happened.

Skrowaczewski had emergency eye surgery the next day. He was fortunate that Dr. Malcolm McCannel, one of the country's top ophthalmologists, practiced in Minneapolis. McCannel's pioneering work in cataract surgery and use of intraocular lenses as well as his publications and humanitarian work throughout the world had earned him an international reputation. McCannel and his wife, Louise Walker, the granddaughter of T.B. Walker, were major supporters of Walker Art Center for many years.[61] McCannel, whom Skrowaczewski described as a "wonderful and charming man," was his eye physician for several decades after the conductor's 1967 eye trauma.

"The morning after the concert, I went to Dr. McCannel," Skrowaczewski said. "At first he thought I might have been exaggerating my condition, but after he examined my eye, he didn't say anything. His hand started to tremble. He knew immediately what had happened." McCannel recommended that one of the top retina specialists in the region, Dr. William Knobloch, professor and head of ophthalmology at the University of Minnesota, operate on Skrowaczewski. A few hours later Skrowaczewski underwent emergency surgery at the university. The operation was successful, but Skrowaczewski had paid a price by conducting the *St. Luke Passion*:

> For a number of years I saw quite well. I could read with this damaged eye. A few weeks after the operation Dr. Knobloch did a procedure on my other eye (left)— the good one—to prevent another detached retina. This second operation was necessary, and thank goodness another detachment never occurred in this eye. Now this eye is the only one I can read with. Many years after my detached retina, the right eye did become distorted. The retina was probably shrinking, and they couldn't help it. As soon as I realized what had happened the day of the concert, I should have gone to the doctor. I didn't realize that all of the motion from my head and body while conducting could aggravate the problem.

Although he was lucky that the delay of his initial surgery hadn't caused permanent vision loss at the time, during the next two decades his right eye progressively deteriorated. By the 1990s this eye barely functioned, and it continued to worsen. "If I hadn't done that concert," he said, "the condition of the eye years later would have been much better. Today doctors have confirmed that my doing the concert was a grave mistake."

The second Minneapolis performance of the *Passion* was canceled, as was the New York premiere at Carnegie Hall, scheduled for the following week. Skrowaczewski wanted his associate conductor, George Trautwein, to take over the Carnegie Hall performance, but he declined. "He was excellent," said Skrowaczewski, "but it would have been too difficult without the proper rehearsals. Penderecki wrote some aleatoric passages for which I had my own method of conducting."

Trautwein, then in his second season with the Minneapolis Symphony, had joined the orchestra after the short tenure of assistant conductor Russell Stanger, who had succeeded Fennell. Skrowaczewski's relationship with Trautwein was similar to the one he had enjoyed with James Dixon, but it was longer and deeper. "He had been with the Dallas Symphony," Cisek said. "When he came here, a wonderful intellectual fusion between Stan and him developed. He was a very talented man and a capable conductor." "He really deserved a great international career," Skrowaczewski stated. "He was sort of a young George Szell, only without his authority." Trautwein had in fact spent 1953 to 1957 playing in the first-violin section of the Cleveland Orchestra.

Disappointment over the cancellation of the New York debut of the *Passion* lingered. Wrote critic John Sherman of the *Minneapolis Tribune*: "This was to have been the Minneapolis Symphony's strongest bid in recent years to national attention and acclaim. We can only blame the wheel of fortune for this unpredictable turn of affairs."[62] The Carnegie Hall performance was rescheduled for the following season, although the delay may have slowed the orchestra's rise to the top and dampened the excitement over the work. A significant column entitled "Big Five Plus One?" appeared in the music section of *Time* magazine a week after the Minneapolis premiere. The article attributed the Minneapolis Symphony's achievement in securing the important premiere largely to the "auspicious strides that Skrowaczewski has taken…in recent years." It continued with a concise view of Skrowaczewski and his orchestra:

> He had made only a handful of guest appearances with U.S. orchestras and was practically unknown in the States. Nowadays his name is not only familiar and esteemed but also correctly pronounced (Skro-vah-*cheff*-ski) throughout the American orchestral circuit. A stern, scholarly type who conducts with angular, stork-like grace, Skrowaczewski takes an approach that is exact and exacting. Starting with a unit that was already a leader in the second rank of U.S. orchestras (behind the "Big Five" of Boston, Philadelphia, New York, Cleveland, and Chicago), he has given it an even finer edge of technical precision. While enriching its sound, particularly in the strings, he has achieved limpid texture that lets the inner architecture of the music shine through. His interpretations, though vigorous and often intense, do not often reflect great emotional involvement—a trait that frustrates some members of the audience and orchestra. "Sometimes," sighs one of his musicians, "we wish he'd let himself go more."
>
> Nevertheless, Skrowaczewski's technique and temper are ideally suited to the complex music of the 20th century. Of all the programming changes he has made in Minneapolis—expanded season, summer "play-ins" for Minnesota high schoolers, more stress on cycles of thematically unified concerts and less on big-name soloists—by far the most significant is the generous sampling of provocative modern works…. Skrowaczewski's efforts have convinced Minneapolis civic leaders that, in the words of one symphony official, "it's now possible for us to have one of the great orchestras of the world." The orchestra has launched a drive to raise $10 million in capital funds, is planning to enlarge from its current ninety-four players to 105, and is already underwriting more tours…. "In a sense," says orchestra manager Richard Cisek, "we're declaring war on the Big Five."[63]

Perhaps more than at any other time in the orchestra's history, it was poised to make the shift artistically and financially to secure its position among the upper echelon of American orchestras. Yet it was at this time that the orchestra's executive committee made the most controversial decision in the organization's history. Unbeknownst to the musicians and even to Skrowaczewski, the ensemble's 1967–68 season was its last as the Minneapolis Symphony Orchestra. When Skrowaczewski returned from his summer engagements in Europe, he would be the music director of the "Minnesota Orchestra."

FIFTEEN

WHAT'S IN A NAME?

The distinctive personal character of the Minneapolis orchestra may well have some underlying relationship with geography and rugged climate, for the organization through all its changes of conductor and personnel has been a lively, quick-learning, adaptable unit, expressing in the spirit of its work a certain "Midwestern" forwardness, candor, and impetuosity. That forwardness in its nature has reflected from its earliest days a dogged will to survive and improve, a conviction of perfectibility.

—John Sherman, *Music and Maestros: The Story of the Minneapolis Symphony Orchestra*

Skrowaczewski had no real rest after his post-*Passion* eye trauma. Despite his doctors' suggestion that he stay put, two weeks after his surgery he was back on the podium making his Symphony Hall and subscription concert debut with the Boston Symphony Orchestra (BSO) in December 1967. Wearing sunglasses at the first rehearsal to protect his eye, he told the musicians that he had to restrict his body motions because he was still recovering.

But Skrowaczewski turned quite a few heads in the orchestra when he began rehearsing a newly discovered score to Mozart's Symphony no. 35 (*Haffner*). The find had prompted him to make amazing changes to the instrumentation, articulations, and musical nuances. The venerable BSO rarely encounters such a startlingly new approach to a familiar piece. Skrowaczewski described his first rehearsal:

> George Szell had just sent me a facsimile of the newly discovered original manuscript of the *Haffner*. It was a big find at that time. I came to Boston with my own materials, the Breitkopf and Härtel edition, with all the changes marked in red ink. Before we started playing I told the orchestra I had studied the original manuscript and put all the changes in their parts because the new score hadn't been published yet. The first movement didn't have many modifications, but there were still some striking differences. For example, some bassoon passages almost seem like mistakes, but they are in fact what Mozart originally composed. The BSO accepted these new discoveries without any problems. There were hardly any alterations in the Andante and Menuetto movements, but then came the finale, the Presto movement.
>
> This movement had the biggest changes. They are completely unusual, and when I first saw them, even I was flabbergasted by the contrast from the version everybody knew and played at that time. The most startling change is in the first violins, after the second repeat. There is a progression that moves chromatically up in the coda. In the standard score it's marked *legato* and slurred, and is relatively easy to play, but in the original manuscript it is marked *staccato* on each quarter note, all with grace notes. With the *presto*

tempo of the movement, it is very difficult technically to play. It sounds funny and seems absolutely like a joke.

When we came to this passage I didn't say a word. I said it was difficult, so we should repeat it again, slower. We did, and it still didn't go well. I said, "Let's try it again," and Joseph Silverstein, concertmaster at that time, said, "Are you *sure?*" All the first violinists looked at me and smiled. They couldn't believe this change was true. "Yes," I said to them, "this is in the original!"

Then I took out my copy of the facsimile of the original score from under my music stand and opened it to the passage. I hadn't shown the score to anyone up to that point. From the first to the last stand of first violins, they all looked at it! I just waited quietly while they took turns passing it along. There was absolute amazement on their faces, and they suddenly became serious and concerned. They just assumed that this particular change was my fantasy and that I was crazy. It was my trick to wait until after they tried to do it before I showed them the original. Had I shown it to them ahead of time, there wouldn't have been such a reaction, which drew attention to this detail. It was a great moment!

Back home with his orchestra, Skrowaczewski collaborated with French pianist and composer Robert Casadesus, performing concertos of Bach, Mozart, and Casadesus himself. Throughout the packed 1967–68 season, Skrowaczewski stayed mainly in Minnesota. At the start of the orchestra's annual monthlong Upper Midwest tour, Skrowaczewski the composer received a boost when the Chicago Symphony Orchestra under music director Jean Martinon performed his Symphony for Strings in early April. It was among the few performances of a Skrowaczewski work by a major orchestra that its composer did not conduct.

Two weeks after the Chicago performances Skrowaczewski was back in Minneapolis preparing for a subscription concert when his second child, Paul—named after Skrowaczewski's father—was born. After Anna's birth, the Skrowaczewskis were tested at the renowned Mayo Clinic in Rochester, Minnesota, where doctors assured them it was safe to have another child. Genetic testing, which might have revealed the potential for inherited birth defects in their future children, was not an option then. However, baby Paul was born healthy, and his parents were overjoyed.

Skrowaczewski's accent and his "interesting" interpretations of English words and sayings had long amused Midwestern colleagues. "After his son was born," remembered associate conductor George Trautwein, "he arrived at the office and was congratulated by the staff. 'What's his name?' they asked. 'Pole,' answered Stan. 'Pole?' 'Yes, Pole.' 'How do you spell it?' 'P-A-U-L,' he said. 'Oh! PAUL!' 'That's right,' he said, 'Pole.'"

The demands of caring for Anna tempered Krystyna's elation over her healthy newborn. At times it took Krystyna an hour's effort before she could get Anna to eat one spoonful of food. Blindness prevented the child from learning by imitation, an essential skill for babies. The combination of her daughter's physical condition, limited mental abilities, and lack of speech made her daily care extremely difficult. After Paul's birth an English nanny was hired to help Krystyna with child care.

Skrowaczewski's guest-conducting schedule had been full since the mid-1950s, but the pace and prestige of the engagements increased dramatically, beginning in the summer season of 1968. He conducted at every major summer music festival in the United States and made his debut at Europe's premier summer event, the Salzburg Festival.

A week after a special fund-raising concert with the Minneapolis Symphony and guest artist Van Cliburn performing the Tchaikovsky Piano Concerto no. 1, Skrowaczewski—joined by his favorite collaborators, Weissenberg and Szeryng—completed two engagements with the Royal Philharmonic Orchestra. Then came three concerts with members of the Philadelphia Orchestra opening the first week at The Robin Hood Dell. Afterward Skrowaczewski returned to Minneapolis to launch the American Music Project, a monthlong festival of contemporary music-reading sessions and seminars held in cities throughout Minnesota.

After completing his final Minneapolis Symphony engagement of the season, a family "dollar" concert in early July, Skrowaczewski and Weissenberg were featured as part of "Slavic Night" with the Chicago Symphony Orchestra at the Ravinia Festival. A week with the BSO immediately followed, during which Skrowaczewski gave the first Tanglewood performance of Lutosławski's Concerto for Orchestra. From the Berkshires of Massachusetts Skrowaczewski headed to Barbados. Frederic Mann, then U.S. ambassador to Barbados, enlisted his help in brainstorming ideas for developing "serious music" programs in the small Caribbean country, newly independent from Britain in 1966.

After Barbados Skrowaczewski led two concerts with the Cleveland Orchestra at Blossom Music Center before making his Salzburg Festival debut on August 15, 1968. His appearance marked the first time a Polish or Slavic native had been invited to conduct at the prestigious festival.

The festival's 1968 schedule included seven operas (four by Mozart), three plays, and eleven orchestral concerts by the Vienna and Berlin Philharmonics led by a who's who of major conductors.[1] The festival's glossy, 320-page program book describes Szell, Karl Böhm, and Karajan as "the three great almost 'old men'" of the podium.[2] Claudio Abbado, Lorin Maazel, Zubin Mehta, Wolfgang Sawallisch, and Skrowaczewski represented the younger generation. "The Chopin records of [Skrowaczewski] and the pianist Alexis Weissenberg have been largely responsible for Skrowaczewski's European fame," noted the program book. "[Skrowaczewski] belongs to that limited group of musicians who take Chopin's orchestral parts really seriously, instead of regarding them as a weak and withered product of a composer for the piano that can be conducted 'with one hand only.'"[3]

His Salzburg engagement and debut with the Vienna Philharmonic gave Skrowaczewski the perfect opportunity to confirm this reputation, for Weissenberg was his soloist. After beginning the program with Lutosławski's Concerto for Orchestra—a first performance by the Vienna Philharmonic—Skrowaczewski led Chopin's Piano Concerto no. 1 and concluded with Dvořák's Symphony no. 7.

The Vienna Philharmonic, one of the few self-governing major orchestras without a music director, is noted for its fastidiousness. Szell, who had conducted a festival concert with the Berlin Philharmonic a few nights earlier, was in the audience for Skrowaczewski's concert. Proud of his "Polish discovery," he invited Stanisław and Krystyna to lunch the next day. Szell shared his observations about Skrowaczewski's Vienna Philharmonic concert. "He was unusually eloquent," Skrowaczewski remembered. "Generally he was not eager to give his opinions, but he was talking a lot about this performance."

> It wasn't the big teaching lesson that Szell loved to do with everybody— he would even teach a waiter in a restaurant how to do certain things. He apparently talked to some members of the Philharmonic and the concertmaster about my work, and they were impressed that I only rehearsed the places in the music that were technically difficult for the ensemble, trusting them for other areas. In the slow movement of the Dvořák symphony, for example, the first horn plays very delicate passages with the first violins that are challenging rhythmically, due to the distance of the instruments from one another on the stage. Even on fine recordings this spot is often not clear. It had to be subdivided, which I did, and it worked. I was also surprised that Szell had so many good things to say about bowings, etc. It was very pleasant for me to hear, of course, coming from him.

Szell felt a kinship with Skrowaczewski, whom he regarded as one of the few conductors of the younger generation who were cast in his mold. "Let me tell you once more what pleasure your concert and our talks in Salzburg gave me," Szell wrote to Skrowaczewski the month following the Salzburg performance.[4]

Trautwein was visiting Skrowaczewski during a rehearsal intermission when the Vienna Philharmonic's concertmaster stopped to ask if the orchestra could have some overtime rehearsal because the musicians hadn't performed the Dvořák Seventh Symphony in a number of seasons. "For heaven's sake, don't mention this to anyone when you get back to Minneapolis!" Skrowaczewski joked to Trautwein after the concertmaster left. The concept of an American orchestra requesting overtime rehearsal was unimaginable. "I don't think they would have suggested further rehearsal if they hadn't liked Stan and wanted to produce a good performance for him and themselves," said Trautwein.

Knowing the lavish festival budget, the Vienna Philharmonic was also savvy in gaining extra pay for its members. Regardless of motivation, a cooperative musical spirit was evident, as Trautwein recalled: "There is a tricky transition in the Scherzo of the Dvořák symphony, at the end of the Trio, at the *da capo*. Stan wanted a bit of hesitation after the upbeats and rehearsed it. The upbeats at the concert were played with a true lilt, *à la viennoise*, and the concertmaster gave his assistant an 'in-the-know' glance of completion as they got back into the Scherzo."

Ronald Wilford—usually reserved towards Skrowaczewski—came to him after his concert, visibly moved by the performance. "I never forgot. He was all honey," Skrowaczewski recalled. "He had tears in his eyes and was hugging me, apparently genuinely overwhelmed by the concert."

Although Skrowaczewski was never invited back to the Salzburg Festival, his success earned him a return engagement with the Vienna Philharmonic the following season. Said one Austrian reviewer of Skrowaczewski's debut, "The Vienna Philharmonic Orchestra is a seismograph for conductors, and this time they played the best of all concerts they performed during the festival at Salzburg."[5]

From Salzburg, Skrowaczewski returned to the United States for an engagement with the Philadelphia Orchestra at Saratoga Performing Arts Center in upstate New York. Guest artist Benny Goodman was the soloist in Weber's Clarinet Concerto no. 1. During the late 1960s the "King of Swing," whose music attracted millions of adoring fans in the 1930s and 1940s, still toured. He also was the first major jazz artist to achieve considerable recognition performing classical literature. In the mid-1930s he made his first classical recording, and during the next decade or so he commissioned clarinet works from Bartók, Copland, and Hindemith. He was a serious, if infrequent, classical soloist and recording artist with major orchestras and chamber ensembles. Goodman performed works by the aforementioned composers as well as Bernstein, Debussy, Milhaud, Nielsen, and Stravinsky, among others.[6] "He played very correctly and smoothly," Skrowaczewski remarked of his one-time collaboration with Goodman. "There were no extravagances."

While in Rome on his last guest-conducting assignment that summer, Skrowaczewski was broadsided by the "name-change bomb":

> An intelligent American girl was interviewing me because she was writing artistic reviews for the *Roma Daily*, a small American paper. When she asked me about the name change of Minneapolis Symphony to Minnesota Orchestra, I was completely shocked. I exploded in anger and said it was absolutely the wrong thing to do. Word got back to the orchestra board about my interview, and they were furious with me. When I arrived in Minneapolis, I repeated these words, and they almost fired me. "Well, I am extremely upset," I told them, "that you did it without any consultation with me, the music director, or with the orchestra."

> All of these friends, members of the board, never told me that this was a possibility. I was very offended. When I asked them why they did it without checking or consulting with me, they answered, "This is a great move for the orchestra. We are adamant. You have to take this decision—like it or not."

I talked to Ken Dayton, my greatest friend on the board, and John Myers, but they had a very stern, firm opinion that they had done the right thing to include St. Paul and the entire state of Minnesota. Their rationale was that the name Minneapolis Symphony Orchestra didn't represent the entire state. But they were wrong, and they never acknowledged that they were wrong, even later. I thought of resigning at that point. I was really hit by this decision. The whole orchestra was shocked by this action. It might have been a good idea if we had all resigned at that time. No more concerts.

Without a doubt, the name change was one of the boldest actions ever taken by the governing body of a major symphony orchestra, but it was not done capriciously. It originated in June 1964 at a special meeting of the MOA's executive committee held in Stillwater, Minnesota. The meeting produced a confidential Outline of Action Program document to be presented to the board of directors in the fall. Among the initiatives cited were to "set a 'target date' for annual employment" and to seek a "new image of the Minneapolis Symphony Orchestra, including [an] accent on identification of the [orchestra] as a 'State of Minnesota' institution.... Who will do this, and at what cost?" the statement asks. Another Stillwater meeting immediately preceded the start of the 1965–66 season.[7]

In fall 1966 the executive committee held its third retreat, this time to assess the progress made since the Stillwater meetings and to chart the orchestra's future course. The list of unresolved issues included financial concerns about the guaranty and endowment funds, union attitudes, acoustics, and the orchestra's growth. Of primary concern was "making the community aware of what we are attempting to do—build one of the best orchestras in the nation and the first regional major orchestra. How do we get this across?"[8]

By the next annual retreat, in November 1967, the orchestra's name change was a foregone conclusion. The issues being discussed at this meeting were the choice of a name and the means of implementing it. Judson Bemis, MOA president, delivered a statement on the objectives: "to place the orchestra on a sound economic basis" and to "make good on our New Dimensions promises to build a truly regional orchestra and to make the Minneapolis Symphony Orchestra one of America's top six symphony orchestras."[9] (The highest budgets at that time were those of the Cleveland, Chicago, New York, Philadelphia, and Boston orchestras).

Although the orchestra had gained unearned income via the guaranty and endowment funds, expenses were increasing faster than the orchestra's earned income, Bemis reported. He cited a Ford Foundation member's prediction that during the next twenty-five years major orchestras would continue to grow and smaller ones would diminish. "The regional orchestra concept is good and needed," Bemis said. "The orchestra can't survive on the Twin Cities' support alone."[10] "It will be easier to induce people outside this area to support this organization under a different name."[11]

The executive committee formed a committee to generate name suggestions and to seek advice from public-relations professionals. The meeting's documentation did not mention the possibility of consulting orchestra musicians or Skrowaczewski about the impact of a name change.

By February Cisek reported to Bemis that the orchestra's public-relations committee agreed on the name "Minnesota Symphony Orchestra." The name change, scheduled for fall 1969, would be followed by three years of promotional activity, including recordings, special concerts, and possibly a foreign tour.

However, the upcoming 1968–69 season included two high-profile performance opportunities: a concert at the United Nations commemorating the twentieth anniversary of Human Rights Day and the New York premiere of Penderecki's *Passion*. With those events in mind, the MOA decided that it would be promotionally advantageous to institute the name change in time for the coming season.

On September 23, 1968, Bemis addressed the orchestra at its first rehearsal of the season. He announced that the board of directors would vote on the proposed name change the next day. The orchestra was stunned, although rumors had been circulating, and music critic Allan Holbert had discussed a possible name change in a *Minneapolis Tribune* article published on September 8.

Bemis brought ammunition with him to the rehearsal: letters of support from the Hill Foundation and Ken Dayton (then MOA vice president)—both strong financial supporters—and from Eugene Ormandy.

"I assure you," Ormandy wrote Bemis, "I am happy to endorse the decision to change the name of the Minneapolis Symphony Orchestra to the Minnesota Orchestra. With this change, an old wish of mine, dating back to my association with your fine orchestra, is coming true."[12] Ormandy framed his endorsement around the issue of gaining support from St. Paul, which had been a concern during his tenure as the orchestra's conductor in the early 1930s. Getting an endorsement from such a beloved figure from the orchestra's past was a brilliant move, but it returned to haunt Bemis.

"I'm completely against this," Skrowaczewski told the orchestra after Bemis left the rehearsal. "I have tried to discuss it with them [because] I still cannot see what purpose it serves."[13]

Orchestra musicians began drafting a petition against the action. After the rehearsal a large group of them met with Skrowaczewski, who lent his support to their efforts.[14] The next morning eighty-three out of ninety-four musicians, including Skrowaczewski, signed the petition. The document expressed their concern that changing the name of the esteemed sixty-six-year-old orchestra could harm its status and make recruiting young, gifted musicians difficult. It refuted the board's claim that serving the entire state required a name based on geography, pointing out that the esteemed orchestras of Boston, Philadelphia, and Cleveland performed throughout their respective home states without resorting to a name change.

Although one could argue that the community and support mechanisms in those cities differ from those in Minneapolis, the petition's last point—one that apparently had not been addressed by anyone—was extremely sound:

This finally brings us to the only reason that is plausible for a name change: the possibility of revenue from people who are unwilling at this time to give to a "Minneapolis" institution. We, of course, do not have access to information on just how much additional money would definitely be forthcoming, but we believe that this amount should be specifically and clearly defined before the organization pays such a dear price. A price tag on such a great name should be astronomical.[15]

The petition was delivered to the board of directors' annual meeting, where the executive committee's name-change proposal was brought to a vote. The petition failed to change the outcome. The board voted unanimously for the action and after much discussion settled on the name "Minnesota Orchestra."

In an effort to acknowledge the orchestra's overwhelming opposition, the board created an ad hoc committee that had the authority to determine the name-change implementation in terms of timing and public relations.[16] This committee met with seven orchestra representatives the next day in a hastily organized early-morning meeting to discuss the implementation and to consider the possibility of damage to the orchestra's reputation. The meeting was a hollow gesture, however; the executive committee's implementation plan was already in motion. Furthermore, the meeting was cut short because the press conference announcing the orchestra's new name was scheduled for 10:00 a.m. at the Minnesota governor's mansion in St. Paul.

"The Orchestral Association is convinced that the future of our orchestra, and of most important orchestras in this country, rests in their development as regional organizations," enthused Governor Harold LeVander, who shared the podium with Bemis. "The Minneapolis Symphony has been a national pacesetter in this kind of regional development. By changing the name of this widely respected cultural organization to 'Minnesota Orchestra,' the association is underscoring the orchestra's continually expanding program of service to audiences in every section of Minnesota."[17]

After the press conference Bemis, Cisek, and two board members drove to Roosevelt High School in Minneapolis, where the orchestra was rehearsing for an evening concert at the school. In their petition the musicians had expressed the concern that "any orchestra that uses a state name is synonymous with a semiprofessional amateur orchestra." To receive the official news of the name change in a high school auditorium further demoralized many orchestra members.[18]

Bemis described the day's early-morning meeting between the musicians from the orchestra and the ad hoc committee as "very constructive" but added that the board's position on the matter would not be altered.[19] He concluded his remarks by noting "Mr. Skrowaczewski, …although still deeply concerned at [the name change]…accepted the decision of the board and would work wholeheartedly to implement [it]."[20] Bemis asked the orchestra to do the same. "We felt like we had just buried a dear old friend," said violinist Herman Straka.[21]

Skrowaczewski and his musicians had no choice but to comply. Although the maestro briefly considered resigning, Wilford advised him against it. Skrowaczewski knew that the other major orchestras had no openings, and although the name change upset him, it wasn't worth giving up what he had built over the past eight years. "Personally, I am sick about the name change," he said in a *Minneapolis Tribune* article the day before the board's vote. "But if it will help the orchestra win more support, if it will help us get a new hall and help us pay our musicians more, I will support it."[22]

Public response to the name change reflected the musicians' attitude. Newspaper editors and the orchestra management received a deluge of letters. Immediately after the press conference an orchestra supporter sent his opinion via telegram. Bemis received it at the Minneapolis Sheraton Ritz, where he and MOA members were about to have a lunch:

> VIENNA PLAYS SALZBURG, STILL VIENNA PHILHARMONIC RATHER THAN AUSTRIAN. PHILADELPHIA PLAYS TEN CONCERTS [IN] BALTIMORE ALONE, STILL PHILADELPHIA. NO BRIBERY WORTH FALSIFICATION OF AN INSTITUTION'S OWN TRADITION. BUILD DECENT CONCERT HALL FIRST. GET GREAT INTERPRETERS LIKE MAAG FIRST. PHONY PUBLIC RELATIONS WILL NOT MASK DISTURBING QUALITY DECLINE, ENDOWED CHAIRS NOT WITHSTANDING.[23]

"Among my friends, there is not one who does not find the change in name repugnant," wrote a symphony patron and music teacher to Bemis. "Are we not to be considered?"[24] "Can one sustain an image by deliberately destroying its primary identity?" wrote Mr. and Mrs. B.F. Cunnington. "Would any other thoroughly established symphonic organization dare risk a name change as the Minneapolis Symphony has done on the eve of its seventieth anniversary? We think not."[25]

A few days before the official announcement of the name change, Ormandy learned from friends in Minneapolis that Skrowaczewski was against it. He immediately wrote a letter to his younger colleague apologizing for the endorsement he had written. Skrowaczewski appreciated the gesture but assured the older conductor that he had done nothing wrong in stating his opinion to Bemis. He wrote back to Ormandy saying that although he had felt "uneasy" about the name change, he accepted the decision. (Privately, Skrowaczewski never changed his belief that the action was a mistake.) "He was extremely apologetic to me," Skrowaczewski recalled. "He was really very angry that they used his words and that he had no idea that I was upset by the name change."

A week after the news conference Bemis wrote to Ormandy explaining that he hadn't anticipated that the press would report that he read Ormandy's letter to the orchestra or that Skrowaczewski would publicly voice his opposition. "Had I really been aware of his feeling," wrote Bemis, "I certainly would not have asked you to express any opinion at all on the name change and thus run the risk of interposing yourself between Stan and the association."[26]

Ormandy promptly responded: "I must admit, very honestly, that I am unhappy about the whole incident and urge you to leave my name out of any further discussion on the name change of the Minneapolis Symphony Orchestra. In all fairness to me, you should have told me that (a) Mr. Skrowaczewski was against it and (b) that you intended to publicize my statement."[27]

Not everyone opposed the name change. The possible financial gain to the orchestra was a leading consideration among name-change supporters, a number of whom were businessmen. In addition, an air of Midwestern inclusiveness and anti-elitism characterized some responses to the orchestra's management and to newspapers. "It is about time that the whole Upper Midwest region should share in the worldwide fame of the orchestra," wrote Gertrude Hill Ffolliott. "Minneapolis has hogged it far too long."[28]

An editorial in the *St. Paul Dispatch* supported the change:

> Sound reasons support the change of the Minneapolis Symphony Orchestra's name change to the Minnesota Orchestra, …sound in the sense of music and sound in the sense of economy. In the first place, the Minnesota Orchestral Association would like to bring more music to a larger audience than that of the metropolitan area. For that reason the 1969–70 season will find the orchestra playing more [frequently] outside Minneapolis than in [the city, reversing] a pattern which has existed since 1903, when the orchestra was founded. To do this, of course, the orchestra will have to broaden its economic base, which can be done more easily by linking it to the entire state instead of with Minneapolis alone.[29]

The need for the Minneapolis Symphony to "broaden its economic base" via a connection to the whole state and Upper Midwest region was clearly a nondebatable point. The orchestra was scheduled to make the jump to full-time, fifty-two-week employment by the early 1970s. The MOA wished to increase the orchestra's size and to build a $10 million endowment fund by 1971. In short, to achieve the goal of being counted among the nation's top five orchestras in terms of size, budget, and artistic merit, the orchestra's expansion demanded financial security.

With all good intentions, the board of directors changed the orchestra's name, but it was clearly a risk. The board had no guarantee from the state, regional institutions, or foundations that funds would automatically increase as a result. It was banking largely on the successful model set by statewide organizations such as the Guthrie Theater and Minnesota's professional sports teams, which appeal to a wider market. No real precedent existed for an organization like the Minneapolis Symphony—with its long history and enviable artistic luster—making such a move.

A few days after the public announcement of the name change, *St. Paul Pioneer Press* music critic John Harvey aptly summarized both sides of the controversy:

> Whether the action proves right or wrong, the decision has been based on considerable study and analysis of the facts. When the board of the Minnesota Orchestral Association, with an overwhelming majority of Minneapolitans, decided to erase the fair name of Minneapolis from the orchestra's escutcheon, one can be sure its members were convinced there were compelling reasons. Still, I believe it was an error to have left the musicians entirely out of consideration in deliberation. They were entitled to know before the irrevocable action was taken and at least to have had the chance to voice

their feelings. And if that had resulted in a public controversy, so be it. The Minnesota Orchestra is a public institution existing on public support, and the public should know what it is up to. You can't be a public institution in the dining room and a private club in the kitchen.

The musicians feel a loss of identity in this change of name. They fear damage to their professional standing—an understandably sensitive point—in playing under their new name, since other orchestras bearing the names of states are not thoroughly professional. "Minneapolis Symphony Orchestra" has become a name respected around the globe. And, as musicians, they know how fragile reputations are in the music world. They fear disappearance of the bright public image associated with the name.[30]

A performance of Skrowaczewski's transcription of Bach's Toccata and Fugue in D minor opened the season's first subscription concert on October 11, 1968, and with the maestro's firm downbeat, the Minnesota Orchestra officially was born.

A new orchestra logo appeared on the program booklet and on all promotional materials. According to the designer, its abstract black-and-white waves were based upon a rolling "M," but it was also intended "to connote sound waves, rolling hills, or just about anything the viewer wishes to attach to it."[31] The MOA was hoping that listeners would soon attach themselves to the Minnesota Orchestra, but the graphic's "rolling hills" foreshadowed the ups and downs of a long journey on the road to acceptance.

After the tumultuous change in September 1968, the Minnesota Orchestra made significant progress during the next six years. Fulfilling the promise of its new name, the orchestra saw the number of Twin Cities concerts double with the advent of a ten-concert series in St. Paul (the first held there since 1930), the addition of shorter series in other Minnesota towns, and an increasing number of run-out concerts.[32] As part of the orchestra's seventieth-anniversary season (1972–73), it performed in Mexico City, the first international jaunt since Doráti's historic Middle East tour in 1957. There also were prestigious concerts, including the 1968 United Nations performance, the long-awaited 1969 New York debut of Penderecki's *St. Luke Passion,* and the 1972 debut at the Kennedy Center for the Performing Arts. By 1974 the summer season expanded to three separate series, including a Beethoven festival—a total of sixteen concerts.

The administrative leadership also expanded. The job of MOA president became a full-time, professional paid position in 1971, the second such position with a major orchestra in the U.S. at the time.[33] Staff increased, and by 1973 eight separate committees under the MOA dealt with issues related to running a major orchestra.

Financially the orchestra had made some strides, but from the 1969–70 season to the 1972–73 season, the reported net loss steadily increased. Yet despite these challenges, after Skrowaczewski's thirteen years of ceaseless lobbying—publicly and privately—for a new concert hall, the MOA decided it was time to act. In the wake of the name-change storm, a dream—decades in the making—would come to fruition.

Everything seemed promising for the "fledgling" Minnesota Orchestra, but trouble was brewing.

Six years after the change, the name "Minnesota Orchestra" remained unfamiliar to the world outside Minnesota, and in some cases it was not recognized even within the state. Examples of misidentification were numerous enough to alarm the musicians. With the opening of the new hall only seven months away, orchestra members saw the event as a prime opportunity to bring back the tradition of the Minneapolis Symphony Orchestra.

The musicians recently had formed an Artistic Advisory Committee (AAC) consisting of "five members elected to represent the players artistically and to offer suggestions and recommendations that may better the artistic presentation of our orchestra."[34] In March 1974 they presented the executive committee of the MOA board with a petition signed by "all of the ninety-seven performing members of the orchestra, the personnel manager, stage managers, librarians, and conductors Stanisław Skrowaczewski, Henry Charles Smith, and George Trautwein."[35] The document included testimonials from every concertmaster of the orchestra, going back to Louis Krasner (who served under Mitropoulos), former music director Antal Doráti, and Swiss conductor Peter Maag, who had recently guest conducted the orchestra.

The petition cited seven reasons for the strong support of the document, the most important being the recurring problem of institutional identity. The orchestra was "constantly being mistaken for the University of Minnesota Orchestra."[36] The powerful petition summed up the issue from the musicians' perspective:

> This committee feels that no group is more capable of assessing the damage done by the name change than the members of our orchestra. All of us have musical friends throughout the world with whom we are in contact. The first question most of us hear is "Why did you change your name?" The name of the Minneapolis Symphony is golden! It has a nearly seventy-year reputation and is backed by eighty-one recordings that are still being pressed, distributed, played on FM stations, and collected. It is known in Europe, Asia, and in the Americas as a great musical organization. *The Minnesota Orchestra can claim none of this.* [italics in the original]
>
> After six years, the name change is no longer news. Despite well-intentioned local and national public relations efforts, the name Minnesota Orchestra simply has not taken! (We have collected dozens of anecdotes and press errors to prove this point.)[37]

The administrative leadership could not ignore the issue. MOA president Donald Engle, speaking on behalf of the executive committee, recognized that there was a problem but made clear in his memo to the MOA that the present name should remain. He also recommended that a committee be formed to include members of AAC (ultimately there was only one musician on it) and members of the board. The committee's purpose was not to consider changing the name back but to "develop specific means of promotion."[38]

Still, the name-change committee, which met during a thirty-day period, created a summary of pro-and-con arguments as well as an extensive document on improving promotional strategies for the orchestra. But after going through the motions, the result was the same. On June 19, 1974, chairman John Pillsbury, Jr., formally told the musicians that the board voted to retain the name "Minnesota Orchestra." He quoted portions of the committee's report that recognized the orchestra's desire to change the name back and acknowledged that "there will continue to be dissatisfaction unless the name Minnesota Orchestra develops prestige and recognition comparable to the name Minneapolis Symphony Orchestra."[39] It also recognized that recordings and touring—both of which were central to establishing the orchestra's new name—were not financially feasible at that time. So it was recommended that a committee be formed to find ways of making recordings and touring feasible in the future.

The general consensus in 1974 was that better promotion, significant tours—meaning European engagements—and recordings were badly needed to establish the integrity of the name "Minnesota Orchestra."

The idea of a major international tour was earnestly explored in winter 1974 along with the possibility of its implementation in fall 1976 or 1977. But the expenses associated with a new hall, longer seasons, and annual deficits, not to mention the inflation of the late seventies, made a major tour impossible. Local, regional, and national touring also decreased. During the 1973–74 season, the orchestra gave twenty-eight non-Twin Cities concerts, most of which were still in Minnesota.[40] By the 1979–80 season that number dropped to nine, with only two in Minnesota. (This figure does not include the longstanding series in Rochester and at the College of Saint Benedict and Saint John's University in Saint Joseph, Minnesota.)[41]

Ironically, the Minneapolis Symphony Orchestra of 1967, which gave almost half of its concerts outside the Twin Cities, fulfilled the MOA's stated goal—"to bring the enjoyment and rewards of great music to increasing numbers of citizens of Minnesota and the Upper Midwest"—to a far greater degree than did the Minnesota Orchestra in 1979.[42] It should be noted, however, that in 1967 the orchestra's season was thirty-eight weeks, in comparison to fifty-two in 1979. And by 1979 various factors converged to make outside activities less cost-effective, including the expense of touring, demands by musician for fewer performances, and the presence of a new venue.[43]

On the recording front, progress had been made. In 1974 the orchestra secured a three-year contract—its first in twelve years—with Vox Productions of New York. By 1980 Skrowaczewski and the Minnesota Orchestra had released twelve long-playing (LP) records. All were for Vox except Penderecki's Violin Concerto (Columbia) and Skrowaczewski's English Horn Concerto (Desto). *Ravel: The Complete Works for Orchestra,* a four-record issue, was the first in the Vox series and received wide critical acclaim. Four more LPs were scheduled to be released in 1981. By the late 1970s, however, Mercury began to reissue the Minneapolis Symphony's celebrated recordings from the 1950s and

1960s. Concerned about confusing consumers, Mercury only listed the Minneapolis Symphony on the reissues. By the early 1980s there were dozens of recordings available on at least five different labels under the two different orchestra names.

Although the musicians had lost their latest battle to reclaim the orchestra's old name, the closing paragraph of their 1974 petition had cautioned: "The question will not fade: as the self-defeating results of the name-change become ever more apparent, feelings will only grow stronger."[44]

The issue resurfaced in the early 1980s, a time when the MOA was about to launch the biggest capital campaign by a U.S. symphony orchestra. Although people within Minnesota had adjusted to the name change after eleven years, the orchestra still encountered difficulties outside of the state.

"On the first night of our tour last week in Midland, Michigan," wrote one board member to MOA president Cisek in 1981, "the presenter explained our pitifully small house (600 of a potential 1,100) as follows: 'You changed your name on us. People still hear the Minneapolis Symphony recordings on the radio and are confused or do not relate to the present name.' It was like a page out of the musicians' book!"[45]

The national and international press still called the orchestra either by the old name or by some fusion of the old and the new, although it happened less frequently than in the early years of the change. Even the orchestra's official logo had an identity problem. In an effort to recognize its heritage—or appease the complainers—the name "Minneapolis Symphony Orchestra," followed by the line "Founded 1903," appeared underneath the boldly printed "Minnesota Orchestra" and the "M" symbol. This odd labeling appeared on official orchestra documents and letterhead in 1968 and continued into the 1980s. (The pairing of "Minneapolis Symphony Orchestra" with the logo eventually disappeared in the late 1980s, but the dated logo design remained attached to the orchestra until 2003.)

The musicians' continuing dissatisfaction forced the MOA board's hand. The executive committee appointed a sixteen-person committee, which included two orchestra members, to reassess the name-change issue again. The new committee embarked on an involved, lengthy analysis of the matter; however, just before the start of the 1981–82 season, it recommended against changing the name, citing "a high probability that a name change would be traumatic to the impending capital campaign and other fundraising efforts."[46]

Among other things, the committee recommended that "the orchestra must develop a national and international reputation of quality to attract and keep well-qualified musicians. The staff and the board must recognize that many of the policies currently in place and contemplated could result in being recognized as a regional orchestra."[47] The minutes of one committee meeting noted the mood of the orchestra as this latest chapter of the controversy ended:

> The reality for the musicians is that no matter what the capital campaign
> hopes to make possible in the future, the orchestra is going to have to see

something soon. They have been waiting for recordings and tours, and they just haven't happened. The drive itself will not be accepted as evidential to the orchestra. It needs to see something tangible.[48]

In 1991 the musicians made their last formal effort to get the orchestra's old name back. A petition from the "committee to reestablish the name 'Minneapolis Symphony Orchestra'" was circulated during the spring. Herman Straka chaired a committee comprised of five orchestra members, most of whom had been around for the 1981 effort. The notable exception was concertmaster Jorja Fleezanis, then in her third season with the orchestra. Both Edo de Waart (now music director) and Skrowaczewski, serving as conductor laureate, signed the petition. The issue may have been old and one that some people considered "water over the dam," but it was still a hot topic for a majority of the orchestra members.

Through a bargaining procedure in summer 1992, the musicians and the MOA agreed to form a joint committee consisting of five musicians and five members of the board and staff, including MOA president David Hyslop, and the chairman. The committee's mission was to "discuss the name of the orchestra and the feasibility or desirability of changing the name, including restoring the name to the 'Minneapolis Symphony.'"[49] The process was well-worn territory for people who had been involved in the issue since 1968. Hyslop brought substantial experience to the issue with a combination of history, freshness, and savvy. He knew quite well that the name "Minnesota Orchestra" was very important to Ken Dayton and that any discussion about it ultimately began and ended with his authority.

Dayton, the architect of a precursor to the name change, had suggested in 1956 that the Orchestral Association of Minneapolis change its name to the Minnesota Orchestral Association "to reflect a new and broader mission for the orchestra."[50] Dayton initiated this shift after completing his two-year service as chair of the board of directors, during which he had overseen two years of balanced budgets after years of deficits. Dayton masterminded the actual name change, which had strong support from Bemis, and Cisek served as a key emissary. The orchestra was the love of Dayton's life, and he was involved in various facets of it from 1947 until his death in 2003.

Dayton descended from a long lineage of successful businessmen with a strong commitment to philanthropy. In the early 1900s his grandfather founded a department store in downtown Minneapolis, and after the death of Dayton's father in 1950, Ken and his four brothers inherited the family business. Under the brothers' leadership the company created a remarkable philanthropic policy—still in practice today at Target Corporation—whereby five percent of the company's pre-tax profits went to the community's charitable organizations.

Dayton's relationship with the Minnesota Orchestra began in 1929 when he attended Young People's Concerts under Henri Verbrugghen, the orchestra's second music director. Later he became an ardent fan of the electrifying Mitropoulos and served on the committees responsible for hiring Doráti and Skrowaczewski. When Dayton was not officially serving on the board, he was working on projects like the orchestra's first endowment fund campaign, the New Dimensions Fund (a collaborative project with the Ford Foundation), and fund-raising for a new concert hall.[51] Over several decades, Ken and Judy Dayton personally donated generously to the Minnesota Orchestra for the endowment, the new venue, commissioned works, tours, and more.

Hyslop understood that he needed Ken Dayton's support for his fresh approach to the name-change controversy:

> I did something that was a little controversial, but it was very helpful. I got together with the board chair, Nicky Carpenter, and said, "We're on tour. Instead of talking to ourselves about this issue, let's get the folks who are out there with all the orchestras to talk to us. So while we were on tour we got Doug Sheldon, who was still at Columbia, Stewart Warkow at ICM, and others who had a great deal of experience to discuss the issue with us. What they said made a lot of sense: "Look, you can call it anything you want; maybe you shouldn't have changed the name in 1968, but what you didn't do was while other orchestras expanded recordings, radio series (Minnesota *did* do that) and toured Europe, you didn't. And you also need to look at where you are going in terms of conductors, because a conductor brings a lot of cachet to an orchestra."

> So I went to Ken Dayton—who is one of the greatest people who ever lived—with this information, and he said, "Why do they always bring up that name change? They are always bringing it up." I took my life into my hands because he could be a tough guy—he was a great man but sometimes a tough guy—you're not a retailer all those years by being a pushover—and I said, "Ken, here's the reality. I agree with you. I don't think we should go back and change the name again, but I do understand the reaction when it took place. The reality now, however, is that we've not delivered on things we promised."

> To get my point about Europe across, I used a baseball analogy. I said, "Put the name aside for a second. You're told you are one of the great orchestras of the world. It's like being the Twins. They won the World Series in 1991. The Twins could say they are the champions of baseball, but if they had never played New York, Chicago, or Los Angeles, what kind of champions would they be? They would feel like they were pretenders, not players." I gave Ken and others a list of orchestras that had been to Europe. It wasn't just New York, Chicago, and Los Angeles. Seattle had played Europe, Indianapolis had, and St. Louis, had several times. It's not just about ego for the orchestra. It gets the name out there, and you get better soloists, better conductors, and all the rest. After all, what we're about is excellence. Ken understood this point, as did many board members. They got it. And the next thing you know, boom, we're off! Recordings came, there were Grammy nominations and other awards, and we went to Europe and Japan. Now there have been several tours, and it's a completely different ballgame.

So was the name change worth it? Skrowaczewski's opinion is clear: "It was a bad decision. We lost a lot. We lost time, and I lost my reputation. It absolutely affected my career. I still feel it all the time."

In her book *More Than Meets the Ear*, violinist Julie Ayer offers her perspective on the difficult transition and its prolonged denouement:

> In March 2004 we returned from our third European tour. Finally, it appears the connection is beginning to be made internationally between the renowned Minneapolis Symphony Orchestra and the Minnesota Orchestra. Receiving rave reviews and acclaim in major European cities is the culmination of years of struggle to reestablish and maintain an international reputation that was diminished by the name change (certainly not by the quality of the orchestra).[52]

The name "Minnesota Orchestra" is more established today than it ever has been, thanks to international tours, recordings, and the conductors most prominently associated with it since 1968. But the intense emotional attachment that some people still have to its former name cannot be dismissed, nor can all the time, energy, and funds expended to rebuild a name that, for all intents and purposes, did not need restoration.

A minority of today's orchestra members either belonged to the ensemble when its name was changed or joined during the early 1970s. These members, Skrowaczewski among them, were deeply wounded by the decision. However, the majority of orchestra members, many of whom joined long after 1968, are not particularly interested in or concerned about the issue.

Fleezanis, concertmaster from 1989 to 2009, conveyed her perspective in 2003:

> No matter what anyone thought were sound reasons to reinvent the name and thus the image of this orchestra, the longevity of a brand name is monolithic—Tide is Tide, Chevrolet is Chevrolet. The inculcation of the name "Minneapolis Symphony" was deep in the psyche of the classical music profession and the greater public, nationally and internationally, through its illustrious music directors, recordings, tours and the continuity brought on by time. In 1989 I joined the orchestra on the strength of its history as the Minneapolis Symphony. The Minnesota Orchestra was a tad over twenty years old then, and I had no sense of its history except the association with Skrowaczewski and Edo de Waart, who hired me to become concertmaster of this infant child—the Minnesota Orchestra—standing on the shoulders of its older sibling, the Minneapolis Symphony. I saw no external signs of recordings or touring to reinforce the current artistic standards of this seemingly new orchestra, but I had heard many positive reports from Edo before I left San Francisco of the strengths of the orchestra. However, for all intents and purposes it still had the air of a provincial orchestra. Within my first two years it became clear that the orchestra's direction and mission had stalled, and in this atmosphere the name change reared up again.

Surprisingly, it took the arrival of Eiji Oue as music director—with his infectious optimism and ambition to elevate his career through the strengths of the orchestra—to begin to lead the way out of the stalemate of our mistaken identity and into the national and international limelight. He convinced people that we should go on tours and start making recordings again. He wanted the orchestra to go to Vienna, and with his efforts and support from the Daytons and private and corporate sponsors, we did. Something very similar happened in San Francisco as well. Edo de Waart was on the cusp of bringing that orchestra to Europe, but it ultimately happened under Herbert Blomstedt's watch. I think the San Francisco Symphony and the Minnesota Orchestra went through similar growing pains, trying to get themselves on the international map. Now they both have.

As to the question of whether the original goals of the name change were achieved, the answer is somewhat ambiguous. When asked about the reasoning behind the name change in 2001, Ken Dayton was clear on the points involved:

I think there were three things. Number one: the recognition that a good deal of our support came from St. Paul, and just to call it "Minneapolis" when we were raising big money in St. Paul didn't make any sense. Secondly: as government support increased, it was important to recognize that it was an orchestra of the whole state and to go to the legislature to ask for money would not be a good thing if they were just giving money to Minneapolis instead of to a statewide institution. Thirdly, and most important: the mission of the orchestra at about that time changed from just being a resident orchestra in Minneapolis to a statewide mission to bring great music to the citizens of Minnesota. All of these led logically to the name change.

On the topic of criticism about the decision, Dayton was equally direct: "It took a long time to prove it to everyone, but it was a wise decision. Now there's no question about it because there are many more recordings under the Minnesota label than there ever were under the Minneapolis label, so it's a dead issue." (As of 2010, 210 works have been recorded under the name "Minnesota Orchestra." The Minneapolis Symphony Orchestra made 250 recordings.)

Within the business community of St. Paul, the ensemble attracted increased donations as the "Minnesota Orchestra," but the extent of the growth is unknown. Figures were not revealed to any of the musicians on the various name-change committees over the years.

The notion that the new name would facilely translate into funding from state government agencies was precarious at best. Such funding is often tied to the political interests of those in power, which of course changes frequently. Even Dayton described government funding as "frightening…because [it] could vanish overnight with a hostile Congress or state legislature."[53] During the last thirty years the Minnesota state legislature frequently has not been particularly supportive of the orchestra, state name or not.

Even as a business decision the name change was flawed. Ken Dayton, the main architect of the change, was one of the most successful businessmen and arts-conscious philanthropists in America. Given his business acumen, it seems odd that he maintained his unwavering stance on the virtues of the name change. Clearly he had a deep and profound love for the Minnesota Orchestra and for Skrowaczewski. The notion that Dayton would lead an action harmful to either is unfathomable. To the credit of both men, the issue did not affect their long friendship. "I was never aware of any animosity between the two of them all through that time," said Judy Dayton, "but it was a tough issue."

A deft financial mindset fused with a strong Midwestern philosophy of inclusion and nonelitism likely motivated Dayton and others to promote the name change. In essence he dreamed of a widespread corporate model for the orchestra. Association members—like shareholders in a company—would represent large populations and thereby increase financial support and visibility for the organization, not unlike what eventually happened with his businesses. Coming from a corporate executive of his stature and experience, it was an interesting, provocative idea for the state's leading cultural institution. But at some point, the drive to serve an ever-broadening constituency may conflict with an organization's artistic mission.

Acknowledging the reality that American orchestras must rely largely on private donations—unlike European orchestras that have state or municipal support—Skrowaczewski frankly addressed the reality of orchestra-concert attendance in the Twin Cities. He cited a statistic published in the *Minneapolis Tribune*: a mere nine percent of the population attended such concerts during the 1967–68 season. In his remarks to the orchestra's New Dimensions Fund donors he said: "Thus, a symphony orchestra still seems to play in a more or less ivory tower for an elite segment of society. And it is probably the same in other American cities and in Europe. But I think there is nothing wrong with this fact, as any art, both in the past and now appeals always to a certain elite."[54]

Acknowledging the importance of attracting as many people as possible to the arts, he said, "We might expect good results only through a wise education, and even then we will never know how much people will turn on or off to the arts."[55]

The long-lasting achievement of the name change—for better or for worse—has nothing to do with funding, status, or recognition but everything to do with the advancement of a particular philosophy of "music for all" and of "access." Rather than building an elite orchestra identified with a major city and its particular culture, a few key figures decided that excellence within a more populist framework was better. "We're not a big-city orchestra," Judson Bemis said in 1974. "We represent and serve a region."[56]

And yet there is something oddly insular about this message of inclusion, a comforting belief that excellence has been achieved among a certain population of people and that "Lake Wobegon is doing just fine, thank you very much." Perhaps there exists an honest reluctance to really stand out as an elite entity, even if singularity is a requirement for true distinction in any field.

More than forty years after the orchestra's name change, Skrowaczewski still takes great pride in his long association with the Minnesota Orchestra and in their joint achievements. His respect for the orchestra and its artistry is unwavering. But he also remains steadfast in his opinion that "principal mistakes" were made by the MOA leadership. For him, it remains an important facet of his and the orchestra's history:

> During the first few years of my tenure in Minneapolis, with our small team of leadership, I thought it was a particularly good combination of people devoted to the arts. They listened to the music director, and we worked together. But soon the number of people involved in the administration grew and grew, and the executive committee—which also became very large—began making decisions without consulting or listening to the music director and the musicians. Mistakes happened, especially the name change. They made our orchestra, which was becoming more and more international, into a provincial one. This decision, at the time, really stopped the orchestra's rise to international fame. It was distressing, unnecessary, and dangerous.

SIXTEEN

REEMERGENCE

There was a black spot in my artistic life. To feel fulfilled I needed to compose again, but no ideas were coming. Then came Stacy.

—Stanisław Skrowaczewski

Skrowaczewski had little time to be preoccupied with the Minnesota Orchestra's identity crisis at the start of the 1968–69 season. Along with the rescheduled Carnegie Hall premiere of Penderecki's *St. Luke Passion*, the orchestra was invited to give a special concert at the United Nations in honor of the twentieth anniversary of Human Rights Day. Skrowaczewski also had a full guest-conducting schedule that included the U.S. premiere of Penderecki's opera *The Devils of Loudun*, his debut with the Berlin Philharmonic, and a planned debut at the Metropolitan Opera, conducting *Eugene Onegin*.

After the most successful summer season of his career, the stress of the name change, and his intense focus on the coming engagements, Skrowaczewski needed a rest before starting his ninth year in Minneapolis. A week of intensive mountain climbing was his chosen respite. "It gives Stan a chance to recharge his batteries, to be fresh and ready for the new season," said Krystyna.[1] Skrowaczewski savored the rigors of mountain climbing:

> Climbing, roped to a guide and reaching for a foothold at a height of ten thousand feet, concentrates the mind wonderfully! Hanging by your fingernails to a vertical two- thousand-foot precipice sometimes makes me tremble with fear, but for me it's the greatest mind-cleanser. Sometimes I'm trembling up there, but experiencing that fear is so important to me. Fear cleanses your mind. Then there is the pride and happiness after accomplishing the climb.

Wyoming's Grand Teton National Park had become a favorite vacation destination for the Skrowaczewskis. The forty-mile-long Teton Range reminded them of Poland's Tatra Mountains, where they first met while skiing in the early 1950s. A journalist-photographer from the *Minneapolis Tribune* accompanied them on the trip for a special feature in the *Sunday Picture Magazine*. "High on a slope in Wyoming's Grand Teton Mountains, the small climbing party came to a halt," wrote Mike Zerby. "Leader of the group, Stanisław Skrowaczewski looked about at the towering outcroppings of sheer rock, the lush forests, and glittering lake below, and the electric-blue sky with its dazzling sun overhead. To himself more than anyone, Skrowaczewski said one word, 'Magnificent.'"[2]

Ken and Judy Dayton, Ken's brother Wallace and his wife, Mary Lee, and members of their families joined the Skrowaczewskis on what was the their fourth Grand Teton trip. After vigorously hiking trails in the park, Skrowaczewski and Krystyna broke off from the party to do some "serious climbing." They sought out guide Herb Swedlund from Exum Climbing School to prepare them to take on the Grand Teton, at 13,766 feet the highest peak of the range. Skrowaczewski was thrilled to learn that Swedlund had been among the party that accompanied Dimitri Mitropoulos on his journey to the peak in 1946. However, Swedlund informed a disappointed Skrowaczewski that there wasn't time to tackle the range's highest peak because it was the end of the season.

In an effort to soak in as much of the mountains as possible, Skrowaczewski decided that he and Krystyna would take one more hike on the last day of their vacation:

Everybody had left. The mountains were devoid of any tourists. By the first of September the season was over. It was a glorious, sunny day with just a little wind. Near Jenny Lake Lodge, where we were staying, the main slope had some very steep trails, so I thought it would be nice to go up one before we left. We went up quite high. Some rock climbing was necessary, and eventually we stopped to take in the gorgeous view. We were on the north slope of the Grand Tetons, and from that side it's difficult to hear a storm coming from the southwest slope. The clouds were starting to become darker, and already there was more wind, so I decided we'd better head back down the mountain. I began down a steep path—there wasn't a formal trail—along a stream that had bountiful bushes with gorgeous raspberries, almost a field of them! Krystyna was about twenty yards behind me, going a bit slower. Suddenly, in front of me I saw a big cloud of dust that seemed to be moving. I had no idea what it could be; I wondered if it was the wind moving. I moved closer, and about thirty feet in front of me was a huge grizzly bear, a massive animal. He was crazed, running from left to right and pulling the little spruces from the earth up into the air, and he was making this cloud of dust—it was an amazing sight! He was totally angered by something; maybe wasps or bees or something had bitten him.

I became scared for our lives because this path was really the only way down the mountain. It was a very narrow valley with vertical rocks on either side that we couldn't really climb. It was quite a dangerous situation. I went back on the path to tell Krystyna about the grizzly and to try to figure out what to do. Almost automatically we both knew what we had to do to survive. *How* we managed to cross the stream going over these steep, vertical wet rocks to go down, I'll never know, but we did it. Fortunately, grizzlies don't see well, and although they do hear well, the wind and sound of the stream prevented him from hearing (or smelling) us. But we had no idea if he would come for us at any point. It was terrifying, because if something did happen, no one would find us until the following season. We weren't on a trail, and the park was empty. When we were about two hundred yards down the mountain I turned back, and he was not following us. As soon as we made it down I called the ranger's station at Jackson Hole. He was aware of one particularly dangerous grizzly bear—he said [it] was from Canada—that had already attacked some campers earlier in the season. We left the next day, but a few weeks later we received a letter from the ranger saying that the bear was tranquilized and sent back to Canada. But I will never forget this incident. You know, the things you do when you are in danger—how we got over those wet steep rocks over this stream is a mystery!

During the calmer moments of the Grand Teton trip, Skrowaczewski studied scores amid the beauty of the mountainous environs. When he was asked to contribute a short essay to the fall 1968 issue of *Symphony Magazine*, he eloquently incorporated that memory while once again stressing the point that Minneapolis lacked a proper performance facility:

The Light of Our Eye

Recently I rested in a sun-soaked valley, high in the Grand Teton Mountains, and opened one of my beloved scores—Stravinsky's *Orpheus*. The poetry of music, accompanied by the silken web of the valley's quiescence, almost stopped my consciousness of physical existence. I passed into that unique atmosphere in which, as we seem to reach the infinite, our perception of art sharpens.

Involuntarily, I thought of the human ability to receive art and of the physical and spiritual conditions which make this reception possible—in our case, the concert hall and the concert itself.

Music is the most mysterious of the arts, veiled by something solemn, far from the realities of life. Its soul is revealed only to those who desire and are willing to go through certain stages of ceremony and mystery to reach it. A concert hall should be the temple where music leads us gradually from the secular life into the realm of the extraordinary, to the life that is innermost....

Our own orchestra, someday endowed with an acoustically proper symphony hall, can provide a Temple for music, musicians, and listeners, where enhanced artistic goals and technical equipment will allow us to encompass a wider variety of musical forms, including the very contemporary.

I dream of such a "Musical Arts Center"—the light of our eye and one of the tools which will transfigure the enormous energy of our chaotic and troubled times into a human renaissance.[3]

During his Grand Teton vacation Skrowaczewski finished an orchestration of Bach's Toccata and Fugue in D minor, a project he had begun at the start of the summer. Although the piece was scheduled to open the Minnesota Orchestra's season, the prospect of that performance—or any other—wasn't his only motivation for orchestrating one of Bach's most popular works: "I adored this work as a boy. At age eleven or twelve, I played the Busoni transcription; it was one of my concert pieces that I did on both organ and piano. I guess I felt that being a conductor and having a good ensemble, I wanted to show how a big orchestra sounded like an organ. My motivation was completely personal, out of my love of this work."

Skrowaczewski was aware of Stokowski's famous transcription of the work that became entrenched in popular culture through Walt Disney's 1940 film *Fantasia*, but he had not performed or formally studied the piece. A week before Skrowaczewski led the first performance of his Toccata and Fugue, he gave reporters more insight into his orchestration of the work:

> There have been several arrangements of the work, but none quite satisfy me. I have tried to make it large but pure, not adding any harmonic embellishment but at the same time making the most of effects implicit in the score.[4] This is not a transcription but an orchestration. Nothing has been added to or taken away from what Bach wrote. There is a marvelous, big, 18th-century organ in Leżajsk, a small city in Poland. One might say the church was built around the organ. It is the sound of that instrument that was in the back of my mind when I was doing this orchestration.[5]

Skrowaczewski's Bach contribution—perhaps the only published version of Toccata and Fugue in D minor for full orchestra other than Stokowski's—placed him in good company. Many major composers and conductors—including Schoenberg, Stravinsky, Webern, Elgar, Klemperer, Mitropoulos, and Ormandy—have transcribed, arranged, or orchestrated works by Bach for full orchestra. Skrowaczewski's orchestration was included on a 2004 Chandos CD with the BBC Symphony Orchestra conducted by Leonard Slatkin, a recording comprised entirely of Bach settings for orchestra conceived by conductors. In 2008 a thrilling, nuanced live recording of the piece with Skrowaczewski conducting the Yomiuri Nippon Symphony Orchestra was released on the Denon label.

Following the performance of Skrowaczewski's Bach Toccata on opening night in 1968, the Minneapolis audience heard a work that was its total opposite, both in subtlety and in ensemble size—Stravinsky's *Orpheus* Ballet Suite, composed only twenty-one years earlier. One reviewer bemoaned this "driest music" of Stravinsky and the uninspired performance he felt it received, noting that a "large number of people in the audience slept during the piece."[6] Another observed that the music required "careful listening rather than raw pleasure."[7] By juxtaposing the piece with the grandiose Bach, Skrowaczewski was making a statement:

> *Orpheus* is a marvelous work but very austere, using a rather small orchestra. It compels the listener to find the beauty in it, even the emotions in it, through the use of one's intellect. It is not an easy piece to digest or to understand. My point is to remind people that beauty and emotion and all the highest characteristics of art do not necessarily reside in loud, grandiose, "lushy" things. What we probably all need is more intellectual work, a preparation to enjoy those more intimate, hidden values in music. So my programming of *Orpheus* is a reaction against, not deterioration, but a certain degeneration of tastes. It is a reaction against a loud, amplified lack of intellectual involvement of various people.[8]

These remarks were not the typical "maestro comments" intended to lure people into the concert hall, but Skrowaczewski rarely spoke or acted like a typical maestro.

The ten-minute Toccata received many performances in late 1968. Skrowaczewski frequently programmed it as an opener on the Minnesota Orchestra's fall tour. Two weeks before the U.N. concert in early December, he guest conducted the New York Philharmonic for the first time since 1961. Having two series of concerts with the Philharmonic, he programmed his Bach Toccata with Chopin's Piano Concerto no. 1 (with Weissenberg) and Shostakovich's Fifth Symphony for the second series. Harold Schonberg dismissed both Skrowaczewski's "linear effects" and Stokowski's "organ-like" approach to the Toccata as "old fashioned.... With the orchestral literature as big as it is, and as relatively unexplored as it is, why waste time with such nonsense? The Bach is an organ piece and should be left as an organ piece."[9]

Perhaps Schonberg's point was valid, but in his first program with the Philharmonic Skrowaczewski conducted some relatively unexplored literature: Lutosławski's *Musique funèbre* (heard only once before in New York, in 1964) and Szymanowski's Symphony no. 2, with Skrowaczewski's own significant cuts and alterations to the orchestration, which he soon ceased to perform.

Coincidentally, a few months before Skrowaczewski's Philharmonic appearances Elliott Carter raised the issue of Bach orchestrations in a letter published in *The New York Times*. Carter objected to a criticism he received from Schonberg and stated that the concertgoing public during Beethoven's time was primarily interested in contemporary music, "a necessity," he said, "for the life of music at all times.... Contemporary music of each new period gives that period a new point about the musical past."[10]

Carter noted that Webern's orchestration of Bach's *Fuga Ricercata* from *The Musical Offering* reflects that composer's interest in small motives and the "inner organization" of the music. To further clarify his point, Carter referred to Skrowaczewski:

> For the musical works of the past cannot fail to be reheard and re-experienced in the light of present musical experience. When contemporary music ceases to be an important part of the musical scene, then older music becomes a dead effigy and loses its life. This is very obvious in the theater and has often been pointed out in literature. It is certainly not by chance that Pierre Boulez, Stanisław Skrowaczewski, and Lukas Foss are considered very important as young conductors today. ...They have a new point of view about the entire repertory—and this point of view was formed by their involvement with "advanced" music, which gives it a cogency, freshness, and vigor that could not have been attained in any other way.[11]

"The more I hear Skrowaczewski conduct, the more I like him," said Winthrop Sargeant in *The New Yorker* review of Skrowaczewski's second set of Philharmonic concerts. "There is nothing of the exhibitionist about him. He is a very serious maestro, wearing spectacles that make him look a little like a schoolteacher, and he knows just about every secret there is to handling an orchestra. Under him, the sound of the Philharmonic is better than it has been in a long time."[12]

Sargeant was among the few New York music critics who had been a professional musician. He played in the San Francisco Symphony during the early 1920s and later in the New York Philharmonic under Toscanini. A critic and music writer since the early 1930s, Sargeant was influential in the New York musical community. Staunchly conservative in his musical tastes, he nevertheless became enamored of jazz and published two books on the subject.[13]

After his last Philharmonic concert on December 9, Skrowaczewski was scheduled to conduct the Minnesota Orchestra at the United Nations the following evening. The orchestra had been chosen to give a special concert commemorating the twentieth anniversary of the U.N.'s proclamation of its Universal Declaration of Human Rights, created in Paris in 1948. Two years later the U.N. General Assembly selected December 10 as Human Rights Day, and ever since, the Universal Declaration has been commemorated on that date through a variety of events. In 1968 the U.N. specified that it wanted to feature an orchestra from the heart of the country at the commemoration. Audrey Michaels, who assisted the orchestra's publicity department, was involved in contacting the U.N. about participation. The concert, which would be videotaped and broadcast nationally by National Educational Television (NET, precursor to PBS), was a prime opportunity to promote the Minnesota Orchestra.

The program's centerpiece was a cantata commissioned at the request of U Thant, secretary-general of the U.N., who chose thirty-eight-year-old Spanish composer Cristóbal Halffter to write the music. Halffter, today considered among Spain's most important composers of his generation, focused on big proportions and effects in *Yes, Speak Out, Yes.*

Writer Norman Corwin crafted the text largely from the articles of the declaration. Dubbed the "poet laureate of radio," Corwin was synonymous in the 1930s and 1940s with memorable radio dramas and programs about important political events. He also wrote extensively for theater, television, and film. He created a series of radio programs for NPR in the 1990s and is still writing and teaching. Corwin celebrated his one-hundredth birthday in 2010.[14]

In addition to a full orchestra, the cantata required two vocal soloists (soprano and baritone), two choirs antiphonally placed, and two conductors to manage the complexities of the music. (Halffter served as the second conductor.) The Augsburg College Choir, from Minneapolis, admirably assisted the orchestra. The youthful choir of robed undergraduates worked hard under the pressure of the event and despite the hot lights required for filming the concert. When a singer fainted in the middle of the piece, two U.N. attendants quickly shuffled him offstage. The program also included Skrowaczewski's Bach Toccata and Fugue and Brahms' First Symphony.

Wrote Minneapolis critic John Sherman: "It was a glossy and momentous occasion attended by an invited audience of nearly 2,400 U.N. delegates and foreign ministries—probably the most international audience the Minnesota Orchestra has ever played to."[15]

Unfortunately the event and commissioned piece did not produce the widespread coverage that the orchestra and the U.N. desired. And it didn't help that *The New York*

Times review called the ensemble the "Minnesota Symphony." Halffter's piece was not an artistic triumph. Although it made a striking first impression, particularly with the chorus and soloists talking and shouting throughout the score, it was destined to be, as Mary Ann Feldman called it, a *pièce d'occasion*.[16]

In 2006 Corwin recalled "only negative memories" of the performance of *Yes, Speak Out, Yes*: "The work was extremely dissonant, so much so that I, who wrote the text, could not decipher a single word when performed. One of the movements was designated to be played in 'aleatory' fashion, which meant leaving what was to be played to each musician's choice. Not Skrowaczewski's fault."[17]

Nevertheless, the fact that the orchestra had been chosen to perform at this prestigious event marks a high point in its history. "All of the musicians who had toured the Middle East [in 1957] and had gone to so many countries were really touched by playing under that big symbol of the United Nations in the familiar General Assembly Hall. It was a thrill," recalled Richard Cisek.

It is not surprising that this anniversary of the Human Rights Declaration failed to attract the American public's attention during a year that ranks as one of the most devastating in the nation's recent history. Tumultuous 1968 witnessed the assassinations of Rev. Dr. Martin Luther King, Jr., and U.S. Senator Robert Kennedy; riots in 125 cities after King's assassination; increasing antiwar sentiment over Vietnam, in part as a result of the My Lai massacre; student demonstrations around the country, including protests that shut down Columbia University; and violent clashes between protestors and Chicago police outside the 1968 Democratic National Convention.[18]

As part of the broadcast of the Human Rights Day concert, NET showed excerpts from interviews the network conducted on the streets of New York City. Ordinary people were asked if they thought a formal declaration of human rights was important. The solemnity of the U.N. concert contrasted sharply with the realities of the "man-on-the-street" interviews. Opinions ranged from disinterest to thoughtful responses. A twenty-year-old black man said, "We need civil rights first, then human rights," and he described the indignities he faced simply in going to a restaurant.[19] A white man, barely out of his teens and clad in a military uniform, explained that he "joined the service for four years to try to protect other people's rights because they will be violated if the Communists come over to this country."[20]

In a little more than two months, the Minnesota Orchestra would give the New York premiere of Penderecki's *St. Luke Passion*, which had been postponed after Skrowaczewski suffered a detached retina in 1967. Before the New York engagement, he led a few concerts in Minneapolis and had guest-conducting engagements in Europe. Skrowaczewski conducted concerts in England, including two with the Royal Philharmonic Orchestra and violinist Josef Suk, the great-grandson of Dvořák, who played his ancestor's 1729 Stradivarius. Next on his schedule was his debut with the Berlin Philharmonic.

Skrowaczewski had met Herbert von Karajan, the imposing music director of the Berlin Philharmonic, at the 1968 Salzburg Festival. He assisted Karajan by monitoring balances during a rehearsal for the Berlin maestro's performance of Bruckner's Fourth Symphony. "It was incredible," Skrowaczewski remembered. "He used a double orchestra. There were nine horns!"

Founded in 1882 and long considered by many to be the world's foremost orchestra, the Berlin Philharmonic derives its prestige in part from its roster of august conductors. Its first maestro was Hans von Bülow, notably associated with Liszt, Wagner, Brahms, and Tchaikovsky. He conducted the premieres of *Tristan und Isolde*, *Die Meistersinger*, the Fourth Symphony of Brahms, and Tchaikovsky's First Piano Concerto. The electrifying Austro-Hungarian conductor Arthur Nikisch, who followed von Bülow, led the Philharmonic for twenty-seven years and established the standard of excellence for future maestros. Before coming to the Berlin, he had been music director of the Boston Symphony Orchestra. Wilhelm Furtwängler succeeded Nikisch, and except for a seven-year postwar hiatus, he stayed with the orchestra until his death in 1954. Karajan succeeded Furtwängler and created unprecedented fame and wealth for the Philharmonic, leading it for a record thirty-four years until his death in 1989.[21]

The weight of the Philharmonic's formidable history did not deter Skrowaczewski from his program choices. In fact, the repertoire for his Philharmonic debut was notable for the challenges it presented the acclaimed ensemble. He opened with William Walton's relatively new *Variations on a Theme by Hindemith*, followed by the European premiere of Elliott Carter's Piano Concerto and Lutosławski's Concerto for Orchestra. It was risky to conduct an all-20th-century program for a debut with the Berlin Philharmonic, which at that time seldom played works by living composers. Although the orchestra was unfamiliar with the Walton and Lutosławski pieces, the work by Carter was the real challenge.

Carter's two-movement, twenty-five-minute concerto, composed in honor of Stravinsky's eighty-fifth birthday, employs "a concertino of three winds and four solo strings mediating between the individualized solo piano part and the orchestral mass."[22] American pianist Jacob Lateiner, who had performed the concerto with Skrowaczewski in Minneapolis after premiering it with the Boston Symphony, also gave the Berlin performance.

"It is by far the most difficult piece of music I have ever known," Skrowaczewski declared a week before he arrived in Berlin.[23] "It was on the basis of the splendid Minneapolis performance of the concerto, second of two so far worldwide," wrote *Time Music*, "that Carter asked Skrowaczewski to tackle [it in] Berlin."[24]

His debut engagement with the Berlin Philharmonic pleased Skrowaczewski:

> They may have played the Lutosławski, perhaps with him conducting, but it would have been a number of years earlier; they didn't know it. However, I knew this piece very well, so it went easily. The Walton was also no problem for them. For normal programs you generally would have three or four rehearsals maximum, but with this program I had five. I was very prepared with the

Carter, but it is a deadly score, just to read and remember it. The notation was crazy; instead of using triplet or quadruplet figures, he just used points. Some pages had hundreds of them (I think he later altered this notation, so it was easier to deal with). The Philharmonic worked wonderfully with quiet concentration and without any dissatisfaction about the music. The solo players in the concertino were terrific.

It is quite rare for me, but I recall that I was pleased with myself, almost proud of the fact that I came to this orchestra with this extremely difficult program, and I made a good impression, enough so that I was invited back. Karajan was not there, but Wolfgang Stresemann, the *orchesterintendant* (orchestra administrator), was on hand. He was a renowned figure with the Philharmonic, highly intelligent and an excellent musician. (His father, Gustav, was the German chancellor of the Weimar Republic and received the Nobel Peace Prize for his efforts in Germany's conciliation work after World War I.) Wolfgang was also a professional conductor. He fled Nazi Germany and settled in America. He was music director of the Toledo (Ohio) Symphony for several years before joining the Berlin Philharmonic. He knew a lot about composers and conductors.

I know that Wolfgang was impressed, because I met with him and other representatives from the Philharmonic. They wanted my advice about their future programming of contemporary music. They took me quite seriously, and for a while I was helping them the way Boulez helped Szell in matters of programming contemporary music. At the time they were presenting concerts like mine, that were all contemporary works. They asked me if I felt it was better to mix new music with more traditional pieces, and of course, I said yes.

After Berlin Skrowaczewski was off to Paris to guest conduct L'Orchestre National de France before returning home for a short tour and a subscription concert with his orchestra before heading to Carnegie Hall for the *St. Luke Passion* performance. The subscription concert was Skrowaczewski's first of two experiences working with cellist Jacqueline Du Pré. Only twenty-four years old when she first played in Minneapolis, Du Pré was already at the height of her short career. At age twenty-eight she was diagnosed with multiple sclerosis, which soon forced her to stop performing publicly. With Skrowaczewski she performed the Elgar Cello Concerto, which had established her fame as a recording artist in 1965.

"I was very impressed by her. Her sound was extremely beautiful, and her involvement in playing somehow did not destroy the overall 'classical' approach. It wasn't over-exaggerated," Skrowaczewski remembered. The following season Du Pré returned to Minneapolis to perform the Lalo Cello Concerto. "It was wonderful again," Skrowaczewski said, "but somehow I felt that maybe she was not herself. It gave me an uneasy feeling." Du Pré suffered a long, arduous decline in her health after her professional career ended. She died in 1987 at age forty-two, but her struggle helped to raise public awareness of the disease.[25]

Following the 1969 Du Pré concert Skrowaczewski and the orchestra performed the *Passion* to great effect in the St. Paul Cathedral. It was a warm-up for their New York premiere of the piece a week later. The night before the Carnegie Hall *Passion* concert they presented another performance in the hall featuring the New York premiere of Symphony no. 2 by Lutosławski, another of Skrowaczewski's Polish compatriots. The thirty-minute symphony, completed in 1967, is a striking exploration of the forces of a full orchestra. "Previously, Lutosławski mixed aleatoric elements into his compositions, but this symphony was the first time he used aleatory for an entire work," Skrowaczewski noted. "The novelty was the complete aleatoric treatment from beginning to end."

The orchestra had presented the work's U.S. premiere on the Du Pré concert in Minneapolis. One critic wrote that it evoked the sonorous worlds of Messiaen and Ives.[26] Skrowaczewski didn't agree with the comparisons: "At that time Symphony no. 2 was very avant-garde, but not of the reigning serial avant-garde. Lutosławski's language was completely his own." Skrowaczewski's inclusion of Debussy's *La Mer* on the program gave the audience an illuminating listening experience of two coloristic, innovative works from different epochs.

The Carnegie Hall dress rehearsal for the *St. Luke Passion* attracted a small New York audience comprised mostly of critics and interested musicians, including Robert Shaw, who was planning to perform the work with his Atlanta Symphony. In an article published in *The New York Times* two weeks before the *Passion* performance, Penderecki remarked that he didn't feel particularly connected to or influenced by another composer, but "if I am closer to any one composer than another in my intent and style, it is maybe György Ligeti—or to Toru Takemitsu."[27] He was quick to dismiss style and language as unimportant in composition. "What counts," he said, "is the amount and quality of information the work gives. Bach and Brahms used quite conservative styles for their times, but their works give exceptional information. I am using the word information in the cybernetics sense, you understand."[28] When *Newsweek* asked Penderecki why he chose the St. Luke text, he said, "Stylistically, it's the most beautiful. It has a broad poetic vision of Christ's suffering. But also it was one text that Bach didn't use. And I didn't want to offer more ground for comparison than I had to."[29]

On March 6, 1969, New Yorkers heard Penderecki's already-celebrated *St. Luke Passion* in a sold-out concert at Carnegie Hall. "At the end of Krzysztof Penderecki's *St. Luke Passion* last night in Carnegie Hall," wrote Schonberg, "there was a moment of silence. Then a crashing burst of applause. Then a couple of resonant, heartfelt boos. Then great applause, which drowned out the boos. Finally the composer made his appearance, and the hall erupted."[30] Bain Murray of the *Cleveland Sun Press* said, "One left the hall feeling musical history had been made and that a profoundly moving musical experience had occurred."[31]

The intensity of the audience's response stunned Skrowaczewski:

To this day I've never experienced such a reaction to a performance. I heard myriad concerts of Boston, New York, Philadelphia, etc., over the years, but all those experiences were not like what happened after the Penderecki that night in Carnegie Hall. This was a triumph. I think this achievement was largely attributed to it being the right piece at the right time.

It came after a period of heavy, crazy avant-garde in Europe and also in America. Heinrich Strobel, the renowned artistic director of the Sinfonieorchester Baden-Baden, told me that when they commissioned young composers they told them their pieces could be no longer than ten or twelve minutes—that's all the public would accept—and just one such piece on a concert.

Even after this heavy period of avant-garde music, there were always struggles programming new music. Much later, when I was conducting the Hallé Orchestra, Clive Smart, the general manager, would tell me to make a long pause after a contemporary piece if it opened the concert because that's when some of the public would show up! And he also warned me to not be surprised if people just got up and left if a contemporary piece was last on a program. And it really happened. At the New York Philharmonic it was especially pathetic because people were often leaving before the end of a concert and making noise, etc., when they didn't like a certain piece. Of course, in Minneapolis my programming included a few of these avant-garde works by composers such as Babbitt, Cage, Ligeti, and Arvo Pärt, who at that time wrote these crazy but wonderful pieces, a symphony only twelve minutes, a cello concerto not much longer. All these pieces were short. Yet in Minneapolis they were disappointing for the public. Some people even threatened to withdraw financial support for the orchestra. I answered dozens and dozens of complaint letters explaining why it was important to play these works; it took an enormous amount of my time. I remember spending some entire weekends with my secretary answering these letters. They weren't just short notes. I went into great detail explaining what was going on in the music world and how I believed performances of such pieces were necessary for the continuation of the development of music as an art and that Minneapolis must be a center for such work.

The year 1968 was really the culmination of [the] unrest of populations in countries all over the world: problems of communist propaganda, Mao's actions causing the Cultural Revolution in China, student riots in Paris and the change of government, the Soviet Union invading Czechoslovakia, and of course in the United States all the large protests against the Vietnam War at universities and in the streets. The world was in chaos.

So Penderecki was genuinely clever. He thought, "Well, this is the period; I'll write a work for an entire evening." And this was an extraordinary idea. It took courage for him to think that all of these rebellious youths and other people trapped in the chaos of the world would suddenly say, "Wait, listen, what is this music?" They wanted something big, long, not a few minutes of funny sounds [and then] it's over, then on to Brahms. The *Passion* at that time offered a place to go, so to speak, for the listeners to reflect and to perhaps heal. Its length and accessibility offered this to people, and they really responded. In looking back on the piece, I feel strongly about it in its historical context. Musically I like it; I respect it because it was really something completely new. There was nothing else like it at the time, and soon after, other composers, like Tavener in England and Henze in Germany, began creating longer similar works.

Critical response to the *St. Luke Passion* and to Skrowaczewski's leadership was glowing. "I had predicted months ago that this would be the most distinguished event of the season," said New York critic Alan Rich, "and I retract nothing.... The performance under Stanisław Skrowaczewski was in all respects the finest work that the conductor has done here, and enough in itself to move him into the front ranks."[32] Even the normally reserved Schonberg lauded the concert: "There can be nothing but praise for the work of Mr. Skrowaczewski, the Minnesota Orchestra, and various participants. He is a brilliant musician, and he had everything in the hollow of his busy hands."[33]

Critical assessment of the *Passion* as a composition varied. Bain Murray proclaimed that the piece "may well be the most important to be written since Stravinsky's *Symphony of Psalms* (1930)."[34] Schonberg remarked cautiously that the work cannot "stand many hearings, for the musical materials are not very strong, [but] at least it attempts a modern solution to an old problem [formulas of dissonant international modernism], and in many respects carries it off."[35] A week later, in a piece entitled "Romanticism Coming Up?" Schonberg continued his evaluation of the *Passion,* noting that "there is no denying the modernism of the score, and yet it does not sound modern.... There is hardly anything in it that, in one form or another, has not been heard in various other contemporary scores since 1950."[36] He regarded the work as a complete break from "post-Webern writing practiced by such exponents as Stockhausen, Xenakis, and a number of the Americans," but he also believed that it would not become a repertory piece.[37] Schonberg's concluding remarks were prophetic:

> [The] *Saint Luke Passion* may yet to turn out to be a significant work for
> another reason. It may be one of those transitional scores that lead the
> way toward a new approach. In this case the approach is away from the
> complexity of the post-serialists into something infinitely more direct. [The]
> audience at the Carnegie Hall concert may have been in on the birth of
> neoromanticism of the 1970s.[38]

During the 1970s Penderecki fully embraced his own neoromanticism and did not look back, as did various composers.

On the heels of Skrowaczewski's recent accomplishments as a conductor, he received an opportunity to revive his career as a composer.

Thomas Stacy, English hornist who joined the Minneapolis Symphony Orchestra in 1962, hadn't heard a note of Skrowaczewski's music, but he knew the conductor's reputation as a composer. A virtuoso on his instrument and one of the orchestra's woodwind stars, the twenty-nine-year-old musician was disappointed by the dearth of solo literature for his instrument. Skrowaczewski said, "He begged me, 'Please, we don't have anything for English horn, only Donizetti for five minutes. Will you write a concerto for me?' He was such a wonderful young player that I said, 'Yes, Tom, but when?'"

Consumed with conducting, Skrowaczewski realized that composing would be difficult after a hiatus of nearly fifteen years. He had completed—and discarded—his last serious composition, the Fourth Symphony, in 1954. He faced a dilemma:

> I was, as always, writing very slowly and rejecting lots of ideas. I couldn't create music that pleased me. I was repeating myself in the mid-fifties. I realized that if I wanted to change my so-called language, I would have to spend a lot of time building a completely different way of expressing myself. When more and more conducting opportunities came to me, I ended my serious composing.

By 1968, however, his dormant creative urges surfaced: "The idea of writing a concerto for Tom brought up my childhood desires that composition was something important that I needed back in my life. Something was lacking otherwise." That same childhood curiosity played a role in bringing this new work to life. After Skrowaczewski agreed to the project, he spent time with Stacy after rehearsals, experimenting with the sound possibilities of the English horn. Stacy recalled this early development of ideas for the concerto:

> I remember the first time we got together on the stage of Northrop Auditorium. I mentioned that I liked the moment in the Goossens Oboe Concerto when a gong sounds and the oboe picks up some of the overtones and vibrations when the gong leaves off. So we experimented with that idea. I also remember that Stan told me he had done a film score in Poland [and] that everyone thought he used very progressive electronics, but really he had just recorded some sounds inside the piano. So we started experimenting with playing the English horn into the piano. We discovered that if I played a low note—where all the sound and air comes out of the end of the instrument—into the soundboard of the piano, and a pianist holds down the sustaining pedal, it creates a fantastic sound!

"The most novel effects in the piece that Tom and I searched for and [that] I eventually wrote were the multichords," Skrowaczewski recalled. "We tried to find a certain combination of notes through various alternate fingerings and manipulation of fingerings and blowing techniques. These multichords ultimately became very important in the piece." Multichords or multiphonics—the effect of single-note instruments playing two or more notes simultaneously—creates a harmonic interval or chord if three or more notes are sounded. Luciano Berio first used the technique most notably with a wind instrument in his *Sequenza* (1958) for solo flute. Skrowaczewski was the first composer to use this technique on English horn in a formal, extended concerto.

Stacy recalled that some of Skrowaczewski's explorations led to compromises:

Later on, when he was beginning to compose the piece, he came over to my house, and we experimented further with some of his ideas. I remember he wrote an outrageously high note in one place. While he was there I could play it, but then after he left I couldn't play it at all! I decided it wouldn't work. I called him up right away and said that the note wouldn't work, so he took it out.

Taking notes out and actually throwing away pages of music has always been part of Skrowaczewski's compositional process. His long absence from composing, combined with his fastidious approach, made the process of creating the concerto especially arduous. A week before the concerto's premiere he told the *Minneapolis Tribune* that after more than a fourteen-year lapse in composing, "it seemed impossible; I almost gave up, but kept struggling."[39]

By June 1969 he nearly had completed and programmed the work for the orchestra's upcoming season. He soon changed his mind, however, and decided that he disliked the composition. Unfortunately his conducting schedule allowed him no time for revising it, and prospects for a 1969 premiere seemed unlikely.

Skrowaczewski spent most of July in New Mexico with the Santa Fe Opera, preparing for the U.S. premiere of *The Devils of Loudun*, Penderecki's new opera. At the end of August he was scheduled to begin rehearsals for Tchaikovsky's *Eugene Onegin* at the Metropolitan Opera in preparation for his New York opera debut in mid-September. But it was not to be.

Skrowaczewski recalled, "On the eve of going to New York, Rudolph Bing of the Met called me and said, 'Don't come; there's been a strike of all the unions of musicians and all other workers at the Met, seven unions combined, and we may not have a season at all.' The strike lasted four months, and I lost *Onegin*."

He had reserved nearly six weeks in his schedule for his work with the Met, and it was too late for him to take any replacement engagements. Upon learning of the cancellation, Stacy immediately went to Skrowaczewski. "Aha! *Now* you have time to compose the piece!" he remarked. "This comment was so nice and direct coming from him," Skrowaczewski remembered.

For the first time in twenty years he had an extended open period that gave him a chance for a fresh start on the concerto: "I threw everything I had done on the piece into the garbage can. That first, terrible effort was something I had to go through in order to 'get in shape,' apparently, after many years of not writing. The second effort was an entirely new experience: ideas and structures began to fit into place, and composing became fun."[40]

Skrowaczewski requires a quiet working atmosphere, and Krystyna often used his extended absences to tackle house projects. Anticipating her husband's long stay in New York, she had scheduled some remodeling work for their Wayzata home. Skrowaczewski escaped the cacophony of hammers and drills by occasionally composing at friends' homes. The retreats helped his focus, and in three weeks he had produced a new eighteen-minute concerto. Refining the orchestration took another week.[41]

"I am fascinated by opportunities in composition to open up the orchestra and expose its insides," Skrowaczewski said.[42] To that end, he used instruments carefully; for example, to highlight the English horn he excluded all woodwinds except for three flutes. "Strings play not as sections but as persons," Skrowaczewski noted. "Much of the time each player is allotted different musical material."[43] He also used a full complement of percussion instruments including vibraphone, conga and bongo drums, and temple blocks. By today's standards this instrumentation is fairly typical, but in 1969 it was seen as a somewhat exotic use of percussion.

Wrote Edwin Bolton of the *Minneapolis Tribune*: "The score is light, open, and lean; there are few *tuttis*."[44] At the premiere Skrowaczewski described the piece as "mysterious, moody, and weird" but added that "wit pops out some places like champagne."[45]

"In a sense," Skrowaczewski later reflected, "I wanted to depart from my former language of avant-garde: clusters, aleatoric devices, and electronic music. So I used a lot of devices as a little joke, to make the piece humorous and something new to me, almost shocking—like the idea that Tom would blow into the piano and get a sound almost like a trombone. This piece unlocked a new language of mine: not a style but a language, which continued in my future works."

Skrowaczewski was inspired by new techniques that Stacy could use in the concerto, such as the multiphonic fingerings that enabled him to play multiple notes simultaneously. He also looked to the past:

> The spiritual climax of the finale breaks into a chorale of four triads, each of three different notes, so that all twelve tones of the octave are used. The choice of these chords is such that any order of them gives the B-A-C-H pattern—a kind of homage to Bach. Nevertheless, the work does not proceed from any particular school or "ism." Whatever aspects of twelve-tone technique it has absorbed are almost accidental, for they function as the by-product of expressive development of melody.[46]

The composer was pleased with his work and with the recognition it would soon receive, but what mattered more to him was the fact that it reignited the first passion of his creative life, composing. Even before the concerto's November 1969 world premiere in Minneapolis, Skrowaczewski was already looking ahead to future projects: "I am thinking of writing a series of 'little concertos' involving instruments for which there is not much literature. For example, how about a concerto for four trombones?"[47]

Skrowaczewski's composing career could not compete with his work as a conductor. During the next fourteen years he wrote only sporadically, composing four orchestral works and two chamber pieces. Nevertheless, this period—which peaked in 1985 with two world premieres a week apart (with the Philadelphia and Minnesota orchestras, respectively)—represented a major step in Skrowaczewski's reemergence as a composer of international renown. From 1985 on, he composed more consistently, and by the 1990s he was less reluctant to conduct his compositions. Although he would never be satisfied with the balance between conducting and composing, the "black spot" in his artistic life had vanished.

SEVENTEEN

BEATING THE DRUM

I'm still optimistic for art. Even the regimes of Hitler and Stalin could not kill it. And maybe art shall have from now on a special destiny: to save us from the technological man of the future. Only if our soul is dead will art be dead.

—Stanisław Skrowaczewski, 1969

The 1969 strike at the Metropolitan Opera gave Skrowaczewski the composer a month free from conducting assignments. Before the strike, however, when he first began sketching the English Horn Concerto, several major conducting engagements forced him to confront the nearly impossible task of balancing his two artistic personae.

Before heading to New Mexico for his major summer engagement—conducting the U.S. premiere of Penderecki's opera *The Devils of Loudun*—Skrowaczewski led multiple concerts featuring pianist Van Cliburn. After performing the Liszt Piano Concerto no. 2 with the New York Philharmonic at the year-old Garden State Arts Center amphitheater, Skrowaczewski and Cliburn collaborated with the Philadelphia Orchestra in a performance of Rachmaninoff's Second Piano Concerto. Skrowaczewski has a lifelong aversion to the Russian composer's music, but the record crowd of thirty thousand at The Robin Hood Dell couldn't get enough of Cliburn's ultraromantic interpretation of the Rachmaninoff concerto.[1]

Eleven years after his much-celebrated triumph at the Moscow Tchaikovsky Piano Competition, Cliburn still held enormous audience appeal. *Symphonie fantastique* opened the concert, and Cliburn's Rachmaninoff was reserved for the finale. Traditionally, a concerto would be placed in the middle or at the beginning of a program—this coveted position in the program signified Cliburn's popularity. The "musical love-in," as one writer called it, went into high gear after the concerto, when a young woman ran to the foot of the stage. Hundreds of young people followed, including the "hips with their Ben Franklin glasses," and Cliburn played a thirty-minute recital as an encore, although the orchestra was long gone.[2]

For his second Dell concert Skrowaczewski conducted a work that sparked a different reaction. "People either walked to the exits, sat in stunned silence, or listened with total fascination as the two movements of the [Lutosławski Symphony no. 2] unfolded," reported Philadelphia's *The Evening Bulletin*.[3] Skrowaczewski was continuing his advocacy for his compatriot's innovative compositions. Personally he was not fond of the piece, but he believed that it represented an important development in Lutosławski's compositional language and in the overall world of composition. Several months later, when Skrowaczewski programmed the work for his second appearance with the Berlin Philharmonic in 1970, one member of the audience did more than merely walk out, as the maestro recalled:

> The first movement, as its title *Hésitant* suggests, has constant breaks. Sometimes the orchestra plays for one or two minutes, and then there is silence for four or ten seconds. Some silences are as long as twenty-five seconds! You can imagine how challenging that was for listeners. I couldn't stand it myself, so I shortened some of them. *Direct*, the second movement, runs straight through for fifteen minutes without any pauses. It's a complex score and a novelty. I didn't like this symphony at all, but I found it fascinating as an example of what a gifted composer can do with complete aleatoric technique. When I later played the work with the Berlin Philharmonic, a man in the audience apparently found the music and all the silences very irritating. During one of the pauses, his loud, drunken voice shouted, "What is it? Is it music, or is it shit?" There was an uproar. He was shouting, and then the public shouted for him to shut up. The police were called. It was a mess.

> We stopped playing when we heard this ruckus, and for a few moments I didn't know what to do, [and] neither did the musicians. We were waiting to see if it would subside before we started the next section. Then I just looked at the concertmaster, Michel Schwalbé, my old friend (who was born in Poland), and I said, "Michel, let's play." He agreed, and we started where we left off. Meanwhile, this drunken man was taken out of the hall. At the next break with silence in the piece, I didn't stop (as Lutosławski instructs). I *did* stop right before the second movement, and the audience was silent. When we finished the symphony, the applause was enormous! I realized that I made the right decision to continue the piece after the incident; otherwise, it would have been the end of the concert.

If some members of the Dell audience suffered through the hesitations and complexities of Lutosławski's Second Symphony, the next night's program offered some of the most emotionally direct music in orchestral literature: Mahler's Symphony no. 2 (*Resurrection*). The ninety-minute, five-movement epic composition for orchestra, large chorus, soprano and contralto soloists, and backstage and offstage brass, is a conducting tour de force. Wrote James Felton of *The Evening Bulletin*: "Skrowaczewski's achievement was nothing short of genius."[4] Perhaps Felton's praise was heightened by the overwhelming effect that the Mahler Second generally has on listeners and by the fact that it had never been heard at the Dell's outdoor amphitheater. Remarkably, Skrowaczewski had conducted the Mahler Second only once before—three months earlier, with the Minnesota Orchestra. He led all three diverse, complicated Dell concerts after having only four rehearsals: one each for the first two programs and two for the Mahler.

During a summer of dramatic events ranging from Neil Armstrong's first step on the moon to the horrific murders by the Charles Manson "family" to the iconic Woodstock music festival, it would seem—as *Newsweek* described it—that the U.S. premiere on August 14, 1969, of Penderecki's titillating opera was a child of its era:

> *The Devils of Loudun* came to Santa Fe, New Mexico, last week with a stage full of young nuns simmering with lust and autoeroticism and in general disporting themselves so blasphemously that superstitious souls might have wondered if this American premiere of Krzysztof Penderecki's opera about erotic diabolism in the 17th-century church might not call down the wrath of God.[5]

At its world premiere two months earlier in Hamburg, *The Devils of Loudun* received poor reviews for being "too subservient to the script and for a general lack of musical eloquence."[6] Penderecki responded by reworking and expanding the opera's ending. He created the libretto based on Aldous Huxley's 1952 book *The Devils of Loudun* and John Whiting's 1961 play *The Devils*, which is based on Huxley's text. Set in 17th-century Loudun, France, it is based on eyewitness accounts of the public execution of a priest wrongly accused of having sex with several nuns. When the priest declines to become the spiritual advisor for the nuns' convent, the prioress—who is in love with him—becomes obsessed. In an effort to excuse her sexual appetite, she tells clerical and government officials that she has been "violated" by a devil that looks exactly like the priest; her fellow nuns echo the claim. Eventually the nuns' accusations are judged to be false, but because the priest is disliked by his peers and the government, he is tried anyway and executed.[7]

Thematically the work resembles Arthur Miller's play *The Crucible*, which also was published in 1952; both works evoke the mass hysteria of the McCarthy "Red scare" era. In the context of the late 1960s, however, some individuals may have perceived Penderecki's *Devils* to be an allegory of sexual liberation, distrust of government, and societal malaise.[8]

In late July 1969 Skrowaczewski arrived in Santa Fe, New Mexico. He had only three weeks in which to assemble an eighty-piece orchestra, chorus, and cast for two performances of the work, the first being its U.S. premiere. The fastidious Penderecki came to New Mexico for rehearsals still angry over bad reviews of the faulty Hamburg production. Mounting the piece with the Santa Fe Opera Company was particularly nerve-wracking because Penderecki altered the opera's ending while it was in production. "He was changing things on the spot," Skrowaczewski remembered. "Day after day, music was sent to New York to produce new parts, and two days later I was rehearsing new music for this opera." One new "addition" resulted in the most powerful and dramatic downbeat Skrowaczewski ever conducted.

Penderecki was particularly dissatisfied with the opera's third act. He made changes at every rehearsal, continually trying to achieve brutal percussion effects using chains, anvils, and large blocks of wood played with hammers. "But still," Skrowaczewski recalled, "Penderecki said, 'It is not enough. Louder, louder!' He simply wanted an enormous sound."

At the second dress rehearsal with the full choir and cast, a powerful storm arose swiftly from the valleys below the hilltop site of the open-air opera house. Some players had to move farther inside the pit to avoid the downpour, but the rehearsal continued. Skrowaczewski was rehearsing the infamous percussion downbeat when Penderecki asked to hear it again. Suddenly, lightning flashed and a massive clap of thunder boomed, perfectly synchronized with the maestro's downbeat. "It was amazing," Skrowaczewski said. "I turned to Penderecki and asked him in Polish, 'Is it good?' 'Yes!' he shouted, and almost in unison we both said, 'This is it! This is it!'"

When the full force of the storm hit, everything halted. Set decorations, some multitiered, came crashing down under the gusting winds. People were shouting and screaming. "It was absolute pandemonium," Skrowaczewski said. The orchestra and chorus fled the stage and headed to the basement for protection. Fortunately there were no injuries. The choir, comprised mostly of young Catholic women, had been offended by what it perceived as the opera's sacrilegious content, which involved misdeeds of priests, including a love scene in a tub. Skrowaczewski overheard some of the choir members whispering, "You see, this is the voice of God showing his disapproval. This opera won't happen!"

Nevertheless, the opera was performed, and most major American newspapers sent critics to Santa Fe for its U.S. premiere. If the assembled critics thought Penderecki's opera would resemble his *St. Luke Passion*—a notion even Skrowaczewski predicted to the Minneapolis press—they were mistaken. Penderecki had reverted to his avant-garde language of the early 1960s for this three-act epic. His libretto bothered most reviewers as much as did the effects of *glissandos*, tone clusters, and choral shrieks and moans. (Skrowaczewski described to *Newsweek* a "scene where the chorus duplicates the sound of breaking wind when the demons announce their presence in the prioress's bowels as 'obscene noise.'")[9]

Lighting director Georg Schrieber had an unexpected "duet" at the premiere. As if on cue, reported *Time*, "precisely at the moment when one of Penderecki's characters shout[s], 'God is dead!' there came a clap of thunder, and a storm enveloped the theater."[10] Just over a year old, the outdoor theater was open on both sides, forcing some audience members to huddle at the rear in order to avoid the torrential rain.

Reviewers generally praised Skrowaczewski's work, with the exception of the *Los Angeles Times*, which said that he concentrated "more on producing clear sounds and precise phrases than on communicating emotions."[11] (Many reviewers identified him as the conductor of the "Minnesota Symphony" or of the Minneapolis Symphony.) Penderecki remembered the event as a "fantastic performance," and the audience gave a tumultuous ovation that mirrored the musical and nonmusical cacophony it had endured. Several months after the performances, Skrowaczewski wrote about the opera in a letter to a colleague: "The premiere went well and certainly was an interesting event for everyone. Personally, however, I was to a certain extent disappointed with the music, and I don't think this work can be compared to the author's *St. Luke Passion,* nor will it be as durable as the other."[12]

Of his three operas, *The Devils of Loudun* became Penderecki's most popular, and it has had many productions in Europe and the United States.[13] In 2007 a DVD of the original 1969 Staatsoper Hamburg production was released.

The forty-seven-year-old Skrowaczewski opened his tenth season with the Minnesota Orchestra in October 1969 with a commissioned work for electronic tape and orchestra by American composer Mel Powell. The Women's Association of the Minnesota Orchestra (WAMSO) commissioned the work in honor of its 20th anniversary. Skrowaczewski also revisited Berlioz's *Symphonie fantastique,* a nod to his Northrop Auditorium debut with the orchestra a decade earlier.

Since 1960 Skrowaczewski had devoted most of his time and energy to developing the ensemble, and the success of his efforts was evident. The orchestra could perform effectively a wider range of repertoire than ever before, the number of musicians had increased, and a year-round season was imminent. The ensemble had earned a solid national reputation—often favorably compared to orchestras of New York and Philadelphia—and certainly it was viewed as a leader among orchestras in such cities as Pittsburgh, San Francisco, and Detroit.

During the late 1960s the state of American symphony orchestras was a frequent topic of arts coverage in the media. The Big Five commissioned a study in 1969 to examine the financial issues facing U.S. orchestras. While smaller, struggling orchestras considered merging (the Buffalo and Rochester Philharmonics were one such example), major orchestras seemingly were doing well in terms of earned income from ticket sales, tours, recordings, broadcast fees, and the like. (One article cited an increase of ninety-two percent since 1965.)[14] Unfortunately, earned income could not match expenses, such as paying musicians year-round salaries and covering the rising costs of soloists and conductors. Recordings, once a profitable item for major orchestras, became more expensive to produce because of new rules regarding overtime pay and length of recording sessions that were established in 1969 by a contract with the American Federation of Musicians. High deficits loomed for a number of orchestras, and even the Chicago Symphony and Cleveland Orchestra were forced to tap their endowments.[15]

However, both *Time* and *The New York Times* singled out the Minnesota Orchestra as a beacon of hope. When the Ford Foundation offered the orchestra $2 million in 1966 if a matching $4 million were raised, the MOA responded with a campaign chaired by Ken Dayton that generated $10 million by 1969. Establishing endowed chairs for the principal players, another Dayton initiative, was touted as a Minnesota innovation. Rotating the position of MOA president and making frequent changes in board membership brought in fresh business perspectives and also expanded community investment in the organization. Pride was another key factor. Dayton told *The New York Times,* "The success of our campaign was the result of our conclusion some years ago that with Stanisław Skrowaczewski as our conductor we wanted to make this orchestra one of the world's greatest, and the community came to our support."[16]

Financial troubles weren't the only challenges that plagued symphony orchestras during the late 1960s. The issue of relevance also became a media topic, fueled by comments from Leonard Bernstein published in *The New York Times*. In an article entitled "Conductor Thinks Symphony Is Out of Date," Bernstein likened the symphony orchestra to a museum, partly out of his frustration over the lack of contemporary works to champion.[17] "The last important symphony I can think of is Stravinsky's Symphony in Three Movements, which was written in 1945. Since the war, there has been virtually nothing important of a symphonic nature."[18]

Bernstein's statements may have revealed more about him than they did about the state of contemporary music at the time, but his comments were widely quoted. Much to his frustration, he was misquoted as saying that "the symphony is dead." This error was compounded by a 1968 interview published in *Time* in which Bernstein reiterated his conviction that the "symphonic form is dead," although he also explained that the masterpieces that sprang from it would live for hundreds of years.[19]

Musical America named Skrowaczewski "Musician of the Month" in its September 1969 issue, which featured a cover story on him. When the interviewer raised the issue of the difficulties facing orchestras, Skrowaczewski referenced Bernstein and the *Time* article with his typical philosophical bent:

> I think there is a big panic over this. You remember three years ago on the front of *Time* magazine it said "Is God Dead?" Now this is very exciting and interesting. It may not be true, but it stirs intellectual people to talk about it, to discuss it, to worry about it. It was the same when Leonard Bernstein said, "The symphony is dead"—or words to that effect, I don't want to misquote him. Everyone gets very disturbed about it. But this is like everything else in life; it goes up and down. If we are in a down period now—and it is true that ticket sales have dropped over the last five years—then we will come up again. But the thing that should be accepted in this country is that up or down, the orchestras should go *on*, like schools or roads or housing. We don't question the existence of these things. And the existence of the orchestra ought not to be in question.[20]

In an interview with John Harvey in fall 1970, Skrowaczewski discussed the media's obsessive desire to question the value of the symphony orchestra and its role as curator of masterworks. His statement makes a timeless case for the continued propagation of musical treasures:

> The great works of the past *do* have relevance to the present. Harold Schonberg of *The New York Times* states that [the] "relevance" concept is constantly cropping up, though I for one entirely fail to see its relevance. Often it is made by people who seem to have little identification with music. Those people do not go around saying that Rembrandt has no relevance today, or Shakespeare, or Proust. It is only against music that the charge is leveled, and

there generally is a corollary to the effect that the only music with "relevance" today is rock or one of its derivatives.

And that, I think, is nonsense. The great music of the past has, in these crazy times, more "relevance" than ever before. It is a healing force, a restorative, and it operates on several levels. It is, on one level, an idealization of what mankind can aspire to. It is, on another, the ultimate triumph of logic. And it is needed today more than ever before. Immersion in great music means contact with extremely powerful minds, minds that worked toward an ideal. Listening to the music of Bach, of Mozart and Haydn, of Beethoven and Schubert, means becoming involved with ethical as well as tonal and aesthetic ideals. One emerges from the experience a better man, a calmer man. This is not escape. It is rejuvenation.[21]

Responding to the notion that orchestras should abandon the standard repertoire to avoid becoming outdated, Skrowaczewski explained the differences between his musical predilections and those of some of his contemporaries:

To throw out two hundred years of tradition and say, "We will have none of it"—this will not work. I want to show audiences not the gaps in music but the bridges. There are very few conductors of my age—they are either much older or younger, even just three or four years younger. This makes a difference. Even musicians who were three years younger than me—eleven or twelve when I was fifteen—were not old enough when the war was over to remember life as it had been before. They had a totally different outlook—in politics, in music, in morals. I want, as much as possible, to bridge the gap.[22]

Although Skrowaczewski embraced the 20th century and thrived in its milieu, he is in many ways a conductor who belongs to the generation preceding his own. After Mahler's death in 1911, the 20th century produced few true conductor-composers, and the new century so far can claim even fewer such artists. Many conductors who predated Skrowaczewski's generation had substantial compositional training and wrote or arranged works.

Although Skrowaczewski does not emulate the tyrannical behavior of some maestros from an earlier era—the idea of him having a tantrum on the podium is inconceivable—his intense self-discipline brings a businesslike, task-oriented approach to rehearsals, a characteristic associated with past conducting titans. In earlier stages of his career, this self-discipline sometimes impaired his ability to communicate his feelings to musicians and audiences.

Perhaps Skrowaczewski's most salient "foot in the past" is his skill as an orchestra builder. While many of his contemporaries were moving from one position to another, Skrowaczewski focused on improving his orchestra and its circumstances, and tending to the myriad details, musical and nonmusical, which that effort required. Although the era of the long-term rule of a music director essentially ended by the late 1960s, he was committed to Minnesota for the "long haul." After Szell's death, only Ormandy and the Philadelphia Orchestra remained as models of an earlier time.

Pianist Leon Fleisher, who began a conducting career in 1967, worked with many of the great 20th-century conductors, including Pierre Monteux and Szell. He believes that Skrowaczewski bridges two eras of maestros:

> Skrowaczewski is a holdover and a throwback, both in the best sense of the terms. Back in the first half of the 20th century, conductors were tyrants, and that was one of the ways they maintained authority and respect. The other was the fact that they knew so damn much. They had come up from the bottom rung, from third assistant choral director in a fourth-rate German opera house, working their way up until they knew just about everything because they had had the experience. Then came Bernstein, who was not only a great musician with extraordinary gifts but also was a totally different kind of personality, one who loved everyone and in return needed love. Until then, all [that] conductors needed was respect. They certainly didn't need anyone's love. But Lenny turned that around. To be a successful conductor you could no longer tyrannize the orchestra. That was a wonderful thing; the orchestra no longer played out of fear but out of respect and affection. And Skrowaczewski was a man who had the authority of the old school because he came up a similar ladder of experience, and just instinctively, as a gentleman and as a man of integrity, he was also a conductor of the new school. One had enormous affection as well as respect for him.

A seismic shift in leadership of American orchestras occurred in the late 1960s. Bernstein, following a celebrated but relatively short tenure of eleven years, resigned from the New York Philharmonic in 1969. Erich Leinsdorf left the Boston Symphony the same year, and with Jean Martinon's departure in 1968, the Chicago Symphony was also without a music director. By the end of 1968 Szell told the Cleveland Orchestra of his impending retirement, and his death in 1970 accelerated the search for a successor. The year 1970 also witnessed the departures of Josef Krips and Max Rudolf from their respective posts with the San Francisco and Cincinnati symphonies. "Never has the American symphony establishment been in such a state of flux and subject to so much speculation," wrote critic John Harvey at the start of 1969.[23] Skrowaczewski became the subject of some of that speculation.

By the late 1960s he was poised to enter another stage of his conducting career. He had achieved national recognition as an orchestra builder and as a gifted interpreter of varied repertoire. His management, both in Europe (Glotz) and in the United States (Wilford), was among the most prominent and, in the case of Wilford, the most influential in America. Skrowaczewski long had had a strong reputation as a guest conductor in Europe, but during the late 1960s he frequented the more elite European podiums, such as those of Berlin and Vienna. He had emerged as a "player" on the international scene. Then in his mid-forties, still young by conductor standards, he already had a decade of experience as head of a major American orchestra.

Few conductors of the titan generation born in the late 1880s were still alive in 1968. They included Stokowski, Szell, Klemperer, Ansermet, and Münch as well as

Ormandy and Sir John Barbirolli (both born in 1899). The next generation, including Karajan, Solti, Leinsdorf, Giulini, and Bernstein, all born before 1920, had established themselves as major international figures. But youth and podium personality, largely driven by Bernstein's enormous success, became the wave of the future for the leadership of American orchestras. His immense musical talent was evident to all, but the "extras" he brought to his role as music director of the New York Philharmonic set the standard for what American musical management and, to a certain extent, what the public expected of a conductor.

In an article published after Bernstein announced his impending retirement from the Philharmonic, Schonberg described the situation:

> Presumably the New York Philharmonic will be looking for certain things in its new conductor. Bernstein has set the pattern. The new conductor will have to have glamour, youth, personality, and projection. Good looks and sex appeal will have to be included in the package. Flair for conducting also will help. I am not being cynical. Box office considerations loom high in any unsubsidized orchestra that has a budget and a schedule as big as the Philharmonic's; and all things being equal, the Philharmonic is going to be forced to select a box office draw. This may not be the way things should be, but in the United States it happens to be the way they are.[24]

The shift from the generally accepted image of a conductor as an elder statesman in the mode of Toscanini, Koussevitzky, and Bruno Walter to that of a youthful figure occurred, not coincidently, with the development of the so-called absentee music director. With the advent of the year-round season, the workload of a music director became an overwhelming responsibility for some. Leinsdorf cited the problem as his primary reason for resigning from the Boston Symphony. If orchestras wanted to retain their music directors, now they had to demand less time from them. Such freedom was a relief to some music directors, allowing them to do more guest conducting; others who possessed the necessary stamina could split themselves between two orchestras. One of the most striking examples, which ultimately did not work, was Seiji Ozawa's simultaneous directorship of the San Francisco and Boston symphonies, which he maintained for four years before relinquishing his West Coast podium.

After the announcement of Bernstein's retirement from the Philharmonic, Szell was chosen to serve as the ensemble's music advisor and senior guest conductor during the search for Bernstein's successor. All guest-conducting appearances with the Philharmonic were considered "unofficial public auditions" for the music director post.[25] Skrowaczewski was a potential contender on a list that included Boulez, Colin Davis, Carlo Maria Giulini, Ozawa, Claudio Abbado, Lorin Maazel and a few others.

"Skrowaczewski garners few bets because he is solidly entrenched in Minneapolis, because he has yet to establish a far-reaching glamour image, and because he leans too far toward the modern repertory," wrote Martin Bernheimer.[26] "Skrowaczewski is considered a very long shot," Schonberg said. "In romantic music he is apt to be bleak and analytical (the same is reported about Boulez)."[27] Perhaps Schonberg was surprised when the Philharmonic ultimately named Boulez as Bernstein's heir, once again following the long-established unwritten tradition of hiring music directors whose personalities differ from their immediate predecessors.

Although Skrowaczewski's name surfaced as a possible replacement for Leinsdorf, it was mentioned more frequently in association with the Cleveland Orchestra. The possibility of Skrowaczewski replacing Szell was not far-fetched. He was a regular guest with that esteemed orchestra, and his appearances were consistently well received by musicians and reviewers. But it was not to be. Cleveland's choice was American conductor Maazel, a gifted violinist with an interest in composition and a rare example of a conducting prodigy. By age eleven he had conducted Toscanini's NBC Symphony in a performance that garnered much praise from the grand maestro.

By the early 1970s America's elite orchestras had secured their new conductors. Ozawa went to Boston, where he stayed for twenty-nine years. After a decade with Cleveland, Maazel was replaced by Christoph von Dohnányi, who remained for eighteen years. Solti went to the Chicago Symphony in 1969 and stayed until 1991. The New York Philharmonic installed three music directors during the thirty years following Bernstein's departure: Boulez, Mehta, and Kurt Masur, respectively. After Ormandy retired from the Philadelphia Orchestra in 1980, Riccardo Muti led that ensemble for a dozen years before Wolfgang Sawallisch took over. From the mid-1960s through the 1980s, Skrowaczewski's frequent guest appearances and tours with the Philadelphia Orchestra made him an unofficial principal guest conductor. Ormandy occasionally mentioned to Skrowaczewski that someday he would like to see him officially connected with the Philadelphians.

If there were a period in his career when Skrowaczewski might have moved to another major orchestra for an extended tenure, the late 1960s would have been the time. That it didn't happen gave Skrowaczewski little cause for concern because he was still in the throes of developing his own orchestra. When a 1969 Paris interviewer broached the subject of his leaving Minneapolis if the opportunity arose, Skrowaczewski replied: "I'm not saying I would never consider taking another orchestra if it were offered, but I honestly do not feel my work in Minneapolis is yet completed. Guest performances with big orchestras are thrilling, but building an orchestra of your own and watching it develop is as satisfying as raising a child."[28]

A month later, having completed a European tour conducting top orchestras in Berlin, Munich, London, Paris, and Helsinki, he stepped to the podium in Duluth, Minnesota, to lead his orchestra in a run-out concert. He told the *Minneapolis Star* that there wasn't "a bit of a step-down from the quality he had just experienced overseas. In these days of roving maestros, [Skrowaczewski said] this experience proved the virtue of permanency in conducting posts. Orchestras can't play well and consistently without it."[29]

Four decades later, in 2009, Skrowaczewski reflected on the factors that kept him in Minneapolis:

> I had several ideas in my head at that time, but I just didn't think it was the right moment for me to leave. I was guest conducting outstanding orchestras

around the world, which was satisfying, as was building my own orchestra. It was also a period of increasing conflicts with unions, management, and the business side of things. I was trying to protect the quality of the orchestra from various forces. I knew that if I went to another orchestra I would be dealing with the same issues, but starting anew, it would be worse. But the most important factor was the prospect of a new concert hall. I knew that the fruit of my work with the organization would eventually be forgotten, but a concert hall would really make a difference to overall history and growth. It had been the struggle of others before: Doráti, Mitropoulos, Ormandy, etc. This goal was much more important to me than leaving for another orchestra, so I never actively pursued one.

Late fall 1969 and early winter 1970 witnessed two births for Skrowaczewski. His English Horn Concerto was premiered in November, and his second son, Nicholas, was born in January.

Star power accompanied the Minneapolis program that featured his concerto's world premiere. Isaac Stern performed Bruch's Concerto for Violin no. 1 and Mozart's Adagio and Rondo. Even with such a popular soloist and concerto on the program, Skrowaczewski's new work was not overshadowed. Thomas Stacy's virtuosity and musical delivery saw to that, as did Skrowaczewski's unique orchestration and the fresh sounds he created.

Critics were intrigued. After describing the various techniques and effects used in the piece, such as multiphonic fingerings, which preoccupied his listening experience, John Harvey wrote: "All of this may be just another case in the current epidemic of phonephilia among composers, but knowing Skrowaczewski's serious approach to music, I suspect there is more to it than meets the ear initially."[30] Another critic agreed, stating that the "materials were picked as part of an overall design," exploiting tonal characteristics and revealing "little-known capacities."[31] The conversational aspects between soloist and orchestra were praised for creating moods ranging from "dry and austere to warm and humorous."[32]

One Minneapolis patron found no humor in the work. At intermission she stalked to the foot of the stage and got the attention of timpanist Robert Tweedy. "It is obscene!" she declared. "It looks like Stacy is imitating making love." Apparently the image of Stacy placing the bell of his English horn into the piano's sounding board, causing sympathetic vibrations in the piano strings when he played, created a disturbing symbolism for this listener.

Skrowaczewski the perfectionist was pleased with the efforts of his wonderful soloist. The day after the premiere, a case of specialty wines arrived at Stacy's house, a thank-you gift from his maestro.

Skrowaczewski fulfilled the request of one critic who had hoped his concerto would receive more performances. In spring he took the piece to New York for the Minnesota

Orchestra's annual Carnegie Hall appearance. He repeated the program format, but this time the big-name violin soloist was Szeryng and the second concerto was by Bartók. Even today a conductor rarely directs his composition with his orchestra and soloist. Thus the concert generated curiosity, especially because Skrowaczewski was not known as a composer.

Schonberg, characteristically blunt, criticized the work as trying to be modern when "the composer simply does not think modern. [Skrowaczewski] used certain contemporary devices in a romantic manner. The music not only refused to gel, it also dissolved into a kind of amorphous mass."[33] But he admitted there was interest in the exotic sounds that Stacy produced and in Stacy himself: "He must be the Heifetz, or maybe the Kreisler, of the English horn."[34] Schonberg disliked Skrowaczewski's interpretation of the Schumann Fourth Symphony, which concluded the concert ("unsettling—stop-and-go"). However, he conceded: "But of one thing there could be no doubt. Mr. Skrowaczewski has made the Minneapolis Orchestra into one of America's greatest ensembles; and whatever reservations there could be to the interpretation, there could be none about the manner in which it was delivered."[35] His fine tribute to Skrowaczewski just missed giving the orchestra's marketing department a gem of a quote: it was marred by the wrong name for the ensemble.

Schonberg's criticism not withstanding, Skrowaczewski had structured the work deftly and confidently. In his program note he explained why he did not offer an analysis of its construction:

> It would be very easy for me to make a formal analysis and put forth my intellectual intentions and bases. Though this might contribute to the general fun of perception, I am in principle against the composer explaining his works analytically—at least before the first hearing. The most important thing about music is not how it looks in the score but how it sounds to the ear.[36]

Skrowaczewski and Stacy continued to perform the concerto into the fall of the next season, bringing it on tour throughout Minnesota. During the next few years Skrowaczewski conducted the work in Philadelphia, London, Paris, Madrid, and Germany, all performances with soloists from the various orchestras. The concerto received additional performances in Europe that Skrowaczewski did not conduct. Stacy was unique in his technical proficiency, tone, and innate musical ability, and Skrowaczewski soon discovered that other performers could not master some techniques of the concerto, such as the multiphonic fingerings:

> It got to the point that some performers were playing multichords that didn't fit as I had intended with the passages that came before and after them. Even though the music was atonal, there are certain relationships that are important to me. But because the sounds were in fact so off the normal tonality and because most players had trouble living up to Stacy's standard, I didn't really care, so I said, "Okay, why not?"

Skrowaczewski's only performance of the concerto with a soloist whose artistry rivaled that of Stacy occurred in 1978 with the Berlin Philharmonic and its renowned English horn player, Gerhard Stempnik. Skrowaczewski recalled:

> Stempnik had recorded all the major repertory for English horn with Berlin and Karajan. I was eager to hear what he would do with my piece, but I was also anxious because you never know how a soloist will react to a new work. I arrived the day before my first rehearsal and went to the concert the evening that Karajan was conducting. As I was waiting in the lobby to get my ticket, someone came from behind me and gave me a big hug. "Herr Skrowaczewski, I love your concerto, and I'm looking forward to playing it!" I turned around, and it was Stempnik. I was so relieved to know he liked it. The performance was truly exceptional, though it was so different from Stacy's. Stempnik's tone was also beautiful, but it was leaner than Stacy's wonderful huge tone. It was more restrained, perhaps more classical. I wouldn't say I preferred this approach to Stacy's, but it was different and convincing. A concerto depends so much on what the soloist brings to it. It was perhaps the only time in my composing career when I had such a different but positive experience with one of my concerto works.

Fortunately, Stacy and Skrowaczewski recorded the Concerto for English Horn and Orchestra. The Desto LP also included two short works by American composer William Mayer. This album was the first recording Skrowaczewski made with the Minnesota Orchestra since its 1962 Mercury contract ended, the first under the ensemble's new name, and the first of a Skrowaczewski composition. Soon after the LP's release in 1972, Stacy became English hornist of the New York Philharmonic, a position he maintained until 2010. Although he auditioned for the position, his achievement with the English Horn Concerto in Carnegie Hall and the reviews his performance earned certainly had attracted the Philharmonic's attention. Stacy's departure from Minneapolis was a bittersweet occasion for him and for Skrowaczewski.

Stacy's positive experience with the maestro inspired him to continue expanding the English horn solo repertory. Over the years he has premiered more than twenty-five works by composers including Gunther Schuller, Vincent Persichetti, Peteris Vasks, and Ned Rorem. Stacy has become perhaps the only English horn soloist to consistently perform internationally, and he has also earned the title of the most recorded English hornist in the world. Several years after Stacy joined the New York Philharmonic, he and Skrowaczewski performed the work with the Indianapolis Symphony. In 1991 the original LP was rereleased by Phoenix on CD.

"Show me my son!" Skrowaczewski exclaimed excitedly to the nurses, a touch of anxiety in his voice. He wanted to hold his newborn son, Nicholas, before he boarded a plane back to New York that evening to conduct his second performance of Mozart's *Die Zauberflöte* (*The Magic Flute*) at the Metropolitan Opera. The new baby's arrival was an especially joyous event for the Skrowaczewskis. After Anna's birth and its complications, they hoped for a healthy baby, and their wish had been granted with Paul, who now had a healthy sibling. This blessing was particularly uplifting for Krystyna. The stress of caring for Anna, age three and a half, and Paul, age twenty months, was mounting. Anna's development had progressed little since her birth. She responded well to sounds and exhibited some musical instincts, but she had no verbal communication skills. With the addition of Nicholas and with Anna's increasingly violent behavior, it soon became impossible for Krystyna to keep her daughter at home. Anna began living with a nearby health-care professional. It was a heartbreaking step for Krystyna, but she had no other option. She has remained a constant presence in Anna's life, and over the years Paul and Nicholas have had as much contact as possible with their sister.

The Metropolitan Opera was just beginning to get back on its feet when Skrowaczewski made his debut at the celebrated opera house, two days before Nicholas's birth. The union strike that had thwarted Skrowaczewski's originally scheduled debut with *Eugene Onegin* continued for three and half months. It was a chaotic period for the Met, which was trying to make up for lost time. Opening night was postponed until December 29, 1969, and seven operas were simultaneously in production during Skrowaczewski's six *Magic Flute* performances.

Skrowaczewski knew *The Magic Flute* well, but he had never conducted it as an opera. To prepare himself, he wisely scheduled a complete concert performance of it with his orchestra in the fall. However, nothing could have prepared him for the situation he faced at the Met:

> It was miserable. First, everyone's morale was low; the long strike had just ended. Second, the excellent singers that were originally scheduled did not all remain with the production because no one knew if the season would happen or not. Many of them took other work, so for most of the six performances at the Met I had different singers, often without the opportunity for rehearsals with them. I had maybe one rehearsal with the orchestra to go over tricky spots when these changes happened. It was a demoralized ensemble at that time, with a number of older musicians who could no longer play well. It was *The Magic Flute,* and the first flutist was badly out of tune. Günther Rennert's production was thought to be imaginative, but it was difficult for the singers and for me. He didn't care about problems for the orchestra; for example, he put three ladies far away in three corners of the big stage, and with quick-tempo arias where they all sing, it was almost impossible to get rhythmic togetherness. It was very hard for me. I couldn't really treat it seriously because it was like a sport, with different singers coming unprepared. They were prepared musically for what they do, but not with me and not with others. It was very dramatic in a sense. At that time in my life, of course, I took it because it was interesting and very challenging. I cannot be proud of it, though. Musically, it was nothing special just to put it

together at the last moment with different people, so I couldn't project any personal ideas into it.

Before Skrowaczewski gave the downbeat for the overture on opening night, there already had been eight changes in the original cast. Essentially the Met was resurrecting its 1967 production of *The Magic Flute*. Rennert had been its producer then, and Marc Chagall was the set designer, as he was in 1970. Six cast members from the 1967 production were also back. Skrowaczewski's six Met performances featured three different singers in the role of Pamina, and only once did the same person perform the role for two consecutive nights. The other key roles—Tamino, Queen of the Night, Sarastro, Pagageno, and Papagena—also had changes during the short run. In the spring, however, Skrowaczewski took the Met's *The Magic Flute* on tour to six major U.S. cities (including Minneapolis) with a stable cast.

Despite Skrowaczewski's frustration with his Met debut, critics largely praised his work. "*Die Zauberflöte* stands apart from Mozart's other operas not only because of its story material, but also because of the wide variety in his instrumental settings for the arias," explained Jack Hiemenz. "Thus it gives a conductor more opportunities to demonstrate his capabilities. Skrowaczewski used them to the hilt."[37] Wrote Arthur Satz, "[He] conducts a musician's Mozart, perhaps not everyone's ideal interpretation, but one so filled with the sense and sensibility of a first-rate musical mind that the entire opera emerges as one piece of music rather than a succession of arias, orchestral interludes, and speech."[38]

Despite his accomplishment at the Met under trying circumstances, Skrowaczewski was never invited back, but he didn't actively seek a return, due to bad memories associated with working conditions at the famous opera house. "Of course, it is a special environment," he later reflected. "But even without strikes, there is always something going on in opera that distracts from the music: singers canceling at the last moment, problems with sets, etc. I find all of these things go against the music. I really had had enough of opera."

For the rest of his career, aside from a production of *The Marriage of Figaro* with an opera company in Philadelphia during the late 1970s, Skrowaczewski's involvement with opera took place primarily in concert format. This approach better satisfied his interest in the purely musical content of opera. He refused opportunities to lead fully staged opera productions, thus freeing his schedule from the multiweek commitments.

Skrowaczewski's English Horn Concerto was not the only important new work featured in his tenth season in Minneapolis. He also conducted the U.S. premiere of *Carré* for Four Orchestras, Four Choirs and Four Conductors by Karlheinz Stockhausen. The event marked the first time that Twin Cities audiences heard large-scale music by Europe's leading avant-garde composer. By the late 1960s Stockhausen had become a cultural phenomenon, particularly for young people. His image was included in the collage of celebrities on the cover of The Beatles' iconic *Sergeant*

Pepper's Lonely Hearts Club Band album (sandwiched between images of Lenny Bruce and W.C. Fields).

Carré proved a bit much for some audience members. Although visually interesting—four conductors augmented by four others who flipped over numbered flashcards to keep the mass vocal and orchestral forces synchronized—some listeners regarded the piece as an unfortunate example of Skrowaczewski's advocacy of new music. But the maestro believed strongly in what he programmed, and his personal feelings about a new work were irrelevant:

> I played lots of new compositions that I considered very important, valuable, and fresh, even if they did not particularly interest me musically. I also rejected dozens of works. If you are music director of a major orchestra, with only so many weeks per season, you must play some of these works yourself, and it's not possible to have a hot-blooded relationship with all of them.[39]

Notable new American music during the 1969–70 Minnesota Orchestra season included works conducted by their respective composers. In his conducting debut with the orchestra, Aaron Copland led a program that included *Inscape*, a twelve-tone work premiered by Bernstein and the New York Philharmonic in 1967. Two weeks later Gunther Schuller led his masterful *Spectra*, also originally commissioned by the Philharmonic.

The season's most explosive program was the last: Mahler's Symphony no. 8 (*Symphony of a Thousand*) a first-time experience for the Minnesota Orchestra and Twin Cities audiences. The scale of the work was memorable, but so was the political context surrounding it. On May 4, 1970, four days before the Mahler performance, National Guardsmen at Kent State University in Ohio killed four student protesters and wounded nine others when they fired shots into a crowd. The students, like thousands of others on college campuses around the country, were protesting the invasion of Cambodia by U.S. military forces the previous week. The Kent State tragedy, emblematic of the country's division over the Vietnam War, launched America's first general student strike. During the next four days, four hundred colleges and universities held strikes, the University of Minnesota among them.

Richard Cisek described the situation:

> Even though our concert, and in fact the orchestra, were formally unrelated to the university, we were still very high-profile occupants of Northrop Auditorium. The students thought of our supporters, financial and otherwise, as being part of the establishment. They wanted to show their anger by not letting the university conduct business as usual. We entered long negotiations with the students. Eventually we convinced them that we were not under the auspices of the university and that the performance of the Mahler would give a message of hope and peace. We pulled off a compromise: if someone [from the orchestra] made a statement prior to the performance that the orchestra was a nonpartisan organization, they would allow it and audience members to cross the picket line. Our principal cellist at the time, Bob Jamieson, who

had sat in on all the negotiations, made the statement at the concert.

Skrowaczewski recalled the concert as a rare occurrence, not unlike the Penderecki's *St. Luke Passion* performance in Carnegie Hall the previous season, when the power of a work became a kind of catharsis for the nonmusical circumstances surrounding it.

After finishing the Minnesota season, Skrowaczewski headed to Europe for guest-conducting engagements that included the Gulbenkian Festival in Lisbon, where he gave his only other performance of Penderecki's *Passion*. Back in the United States, he conducted the Philadelphia Orchestra's last three concerts of its Robin Hood Dell series, which drew massive crowds. "Both public and players greeted the return of the Polish-born conductor of the Minnesota Orchestra as an old friend, which he has become, both at the Dell and at the Academy of Music," noted *The Evening Bulletin*.[40] A crowd of twenty-four thousand turned out for Skrowaczewski's first concert, which featured his old friend Szeryng.[41] The final concert reprised the popularity of the previous summer's performance by Van Cliburn, who this time played Brahms' Piano Concerto no. 2. A record crowd of thirty thousand turned out for the concert, and again Cliburn gave his fans an extended encore of solo pieces for half an hour. The sight of teenage girls rushing to the stage carrying red roses for their idol, a classical musician, was an act of adulation from another era—one that would become increasingly rare in the coming decades.[42]

A few days after closing the Philadelphia Orchestra's Dell season, Skrowaczewski was back with the ensemble to open its series of concerts at Saratoga Performing Arts Center. The gala concert of Beethoven's Ninth Symphony opened with a performance of Copland's *Lincoln Portrait* featuring the celebrated American contralto Marian Anderson as narrator.

Skrowaczewski lost perhaps his most important advocate and colleague in America when George Szell died at age seventy-three on July 30, 1970. Richard Vincent of *The Plain Dealer* ended his Szell tribute article by offering two suggestions for successors: Karajan and Skrowaczewski. He described the "severe, even grim dedication to [their] professions" as one of several traits that Szell and Skrowaczewski shared.[43]

Rafael Druian, Szell's concertmaster from 1960 to 1969, told Skrowaczewski about an incident that demonstrated the maestro's devotion to his art, even under trying circumstances. Just before the end of the Cleveland Orchestra's Japan tour, the musicians came through Seattle, where they gave a concert just a few months before Szell's death. Already very weak and pale, the maestro could hardly move. After the concert he and Druian happened to meet in the hotel elevator. The concertmaster said to Szell:

> "One more concert, and then we are home. Just one more downbeat from you maestro tomorrow, and we're on our way." "Not a downbeat!" Szell blurted out. "The downbeat doesn't mean anything! Only the upbeat gives you the tempo, articulation, and character." The door to the elevator opened,

and Szell, now full of life and energy, proceeded to give Druian a lecture on the importance of the upbeat!

Two weeks after Szell's death, Skrowaczewski led the Cleveland Orchestra at Blossom Music Center in a Szell-like program of Beethoven, Mozart, and Schumann. Beethoven's *Leonore* Overture no. 3, which opened the program, had just been performed by the orchestra at the memorial concert for its deceased maestro. "Skrowaczewski certainly should be one of the most serious contenders for the directorship of the Cleveland Orchestra," wrote one critic, "if his interpretation of Schumann's Fourth Symphony has any bearing at all…. His two performances this season and last leave few doubts about his remarkable abilities as a conductor and a gentleman."[44]

Moments after Skrowaczewski briskly launched into "The Star-Spangled Banner" to open the Minnesota Orchestra's 1970–71 season, he was startled to hear the audience burst into song. His instincts took over, and he turned around to lead the impromptu mass choir. It wasn't merely patriotism that caused the audience to seize the moment. This concert was the first in O'Shaughnessy Auditorium, a new hall on the campus of the College of St. Catherine, and the occasion also marked the first formal Minnesota Orchestra concert series in St. Paul since 1930.

When it became known that the College of St. Catherine was including a 1,800-seat auditorium in its new fine-arts center, Cisek recognized an opportunity to create a concert series in St. Paul. The number of subscription concerts immediately doubled (twenty at O'Shaughnessy and twenty at Northrop). The move automatically increased subscription income while giving St. Paul donors a sense of ownership of the orchestra. (One wonders if this series in itself would have made the name change a moot point in terms of St. Paul financial backing.)

The orchestra's opening concert in O'Shaughnessy, the most newsworthy event of its season, attracted national critics. Although the new hall offered a much-welcomed and overdue alternative to Northrop, it was not a vast improvement. Most local listeners were grateful for any venue other than Northrop, but all visiting critics, orchestra musicians, and Skrowaczewski recognized that O'Shaughnessy had serious failings.

Acousticians from Bolt, Beranek, and Newman, the same team that designed New York's flawed Philharmonic Hall in 1962 (now Avery Fisher Hall), were hired for the design of O'Shaughnessy Auditorium. Northrop and O'Shaughnessy shared the overriding problem of being a multipurpose facility used for speeches and lectures as well as arts events. To ease problems with the space, acoustic consultant George Izenour, the orchestra's go-to person during the attempts to improve Northrop years earlier, installed a steel-and-concrete shell that unfortunately produced a dry, bright, and hard sound. The orchestra had to wait until the mid-1980s, when Ordway Center for the Performing Arts opened, to have a better acoustical venue for its St. Paul concert series. (Ironically, the orchestra currently has no concert series in St. Paul.)

Not long after the opening concerts at O'Shaughnessy, another Minnesota Orchestra performance there gave Skrowaczewski a long-lasting memory:

> After our first concerts, the hall was still not completely finished. There were no sidewalks yet around the building, and you could still smell glue and other materials inside the auditorium. No one really cared because we were so thrilled just to have a fine performing alternative to Northrop.
>
> We were playing Wagner's Prelude to *Tristan und Isolde,* and just as we started *Isolde's Liebestod,* the lights went out. It was completely black, no emergency lights or anything. I kept conducting, and the orchestra kept playing. We had played the piece often, and they knew it very well. Lea Foli, concertmaster then, said he could feel that I was still conducting. We played for about a minute, completely perfectly. Suddenly the lights came back on. Everyone was relieved. The audience remained silent, as if nothing had happened. We played for about four or five minutes more and again, a blackout. The complete darkness remained for the rest of the piece. Again, the orchestra played flawlessly. The audience applauded, and ushers came with candles. There was no panic at all. People simply left, guided by candles. No one knew why this happened.
>
> It turned out that the electrical circuitry to the auditorium was connected to a nearby chemistry building. Apparently a professor had finished teaching his class, shut the lights off in his room, and automatically our lights also went off. It happened to be raining, so he went back to his classroom, turned the lights on again to find his umbrella, so our lights went on again. Then he left, shut the lights off, and we finished the concert in the dark. I loved this explanation! Later I thanked the orchestra and joked that they apparently didn't need me. They agreed! There was a very good atmosphere between us at that time.

Despite the publicity and short-term excitement over O'Shaughnessy Auditorium, Skrowaczewski remained adamant about the orchestra's need for a new home. Since the early 1960s he had been hammering the point to anyone who would listen. He broached the issue nearly every time he was interviewed, as Cisek remembered:

> After Stan had been here for a few years, and the two attempts to improve Northrop with acoustical shells failed, he felt comfortable enough to lose his subtlety and really begin to champion a new hall. I tried to hold him back, saying, "Stan, you can't damn Northrop every time you're on television or on the radio and then have me go out and sell tickets to come to it!" But he would see the larger picture: this was what *was* going to sell tickets and what was going to really bring the orchestra into its own. He single-handedly just kept convincing people until it became a reality. He urged people to travel with us, to come to Carnegie Hall, to come to other places we played that had better halls. Even when he guest conducted orchestras, like the Pittsburgh Symphony, that had a new hall, he would say, "Come here, see what this is like. Hear the difference." I remember Sandy Bemis, who was president of the

association when I first became manager of the orchestra, saying to me one day, "You know, Stan has convinced me. We do need a new hall, and we do have to start thinking about what our possibilities are."

Skrowaczewski's persistence ultimately would lead to his greatest accomplishment as music director of the Minnesota Orchestra.

EIGHTEEN

MODULATIONS

One of the major problems of the conductor is the living contradiction between excitement and control of what is going on. If you are all "control tower" you maybe lose flair and excitement about a work, which is somehow contagious to the musicians and the audience. This control—it is the eternal problem for every conductor.

—Stanisław Skrowaczewski

Guest-conducting engagements offer musical experiences unencumbered by the responsibilities and obligations of administrative leadership. If the relationship between a guest conductor and an orchestra lacks chemistry, the experience is over in a week. When it goes well, however, the guest forms a positive, instant connection with musicians and management, and a return engagement is likely. The determining factors usually include an absolute command over the interpretation of the music (and the gravitas to back it up), the ability to communicate that interpretation, and a mysterious quality that can best be described as the power of personality. Composer John Harbison uses the word "profile" to describe the aggregate characteristics of a given maestro. Every major conductor or musician has a distinctive profile: artistic background and tastes, personality, and imagination. "Profile" is the reason one wants to hear the same Chopin concerto played by Rubinstein, Weissenberg, and Zimerman.

Skrowaczewski's profile, particularly during the 1960s and 1970s, often was considered to be that of an introverted disciplinarian, "apt to be bleak and analytical in romantic music," as Harold Schonberg wrote.[1] On the podium Skrowaczewski does not outwardly express his feelings for the music he conducts, but any orchestra he leads cannot help but sense his total dedication and commitment to his art. His perspective as a composer and his deep knowledge of the score also are evident. Sensitive musicians who make an effort to understand Skrowaczewski's musicianship and interpretive ideas can perceive his deep passion for conducting. Some musicians may not find his communications inspirational, but nearly all respect his preparation for and command of the music.

The New York Philharmonic of the 1960s and 1970s may have been the most challenging orchestra Skrowaczewski ever led as a guest conductor:

> It was a very hard orchestra. I was always so tired after those rehearsals. It was without discipline in that era. After coming from the Cleveland Orchestra, I found a huge difference in attitude. The Philharmonic had wonderful players with fantastic technical facility, but somehow they had a permanent dissatisfaction about something. They were perhaps spoiled by their image.

For years the Philharmonic typically bore an antagonistic attitude toward some conductors. Having been led by some of the greatest maestros in music history (Mahler, Mengelberg, Toscanini, Walter, etc.), the musicians had little patience or tolerance for conductors who did not instantly command their attention or who were not strong-willed enough to rein them in. "They are a difficult orchestra, those New Yorkers," Bernstein admitted. "They play only as well as you can conduct or force them to play. If you let go even a wee bit, the whole thing falls apart."[2]

Skrowaczewski witnessed what was possibly the nadir of the Philharmonic's behavior when he attended a rehearsal that Mitropoulos led of Mahler's Fifth Symphony in late December 1959. "This poor man, a wonderful musician with immense knowledge and communicative skills, and he couldn't get through to them. They really behaved like pigs to him, being noisy, talking, with no attention." It was the last time Mitropoulos led the Philharmonic.

The early 1970s were challenging for all American orchestras. The Philharmonic faced financial difficulties and union contract situations, but it also was in a state of transition from 1969, when Bernstein left, to 1971, when Boulez entered as music director. Szell and Skrowaczewski each had been scheduled to lead five weeks during the 1970–71 season, but after Szell's death the Philharmonic turned to Skrowaczewski and other guests to fill those conducting engagements. Although Skrowaczewski could add only one more week, he ultimately spent more weeks with the Philharmonic that season than did anyone else.

The breadth of the repertoire he conducted over a total of six weeks (three in winter, three in spring) was impressive: from Mozart, Haydn, and Mendelssohn to Schumann, Dvořák, and Sibelius, whose music Skrowaczewski rarely conducted. Twentieth-century music was amply represented by the rarely heard *Stabat Mater* of Szymanowski, the *Mandala* Symphony by Japanese composer Toshiro Mayuzumi, and the first New York performances of Ginastera's *Estudios Sinfónicos* and Peter Mennin's *Sinfonia*. Skrowaczewski also conducted music of William Schuman and Samuel Barber on a program honoring their sixtieth birthdays. The composers were present and seated together at the event.

A week before Skrowaczewski began the spring segment of his New York Philharmonic engagements he conducted the Minnesota Orchestra at Carnegie Hall with soprano Leontyne Price as soloist. "She has such discipline, and she works so well with the orchestra," Skrowaczewski said. "She proves it—the greater the artist, the less a prima donna."[3]

Strauss' *Four Last Songs*, the program's featured work, was dedicated to the memory of civil-rights leader (and former University of Minnesota graduate student) Whitney M. Young, Jr., who had drowned while swimming with friends in Nigeria the previous week. The concert was Price's only New York appearance for the season, and the hall was packed. Lea Foli, then in his second season as the orchestra's concertmaster, was with Skrowaczewski looking out at the audience while Price received prolonged acclamation for her performance.

"The crowd went nuts: great cheers, flowers, bouquets, the whole bit," said Foli. "I remember Stan looking out and saying, 'I wonder if anyone will stay to hear the symphony.' The Brahms Second was closing the program. He was both serious and kidding at the same time—his unique Polish humor."

The following night, as the Minnesota Orchestra continued its East Coast tour, Garrick Ohlsson made his debut with the ensemble, performing Chopin's Piano Concerto no. 1. A few months after his tour with the orchestra, the relatively unknown Ohlsson became the first and only American to win the top prize at the Fryderyk Chopin International Piano Competition. During the next three decades Ohlsson became one of Skrowaczewski's most treasured collaborators.

The pianist described his first experience working with Skrowaczewski:

> I was a struggling young pianist who hadn't yet won the Chopin competition, and my manager had me audition for Stan. I was booked to do a couple of tour concerts with the Minneapolis Symphony. In some ways, nobody does the Chopin concertos better than he does. Not only did he grow up in Poland and is a wonderful conductor, but also he actually loves the music, which is not something that can be said for all maestros. Because I was young and inexperienced, I don't recall whether I heard any of the subtle retouching he does with the orchestration just to clarify certain lines, but I knew it was wonderful accompaniment. I didn't have vast experiences with major orchestras, but it made me feel like I was walking on air!

During Skrowaczewski's rehearsals for his last series of concerts with the New York Philharmonic in April 1971, Igor Stravinsky died in New York City. Several prominent musicians were asked to comment on the composer's legacy. Skrowaczewski offered the following: "The death of a genius like Stravinsky would be a cosmic tragedy to mankind if not for the fact that his works will always live with us, ever fresh and meaningful. To me, personally, he is the greatest composer since Wagner."[4]

Along with his brief encounter with Stravinsky at Nadia Boulanger's apartment in the late 1940s, Skrowaczewski's only other contact with the 20th-century master was in Venice in 1958. He recalled the occasion:

> I was guest conducting the Orchestra Opera di Venezia, and Krystyna and I were staying in the same hotel as Stravinsky and his wife, Vera. We saw them several times throughout the hotel. Our rooms happened to be adjacent. A couple of times Vera knocked on our door looking for cognac "because Igor wasn't feeling well." They were in our room for a moment at one point. They were both so charming. I remember attending the world premiere of Stravinsky's *Threni: id est Lamentationes Jeremiae Prophetae*, his biggest serial work. He conducted it in the upper chamber of the Scuola Grande di San Rocco.

Skrowaczewski's extensive work with the New York Philharmonic during the 1970–71 season put him under the microscopic scrutiny of the New York press more than at any other point in his career. Wrote Winthrop Sargeant: "Mr. Skrowaczewski is a mature conductor with an expressive beat, a scholarly look, and a scholarly temperament. Charisma? Well, enough of it to get by."[5] Critics at *The New York Times* often recognized that Skrowaczewski possessed various assets and virtues, among them a no-nonsense approach to conducting, but they were also quick to point out his lack of a romantic sensibility in repertoire that required it.

Ironically, in his post-Minnesota career as a guest conductor, he became increasingly identified with the romantic repertoire. Longtime observers of Skrowaczewski have noted his enhanced ability over the last decade or so to communicate this affinity with a greater openness on the podium. To some extent, U.S. critics unfairly stereotyped him early as primarily an objective conductor. Certainly there still is some truth to this point, but Skrowaczewski always has had a feeling for the romantic repertoire. He explained his frustration with the stereotype:

> From the beginning of my career Harold Schonberg constantly pigeonholed me as a cold conductor because I conducted a lot of contemporary music. He was rather strange in this regard towards me in print. In America, especially at that time, critics loved to use labels. It was ridiculous for them to call me a contemporary-music conductor, which automatically excluded me from being romantic. It was stupid, because from my childhood I was super-romantic with everything! My sober gestures were misleading to the public. In comparison to Bernstein or Thomas Schippers, I seemed stern. Because I didn't jump on the podium or cry on stage or something like that, they called me cold. It was taken as a lack of romantic sensibility. Later, in the 1980s, I didn't change much, but the times changed. Then this criticism didn't happen anymore. In Europe they would never criticize me for this, but in America it happened, mostly because I performed contemporary music.

Although Skrowaczewski's physical mannerisms on the podium may not have changed much from the 1960s through the 1980s, his approach to rehearsing an orchestra did: "There were certain years that I found myself too much of a teacher towards the musicians, but then I got out of this approach beginning in the late 1970s and then completely away from it by the 1980s."

Skrowaczewski's approach during his six weeks with the New York Philharmonic that season apparently satisfied some critics and some musicians of the orchestra. It earned him an invitation to return for three weeks during the 1972–73 season. However, some rehearsals for those engagements brought challenges:

> I remember playing Weber's *Freischütz* Overture. It's not an easy overture. It requires great precision and sudden changes of moods and tempos. A slightly free interpretation is necessary. After an hour of hard rehearsing and digging in like one needs to do with a school orchestra, the concertmaster came to me and said, "I have to congratulate you. This was the best Weber I ever played." There were other moments like this, when players came to me with kind comments, but I remember it was a big challenge to really make them rehearse. Now it is a completely different orchestra. They are lovely to rehearse. Why? Because the older, complaining people retired and were replaced by excellent young people from the best music schools. Now they

have their own discipline. But at that time I was a younger conductor, and
they probably thought they didn't have to behave.

In the coming decades Skrowaczewski's return engagements with the New York
Philharmonic were sporadic. He conducted the Philharmonic only a few times during
the 1980s and not at all during the 1990s; his last engagement was in 2001. During the
last twenty-five years he appeared more often in New York with the Juilliard Orchestra
than with the Philharmonic. Beginning in the 1980s, his success at Juilliard opened
up a side-career as one of the most popular guest conductors of America's elite music
schools and conservatories.

By the early 1970s Skrowaczewski's programming of contemporary music had
become such a normal part of Minnesotans' concert life that if several new works
were not featured in a season, it was newsworthy. Such was the case for the 1971–72
season. Perhaps Skrowaczewski and the orchestra's management were taking a more
conservative approach to programming, given the negative response of some audience
members to contemporary music—particularly to Stockhausen's *Carré*, performed in
1970. It was more likely, however, that the small number of new pieces (three) in
comparison to previous years was merely the natural result of Skrowaczewski's balanced
programming. He didn't seek to fill a season with music from any particular era.

His discerning ear carefully chose from among dozens of scores sent to him each year
by composers and publishers or from live performances he had heard. In a season-preview
article, Skrowaczewski revealed that of the estimated 150 new works he received in any
given year, only one or two sustained his interest. "Not everybody's a genius," he said.[6]

His receipt of scores was the impetus of an often-told anecdote in Minnesota
Orchestra lore. A reporter, curious about the maestro's source of so many contemporary
scores, asked him, "Where do all these scores come from?" Perplexed by what seemed
to be such an obvious question, Skrowaczewski paused for effect and humorously
replied, "Well, they come in the mail."

Luciano Berio's *Sinfonia* for Eight Voices and Orchestra was the most provocative
new work Skrowaczewski programmed for the 1971–72 season. "It's an example of
where a very gifted young composer of the avant-garde is right now, [in] the crisis of
the avant-garde," Skrowaczewski observed a few months before he conducted the work.[7]

Responding in part to the avant-garde tumult of the late 1960s, Berio used
a complex montage of musical quotations from the past and numerous texts from
various sources, including Claude Lévi-Strauss and Samuel Beckett. The second part
of the hour-long piece pays tribute to Dr. Martin Luther King, Jr., by incorporating
the phonemes of his name spoken by amplified voices. (King was assassinated six
months before the New York Philharmonic premiered *Sinfonia*, with the composer
conducting, in October 1968.) The piece is best known for superimposing verbal and
musical quotations over the entire Scherzo movement from Mahler's Symphony no. 2.

"[It] is a tribute to Gustav Mahler," wrote the composer, "whose work seems to carry all the weight of the last two centuries of musical history."[8]

Skrowaczewski's performances of Berio's *Sinfonia* with the Minnesota Orchestra in fall 1971 occurred a year after Bernstein and the New York Philharmonic gave the first performance of an expanded version of the score. Like others who performed the piece at that time, Skrowaczewski collaborated with the Swingle Singers, the French *a cappella* group that became popular in the 1960s for fusing jazz and classical styles— most notably by scatting to works by Bach. The Swingle Singers performed *Sinfonia* more than 200 times from 1968 to 1985 with orchestras from around the world.[9]

In addition to encountering the latest work by Italy's most prominent contemporary composer, Minnesotans also heard a new concerto by Skrowaczewski's esteemed compatriot Lutosławski. With Mstislav Rostropovich as soloist, Skrowaczewski gave the U.S. premiere of Lutosławski's Concerto for Cello in early 1972. Rostropovich premiered the concerto in 1970 with the Royal Philharmonic, which commissioned the piece. Haydn's C major Cello Concerto and Shostakovich's Symphony no. 8, new to the orchestra, rounded out the program. (The Haydn Concerto, also a first American performance, was discovered in 1961 in the Prague National Library.)[10]

At the first Minnesota performance audience members filled the aisles of O'Shaughnessy Auditorium to hear Rostropovich tackle the two diverse concertos. "Slava always played with great imagination," Skrowaczewski said. "He would create stories about the music he played; often they had sexual references." He continued:

> We took the concerto on tour in Germany with the Bamberg Symphony for about six or seven concerts. It was still during the communist era, and Rostropovich had a funny political explanation. In the beginning there's this permanent three note gesture "*D D D.*" "It's like a Soviet official in an office," he said, "not doing anything, just like 'ah, ah, ah.'" And then the music moves, so he had some other explanation, but it was all very anti-Soviet, which you can expect from Rostropovich. Otherwise, musically the concerto is an aleatoric piece—nothing exceptional, really. But as with all Lutosławski, it's very well constructed and organized.

A week later Skrowaczewski gave a special concert with one of America's most beloved classical musicians, Artur Rubinstein. The appearance of the Polish-American pianist in Minneapolis was not that rare. He performed regularly with the orchestra beginning in 1921, and since 1960 he had appeared with Skrowaczewski on three series of concerts. However, the fact that Rubinstein would celebrate his eighty-fifth birthday just six days shy of the concert made the evening noteworthy. The pianist was a passionate performer, and his last Minneapolis concert with Skrowaczewski was no exception. He played with the same freshness and sheer joy he brought to every performance.

In a television interview a few years before this Minneapolis concert Rubinstein described the thrill of performing: "I go to [a] concert with a feeling of really [my] heart beating. Do I own the piece or not? What will happen? And this [feeling] is all for the good because it is that promise, that new approach, that mystery about it which the public feels [I also feel]. And *that* makes it alive."[11]

Rubinstein played Mozart's Piano Concerto in D minor, no. 20, and the Schumann Piano Concerto with the Minnesota Orchestra for his eighty-fifth birthday concert on January 22, 1972. "I have never felt more ill, and I have never played better," Rubinstein said a few days later. "At the piano, my sickness goes away."[12]

Skrowaczewski recalled the event a few years later:

> It was an incredible delight to me to hear him on that day. As he has grown older, I think there has been a trend to simplicity in his interpretations that is beautiful. He plays like a young Mozart in a tone that is incomparable for pianists. Even now I wonder how he does it. You know a keyboard can be so unfriendly. On that day, for his birthday concert, his touch was almost a mystical thing. He knew how well he played.[13]

Unfortunately Skrowaczewski could not fully enjoy his last concert experience with Rubinstein in Minneapolis. Like the pianist, he also was ill. "I barely made the concert," Skrowaczewski remembered. "I was feeling sick, so Krystyna drove me home immediately after this little ceremony with a cake we had on stage for Rubinstein after the concert. I threw up in the car on the way home." Skrowaczewski was due to leave in a few days for a monthlong European tour that included several important guest-conducting engagements:

> I was supposed to fly from New York to Munich, but I became so sick on the plane that they brought me back to Minneapolis. I was in a wheelchair when Krystyna met me at the airport with Dr. Frost, head of one of the hospitals in St. Paul. I was practically in bed, half-sleeping and half-conscious for a long time. It was difficult to walk, and my balance was disturbed. I had all kinds of tests, doctors came to the house, and no one could figure out what was wrong with me. So the whole tour, four weeks, was canceled, and I was home. Slowly I began to feel normal again, but when I started to conduct, I was quite insecure in standing and in concentrating.

Skrowaczewski's Minneapolis schedule for spring 1972 did not permit him to ease back into work. After a month of subscription and run-out concerts, he went on the road with the orchestra for a monthlong, eighteen-city national tour that included Chicago, New York City, Washington, D.C., Ann Arbor, Toledo, and Memphis. The major work for the tour—Mahler's *Das klagende Lied* (Song of Lamentation)—was heard for the first time in its complete version in all cities where the orchestra performed.

Mahler began composing the work at age nineteen and completed it a year later. It failed to win the Beethoven Prize in Vienna (Brahms was one of the judges), and after Liszt rejected it for a performance at the Altgemeiner Deutscher Musikverein festival, Mahler withdrew it. He made several revisions that eliminated one of three parts and then conducted the premiere in 1901. The two-part version was published but seldom performed. The first complete performance of all three parts was heard on a Vienna radio broadcast in 1935. Mahler's nephew conducted the broadcast and then withdrew this version of the piece. The manuscript surfaced only in 1969, when Yale University obtained it, and the American premiere of the complete version was presented there early in 1970. Minnesota was among the first major orchestras to perform the work.[14]

Mahler derived his inspiration for the hour-long cantata from a Brothers Grimm fairy tale and based its setting on his memory of a childhood story. He considered the work to be the first expression of his true voice. The quality of the Wagner-influenced piece does not stand alongside Mahler's symphonies, but forces for the original version—large orchestra with an offstage military band, chorus, two boy singers, four adult soloists, and six harps—foreshadowed the compositional proportions of the composer's maturity.[15]

Skrowaczewski's performances of the novel Mahler work were well received by audiences and critics throughout the orchestra's tour. "The drama of the music was always there," said one New York critic. "What the conductor and his orchestra by their skill made us never forget was the youthful flame of [Mahler's] genius, aware and burning bright."[16] Another critic described Skrowaczewski's programming of excerpts from Berlioz's *Roméo et Juliette*, which followed the Mahler, as "musically shrewd" because the narrative nature of that work had influenced Mahler's approach to *Das klagende Lied*.[17] Perhaps even more astute was Skrowaczewski's choice of soloists: Canadian contralto Maureen Forrester, still in her prime, had long been considered a gifted Mahler interpreter, and soprano Phyllis Curtin, along with baritone Brent Ellis—then a twenty-six-year-old newcomer—gave the solo voice parts a heightened atmosphere.

The orchestra's New York performance was part of Carnegie Hall's International Festival of Visiting Orchestras. The week's schedule also featured the Philadelphia and Chicago orchestras. Coincidentally, the Chicago Symphony under its relatively new music director, Sir Georg Solti, performed Mahler's penultimate work, *Das Lied von der Erde*. Critics could not avoid comparing the three venerable ensembles heard in the same acoustically pristine environment. Although the strings of the Philadelphia Orchestra stood apart for one writer, he also remarked that "the playing of the Minnesota Orchestra, which has been burnished to a new sheen of metallic brilliance by Skrowaczewski, was a reminder that there are great orchestras beyond the East Coast, beyond the Alleghenies, even beyond the Mississippi."[18]

A few days after the Carnegie Hall performance the Minnesotans made their debut at the John F. Kennedy Center for the Performing Arts in Washington, D.C. "Dust had scarcely coated the chandeliers at the Kennedy Center," wrote Mary Ann Feldman, "when the [orchestra] played in the new concert hall."[19] Barely more than seven months old, the hall had opened to much fanfare with the premiere of Leonard Bernstein's *Mass*. The two-hour *Theatre Piece for Singers, Players, and Dancers*, as Bernstein subtitled it, was commissioned by Jacqueline Kennedy Onassis in memory of John F. Kennedy.

The orchestra enjoyed a warm welcome at its Kennedy Center debut on April 21, 1972. The event was a source of great pride for several prominent political figures from Minnesota, including U.S. Supreme Court Chief Justice Warren Burger, Associate Justice Harry Blackmun, Secretary of Labor James Hodgson, U.S. Senator Walter Mondale, and the state's governor, Wendell Anderson, all of whom attended the concert. The chosen program—symphonies by Mozart and Schumann and excerpts from Berlioz's *Roméo et Juliette*—took full advantage of the Kennedy Center's fine acoustics.

Skrowaczewski used the event to reiterate his persistent message about the orchestra's need for a real concert hall. "You can't believe how we all feel every time we play in a great hall," he told a reporter after the concert. "We only wish the conditions could be as good at home."[20] At a postconcert reception, Justice Burger—whose own artistic talents included sculpting and painting—said the concert reminded him of the excitement he had experienced while listening to the orchestra during Ormandy's tenure. Skrowaczewski's predecessor on the Minneapolis podium, Doráti, was also on hand to hear the concert. Doráti was then in his second season as music director of the National Symphony Orchestra, and the Kennedy Center was its new home.

Skrowaczewski spent the first part of summer 1972 guest conducting in Europe before settling into a three-week stay at Tanglewood, where he was an artist-in-residence. He taught the conducting seminar and conducted a concert with the Boston Symphony. Koussevitzky's renowned summer music school, the Berkshire Music Center (today the Tanglewood Music Center), was in its third and final season under the leadership of artistic directors Seiji Ozawa and Gunther Schuller and artistic advisor Leonard Bernstein, who was not at Tanglewood that summer. Ozawa became the Boston Symphony Orchestra's music director in 1973, and Schuller headed the center until 1984. At Schuller's request, Skrowaczewski was invited to teach at the school. Leading the seminar was the first time he had taught conducting since his student days in Kraków.

After coming to the United States Skrowaczewski had refused to teach in order to protect his time. However, Tanglewood's special atmosphere and history, Schuller's invitation, and the opportunity to conduct both the Boston Symphony and the student orchestra enticed him to accept the invitation. This commitment was one of the few times that Skrowaczewski ever formally taught conducting in the United States.

In some respects the infrequency of Skrowaczewski's teaching is regrettable, in light of his recognition at Tanglewood in 1972 and 1973, his vast professional experience, and the popularity of his work at The Juilliard School, Curtis Institute of Music, and New England Conservatory of Music. However, he was well aware of the time that teaching demanded, and he knew it would impinge on the time he needed for conducting and composing. His experiences teaching at Tanglewood, however, were illuminating, as he explained:

> It was my principle in teaching to never discuss my personal approach to interpretation. I tried to be objective as to what was not appropriate musically in their conducting. I would explain what the mistake was and why it was not good. It was also important to tell them what was very good and why it was good.
>
> The challenge of conducting is incredible—to convey immediately to the orchestra not only your knowledge of the score but also your feelings

about it and your interpretation. Knowledge of the score is one thing, but interpretation is a very different matter—it comes from this knowledge, but not fully. Yet it must be there before you can begin to form an interpretation.

At Tanglewood I had interesting experiences with some student conductors who were already conducting good orchestras in Europe. I would ask them about their knowledge of the score when they would try to do certain elements by heart. I would say, "Do you know [the score]?" and they would say, "Oh, yes, we know it." "Well, tell me what the horns do in such and such a place." And they wouldn't know. And I am talking about well-known music like symphonies by Mozart, Beethoven, or Brahms. They would know the melodies but not necessarily the instrumentation up to the point of exactly what each instrument does. If it doesn't sound right, they can't correct immediately why certain things don't come. They don't know exactly which sections are guilty. If the musicians don't play exactly the dynamics necessary, for example, they can't correct them. And then to hear it—to hear the instrumentation of the chord, to be able to hear what is lacking and to know which notes are too loud, and so forth. These elements are so important.

When I had these experiences at Tanglewood, I remember being reminded that whatever you do later with interpretation, you absolutely must have perfect knowledge of the score. From this you develop your own sound of the music, of the chord, etc. This knowledge is the first duty of a conductor. Then comes interpretation: line, tempo, dynamics, etc. These issues are great challenges every time one conducts. And implementing your interpretation will change as you go to different orchestras because they will have different sounds, different approaches, etc. Even many of the best orchestras are not necessarily prepared. Even with music they know very well—it doesn't mean that they will necessarily produce a sound that is proper.[21]

Among Skrowaczewski's students at Tanglewood in 1972 who did know his scores was Bruce Hangen, who won a prize for his work that summer. "I remember we were all watching him rehearsing with the BSO," Hangen recalled. "He was definitely very musical, but we were all trying to figure out where his beat was. It was unique." The class was eager to understand how Skrowaczewski learned a score but hesitated to ask him:

We were all in awe of his deep knowledge of scores. He really knew the ins and outs: the social context of the piece, the cultural environment at the time a work was composed, etc. I still use his knowledge of a score as inspiration whenever I'm learning something new. One day in class we worked up the courage and just blurted it out, "Maestro, how do you learn a score?" After much hemming and hawing, his response was, "Well, how do *you* learn a score?" That's been my answer to students over the years.

One of Hangen's fondest memories of that summer was the time he had coffee with Skrowaczewski:

I worked up the nerve to ask him to join me for a coffee. To this day I cannot really remember what I asked him or what he told me. I just remember being so young and thinking [about] what an experience it was to be one on one with a major conductor. I do remember he spoke about how there was a special market in Lenox where he got his natural foods. That inspired me. It showed me again that this man is an artist and a gentleman, a very clean person with great wisdom and sincerity. I don't think you could find a more genuine person in the music field.

Before summer 1972 ended, Skrowaczewski conducted the Monaco National Orchestra at the Monte Carlo palace of Prince Rainier and Princess Grace (Kelly). He and Krystyna, who joined him on the trip, were charmed by the royal couple's regal warmth and generosity at a reception they hosted for the visitors. After the Monaco engagement Skrowaczewski made his debut with the Swiss Festival Orchestra at the Lucerne International Festival. Nello Celio, president of the Swiss Republic, also hosted a reception in honor of the Skrowaczewskis.

At the start of the Minnesota Orchestra's 1972–73 season, its seventieth anniversary, Skrowaczewski had much to anticipate: his first international tour with the orchestra (to Mexico); performances of his music; important European engagements; and an extended tour with the Cleveland Orchestra. But amid this artistic prosperity he faced a crisis in his career.

By late 1968 Skrowaczewski was increasingly dissatisfied with Columbia Artists and with the scarcity of his guest-conducting engagements in the United States. When he was in New York, Skrowaczewski met with his American manager, Ronald Wilford, to discuss his concerns. Their meeting marked the beginning of Skrowaczewski's tumultuous relationship with the artists' management mogul.

Beginning in 1969, Skrowaczewski had noticed that Wilford, then vice president of Columbia Artists Management (CAMI), was devoting considerably less time to him. He also was disappointed with the quality of service he received. By the early 1970s Wilford's secretary, Judie Janowski, handled many of Skrowaczewski's guest engagements, and although she was excellent, she was not Wilford. With more than a decade's experience of leading a major U.S. orchestra and securing important European engagements, Skrowaczewski believed that Columbia was not investing in him appropriately.

"I *am* absolutely ruthless if it comes down to telling an orchestra to go to hell if I feel something is unfair to an artist of mine," Wilford said in a 1971 article in *The New York Times* entitled "Muscle Man Behind the Maestros." "I really don't care, because if I have an artist they want, they will have to book him."[22] By this time Wilford, age forty-three, was the youngest president of CAMI in its history. He was fiercely loyal to a handful of his conductors, principally Ozawa, Levine, Previn, and Karajan. Those not on his "A" list, like Skrowaczewski, were not a priority. Wilford's instincts regarding Ozawa and Levine, whose careers he had guided since the beginning, were clearly good. Based on his past accomplishments, he had reason to be confident in his ability to discern talent; however, his subjective judgment regarding an artist's worth and suitability for a particular engagement or position was not flawless.

Rather proud of not being a musician, Wilford believes that it has been an advantage to his career. In a 2005 interview he claimed that he lacks the bias inherent in a formal education in music and that he prefers to be in the "I know what I like, I like what I know" camp, based on his numerous years working in the arts.

Skrowaczewski's approach to his art differed from that taken by most of Wilford's other conductors. He is more introverted, probing, and perhaps less flamboyant, and the manager could not relate to Skrowaczewski as easily as he did to other conductors. At the few Skrowaczewski performances Wilford attended, he did not witness the typical audience response that his star conductors received; consequently, he ranked the maestro at a certain level and did not seem to invest fully in him.

Skrowaczewski may not have consistently elicited the visceral reactions that Wilford so admired, but his artistry merited greater attention. In 2005 Wilford acknowledged that few people can properly judge the quality of a conductor, which is to some degree a subjective matter; nevertheless, he clearly believes that Skrowaczewski is not one of the great conductors of his time.

Michel Glotz, in some respects Wilford's opposite, was a trained pianist and a recording producer. He recalled an incident that happened when he was with Wilford and Karajan. Wilford brought up the point that no one can fully assess a conductor's ability. Karajan quickly responded that Glotz was qualified to do so but that Wilford was not.

Glotz once had been very close to Wilford, particularly with Karajan as their commonality. Wilford advised Glotz to become Skrowaczewski's European manager. "At the time [late sixties] he was very much in favor of Stan," Glotz recalled, "but Mr. Wilford is somebody who changes like a chameleon." When Skrowaczewski first told Glotz of his concerns about Wilford, Glotz tried to serve as a diplomatic mediator between the two. Alexis Weissenberg, one of Glotz's closest clients and friends, was also under Columbia, and he, too, was disappointed with Wilford's work. He left and went to Columbia's primary competitor, Sol Hurok. Glotz and Wilford soon fell out of favor with one another.

Skrowaczewski tried to avoid leaving Columbia. In 1970 he spoke with Wilford about his career and his goals for the future. Skrowaczewski explained that he had devoted "much time" to his "thorough growth as an interpreter" and that his self-criticism allowed him to "compare his artistic results with the rest of the world."[23] He sought Wilford's opinions and advice on improving his career opportunities. It was the first time since their relationship began in the early 1960s that Skrowaczewski had raised these issues; nevertheless, this discussion and several subsequent conversations offended Wilford. Despite the respectful manner with which Skrowaczewski inquired about the future of his career, Wilford viewed his concerns as criticism.

The situation came to a head in early January 1972. While guest conducting the Philadelphia Orchestra, Skrowaczewski met with Wilford in New York. Wilford reminded Skrowaczewski about plans for a two-week engagement with the Philadelphia Orchestra during the upcoming 1973–74 season. By this time, however, Skrowaczewski was simply not satisfied with CAMI. In a friendly and professional manner he expressed his doubts about his future with Wilford, who became angry. According to Skrowaczewski,

Wilford assumed that the conductor wanted to end their business relationship and in effect stopped working for him after the meeting—without Skrowaczewski's knowledge. Three weeks after the meeting, Skrowaczewski learned that the Philadelphia engagement had been canceled. He believes other engagements were also lost.

The two had agreed to meet again in New York a few weeks after the January meeting, when Skrowaczewski would be en route to Europe, and at that time they planned to discuss his new contract with the Minnesota Orchestra. However, the illness that forced Skrowaczewski to cancel his European tour also prevented him from meeting Wilford as planned.

Wilford and Skrowaczewski finally connected by phone almost two months after the January meeting. Wilford accused Skrowaczewski, who was at home still recovering from his illness, of playing games with him, and he admonished the conductor for not having the courtesy to call him. Skrowaczewski was taken aback by his manager's attitude. The next day he wrote a letter to Wilford in which he recounted his perspective on the situation in detail. The letter, referencing Skrowaczewski's discussions with Wilford about his career, concluded:

> I was and am sorry that I have evidently hurt you, but certainly I did not mean it. I have never questioned or criticized your abilities as an outstanding impresario. Once more, when I feel that something has been lost or failed in the past, my nature usually goes all out to criticize and blame first myself. However, your repeatedly same reaction—that what you do is right and the best of all existing possibilities, and whatever doesn't come through is my personal failure—did not quite answer my questions. Certainly, I am sure, what you say is right in several cases but maybe not in all of them. However, the gist of the matter here for me is that your answers and reactions indicate that you have somehow put me in a certain "category" of artistic value and ultimately this differs from my opinion. In other words, you don't believe what I believe. By this I mean no conceited thoughts of my own possibilities or talent but rather a vast and objective evaluation of musical life nowadays. Here I see a gap between us, and as much as I like you personally, and I am grateful for all the good you have done for me, I think we should discontinue our business relationship.[24]

Skrowaczewski was the first major conductor ever to leave one of the most powerful artists managers since the days of Arthur Judson (the man who first signed Skrowaczewski to Columbia twelve years earlier). On Glotz's advice, Skrowaczewski joined the office of eighty-four-year-old Sol Hurok in spring 1972. "We went together to [Hurok's] office," recalled Skrowaczewski. "He was, of course, the most famous manager in America. His agency was smaller than Columbia's but still powerful. He accepted me with great promises for the future. But two years later he died."

Fortunately, when Skrowaczewski first joined Hurok's office, it was under the care of Sheldon Gold, who previously had worked for Columbia until Hurok stole him away. "He was then Hurok's right-hand man," said Skrowaczewski. "He was young, just forty-two at the time, and energetic. I knew that he liked me. He said, 'Listen, I'm trying to do the finest things for you possible.'" Gold became Skrowaczewski's U.S. manager under contract from March 1972 through June 1974.

After Hurok's death in 1974 chaos erupted within his company, and legal battles ensued over contracts, representation, and related matters. In May 1976 Gold was abruptly fired from the company. According to *The New York Times*, a possible reason for Gold's dismissal was the major financial loss that resulted from his bringing the Bolshoi Opera to the Met (a dream of Hurok, Gold's mentor and predecessor).[25] It didn't take Gold long to bounce back. A week later he was appointed president of ICM Artists, a newly formed classical music and dance agency under the auspices of Hollywood's conglomerate International Creative Management (ICM).

Skrowaczewski wanted to leave Hurok Concerts, Inc. and sign with Gold; however, a lawsuit brought against Gold by Hurok, Inc. over contract and representation disputes made it difficult for the maestro to join ICM. If he did, he risked becoming involved in the litigation process against Gold. Charlie Bellows wrote to Skrowaczewski: "Either you should represent yourself, as you are now doing with me as your attorney in negotiations with the Minnesota Orchestral Association, or you should secure representation by some corporation person other than Gold-ICM."[26]

It was now late August, and Skrowaczewski had been in managerial limbo since May. Work on his guest-conducting engagements and his negotiations with the MOA needed attention.

Glotz foresaw that the Hurok empire "was going to break down," and without ICM as an option at the time, he advised Skrowaczewski to consider going back to Wilford at Columbia. "I didn't say he should necessarily do it," Glotz said, "but I said that I could mention the situation to Ronald. We were not as friendly as in the past, but we were still on speaking terms. I spoke to Ronald, and he welcomed Stan back, and also Alexis and other artists of mine."

"We were accepted by Wilford with open arms, Glotz and I," Skrowaczewski said, "but it was completely the wrong move on my part. For Glotz, I don't know. They had to work together because of the artists they had in common." A major conductor leaving Wilford was unprecedented; one coming back a second time was unimaginable. A difficult working relationship persisted until 1985, when Skrowaczewski finally ended his Columbia contract and joined Gold at ICM. Three months into the contract, Gold died of a heart attack at age fifty-five.

Throughout the mid-1970s to the early 1990s—and to a certain extent, even a decade later—Skrowaczewski struggled with management problems. "I could be more clever in this area," he admitted in 2002, "but I don't like that manner of being." He continued:

> I let many things go about my own career and situation. I do what I like to do, and at that time I took the advice of Glotz, thinking that it would be okay. Given my nature, I don't always see the reason for someone to hate me or spoil my career. It's not something I would ever do myself, so I wouldn't imagine anyone else would. I'm not too clever in this regard, but I don't want to be clever in life. The politics! I hate to care about a relationship if there is no reason, no pleasure. I value a relationship where there is the satisfaction of an exchange of ideas, common goals. Fine. But otherwise? For pure politics? To be a Republican, another year a Democrat, it is not for me.

NINETEEN

Allegro energico, ma non troppo

I tried to do too much before. It is contagious, jumping from plane to plane, conducting a different orchestra every night. But it is not wise. Do it, and you don't read enough, you don't think enough, you don't live enough. Now, if the invitation is not exciting artistically, I refuse to go.

—Stanisław Skrowaczewski, 1972

Skrowaczewski made the above statement a month before beginning his thirteenth season with the Minnesota Orchestra. He expressed concern over how he was leading his professional life, which related to the conversation he had with Wilford about improving his career opportunities.

In the early 1970s some of Skrowaczewski's colleagues had settled into a professional lifestyle with dual music directorships on different coasts or continents. Some musicians and critics worried about the effect of this professional lifestyle on orchestras and on their conductors' personal growth as interpreters. Several factors accounted for the loss of the steadfast leadership maintained by maestros like Koussevitzky, Stokowski, Szell, and Toscanini. Most major orchestras moved towards longer seasons in the late 1960s and early 1970s. This change provided musicians with full-time jobs, but it also dramatically increased the conducting responsibilities of music directors. As a result, more guest conductors were hired, and most music directors led only about half a season's worth of concerts. Instead of using their extra time for study, reflection, and personal growth, many conductors of this era simply took on other music directorships or principal guest-conducting positions. This practice may have offered audience members more variety, but some observers believed it significantly diminished a music director's ability to create a cohesive ensemble.

"You *need* someone in charge," said recording producer Paul Myers:

> Szell had a "hobbyhorse" he used to ride regularly with me, and that was that the seventies and eighties would see the dissolution of the great orchestras. He said that (a) there was too much democracy and (b) that conductors wanted to be superstars and wanted to tour around like virtuoso pianists and conduct a different orchestra every week. He would say, "Someone has got to stay home and do the five-finger exercises."[1]

Skrowaczewski "stayed home" with his orchestra more often than most maestros did, and he turned down opportunities to hold multiple posts when they arose.

Throughout his professional career Skrowaczewski has publicly expressed his opinions on a wide variety of subjects. By the early 1970s, secure in his position in Minneapolis and his international standing, he became more open in the few interviews he gave. In almost every extended interview from 1960 through 1974, he expressed his disdain for Northrop Auditorium. "That hall does not inspire me to create or re-create," he said in 1972. "I'm certain it turns off the young listeners because it's too establishment, too square. We need a place to lure people away from their TV dinners."[2]

In an interview published in *The Minnesota Daily*, Skrowaczewski declared that the orchestra's departure from the campus would not sever its relationship with the university, despite his displeasure with Northrop. Yet the university had never fully capitalized on having a major orchestra in residence. When Skrowaczewski learned in 1960 that the orchestra performed on a university campus, he assumed that concert audiences would be full of students and that he might present special concerts for the university, perhaps even collaborate with the music school's ensembles.[3] But this relationship never developed. "I expected to be asked by the university to do much more," Skrowaczewski said in 1973. "I was ready to offer more. I would like to see lots of students at dress rehearsals. We made a lot of moves in this direction, yet somehow I don't feel that at present the orchestra means too much to the university."[4] The summer Contemporary Music Workshops of 1966 and 1967 were basically the only substantial collaborations between the university and the orchestra during Skrowaczewski's tenure.

"When university president O. Meredith Wilson left office in 1967, that was the end of our collaboration," Skrowaczewski noted. "The next presidents didn't respond. Wilson was really the only hope for a true partnership, and the only one who knew that this relationship was important for both sides."

Concerns about education and the proliferation of the electronic age became themes Skrowaczewski revisited during the next thirty years. "Music education is [scandalous], even at [the] university," he said in 1972. "How much musical participation expands in America depends on how much college and high school students are involved. This is an area of education left completely alone for numerous years, and the result is certainly not good."[5]

His observations were remarkably prescient:

> We must know that education in art is just as important as education in science. To put arts education on the same level as a sport like football is wrong. I have nothing against football, but all this attention to it at the expense of art is unbelievable. We must reach a balance in education. It is like food for the body—you might grow a monster if you treat food in a certain way, if one does not preserve a balance in one's [diet].[6]

Worried about the media's influence on children, Skrowaczewski warned of a "push-button" lifestyle:

> "Leisure doesn't mean sitting in a chair, pushing a button doing nothing," said Skrowaczewski, getting excited. "Even listening to the orchestra should

not be relaxing. It should stimulate the spirit just as reading a good book does. Who reads anymore? If television wanted to do it, it could spend more time on creative and exciting programs to stimulate creativity in us. And they could show commercials that do not kill us with stupidity. How can a passive people create anything in the future?"[7]

"In every kindergarten, the children should create some music themselves," he said. "They should be provided with very simple instruments, and without teaching, the teachers should just let them play. Children love to make noise."[8]

Skrowaczewski's belief in exposing children to music at an early age extended to his family. "They make some noises now, but we don't know yet if they're musical or not," he said nine months after Paul was born. "If they respond to it, okay, but if they don't, I won't force them."[9] Although Anna could not vocalize, Krystyna noticed that she did respond to music. Her physical activity with toy instruments, although often violent, did demonstrate some musical instincts. By the time Paul was a preschooler, his sensitivity to music was evident, as Skrowaczewski described in 1972:

> Paul, who is four, is in his Stravinsky period right now. He was addicted to Mozart, but now he plays *The Rite of Spring* over and over and will even play passages repeatedly. And mind you, he has hundreds of pop and children's records. But he picked Stravinsky. I don't know what it means. But I will never push him into music or anything else. Even with great talent, one must have the dedication that is stronger than life.[10]

Paul's particular fascination with the driving rhythmic ostinatos of *The Rite of Spring* may have foreshadowed his later ventures in music. By the early 1990s he was leading Psykosonik, an electronic-rock band that had a strong following in techno-pop music circles.

Skrowaczewski's societal concerns over media influence extended to his profession. "The last few seasons have witnessed a constant deterioration of the level of [music] criticism in Minneapolis papers," he wrote to the Minnesota Orchestra's leadership in 1972.[11] After the death of longtime music critic John Sherman in 1969, the *Minneapolis Star* experimented with a "democratic approach," as Skrowaczewski described it, by "using a large spectrum of concertgoers (musically educated or not) as an ever-changing panel of reviewers."[12] Writers for the paper told Skrowaczewski they wanted to see a permanent music critic. The maestro realized it wasn't his place to tell the city's newspaper how to conduct its business, but he was "worried about the impact of the written word on the large majority of [the orchestra's] less knowledgeable or potential concertgoers and supporters."[13] He wanted the MOA to privately bring "enlightenment and advice" to the paper. It is uncertain whether it did or not, but by 1971 the *Minneapolis Star* hired Michael Anthony, who would be the paper's principal classical-music critic for the next thirty-six years.

The only musician other than Skrowaczewski to ever hold the title of "laureate" with the Minnesota Orchestra is composer Dominick Argento. Skrowaczewski presently retains the title of conductor laureate; Argento is composer laureate (his honorific was the first ever created for a composer by a major American orchestra). The laureate honor for both musicians is quite fitting, considering their longevity as Minnesota residents and their consistent, significant presence on the international music scene. Their combined artistic achievements have dramatically influenced the Twin Cities' cultural landscape from the 1960s to the present.

Argento was a teenager when he heard his first symphony orchestra, the Minneapolis Symphony under Mitropoulos, when the "orchestra-on-wheels" rolled through his hometown of York, Pennsylvania, during the early days of World War II. Nearly twenty years later the ensemble became Argento's home orchestra after he accepted a position in 1958 as a professor of composition at the University of Minnesota. Cofounder of Center Opera Company (today the Minnesota Opera), Argento was a driving force behind the development of opera activity in the Twin Cities during the 1960s. He also contributed numerous scores for productions at the Guthrie Theater, collaborating with Sir Tyrone Guthrie and Douglas Campbell.

Argento made his mark as a major American composer in vocal music and lyric opera. After his 1971 opera *Postcard from Morocco* won national recognition, arts leaders in Minnesota realized that Argento's stock as composer was on the rise. It was no surprise when the orchestra commissioned him for a new work honoring its seventieth-anniversary season. Skrowaczewski opened the 1972–73 season with Argento's *A Ring of Time* and later took it on tour, and also led it with the New York Philharmonic the same season. "Stan really was the first big-time conductor who ever looked at my music," Argento said, "and he did wonderful performances. He was always concerned in rehearsals with my thoughts about how the piece was going. He never tried to impose anything on my music."

Two years after the premiere of *A Ring of Time* Argento won the 1975 Pulitzer Prize for *From the Diary of Virginia Woolf*, a song-cycle premiered by Dame Janet Baker in a Schubert Club Recital Series concert in Minneapolis. Over the next thirty years Argento received numerous important commissions and awards for his compositions. His works continue to be performed throughout the world.

In 1977 the orchestra turned again to Argento for a new work to commemorate its seventy-fifth anniversary. The result, *In Praise of Music: Seven Songs for Orchestra*, provided the composer with a unique rehearsal experience with Skrowaczewski. Argento reflected:

> Each of the seven pieces honors a "god" of music, and the last one is a tribute to Mozart. It was in a Mozart style but also clearly modern. It's scored for solo violin, no harmony. At the rehearsal, when they got to that movement, Stan suddenly started conducting it, and I thought I was losing my mind. It didn't sound like my piece, but I couldn't figure out what was happening. Well, he

had substituted a real Mozart piece and had the orchestra play it as a joke. He had me thinking for about eight measures that I was crazy. Then he turned around and laughed. For years I never thought Stan had a strong sense of humor, and I certainly had never seen him do a practical joke like that, but after that rehearsal I saw a side to him that was brand-new to me.

Argento's relationship with the orchestra continued to prosper under Skrowaczewski's successors, who also have programmed or recorded his music. Nearly five decades of observing Skrowaczewski's work gave Argento insight into his "laureate" counterpart:

Stan's dominating characteristic for me is courtliness. There's something quite aristocratic not only in his background but also in the way he approaches music, the way he writes music, and the way he presents music to others. You are in high-toned company when you are working with Stan as a composer or as a player. I've lived through six conductors now with the Minnesota Orchestra, and Skrowaczewski is by far the most aristocratic. I don't mean that in a bad sense. I mean he has a reserve and a polish and an education that just shines through in every performance.

Stan had a way of introducing beautiful new music, like works by Lutosławski and other such colleagues. He meted them out very carefully. He never made entire programs of contemporary music, and the works fit so well with the other pieces. Some conductors who set out to educate an audience end up driving them away. As a composer I admired his approach to introducing audiences to new music. It was done in such a satisfying and pleasant manner. I would put Stan very close to the top of the people who have influenced the cultural landscape of the Twin Cities, and I regard him as one of the principal reasons why it is so attractive.

After Skrowaczewski spent a week getting the anniversary season's first two series of subscription concerts off the ground, he headed to New York for the first of three weeks of concerts with the Philharmonic. Each program featured something fresh for the New Yorkers. Despite having been on the international circuit since the late 1950s, cellist János Starker made his belated debut with the New York Philharmonic performing Haydn's Cello Concerto in C (the work discovered in 1961), which Skrowaczewski previously had performed with Rostropovich in Minnesota.

That series of concerts also included Bruckner's Fourth Symphony. Harold Schonberg questioned some of Skrowaczewski's tempos in the Austrian's massive symphony, noting that the pacing was majestic but the interpretation lacked imagination and "the spacings and turns of phrase that other conductors have brought to it."[14] If Skrowaczewski's Bruckner interpretations then were not of the stature they have today, another New York critic recognized that as a "composer-conductor [he] knows how to project structure." This same critic possibly sensed the result of Skrowaczewski's efforts to slow the pace of his professional life. "He was relaxed," wrote Harriett Johnson of the *New York Post*. "The almost unbearable tension that once characterized his conducting has disappeared. Now his extraordinary musical qualities have no static to interfere with their projection."[15]

The following week Skrowaczewski gave the New York premiere of Szymanowski's Violin Concerto no. 2, the composer's last major work before his death in 1937. Henryk Szeryng was the soloist. After the New York concerts Skrowaczewski returned to Minneapolis for performances that gently flexed his compositional muscles with *Rameau Suite* from *Six Concerts en Sextuor*. Skrowaczewski arranged five pieces for string orchestra from Rameau's original work for string sextet.

"The pieces are elegant bits of French Baroque," wrote critic John Harvey. "No notes have been changed, lines and textures are clear and unmuddied, and the full string tone gives an agreeable richness of sound. In sum, a fine concert piece."[16] Skrowaczewski paired the Rameau arrangement with another interesting "first" for the orchestra. In the late 1960s Szeryng had cajoled the great-granddaughters of Niccolò Paganini to allow him to perform the Violin Concerto no. 3, a work once considered lost. With the family's blessing, Szeryng gave the first modern-day performance of the forgotten piece in this 1972 concert with the Minnesota Orchestra.

Skrowaczewski's Rameau arrangement, like his Bach transcription a few years earlier, exemplified his desire to become closer to certain pieces and to share them via the orchestra:

> I just did them for myself; there was no commission. I love the *Concerts en Sextuor,* and I chose to set those five pieces from it because of their special character and beauty. Most striking to me is the harmonic richness of the modulations, anticipating Wagner's *Tristan und Isolde.* One of the movements is particularly rich, so I repeated some moments in a different key. It didn't alter the piece. It just illuminated the quality of these amazing modulations. I also found these pieces very useful as an opener for programs featuring only string orchestra.

Years later Skrowaczewski's desire to set existing pieces for orchestra surfaced again with the music of Gesualdo (a setting of madrigals for string orchestra) and with his beloved Bruckner (the Adagio from String Quintet in F major for string orchestra). Music history offers numerous examples of composers and conductors paying similar homage to past deities of composition by expanding some of their chamber works for the orchestra. Mahler and Furtwängler performed string quartets with full string orchestra; Mitropoulos set Beethoven's arduous quartet, op. 131, for full string orchestra; and Toscanini did the same with two movements of op. 135.

After introducing his Rameau pieces in Minnesota, Skrowaczewski took them to New York for his final week with the Philharmonic. "Rameau's music doesn't get played in symphony concerts," wrote a critic in *The New York Times*, who noted that the 18th-century composer's genres were solo and chamber music. "It was good to hear some of these pieces because they can be full of startling harmonies."[17]

Although the Rameau pieces were Skrowaczewski's only compositional work since the 1969 English Horn Concerto, appreciation of him as a composer slowly increased. The second New York hearing of the concerto came at the end of the 1972–73 season. Thomas Stacy, in his first year as English hornist with the New York Philharmonic, chose the work for his first solo outing with his new ensemble. Italian conductor Aldo Ceccato led the Philharmonic. Donal Henahan of *The New York Times* heard the piece as "conductor's music… [an] expertly scored but derivative work."[18] Although Henahan didn't think much of the piece, citing as its major weakness the lack of a robust solo part for Stacy, others did. Reviews for the Minnesota Orchestra's recording of Skrowaczewski's Concerto for English horn began to surface in late summer 1972.

"Of the many times I've listened to this piece," said Lyn Farmer of *Classic Currents*, "the sound is never quite the same from time to time; each listening bringing some new discovery to my ears."[19] The *Buffalo News* noted that the concerto "represents an unusual light-textured, melodically exotic adaptation of the standard Honegger and Martinů-influenced Eastern European idiom."[20] In *High Fidelity*, Alfred Frankenstein wrote, "This is the Record of the Month so far as this reviewer's assignment is concerned, and one of the very great records of the year, thanks entirely to Skrowaczewski and Stacy. The Concerto for English Horn seems to be the first composition by the distinguished conductor of the Minnesota Orchestra to reach American discs, and it is a masterwork."[21]

Skrowaczewski began 1973 with another new experience for his orchestra: a complete concert-version performance of Wagner's *Tannhäuser*. Cast in the demanding lead role was tenor Richard Cassilly, then in his prime. His engagement was a coup for the orchestra. A week after Cassilly starred in the three-and-a-half-hour concert production in Minneapolis, he made his Met debut as Radames in *Aïda*. He would later perform in several *Tannhäuser* productions in Vienna and at the Met, solidifying his stature as an operatic tenor.

In February 1973, after a decade of requests, Skrowaczewski finally succeeded in engaging Ormandy to guest conduct the Minnesotans. "The orchestra to me seems even more homogenous and better balanced than the last time I was there," Ormandy wrote Skrowaczewski after the engagement.[22] Krystyna was a gracious host to Ormandy and his wife, Gretel, during their stay in Minneapolis. Regrettably, Skrowaczewski was out of town conducting in Paris, leading a twelve-concert series on tour with the Israel Philharmonic Orchestra.

During his Minnesota homecoming Ormandy had his first experience conducting in O'Shaughnessy Auditorium. "The hall in St. Paul seems to me far better than the terrible Northrop Auditorium," he wrote to Skrowaczewski. "I was literally suffering during Friday's concert."[23]

Ormandy was responsible indirectly for one of the most humorous Minnesota Orchestra performances that occurred during Skrowaczewski's tenure. Ormandy first invited entertainer Danny Kaye to conduct at a benefit for the Philadelphia Orchestra in 1957. During the next twenty years Kaye conducted orchestras as part of his multifaceted career. Although some of his podium antics included conducting Rimsky-Korsakov's *Flight of the Bumblebee* with a flyswatter and lying on the podium keeping time with his feet, Kaye possessed sound musical instincts. He also worked well with conductors when he sang and performed comedic routines. In 1973 the Minnesota Orchestra invited Kaye to help celebrate its seventieth anniversary.

"As a singing comedian, Danny Kaye has no peer," said longtime orchestra member Henry Kramer. "Although he is very funny in the movies, [and] there is a great deal of slapstick humor in them, his true personality as a comedian doesn't come through as it does 'live' on stage. When you sit four feet away from him as I did, there is an electric current between him and the conductor that spills over to [everyone]."[24] Skrowaczewski was equally taken with Kaye's talent: "He was an excellent conductor. His gestures were magnificent. They worked with the orchestra immediately, and it was stupendous what he achieved. I wish many conductors had his gift for gestures! He was so funny. Of these types of events, his was the best we ever had. Danny Kaye was simply incredible."

During spring 1973 Skrowaczewski began a nearly monthlong tour that ended with a week of concerts in Mexico City. The tour included a Carnegie Hall performance in which New Yorkers heard Szymanowski's popular Symphony no. 3, *Song of the Night*, for the first time. It also marked the Minnesota Orchestra's first experience with Szymanowski's penultimate symphony. Persian melodies are infused in this cantata-like symphony with a large orchestra, chorus, and tenor soloist. Skrowaczewski's New York performance of the work—along with various other Polish compositions he introduced in America—was a source of pride for Poland and the Polish artistic community in the United States. The Polish-American press covered the concert, and Skrowaczewski was hailed for his advocacy of music from his homeland as well as for his efforts in building his orchestra.

Although his life in Poland had ended some thirteen years earlier, Skrowaczewski felt gratified to be recognized for his consistent efforts on behalf of Polish composers. Several years elapsed before he would return to Poland and experience firsthand the pride his fellow Poles felt about his achievements in the West. Aside from Leopold Stokowski (born in London of Polish and Irish parentage), who conducted the Philadelphia Orchestra for twenty-six years, no Polish-American conductor to this day has led a major American symphony orchestra longer than Skrowaczewski's nineteen years with the Minnesota Orchestra. Artur Rodziński served for eighteen consecutive years as music director of three major American orchestras (Los Angeles Philharmonic, Cleveland Orchestra, and the New York Philharmonic).

Not since its 1957 Middle East tour under Doráti had the Minnesota Orchestra traveled internationally. To celebrate its seventieth anniversary the ensemble would perform outside the United States for the first time in sixteen years. Although performances in Mexico during the orchestra's spring 1973 tour did not carry the same artistic weight as those in Europe, the tour nevertheless was a chance to polish the ensemble's reputation under its new name and, to some extent, reclaim its international stature. The effort failed miserably.

The confusion over the orchestra's 1968 name change continued to plague the organization. The tour got off to a sadly prophetic start when it was announced over the Minneapolis airport intercom that boarding for the University of Minnesota

Orchestra was commencing.[25] If that mistake demoralized orchestra members, it paled in comparison to the ill feeling some of them experienced upon arriving in Mexico City. "They held us on the plane and sprayed the interior with something terrible," Skrowaczewski remembered. "It was foul smelling, and my eyes and nose were running for quite some time. The orchestra was furious. They opposed the action, but the Mexican authorities said that this was the law." Skrowaczewski speculated that a DDT-like pesticide was used. Although DDT was banned in the United States in 1972, it may have been used on planes to kill malaria-carrying mosquitoes. It is still used in agriculture and disease-control in Mexico and around the world today.[26]

The orchestra's opening concert took place at the Teatro de Bellas Artes, a theater and concert hall within the Palacio de Bellas Artes (Palace of Fine Arts) in Mexico City. The theater has an audience capacity of 3,500, and the entire complex is so big and artistically opulent that it took thirty years to complete. Built of Carrara marble, the weighty structure has sunk at least twelve feet since construction began in 1901.

When Skrowaczewski and his players looked out to see an audience of only 379, they no doubt suspected that their first international outing as the Minnesota Orchestra was doomed. "I was angry and depressed because of this empty hall," said the maestro. "Everyone blamed it on the confusion over our still relatively new name."

"It was a disaster. It was like the end of *Laugh In*," recalled former concertmaster Lea Foli, referencing the television comedy series that concluded each episode with a blank screen and the sound of one person clapping. "Nobody knew who we were," he said. "They thought it was the University of Minnesota Orchestra. At the first concert we had just a few hundred people in the audience, and lots of them had come from Minneapolis! They were from the board [or were] family members of the orchestra."

Mary Ann Feldman, who was on the tour, explained that most concertgoing Mexicans and music critics did not understand that this orchestra was in fact the famous but renamed Minneapolis Symphony Orchestra. The inclusion of the word "Minnesota" in its title led most Mexicans to assume the group was the university orchestra or band. According to Richard Cisek, Bellas Artes failed to properly advertise the orchestra's concerts. He and Feldman worked hard to spread the word, and by the fourth and final concert an audience of 1,400 gathered to hear the performance.[27] Nevertheless, the trip lowered the orchestra's morale for years to come.

Skrowaczewski followed the unpleasant experience in Mexico with a two-week engagement with the Philadelphia Orchestra. Ormandy's regard for Skrowaczewski was the most important factor in the Minnesota maestro's recurring engagements with the ensemble. By now his relationship with the Philadelphians was a decade old, and they admired and respected his musicianship. They expected no-nonsense, refined music making from Skrowaczewski, and they got it. Ormandy gave his colleague the freedom to program almost anything he wished. Skrowaczewski elaborated on the quality of the Philadelphia Orchestra during his spring 1973 guest-conducting stint:

> The longer I live and work, the more I can really appreciate this orchestra. They play so well, they're so flexible…so beautifully elastic. They follow you so perfectly it's dangerous, because if you are not in the mood they'll play flat. And they catch on so quickly. Ten years ago, when I first came here, I didn't realize how good they were, but now I know.[28]

The Philadelphians also saw a side of Skrowaczewski of which most Minnesotans were unaware. Near the end of his two-week engagement, he and members of the Philadelphia Orchestra participated in an outdoor concert and rally protesting the treatment of Jewish musicians, artists, and writers in the Soviet Union. "We must raise our voices in protest against such cruelty," he exclaimed to a crowd of a thousand people.[29] When *The Sunday Bulletin* interviewed Skrowaczewski after the event, he was asked about his homeland. His anger over Poland's treatment by the United States during World War II was still palpable: "A terrible situation! Roosevelt sold Poland to Stalin at Yalta."[30]

Skrowaczewski's closing programs of his orchestra's seventieth-anniversary season featured some of the finest new American music. Minnesotans heard *Windows*, the 1972 Pulitzer Prize-winning work by Jacob Druckman, and Karel Husa's *Music for Prague 1968*. Also a Pulitzer Prize recipient, Husa received the coveted award in 1969 for his String Quartet no. 3. Skrowaczewski's performance of *Music for Prague* reunited him with Husa for the first time since 1948. "I found your interpretation of my music one of the most powerful I have heard," the longtime Cornell University professor wrote Skrowaczewski soon after attending the Minnesota performances.[31]

Music for Prague is Husa's most-performed work, having received more than ten thousand performances worldwide by wind ensembles and orchestras. (It is one of the few pieces originally composed for wind ensemble that was transcribed for orchestra.) Husa completed the work seven weeks after the Soviet Union invaded and occupied Czechoslovakia in August 1968. The composition was not heard live in Czechoslovakia (now the Czech Republic and Slovakia), until 1990. Husa returned to his homeland after more than forty years in exile to conduct the Czech premiere of *Music for Prague*, which was broadcast nationally on radio and television.[32]

At the Minnesota Orchestra's first concert featuring *Music for Prague*, Skrowaczewski received Columbia University's Alice M. Ditson Conductor's Award for 1973. Created and given annually since 1945 to honor conductors committed to the performance of American music, the award placed Skrowaczewski in an elite group of conductors that includes Stokowski, Bernstein, Schuller, Ormandy, Rostropovich, and Christoph von Dohnányi. "It is to the heartland of the United States that you have brought the maturity of your talents," the citation read. It continued:

> We honor you today as a musician who has generously and consistently conducted orchestral works of other composers of your own time, in particular

the music of American composers. That these have been consistently of high quality is perhaps a reflection of your own high standards as a composer. That they have been performed from no motive of parochial expediency is clear from your championship of European composers of quality and seriousness.[33]

Not long after Columbia University award bestowed this award on Skrowaczewski, Macalester College, a St. Paul institution, presented him with an honorary doctorate.

Skrowaczewski ended the orchestra's seventieth season with the most important "downbeat" of his entire career as music director. In late June he "conducted"—baton and all—city and orchestra officials in the groundbreaking ceremony for Orchestra Hall, where sixteen months later he would lead the orchestra's debut concert in its new home. Skrowaczewski had no time to savor the fulfillment of this long-awaited dream. Days after shovels turned over the soil for a new era in his orchestra's history, he undertook a substantial summer season of guest conducting.

It began with two Philadelphia Orchestra concerts at The Robin Hood Dell, one featuring tenor Richard Tucker and baritone Robert Merrill. The two veteran Metropolitan Opera stars drew a capacity audience of nearly twenty-five thousand for a program of arias and duets. "The orchestra accompanied the singing manfully under the baton of Stanisław Skrowaczewski," wrote one critic, "but without great flexibility. Balances were orderly, but an ease of movement was not apparent."[34] With two big personalities performing mostly operatic excerpts with limited rehearsal time, Skrowaczewski felt he did well navigating his soloists' idiosyncratic tempos. It was not the kind of musical experience he enjoyed.

From Philadelphia he headed to the Berkshires for a monthlong stay at Tanglewood, where he served as conductor-in-residence. He led conducting seminars at the Berkshire Music Center, rehearsals with the student orchestra, and two programs with the Boston Symphony Orchestra. Skrowaczewski's first concert, an all-Mozart program, followed the opening-night performance of Haydn's epic *The Creation*, led by the orchestra's thirty-seven-year-old music director-designate, Seiji Ozawa. Skrowaczewski's Mozart concert elicited this thoughtful response from one reviewer:

> The glamorous, hair-flying-in-the-face, pleading conductor [Seiji Ozawa], whose pyrotechnics are the talk of the music world, is no stranger to American audiences.... Stanisław Skrowaczewski is an interesting change from this melodramatic conducting epoch. In addition, he is capable of eliciting a remarkable performance from the Boston Symphony, an orchestra that does not always play remarkably well. Ramrod straight on the podium, crisp-gestured, saving extravagances for special occasions, he is definitely not a distraction from the music.... [He] led the highlight of the Tanglewood concert Saturday night, the *Haffner*, at a brilliantly conceived pace. The result was one of the most articulated performances I've heard the Boston Symphony give in recent years.[35]

Two weeks later Skrowaczewski and Ormandy led concerts that were part of a weekend-long Beethoven festival, which drew a record 42,604 concertgoers.[36]

Ormandy, whose regular appearances at Tanglewood had become much anticipated by the musicians and the public alike, conducted the first two concerts.

More than 14,000 people packed Skrowaczewski's Sunday concert. "Audiences experienced two widely contrasted approaches to Beethoven's music," wrote one reviewer. "Ormandy's Beethoven was great oratory; Skrowaczewski's was calculated, precise, mathematical."[37] Another writer noted that Skrowaczewski "delivered [the Funeral March from the *Eroica*] with 'spine-tingling effect,'" adding that "…it is seldom that music so familiar can re-create the effect it had before it became too familiar."[38]

Just days after his Beethoven triumph at Tanglewood, Skrowaczewski was at Severance Hall rehearsing the Cleveland Orchestra for two performances at Blossom Festival. Nearly the entire repertoire was strategically scheduled for use on the orchestra's monthlong tour to Hawaii, New Zealand, and Australia. Skrowaczewski shared conducting duties on the tour with Erich Leinsdorf and Lorin Maazel, the Cleveland Orchestra's new music director. Amid the standard repertoire on Skrowaczewski's Blossom Festival concerts, a seldom-heard work—Szymanowski's Symphony no. 4 (Symphonie Concertante)—stood out as surprisingly popular. Eugene Istomin was Skrowaczewski's soloist for this hybrid piano concerto-within-a-symphony. "It is an ungrateful piece for the pianist," Skrowaczewski told an interviewer, "but [Istomin] is such a fine musician, he recognizes the beauty that is in it. This is twenty-one minutes of music, but today we spent two hours on it. There are too many strands of polyphony, too much you have to get through to get at the real core of the music."[39]

Bain Murray of the *Cleveland Sun Messenger* called Skrowaczewski's performances "the two best concerts of the season thus far," noting that "the Cleveland Orchestra has not sounded this splendid since George Szell died."[40] Such praise can always be taken with a grain of salt, but Murray brought considerable experience to his critical assessments. A recognized composer and a Polish-music scholar, he headed the theory and composition department at Cleveland State University; Piston, Boulanger, and Randall Thompson were among his teachers. Murray, a perceptive observer and reviewer of the Cleveland Orchestra for several decades, described Skrowaczewski's Blossom Festival performance of Shostakovich's Fifth Symphony as the finest he had heard since one led by Rodziński at Ravinia years earlier.[41]

After completing his orchestra's season and then guest conducting three major orchestras consecutively, Skrowaczewski took a break by fulfilling a longtime ambition: climbing the highest peak ["The Grand"] of the Grand Tetons. With a guide and a group of eight climbers he reached the 13,766-foot peak on a gorgeous, clear day. The journey to the top was an involved process. After reaching a preliminary spot, the climbers made camp on a ledge. At 4:00 a.m., under the light of the moon and with flashlights, they undertook the last leg of the climb. The early start was timed for their arrival on the peak at sunrise. Skrowaczewski was the best climber in the group, and the guide relied on him to help a young woman who was inexperienced and frightened. "She was a scientist from Los Angeles," Skrowaczewski recalled. "On the difficult spots

I just pulled her up, not all the time, but on the steep walls of the mountain that are practically vertical. You have to be a skilled climber to manage them."

After the climbers reached the summit, they enjoyed the morning, taking photos and savoring the magnificent view. Skrowaczewski was eager to register his achievement. A small canister fastened to a rock contained a ledger listing the names of former climbers. The maestro's penultimate Minnesota predecessor, Mitropoulos, had signed the ledger in 1949, the year he left Minneapolis to take over the New York Philharmonic. Skrowaczewski removed the ledger from the misshapen canister, warped by decades of lightning strikes, and signed his name. Under the cobalt-blue sky he soaked in the view and reflected on his personal triumph. A few days later he was on a plane to Hawaii to conduct the opening concert of the Cleveland Orchestra's tour.

Skrowaczewski's monthlong tour with the Cleveland Orchestra in September 1973 was the first coup for Sheldon Gold, his new manager from Sol Hurok's office. "He was quite proud of this accomplishment for me," Skrowaczewski remembered. "Maazel couldn't do the entire tour, so Leinsdorf and I were asked. We each did one concert in Honolulu, then Leinsdorf did New Zealand, and I did Australia. Leinsdorf was supposed to do part of Australia, but when he became sick I took over his concerts without any rehearsals. At the end of the tour Maazel came for concerts in the brand-new Sydney Opera House."

Before the Cleveland Orchestra left Honolulu, it coincidentally met up with the Philadelphia Orchestra, then en route to China, the first America orchestra ever to tour that country. "It was a marvelous meeting," Skrowaczewski recalled. "Here were two of the finest orchestras in the world having a chance meeting. There was a lovely party in the ballroom of the hotel where everyone was staying. All the musicians socialized and were happy to be in each other's company." Skrowaczewski reconnected with his other "orchestra family" before the Cleveland contingent boarded its plane to New Zealand. Onboard, the Cleveland Orchestra musicians distinguished themselves by breaking the airline's existing record for alcohol consumption on a trip. According to the airline, the record had been previously held by a flight filled with Australian soldiers.[42] Leinsdorf led concerts in Auckland, Wellington, and Christchurch before the troupe headed to Australia.

Skrowaczewski had acoustics on his mind when he arrived in Brisbane to lead the tour's first Australian concert. Construction of his orchestra's new home was underway, and now he would have the chance to hear the sound of the Sydney Opera House later in the tour. "Acoustics are as important for the orchestra itself as for the audience," he told his Brisbane hosts. "If you don't have the best, the result is rather like frozen food. You don't get the real tone or flavor."[43] The Brisbane concert, as well those Skrowaczewski led in Adelaide and Melbourne, received rousing receptions, with three or four encores after each performance: "The people would not leave their seats until I took the concertmaster by the arm and we would walk offstage. It was thrilling."[44]

In Brisbane Skrowaczewski visited Lone Pine Koala Sanctuary, the first and largest of its kind in the world. "I fed kangaroos, hugged a koala bear, and had a photo taken with a python around my neck," he said proudly. "I did it just so I could tell Paul and Nicholas about it." In Canberra, the capital city, Prime Minister Gough Whitlam hosted an afternoon party for Leinsdorf, Skrowaczewski, and others. Skrowaczewski enjoyed talking with Whitlam and learning about Australian politics.

On arrival from Canberra Skrowaczewski was reunited at the Adelaide Airport with his cousin Witold Kropiński, whom he hadn't seen in thirty-four years. Kropiński fought in the Polish Army during World War II and settled in Australia soon after 1945. He and Skrowaczewski had been close friends while growing up in Lwów. Witold attended his cousin's concert, and for a period the two corresponded but eventually lost touch.

"Wonders were expected, and wonders there were in abundance," wrote a critic about one of Skrowaczewski's three Melbourne concerts with the Cleveland Orchestra. "It was the finest display of virtuoso playing I have ever heard."[45] Indeed, the orchestra was still the polished gem Szell had left upon his death in 1970. With good chemistry between conductor and orchestra—which Skrowaczewski had—the Cleveland Orchestra could still deliver an almost otherworldly performance.

Leinsdorf, of course, also was experienced in "playing" this great orchestra, having been its music director for three years before Szell took over in 1946. Eleven years older than Skrowaczewski, Leinsdorf had a slightly paternal attitude towards his younger colleague on the tour. During their long hours of travel together, the pair spoke often about music. A rather cerebral and erudite musician, Leinsdorf had interesting methods of conducting one of the tour works, Beethoven's Fifth Symphony, as Skrowaczewski observed:

> He was a fascinating musician. I observed his first rehearsal of Beethoven's Fifth. He told the orchestra that the fermatas at the beginning of the first movement would be measured. The first fermata would be held four or five measures and the second, nine. It didn't sound natural to me, but somehow he made it work. But what was more surprising to me was his interpretation of the well-known dotted 32nd-note figures against the triplet figures at the end of the first phrases of the opening of the second movement (measures fourteen and eighteen). He told them to do both figures the same, as triplets, negating the 32nd-figure altogether, saying that Beethoven didn't write it methodically, and he meant it to be the same. How did he know this? I have no idea. And yet the three against four that is created when these figures are done as written is beautiful (especially at a slower tempo, because at a fast tempo it doesn't work). The character changes completely by making it the same! In fact, later in the second movement, when the strings play triplets and the trumpets, horns, oboes, and timpani have the 32nd-figure against them, I always ask these instruments to be very precise, so that they fall a little after the triplet [and] this effect of three against four is preserved. It works well and sounds natural. But Leinsdorf had his own theories on such topics. His book, *The Composer's Advocate*, is very interesting, but I find many of his ideas strange. I find myself asking, "Why?"

From Melbourne Skrowaczewski went to Sydney. He didn't plan to stay long, but he left even sooner when he discovered there were problems with airline strikes. He managed to get the last plane to Melbourne and eventually back to the States before an airline shutdown. Before he left, however, Skrowaczewski heard Maazel rehearse the Cleveland Orchestra for the opening concert of the Sydney Opera House Concert Hall. "The Cleveland," as the Australians dubbed the orchestra, was the first visiting ensemble to perform in the new space. Queen Elizabeth II officially opened the Opera House two weeks after the orchestra's fourth concert.

Skrowaczewski arrived home in time to celebrate his fiftieth birthday at an elegant party hosted by Krystyna. Close friends and associates of the orchestra attended the gathering at the couple's comfortable Wayzata home. Three days later Skrowaczewski was back leading the Minnesota Orchestra. After two run-out concerts, the ensemble played the first subscription concert of its last season scheduled at Northrop Auditorium. No tears were shed during the last opening night in the "great barn."

The next six years would encompass the greatest triumphs and difficulties of Skrowaczewski's tenure in Minnesota. Major orchestras across the United States continued to face the financial realities of year-round seasons, and they implemented new administrative, marketing, and programming strategies that now are commonplace. The era did not suit a musician like Skrowaczewski, for whom music is an artistic entity with values that transcend the business of the art.

TWENTY

RESURRECTION OF THE INVISIBLE

This hall will stimulate our awareness of art and sharpen our sense of life. We should regard this place not as an arena for competition between stars but as a temple of mystery and contemplation in which the dialogue with the unknown will continue....

—Stanisław Skrowaczewski, 1974

Looking a decade younger than his fifty years, Skrowaczewski strode briskly to the Northrop Auditorium podium at the Minnesota Orchestra's opening-night concert on October 11, 1973. His three quick, circular gestures signaling the start of Mozart's *Jupiter* Symphony were especially ebullient. Having completed a summer of prestigious guest-conducting engagements, he looked forward to a brilliant season with his own orchestra, interesting international guest-conducting assignments, and a new concert hall finally under construction.

"The Minnesota Orchestra under Stanisław Skrowaczewski is one of the finest in the country," reported *Time* magazine in an August 1973 feature story trumpeting "The Good Life in Minnesota" on its cover.[1] A few months earlier the magazine had rated the Minnesota Orchestra in the same category as the Boston, Cleveland, and Pittsburgh orchestras—seventh overall—with Chicago, New York, and Philadelphia as the top three. Generally speaking, such ratings are subjective and influenced by the histories, locations, and budgets of the orchestras ranked. However, the national media's positive coverage of the orchestra during the mid-1970s—preceded by the critically acclaimed premiere of Penderecki's *St. Luke Passion* in the late 1960s—gave the Twin Cities their due as a cultural force in America. The *Time* cover story, "Minnesota: A State That Works," extolled the qualities that made the state an ideal place in which to work and live: a rich and varied natural environment, a thriving business community, a major research university and excellent medical facilities, a low crime rate, the lowest high school dropout rate in the country, largely untainted politics, popular sports teams, "Minnesota-nice" friendliness, and strong community involvement with the arts.

"California is the flashy blonde you like to take out once or twice. Minnesota is the girl you want to marry," said Chuck Ruhr, a Minneapolis advertising executive featured in the *Time* article.[2]

Although Skrowaczewski had the advantage of developing his career from a home base that suited his temperament, the imbalance between his productivity as a composer and his conducting activity persisted. Although his stature as a conductor was well established by the mid-1970s, his life as a composer once again had stalled.

The Concerto for English Horn and Orchestra had not rejuvenated his composing as he had hoped it would.

"The whole concerto was a little joke for me," Skrowaczewski wrote to Philadelphia music critic Peter Chrisafides. "What else and how else could I come to composing after something like sixteen years of intermission?"[3] After hearing three radio broadcasts of the piece, Chrisafides attended its first performance by the New York Philharmonic in April 1973. He was so taken by the work that he sent Skrowaczewski his brief analysis of it. "It is a sad and wasteful thing that you do not compose actively," Chrisafides wrote. "After the concert, others said as much, particularly Hanna Lachert."[4] The Polish-born Lachert, a new member of the New York Philharmonic's violin section, performed frequently as a soloist who championed contemporary music for her instrument.

Other musicians contacted Skrowaczewski about composing for them. Oboist and composer Larry Singer suggested the possibility of a concerto for oboe and English horn (one player), and distinguished bassist Gary Karr also asked Skrowaczewski to compose a concerto for his instrument. Karr, who made his Minnesota debut with Skrowaczewski in 1967, had established an international career as a double-bass soloist, the first ever in music history.[5] When Karr contacted Skrowaczewski in 1973, Henze and Schuller, among others, had already composed works for him. The maestro wrote Karr that he had been thinking of a work for contrabassoon and orchestra, so the idea of a bass concerto also appealed to him.

"Let's hope during a summer I could [write you a piece]," he told Karr. "In such a case, and if I find my ideas worthy of distributing to anyone around me, I will certainly send it to you...."[6]

"I am so enthusiastic about your English horn concerto," Karr responded, "and if this is an indication of your compositional development, I shall wait twenty years with the same enthusiasm for you to write a work for my instrument."[7]

It never happened, although the genre brought Skrowaczewski back to composing within a few years, when he wrote *Ricercari Notturni*, a concerto for soprano, alto, and baritone saxophones, all played by one musician. This piece received its premiere in 1978, the same year that the first French horn and first clarinet players of the Berlin Philharmonic asked Skrowaczewski if he would consider writing separate works for them. Unfortunately his time and the opportunity for the projects slipped away.

He accepted his fate of being a conductor first and a composer second. "I would really love to be able to come back to composing," he wrote Singer in 1973, "but I don't see any time and concentration possibilities right now."[8] He knew that it would take substantial time for him to compose a work that represented his new voice. "I don't think I'd continue the kind of music I wrote in the English horn piece," he told a Philadelphia reporter. "When I did that, I was unprepared for composition; I was trying to get back to my music of the 1950s. I wouldn't do that again."[9]

After 1979 he begin to compose somewhat regularly. From 1980 to the present he has produced on average at least one work every two to three years, composing between guest-conducting engagements.

With the promise of Orchestra Hall as a backdrop, Skrowaczewski's tenure in Minneapolis experienced a kind of second honeymoon in the mid-1970s. His relationship with the ensemble varied during this period, but the musicians, the MOA, and the public generally recognized that he was largely the force behind the hall's creation. Many people also appreciated that he had elevated the orchestra's quality and greatly expanded the breadth of its repertoire.

He was not a person to rest on his laurels. He knew that a new hall was but one essential step toward bringing the orchestra to its full potential. With renewed energy and hope he began pushing old and new agendas with vigor. "A lot of people know how much Skrowaczewski pushed himself, but few knew how much he pushed others to excel," said Richard Cisek in *Thank You Maestro*, a television special broadcast in 1979.[10]

The maestro had long advocated for improved conditions for his musicians. During his second season in Minneapolis he gave a talk to music journalists from around the country about the key barriers to progress for symphony orchestras. A short season meant that musicians were underpaid, he explained, and consequently they lacked sufficient Social Security benefits when they needed to retire. "All this makes the union of musicians struggle for better job security, and this is naturally all right," he said. "But the trouble starts when this battle interferes with the other struggle: the one for artistic standards, which is led only by a musical director alone!"[11]

Despite the excitement over the new hall, Skrowaczewski's fourteenth season, which began in fall 1973, was somewhat rocky. It was almost postponed due to a contract dispute between the orchestra and the MOA. Just hours before rehearsals for the first subscription concert began, an agreement was reached on a new three-year contract. The musicians were guaranteed a longer season (from forty-eight to fifty weeks, beginning in 1975–76) and improvements in medical benefits, vacation time, rehearsal schedules, and other details. The musicians agreed to more radio and television broadcasts without additional fees. They also consented to increased scheduling flexibility for educational outreach and special projects such as "Explorations with Skrowaczewski," a new concert series devoted to rarely heard chamber orchestra works.

However, the resolution that ultimately settled the dispute was the end of a mutual-benefit fund originally established to aid musicians in emergency health and leave situations. The musicians had won improved sick-leave benefits, which made the mutual fund unnecessary. They voted to release the fund to MOA's pension fund, a step that permitted an increase to the musicians wage packages. It was a controversial move but one that has resulted in helping all musicians, according to violinist Julie Ayer.[12] The orchestra was fortunate to have reached an agreement so quickly. The New York Philharmonic's dispute over its contract, concurrent with Minnesota's, caused a strike that lasted ten weeks.[13]

Skrowaczewski's strategy for moving the orchestra to the next level of artistry also caused disputes. The new concert hall would change and shape the sound of the ensemble, but replacing musicians who were past their prime was an inevitable part of improvement. "It has to be done," said former MOA president David Hyslop, "because if you don't do it, there's a danger of other players going downhill as well." Skrowaczewski did not undertake the responsibility lightly. "He didn't deal with that task willy-nilly," recalled Hyslop. "It wasn't like with some conductors, who immediately come in and start firing people. Stan is from the European system; he's more formal."

Rather than take immediate action when a musician played poorly, Skrowaczewski kept notes. In the case of one musician whose playing disappointed certain colleagues as well, he presented the union with a five-page memo containing no less than thirty-six specific examples of faulty playing dating from 1960 to 1972. "I feel obliged to mention that I have not been keeping a lot of notes about musicians generally speaking—only the cases that I consider grave and disturbing to the level of the orchestra," his memo stated. "You would be interested to know that for the twelve years as music director, I have some notes about only twelve musicians in all. It is remarkable, to me at least, that [this musician] caused me to write more notes than any other musician."[14]

Despite strong grounds for having the musician fired, he lost the battle. "I flew back to be a witness," remembered Hyslop, by then working as general manager of the Oregon Symphony. "When the arbitrator asked our associate conductor if the musician's playing was inadequate, he said it was, but then [the arbitrator] asked him if it was any better since the last complaint. He said it was a 'little' better but that it still was not up to the caliber of the orchestra. The ruling was that if the playing level was better after nineteen years, then the musician could remain in his position. He ended up playing for many more years."

Skrowaczewski had no patience for such nuanced legalities. "The situation was one example of how insistent and difficult the union could sometimes be," he said. "And the arbitrator, from Boston, was not a musician. He probably hadn't been to a symphony orchestra concert in his life. It was scandalous, in my opinion, and unjust. The management was weak in agreeing to use such an arbitrator."

Although Skrowaczewski had difficulties making orchestra personnel changes during the latter part of his tenure, he continued to push for additional musicians. He wrote to the executive leadership in 1974: "We have always been short of the proper number of string players in all sections in comparison with about ten other major orchestras in the States."[15] He sought only one more player per section, but he knew this step would be an important, albeit subtle, enhancement to the overall sound. Such numbers were more in line with those of the most elite orchestras, including New York, Cleveland, and particularly Berlin and Vienna. "There has always been a great problem finding good string players in America," he observed in his memo. "If an opportunity occurs, we should try to grasp immediately a fine player, as numerous orchestras have vacancies in strings, and sometimes we have to wait two or three years for the right person."[16] By 1979 Skrowaczewski had only two of the five string sections at the numbers he wanted. Although not ideal, the Minnesota numbers were on par with most major U.S. orchestras.

Budget deficits in early 1974 forced hard choices on the MOA. The decision to cancel the orchestra's annual Carnegie Hall concert did not sit well with Skrowaczewski, who immediately fired off a memo to the chairman and executive committee:

> I understand *very well* the burden of the financial stress and deficit. However, I cannot forget that some years ago our association, facing the unknown deficit and risk, decided to send the orchestra to New York and other cities every season and to enlarge the personnel with the best available (therefore costly) musicians—all this in order to make it better. The recent marvelous decision and effort to build the concert hall speaks for itself as a reflection of deep civic care and vision of the development of this community.
>
> It takes years to improve the orchestra. It has already taken a lot of money to afford the new good musicians, and it took thousands of hours for us to audition and find [them]. I am afraid that one hastily taken decision may spoil years of such efforts. The concert tour to New York may seem to some to be a minor event; indeed, it would amount hardly to one percent of the budget. However, because of 1) comparison with other American orchestras (even less good) that have national and international tours; 2) the finally achieved pride of our leading musicians and their high evaluation of the orchestra's level; 3) the fact that the cancellation of the tour suddenly withdrew this only major artistic exposure our musicians used to have, all this becomes a matter of symbolic importance and as such, if not solved, can produce a detrimental effect and undercut the rising level of the orchestra.[17]

The Carnegie Hall concerts were reinstated. The Oakleaf Foundation, a philanthropic organization headed by Ken and Judy Dayton, covered the costs.

Skrowaczewski had not given up on the idea of a European tour, either. He arranged for a meeting between Glotz, Engle, and Cisek to discuss the possibility for spring 1975 or fall 1976. With his command of the European concert scene and his experience as Skrowaczewski's European impresario, Glotz was ideally suited to design an effective itinerary for the Minnesota Orchestra's European debut. But the effort was perhaps doomed before he even tried. Skrowaczewski later recalled, "They all said, 'We can only do one thing at a time,' and I said, 'Do the hall.'"[18] No music director before or after Skrowaczewski had done more to earn the honor of performing in major European capitals. "I felt badly for Stan," remarked Hyslop. "With his reputation and international career, I wish he had toured Europe with Minnesota."

Skrowaczewski continued to seek the best international conductors for guest engagements. He knew that outstanding guest conductors furthered the orchestra's development and its reputation. However, he faced at least two obstacles to this goal: the availability of top conductors for so few spots (Skrowaczewski conducted half of the subscription concerts) and the refusal of some management firms—namely Columbia Artists—to book their top conductors with orchestras they did not rank among the world's elite.

Nevertheless, he secured notable maestros for guest engagements. Venerable masters of the podium included Ormandy, Leinsdorf, Doráti, and Peter Maag. Copland, Gunther Schuller, and Lukas Foss represented the composer-conductor contingent, and Yehudi Menuhin and Alexander Schneider, the violinist-conductor faction. Notable guests closer to Skrowaczewski's generation included Austrian conductor-composer Michael Gielen, Robert Shaw, and Rafael Frühbeck de Burgos. Five maestros appeared who would figure importantly in the orchestra's future: Marriner, Edo de Waart, Klaus Tennstedt, David Zinman, and Leonard Slatkin. Along with Slatkin and Zinman, the other young guest conductors included Dennis Russell Davies, Sir Andrew Davis, Michael Tilson Thomas, and James Levine.

"Why don't Minneapolis and St. Paul have visits by other major U.S. orchestras?" asked an audience member in a survey conducted by the MOA. Skrowaczewski also noticed this gap in the Twin Cites' musical scene. He wrote to Cisek and Engle, then MOA president:

> It is with rather great sorrow that I do not see any visiting guest orchestras in the Twin Cities. I know that a number of great orchestras come almost every year to areas very close to us, such as Madison (not to speak of Chicago); Ames, Iowa; Iowa City, etc.... Whatever the financial problems and risks [there] may have been in the past, I would like to see our association somehow not be impervious to this very important factor in our musical life—the comparison with some other great orchestras."[19]

In early 1973 the maestro called a meeting to discuss the sponsorship of future concerts by visiting orchestras and the creation of a series coordinated with community organizations. Thus, between 1974 and 1979, on a series entitled The Great Performers, Minnesotans heard the Chicago Symphony under Solti, the Los Angeles Philharmonic under Giulini, and Amsterdam's Concertgebouw Orchestra under Bernard Haitink. Later the Cleveland Orchestra conducted by Maazel performed in Orchestra Hall.

In spring 1973 the MOA distributed a survey to audience members at two concerts with contrasting programs. Over 1,700 people responded to a variety of topics that provided a barometer of views on Skrowaczewski's programming. Essentially the opinions were divided among three camps. Opinions ranged from calls for "More 20th-century music!" to "I like some contemporary music, but please spare us the ones that are merely experimental *contrived* dissonance" to "Modern composers' premieres drive me nuts! Why foist them on us?"[20]

Skrowaczewski spent long hours answering dozens of letters about his programming. The following letter from 1974 is typical of what he wrote to audience members who were fed up with contemporary music:

> Dear Mrs. Power:
>
> Thank you for your letter of January 13 concerning our programming. I have always been glad to receive opinions and criticisms from our audience, as this is a very interesting and necessary dialogue between the performer and listener.

I always take these listeners' opinions very seriously, as I definitely feel the great importance of reaching the widest possible segment of the public through our concerts and not attempting to create an isolated tower for a select few.

Please do not think that I will try to defend my position on the matter of programming. I will rather try to discuss those factors which have led to my position.

As you can imagine, any performer responsible for programming can always be criticized from at least two sides: the more conservative public may charge him with playing too much contemporary music, and the other side for always playing "the old warhorses."

I understand well that a composition may sound incomprehensible, irritating, or simply ugly. Being honest, we may do anything we find suitable—we may restrain from applauding or even "boo"—any fresh manifestation of our feelings is always better than a lukewarm response. But we must not forget that our neighbor may have opposite feelings, and in such a case tolerance may give the best results.

You may be surprised to know that my personal penchant, what I like to play myself, is definitely 19th-century classical or romantic music. But I try to create a certain balance between the known and the unknown in our programs, as I strongly feel that the common division between contemporary and old music is really artificial and wrong. There is bad and good music at every time and in every epoch. We play the great composers of the past and the great composers of this century. In fact, I couldn't imagine any artistic organization limiting itself to a certain date in the history of art. What would we lose, for instance, if we couldn't see any paintings after 1900, or couldn't read books written in the last fifty years, or were deprived of theater and film activity and artistic results within the last half century?

What I would most like to achieve is to convince you, and other listeners with similar reactions to our presentation of the works of our great modern composers, that a variety of styles is really psychologically necessary in our appreciation of music. Very often a new, unknown work illuminates in a retrospective way the older, well-known compositions. It is fascinating to see the changes in musical thinking and language occurring over at least the last three hundred years, and occurring also within the lifespan of one composer. This history gives us an overwhelming testimony that the composers of the past whom we today consider the great ones were great in their own day and withstood the test of time only because they brought to their music a fresh and new approach—if not revolutionary changes!

Last, but not least, I would like to note that in the totality of the orchestra's programming, we play something like fifteen to twenty percent of more or less new music. Do please look into our programs of this or past seasons, and you will find all of the great classical or romantic symphonies and concertos.

I hope that you will find indeed a lot of beauty and artistic excitement in our future programs.

Sincerely,
Stanisław Skrowaczewski
Music Director [21]

When another letter writer postulated that American orchestras programmed more contemporary music than European ensembles did, he disagreed: "Our programs could even perhaps be classified as more conservative in many cases."[22]

Some Minnesotans agreed that the orchestra's programs *were* too conservative. "I feel the orchestra should play more contemporary works," wrote another audience member. "I recognize that the age profile of the typical concertgoer is older; however, if new, more modern pieces are not presented, the younger patrons will not get into the concert habit. A trip to the concert is like a visit to the Minneapolis Institute of Arts—there should be an element of going to the Walker [Art Center] in that same experience."[23]

On the topic of standard orchestral repertoire, Bruckner's name surfaced often on the surveys. Although some respondents called for more Bruckner, others had had enough of the Austrian composer. "I dislike Bruckner symphonies, and there are many who share my opinion," a patron stated. "If they must be played, one per season is quite enough."[24] Over the course of his nineteen years as music director, Skrowaczewski conducted all nine Bruckner symphonies, four of which—the First, Second, Third and Fifth—had never been performed by the orchestra previously. Performances of these symphonies were spread over twelve seasons.

Skrowaczewski programmed two Bruckner symphonies—the First and the Eighth—during the orchestra's last season in Northrop Auditorium. Nevertheless, in its diversity and balance of musical styles, eras, and genres, that season's overall programming may have been the finest of his entire tenure. Patrons seeking more contemporary music must have been pleased with the works included: a world premiere by Druckman, U.S. premieres of Górecki's Symphony no. 2 and Ohana's *Chiffres for Harpsichord and Orchestra*, and works by Carter, Ives, Ruggles, Foss, Webern, and Schoenberg. Other works performed for the first time by the orchestra were a balanced selection from various periods: Tchaikovsky's Symphony no. 7 (unfinished by the composer but completed in the mid-1950s by Semyon Bogatïryov), Bruckner's Symphony no. 1, Mahler's Sixth Symphony, Lutosławski's *Livre pour Orchestra*, Messiaen's *Celestial City*, and Shostakovich's Symphony no. 14, composed only four years earlier.

Based on poems related to the anguish of death, Symphony no. 14 is a cantata-like work for soprano, bass, and a chamber orchestra of strings and percussion. Shostakovich composed the eleven-movement, fifty-minute work from his hospital bed in 1969. It was premiered in Leningrad a few months later. In 1971 Ormandy and the Philadelphia Orchestra gave the U.S. premiere of the symphony with soloists Phyllis Curtin and Simon Estes. Skrowaczewski chose the same duo for Minnesota's first performance of the symphony, early in the 1973–74 season. It would be his last collaboration with the esteemed soprano. "She was always a wonderful artist to work with," he remembered, "so deeply musical. I have the greatest respect for her. I was sorry that I couldn't do more with her, but my possibilities were limited."

Although they only collaborated on five occasions (Britten's *War Requiem*, *Salome*, Mahler's *Das klagende Lied*, *Scheherazade* at Tanglewood, and the Shostakovich 14th), their artistic relationship was symbiotic. "There's something about him as a man that appealed to me right away," Curtin recalled. "There sometimes are people that you just make music with and it works, and that's how it was every time with him." She sang the title role when Skrowaczewski led a complete concert performance of the opera *Salome* in Minneapolis in 1966. She recalled the experience: "I don't remember that we had anything to work on with *Salome*; we just did it. From the first rehearsal it worked well. I don't remember his asking me to change anything or to look out for this or for that. We simply took a breath and made music."

Curtin performed the Shostakovich's 14th Symphony dozens of times—"I adore it, a major work that has always deeply moved me"—but she regarded her collaboration with Skrowaczewski to be unique:

> As far as I know, he was probably the only conductor that I sang it with who spoke Russian. When I mentioned that I wanted to do the piece with him, he said, "I don't think it should be sung in Russian. It should be done in English, so people really understand it." So I called Boosey and Hawkes to obtain a score to do my own translation. They told me they had one. It was by someone from England, but it was a very 19th-century romantic translation of this poetry, which is the wrong character. So I did my own, and we performed it in Minneapolis. I never did it in English before or since. Not all conductors are keyed in to text, but Skrowaczewski certainly was. As far as I'm concerned, communicating the text is the only reason to sing.
>
> Skrowaczewski and Carlo Maria Giulini were the only conductors who ever asked me a really deep question about the music. I treasured those two gentlemen for that more than you can know.

Jacob Druckman was a popular American composer during the 1970s and early 1980s. Having studied with Copland at Tanglewood and with Persichetti, Mennin, and Bernard Wagenaar at Juilliard, he was among the most important composers trained by major American composers born in the early 20th century. After winning the 1972 Pulitzer Prize for *Windows*, his first large-scale orchestral work, he attracted greater attention from major orchestras. Skrowaczewski admired his gift for color and orchestration and for his rigorous compositional technique. In the late 1960s Druckman's compositional interest shifted from serialism to electronic music. Aspects of his music were realized at the Columbia-Princeton Electronic Music Center; beginning in the 1970s, he headed the electronic music program at Yale University, where he also led the composition department. Beginning with *Windows*, his orchestral music embraced a "new romanticism"—his term—that incorporated quotations from older music. It also employed unusual percussion instruments, such as a steel drum, a spring coil with sizzles, and a saw.[25]

After introducing his Minnesota audiences to *Windows* the previous season, Skrowaczewski gave the world premiere of *Incenters* in November 1973 and subsequently the first New York performance in Carnegie Hall. The piece was an expansion of an earlier chamber ensemble work. Druckman, a skilled jazz trumpeter, incorporated improvisation for players and conductor in the piece, which also quotes chords from the Coronation Scene from Mussorgsky's *Boris Godounov*.[26] The Minnesota Orchestra was the first major ensemble to present Druckman's orchestral music, and other orchestras soon followed suit.

Less than a week later Skrowaczewski premiered Henryk Górecki's *Copernicus* Symphony no. 2. The Kosciuszko Foundation of America commissioned the piece in honor of the 500th anniversary (1973) of the birth of Nicolaus Copernicus, the great 16th-century Polish astronomer. The two-movement symphony calls for a large orchestra, mixed choir, and soprano and baritone soloists. Its text comes from Psalms 145 and 135 as well as an excerpt from Copernicus' Book 1, *De revolutionibus Orbium Coelestium*.

The Minnesota Orchestra issued a press release announcing its world-premiere performance of Górecki's Symphony no. 2. Two weeks after the announcement, the symphony's actual premiere occurred in Poland's capital city by the Warsaw Philharmonic. This situation no doubt made for an awkward telephone call from Cisek to the Kosciuszko Foundation of America.

Górecki's avant-garde music of the 1950s and 1960s was influenced by Boulez, Xenakis, Nono, Stockhausen, and Penderecki. Not unlike Penderecki—who was born the same year—Górecki shifted from the avant-garde to a more consonant style embracing minimalism. *Copernicus* bridged the two styles. The piece has qualities of synthesis similar to Penderecki's *Passion*. It uses a 15th-century choral antiphon, for example, and like the *Passion* it exposed Górecki to an international audience, although that exposure was not as wide or as rapid as was Penderecki's.

It wasn't until 1992 that Górecki became a worldwide phenomenon. The catalyst was the release of the fourth commercial recording of his Symphony no. 3, *Symphony of Sorrowful Songs*, by soprano Dawn Upshaw and the London Sinfonietta conducted by David Zinman. In part his fame stemmed from a mistake made at a record shop in London. Skrowaczewski relates the little-known story:

> This situation was, at first, completely by accident. The Zinman-Upshaw recording went to a huge record shop on Oxford Street in London, and by accident it was filed in the pop-music room. Of course, a lot of people will buy something that is unusual and has novelty. People began buying this CD initially because of their curiosity, and then they really loved it, and the word spread. The symphony soon got extensive airplay and sold like crazy.

Górecki himself was amazed by its success. The piece was already sixteen years old when this Nonesuch CD came out! The other side of the story is that obviously, this kind of a piece—quiet, repetitive, soothing, all tonal chords, simple development of lines, etc.—was enormously appealing to the general public, especially nonmusicians. It's funny to think that this misplacement had a role in the popularity of the recording. Ultimately, millions of people enjoyed being exposed to something new, and it stuck with them. It made me wonder what would happen if CDs of my music were put in the pop section of stores. They would probably not have the general public appeal of Górecki's symphony.

Górecki's wildly popular Symphony no. 3 (1976) was a follow-up work and continued stylistically where his earlier symphonies left off. It placed the composer in a musical world that included Arvo Pärt and John Tavener. Conducting Górecki's Symphony no. 2 was Skrowaczewski's first experience leading a work that partly embraced minimalism. As the genre became more widespread during the late 1970s and beyond, he occasionally expressed his disdain for much of it. To minimize the repetition in Symphony no. 2 that he deemed unnecessary, he made cuts that shaved about six minutes from the work. Górecki was one of the few major Polish composers whose music Skrowaczewski did not embrace and perform frequently.

If the premiere of Górecki's *Copernicus* Symphony left the maestro momentarily unenthusiastic about presenting certain new works to the public, his two concerts entitled "Explorations with Skrowaczewski" offered effective antidotes.

"Skrowaczewski talks!" reported Roy M. Close in the *Minneapolis Star*. "That's the most refreshing note—of several—to come out of last night's first 'Explorations with Skrowaczewski' concert…. [He] has never been especially comfortable speaking to audiences. Last night, however, armed with a sheaf of notes, he devoted more than forty minutes to his remarks about the concert works, which were both instructive and entertaining."[27]

The short series exposed audiences to rarely performed chamber ensemble works in an informal atmosphere. Skrowaczewski conducted and acted as master of ceremonies. Wine was served during intermission, and after the concerts ended, audience members were invited on stage to discuss the program with him and the other musicians. In an effort to connect more with audience members, orchestras around the country began using similar formats for some concerts. One thousand people appeared at the first Explorations program, and the maestro "turned out to be an affable, even entertaining host for the evening," according to critic Michael Anthony.[28]

Within the informal setting and without the burden of leading the entire orchestra, Skrowaczewski gave audiences a glimpse of his more relaxed and witty side, so familiar to his close friends. They also heard him explain his philosophical approach to music. "Any contact with art," he told his audience at the first concert, "should involve an open and searching mind. Here I see the salient meaning of great art as an antidote to the flood of the prefabricated, frozen, canned, ready-to-eat slogans, habits, and banalities of our modern times. Every concert is a sort of exploration with composers, with performers, with the public, with oneself."[29]

Although he presented an eclectic mix of old and new music in his programs, the audience nevertheless heard important firsts for the musicians: the Berg Chamber Concerto, Schuller's Quartet for Four Basses, and Henze's Double Concerto for Oboe, Harp and Strings. Mary Ann Feldman assisted Skrowaczewski with commentary at the second Explorations program, which concluded with Mendelssohn's Concerto in A minor. Mendelssohn composed the concerto at age ten, but it was not heard in public until 1960, when a copy was obtained from the International Mendelssohn Society in Basel.[30]

Unfortunately, like the short-lived Sinfonia ensemble that Skrowaczewski created in the mid-1960s, Explorations survived only one more season. A single concert, then repeated, was cosponsored by and performed at the Guthrie Theater. He conducted and commented on Stravinsky's *L'Histoire du Soldat* and *Les Noces*. Robert Benedetti directed *L'Histoire,* which was billed as "an entertainment with music, mime, and dance." Skrowaczewski's enthusiasm for Stravinsky illuminated his opening remarks:

> Stravinsky, the teller of tales, the remaker of myths, the evoker of legends! How romantic it sounds of someone who can be considered the most classic of masters. This is what makes Stravinsky such an extraordinary personality to explore, for his works also explain not only changes in music of the 20th century but somehow also condense the entire history of art. Someone said that Stravinsky was the greatest music historian because through his ears and mind we hear the ages of our civilization. We are forced to understand that music is an organic art, constantly undergoing evolutionary processes.[31]

Conducting Stravinsky's *Petrushka* with Rome's Santa Cecilia Academy Orchestra in spring 1974, Skrowaczewski did not have enough time for the musicians to contemplate the "evolutionary processes" of Stravinsky's "organic art." A musicians' strike cost him a rehearsal, a significant problem, given the difficulty of *Petrushka* and Shostakovich's 14th Symphony, which also was on the program. It didn't help that the back of the Santa Cecilia Academy Auditorium's stage had a heavy curtain that caused disastrous acoustics. Even getting to the concert was a problem; student protests against the government's new voting policies blocked city streets. The maestro maneuvered his way on foot through dark backstreets in Rome in order to arrive at concert time.

Working with the Academy Orchestra always required an extra effort from Skrowaczewski. The ensemble was not the most disciplined of organizations then, but still he returned regularly to lead it. After conducting the orchestra in 1956 to win the International Competition for Conductors, he felt emotionally connected to the ensemble and took pride in training it. "Usually it is very hard to get them working well, just because of their temperament," he told a reporter in Rome, but he was pleased that they had done "the maximum they could" with the demanding program.[32] When asked about the progress of his own orchestra, Skrowaczewski was modest about his contributions but pleased with the ensemble's progress since 1960. He also condemned the orchestra's name change, a subject he would not drop.

The Rome concert was the first leg of a brisk monthlong European tour that also took him to Berlin, Paris, Munich, and Madrid, where he gave the first European performances of his Concerto for English Horn and Orchestra. Back home in Minnesota, he had three more subscription concerts featuring works new to his and/or his orchestra's repertoire. A particularly intriguing program opened with *Oraison Funèbre*, the second movement of Berlioz's rarely heard *Symphonie Funèbre et Triomphale*. Associate conductor Henry Charles Smith as trombone soloist "orated the sermon." Scored for a massive military band and choir (employed only in the last of three movements), the piece was composed a decade after *Symphonie fantastique*. Skrowaczewski followed the Berlioz with another rarity, Webern's *Im Sommerwind*, an Idyl for Large Orchestra, before concluding the program with Mozart's Requiem.

Composed in 1904 when Webern was just twenty-years-old, *Im Sommerwind* hints at the composer's style that was to come, yet it is influenced primarily by the late romanticism of Wagner, Mahler, and Strauss. *Im Sommerwind* was heard for the first time nearly sixty years after it was composed. Webern fled when Russian troops invaded Vienna in 1945, but first he buried important possessions, among them a stack of scores that included *Im Sommerwind*, under his garden house. Soon afterward he was mistakenly shot and killed by an American soldier. Webern's widow retrieved his buried possessions but was too distraught to sort them, so she stored them in her mother's attic. They remained there untouched for twenty years until Webern's biographer, Hans Moldenhauer, discovered them. In 1962 the Philadelphia Orchestra under Ormandy presented the world premiere of *Im Sommerwind* in Seattle as part of the First International Webern Festival.[33]

A week after the composer finished *Im Sommerwind* he met Arnold Schoenberg, who became his teacher. Webern showed the thirty-year-old master composer his new score, and Schoenberg advised him to avoid using such a large orchestra to express his ideas. Ironically, Schoenberg himself had already finished composing one of the most massive scores of 20th-century orchestral-choral literature, *Gurrelieder*.[34] This masterpiece, never before performed by the Minnesota Orchestra, closed the 1973–74 subscription season.

Before tackling this Schoenberg epic, Skrowaczewski had made his Philadelphia opera debut with a most intimate work, Mozart's *The Marriage of Figaro*. "He began tensely, rushing things," wrote Max de Schauensee of *The Evening Bulletin*, "but soon settled into a groove that broadened into fine balances and an instinctive feel for the Mozart idiom which is something *sui generis*."[35] Even the maestro was pleased with the results, and the experience renewed his interest in opera. "It went really well," he wrote to Michel Glotz, "and I adored doing an opera which I like more and more."[36] Glotz's efforts to jumpstart his client's career as an opera conductor did not produce results. *The Marriage of Figaro* with the Philadelphia Lyric Opera was the last fully staged opera he conducted.

Like Mahler's Eighth Symphony, Schoenberg's *Gurrelieder* is one of those works that a music director usually can program only once during a given tenure. Among the most expensive works for an orchestra to mount, *Gurrelieder* requires extra rehearsals (Skrowaczewski had three on top of the standard three); its orchestration demands twenty extra musicians beyond the proportions of a typical professional orchestra plus five vocal soloists, a narrator, and large chorus. In his review of the first concert Michael Anthony wrote, "This performance, [with] five soloists, an orchestra augmented to 122 players, plus a chorus of 173—[made] the stage look like a poster for Zero Population Growth."[37] The limitations of O'Shaughnessy Auditorium created some balance problems in Skrowaczewski's first performance, yet critics recognized the qualities he brought to the massive work and noted that the presentation was a performance landmark for the Twin Cities.

Focused on the mental, physical, and spiritual involvement necessary to conduct *Gurrelieder*, he forgot that the second performance of the work would be the orchestra's final subscription concert in Northrop Auditorium. He realized this fact only after he walked into Northrop's "gray room," as he jokingly called the green room, to change for the concert. There he found two enormous bottles of champagne—a gift from Ken and Judy Dayton to mark the occasion. He wrote to the Daytons, "I appreciated it in direct proportion to my dissatisfaction with the Northrop acoustics."[38]

Several years earlier Skrowaczewski and George Trautwein, the orchestra's former associate conductor, had attended a rehearsal of *Gurrelieder* by the Los Angeles Philharmonic Orchestra. Trautwein said the rehearsal provided a striking example of the acuity of the maestro's ear: "Looking over the shoulder of the assistant conductor, who was holding a score of the piece, Stan kept a running litany of all the wrong notes he heard coming from the stage. No one else mentioned them. Even more surprising, I don't believe he had ever conducted that piece before."[39]

The year 1974 marked the 100th anniversary of the births of Schoenberg and Charles Ives, which were celebrated by concerts worldwide. Schoenberg's *Gurrelieder* and his Violin Concerto with soloist Joseph Silverstein were featured early in the Minnesota Orchestra's season. Skrowaczewski and Edo de Waart led major works by Ives in honor of America's maverick composer. Cisek, enticed by the occasion of Schoenberg's anniversary, wanted to achieve another performance coup like Penderecki's *St. Luke Passion*. Despite the work's proportions, he sought to take *Gurrelieder* to Carnegie Hall. A handful of other orchestras had scheduled performances of the epic piece between 1973 and 1975, but none planned take it to New York. Ultimately the bottom line won out, and the idea was scrapped.

Skrowaczewski's summer 1974 engagements included working with a variety soloists at festivals in the United States and Europe. He led the Pittsburgh Symphony in an all-Wagner program with soprano Eileen Farrell, and a second concert featured actress Cicely Tyson narrating *Lincoln Portrait*. The stunning array of his piano soloists that summer included Jörg Demus, André Watts, Eugene Istomin, Alexis Weissenberg, and Claudio Arrau. In Minneapolis he was reunited with former concertmaster

Norman Carol to perform the Beethoven Violin Concerto as part of a three-night, all-Beethoven festival. After the festival the pair headed to Saratoga Springs, where Carol resumed his role as concertmaster of the Philadelphia Orchestra and Skrowaczewski guest conducted.

Before the maestro undertook summer engagements in the United States, including a performance with the Chicago Symphony at Ravinia, he was briefly in Switzerland and Germany. With the help of a concert agency in Zürich, he brought Krystyna's parents from Poland so they could meet Paul and Nicholas, then ages six and four, respectively. The complicated process required six months of planning. The agency had to send the Jaroszs' certificates to apply for Swiss visas and also cover their travel expenses until Skrowaczewski could reimburse them after their arrival in the country. "If we [pay] it from here," he wrote the agency, "it will produce suspicion from Poland."[40] The brief reunion would be the last time the Skrowaczewskis as a family would see both Jaroszs. The trip is a joyous memory:

> The boys were so excited about this trip. It was their first time overseas. We stayed in a fabulous hotel in Zürich, high on a hill in the woods. Paul and Nicholas were hunting escargot in the little paths in the woods. They wanted to eat them! There were also fascinated by the hotel's elevators. Every time we couldn't find them, they were on the elevators. It was very touching, waiting for Krystyna's parents at the railway station. We had a wonderful time. It was the last time we saw her parents together. Krystyna's mother survived her husband by a number of years. Krystyna, Nicholas, and I visited her in Poland in the late 1990s. She lived into her nineties, and she was in wonderful health when we last saw her.

In late August the maestro was in Switzerland to open the Lucerne Festival with Yehudi Menuhin. Another part of his European summer schedule included a Radio for Berlin recording session of Beethoven's Fifth Symphony and Lutosławski's Concerto for Orchestra. Skrowaczewski thrived on running from one program to the next: "Changing programs keeps me alive. It's like changing spiritual food."[41]

The final steps toward the creation of Orchestra Hall moved relatively quickly, considering Skrowaczewski's longtime push for a proper home for his orchestra. His consistent comments to the press received more attention.

By 1969 he had refined his advocacy for a new hall:

> Since my first visits to America I've been incessantly asked my opinion about the U.S.A. being a "materialistic" country in comparison to the "spiritual" traditions of Europe. Very shortly I became convinced that I feel almost the opposite. Whatever history might say of the past, in my opinion, the last war's destructions and ordeals of Europe put its reconstruction years on a very materialistic course. While here, a sooner-achieved high standard of living gave to numerous Americans an incentive to look beyond that, to an

awareness of metaphysical goals. I've always considered the Twin Cities one of the most cultural places in America. Therefore, it is now time to understand that a beautiful orchestra like ours, homeless for its sixty-seven years, is only a partial success and that this situation for a long time has shadowed not only our artistic possibilities but also our cultural status. "People have what they deserve" is not always true about individuals, but it seems to have sense in a case of a powerful, resourceful, and *free* country like ours.

Do you realize what a minuscule fraction of our state budget in this century would cover the cost of a new hall? Probably a small tax on liquors or cigarettes during one year would build it the next year. This lies simply in the hands of our people. We need good leaders to enlighten those who are ignorant. What a beautiful goal for any politician or anyone else who would feel like making history.[42]

In spring 1969 Skrowaczewski urged *Minneapolis Star Tribune* music critic Peter Altman to write about the issue. Altman produced a five-part series of articles on "the options open to the Minnesota Orchestra in its search for a suitable home."[43] The first article profiled seven U.S. concert halls in photographs that covered an entire page, ending with a shot of Northrop Auditorium with the caption "And this is the dreary home of our orchestra."[44] The article examined all the problems with the space: acoustics and atmosphere, availability, access, facilities, and more. "Northrop Auditorium is the largest concert hall in the country and quite possibly the worst," wrote Altman. "For forty years it has been the home of an orchestra that despite its setting has earned a place among the nation's six best symphonies. But this is about to change. Either Northrop will be radically remodeled, or the Minnesota Orchestra will build itself a new home. If not, the orchestra will be faced with a crisis in maintaining its quality."[45]

The University of Minnesota took the first step by hiring acoustical consultant Paul Venaclausen to examine the possibility of renovating the auditorium's interior. If the university decided to renovate the venue, then the orchestra would have to decide whether to support it or to examine other options. Skrowaczewski never threatened to resign over the issue of a concert hall, but after ten years of tolerating Northrop Auditorium, his patience was wearing thin. Altman's final articles made the case for building a real concert hall in downtown Minneapolis.

The timing of the articles successfully planted the idea of a new hall in the public's consciousness. In 1969 the MOA had created a house committee to see what might be done to improve issues like parking and building maintenance at Northrop. Two years later the Lyceum Theater, located in downtown Minneapolis, went on the market. At the time, an evangelical church called Soul's Harbor owned the building. The house committee discovered that the 1905 theater, which had been modeled after Boston's Symphony Hall, had been one of the first performance halls for the Minneapolis Symphony. The committee members thought the old theater might be an answer to the orchestra's search.

Acoustician Cyril M. Harris was hired near the end of 1971 to determine the feasibility of renovating the 1,800-seat Lyceum. Renovation seemed to be a realistic option, so the orchestra bought the building. In 1972 the MOA received a cost estimate of $6.5 million for the proposed renovation. The work would involve gutting most of the original building, but it did not include needed support space. Further investigation determined that the MOA could build a new hall on the site for a similar price (it ended up being more than double that amount). Thanks to an initial gift of $2.5 million from Ken and Judy Dayton and other gifts from John Pillsbury, Jr., and local foundations and trusts, the MOA already had raised nearly $5.5 million by the end of 1972 for the original plan, renovating the Lyceum Theater.

By early 1973 the MOA had a new plan: raze the Lyceum Theater and all other buildings on its block to make way for a new concert hall, a city park, and a municipal parking garage. It reached an innovative agreement with the City of Minneapolis whereby the city would buy the hall and lease it back to the association for a thirty-year period. In return, the association's income from the sale helped finance the park and other expenses owed to the city.

In early June 1973 the MOA approved the new concept, a new fund-raising drive of $13.5 million was in place, and Skrowaczewski gave a downbeat at the groundbreaking ceremony. Just sixteen months later he triumphantly gave another downbeat for the Orchestra Hall dedication concert.

With more than a decade of advocacy invested in the project, Skrowaczewski stayed involved in the evolution of Orchestra Hall. In December 1972, after the MOA officially approved a plan to build a new hall, he immediately sent a memo to the executive committee in which he outlined in detail his concept of the structure, which focused on acoustics and appropriate space for performing flexible repertoire. He envisioned rehearsal facilities for concurrent sectionals and for choirs, sound systems for electronic-music performances, and temperature control of all spaces. His ideas synthesized thirty-plus years of experience with the world's finest (and not so fine) concert halls. In some respects he was ahead of his time. His vision describes a facility quite similar to Walt Disney Hall, home of the Los Angeles Philharmonic, which opened in 2003. His primary concern—acoustics, as outlined below—was achieved, for the most part:

> The audience should get at every place the full range of volume in gradation, from the most ethereal *ppp* to the almost unbearable *fff* and the full range of differentiation of tone color varieties and subtleties. The "one-room concept": a low stage should bring the orchestra physically and mentally to the public as close as possible. The inner design of the hall and the accent on acoustically proper materials (wood) should produce the richness but also mellowness of tone.

> For the musicians and conductor on the stage, the above [requirements] should be extended and enhanced by the clearness of good hearing between the sections and between singular musicians. This demand on physical (visual and oral) contact between the musicians would be enhanced by a set of risers (easily movable) being done like wooden boxes, which would eventually help to resonate the tone of some instruments and could be rearranged to

meet all demands of different sets of the orchestra for different works. As much as the brightness of tone and long reverberation are good for the public performance, there should be a device (probably a curtain) to make the acoustics drier, if necessary, for certain rehearsals (or at least to balance the muffling characteristics of a full audience).[46]

While Skrowaczewski focused on the musical aspects of the hall, Ken Dayton crafted a five-point "Design Philosophy," approved by the board of directors, "to serve as a basis for all architectural decisions on the project."[47] The well-articulated philosophy was, in effect, an official way for Dayton to ensure, true to his own values, that the hall was about access, not elitism. "The building should be designed to serve the concertgoing audiences of the future rather than to reflect old world elegance," he stated. "It should be an honest building, conveying a sense of dignity, simplicity, and eye-satisfying proportion…. The emphasis should be on the concert rather than on the building itself."[48]

These principles ultimately extended to the naming of the hall, a complicated process that involved a committee, research, and even solicitations for ideas from the public. No single individual was funding the majority of the hall's expense, so the idea of naming it after a donor was dismissed, although considering Ken and Judy Dayton's overall contributions to the orchestra, it could have easily been named in their honor. But the Daytons neither sought such overt recognition nor believed that it was appropriate.

Ken Dayton suggested the name "Conductors' Hall," a designation that would honor the orchestra's maestros. He envisioned the building becoming a conductors' hall of fame, an international attraction that housed mementos and archives of eminent conductors. An invitation to conduct there would serve as "part of their admission to the hallowed rostrum."[49]

Ultimately the committee chose the generic but appropriate name "Orchestra Hall." The rationale for that choice, as MOA president Engle told a patron, was that "it would call attention to the fact that the Minnesota Orchestral Association was constructing and funding this new facility" and that it was the orchestra's permanent home. As such, it was designed specifically for a symphony orchestra. The committee also liked the fact that the only other major orchestra to use the same name was the Chicago Symphony.[50]

The pending debut of Orchestra Hall stirred a palpable buzz of excitement in the Twin Cities. For the first time in seventy-two years the orchestra would have a permanent home of its own. "Dreams Really Do Come True," declared a half-page ad sponsored by Dayton's department stores, included in a special sixteen-page pullout feature published by the *Minneapolis Star* three days before the dedication concert. In the aptly titled lead article, "Hall's Opening Climaxes Decades of Hopes, Labors," writer Peter Altman described the important role that the city, the Daytons, Pillsbury, Cisek, Engle, and other leaders had in making Orchestra Hall a reality. Since the beginning of Skrowaczewski's tenure, Dayton continually funded efforts to explore acoustical improvements in Northrop and later to search for sites for a possible hall, keeping the prospect of change alive.[51]

"Musicians have been important in creating the hall," Altman said, "particularly Skrowaczewski, who has pushed harder and more determinedly than any other maestro in orchestra annals, and must be noted as having brought Orchestra Hall into being. When many people around him thought it would be wiser to duck the question of the orchestra's playing base, Skrowaczewski persistently and emphatically dramatized the urgency of resolving the issue."[52]

On the day of the groundbreaking ceremony in summer 1973, the maestro wrote to Cisek and Pillsbury, acknowledging their contributions to the achievement. "In truth," Cisek wrote Skrowaczewski, "it was your leadership and uncompromising and persistent effort—sometimes at the risk of personal popularity—which was the greatest catalyst in the effort to get a new building for the orchestra's new home."[53]

Skrowaczewski was "like a kid in a candy store" during the period leading up to the opening of Orchestra Hall. Even before the chairs were mounted in the hall he was inside it, testing the acoustics with various instruments, playing some himself, and having individual musicians do the same. "We were utterly flabbergasted at how wonderful the sound was," he remembered. "It was a quick reaction."

The orchestra gave a week of run-out concerts before the hall was ready for its first rehearsal, the real test of the acoustics. "I remember it was very moving," he said, "because you could see the faces of the musicians, their emotions of the moment." *Minneapolis Tribune* columnist Barbara Flanagan was at the first rehearsal, along with the Daytons and others, when the first notes of Skrowaczewski's orchestration of Bach's Toccata and Fugue sounded. "So many of our friends had tears in their eyes," she recalled.[54]

Three days before the official dedication concert the orchestra gave a special performance for the 350 workers involved in building Orchestra Hall and for their families. The walls were still wet with paint and the hallways unfinished, but the orchestra played Ravel, Strauss, Beethoven, and Ives as it never had before in its hometown.

For the Orchestra Hall dedication concert on October 21, 1974, Skrowaczewski served up four sonic delights: Bach's Toccata and Fugue in D minor, Stravinsky's Suite from *The Firebird,* Beethoven's Fifth Symphony, and Ives' *Decoration Day* (the previous day marked the 100th anniversary of Charles Ives' birth). After intermission, MOA board chairman John Pillsbury, Jr., Minnesota governor Wendell Anderson, Minneapolis mayor Albert Hofstede, and the president of the Minneapolis City Council presided over the dedication ceremony.

Skrowaczewski beamed throughout the concert, which was broadcast live locally and nationally and taped for local and national TV. The event was both a pivotal moment in the history of the Minnesota Orchestra and his greatest accomplishment as its music director. The achievement gave him pause for reflection and contemplation. He expressed his thoughts elegantly in "The Resurrection of the Invisible," a short essay he wrote for the special dedication issue of the orchestra's *Showcase* magazine:

We all rejoice at this handsome and indispensable edifice, completed only two weeks after the reopening of the Art Institute. My own happiness, however, goes far beyond the realm of the tangible. For this hall is the visible symbol of the never-ending search for the invisible, the infinite, which—pervading and ennobling all conscious and unconscious human desires—is the wellspring of artistic imagination and creativity. What I therefore find most important about the hall is the enlightenment and the effort of the people who donated it. Their understanding of the priorities of life speaks for itself: art is inherent in human nature and, together with religion and science, is a precondition of human transformation and ascent.

To me, art is a dialogue with the unknown. This dialogue encompasses all fundamental human concerns—such as the meaning of life and death, love and cruelty, sacrifice and redemption—in the constant hope to know that which cannot be known. Art thrives on metaphysical ideas, which I believe are as old as human consciousness. A great work of art, reflecting the powerful intellect and the compelling imagination of its creator, elicits from us a metaphysical shiver as it confronts us with a vision of ultimate reality. This vision can liberate us from the mediocrity of everyday situations, thoughts, and feelings by lifting us onto a higher, more spiritual plane of being. And while doing so, it has the capacity to bemuse, delight, heal, and ennoble us. Thus art is a powerful antidote for the spiritual ills of our chaotic, violent, and troubled times.

This hall will stimulate our awareness of art and sharpen our sense of life. We should regard this place not as an arena for competition between stars but as a temple of mystery and contemplation in which the dialogue with the unknown will continue....[55]

As proclaimed by its season brochure, the orchestra presented its "Stars of the Inaugural Season" in 1974–75, but the real star was Orchestra Hall. The dedication concert received national media attention, and the overwhelming acclaim for the hall's acoustics was unanimous. "In Minneapolis, the Acoustics Are Almost Too Good to Be True," declared the second of two lengthy articles in *The New York Times* that Harold Schonberg devoted to Orchestra Hall.[56] "The world's worst concert hall gives way to one of the best," announced *The Boston Globe*.[57]

After the first Friday-night subscription concert in Orchestra Hall, two unexpected visitors came backstage to greet Skrowaczewski: Carlos Moseley, chairman of the New York Philharmonic, and Avery Fisher, the Philharmonic board member who largely funded the 1962 concert hall that bears his name. "They congratulated me on the concert and the new hall," the maestro recalled. 'We are very excited to be in this new hall,' they said, 'and tomorrow you will read on the front page of *The New York Times* that the New York Philharmonic has decided to redo its hall!' And sure enough, it appeared in the *Times* as they said the next day. I was flabbergasted." Cyril Harris was soon enlisted to renovate the acoustics of Avery Fisher Hall.

"The term for the way in which a stage projects sound in an auditorium is 'throw,'" noted *Time* magazine. "Orchestra Hall has a throw that even Tom Seaver might envy."[58]

Indeed, the hall came off as a powerhouse: "Tonally," wrote Schonberg, "it is one of the most remarkable concert halls in the world. Mr. Harris believes, and there are few experts who will disagree with him, that no hall anywhere has such power. Sound comes off the stage in unprecedented volume."[59]

The hall's amplification was evident during the dedication concert—producing at times a volume that was almost painful to some listeners—but so was its evenness. The most delicate *pianissimos* were clear as a bell, and the details of the orchestra's playing were easily delineated. The basses, a section of instruments that often struggles acoustically in many concert halls, were heard clearly by most listeners. The woodwinds, accustomed to the deadness of Northrop where, as one bassoonist quipped, they had to "whittle reeds out of two-by-fours" to blast their sound to get it off the stage, now had to learn restraint.[60]

A concert hall itself is an instrument, and Skrowaczewski and his musicians would learn how to "play it" eventually. Brass sonorities in Orchestra Hall could be overwhelming, and all conductors still wrestle with that issue today. Nevertheless, the acoustics were a triumph.

The hall's creation remains the most important development in the orchestra's artistic advancement throughout its entire history. "Stan forced us to do it," John Pillsbury, Jr., told the *San Francisco Examiner & Chronicle*, only half joking.[61] "That it was built at all," wrote Dayton to Skrowaczewski soon after the hall's opening, "and that it turned out so well is due to your inspiration more than any other factor. So it really is your child! And what good hands it is in."[62] Judson Bemis, president of the MOA when the decision was made to build the hall, recalled Skrowaczewski's passionate advocacy for a new venue:

> I can well remember when I had agreed to take the responsibility for funding the new hall. I had a call almost immediately from Stan. He happened to be home ill. I knew that, and he said he wanted to come immediately to see me that afternoon. I said, "But Stan, you've been ill, let me stop by on my way home." "No," he said, "I want to come and see you." So he got up out of his sickbed and came down for the purpose of telling me what a vital decision this was and how extremely important [it was] that there be a new hall [equal] to the quality of the orchestra. He said, "I've taken this orchestra as far as I can, given the present facilities, and the only way it can improve is with a hall of top acoustical quality.[63]

Luck had little to do with the hall's acoustical triumph, although a bit of good fortune is needed for the precarious task of building concert halls. Minnesota had a secret weapon in Cyril Harris, who came to the project with a stellar track record as a consultant for more than one hundred halls, including the Kennedy Center, the Metropolitan Opera House, and Powell Symphony Hall, home of the St. Louis Symphony. "Wood, not concrete. I like the feeling of it under my feet," said Harris in an article by Mary Ann Feldman. "After all, you can experience music not only through your ears, but [you] feel it as well. Unlike concrete, wood vibrates. It helps to provide an optimum acoustical environment."[64]

However, it wasn't just the hall's wood floors and panels that created its acoustical character. Giant plaster cubes of varying sizes—113 in all—protruded from the ceiling and tilted at different angles; another fifteen massive cubes were set into the wall behind the stage. The cubes are largely responsible for Orchestra Hall's enormous "throw," and they create a visual effect that a few critics nicknamed "the nuclear explosion in a sugar-cube factory."[65] Some people thought the cubes on the back wall made the orchestra look as if it were playing on a stage set for *Romper Room* or in a gaudy Las Vegas venue, while others likened the plethora of cubes to modern art.

Harris took his design cues from 19th-century classic shoebox-style concert halls, most notably Vienna's Musikverein and Boston's Symphony Hall, but he applied modern technology to the acoustics of the space. To prevent seepage of extraneous noise from the lobby, offices, and the building's mechanical and electrical equipment, a one-inch buffer filled with sound-absorbing material is wrapped around the performance space, isolating it acoustically from all other areas of the building. Harris also ensured that a minimum amount of plush upholstery and carpet was used in the hall. The oak chairs matched the floor and side panels, and Harris tested foam cushions to determine their sound absorbency. He had lockers installed in the corridors to encourage people to leave their wool, fur, and velvet items outside the hall. The twenty-five-cent fee for locker use was "a lot more convenient than a checkroom where you have to wait in line," Harris remarked, and it certainly was in line with the anti-ostentatious objectives implicit in Ken Dayton's "Design Philosophy."[66]

"We put all the money into the auditorium, so we couldn't afford elegant lobbies," Cisek explained to the *Toronto Star*. "I know the result is controversial—I was just horrified by the funnels at first—but I have come to love it all. It's a fun place rather than a temple."[67] The "funnels"—large, bright-blue air exhausts and intakes on the building's exterior—evoke the image of a huge ocean liner, as several critics observed. "We wanted the new hall to impress people as a mystery," said Hugh Hardy, one of the architects. "It is completely inert from the outside. There are no windows. We wanted people to ask, 'What is it?'"[68]

Orchestra Hall is an odd hybrid: a white façade of steel and glass fronting a brick auditorium that houses the performance space. Taken as a whole, the facility resembles a biotechnology lab. Its architects likely were influenced by the design of the Pompidou Centre, which was constructed in Paris from 1971 to 1977 and which shares characteristics with Orchestra Hall's exterior and interior.

The building's interior offered another striking contrast to any other concert hall of the time: the absence of chandeliers, red carpets, and elaborately decorated foyers. With its shades of magenta, green, and yellow, the lobby "combined the attributes of a greenhouse and a boiler room, with exposed yellow and blue pipes running across the ceiling and through the floors (yellow for air, blue for fluids)."[69] Indeed, the lobby was a "rebuke to red velvet," as one article on the design was entitled.[70]

"All too often, when people decide to build a concert hall, they start with creating a monument to culture, and acoustics come in second," said an MOA board member. "With Orchestra Hall we began with the premise that acoustics should have first priority."[71] Skrowaczewski had insisted upon this priority from the beginning, and Dayton took it seriously. Longtime *St. Paul Pioneer Press* music critic John Harvey thought the lobby felt like being in "a huge piece of environmental sculpture. It's open, simple, honest, and above all, lively. There's no hint of the stodgy ostentation found in so many of our American temples of culture."[72]

"It is such a mad, marvelous facility," commented Barbara Flanagan to Skrowaczewski while they stood outside Orchestra Hall in front of the four blue exhaust pipes, waiting to film a segment for *Thank You Maestro*. "People have complained that it doesn't look dignified enough. What do you think?" "Well," the maestro replied, "I think it's a great and wonderful contrast."[73] He continued:

> I'll never forget the first impression—and I've felt it often since—when entering through the lobby I would go through those gray hallways around the hall with closed doors. Everything is gray, and you don't get the impression that this is a symphony hall. Suddenly, you open the door [and] this wonderful warm, red color strikes you and the wood of the walls and stage. This contrast makes an incredible impression![74]

"Orchestra Hall is but the latest symbol of the flourishing cultural life in the Twin [Cities]," reported *Time* two weeks after the dedication concert. "The public continues to flock to established arts institutions like the Walker Art Center and Guthrie Theater."[75] The Twin Cities' cultural stock continued the upward trajectory that began in the mid-1960s. In 1973 Walker Art Center reopened with a new wing, and two weeks before the debut of Orchestra Hall, the Minneapolis Society of Fine Arts Park opened. The St. Paul and Minnesota opera companies flourished, and the Saint Paul Chamber Orchestra, under the leadership of the innovative Dennis Russell Davies since 1972, was being hailed for its diverse programming. The Minnesota Orchestra had a sold-out inaugural season in Orchestra Hall, and its series in St. Paul at O'Shaughnessy Auditorium, now five years old, continued to pack in audiences.

"This is a city in which one senses extraordinary energy, vitality, and pride," wrote Michael Steinberg in *The Boston Globe*. "When the orchestra appeared on stage [at the dedication concert], the very classy audience erupted into a prolonged standing ovation. I had never seen that before, and I can't imagine it happening in many places."[76]

After the final notes of Beethoven's Fifth Symphony concluded the dedication concert, the force of the applause kept Skrowaczewski, his hair slightly disheveled, on the podium. After acknowledging the orchestra several times, he threw up his arms in jubilant tribute to Orchestra Hall. The audience's enthusiasm persisted, and the maestro flashed a 'V' sign. For the generation that lived through World War II, the gesture symbolized resistance to the enemy, and in Morse code the famed opening notes of the Fifth Symphony translated (three dots and a dash) to "victory." As Michael Anthony noted in his *Minneapolis Tribune* review of the historic concert, the building of Orchestra Hall wasn't a victory on the scale of World War II, yet it was the perfect complement to the occasion. It signaled the maestro's Churchillian confidence and symbolized a victory for everyone present that night as well as a promise to future generations. When he finally left the podium, Skrowaczewski experienced a fleeting sense of disbelief—he was actually walking off the stage of the resplendent Minnesota concert hall whose creation had been his dream since 1960.

Three-year-old Staś in a familiar pose.

Photo courtesy of the Skrowaczewski family.

Zofia and Paweł Skrowaczewski, circa 1913.

Young Staś poses with his mother, Zofia, and sister, Krystyna.

Photos courtesy of the Skrowaczewski family.

Groupe Zodiaque in Paris, 1948. From left: Alain Bermat, Maurice Ohana, Pierre de La Forest-Divonne, and Skrowaczewski.

Greeting well-wishers after winning the 1956 International Competition for Conductors, Rome.

Photos courtesy of Stanisław Skrowaczewski.

George Szell in conversation with Skrowaczewski in Warsaw, 1957.

Guest conducting the Cleveland Orchestra, 1959.

Photos courtesy of Stanisław Skrowaczewski.

Stanisław and his wife, Krystyna, in
Poland, the late 1950s.

Stanisław, Krystyna, Paul, and Nicholas
at home in Wayzata, Minnesota, 1970.

Photos courtesy of the Skrowaczewski family.

Dmitri Shostakovich and Skrowaczewski in Moscow, 1959.

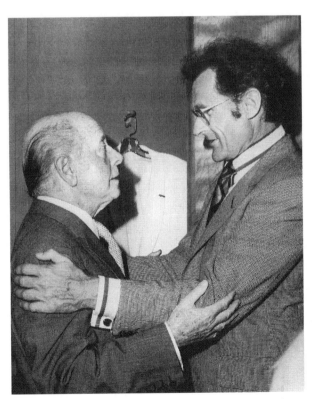

Greeting Eugene Ormandy in Minneapolis, the 1970s.

Photos courtesy of Stanisław Skrowaczewski.

In the nearly completed Orchestra Hall, Minneapolis, 1974.

Skrowaczewski with his two Minnesota Orchestra concertmasters,
Lea Foli (left) and Norman Carol.

Rappelling a near-vertical cliff face in the Grand Tetons, Wyoming, 1973.

Photo courtesy of the Skrowaczewski family.

Kenneth Dayton, Krystyna Skrowaczewski, Judy Dayton, and Stanisław at the Daytons' home, early 1990s.

Stanisław and Krystyna in the Sawtooth Mountains, Idaho, the 1990s.

Photos courtesy of the Skrowaczewski family.

Scaling a jagged peak in Idaho, the late 1980s.

Postconcert 80th-birthday celebration with Krystyna, Paul, Melissa, Madeleine, Mia, and Nicholas at Orchestra Hall, 2003.

Nicholas Skrowaczewski (left), Stanisław, and the author in Kobe,
Japan, after a Yomiuri Nippon Symphony Orchestra concert, 2009.

Photo credit: Susumu Nakano

Skrowaczewski visiting Anton Bruckner's tomb for the first time, 2010.
The tomb is located in the Abbey of Saint Florian Monastery,
Linz, Austria.

Photo credit: Daniel Schröter

A page from Skrowaczewski's handwritten score of *Music for Winds*.

Courtesy of Boelke-Bomart.

TWENTY-ONE

ENDING WITH A BEGINNING

What we call the beginning is often the end
And to make an end is to make a beginning.
The end is where we start from.

—T.S. Eliot, "Little Gidding"

By the end of 1972, after it became certain that Orchestra Hall would be built, Skrowaczewski contemplated the future of his career. At fifty-one he was still relatively young, given the usual longevity of conductors and their careers. He had various possibilities: he could take a post in Europe, reduce conducting engagements and focus on composing, or embark on a freelance career in the United States and abroad. However, Krystyna suggested that he continue in Minneapolis for a few more years and enjoy everything he had worked so hard to achieve. With a new contract in hand that extended his tenure through the 1976–77 season, Skrowaczewski opened the Minnesota Orchestra's inaugural season in Orchestra Hall in fall 1974. The orchestra, too, had a new agreement in hand. After more than a decade without a recording contract—and now with the prospect of a fine hall in which to record—it had an agreement with Vox Productions for a series of recordings. The first project would be a four-LP Vox Box of Ravel's complete works for orchestra, timed for release in 1975, the centennial of his birth.

Even as he entered his fifteenth year as music director, most Minnesotans—and even many musicians—still knew very little about him beyond what they saw and heard from the podium. It didn't bother the maestro at all. "The only image an artist should have is the work he is doing," he told an interviewer in spring 1974.[1] Skrowaczewski the artist and the man were portrayed in an article entitled "Skrowaczewski at Ease":

> Onstage, Skrowaczewski has all the bearing of a Baltic baron. He wears formal attire easily and naturally, and manipulates his instrument, the Minnesota Orchestra, with a thoroughly impressive dexterity and élan through interpretations that more often than not border on pure wizardry—factors which understandably can make him appear rather formidable. Offstage, however, Skrowaczewski is totally disarming and not at all intimidating. Despite his princely physiognomy and diplomatic demeanor, there is an impish glint in his merry eyes reminiscent of a mischievous Polish gnome. He is warm, witty, quick to smile, and in other respects, quite satisfactorily human.[2]

"I happen to like the man," said concertmaster Lea Foli at the time of Orchestra Hall's opening. "He's not what you'd call a beaming person. Skrowaczewski doesn't jump up and kiss you if you do something properly. But compared to some of the buzzards I've worked with in the past, he is a creampuff. What more do you want from a conductor than a man who treats you with respect and knows his music?"[3]

Some musicians wanted more. They included players who continued to be dissatisfied with Skrowaczewski's rehearsal style and interpretations, and others who respected him greatly but yearned for an overtly emotional, inspirational approach to making music. Henry Kramer had long been in the latter camp. In his eyes, no one could match the charisma of Mitropoulos, his first Minneapolis maestro. Kramer also broke through Doráti's exterior and developed a personal relationship with him. Doráti's moments of inspiration and his orchestra-building skills were enough to keep Kramer content through the tumultuous periods of the Hungarian conductor's tenure. But working with Skrowaczewski was an entirely different experience for Kramer, who found him to be a rather detached, obsessively objective presence on the podium:

> Skrowaczewski had all the potential for being one of our greatest conductors if only he had some of Mitropoulos' subjective "warmth" in his conducting and had been less impersonal in his dealings with the orchestra.... It was as if a board stood between him and the ensemble.... He was so formal and cold in his attitude towards us. Yet backstage I could hear Skrowaczewski being addressed as "Stan" by board members and well-wishers after a concert, and his expression would be one of delight and full of humor.[4]

Kramer struggled to reconcile the two Skrowaczewskis. One incident exemplified the negative effect Skrowaczewski's objectivity could have on him:

> We had played what I thought to have been an exceptionally fine Friday-night concert at Northrop. Skrowaczewski was still backstage when I came offstage myself at the end of the program. I was full of the delight and uplift that came from having played an exceptionally fine program of great music. I went up to Skrowaczewski, on his way to the green room, and congratulated him on having presented such a splendid concert. Looking at me without any overt enthusiasm for my remarks, he said, "Yes, but it could have been better." I was shocked by this very negative response to my enthusiasm: it was like taking a cold shower. Of course, it was a perfectly objective statement on his part, as something can always be better. But I felt like screaming at him: "Better for whom?" The audience? Himself? The orchestra? Or the dead composers whose music we had just played?[5]

From 1971 to 1979 former associate conductor Henry Charles Smith was Skrowaczewski's second pair of ears. He continued to serve the orchestra in that position until 1988. The maestro's fastidiousness impressed Smith:

> Stan's ears didn't miss a speck. When we rehearsed Bartók's Music for Strings, Percussion and Celesta, I played the celesta part. You wonder, "Maybe the conductor doesn't hear everything." I made a little slip in one measure, a

very wispy little part, and I had one wrong note. Stan heard it! I couldn't get away with a thing! And when I was listening to the orchestra in the hall at rehearsals and concerts for him, he expected the same kind of detailed hearing from me.

The amazing thing was, even after the sixth performance of a program, even after that, he'd still want feedback—even though it was the last concert. I remember one night [when] he was particularly discouraged. I went backstage after the last performance, and he said, "Tell me at least six things that were horrible about this concert." I could only think of three. He was obviously looking for something. It's that quest—it never ends for him, even after the last performance.

This quest, as Smith called it—seeking the infinite possibilities of art—is at the heart of Skrowaczewski's approach to conducting and composing. What some people perceive as his emotional blockage and personal detachment might best be explained in Skrowaczewski's own words. Early in his tenure, before beginning the season's first rehearsal, he spoke to the musicians about his goals for them. He first listed such external objectives as more concerts, higher salaries, and a new hall, and then he spoke of his internal goals. The statement perhaps best represents his philosophy of conducting:

As a conductor and musician I am even more deeply concerned with the question: "What is the real interior goal of our music making?" Obviously, this goal is, or should be, to satisfy our hunger for aesthetic truth. But…how are we to find this satisfaction? Whether we know it or not, the satisfaction of this hunger is the controlling principle of our lives as artists. May I submit to you that the achievement of this interior goal depends upon a sense of permanent artistic responsibility and upon absolute musical integrity in our playing. Musical integrity means not only technical perfection but also, in the words of Casals, "The ability to bring to life what is written." To me, to solve technical problems is important, but acquiring and maintaining this integrity is even more important! And I should like us all not only to display virtuosity but also to develop a passion for permanent integral musicianship. If this happens, the first people to enjoy it will be ourselves.

In achieving this interior goal, the purposes of the conductor are identical and coterminous with those of every musician of the orchestra. I would like to emphasize this point because the purposes of the conductor and the orchestra are commonly said to be opposite of each other. Needless to say, this historical fallacy has resulted in a grave confusion [over] artistic purpose. As a matter of fact, my desire and plea to you for developing the artistic qualities I have just mentioned go a long way towards explaining the strange but wonderful words of Franz Liszt: the real task of the conductor consists in making "himself quite useless!" Before it happens, however, I am happy to be with you, and if my words sound serious and tragic, this is partly because we are about to start the first movement of Beethoven's Fifth.[6]

In *Beethoven: His Spiritual Development*, J.W.N. Sullivan emphasizes the necessity of a "rich and profound inner life" to the development of a personality.[7] In the book's final pages Sullivan describes Beethoven's spiritual development in the context of the composer as an explorer:

> What we may call his emotional nature was sensitive, discriminating, and profound, and his circumstances brought him an intimate acquaintance with the chief characteristics of life. His realization of the character of life was not hindered by insensitiveness, as was Wagner's, nor by religion, as was Bach's. There was nothing in this man, either natural or acquired, to blunt his perceptions. And he was not merely sensitive; he was not merely a reflecting mirror. His experiences took root and grew. An inner life of quite extraordinary intensity was in process of development till the very end.[8]

Skrowaczewski's intense interior life was such that some people had difficulty understanding him. He was sometimes seen as aloof; however, for people close to him personally or professionally—and in some cases, even musicians seated near him in the orchestra—his deep sensitivity and inner feelings were clearly evident.

As Foli told the *Minneapolis Star* in 1974, he was certain that Skrowaczewski was immensely proud of the orchestra and its musicians. "He's never really verbalized it," Foli said, "but I think he feels it very deeply. He's a very sensitive man."[9]

The tragic aspects of Skrowaczewski's life have deeply influenced his artistry, but he keeps them almost entirely to himself. "There has been a lot of hardship and suffering in his life," noted Jorja Fleezanis, another Minnesota concertmaster. "It keeps him humble, appreciative, and concerned about people. The depth of his life experiences permeates every piece he conducts."

When Kramer retired from the orchestra in 1976, he received a silver and lacquered-enamel bowl and a personal letter from Skrowaczewski. "You have been not only one of the most leading and exemplary musicians of our orchestra," Skrowaczewski wrote, "but also a personal source of inspiration to me."[10] In these words Kramer found affirmation in the unspoken regard that Skrowaczewski had for him and his musicianship over their many years together. He was so moved by the letter that he had the bowl engraved with his and Skrowaczewski's initials and then told the maestro what he had done. Skrowaczewski wrote back: "I thought of engraving our first names on it before giving it to you but thought it might be presumptuous to do so."[11]

More than two decades later, Kramer described the impact that Skrowaczewski's letters had on him:

> Over the years since I retired, these two letters were as if I had been talking face to face with Skrowaczewski, a conductor who seemed so remote on the podium— and I have never been so deeply moved as with this personal relationship with a conductor. For an orchestra musician it was an ennobling experience to be thought of this way by a great conductor. To say that I, one of ninety other musicians in his orchestra, was a "personal source of inspiration" makes me feel that my career in Minneapolis as a symphony player was worth all the effort I put into it.[12]

As a man and a musician, Skrowaczewski is the antithesis of superficiality. It takes time and effort to get to know him, his artistic personality, and motivations. His love of the music of Bruckner and Mozart is emblematic of his character. Both composers embody a classicism and spirituality that resonate deeply within Skrowaczewski:

> Mozart is subtle, sublime, and transcendental. To me, his music comes as not from this world; its beauty [and] organization of elements is eternal, as if beyond us. Even when his music is gay, cheerful, and serene, its content [seems] sad, tragic to me, as if [it were] a presentiment of his untimely death or, in general, a feeling of the tragic fate of human beings. However, Bruckner's deep faith often turns this tragic fate into a glory for God.

> The "metaphysical shiver" I feel from Mozart's music, I also feel from Bruckner, Beethoven, Schumann, Wagner, and sometimes from Alban Berg. To me, Bruckner is one of the greatest composers. He is another Mozart: his music is magical. Of course, there is the sheer beauty of harmony, instrumentation, polyphonic patterns, and grandeur of architecture that engages and challenges our entire mind. But his music is also full of the deepest content. Its message speaks about the infinite, transcendental cosmos, God, timelessness, love, and tragedy. All these metaphysical ideas touch us deeply, bringing forth our spiritual attributes.

> I view Bruckner's music as a continuation of the Viennese classical tradition of Mozart, Beethoven, and especially Schubert, as a music that is not disturbed by human problems. The music of Mahler, in contrast, is disturbed by these problems all the time. He is easier to understand because he is, to me, "human" (often too human). When Mahler is sad, he's sad; when he's happy, he's happy—sometimes even too happy, approaching vulgarity. You can never find this quality in Bruckner, Mozart, or Beethoven, whose classicism is transcendental, less human, and more godlike. Bruckner's music leads toward a mystical, metaphysical meaning beyond human nature. It points to something higher, to something like religion. Bruckner himself was a very religious man. His music floats above us in heaven somewhere.

A soloist was not featured in the 1974 dedication concert, whose focus rightly was on the orchestra itself. Cellist Lynn Harrell had the honor of being the first soloist with the orchestra during the hall's inaugural season. Originally Skrowaczewski had a soloist in mind for the first concert. After speaking to Artur Rubinstein's wife and following up with a letter, Skrowaczewski received a letter from Paris in which Rubinstein expressed his regret that he couldn't accept the invitation:

> Nothing could give me more pleasure than to accept your proposition, but, as you may know by now, I have decided to stop my concert activities, except for a few in Europe, and, of course, on the condition that I can cancel any concert shortly before the date set. At my ripe age of eighty-seven I have no

right to plan a year ahead for anything…. Frankly, I believe that the time has come when I ought to cede my place to the younger generation, who shows so much talent.[13]

It would be two more years before Rubinstein, then almost ninety, officially ceded to the younger generation in 1976 with his last public concert in London. Not long before, Skrowaczewski collaborated a final time with the legendary pianist. The Paris concert left Skrowaczewski with a sad, final memory of his famous compatriot:

It was in La Salle de Congrès with Rubinstein playing the Brahms D minor concerto, one of the last concerts of his life. The hall was created for L'Orchestre de Paris and L'Orchestre National de France. It was the first concert opening the hall, and the musicians cried. It was just horrible. It was a huge hall with over three thousand seats that were like first-class in Lufthansa, huge and soft, for congress members. They destroyed the sound. In the middle of the hall we couldn't hear anything. It was much worse than Northrop. After a few concerts no one ever played there again. After the concert Rubinstein said to me, "You know, during the piece I was thinking I wanted to die on stage with this concerto." When he had been in Minneapolis in 1972 for his eighty-fifth birthday concert, he didn't complain about his eyes, but now he was having great difficulties. On fast passages he played wrong notes because of his poor sight. He was very emotional, not disturbed, but rather serene with a feeling of "this is the end."

Rubinstein died in 1982. His was among the most extraordinary performing careers in music history. He had made his professional debut in 1894, three years before the death of Brahms.[14]

The music of Ravel put the Minnesota Orchestra back on the recording map in 1975. "No one who spends any time with music needs the occasion of a centenary as a reminder of the genius of Ravel," wrote Richard Freed, but the occasion of Ravel's centenary certainly didn't hurt the prospects for the orchestra's first major recording since the Mercury years.[15] Timed for release on Ravel's 100th birthday, the four-LP set was actually the first recording of the composer's complete orchestral works made outside of France. It was also the first time these pieces were recorded in quadraphonic sound, a relatively short-lived format served best by listening with four speakers—an early form of "surround sound." The Vox Box, as the set was marketed, included Fanfare for the ballet *L'Eventail de Jeanne*, at the time the second known recording of that brief work.

Microphones went up in Orchestra Hall during the first subscription concert of the 1974–75 season in preparation for the upcoming quartet of four-hour recording sessions, the next test for the venue to pass. "It's a hell of a good hall," said Marc Aubort, who coproduced the sessions. "You really can hear everything, noises and all."[16] Skrowaczewski heard too much:

The cubes behind the orchestra projected the brass too loudly in different directions. For the recording I wanted to use a curtain, but the engineers wouldn't do it. They wanted the long reverberation, and they were right, but without the public absorption it was too loud. It was hard to get right balances with percussion, brass, low and high frequencies, especially the high violins. Live in the empty hall, it sounded powerful, but when I went to hear the playback, the sound was somehow thin. I was a little dissatisfied, so I tried to help them as much as I could.

Ravel's orchestral music, a bounty of masterful orchestration and colorful hues, was in good hands with Skrowaczewski on the podium. His exacting labors paid off. The Ravel set was a strong critical and commercial success, widely praised in the United States and abroad.

"Skrowaczewski has managed for the most part to create a perfect Ravelian orchestral ambience," said *High Fidelity Magazine*.[17] A French critic described Skrowaczewski's "very personal intentions which give us a Ravel which is secure, extremely subtle, and distinguished, with an accent of lyricism, of tenderness which surprises lovers of 'the Swiss watchmaker' (Stravinsky's nickname for Ravel, who was noted for the precision of his scores)."[18]

"It is hard to name a composer who was more meticulous and detailed in his musical notation than Maurice Ravel," wrote Gunther Schuller in *The Compleat Conductor*.[19] In 1975 Schuller wrote Skrowaczewski, praising the Ravel LPs: "The Ravel recording is really terrific. You have brought out things in Ravel's scores that I have been waiting decades for conductors to do."[20] (In *The Compleat Conductor* Schuller presents a highly detailed comparative analysis of fifty-four recordings by major conductors and orchestras of *Daphnis et Chloé*, Second Suite. He cites several commendable qualities of Skrowaczewski's recording of the piece.)

By the end of the orchestra's 1974–75 season, the LPs were on *Billboard's* bestsellers chart, amid competition that included new Ravel recordings by Boulez and the New York Philharmonic, Maazel and the Cleveland Orchestra, and Ozawa and the Boston Symphony. Critic Bob Epstein offered a comparative view:

> These [Minnesota Orchestra] recordings are perhaps closest to the cultivated, subtle, and idiomatic performances of Boulez that are so miraculous and in their own way incomparable. If Skrowaczewski is not always up to Boulez's very high standards, this Vox set often holds its own and occasionally even surpasses the Boulez. Skrowaczewski has the most success with the rapt, poetic world of Ravel, and his reading of *Ma mère l'oye* is the finest in the set and arguably the best presently available.[21]

Critics took issue with the fact that the Vox Box was billed as Ravel's complete orchestral works but also included the two suites from *Daphnis et Chloé* instead of the complete ballet music. Four months before any tape was laid down for the recordings, Skrowaczewski anticipated this criticism and raised the issue with Cisek before the orchestra made its final commitment to Vox. Nevertheless, Vox and the orchestra included only the suites, primarily because of time and financial constraints. More than thirty years after their initial release the Ravel recordings on Vox remain available, and several recording companies have reissued them on CD.

Skrowaczewski and the orchestra followed their fruitful Vox Ravel recordings with Wagner and Handel LPs, released in 1976. The movement to perform early music on period instruments and with strict performance practices was gaining popularity. Christopher Hogwood attracted attention in classical-music circles in 1973 when he founded the Academy of Ancient Music in London; Sir Roger Norrington, Sir John Eliot Gardiner, and Nikolaus Harnoncourt were also innovators in this area of performance. Although Skrowaczewski has studied performance practices, he has never felt straitjacketed by them interpretively. In preparing to record Handel's popular *Water Music Suite* and *Royal Fireworks Music,* however, he consulted Handel's final editions of the masterpieces, and he spent substantial time with his string players on producing bowings that he believed would deliver the composer's proper stylistic language. Critics praised his interpretive efforts, noting that the LP offered a contemporary-sounding alternative to recordings that were restricted to authentic baroque performance practice.[22]

Along with new recordings and concert series, Orchestra Hall's inaugural season brought two commissioned works planned to mark the occasion. Gunther Schuller was unable to accept his offer, but Minnesota composer Eric Stokes contributed *The Continental Harp and Band Report: An American Miscellany.* Looking for a piece with a distinctively American quality that would highlight the hall's acoustics, Skrowaczewski specifically requested a piece from Stokes that would not feature any strings. Initially the request depressed Stokes, who was eager to compose a piece for the full orchestra. After some consideration, however, he saw the request as a gift: "It meant that I could make a piece of music starting from the values and the experience that I know, without any of the baggage of European symphonic implications," he said.[23]

The United States would mark its bicentennial slightly more than a year after the 1975 premiere of Stokes' piece, and the composer said he "viewed this piece also as a bicentennial commentary."[24] The title of the nine-movement, forty-minute work was inspired by a collection of old American music: a miscellany of dances, tunes, songs, and marches. The title derives "continental" from the Continental Army of 1776; "harp" from *The Sacred Harp,* the title of an old American song; and "band" from the scoring without strings.[25] The work is reminiscent of Ives in its musical quotations and augmented instrumentation, which includes a bass trumpet, Wagner *tuben* quartet, a washboard, and a cash register.

The orchestra achieved a much-coveted bicentennial coup by engaging Aaron Copland for concerts on the Fourth of July in 1975 and 1976. "The bicentennial concerts I conducted with the Minnesota Orchestra on July 3, 4, and 5, 1976, left a vivid impression with me," said Copland.[26] He continued:

Although I have conducted numerous orchestras in different parts of the world, I have rarely encountered so responsive and involved a public as was true on that memorable occasion. The unconventionality of the audience and its spontaneous reaction to the program seemed to have given a special flair to the playing. From my own standpoint, it was an unforgettable concert, one that I much enjoyed watching and hearing again when it was presented on television.[27]

During his historic 1976 Minnesota engagement, another unconventional and spontaneous reaction to Copland came from six-year-old Nicholas Skrowaczewski. His father related the story:

Copland was Nicholas' god at the time. He heard records of his music, and nothing else interested him from when he was four or five. So when Copland gave the Fourth of July concert [in 1976], of course Krystyna and I took both Paul and Nicky to the program, which, by the way, was very good. He conducted efficiently at that time, not only his works but also other American works. Being the music director, I was the ex-officio [host], receiving Copland after the concert. We all went backstage to congratulate him, and suddenly Nicholas says, "Mr. Copland, I am one of your very few admirers." We froze and said, "But Nicky, you ought to say you are a *great* admirer." "Yes," he said, "but one of the very few." Copland became red and burst into laughter. But we felt miserable because the implication was that the child must have heard this from somewhere, but from where and from whom? We never said it. We absolutely adored his music.

We had a principle that we never said to the children, "Listen to this, it is good, or don't listen to this, it's bad." Never! We never said, "This is black, this is white." [Instead it was] "You choose what you like, you are free." We didn't indoctrinate our children. Why had he said it? We don't know. He didn't know later. He presumed that Copland didn't have many admirers. I tell this story to demonstrate that children, at a certain point, if they are artistically sensitive they will show a special predilection. Their inner paper is not written on. They are not contaminated. They are an all-white page. They will write something on it eventually, but there is nothing written on this page in the beginning.

Copland's Fourth of July concerts in 1975 were preceded by pops events and Rug Concerts, the latter a new series led by thirty-year-old American conductor Leonard Slatkin. A rising star and an associate principal conductor of the St. Louis Symphony, Slatkin was named the first principal guest conductor of the Minnesota Orchestra, beginning with the 1974–75 season. After eight seasons as the orchestra's associate conductor, George Trautwein decided it was time to find an orchestra of his own and left his position in 1974. Skrowaczewski was saddened to lose his close colleague, but he understood his situation. "You were one of the few people here with whom I could discuss all sorts of musical matters thoroughly and frankly, with this unique and rare feeling of understanding and trust," Skrowaczewski wrote Trautwein in fall 1974. "Your departure left a major void."[28]

Henry Charles Smith, who began as an assistant conductor in 1971, assumed the title of associate conductor, filling the day-to-day conducting tasks as needed. With Slatkin on board, a team of three conductors remained intact. Slatkin was the principal guest conductor (a new titled post for the orchestra) for four years, through the remainder of Skrowaczewski's tenure as music director.

Rug Concerts gained a following with the New York Philharmonic in the early 1970s, when Boulez instituted them soon after becoming its music director. The Minnesota Orchestra established its own series, which had a four-year run. Encouraged to bring their own pillows, audiences sat on large rugs on the floor of Minneapolis' Orchestra Hall. The repertoire comprised unique contemporary pieces combined with traditional repertoire, and Slatkin offered commentary. "The audience was young, the hair was long, and the whole thing was loose and very 1970s," said Brian Newhouse.[29] Slatkin described the series:

> Crazy! It was nuts, actually. It was a time of experiments. It was the last period of the avant-garde, which was about to end. There's nothing like that now. Today people are not playing a piece for one hundred metronomes, and the experiments with electronics and orchestra faded. I think Stan was intrigued because I was programming music that made him interested. He came to the concerts. Minneapolis was an unusual city because it supported its arts in a way that very few cities were able to do. The Children's Theatre was there, and the Saint Paul Chamber Orchestra was going strong. It was a hotbed of re-creative activity [and] creative activity as well, because the area was producing fine local or Minnesota-area composers. I conducted a number of works by Paul Fetler, for example, at the time. The Rug Concerts were good. They ran their course, things changed, and we came up with Sommerfest.

Following the Rug Concerts and Copland's Fourth of July concerts, Skrowaczewski led a three-day Mozart Festival with the Minnesota Orchestra. The festival continued for two more summers and added some of Haydn's music to the mix. Skrowaczewski remembered the 1976 festival, which included a complete concert performance of Mozart's opera *Idomeneo*—a first for the Twin Cities—along with symphonies, concertos, and small works by Mozart and Haydn:

> I had four concerts, different programs, in four days, with sixteen rehearsals (we divided the orchestra in two). All I did from 8:00 a.m. until 11:00 at night, for six days, was rehearse and perform this music. The schedule looked inhuman, but I was so exhilarated by Mozart's music that I was perfectly fine. There was a certain feedback from the music. I didn't need coffee or vitamins.[30]

After Skrowaczewski's first Minnesota Mozart Festival in July 1975, Slatkin led a four-day Beethoven Festival. As a guest conductor Slatkin spent considerable time around the orchestra and Skrowaczewski during those years. He recalled his memories of the maestro:

> I always had a great time with Stan. I learned a lot from him. He has a real sense of discipline and commitment to the music, and because he

operated—and still does—as a composer, I always felt he was looking at a composition through the eyes of a composer, as if he had created it himself. So if it was Bruckner, Beethoven, or whoever, there was always the touch of the composer's hand in his conducting. I was always impressed by his ability to balance and to clarify aspects of orchestration. He was always keenly aware of sound quality. Very few conductors thought about it, but he did. Those are hallmarks of Skrowaczewski performances for me.

While Slatkin was conducting Beethoven in Minneapolis, Skrowaczewski was conducting Ives and other composers in Detroit with the Detroit Symphony at the Meadow Brook Festival. Skrowaczewski debuted at Meadow Brook in 1974, drawing a record audience of twenty-five thousand. Friends of Polish Arts of Detroit and the national music chairman of the Polish American Council of Cultural Clubs received Skrowaczewski during that visit. The city's large Polish community took great pride in the maestro's achievements. The Detroit branch of *Dziennik Polski* (The Polish Daily News) ran a preview piece on Skrowaczewski for his 1975 Meadow Brook concerts, noting that he had received the 1970 Man of the Year Award of the American Council of Polish Cultural Clubs.

Skrowaczewski was guest conducting the Philadelphia Orchestra at Saratoga in August 1975 when he learned of Shostakovich's death. Speaking to Michael Anthony soon afterward, Skrowaczewski said that he regarded the Russian composer as a continuation of Bruckner and Mahler and perceived the commonality of the three composers' "monumental feeling of deep, profound human expression. In fact, in multiple works they share a similarity of form. But Shostakovich is more similar to Bruckner in that they both have long thematic sections in their symphonies. Mahler tends to be more choppy in his form."[31]

Before his August engagements Skrowaczewski squeezed in his annual mountain-climbing sojourn. Sun Valley, Idaho, was his choice that summer. "It's like my vitamins. I have to have it once a year: skiing in the winter and mountain climbing in the summer," he said. "I get high just to see the mountains, the meadows covered with colors."[32]

After completing a late-summer guest-conducting tour in Europe, Skrowaczewski began work on his saxophone concerto commission, scheduled for performance in 1978. While writing this piece he established a new pattern—which continues to this day—of composing in small spurts when he has time off from conducting.

The Minnesota Orchestra was a confident organization as it headed into its second season at Orchestra Hall. The ensemble had completed its longest (eight weeks) and most prosperous summer season. Subscription concert sales were up by fifty percent, and the 1975–76 season launched a fifty-week season, a first for the organization. Artistically the Ravel recordings boosted the orchestra's reputation, and the ensemble won another award from the American Society of Composers, Authors and Publishers (ASCAP) for adventuresome programming of contemporary music.

Orchestra Hall continued to be the talk of professional orchestras and critics throughout America. For the musicians and Skrowaczewski, however, the honeymoon period with Orchestra Hall was over. After a full season of concerts they were still working hard to learn how to "play their new instrument" and to cope with its quirks. But these issues didn't diminish the intense appreciation everyone felt for the orchestra's new home. In one of many such letters, Skrowaczewski expressed his gratitude to John Pillsbury, Jr., chairman of the MOA board, who left his post a few months into Orchestra Hall's inaugural season:

> There aren't words to reflect the change in our musical life because of Orchestra Hall, both for the public and for the performers. I am glad to report to you that during the last two months of our new season I have distinctly felt a change in attitude, pride, and production on the part of so many musicians— and they don't react only to the fact of better acoustics. They feel happy and important because of their newly won social status and because of the profound concern the association and our city officials have shown for the message of art. It all happened under your dedicated leadership, and to my personal feelings of thanks I can add those of our orchestra members. But as I said, words are limited in regard to human feelings, and I would rather express myself in music. I am hoping to do this by writing a special work dedicated to the Minnesota Orchestra.[33]

The piece to which Skrowaczewski referred—what would become his Concerto for Orchestra—would have to wait until 1985 and the tenth anniversary of Orchestra Hall. "Your expression of what the new hall means to you and the musicians of the orchestra…is just terrific," wrote Pillsbury to Skrowaczewski. "English is not your 'mother tongue,' but when you write it you are much more articulate than most Americans I know."[34]

Skrowaczewski's commitment to improving Orchestra Hall's main flaw—the over-projection of the winds and brass—began almost immediately after the dedication concert. Distinguished visiting musicians sympathized with Skrowaczewski's acoustical concerns. "The hall is a beautiful one, and I believe acoustically is very good," wrote Yehudi Menuhin to Skrowaczewski after guest conducting the orchestra. "The only reservation I have is that the winds, as you rightly warned me, are inclined to be too resonant. I could never get a real *pianissimo* from the woodwinds or the brass, but their quality and musicianship were overwhelming."[35] Isaac Stern, praising the hall, described it as being "a little bright, so that you have to be careful how hard you push—because the hall takes [the sound] away faster than some. It doesn't have the patina of Carnegie Hall. That's bathed in old brown wood like a well-aged liqueur. But it will age."[36]

However, the building had structural issues that time would not improve. The lobby, mechanics, and facilities of Orchestra Hall had taken a backseat to acoustics in planning and financing the building. The stage was a bit small; the string players in particular complained about not having a comfortable amount of individual bowing space. And the musicians' locker/dressing rooms were modest in size. Of greater concern were problems with the building's heating and cooling system.

Still, the orchestra's new home was a world of improvement over Northrop Auditorium, and everyone would have to adjust to Orchestra Hall. Skrowaczewski eventually had a rehearsal curtain installed, which helped suppress the live nature of the hall, but his main objection, the four lower cubes on the back wall, remained. (They finally were removed in 2002.)

Nearly thirty years after he gave his first downbeat in Orchestra Hall, Skrowaczewski reflected on its strengths and shortcomings:

> It is impossible to rate by numbers, but it is one of the best that exists. When I was coming from Vienna, Amsterdam, or Boston, I really liked this hall more. It is on the same level. There are some small mistakes for the public for viewing; for example, the second row of balcony [seats] on the side can see only half of the orchestra, so Cyril Harris corrected this point when he built the analog hall in Salt Lake City. That hall is an exact copy of Orchestra Hall, with improvements for the public and with a different lobby, and so forth.

"Dear Listener," Skrowaczewski wrote to the 1975–76 season subscribers, "those 'shivers' of excitement we feel upon the spiritual impact of music are generated as much by thoughtful programs as by the best performances."[37] For the first time, subscription concerts were titled under four themes: Classical Tradition, Romantic Imagination, Great Symphonies, and Festival Concerts. While the concept of a thematic season was not new—Bernstein had good luck with it during his New York Philharmonic tenure—Skrowaczewski's approach paired works from contrasting epochs within a particular theme, thus "enabling [the listener] to perceive the entire art as one human expression towards the infinite."[38] Although the programs were extremely well balanced, some older, more conservative listeners still believed there was "too much contemporary music."

Skrowaczewski's juxtaposition of works made for fascinating listening. One Classical Tradition program, for example, offered a Bach Brandenburg concerto with Mozart's Bassoon Concerto, de Falla's Harpsichord Concerto (a first for the Minnesota Orchestra), and Bartók's Divertimento for Strings.

The Festival Concerts offered special programs, often with chorus, and new works celebrating the nation's bicentennial. *Echoes of Time and the River* by George Crumb caused the greatest stir. Crumb won the 1968 Pulitzer Prize for the composition, a work that involved theatrical elements and new performing experiences for the Minnesota musicians. String and wind players play small percussion instruments and some vocalize frog croaks. One movement calls for three musicians—first trumpet, first trombone, and one percussionist with a drum on a sling—to march around the stage in front of the orchestra whispering, "*Montani semper liberi?*" ("Mountaineers are always free?"), the motto of Crumb's home state, West Virginia. The piece was surprisingly popular with audience members, and the musicians brought the right spirit to their extramusical tasks. "I know that musicians elsewhere have felt rebellious when confronted by the challenges this score brings, and they haven't wanted to be actors as well as players," wrote Mary Ann Feldman in a letter to the entire orchestra. "Therefore, I'm especially impressed by [your] goodwill that makes it possible to bring the whole thing off."[39]

All of Skrowaczewski's avant-garde programming since 1960, along with Slatkin's more recent popularity with Rug Concerts, no doubt prepared musicians and audiences for the "anything goes" quality inherent in works of the late 1960s and 1970s. Feldman happily reported that a number of the Coffee Concert attendees, mostly older people, asked her how they might obtain recordings of Crumb's music.

Metaphorical theatrics were evoked by the orchestra's formal bicentennial commission and the season's only world premiere. Skrowaczewski and the orchestra had performed a work by American composer Michael Colgrass four years before the world premiere of his *Theatre of the Universe* in March 1976. Colgrass, an eclectic musician whose teachers included Milhaud and Riegger, worked professionally as a percussionist with the New York Philharmonic, the Metropolitan Opera, Dizzy Gillespie, and the Modern Jazz Quartet. He performed on the Columbia Recording Orchestra's *Stravinsky Conducts Stravinsky* series and with the original *West Side Story* orchestra on Broadway.

"Accessible without seeming shallow," wrote Michael Anthony in his review of *Theatre of the Universe*; similar descriptions were attributed to Colgrass's music over his long career.[40] The full-orchestra piece with chorus and soloists uses text from seven Colgrass poems about "the alienation of human feelings in a fast-changing world," certainly a sentiment that resonated with Skrowaczewski.[41] In 1978 Colgrass received the Pulitzer Prize for *Déjà vu*, a commissioned work for the New York Philharmonic.

Colgrass described his first experience working with Skrowaczewski in 1976 and again ten years later:

> I was very impressed by his attention to detail, his excellent ear, and his feeling overall for the music. He was the consummate professional, and he had a quick understanding of the composer's intent. Personally, he was very formal—respectful, attendant to my every request, but still emotionally detached. I found him to be the archetype of "the perfect gentleman": tie always in place, speaking only when absolutely necessary. Stan conducted performances of my *Déjà vu* with the Hallé Orchestra in Manchester in 1986. Again, he was formal, detached, and extremely efficient. At one point I commented on something that made him say, almost apologetically, that he had had a headache all day. But you would never know it from his demeanor, comportment, or his work on the podium. He is an extremely self-controlled person.[42]

The concerts that included *Theatre of the Universe* also featured Argentine pianist Martha Argerich playing Chopin's Piano Concerto no. 2. Skrowaczewski had collaborated with her several times since her Minnesota debut four years earlier. Argerich is among the most gifted musicians of the second half of the 20th century, and her deeply imaginative, technically brilliant playing has been heard live and on recordings since the 1960s to the present. She also has been a troubled and unpredictable artist, suffering at times from depression and intense stage fright, both of which she overcame.

Uncompromising artistically and professionally, Argerich records with any labels and artists she wishes and limits her public performances. She has a long history of canceling engagements, often because she abhors the routine of performance. *The New York Times* review of a 2002 documentary on Argerich describes the extreme circumstances of her first professional concert cancellation:

> Ms. Argerich, whose last-minute cancellations have disappointed fans, describes her first cancellation, at seventeen in Florence. She was not unwell, she says, but thought she "didn't want to play." So she sent a telegram to the concert organizers saying she had hurt her finger. She then took a knife and cut her finger, so "it would be true." The wound was so bad it also prevented her from playing a concert the next week.[43]

Skrowaczewski related his own experiences with Argerich's ironic relationship with public performance:

> We first performed together in 1968, with the Österreichischer Rundfunk of Vienna. She won first prize in the Chopin Competition in Warsaw three years earlier. Then I asked to have her play in Minneapolis. We played Liszt Piano Concerto no. 1 the first time, and she was astonishing. In the mid-1970s we were together with the Israel Philharmonic Orchestra. Engagements with this orchestra would often last at least two or more weeks, so artists stay at the Israel Philharmonic Guest House, located a little outside of Tel Aviv. It's a lovely home with a big conductor's suite and another room for the soloist. I was in my room and Martha in hers, waiting to get picked up to go to the concert.
>
> Often with the Israel Philharmonic, the conductor leads the same concert for two or three weeks, maybe with just a change of the overture. The guest pianist might change concertos, but there is a lot of repetition. There might be six or seven performances of one concerto one week and another concerto the next week. So we played the First Beethoven Concerto. The first night: wonderful. The second night: wonderful. Third night: wonderful. Then there is a day off, and the cycle starts again. On the night of the fourth performance, I was in my room, dressed and waiting for the car. The chauffeur came and said, "Mr. Skrowaczewski, we have a problem. Ms. Argerich is in her bed and says she cannot play tonight. She's tired and angry and will not go." So I said to myself, "Oh, my god, typical Martha." Just a few years before, she had been our soloist with the Minnesota Orchestra for a concert in Carnegie Hall, and right before the concert she disappeared. We couldn't find her anywhere. She finally showed up just as the first piece ended. This is Martha.
>
> So I went calmly to her room and said, "Martha, good evening. I hear you are not willing to come tonight. Why?" And she said: "It is inhuman, it is impossible. They cannot force artists to play every night the same piece. It's not good. I cannot play tonight." And she was very angry and still in bed undressed. I sat on the bed and said very quietly, "Martha, you know, we *all* do it. The artists before you and the artists after you do it. It is hard, I know. For me, I have to do the same symphony more than you have to play the

concerto. Finally, we are professional people, and we must be professional and behave as professionals. There is no reason for you not to play. No one will accept this excuse. They will understand emotionally that you feel too tired to repeat, but you are professional enough to do it well. Even if you are not in the mood." She said, "Yes, I understand you, but I will not go."

So then I said, "Martha, why don't you get dressed and come with me and just feel the atmosphere of the concert hall, the people, the excitement, the orchestra. I'll play the first piece and…" "You can play something else!" she interrupted. I said, "I can't, Martha. I don't have anything else prepared with the orchestra except my program. I cannot play just anything without rehearsing." "Yes, I understand," she said, "but I will not go." Finally, I managed to get her in the car with me. She was in her robe, and she brought her dress on a hanger in the car. We arrived at the hall late. I didn't tell anyone what was going on.

I conducted the first piece. Then came the Beethoven concerto. Martha walked on to the stage. She was dressed and had an angry look on her face. She hardly bowed to the public. She played the first movement, and it was perfect! It was extremely beautiful and probably the best of all four that she played. The stage at Mann Auditorium is very low. You practically step down from it right to the public. The first few rows sit right on top of the orchestra and soloists. The first row is almost touching the stage. So we finished the first movement, there was the typical audience noise, and latecomers were seated. Then, right in the silence after these sounds finish, Martha turned to me and said—very loudly, almost shouting: "Wasn't that horrible?"

You can imagine the consternation of the first rows of people, of the members of the violins of the orchestra, all thinking "What does she mean? What is wrong with her?" Then I said only, "Shut up." I don't know if the audience heard me or not. We started and played to the end very well. There was huge applause. She smiled, thanked me, and that was it. The next day was fine. No problems.

We played again in Minneapolis and later in the 1990s in Warsaw. She's an incredible talent. With her temperament she can go to the extremes of beauty and also not so. It depends on the day. She's not even. As a conductor, you have to be very careful because she may suddenly do something new, unexpected, but usually the spontaneity of her playing is fantastic.

About a month after the Colgrass premiere and Argerich concerts, Skrowaczewski and the Minnesota Orchestra toured Florida with cellist Lynn Harrell as soloist. Two years earlier, Harrell, then thirty years old and newly embarked on an international solo career, had performed in Minneapolis. That engagement had been his first time collaborating with Skrowaczewski as a soloist, although he had previously worked with him when the maestro guest conducted in Cleveland. At age eighteen Harrell became the youngest member of the Cleveland Orchestra at the time, and he served as principal cellist under Szell from 1964 to 1971. Harrell remembered his 1974 collaboration with Skrowaczewski:

I played the Haydn D major during the opening week of Orchestra Hall in Minneapolis. I was so excited to play such a delicate, introverted piece in such a magnificent acoustic. The orchestra was able to play in the refined classical sense and awareness without being dry and lacking in imagination. It was a particularly awesome experience. I don't think I have played the Haydn D major with anyone else since then, on that level. I had not performed with someone who was that much older than me who didn't give me the feeling that I still had a long way to go, still had a lot to learn. I was taken aback as a young soloist that Stan gave me so much respect. I think the Haydn we played later with the Hallé Orchestra in the late 1990s was certainly more deeply conceived artistically through my own work, but it was again a collaboration full of enthusiasm and mutual respect.

Their mutual admiration and affection solidified during the Minnesota Orchestra's Florida tour in spring 1976. Skrowaczewski described the qualities of Harrell's playing he most admires:

He has a wonderful tone, expressive but very clean and with clear intonation. There is a classical organization of his musicianship; nothing is overdone or overextended. The last time I did the Schumann concerto with him, it was beautiful, very romantic, but within a classical framework: no exaggerations, rubatos, etc.

Harrell remembered an apparel incident during the Florida tour:

Stan was very much of the old European school with concert dress. He wore custom-made tails: not a wrinkle in them, stiff collar like the turn-of-the-19th-century, expertly self-tied white tie, and a magnificent vest. The wardrobe truck didn't make it on time for one of the concerts. All the instrument trunks had space for musicians' frocks, so everyone was dressed normally for the performance except Stan, which was so cute because he was the one who took that aspect of concert work so much more seriously than any single member of the orchestra or myself as a soloist. He had to conduct, perhaps even in just a shirt. I don't think he even had a suit. Normally the best-dressed person in the concert, he now was the most casually attired of one hundred people onstage.

One of the reviews during the tour observed that although Skrowaczewski looked young, his gray hair was already showing. The remark surprised the maestro, who believed that he had few gray hairs. In a rare moment of vanity he asked his tour manager, Charles Fullmer, if he would sit down with him and pluck his "few" grays out. "Oh, Stan," the good-humored Fullmer replied, "if I did that, half of the hair on your head would be gone!" The pair got a good laugh from the incident for years afterward.

Harrell was among the soloists with whom Skrowaczewski worked most frequently during his post-Minnesota career. The cellist reflected on Skrowaczewski's qualities:

Part of his musical persona [includes the humility that] is at the very highest level of all things needed to being a concert performer. You have to be artistically and musically sensitive. You have to be bright and well read and well trained. You have to know the craft of what you are doing—playing the cello, piano, or conducting. You've got to know the musicians psychologically, what they need, what they think they need and you know they don't—leadership qualities that you find with any great leader. Stan had all those things. But most important to him was, no matter what, "we are not as good as the music is"; therefore, we have to work particularly hard and afresh each and every single time. Most conductors don't live life that way. The fact that I had this long relationship with George Szell, and then I met Stanisław and was able to make music with him for a number of years, is one of the most lovely and educational aspects of my growth and development.

In Israel, where we played together in the late 1970s, we played six nights in a row, and we were together for a few days before that. At that time the Israel Philharmonic Guest House was the preferred location for artists, so we had breakfast, lunch, dinner, and postconcert dinners every day, like suddenly living together. That experience was also just so lovely. I got to realize that this man is not only a great artist and great conductor but also an enthusiastic, lovely, warm human being. His demeanor sometimes on the podium to orchestra musicians might seem as though he is really an uptight, rather tense guy, but underneath that there beats a really warm heart for friendship, under that certain kind of European demeanor, oftentimes found among people born before 1935. I think [that] giving up your homeland and the very center of your being—which is the music and making music in your country—and coming to a raw Western country, which was the United States at that time, and then having to rebuild your life, affects a person. Stanisław is one of those people, along with Steinberg, Ormandy, Reiner, and Szell, and we have the benefit. Today the American orchestras are the best trained and the best sounding in the world.

Harrell, along with Szeryng and Weissenberg, was among the soloists with whom Skrowaczewski was most artistically aligned. Each possesses a perfection of technique and "classicism" in his approach to music making that resonates with the maestro.

Skrowaczewski closed the orchestra's seventy-third concert season with the Berlioz Requiem. Although it was his first time leading the massive work (the expanded one hundred-member orchestra used a chorus of three hundred singers from the University of Minnesota), Skrowaczewski had a long performing history with the French master's music. He also had closed the previous Minnesota season with a large-scale Berlioz work, a complete performance of *Roméo et Juliette*. "Berlioz has come of age in America," reported the *Berlioz Society Bulletin* in fall 1975, recognizing that because of Skrowaczewski's consistent programming and excellent performances of the composer's music, Minneapolis was becoming another city known for performing Berlioz's music, alongside Chicago, San Francisco, and Boston.[44]

In early summer 1976 Skrowaczewski was among a select group of musicians, including Kubelik, Rostropovich, Rudolf Serkin, and Jean-Pierre Rampal, who were invited to participate in the Festival Casals, held in Puerto Rico. That year the annual festival, founded by the renowned Spanish cellist in 1957, was celebrating Casals' centenary. Later that summer Skrowaczewski led two particularly effective programs with the Cleveland Orchestra at the Blossom Festival. One concert featured Isaac Stern's Blossom Festival debut; the other spotlighted American-Czech pianist Rudolf Firkušný, with whom Skrowaczewski had worked only twice before, in 1970 and again several months before their Cleveland engagement.

Skrowaczewski's 1976–77 concert season followed a characteristic pattern: diverse repertoire, new and rarely performed pieces, favorite guests, and a few new faces. Among the latter were Beverly Sills and Rampal, both of whom had rarely performed with the orchestra. Another season highlight was a performance of Mahler's Second Symphony (*Resurrection*). The mammoth piece did not have a long performance history in Minneapolis. Ormandy led the work twice during the 1934–35 season, Doráti conducted it once in 1954, and Skrowaczewski's previous Minnesota performances dated back to 1969 and 1975. Although not known as a Mahler conductor, Skrowaczewski had an affinity for this work, among the most emotional of the Viennese composer's extended symphonies.

After leading the work in a pair of highly praised performances in Minneapolis, Skrowaczewski concluded the orchestra's 1977 spring tour with the Mahler symphony at the Kennedy Center. Collaborating with a chorus from the University of Maryland, Skrowaczewski shaped a performance that still resonates in the memories of those who attended. "Skrowaczewski made Washington's music fanciers even more than ever conscious of the hairline which separates the so called 'Big-Five' [*sic*] from the country's other major orchestras in quality," reported the *Washington Star*: "[The concert] was one of the high points of the season."[45]

While Skrowaczewski was scaling the emotional heights of Mahler at the end of the season, he was unaware of a difficult situation that was brewing within the MOA. In fall 1975 its executive committee authorized a one-year extension of his contract as music director beyond its designated end in August 1977. He agreed to the extension, which guaranteed his position through the 1977–78 season. A year before the conclusion of Skrowaczewski's current contract, some executive-committee members and others with strong influence on the orchestra saw an opportunity for change.

Most of the major concert series in Minneapolis and in St. Paul were sold out from the time Orchestra Hall opened through the end of the 1976–77 season. Nevertheless, the orchestra was on the verge of performing year-round, and the administrative structure had ballooned to forty-two full-time and 105 part-time employees. Marketing studies predicted the challenges to audience development that soon materialized in the late 20th century. The Minnesota Orchestra was looking toward its future, and certain segments of the organization felt that a change of leadership was necessary for renewal.

Several factors led to their conclusion: on the part of some musicians, a strong dissatisfaction with Skrowaczewski's rehearsal style; a lack of support from key board members; and a general sentiment that, though very successful, his work with the orchestra had come full circle. Consequently, the leadership of the MOA believed it was time for him to move on.

"I did everything I could to prevent Stan's departure from Minneapolis," said Michel Glotz. "I thought that Stan, besides the fact that he was living in Minneapolis, was the ideal long-term conductor for that orchestra."

Ken Dayton, like Glotz, also believed that Skrowaczewski was the orchestra's ideal music director, but he realized that the groundswell of forces against his close friend was too strong to overcome. Skrowaczewski had seriously considered leaving his position ever since Orchestra Hall had opened, but nevertheless he was taken aback when Dayton reluctantly came to his home in spring 1977 and quietly suggested that it was "time to resign."

The obstacles Skrowaczewski faced in trying to raise the orchestra to the next level, combined with Dayton's prompting, brought him to the conclusion it was time for him to leave, and he chose to resign.

On June 24 Skrowaczewski mailed a letter of resignation to George T. Pennock, chairman of the MOA board, in which he explained that the decision resulted from his desire to "be independent of the stringent demands, limitations, and responsibilities of directing an orchestra, so that I may freely pursue my career as a conductor and composer."[46]

His contract was extended an additional year to provide time to find his successor and manage an orderly transition. At the conclusion of the 1978–79 season he became "conductor laureate" of the Minnesota Orchestra, the first and only person to hold that title with the organization. In his first season as a laureate conductor he led three weeks of subscription concerts, and he has conducted at least one week every season since then.

Skrowaczewski was relieved that he would soon relinquish the responsibility of being music director, but he also felt a sense of bitterness. He was proud of his achievements in Minneapolis, and he valued the relationships he fostered and the good friends he had made. By the end of his tenure, however, he believed that his continuing efforts to develop and elevate the Minnesota Orchestra and its reputation were not fully supported. Although this conviction lingered, his "second life" with the orchestra as conductor laureate would unlock many opportunities for the musicians, MOA, and public to express deep appreciation of their maestro.

TWENTY-TWO

TOWARD NEW VISTAS

He turned an already good orchestra into an even better instrument, well disciplined and thoroughly professional. He expanded the musical horizons of audiences. And he prodded the community into giving the orchestra one of America's finest concert halls. Skrowaczewski's future includes a busy round of conducting in the U.S., Europe, [Japan, and Australia], and renewed emphasis on composition. But he plans to keep his home here, and he will take up the baton in Orchestra Hall from time to time, as conductor [laureate]. Thus farewells, after all, are inappropriate: Skrowaczewski will continue to enrich this area's musical life.

—*Minneapolis Tribune*, 1979

Skrowaczewski's resignation from the Minnesota Orchestra shocked some musicians and outside observers. Although he had considered resigning after the creation of Orchestra Hall, he did not discuss the subject openly with anyone other than Krystyna. Composer William Schuman wrote to Skrowaczewski after he learned the news:

> I was astonished to read in the June 29 edition of *The New York Times* that you are going to give up the wonderful orchestra that you have developed so marvelously at the end of the 1978–79 season. My reaction to the announcement was mixed. From your point of view, I can understand your desire to have more time, not only for composition, but to take on a number of guest engagements rather than the full responsibility of directing one orchestra. As a composer, of course, I cannot help but be disappointed. You are one of the few conductors in our country who directs a major orchestra without forgetting his responsibility to the music of his own time. It is really surprising how few of you there are who have this true conviction.[1]

"The Polish-born musician is leaving the Minnesota Orchestra to return to his first love, composing," reported *The Bulletin* of Philadelphia. "At fifty-six he is at the height of his magnetic powers, a man who towers on the podium with a profile resembling Mahler's. It's rare if not unique for the conductor of a major American orchestra to resign such a post in midcareer."[2]

Some Minnesota Orchestra members, particularly the younger musicians who had been hired by Skrowaczewski, felt a particular sense of loss when their maestro shared his resignation letter with them at a summer festival rehearsal three days after the MOA received it. "You shocked me and surely many others today when you read your letter of resignation," wrote tuba player Ross Tolbert. "I feel you have devoted yourself unselfishly to the highest aims. In the ten years I have been here, gigantic strides have been taken, and your responsibility in the success has been outstanding."[3] Wrote oboist

Basil Reeve, "As I look back over the numerous fine concerts you have conducted since I have joined the orchestra, I couldn't help but feel that we will suffer a great loss by your departure."[4]

Musicians also wrote to Skrowaczewski about his personal acts of kindness and his support of their individual efforts. Whether it was his confidence in a musician, exemplified by not pointing out a missed entrance during a rehearsal, or his interest in their careers, the gestures were often subtle and without fanfare. But they were nonetheless strongly felt by some players. "I was especially touched by your efforts in regard to my title," wrote Reeve, "but I am even more grateful for the constant interest and confidence you have shown in me throughout the past six years. Your attitude has done more than anything else during that time to further my artistic growth."[5]

Some letter writers paid tribute to Skrowaczewski's sensitivity and insight. "You are a spiritual man, and this is what I admire so much," wrote bassoonist John Miller.[6]

"You came to America at the very time that Bernstein's instinctive flamboyance so captivated the media and the masses," wrote Mary Ann Feldman, "sometimes overshadowing musical qualities such as yours, with its profundity cum style. Seldom have the critics captured in words (how impossible, I realize) the depth and moving quality of many of your performances."[7]

Skrowaczewski was overwhelmed and surprised by the thoughtfulness of the letters he received. He responded to them all. He penned a revealing letter to Tolbert:

> Your beautiful letter moved me to tears. In the final account, there is nothing more important to me than the spiritual communion between musicians and [conductor] while making music. Without the emotional and moral aspect, the finest technical results seem to me cold and empty and do not completely satisfy my artistic endeavors. I realize that I have at times almost overemphasized the technical aspects of preparing works; as a result, many musicians could not understand that this "disciplinarian approach" was only to build a fine basis for artistic freedom, expression, and depth. Your words now and your own musical activities speak so fully to how well you have understood me; this makes me happier than anything else. Your partnership in our difficult profession has been just wonderful to me, and I thank you for everything. I am deeply saddened to have to leave a colleague such as you.[8]

"Few people genuinely believed [Skrowaczewski] would give up the music directorship to [devote more time to composing and guest conducting]," noted Roy Close in a *Musical America* article about the orchestra's seventy-fifth anniversary. "There has even been speculation—fostered in part by an article in a Minneapolis magazine—that Skrowaczewski didn't really want to resign but did so because the Orchestral Association's board of directors made it clear to him that it wanted a new captain at the helm. There's no evidence to support that allegation, however."[9]

The September 1977 issue of the orchestra's *Showcase* magazine focused on the upcoming gala seventy-fifth anniversary concert but also included an interview with Skrowaczewski. "It was time to go," he stated. "I was thinking of it for a couple of years. Any decision like that is difficult—though, from the other point of view, if it seems necessary, then you don't think it's difficult."[10]

Leaving did seem necessary to Skrowaczewski, regardless of Dayton's prompting. Tensions involving the MOA, the difficulty of removing musicians who performed below the orchestra's standards, and an approach to his position that diverged from the board's vision for the orchestra's future—all were factors. Skrowaczewski explained his frustration with the MOA's style of leadership:

> During my last years, especially when the MOA hired Don Engle as its first professional president in 1971, I was dealing with an unresponsive administration. It was frustrating, especially with key issues affecting the development of the orchestra, such as changes in personnel. When Engle was new to his position, I would be shuttled between him and Richard Cisek, then vice president and managing director, for answers, often without resolution.

"There was an emerging view," explained a former MOA officer, "that perhaps the rigidity that came from Maestro Skrowaczewski's 'Old World' approach was going to be less and less effective with younger generations of musicians and audiences. We needed to become more inclusive and collaborative as the orchestra faced future financial pressures. Having a music director who was more accessible became important."

"I saw year after year the work and the extraordinary passion of Stan," said Michel Glotz. "He is inflexible, extremely stubborn, but fantastically devoted and passionate. If one doesn't understand that, one misses completely the personality of Stan." Of all Skrowaczewski's managers, Glotz was the most musically astute and appreciative of the maestro's gifts, yet he occasionally differed with his client's firm positions.

"I begged him to do Rachmaninoff with Alexis [Weissenberg] because he was playing all over the world," recalled Glotz. "I wanted to hear Rachmaninoff's Piano Concerto no. 3 by the two together, so I continued pestering him, saying, 'If you don't do it for the public, for Ken, for Alexis, do it for me!' Finally he did it, and it was a triumph in the new hall. But it was a concession that he would do only once."

The artistic idealism and integrity that Skrowaczewski brought to his position as music director became increasingly at odds with the attitudes of some concertgoers of the late 1970s. Feldman described the situation:

> Finally, after about twenty years of rock and roll, the handwriting was on the wall: the widening gap between the popular culture and the classical music scene. Music is the vehicle of pop culture, the drug scene, the sexual revolution. So here was Skrowaczewski. He was not well prepared to deal with that and to come to terms with it. You have to have visual images, let the audience lie on the floor if they want to; you have to talk from the stage—doing everything desperately to try to get new young audiences. None of that works at all. You have to grow audiences; you have to *make* listeners. Then they can sit in their seats, and they can shut up and enjoy music without having to have video screens popping images at them. That's my opinion. Stan had misgivings about all the hoopla for the methods and messengers the

orchestra used to appeal to the younger generation. It was hurtful to him, but he handled it with grace over the long run. He never lost his dignity through this period, and he let people do what they thought they needed to do. But I think it was hard for him.

Skrowaczewski became convinced that few on the executive committee or board of directors appreciated the high quality of his interpretations and his development of the orchestra for nearly two decades. He also believed the MOA's focus on the orchestra's income was not balanced by a deep interest in its artistic progress.

He did not air his opinions publicly when he resigned or even after he left in 1979. He did, however, voice his concerns about the outlook for concert life in the September 1977 *Showcase* interview. His cautionary views described the future that he and classical music in general confronted: an audience that was less educated in music and an administrative leadership that would cater to this audience.

> A concert is no longer an affair between a small chapel full of people who gather every first or second week for one concert. Now you have multiple concerts every week. They reach ten thousand to twenty thousand people sometimes. Twenty years ago those one thousand to two thousand people who came to those few concerts a year were probably much better prepared. They were coming mostly because they connected with music, were educated in music, or just lived with it for decades. They represented perhaps a higher level of listener.
>
> Of course, if you go into the masses you have the freshness, the spontaneity of approach. Maybe, you think, a lot of them are hearing the orchestra for the first time. Their reaction is very peculiar sometimes, very unexpected. They don't know about the music [or] about the details. They cannot compare you with some other conductors because this is a language that is still [unknown]. They react particularly to certain parameters like energy, precision, involvement of the orchestra, the behavior of the conductor. [These factors] can be [misleading] because some performers can be very exciting to watch but may produce music with the wrong approach. Maybe with time, the emulation and improvement of tastes will appear on a large scale. This would be marvelous. There's no other way to go.[11]

During his tenure concertgoers gradually showed increased interest in new or unfamiliar compositions. "Our programs at that time gathered some people who were somehow immune to what was happening with pop music," he reflected. "They were a devoted public dedicated to the continuation of symphonic music." Years later Skrowaczewski was pleased to learn that he had educated the public over the years, as was verified by the letters he received (including some from a few board members) saying, "Where are your programs? We miss them."

"In a sense," he said, "I was proud that I kept my line very stern. I told the association that we did not need to succumb to the methods of pop culture to attract audiences." Changing the attitudes of an audience, even a portion of it, takes patience, sturdy dedication, and persistence. That Skrowaczewski made progress on this front was a testament to his steadfastness.

New music generally comprised only fifteen to twenty percent of Skrowaczewski's overall programs, yet for some audience members and orchestra contributors his image as music director had become synonymous with "new" and "experimental music" as well as "nonpopulist" music, such as the Bruckner symphonies.

In his role as vice president and managing director, Cisek was the intermediary who dealt with issues concerning the maestro's programming. He explained the dilemma:

> Board members, for the most part, were supportive of Stan's programming. There were some who were heavily involved in fund-raising who were saying, "If I can't stand coming to the concerts, why should my corporation give money to something even I can't stand? How can I justify this?" A specious argument, but nevertheless those are the pressures that some of our key fund-raisers were facing: looking for that idea of balance—that is, box office potential; what balanced with new music and also how guest artists balanced with those works; recognizing there are times you want an Isaac Stern to play a Penderecki concerto. But by and large, such an artist can easily fill a house, so if you don't do Mozart or Brahms with them, you are really tossing something away financially. But Stan was very good about recognizing this factor and dealing with alternatives. I tried to juxtapose alternatives: "Look, if we do this, we can easily give you that." He was always stubborn and would take his time, but we managed to work these things out because he wanted full houses, or at least not bad houses. But he also stood his ground frequently on certain things he insisted be heard—and he got them. We spent a lot of time and money, for instance, on the Penderecki *Passion*, which only after the work was performed was really appreciated for what it was.

Skrowaczewski disagrees that board members during the last years of his tenure generally supported his programming. "When the executive committee swelled to nearly twenty people," he said, "this move was probably good for the orchestra financially but not for making decisions on artistic policies. Very few members of the committee had real knowledge about music, yet some were calling my programming too elite, too serious, too contemporary, etc."

Some members of the burgeoning executive board had no history with the orchestra "and never really understood it," acknowledges Cisek. Nevertheless, he maintains, "The MOA has always had an unwritten policy of not interfering with a music director's programming. In fact, it's something they've taken pride in since the tenure of Mitropoulos, who programmed a lot of contemporary works."

Although Skrowaczewski was not forced to alter his programs throughout his tenure, criticism of artistic matters by nonmusicians still frustrated him during his last years as music director. The Minnesota Orchestra was about to embark on a new era, one in which nonmusicians increasingly influenced some artistic decisions.

In a 2003 extended article for the orchestra's centenary, Roy Close summarized the shift the organization had made by the late 1970s. In a segment titled *The Corporate Era* he wrote:

> By the end of the 1970s the Minnesota Orchestra had embarked on the course it has maintained ever since: that of a large cultural institution serving both a metropolitan area and the surrounding region with a variety of programs designed to appeal to a broad spectrum of public taste. If that sounds a little corporate, why shouldn't it? Today's Minnesota Orchestra is a nearly $30 million annual operation. It is Minnesota's largest nonprofit performing arts organization by a considerable margin. It has a large administrative staff that has a great deal of leverage to influence any artistic decision with financial implications—as all artistic decisions do.[12]

Skrowaczewski was completely at odds with the Minnesota Orchestra's corporate era:

> In the early 1970s the management invited a special team from the Dayton Hudson Corporation to help the orchestra deal with the deficit and other such matters. This was a popular practice at this time, to bring in outside consultants for help. But these people had no experience with artistic institutions, only with businesses, and they said we needed more development. The management took a great interest in their advice, and soon they doubled or tripled the staff, and the executive board grew to become a crowd. They began interfering in artistic matters, something they knew nothing about.
>
> "We need better business," the team said, but these people were giving the same advice to us that they gave to toilet paper development. It did not matter that we were an artistic organization. The Minnesota Orchestra was one of the first major orchestras to expand its administration on a large scale. They didn't need this firm to tell them what to do. They knew how to develop on their own. At the time I would travel around the country guest conducting, and people would say to me, "What did you do? Your management now is incredibly large, with extra secretaries, assistants, new directors, etc." And it has stayed this way to this day. Now, probably all orchestras have this model, but in my opinion it is wrong.

The year-round employment of the orchestra, along with the increasing costs to maintain it, partly may have necessitated the shift to a corporate model. But it was the conflict of this model with artistic considerations that Skrowaczewski would not accept. "No true conductor would," he said. His last two years as music director were exciting, substantial seasons designed without compromising his integrity.

Before Skrowaczewski began the orchestra's seventy-fifth anniversary season, he made his conducting and compositional debut at Cabrillo Music Festival in Santa Cruz, California. Founded in 1963, the festival was an expansion of the Sticky Wicket Concert Series led by composers Robert Hughes and Lou Harrison. Today the Cabrillo

Festival of Contemporary Music is one of the most prominent such festivals in the United States. It has presented eighty-four world premieres, fifty-two U.S. premieres, and numerous West Coast and local premieres by major composers including Copland, Carter, Cage, and Carlos Chávez, who served as the festival's second music director.[13] Dennis Russell Davies followed Chávez in 1974 and led the festival until 1990.

Davies invited Skrowaczewski, his Twin Cities colleague, to participate in the 1977 festival. That summer, composer-in-residence John Cage had performances of his music from the 1930s and 1940s and the premiere of *Quartets for 41 Instruments*. "Of the seven world and seven West Coast premieres, the most successful was Stanisław Skrowaczewski's *Music at Night*," noted one critic.[14] Reported another reviewer, "It is an engaging piece, which along with Lou Harrison's Suite for Violin, Piano and Small Orchestra, is the best of the contemporary music played in this year's festival."[15] The first performance of a revised *Music at Night* was received extremely well by both the audience and the orchestra.

While in California, Skrowaczewski took advantage of the northern side of Monterey Bay, where Santa Cruz is located, and went for an afternoon swim before his concert. He was alone in the water, which in itself was a bit risky due to the Pacific Ocean's shifting currents. "Suddenly I heard this huge roar behind me," Skrowaczewski remembered. "It was very musical!" He turned around and came face-to-face with a toothy California sea lion, only two feet away from him. Skrowaczewski swam away, but the 800-pound marine mammal continued to follow him for a bit. "He probably just wanted to play," Skrowaczewski said, "but I was scared like hell."

He returned to Minneapolis for the gala opening concert on September 23, 1977, which celebrated the Minnesota Orchestra's seventy-fifth anniversary. The program featured the world premiere of Dominick Argento's *In Praise of Music: Seven Songs for Orchestra*. "Your understanding and sympathetic reading of the piece far exceeded my highest expectations," Argento later wrote to Skrowaczewski.[16] The concert, which paired *In Praise of Music* with Beethoven's Ninth Symphony, was broadcast nationally over public radio and television, and Argento's ingenious work was widely admired by critics and the public.

Beethoven's works also were a focus of the celebratory season. The 150th anniversary of his death coincided with the orchestra's seventy-fifth anniversary, and all nine symphonies were performed throughout the season. Skrowaczewski led four of them, along with the *Missa Solemnis*, four overtures, and the rarely heard cantata *Calm Sea and Prosperous Voyage*.

At the season's first subscription concert he dedicated the orchestra's performance of *The Rite of Spring* to the memory of Leopold Stokowski, who had died two weeks earlier at age ninety-five. Stokowski had led the U.S. premiere of Stravinsky's masterpiece in 1922, and he conducted his last public concert in 1975 at the age of ninety-three. Two weeks later Skrowaczewski conducted a program that the ever-innovative Stokowski might have enjoyed conducting himself.

The program opened with Beethoven's *Egmont* Overture, and then Les Percussions de Strasbourg, the six-member percussion ensemble from the capital city of France's Alsace region, took over. Founded in 1962, the first such ensemble of its kind, Les Percussions de Strasbourg has commissioned dozens of works by such composers as Cage, Xenakis, and Harrison Birtwistle.[17]

"In combining for one of the most fascinating and daring Minnesota Orchestra programs in years," reported Bob Epstein, "Skrowaczewski and Les Percussions de Strasbourg offered six works without an ounce of fat or swoonish lushness, five written in this century. Boulez would've been proud."[18]

After performing a short work by Czech composer Miloslav Kabelac, the maestro and thirteen Minnesota Orchestra string players presented the North American premiere of Maurice Ohana's *Silenciaire*, a piece premiered by the Strasbourg percussion ensemble in 1969. Prokofiev's Suite no. 2 from *Romeo and Juliet* followed, and then the concert concluded with Edgard Varèse's *Intégrals* (adding eleven wind players to the percussion group) and *Ionisation* for lone percussion ensemble.

The seminal percussion piece is scored for thirteen players, but Les Percussions de Strasbourg performed a revised version for six percussionists that Varèse approved before his death in 1965. For logistical reasons the concert ended with the Varèse pieces instead of the more obvious choice of the Prokofiev; *Ionisation* requires thirty-seven different percussion instruments. When some unadventurous patrons saw the announcement of the change in the program order, they fled the hall after the Prokofiev. "Probably because of this kind of thinking, the audience was one of the smallest to hear the Minnesota Orchestra at Orchestra Hall," wrote Epstein. "But the new works were not nearly as intimidating as their reputations may have made them appear."[19] Today, given the proliferation of percussion ensembles and commercial enterprises such as Blue Man Group and *Stomp*, a similar concert would likely attract a much larger audience.

The second world premiere of the anniversary season was written by Gottfried von Einem, then Austria's most famous composer. Born in 1918 in Switzerland, where his stepfather was the military attaché at the Austrian embassy, Von Einem spent the prewar years and most of World War II in Berlin. In 1938 the Gestapo arrested and imprisoned him for a short time. He was aggressively interrogated about his political leanings (he was not a member of the Nazi party) and his friendship with the Wagner family. Von Einem made his name as an opera composer. His *Der Besuch der Alten Dame* (The Visit of the Old Lady), a setting of the play by Friedrich Dürrenmatt, was among the most frequently performed operas of the 1970s.[20]

Von Einem got to know Skrowaczewski when the maestro conducted in Vienna and subsequently dedicated his *Wiener Symphonie* to him. Two months after the Minneapolis premiere of the symphony, Skrowaczewski conducted the piece with the Vienna Symphony in its European premiere. The work received both praise and criticism for its obvious allusions to the German and Austrian masters Beethoven, Bruckner, and Mahler. "It was extremely well written," Skrowaczewski recalled, "but very much in a tonal, 19th-century tradition." The *Wiener Symphonie* was Von Einem's last orchestral work.

Ormandy made a guest appearance with the Minnesota Orchestra in honor of its diamond-jubilee season. His "homecoming," like his rare return visits, was well received by the musicians and the public. The seventy-eight-year-old maestro was amazed by the size of the administrative staff that greeted him at a luncheon in his honor. "We must be doing something wrong in Philadelphia," Ormandy announced. "We only have a music director, general manager, personnel manager, and two secretaries to run our orchestra. And we have a *pretty good* orchestra."[21]

He did not understand why the MOA would allow Skrowaczewski's impending departure as music director. "It is our hope that Ronald [Wilford] is coming here to tell those who make decisions that there is no better available conductor for this post," Ormandy wrote Skrowaczewski before he left Minneapolis. "They should beg you to stay. You built this organization to be a major orchestra, among the top eight or nine."[22]

The anniversary season also featured new recordings, a publication, and a film. Continuing with the Vox series, Skrowaczewski and the orchestra released an LP of Bartók's music to rave reviews, and recordings of Stravinsky, Beethoven, and Prokofiev followed before the maestro stepped down as music director.

In 1977 the orchestra published the first significant document about its history since John Sherman's 1952 book *Music and Maestros*. Described as a photo-documentary history of the orchestra, *Ovation* by Barbara Flanagan is a commemorative book with a two-record album of performances from 1928 through 1977. The recordings, which include works led by all of the orchestra's music directors but Oberhoffer, are important historical documents. The second LP, conducted by Skrowaczewski, was a new recording of Stravinsky's *Petrushka* (the complete ballet of 1947) and the Suite from *The Love for Three Oranges* by Prokofiev.

A documentary about the orchestra entitled *Celebration: A Community and Its Orchestra* was shown in local theaters and colleges in Minneapolis and St. Paul during the autumn of the anniversary season. Narrated by Isaac Stern, the thirteen-minute documentary was also submitted to film festivals. In further commemoration Skrowaczewski initiated a composers' competition for a new work to be premiered. Copland, Schuller, Argento, Dennis Russell Davies, Slatkin, Henry Charles Smith, and Skrowaczewski served as judges.

The maestro took advantage of Orchestra Hall's acoustics by programming works that would have been difficult to perform in cavernous Northrop Auditorium. The Minnesota Orchestra Chamber Ensemble gave a series of programs during the 1977–78 season that featured music from the baroque, classical, and early romantic periods. Skrowaczewski led Bach's Brandenburg Concerto no. 2, Mozart's Horn Concerto no. 1, and Scottish composer Thea Musgrave's Horn Concerto, composed in 1971. British musician Barry Tuckwell, arguably the greatest French horn soloist of his generation, performed both works.

Before Skrowaczewski began 1978 with the anticipated American premiere of Penderecki's Violin Concerto, he conducted the world premiere of the Cello Concerto by twenty-eight-year-old African American composer Primous Fountain. Composer and recording producer Quincy Jones was Fountain's patron early in his career. Michael Tilson Thomas also was an early advocate of Fountain, whose influences include Stravinsky, Miles Davis, and the music of West Africa.[23]

In spring 1977 Isaac Stern phoned Skrowaczewski from Switzerland, where the celebrated violinist had just played the world premiere of Penderecki's Concerto for Violin and Orchestra with the Basel Symphony. "I love it!" exclaimed Stern. "It's a great romantic concerto!" Although the composer had promised Stern he would create a lyrical work, the violinist had his doubts. "Before Isaac first played the piece," Skrowaczewski remembered, "he told me he was concerned that Penderecki still might write something avant-garde, so he was thrilled when he called me that spring after the premiere."

"I had known Isaac for a long time, and I decided to write something that really enjoys the instrument," Penderecki said.[24] The Polish composer had already shifted to his new language, so he had no problem delivering what Stern wanted. "Critics were terrified," Skrowaczewski recalled. "They wanted to know what had happened to Penderecki: 'He's become a 19th-century composer imitating Tchaikovsky and later Shostakovich.' But his more tonal and emotionally direct style of writing really began with the *St. Luke Passion*." Penderecki's comment—"We can still use old forms to write new music"—was widely quoted at the time of the premiere.[25]

Some critics accused Penderecki of fleeing the avant-garde movement of which he had been a part in the 1960s. Others, including some members of the public, welcomed his new language but felt that the forty-minute concerto simply was too long. Skrowaczewski generally did not heartily endorse Penderecki's stylistic shift, feeling it went too far in the neoromantic direction, a trend the composer has continued. "Some of the recent pieces are too dependent on 19th-century music, not as far as Górecki's has gone, but still a bit too much for my taste," he remarked. "I would like to see more development in his works as in his brilliant earlier years."

The U.S. premiere of the concerto and its subsequent New York premiere in Carnegie Hall did not attract the same international acclaim that greeted the orchestra's performances of the *St. Luke Passion* a decade earlier. Still, the events were a major artistic coup for the ensemble and Skrowaczewski. They received strong local, national, and international coverage. Roy Close of the *Minneapolis Star* noted the significance:

> Last night's performance was the most noteworthy event of the Minnesota Orchestra's 1977–78 season—the U.S. premiere of a major new work by an important composer, interpreted by one of the foremost artists of the day, violinist Isaac Stern. The significance of the occasion was underscored by

the presence of representatives of Columbia Records, which will record the concerto next week when the orchestra is in New York, and of a film company that will videotape one of the orchestra's two Carnegie Hall performances of the concerto for international public television.[26]

Skrowaczewski and Stern had the benefit of recording in the acoustics of Carnegie Hall, but the rumble of subways necessitated some retakes. Sony Classical rereleased the recording in 1995 as part of the *Isaac Stern: A Life in Music* CD series.

The concert's national television broadcast included a conversation between Skrowaczewski and Stern, an addition that entailed cutting some music from the final tape. "What you had to say about 20th-century music in your conversation with Isaac seemed to me to be so important to a viewing audience that we included all of it in the finished program," the executive producer of *Tonight at Carnegie Hall* wrote Skrowaczewski.[27]

Penderecki joined the two artists in another conversation included in the television program. Stern acknowledged Skrowaczewski's efforts: "I must thank you especially, Stanisław Skrowaczewski, not only for being willing to do the work but also for taking the trouble to *really* know it so beautifully and exert a mastery over it." Skrowaczewski smiled modestly and replied, "Well, this is the normal duty."[28]

On the heels of this major premiere, Skrowaczewski followed with one of his own, *Ricercari Notturni* for Saxophone and Orchestra, his first composition since the 1969 Concerto for English Horn and Orchestra. The premiere of *Ricercari Notturni* was only the third time that the maestro programmed his music in eighteen years as music director.

Like his 1969 concerto, this work arose out of unique circumstances: specifically, the presence of a talented soloist. In spring 1974 the College of St. Benedict, located in St. Joseph, Minnesota, awarded Skrowaczewski its President's Medal for his artistic leadership and for a decade of conducting concerts at Benedicta Arts Center.

The college also commissioned him to write a work honoring the tenth anniversary of Benedicta Arts Center and featuring Jerry D. Luedders, a saxophonist who was then dean of fine arts at the college. Skrowaczewski wrote a challenging composition for a soloist capable of playing soprano, alto, and baritone saxophones:

> It was a strange situation—at first they wanted a composition for a saxophone quartet. Because I'm not too fond of the saxophone I said, "Quartet? That's not for me." They insisted, so I said, "I will write for one player (especially because I knew [Luedders], who was very good, very musical), but could you use three instruments in one piece? In this case, soprano, alto, and baritone, because those instruments seem to be characteristically strong. The low notes of the baritone are marvelous, and the upper register of soprano is also peculiar, and the alto is often used with a very wide range." And [Luedders] said, "Well, it is a great challenge; I will try." So I wrote, and I worked with him, with all instruments, especially the alto, risking certain ideas in this concerto. It is quite difficult to perform because not all saxophonists can play

all three instruments. Very few would do it. It was a new idea; no literature such as this existed. It is like writing a concerto for viola and violin for one player, I don't think even Zukerman would do it.[29]

Apart from the commission, Skrowaczewski also felt an obligation to the College of St. Benedict: "Every time the Minnesota Orchestra performed at Benedicta Arts Center, I was praising it. Coming from Northrop Auditorium (prior to the creation of Orchestra Hall), the orchestra finally had a place to breathe acoustically. The fact that they built this hall and because it gave us a welcome outlet for concerts, I really felt gratitude towards the institution and the nuns who led it."

As he had done with Thomas Stacy, Skrowaczewski met with Luedders to explore the possibilities of the alto saxophone. "I spent about an hour or so showing him what I could do," Luedders said. "He wanted to hear the instrument in all dynamic, tonal, and pitch ranges. I also showed him extended techniques such as *altissimo* range and multiphonics. Although we talked about soprano and baritone saxophones, it wasn't until the first rehearsal that he heard me play those instruments."

Later he was surprised by Skrowaczewski's determination to improve the piece right up to the last minute:

> We rehearsed the piece in Minneapolis, but the actual premiere was done on a run-out concert to Rochester, Minnesota, before the first "official" performances in Orchestra Hall and at St. Benedict. Stan had never heard the cadenza until just before we left for Rochester. He didn't like what he had written, so en route from Minneapolis to Rochester he sat in the back seat of the car and wrote a new cadenza. I suggested I would practice it, and we could do it on a subsequent night, but he wanted it played that night. So I practiced it backstage during the first part of the concert and played the new cadenza that very night. It's the one that is published now with the piece. He either had a lot of confidence in me or was very displeased with his original cadenza, or a combination of both![30]

Just four days before the world premiere of *Ricercari Notturni* on January 18, 1978, Dennis Russell Davies led the Saint Paul Chamber Orchestra in the Twin Cities premiere of *Music at Night*. These concerts marked the first time audiences anywhere had the opportunity to hear Skrowaczewski's earliest and latest pieces performed so close together.

Feldman's original program note for *Ricercari Notturni* is a descriptive introduction to the work:

> The *Ricercari* of the title has nothing to do with the learned instrumental forms of the 16th and 17th centuries, but rather goes back to the origin of the term, which means "to search for." Thus these are nocturnal quests, the title evoking the visions of the music. In composing the work, Skrowaczewski abandoned his original concept of a concerto that would exploit the saxophone for a more provocative orchestral score using a large body of instruments minus those winds that might dilute the unique color of the soloist. It incorporates a

gleaming battery of percussion, much of it pitched: tubular chimes, marimba, vibraphone, four gongs (high to low, one of them a water gong), three tam-tams, six Chinese temple blocks, two bongos, three congas, and a bass drum. In addition, there are timpani (five drums in all) and amplified harpsichord.

This is not simply an abstract work, the composer stresses. "Somehow I thought of things that would fascinate the listener and offer surprises. There is no underlying program, of course, but there are images," Skrowaczewski has said. "The whole development of ideas is classical rather than free. I start with musical laws and progress logically, even if—fortunate for the music—the laws are to be broken from time to time."[31]

Skrowaczewski built upon some aspects of his English horn concerto in creating *Ricercari*, such as exploring the outer ranges of the three saxophones and the instrumentation of the orchestra. It featured judicious scoring for woodwinds—only piccolo, three flutes, and two bassoons; an expanded percussion section; and an amplified harpsichord, Skrowaczewski's first use of the instrument in a composition.

"Skrowaczewski's writing for sax gnaws at you hauntingly, somehow creeping its way under your skin," noted the *Minneapolis Tribune*. "At times it is full of a distant beauty, weaving its way through slow, pensive melodies which are quite likeable and not at all foreboding."[32] Cast in the traditional three movements, the piece revels in contrasts, both in the form—the second movement is entitled Passacaglia—and in the saxophone's ranges and timbres. The third movement even flirts briefly with jazz, the only time Skrowaczewski has directly referenced the idiom in a composition.

Although Skrowaczewski does not consider the piece a central part of his output, it provided a key breakthrough in his life as a composer. Six months after its premiere he received word that *Ricercari Notturni* was one of ten works under consideration for the first Kennedy Center Friedheim Award. (George Sturm, Skrowaczewski's composition manager, had nominated the work for the award.) *Ricercari* was one of five finalists, which coincidently included Concerto for English Horn and Orchestra by Vincent Persichetti, which Thomas Stacy had recently premiered with the New York Philharmonic.

Skrowaczewski won the Friedheim Award, and his first-prize honors included a performance at the Kennedy Center by the Peabody Institute Orchestra led by Frederik Prausnitz. The other finalists' pieces also were performed in the concert, which was broadcast live nationally on NPR and abroad by the Voice of America.

Despite *Ricercari's* strong reception and the lack of existing solo literature for saxophone and orchestra, the work has had few additional performances. Luedders performed it again in 1982 with the San Antonio Symphony, and in the same year saxophonist Iwan Roth gave the European premiere with the Swiss Radio Orchestra. Skrowaczewski did not conduct these performances. The piece was also performed at Temple University not long after the Minneapolis premiere. The paucity of saxophonists willing and able to play all three saxophones may account in part for the work's infrequent performances. *Ricercari* may be one of the few such pieces in existence that requires the doubling of saxophones within a single movement.

Skrowaczewski's receipt of the first Friedheim Award sparked a renewed interest in his compositions. Coincidently, the announcement of the award occurred in the midst of several previously scheduled performances of his music. A few weeks after the premiere of *Ricercari Notturni*, he led the Berlin Philharmonic in his Concerto for English Horn and Orchestra, which he conducted again the following season in Ottawa. *Music at Night* received its first Minnesota Orchestra performance in November 1978, and a month later he led the piece for the first time with the Philadelphia Orchestra. Later that season he conducted it again with the Munich Philharmonic. The reception in Philadelphia for *Music at Night* was so positive that the orchestra included the piece on tours in the United States and Mexico that were led by guest-conductor Skrowaczewski in spring 1980.

"Write on, Stanisław, write on," exhorted a *Minneapolis Star* headline of a concert review praising *Music at Night*.[33] In Philadelphia, James Felton of *The Bulletin* wrote:

> There is a richness with a taut and knowing quality to this score. It alternately flashes bright with harp, alto saxophone, and other reed instruments, plus dark mysterious moments enhanced by harmonics, densely low chattering and other effects in the strings. The score's sinewy strength seems to spring from a Central European expressivity with roots in Bartók, plus eclectic accents from Stravinsky and Germanic chromaticism. Yet the language is Skrowaczewski's alone, and it speaks with convincing eloquence and interest in a consistent creative mold.[34]

The international praise for both *Music at Night* and the Concerto for English Horn gave Skrowaczewski the confidence and impetus to compose more and to conduct his works more often. From 1977 to the present he has produced a new work every two to three years, on average—a body of nineteen compositions. Although a seemingly modest output over the course of thirty-plus years, it nevertheless is impressive, especially considering his demanding conducting schedule during that time.

Skrowaczewski's final two seasons with the Minnesota Orchestra included dozens of guest-conducting engagements that helped to build his second career as a freelancer. His schedule was so full in winter 1978 that he had to decline an appealing invitation from President and Mrs. Carter to attend a gathering at the White House: a meeting with prominent Polish-Americans to discuss the president's recent trip to Poland.

Early in 1978 Skrowaczewski conducted the Berlin Philharmonic in an exclusively 20th-century program that included his English Horn Concerto and Crumb's *Echoes of Time*. A year later he returned to lead the Philharmonic in Beethoven, Bartók, and the Liszt Second Piano Concerto with Polish pianist Krystian Zimerman.

Performing *Echoes of Time* with the Berlin Philharmonic differed greatly from Skrowaczewski's first experience with the piece in Minneapolis:

> When I conducted the Crumb piece in Minneapolis, our first trombone player, Steven Zellmer, warned me that if we did the procession he would burst into laughter. Crumb specifies that two brass players and a military snare drummer march in front of the orchestra in one section of the piece. The brass players blow into their instruments without tone, only making air and mouthpiece sounds. Zellmer's face kept getting redder and redder, and he finally did burst into laughter, puffing without any tone coming out of his trombone, but it didn't spoil the piece at all. I was laughing myself, but no one in the audience could see me.
>
> When I did the piece with the Berlin Philharmonic, Wolfgang Stresemann, the much-respected *orchesterintendant* of the Philharmonic, asked me to not do the procession. They only wanted to play the music. I mentioned this to Crumb on the phone, and he said, "Oh, please do it. I insist; it is part of it." I said, "Listen, I agree with the request not to do it because the procession, for the public, completely distracts from the music. They think this is a circus, and they start to laugh. And then, where is the music?" Well, Crumb didn't agree. He wanted it. But I didn't do the procession in Berlin or any other time I conducted the piece. Only in Minneapolis did we do it. The quality of the Berlin performance was excellent. I had a little talk with the string players, who had to play small bells hanging from their stands, and also at the end of the piece, they had to whistle, in tune, in fourths, very high. This whistling was done the best in Berlin. They were smiling when they did all of these things, but they did them very conscientiously.

Skrowaczewski invited Crumb to the Minneapolis performance and also to Berlin, but the composer didn't attend performances of his music. "I met him just once, in 2005, when he gave a master class at the MacPhail school in Minneapolis," Skrowaczewski said. "He looked so completely different from what I imagined, because on the phone from Berlin he was so stern, but in this meeting he was quite jovial."

Fond of Crumb's music, Skrowaczewski programmed *Star-Child* during his last season as music director. "He wrote it as though with a microscope," Skrowaczewski remarked. "Every note has such meaning."[35] He continued performing Crumb's music sporadically during his career as a guest conductor.

During Skrowaczewski's last two years with the Minnesota Orchestra and into the 1980s, Glotz worked extensively to secure excellent European engagements for his client. Soon after the announcement of Skrowaczewski's resignation, Erich Leinsdorf wrote to the maestro and recommended that he consider becoming principal conductor of the Deutsches Symphonie-Orchester Berlin, a position Leinsdorf had accepted and then resigned before he began his duties.

"It would be a great break for the orchestra for someone like you to make their [*sic*] headquarters there," he wrote.[36] Anticipating his upcoming freedom as a freelancer, however, Skrowaczewski did not want to assume a new position so soon after leaving the Minnesota Orchestra.

Other important European engagements during this period included concerts with the Vienna Symphony, the Société Philharmonique de Bruxelles (with Emil Gilels as soloist), and return engagements with the Hallé Orchestra.

He continued to be popular with the Hallé Orchestra. "If Stanisław Skrowaczewski, the gifted music director of the Minnesota Symphony Orchestra [*sic*], has not achieved the prominence of certain spotlighted celebrities in the bigger American centres," wrote one *Daily Telegraph* critic, "the quality of his musicianship, at least, is on no less lofty a plane, and, in many respects surpasses that of his more widely publicized colleagues."[37]

Reported another critic, "Anyone who can get the Hallé to play as brilliantly as in last night's Free Trade Hall concert is clearly exceptional. Rarely does the Hallé play so well." But the same critic also found Skrowaczewski's interpretation of Brahms' Third Symphony lacking in "brio and warmth."[38]

Skrowaczewski renewed his relationship with the Pittsburgh Symphony Orchestra and led concerts with the Baltimore, Seattle, and National Symphony orchestras, among others. In summer 1978 he enjoyed a particularly rewarding engagement at Tanglewood with the Berkshire Music Center Orchestra. His long-term relationship with the Philadelphia Orchestra continued through the late 1970s but waned after Ormandy's retirement in 1980.

Similarly, without advocates in the other Big Five orchestras—and his U.S. management's seeming lack of interest in promoting him—Skrowaczewski's engagements with these orchestras were infrequent and eventually became rare. However, other American major orchestras extended invitations, and consequently Skrowaczewski developed fruitful, extended relationships with them.

Before closing the 1977–78 Minnesota season with Haydn's oratorio *The Seasons*—the orchestra's first performance of the seminal composition—Skrowaczewski led other firsts for the orchestra: Beethoven's *Calm Sea and Prosperous Voyage*, Cantata for Chorus and Orchestra, and Schuller's Concerto no. 2 for Orchestra.

During his final season Skrowaczewski invited Schuller to lead a subscription concert. Only the polymath Schuller could lead a program entitled "Rags, Jazz & Nostalgia," which featured works by nine diverse composers, including George Antheil, William Thomas McKinley, Ellington, Joplin, Sousa, and Schuller himself.

In the first *Showcase* issue of the seventy-fifth anniversary season, Skrowaczewski restated his rationale for programming contemporary works:

> Encountering contemporary music scores, we must remember that there is,
> and has always been, both good and bad music. History itself has wisely

eliminated most of the bad. In approaching the works of our own times, however, we lack the historical perspective and are not only prone but entitled to errors in evaluation. What matters is that we maintain our spirit of adventure—in short, that we preserve a youthful curiosity about the music of our century.

This season's programs, like those of the past, do not necessarily reflect my personal predilections but rather my conception of the role of a major symphony orchestra. Like a great museum, we choose from masterpieces of the past and present them to their best advantage. But at the same time, we are committed to understanding what is happening nowadays. If an orchestra, no matter how great, confines itself exclusively to the beloved treasures of the past, admitting nothing of its own time, then it is not even a museum. It is a tomb.

Let this anniversary season remind us how glorious and rare, viewed in perspective of the world's orchestras, our programs have been from the very beginning. I speak of this because a few listeners sometimes react angrily to the performance of contemporary works. Examining the role of an artistic organization such as ours, however, we may cultivate not only tolerance for the new but pride that our musical community has always been receptive to it.[39]

By the late 1970s his reputation as an important proponent of new music from America and Europe was firmly established, although he sometimes was stereotyped because of it. His consistent advocacy and performances of the best contemporary works were responsible in part for giving the Twin Cities an artistic luster and reputation it retains today. By the end of his Minnesota Orchestra tenure, Skrowaczewski had won five ASCAP awards for his promotion of new music.

Although his name was closely associated with Polish composers Penderecki and Lutosławski, Skrowaczewski also was aligned with the most important American composers.

"Conductors who learn Carter scores tend to use them a lot," wrote critic Martin Mayer in a 1978 article. "Solti, Bernstein, Boulez, and Skrowaczewski, among others, have taken Carter pieces on lengthy tours."[40] He referenced Carter's prize for his first string quartet: "Mr. Carter is amused and touched by Mr. Skrowaczewski's consistent sponsorship of his music because the Polish composer-conductor was the disappointed author of the Quartet [sic] that finished a very close second in [the 1953] competition in Liège."[41]

Skrowaczewski did not neglect works by more conservative American composers. His penultimate subscription concert as music director opened with Peter Mennin's relatively new Symphony no. 8, and during his last season he included William Schuman's Symphony no. 10, *American Muse*, on subscription concerts and on tour.

Early in 1979 Skrowaczewski received a letter from Bernstein inviting him to join a committee to honor Schuman's seventieth birthday and requesting that he perform one of the composer's works during the upcoming season. Skrowaczewski replied that he already had scheduled performances of the Tenth Symphony, including one at Carnegie Hall.

His performance of the New York premiere of the Tenth Symphony in April 1979 prompted an interesting correspondence between the two composers:

Dear Stan:

You have been very much in my thoughts ever since your performance of my Tenth on April 20th. It was an extraordinary experience for me because I really had not had an opportunity before of absorbing the work as a composer listening to his product. You, as a composer yourself, will certainly understand what I am trying to say.

At the first performance in April of 1976, on an entire evening of my own music, with three new works, I was so preoccupied with the details of the premieres that I was just content to get through the experience in one piece. When the Tenth was performed shortly afterwards by the Chicago [Symphony] Orchestra, I still had not had the time for reflection. Now, hearing your performance three years later, I know that the work has very deep meaning for me. A layman would ask, doesn't every work have a deep meaning for its composer? My answer would be, at the time of completion and composition, yes, but after time—at least for me—there are some works that I feel close to and others about which I have many reservations. The Tenth, for I can't and needn't try to explain, evokes a strong visceral response.

Your performance was for me an immense achievement. I know that you were dissatisfied with certain aspects of the second movement, which you felt you had not yet fully realized. From my point of view, the overall effect was superb. You do not want my thanks, I realize, but I hope you will accept my admiration for you, not only as an artist but as a sympathetic colleague to whom one can speak intelligently without the slightest fear of ego impairment. It is good to know that, after next season, you will be spending more time in New York City, and I very much look forward to more frequent meetings with you.

On my study wall in New York I have pictures of some conductors and other colleagues with whom I have had a special affinity, starting with my youngest days when I was championed by Serge Koussevitzky. If you would care to send me your inscribed photo, it would be most welcome.

Forgive my delay in sending you this letter, which I mentioned, but I did want time to think.

Faithfully,
Bill Schuman[42]

Dear Bill:

How terribly kind of you to write me such a dear letter. You couldn't have made me more happy in explaining to me how important to your own perspective as a composer was our performance of your "Tenth." I understand it so well because in performing the work of another composer, I usually go through various stages in trying to digest and re-create the composer's idea. This goes, of course, through the prism of my mind with a succession of all sorts of illuminations and doubts that would eventually change the interpretation from one performance to another. Therefore, I have mentioned to you that in spite of several performances of your "Tenth," I was not quite happy with solutions of mine—this makes, however, a pleasant feeling for the possibility of a new approach in the future.

I am grateful to you for giving me the opportunity to play your symphony as the first New York premiere. It is a masterful composition, and the challenge of both artistic values and technical difficulties gave me a unique pleasure and excitement.

I was only sorry that our crazy schedule in New York, with two different programs day after day and rehearsals, didn't give me the opportunity to sit with you for a moment and chat, but this, I hope, can happen when I will be in New York for a little longer.

You make me very happy and honored by asking for a photo, which I am including with this letter.

With all my heartiest congratulations and my deep admiration for your music and with all my warmest regards and wishes.

Very sincerely,
Stan[43]

During Skrowaczewski's nineteenth and final season as music director, he programmed three of Schubert's symphonies in 1978 to mark the 150th anniversary of the composer's death. He led two of them as well as the Mass no. 5 in A-flat major, a first performance for the orchestra. His only personal indulgence during his last season was the performance of three Bruckner symphonies: the Eighth, Fifth, and Seventh. In spring 1979 he took the Seventh Symphony on his final tour as music director, which included back-to-back concerts in Carnegie Hall.

The tour concert that has remained in the orchestra's lore occurred after the Carnegie concerts. On March 28, 1979, at Three Mile Island nuclear power plant in Pennsylvania, a partial meltdown of a nuclear reactor core caused small off-site releases of radioactivity, the worst such accident in U.S. history.[44] The releases were of enough concern to the Nuclear Regulatory Commission (NRC) that the governor of Pennsylvania advised those who were most vulnerable to radiation to evacuate the area within a five-mile radius of the plant.[45]

As part of its spring tour the orchestra was scheduled to perform at Lancaster, Pennsylvania, located twenty-five miles from the Three Mile Island power plant. Two weeks before the orchestra was scheduled to leave on tour, the crisis at Three Mile Island subsided; however, lingering concerns over the effects of radiation exposure and widespread media reports made everyone uneasy. Management assured the musicians that bringing them to the area would not endanger them; orchestra administrators said they didn't have enough information at the time to justify canceling the concert. One musician, unbeknownst to his colleagues, told management that he refused to play unless the reactor was in "cold shutdown."[46]

As the concert date approached, more musicians became concerned about the situation. Julie Ayer, a member of the musicians' committee, was in daily contact with an NRC representative, but she and the committee were not satisfied with the reliability of the information the agency provided. Things came to a head on the morning of the concert. Management told the orchestra that it was comfortable with the information from its sources. The concert would be held, and musicians who refused to perform might be dismissed for insubordination. Twenty-three musicians chose not to play: all musicians voted to waive a contractual stipulation so that management could find them a hotel that was not near Three Mile Island.[47] Sixty-seven orchestra members performed the concert; those who didn't play were penalized by having their pay docked for the missed concert.

The Lancaster concert was especially memorable for Eric Sjostrom, then in his second season as the orchestra's librarian. The operations manager asked Sjostrom, a native of the East Coast, if he would drive Skrowaczewski to concert locations on the tour so the maestro could avoid bus travel. "It was interesting for me, being twenty-three or twenty-four years old at the time, driving in this rental car with Stan in the passenger's seat studying his scores and conducting away," Sjostrom said. "It was quite a sight for people passing us, wondering what was going on."

The postconcert trip gave Sjostrom his most memorable Skrowaczewski anecdote:

> I knew the [Pennsylvania Turnpike] took us past the [Three Mile Island] nuclear plant, and I didn't necessarily want to do that. I got out my Pennsylvania map and figured out the best way to get around that area.
>
> So we're driving, and up to this point we had done mostly interstate driving, and now we're on back roads. But I knew exactly where we were going. Stan had asked me how was I going to go and what roads I was taking. He asked if I had a map. I gave him the map and turned on the dome light so he could see. He said, "Eric, I think this is fifty miles out of the way." I said, "Maestro, it may be ten or fifteen miles out of the way, but I don't really care to go near the nuclear plant. He said, "Don't worry, it's okay, we'll be driving fast!"
>
> We ended up taking my route. It was 2:30 or 3:00 in the morning, but that was the modified plan: not to stay in Lancaster at the hotel but to leave and go to State College, so it ended up being a very late night. That's my famous story, and so when people backstage need to get somewhere, they'll come up to me and ask if I have a map. If I tell a story about going somewhere, they'll ask if I am going fast. So the basis of that story gets transferred to just about every other story that's told!

In 1997 an article was released in *Environmental Health Perspectives*, the journal of the U.S. National Institute of Environmental Health Science, concluding that more radiation than previously believed was released in the 1979 accident, citing the increase in cases of lung cancer and leukemia near the plant as a possible effect. Columbia University disagreed with the findings, and the issue remains controversial to this day.[48]

During his last season Skrowaczewski gave yet another program of firsts for the orchestra. After introducing two never-before-heard incidental pieces by Beethoven, he conducted the first Minnesota performance of *Quatrain* for Clarinet, Cello, Piano and Orchestra by Toru Takemitsu. The piece was composed for Tashi, a chamber ensemble of budding classical music stars which performed with the orchestra: Peter Serkin, piano; Ida Kavafian, violin; Fred Sherry, cello; and Richard Stoltzman, clarinet.

The tributes to Skrowaczewski were modest as he headed into his last subscription concerts. "There will be no lavish public farewells this week," noted the *Minneapolis Tribune*, "as Stanisław Skrowaczewski conducts his final programs as music director. 'Stan wants it to be low-key,' explained an orchestra staff member."[49]

His desire for the future was clear—to focus purely on music:

> Of course, I want to keep as active as I can, but the activity will be purely music. I won't lose time with the whole business of being music director. It is an enormous amount of time if you take even just one aspect of it: auditions. I never counted, but for those nineteen years I probably spent six months of my life auditioning musicians—not conducting, not learning, not composing, not resting or having fun, but auditioning.[50]

He was more than ready to be freed from the responsibilities of being a music director, but nevertheless his orchestra continued to inspire him, and he publicly advocated for its development:

> Morale—no small factor in the day-to-day workings of any orchestra—would be helped, Skrowaczewski feels, were the orchestra to increase the amount of international touring it does, especially to Europe. "I had to struggle with this from the beginning," he said. "A few years ago, the idea of touring was put under great criticism by the association's board, and I had a very hard time convincing them that touring is of extreme importance. When we do our tour nowadays, we don't usually go to the big cities, and we don't go abroad. If you compare this with six or seven other [major] orchestras, they all go abroad. They find means and sponsors, and we could easily find means and sponsors here if they would try it. The orchestra needs this. They need that sort of acclaim.
>
> Look what happened to Chicago. They went to Europe and got rave reviews, and suddenly Chicago was interested in its own orchestra. This is very psychological. Sometimes, after a superb concert here or in St. Paul,

the orchestra receives polite applause, whereas if it were a guest orchestra, it would have received a standing ovation. This is depressing. But I don't blame anyone. This is normal. They have us every week."[51]

Even George Szell dealt with this problem in Cleveland. He told me at least twice that the Cleveland public didn't really appreciate that he had built this wonderful orchestra until after it completed its first European tour and received rave reviews. Only then, Szell said, did Cleveland start to consider its orchestra important. He was bitter about this point.

In an article published by the *Minneapolis Tribune* on the day that Skrowaczewski undertook his last subscription concerts, Roy Close wrote: "The one significant shortcoming of [his] directorship has been his inability to maintain a positive morale among the musicians."[52] Close, who acknowledged Skrowaczewski's "historic legacy" with the orchestra, went on to say that the maestro "does not have the unalloyed respect of all his players." Clearly some musicians liked and respected their maestro; for various reasons, others had "little incentive to give their best for him on a consistent basis."[53] Dissatisfied or not, the musicians played for a maestro whose fealty to the score and to his ideals eclipses all other considerations.

Skrowaczewski's choice of Bruckner's Symphony no. 8 to close out his last season was symbolic. "The Symphony no. 8 is a fitting finale to his tenure of nineteen seasons," wrote Feldman in her program note for the piece. "Upon its premiere in 1892, composer-critic Hugo Wolf hailed it with unstinting praise: 'This symphony is the creation of a Titan, and in spiritual vastness, fertility of ideas and grandeur even surpasses his other symphonies.'"[54]

The eighty-minute work, Bruckner's longest and perhaps most demanding, was in a sense analogous to Skrowaczewski's years as music director. In a *Showcase* tribute by Cisek, then president of the MOA, one paragraph summarized Skrowaczewski's tenure:

> In all of his pursuits he consistently expressed a restless quest for excellence. In this respect he not only exerted himself, but he pushed us all as well. The musicians of the orchestra, the administrative staff, even the audience, and the association's board members—none were spared the sometimes exhausting, frequently exhilarating sweep of his vast musical output and broad artistic idealism. We were driven to participate with him in his vision of a higher attainment for us all.[55]

With his characteristic dignity Skrowaczewski walked swiftly to the podium for his last subscription concert as music director. Despite his preparatory stance, the audience kept applauding. Caught off guard by the response, he quickly motioned for the entire orchestra to stand and share in the acclaim that was clearly intended for him. He conducted the performance without glasses, a small gesture of vanity: the concert was being filmed and distributed on public television, along with a thirty-five minute documentary entitled *Thank You Maestro*.

His gestures were introverted and reposed when the music demanded it and extroverted in moments such as the climax of the Adagio, third movement. At that instant Skrowaczewski exhibited a rare gesture and facial expression of simultaneous exuberance and angst. After the final chords of the triumphant Finale, the bravos echoed throughout Orchestra Hall and the curtain calls began. After his fourth he returned and immediately commanded his ensemble to stand—which they had refused to do after the third curtain call. Their refusal was the ultimate compliment an orchestra can pay a conductor.

Concertmaster Lea Foli quickly stood and motioned for the audience to be silent. He thanked his maestro on behalf of the orchestra for his "dedication throughout the years" and presented him with a letter written in French by Ignacy Jan Paderewski, the Polish pianist, composer, and politician. Hands clasped, his arms up in a frozen stance of thanks, Skrowaczewski listened to the presentation wearing a wide and grateful smile.

A few days after the concert he wrote a thank-you letter to the chair of the orchestra committee:

> I would like to tell you how much I was moved by your very special and unique gift—an original letter of Paderewski, which you presented to me. My last two weeks of subscription concerts were highly emotional for me, both because of the type of music we played and because they were my closing [of a] long period of directorship. But your gift, and your thoughtfulness of having presented me with something that I will always hold dear, was certainly a moving climax of those last days.
>
> Needless to say, how wonderful your choice was! This letter of Paderewski would always by itself have a great value, but given by this orchestra, it acquires a very special and unique meaning to me. Paderewski was not only a fascinating musician, but also a great statesman, fighting all his life uncompromisingly for the highest human ideas.[56]

Skrowaczewski fought uncompromisingly for the highest artistic ideals throughout his entire tenure in Minnesota. He left behind an orchestra more sophisticated, experienced, and musically and technically proficient than the one he inherited in 1960. He also left it with a permanent home. Less tangibly, Skrowaczewski left an unprecedented artistic mark on the Twin Cities. He educated a community through his programming, leadership, and the quality of his interpretations. He brought an international luster to the state of Minnesota that it has enjoyed ever since.

TWENTY-THREE

HOMECOMING

It was pandemonium! They greeted me, they embraced me, they cried. I was a hero because I came. They said, "You are number two." I asked who is number one, and they said, "The Pope."

—Stanisław Skrowaczewski, on his 1981 trip to Poland

Freed from the day-to-day responsibilities of a music director, Skrowaczewski faced—for the first time since 1946—a career solely as a freelancer. "With a few exceptions, my tenure here has been one of the longest of any director of a major American orchestra," he said in his resignation letter to MOA. "Since I was twenty-four I have been continuously committed to work as music director of a major orchestra."[1] Now able to pursue his career independently as a conductor and composer, Skrowaczewski thought his artistic life would bring more freedom, but its pace was as intense as ever. "I thought I would do more composing and choose my guest conducting more carefully," he said, "which I tried to do. But an avalanche of invitations came. I went to orchestras I had never before conducted—St. Louis, Seattle, Phoenix, Atlanta, etc., and they were wonderful. I found it exciting working with all these new people."

Without a music director's secretarial support, Skrowaczewski needed administrative assistance with his "new" career. Krystyna, along with raising two preteens and maintaining the household, pitched in as an efficient assistant to her husband. She always had helped him, but now there was more to do.

In his first season as a freelancer, 1979–80, Skrowaczewski had twenty-seven engagements with twelve American orchestras and eleven from Europe and Israel. They included five weeks of concerts with the Philadelphia Orchestra, including tours of the West Coast and Mexico City; three weeks with the Minnesota Orchestra in his new role as conductor laureate; six concerts in the Netherlands with the Rotterdam Philharmonic; and summer festivals in Lucerne, Detroit, and Cleveland. Aside from brief intervals here and there, he was on the road from September to August, a schedule he maintained for the next thirty years.

To the elite major orchestras with whom he maintained relationships in the United States and Europe, Skrowaczewski remained a reliable and highly gifted interpreter. Less-recognized orchestras often received him as a superstar. Although he urged his management to seek high-profile engagements, he rather enjoyed his newfound status with other orchestras.

When the Utah Symphony opened its new concert hall in September 1979, the ensemble turned to Skrowaczewski to lead its first concerts there. "This orchestra, this wonderful hall—this man made it!" Skrowaczewski exclaimed to the enthusiastic audience at the end of the gala opening concert, singling out Maurice Abravanel, who was present in Symphony Hall.[2] The Utah maestro had retired from the music directorship of the Utah Symphony the previous season, after leading the orchestra since 1947. Like Skrowaczewski in Minneapolis, he had been the driving force behind the building of a new performance venue. In 1993, the year of Abravanel's death at age ninety, the symphony named its concert hall after him.

Skrowaczewski felt at home conducting in the new hall, which Cyril Harris had designed. Essentially it was a replica of Minneapolis' Orchestra Hall, although Skrowaczewski noted, "In my opinion it is an improvement over our hall because the balconies are designed so that the orchestra is more visible. It also doesn't have the problem of the brass sound coming out too strongly, as sometimes happens in Minneapolis."

Before Skrowaczewski headed to Europe for his fall 1979 engagements, he led the Saint Paul Chamber Orchestra (SPCO) for the first time. "They all performed extremely well under Skrowaczewski," wrote Michael Anthony, "and afterward were ebullient in their comments about him. 'It's nice to work with someone you really feel you *can* call 'Maestro,' said one, a comment meant perhaps not to slight the musicianship of either [Dennis Russell] Davies or associate conductor William McGlaughlin but simply reflecting Skrowaczewski's more advanced age and experience."[3]

Surprisingly, Skrowaczewski had not conducted the SPCO previously, for he always admired and supported the ensemble. However, during his early years in Minneapolis the SPCO was new, and the Minneapolis Symphony Orchestra's management regarded it as a competitor, so guest conducting the ensemble was impossible. With the arrival in 1972 of Davies, the SPCO's second music director, a relationship developed between the two conductors after Davies led Skrowaczewski's Symphony for Strings with the chamber orchestra.

Skrowaczewski, who admired Davies' programming and his work with the SPCO, in turn invited him to conduct the Minnesota Orchestra. One of the few conductors to perform his colleague's music, Davies left the SPCO in 1980. In a tribute letter Skrowaczewski wrote the following:

> The Saint Paul Chamber Orchestra under Dennis Russell Davies has always been to me one of the brightest lights, not only in the cultural life of the Twin Cities but also in the entire country. The artistic impact of this organization has come from two important dimensions: on the one hand, the bold, highly intelligent, and interesting programming, and on the other hand, the high quality of performances that Dennis Russell Davies has consistently imprinted by his interpretations.
>
> I have always felt that the existence and the success of the SPCO has spurred the development of the Minnesota Orchestra by exposing the musical public to imaginative programming, to excellence in technical approach and—not the least—by offering works that are chamber music par excellence and therefore not in the repertoire of the symphony orchestra.[4]

Days after leading the SPCO, Skrowaczewski received an honorary doctorate from the University of Minnesota. This award was particularly important to him because of the university's standing as Minnesota's flagship academic institution, its prestigious reputation in the United States, and its connection with the Minnesota Orchestra over the years. In his acceptance remarks Skrowaczewski revisited one of his old themes, but never so eloquently:

> There are obvious differences between science and art: the aim of science is knowledge; the aim of art somehow escapes verbal definition. In confronting art we feel as if we are standing in front of a veiled mystery: the more we try to unveil it—the more ineffable it remains. The very gist of art, its value, its *raison d'être*, seems to lie in this mystery. That is why there are so many different points of view concerning the essence of music, this most abstract of arts: from the ancient Greeks, who thought that music symbolized the harmony of the universe, to Schopenhauer, to whom music directly expressed the very core of our existence, to Stravinsky, who loved to shock people by saying that music does not express anything else but itself. Stanisław Witkiewicz, a Polish writer from the beginning of this century, spoke of music producing "metaphysical shivers."

> Yet what has always fascinated me is that science and art—on the surface, [such] disparate antipodal areas—are, at bottom, fundamentally and inextricably linked. First, I believe that art and science are engaged in identical attempts to apprehend reality, to answer the eternal question: what is the universe and the significance of our existence? Science does it by a discursive method of building a logical, unifying structure of knowledge. Music uses a more intuitive method, although it is based on sound and time—two fundamental categories of reality. Nevertheless—and this is my second point—science and art are in need of both inspiration and intellectual elaboration.

> Numerous great discoveries in the history of science were the result of inspiration that enabled the scientist to perceive old things in a new conceptual framework or new things in an old conceptual framework. In art there cannot be a great work without an inspired perception of novel content or novel form. However, the full success occurs when this inspired perception entails intellectual knowledge and skillful manipulation of the artist's chosen medium. Thus, both science and art require not only the inspiration, this "flash of genius," this "divine spark," but also the intellect: "inductive and deductive reasoning" in science and "conscious craftsmanship" or "technical mastery" in art.

> Third, the achievement of both science and art is an understanding of the self as well as the nonself in the context of reality. This understanding coming from genuine science and genuine art, in any society and any age, is intellectually and emotionally satisfying and spiritually uplifting. I believe that this thirst and appreciation for this understanding distinguishes us from all other animate creatures, and gives our lives meaning, purpose, and dignity.

> I have recently found an extremely striking sentence in one of Mozart's letters. He writes: "We live in this world in order to learn all the time, to enlighten

each other, to exchange ideas, and we should always strive to advance further in science and arts." (He even put science in the first place!)

It is with this idea of the nature of art and of its relationship to science that I gratefully accept this award. I am happy and proud to have been inducted into your academic community. Thank you.[5]

The honor from the University of Minnesota was a fine coda to Skrowaczewski's other prestigious recognition from his home state. After his last official concerts with the orchestra in August 1979, he was the guest of honor at a state dinner hosted by Albert Quie, governor of Minnesota. He received the Minnesota Medal of Appreciation and a state senate resolution honoring his contributions to the arts.

By the end of the busy fall season, Skrowaczewski had begun to adjust to his new life as a full-time guest conductor. He pondered the transition and his future, as reflected in a letter he wrote to Michel Glotz in December 1979:

This last tour and the entire last year or two have given me a reconfirmation of positive changes in my approach to my profession (these changes are rather psychological and not necessarily musical). At the same time, I'm pleased to provide you with a foundation of artistic experience to develop bigger opportunities, which I know you find as an interesting challenge rather than a burden.

I also know that this is not an easy task for you, as my former Minnesota Orchestra directorship does not have strong international impact, and my name has never reached a "hot level." It seems to me, therefore, that reaching for the biggest opportunities and reinstating certain high points that we already had before (like Salzburg, Vienna Philharmonic, recordings, La Scala), we have to start almost from the beginning. The advantage, however, now lies in my experience and level, and in your opinion and position of enormous weight and prestige.[6]

Skrowaczewski's appeal to Glotz for help in obtaining the "bigger opportunities" came at a time when he felt confident and deserving of career advancements. By 1979 Lorin Maazel had announced that he would be leaving Cleveland after a decade as music director. Skrowaczewski asked Glotz to speak to Wilford on his behalf as a candidate to succeed Maazel. He was not eager to take on another major position so soon after leaving the Minnesota Orchestra, but his admiration for and past relationship with the Cleveland Orchestra made the idea attractive. Indeed, he would have been an excellent choice for Cleveland, but without interest from them and Wilford's direct support (Judie Janowski had become the maestro's *de facto* manager at Columbia Artists), it was highly unlikely. After a two-year period without a music director, Cleveland chose Christoph von Dohnányi, who stayed for eighteen years.

Returning to Orchestra Hall, Skrowaczewski led Mozart's Symphony no. 39 and Shostakovich's Fifth Symphony—among "Skrowaczewski's greatest hits," as Michael Anthony pointed out in his review—and Webern's Six Pieces for Orchestra. "The score was Coughers 6, Webern 0," noted Anthony. "The shimmering, ghostly effects of this fabulous score were no match in volume for the less musical strumming of the audience's catarrhs."[7]

Skrowaczewski followed this program with Mahler's Ninth Symphony, a work he had introduced to the orchestra and rarely conducted. Over the years, in his new capacity as conductor laureate, he continued to program contemporary or infrequently played pieces, particularly works by his beloved Bruckner. (He gave the first Minnesota Orchestra performance of Symphony no. 0 later that season.) His predilections often balanced those of Marriner and the orchestra's subsequent music directors. Recognizing the quality of Skrowaczewski's interpretations of Bruckner's music, the Mahler-Bruckner Society awarded him its Gold Medal in 1979.

It was a poignant experience for Skrowaczewski to be a guest conductor on the Philadelphia Orchestra's spring tour in 1980, when Ormandy was in his last season as music director. No other major conductor had befriended and given Skrowaczewski as many conducting opportunities as had Ormandy. At the conclusion of the 1979–80 season, the eighty-year-old Philadelphia maestro stepped down from the position he had held for a record forty-four years, ending an era in American orchestral leadership. Ormandy maintained his relationship with the Philadelphia Orchestra as conductor emeritus for five more years, until his death in 1985. Skrowaczewski is the only conductor to have a formal affiliation with a major American orchestra that exceeds Ormandy's forty-nine-year relationship. Skrowaczewski marked the fiftieth anniversary of his relationship with the Minnesota Orchestra in 2010.

Aside from a single concert led by Ormandy's longtime associate conductor, William Smith, Skrowaczewski and Ormandy split the four-week West Coast and Mexico tour, with Skrowaczewski leading all concerts during the tour's last week and a half.

On May 18, 1980, one week into the tour, Mount St. Helens in Washington State erupted for nine hours, the most devastating volcanic event in U.S. history. Nearly 230 square miles of forest were decimated, 250 homes and 185 miles of highway were destroyed, 57 people were killed, and at least 7,000 big-game animals perished. Ash, traveling at an average speed of sixty miles per hour, reached Idaho less than four hours after the eruption.[8] Two days later Skrowaczewski arrived in Salt Lake City with the Philadelphia Orchestra. "I'll never forget," he said. "We flew into a dark cloud, and when we came to the city, everything was gray and covered with ashes. It was thick, on cars, in the street, up to an inch."

Skrowaczewski's career as a recording artist with the Minnesota Orchestra, reborn with the release of the 1975 Ravel recordings, flourished even after he left his post as music director. Some recordings from his last two years with the orchestra were released and reviewed into the early 1980s. Recordings of *The Rite of Spring* and Suite no. 2 of Prokofiev's *Romeo and Juliet* were listed on *Billboard*'s recommended classical LPs in 1979, and other records were included in top-pick lists. "Here is a brilliant performance of *Le Sacre*. Skrowaczewski is one of the most intelligent, probing conductors around today," noted *Fanfare*, "and his leadership [of the Minnesota Orchestra] produced one of the more artistically constructive, if less publicized, partnerships of the past couple of decades. Anyone who questions this assertion can sample the recording at hand as evidence."[9] All reviews were positive, and several were glowing, particularly in the case of the three-LP set of Beethoven's overtures and incidental music. "The performances are nothing short of a revelation," noted the *FM Guide*. "This record shows that the Minnesota Orchestra is one of the finest on the continent. They abound in nuance, subtlety, and dynamism."[10]

Unfortunately problems with distribution and marketing meant that Skrowaczewski and the orchestra did not benefit from these recording achievements as much as could be expected. In one of his last letters as music director, Skrowaczewski wrote to the Moss Music Group, which distributed the records:

> In most European countries, [our recordings] are not at all available in record shops. Every year I conduct extensively in Western Europe, and I check this situation on every occasion. Of course, the damage done to the selling of our records is enormous, and what makes me even sadder [is that] many of these recordings were appraised here and in Europe as among the finest made.[11]

The importance of basic publicity work, such as placing ads in program books and promotional displays in locations where Skrowaczewski conducted, seemed lost on his distributors. Such efforts would have increased sales and heightened the recognition of the Minnesota Orchestra and Skrowaczewski.

In Manchester, England, his return engagement with the Hallé Orchestra in November 1980 again greatly impressed the musicians, the public, and the critics. Performing Deryck Cooke's realization of Mahler's Symphony no. 10, a work new to the orchestra, was a brave venture for a guest conductor, but Skrowaczewski succeeded admirably. Wrote Sir Michael Kennedy in *The Daily Telegraph*, "I am happy to acclaim a profoundly moving and distinguished interpretation of this wonderful symphony under Stanisław Skrowaczewski, who rightly received an ovation from audience and orchestra."[12]

Although Skrowaczewski had a number of musically satisfying engagements during the 1980–81 season—including the premiere of his Concerto for Clarinet—nothing compared emotionally to his weeklong engagement with the Warsaw Philharmonic in February 1981. It was the first time he had set foot in Poland since he and Krystyna secretly fled the country in winter 1960.

His visit occurred during a key period in Poland's history. Still under communist rule, Poland experienced a loosening of the Soviet Union's grip after the "Bread and Freedom" riots of 1956, which catapulted Władysław Gomułka into the position of first secretary of the Polish United Workers' Party. At this time "the Polish People's Republic ceased to be a puppet state," notes Polish historian Norman Davies, "and became a client state."[13] Certain internal freedoms were granted to citizens. In 1968 the mood of freedom eroded when student protests were silenced, and citizens witnessed Poland's participation in the Soviets' invasion of Czechoslovakia. By 1970, discontent over high food prices led dockworkers to strike in the port cities of Gdańsk, Gdynia, and Szczecin. In its efforts to quell the strikers, the Polish military killed nearly fifty people. Edward Gierek, a former miner and strong Communist Party boss from Silesia who was sympathetic to the needs and concerns of Poland's working class, replaced Gomułka.

"The rise of Gierek in 1970 seemed to offer new hopes for a more constructive relationship [with the United States]," explained Yale University history professor Piotr Wandycz. "Nixon's visit to Warsaw in 1972 and Gierek's to America in 1974 were taking place in the aura of East-West Détente [*sic*]. If massive economic investments in Poland temporarily improved living conditions, they did not resolve the mounting political crisis."[14]

As a prominent Polish-American, Skrowaczewski was invited by President Gerald Ford to attend a reception for Gierek during the Polish leader's 1974 visit to America. The occasion was the genesis of Skrowaczewski's return to Poland. He related:

> Since I left Poland in 1960, I had practically no contact with the country except privately with Penderecki and Lutosławski, basically just those two. In the early 1970s, after ten or twelve years of complete silence, I received an invitation from the minister of culture and the Warsaw Philharmonic saying they would like me to come and conduct. At that time I said I was willing, but they asked for dates very late, and in Minnesota we always had plans scheduled two years in advance. So I said I was sorry, but it was not possible on such short notice. This happened twice.
>
> Then Krystyna and I were guests of President Ford's at a White House reception for Edward Gierek. He wasn't a strict Stalinist; he was already a bit loose towards the arts. "Listen," he said to me, "they wait for you in Warsaw. Why don't you come?" I said, "Mr. Secretary, I would very much like to come, but the Philharmonic always asks me too late." "Please," he said, "give us *any* date in the future that you would like to come." February was always my month free for Europe when I was with Minnesota, and Glotz would arrange trips. So I said, "Okay, February 1981."

Extraordinary events occurred during the intervening years. In fall 1978 Cardinal Karol Józef Wojtyła, the bishop of Kraków (one of Krystyna's college professors), was elected pope, taking the name John Paul II. The historic event sparked immense pride in predominantly Catholic Poland. Davies explains the impact on the country:

The pope's election in 1978, and even more his triumphal visit to his homeland in June 1979, created a psychological uplift, which broke the chains of fear and anxiety preventing ordinary Poles from being themselves. The pope made no overt comments on the political scene, but the blatant contrast between the authentic, spontaneous authority of the Church and the artificial authority of the Party were exposed to the full view of the television cameras. After that, the die was cast. The crack in the crust of the Polish communists' world had been opened. Only one small disturbance was needed to release a pent-up eruption of popular resentment.[15]

That small disturbance came in the form of an increase in food prices. After a number of strikes threatened to bring the country to a standstill, the situation came to a head on August 31, 1980, in the Lenin Shipyards of Gdańsk. Workers there signed an agreement with the government that ended their strike, allowed them to strike in the future, and, most importantly, granted them the right to organize themselves into a federation of free and independent trade unions. The organization was called Solidarity, and Lech Wałęsa, a thirty-seven-year-old electrician and strike leader who had headed the effort in Gdańsk, was eventually named its chairman. The Solidarity movement spread throughout Poland. Weakened by the political situation and by criticism of his leadership, Gierek was replaced as first secretary by Stanisław Kania in September.

Concerned by Solidarity's power, the Soviet Union launched a massive military buildup along Poland's border in December 1980. Calls between the White House and the Vatican ensued, as Zbigniew Brzezinski, President Jimmy Carter's national security advisor, and Pope John Paul II discussed the volatile situation.[16]

These were the circumstances in Poland that Skrowaczewski faced in accepting an engagement with the Warsaw Philharmonic the week of February 23, 1981. U.S. Senator Dave Durenberger of Minnesota wrote to the American Embassy on Skrowaczewski's behalf. "Given the past reluctance of the Polish Government to invite Western conductors into the country," wrote Durenberger to the U.S. ambassador, "and due to Mr. Skrowaczewski's early years in Poland, this experience should prove to be very significant. I hope the Embassy may extend its fullest courtesies to him for this trip."[17]

Durenberger gave a copy of the letter to the maestro's lawyer, Charlie Bellows, with the note, "I hope that this does the trick."[18]

It did, and the trip was indeed "very significant," as Skrowaczewski recalled:

The pope had been elected, and this was six months after the strike starting Solidarity in Gdańsk, and of course with Solidarity came a very strong wave of liberty. There were strikes all over Poland, and a lot of big tension because at any moment the Soviet army was all around, and the possibility of them invading was quite high. So Glotz begged me, "Please, don't go, this will be a bloody war, it will be terrible, and you'll never get out of there! I can find a doctor who will say you are ill so there's an 'official' reason." I said, "Listen, if this was any other country, I would not go, but to Poland I really feel I have to go."

I had concerts in Brussels, and from there I had a nonstop flight to Warsaw. It was a gloomy night with very bad weather, but it was just a two-hour flight. In the middle of it the stewardess, speaking in Polish, told us that we could not land in Warsaw because they had a snowstorm, so we would have to land in Kraków. I wasn't happy about this because the next day I had a rehearsal in the morning. Of course, a number of the passengers were English, Belgian, French, American, etc., and they didn't understand what the stewardess said, so they asked me to translate. They were afraid that the whole revolution and Soviet attack had started, so the atmosphere on the plane was tense.

We landed in gloomy Kraków. At that time they were not prepared for receiving any international flights, so they put all of us in a barn. It was terrible, without food or drinks, and they told us they didn't know what to do because we could not fly into Warsaw. This was 10:00 p.m. or later, and the atmosphere was not pleasant. After one hour of waiting with no one coming or giving us news, we all thought, "Oh no, the revolution has started, and this is it." Suddenly a military person came into the barn and said, "Where is Mr. Skrowaczewski? He has a telephone call." So I ran to the telephone, and it was a representative from the Polish Union of Composers. "We are so sorry," he said, "we really did have a snowstorm, and the airport is closed. But the storm is over, the airport is clearing, and you'll be coming." I finally arrived at 3:00 a.m., and an entire delegation with television cameras and flowers was there. They had waited and waited to be there to greet me. It was extremely moving.

They took me to the hotel, and I had a 9:00 a.m. rehearsal, so I just showered, unpacked a little, and then went to the rehearsal. And it was pandemonium! They greeted me, they embraced me, they cried. I was a hero because I came. I became a kind of legend to them because they thought I was so brave to come because all foreign artists that season didn't go to Poland. They said, "You are number two." I asked, "Who is number one?" and they said, "The pope."

We played a wonderful program: Webern, Six Pieces for Orchestra, Mozart Symphony no. 39, and Bruckner Three. I recorded the Bruckner, which went on an LP, but their equipment was not very good, and distribution was limited. The orchestra was in good shape, and they had such a spirit for doing this concert. It hadn't changed much since I had last conducted it in 1960. Some older members had retired, but probably seventy-five percent of the ensemble was the same. They played as best as they could. Every day was moving, because in between and after rehearsals, all my Polish friends came to greet me, embrace me, and kiss me. Even people I never met were coming to see me. Some came by train from other towns, all of them saying that I was "great for coming to Poland."

In the shops there was nothing to eat. So they got a little milk for me; they hardly had any for the children. Imagine. The shop in front of Philharmonic Hall that carried alcohol was closed. They said, "We don't drink, we pray." Can you imagine such an atmosphere? The tension was astonishing. They expected at any moment that the Soviet army that was around Warsaw and other cities was ready to take over.

Finally came Friday's concert. There was electricity in the air. The public gave an ovation before we even started to play! Old composer friends like Lutosławski, Penderecki, Włodzimierz Kotoński, Perkowski, Zbigniew Turski, and others from Krenz's generation, such as Baird and Sikorski, came. Even younger composers at that time, like Wojciech Kilar and Górecki, they all came. It was very touching. They lived in other cities, but they came to see me. Because of the rehearsals, recording, and concerts there was no time to visit with friends, so they came to the hotel to eat something with me or even to talk to me while I was in the shower because there was so little time and so many of them to see.

After the second concert I flew to Frankfurt and then took a train to Strasbourg, where I had a concert. I fell asleep so soundly on the train. The whole week in Warsaw I didn't sleep, maybe two or three hours a night, not more. And all this tension from the possible dangers and the euphoria of the trip exhausted me. I completely collapsed on the train. I was lost in tiredness. But later the next day I was okay and with a new orchestra. I told them about this incredible experience I had had in Poland, and they could understand because all of Europe was awaiting something terrible, eventually a third world war. This was a possibility.

So this was my first visit to Poland after twenty-one years.

In the months that followed, Solidarity grew to nearly ten million members. It held its first national congress in September 1981, at which Wałęsa was elected the union's national chairman. First Secretary Kania, while always maintaining the communist line, had acknowledged problems in the Polish government and met with Wałęsa in the spirit of cooperation. Amid growing extremist factions in the Polish government, between hard-line and more liberal communists (even the Polish military eventually began demanding a trade union branch), and under pressure from the Soviets, Kania was removed from office after slightly more than a year as first secretary. Woiciech Jaruzelski replaced him.[19]

In early December 1981, feeling increasingly frustrated by the government's inability and reluctance to make progress on its reforms, Solidarity's executive committee called for free elections and a referendum on Poland's alliance with the Soviet Union.[20] This was the last straw for the Polish government. On December 13, First Secretary Jaruzelski declared a "state of war" within his own country, and martial law was imposed on Polish citizens. Unarmed and nonviolent in their principles, Solidarity members faced riot police charged with destroying the union. "Virtually all Solidarity leaders and many affiliated intellectuals were arrested or detained," noted the U.S. State Department. "The United States and other Western countries responded to martial law by imposing economic sanctions against the Polish regime and against the Soviet Union."[21]

Jaruzelski claimed that the declaration of war was intended to prevent an attack by the Soviet Union. According to Russian documents released years later, Jaruzelski apparently had asked the Soviet military to help crush Solidarity in 1981, but it refused.[22] And despite their show of force on the Polish border in December 1980, there is evidence that the Soviets did not intend to invade Poland but planned instead to wait and allow the Polish government to do their work for them, as Davies has noted.[23]

Skrowaczewski was conducting the Saarbrücken Radio Symphony Orchestra on December 13, 1981. He described how the turmoil in Poland affected him:

> I had a matinee concert on Sunday. I had programmed a work by my old friend Kotoński. It was a very pleasant work inspired by aurora borealis. He wrote electronic music, but this was only for the orchestra. He came to Saarbrücken for rehearsals and the concert. Sunday morning I was still asleep at 6:00 when the phone rang, and it was Kotoński. "Did you hear? There was a military coup, a state of war, and everything is closed." I had no idea this had happened. Of course, the entire world was concerned over this action.
>
> At 11:00 a.m., when I entered the hall for the concert, the public immediately rose up. This support of Kotoński and me was very special. It was a terrific concert. Kotoński was worried because his wife was in Poland, and he couldn't fly back because of the situation. But taking the train was possible. I had an engagement in Frankfurt, so we went there together by train. He didn't have any money, so before he made the next train to Poland, I gave him some money, some sandwiches, sausages, bread, and fruit for the trip back. When I got to the hotel in Frankfurt, who do I see in the lobby? Elzbieta Penderecki, the wife of Penderecki. She was terrified. "Stanisław, I just came back from America. What can I do? How can I get back home?" Penderecki had been teaching at Yale for a couple of years. She had gone back to Connecticut alone to sell the house. "Listen," I said, "I just sent Kotoński back on the train. Maybe this will work for you." Because of Penderecki's fame as the number-one Polish composer, a special plane was arranged for her, and she got back safely. The whole situation was a continuation for me of February in Warsaw: these feelings of worrying about the military and the uncertainty of the future of Poland.

Poland's political fate remained uncertain for a number of years. Although the "state of war" was suspended by the end of 1982, hundreds of political prisoners remained in jail, and Solidarity stayed underground for several years. Eventually, a few years after Mikhail Gorbachev took the reins of the Soviet Union, political change in Poland occurred. Pressured by the strikes, the Polish Communist Party finally entered into negotiations with the leaders of Solidarity. Three months of roundtable talks in 1989 ultimately led to the creation of a political structure comprised of a bicameral legislature and a president as chief executive. In December, Lech Wałęsa was elected president of Poland.

Because of the political unrest in his home country, Skrowaczewski didn't return there to conduct until 1986. A year after that visit, another tour of Poland would rival the emotional intensity he experienced in 1981.

TWENTY-FOUR

CALL FROM ACROSS THE POND

Ever since the death of Barbirolli there has been talk of the Hallé's resurgence. Maybe the time has at last arrived when the prophecy can be made with confidence as well as hope. For in revealing the quality of Bruckner's Third Symphony, Stanisław Skrowaczewski and the orchestra scored a triumph against all the odds.

—David Fanning, *The Guardian*, 1983

Though Poland's fate occupied Skrowaczewski's mind throughout 1981, he focused all his energies on his conducting engagements and his renewed drive to compose.

Not long after the 1978 premiere of *Ricercari Notturni*, he told Joseph Longo, his friend and co-principal clarinetist of the Minnesota Orchestra, that he wished to write a concerto for him—featuring the A clarinet, E-flat clarinet, and bass clarinet. "I had to be very diplomatic," Longo recalled. "I jokingly said, 'You do want some performances, don't you?'" Skrowaczewski ultimately agreed that the model of the three-instrument usage in *Ricercari Notturni* was not appropriate for this concerto.

By June 1979 he secured an agreement for a performance date with the Minnesota Orchestra for a clarinet concerto, and he applied to the new commissioning program of the Minnesota Composers Forum (now the American Composers Forum) for a grant. He received the commission from the Forum with funding from the Jerome Foundation of St. Paul. He had just enough time to write the piece, working on it intermittently over the course of two years. He finished the Concerto for Clarinet in A and Orchestra in Frankfurt, where he was guest conducting in January 1981, just weeks before he visited Poland. Four months later Skrowaczewski and Longo premiered the work with the Minnesota Orchestra.

"The short list of twentieth-century woodwind concertos has obviously increased its numbers by one, and an auspicious one at that," wrote Michael Anthony after the concerto's first performances.[1] Skrowaczewski's new piece had a terrific "birth" in Minneapolis. The outstanding performances by Longo and the orchestra gave him an excellent demo recording of the new composition.

Soon after the world premiere of Concerto for Clarinet in A and Orchestra, Skrowaczewski led its European premiere with the Saarbrücken Radio Symphony Orchestra and its principal clarinetist, Dietrich Fritsche. One of the reviews in Saarbrücken amused Skrowaczewski because it interpreted the "A" in the work's title as a reference to the key of A major rather than the instrument, the A clarinet. He had not composed a piece in one clearly discernable key since his youth. In 1983, Concerto for Clarinet had performances in New York and in Manchester, England. New York

Philharmonic's principal clarinetist, Stanley Drucker, gave the New York premiere with the Juilliard Philharmonia, led by Jorge Mester, as part of Juilliard's Festival of Contemporary Music.

Despite the concerto's enthusiastic reception at its premieres and the dearth of solo literature for clarinet with orchestra, ensembles did not perform the piece again for nearly twenty years. (Some collegiate music faculty and students performed it in its solo clarinet and piano reduction.) Part of the problem was—and still is, to some extent—that professional orchestras seldom perform a clarinet concerto, and when they do, it is usually Mozart's composition.

Furthermore, a contemporary concerto seldom receives multiple performances unless a major soloist initiates and promotes them. (Benny Goodman is a notable example among clarinetists.) During the early 1980s major solo clarinetists such as Richard Stoltzman, Sabine Meyer, and Charles Neidich were only just emerging. Skrowaczewski's Concerto for English Horn and Orchestra benefited greatly from its recording by the Minnesota Orchestra and soloist Thomas Stacy, and the maestro wanted the same exposure for his clarinet concerto. He sought funding for a recording, but it was too expensive to secure a major American orchestra to do it. He had to wait twenty years before Concerto for Clarinet in A and Orchestra received a professional recording (the first CD of all-Skrowaczewski orchestral works); the orchestra was the Saarbrücken Radio Symphony, and the soloist was Stoltzman.

Skrowaczewski sent Stoltzman the concerto after it was published, but the busy clarinetist was already committed to other projects. Years later, through his and Skrowaczewski's relationship with the Saarbrücken Radio Symphony Orchestra and its artistic director, Dr. Sabine Tomek, the pair performed and recorded the work in Saarbrücken.

Stoltzman remembered the first time he heard the concerto:

> I listened to the tape of Joe Longo's performance, and it was fantastic! I thought, "I could never play this piece. It's really hard." Also, I thought it was unique. He used some orchestral colors I had never heard before. In fact, I couldn't figure them all out at first because Mr. Skrowaczewski sent me only the piano reduction, not the full orchestral score. I later realized that one of the sounds I was hearing was an amplified harpsichord, something I had never heard in a composition before. The effectiveness of his instrumentation is really stunning. It creates phantasmagoric colorations. He relishes the evocative and eccentric sounds that can come out of a percussion section, such as playing a gong as it moves into a tub of water. One can make light of an effect like that, but when it is heard at just the right moment it sends chills up your spine!
>
> What really intrigued me as a clarinet player was that he understood the *chalumeau* [low] register of the clarinet, which few composers appreciate or know how to frame so that it really is handsome. He certainly did. I marveled at that. He understands the instrument very well. The colorations of tones

by using different fingerings to create a special kind of shading from one moment to the other on the same pitch, for example, is something that not a lot of composers understand.

Skrowaczewski recalled, "I had never played the instrument myself, but as I was composing, I began to breathe with it, to feel as if it were part of me. It was as if the ideas came right from inside."[2]

Indeed, the piece likely is Skrowaczewski's most personal, emotionally direct concerto composition. As Roy Close noted, its "immediate and powerful appeal"—due in part to its coloristic and tonal qualities—does not diminish its artistry.[3] "Stanley Drucker's performance of the fierce and meditative solo part made the work eminently accessible and affecting, yet thoroughly free of condescension or banality," wrote *The New York Times* critic Edward Rothstein of the New York premiere.[4]

Stoltzman elaborated on the concerto's qualities:

> It reminds me a little, at the beginning, of the opening of the Alban Berg Violin Concerto, where these wide arching leaps—which the clarinet is so good at—occur. Something that is very satisfying for musicians when they play a work is when it is tightly composed, and they feel that all the notes are an integral part of the total composition. In Stanisław's concerto, whether there are extremely fast notes that are zipping by so that you can hardly tell one from the other or very slow notes, there is meaning. When you begin to play the piece enough you realize, "Oh, the fast notes are the slow notes sped up." Then you realize, "I really have to play exactly what is written because it means something. It's not just one chromatic note after another." Because he knows all the orchestral instruments so well he is able to compose moments that are extremely loud or extremely soft—both for the soloist and the orchestra—and nothing comes unglued or obliterated or unintelligible. That is the mark of very gifted writing.

As in his previous concertos Skrowaczewski achieved artistic restraint through his instrumentation. Oboes, trumpets, and clarinets (except a bass clarinet) are absent. A large percussion section of drums, gongs, and wood blocks, and an array of mallet instruments are used judiciously. In the second movement, Nocturne, Skrowaczewski for the first time formally employs aleatoric technique. This rhythmic freedom complements the Nocturne's character. Mary Ann Feldman describes the movement:

> Typical of Skrowaczewski's penchant for night images, the spare instrumentation renders the cool blue luminosity of moonlight, out of which the clarinet, tentative at first, undertakes its recitative. The heart of the movement dwells upon a broad theme from the soloist, soon joined by the alto flute; other dark-toned instruments—bass clarinet, contrabassoon, a single cello—are drawn into the episode. The opening strain returns, quite solitary, to conclude the reverie.[5]

"The role of the bass clarinet is strange in many places," Skrowaczewski said. "It is like a *doppelgänger*. I thought it would be witty to have it sneeringly repeat what the solo clarinet was doing."

His reputation as a composer grew steadily after his departure from the Minnesota Orchestra. In 1980 George Sturm wrote to him: "In all the many years of personal involvement with bulk mailings, I have never witnessed (or even heard of) a response as massive as the one I am having to my letter to radio stations, which offers the use of your English Horn Concerto recording. I'm simply overwhelmed."[6]

For the first time since the 1950s Skrowaczewski consistently lived an artistic life as both conductor and composer. Conducting would always win his time and energies, but composing was closer to his heart.

Though he still preferred not to conduct his own works, he now complied with such requests, as he did for his debut concert with the Buffalo Philharmonic Orchestra in 1982. A reporter from the *Buffalo Courier-Express* discussed the maestro's reluctance to conduct his music:

> Skrowaczewski said he is [hesitant] to let himself go while conducting his own music. "I feel stupid on stage if I get excited about my own music in front of people," Skrowaczewski said. No, he is not timid. But if he did get worked up about his own music, he said, wouldn't that show "lack of taste? I can make it in Bruckner, but not in my own music. I give my own music more classical performances than other people will."[7]

By fall Skrowaczewski had completed his first chamber piece in decades, Trio for Clarinet, Bassoon and Piano, written for the Philadelphia Orchestra Chamber Players. He also had two major commissions lined up: a violin concerto for the Philadelphia Orchestra and a concerto for the Minnesota Orchestra in honor of Orchestra Hall's tenth anniversary.

In 1982 George Sturm's Music Associates of America published Skrowaczewski's orchestral arrangement of "The Star-Spangled Banner," originally written for Orchestra Hall's dedication concert in 1974. Sturm noted how singable and "particularly effective it is in A-flat, thus enabling people to join in far more lustily than the customary B-flat version, which lies too high." Skrowaczewski commented on the arrangement:

> I was dissatisfied with the instrumentation and the B-flat key of the standard arrangement the orchestra used to play. It was very poor, and with the public trying to sing the high F, it was horrible. Either Ken Dayton or a board member suggested I create my own version for the opening of the hall. We already had quadruple woodwinds, and I wanted to use everyone, so I just tried to improve it. Frankly, I liked the piece very much, and I discovered it was open to a nice flow of vertical harmonies. Towards the end I introduced some polyphonic aspects. Everyone loved it, and people suggested I do the Polish anthem, French anthem, etc.

The highlight of summer 1981 was a concert of Bruckner's Seventh Symphony and Mozart's "Turkish" Violin Concerto in A with the Philadelphia Orchestra at Saratoga Performing Arts Center (SPAC). "In the sixteen years that I have attended SPAC concerts," wrote Garry Spector, "I do not recall ever hearing the Philadelphians play with the precision and splendor they demonstrated Friday."[8] Skrowaczewski loved pairing Mozart with Bruckner on the same program. "Bruckner is Mozart one hundred years later," he has said.

The Philadelphia Orchestra's affection for Skrowaczewski developed over the course of nearly twenty years of working together. They called him "Mr. Pianissimo," a name he earned in Minneapolis for his insistence on the softest dynamics in rehearsals and performances. Skrowaczewski elaborated:

> After Orchestra Hall was built I was working, in a sense, again on the Minnesota Orchestra's sound. Because of those cubes I had to rework the sound of the brass in particular, asking them often to be more *pianissimo.* For a while they called me Mr. Pianissimo. Well, it was spreading all over the country. When I went to Philadelphia, I always asked for *pianissimo.* Ormandy loved the lush, big sound for everything, which I loved, too, but for certain classical works by Haydn, Beethoven, and Schubert, for example, I like the sound more lean, more balanced. And with a smaller string section, the brass often need to be *pianissimo.* Here in Minneapolis I was constantly fighting to balance the winds. It was like this, to a great extent, all over the country and in Europe. All these orchestras always played with a huge tone. When they got down to a true *pianissimo,* it was a big achievement because it was practically nonexistent at that time. There were exceptions, especially the Berlin Philharmonic, which could play the most beautiful *pianissimo* in the world. This was forever my obsession. It came from my European experiences. I've always loved the hushed sound of strings. In 2007 the Saarbrücken Radio Symphony Orchestra presented me with a sweatshirt with my caricature conducting [and] the caption "shhh, quiet" and then "*ppppp.*"

The Philadelphia Orchestra and Skrowaczewski had shared a special chemistry ever since their concerts and tour in spring 1980. He wrote to Wilford reminding him of their 1979 conversation about the manager's idea for an official affiliation with the orchestra as a permanent guest conductor. With Ormandy's departure in 1980, this step would have been a way to continue Skrowaczewski's long and successful relationship with the ensemble.

After Riccardo Muti was appointed to the orchestra, Skrowaczewski's appearances were less frequent until early winter 1983, when Muti fell ill before starting a five-week stint with the Philadelphians that included a Carnegie Hall concert. The orchestra turned to Skrowaczewski on short notice to replace Muti in concerts in Philadelphia and in Carnegie Hall, where Weissenberg was to perform Brahms' Piano Concerto in D minor.

"Skrowaczewski has such a hyper-intense musical temperament," noted *The Philadelphia Inquirer,* "that he makes even Klaus Tennstedt seem laid-back."[9] Although criticized by some, this intensity no doubt was a factor in the frequent choice of Skrowaczewski as a last-minute replacement for ailing maestros. A few months after he replaced Muti, the Philadelphia Orchestra turned to him again, this time to replace Andrew Davis for two summer concerts, one of which featured Rostropovich playing the Shostakovich Cello Concerto no. 1.

The maestro's particular relationship with the Philadelphia Orchestra was acknowledged formally in 1982, when he received the City of Philadelphia Medal of Appreciation. Detroit also bestowed its equivalent of the award on him that year. He also won Poland's 1982 Karol Szymanowski Medal, the first honor he received from his homeland in nearly thirty years.

Toward the end of summer 1981 he had the rare opportunity to conduct two Mozart operas, both semi-staged, which freed him from logistical issues. He closed the Festival Ottawa 1981 season leading the National Arts Centre Orchestra in two Mozart operatic oddities: *Bastien et Bastienne*, the composer's *opéra comique* written when he was twelve, and *The Impresario*, composed during the same time as *The Marriage of Figaro*. According to one critic, Skrowaczewski met the challenge of presenting two Mozart operas on the same program:

> The lightness of the sound [in *Bastien et Bastienne*], the simplicity and sensitivity with which each musical phrase was shaped—these were a source of constant pleasure. [With *The Impresario*], the sounds the conductor drew from the orchestra were much more robust, more sonorous, yet so marvelously transparent in texture that one could, for example, hear the sound of the bassoon through the rest of the ensemble at all times, without bringing it forward and distorting the essential character of the music. It was an object lesson in making the distinction between early and mature Mozart clear to an audience, without double crossing t's [sic] and dotting the i's [sic]. Skrowaczewski [is] a man of impeccable taste and discernment.[10]

Skrowaczewski returned to Festival Ottawa the next season, again with two infrequently performed works: Szymanowski's *Stabat Mater* and Haydn's two-act comic opera *L'infedeltà Delusa*.

As a guest conductor Skrowaczewski often had the option of choosing his favorite music without the necessity of balancing an entire season. "My repertoire covers practically the entire second half of the 18th [plus the] 19th and 20th centuries," he told an inquiring Italian orchestra manager in 1979, "with a special predilection for German classical and romantic music. Operatic repertoire consists of all Mozart, Beethoven, Weber, Wagner, some Tchaikovsky and Mussorgsky, also Stravinsky, and Alban Berg."[11]

Skrowaczewski elaborated on his freedom of repertoire:

In Minneapolis, where I had a dozen or more subscription concerts year after year, I tried not to repeat any pieces within two or three years, so I did a lot of music for the first time, which increased my repertoire. Of course, I had to learn all of this new music. Sometimes it was necessary to play works that I might not normally program. Sibelius' music, for example, was never my delight, but I still considered him a very specific and fine composer. And of course, with the Scandinavian public in Minnesota, I did several Sibelius symphonies. Tchaikovsky's First Symphony is charming but not really great Tchaikovsky; neither is the Third Symphony. Still, I played them. Why? Partly it was to avoid overplaying his more popular Fourth, Fifth, and Sixth Symphonies. But my main reason was to show his development as a composer. I wanted the audience to experience Tchaikovsky's changes from a young composer to a mature one. I did the same with other composers. Also, it's important for the public to hear the style of composition from different eras of music history and how composers reflected those trends.

Certainly it was refreshing when, as a freelancer, I could choose programs that I had already done or repeat certain compositions for a second, third, or fourth time. This luxury was something I could never do in Minnesota. It was also a great relief for my amount of preparation time.

In fall 1981 he made his debut conducting an Australian orchestra, the Sydney Symphony Orchestra. The three-week tour of Australian Broadcasting Commission subscription concerts with the orchestra was his first time back in the country since his 1973 tour with the Cleveland Orchestra. "How can we involve Skrowaczewski as conductor regularly and fundamentally in orchestral performance in this country?" asked one reviewer, who said Skrowaczewski "inspired the members of the Sydney Symphony Orchestra to some of the best playing of their collective career."[12]

Throughout the 1981–82 season he had outstanding engagements around the world, but his week at Juilliard in late January 1982 was the most refreshing experience.

The occasion was Juilliard's Third Festival of Contemporary Music. Louis Brunelli, the school's associate dean and director of performance, invited Skrowaczewski to conduct a formidable program, even for a seasoned professional orchestra: Carter's Variations for Orchestra, Crumb's *Echoes of Time and the River*, and Symphony no. 8 by Peter Mennin, Juilliard's president for twenty-one years.

The maestro recalled his first experience with the Juilliard Orchestra:

> I was amazed how good they were. The program: Carter, Mennin, Crumb! Imagine the difficulties of this program, and the kids did it! I said to them, "Listen, in five days with five rehearsals, I don't know if any professional orchestra like the New York Philharmonic or Chicago or Cleveland could do this so well." I was completely praising the Juilliard students' commitment and skill.

At the end of the concert he received an enthusiastic display of clapping, stomping, and cheering from the students. The stage was set for a long-term relationship throughout the 1980s and early 1990s.

One of the students in the Juilliard Orchestra—and author of the concert's program notes—thirteen years later became vice president and general manager of the Minnesota Orchestra. Clarinetist Robert Neu, who had graduated from Juilliard's master's program in 1981, was working as an administrator in the school's concert department and also played in the orchestra. He recalled that first experience playing for Skrowaczewski:

> I remember him being one of my two favorite conductors, just because it was no-nonsense, electrifying, and you knew there would be no bullshit. It was *about* the music and playing well. The end. And I think at Juilliard, especially—which can be a very difficult and highly competitive environment that often doesn't have to do with making great music, as opposed to politics and just trying to keep your head above water—this was important. At his rehearsals you could just think about music and nothing else.

The maestro's summer 1982 season began in Brazil and then moved to New York, where he opened the thirty-seventh annual Caramoor Festival. He then worked with Jean-Pierre Rampal and the Detroit Symphony Orchestra at Meadow Brook and with an emerging star, cellist Yo-Yo Ma, at Blossom Festival with the Cleveland Orchestra. It was the twenty-six-year-old cellist's debut at the festival.

The summer season was not as hectic as the previous three, but Skrowaczewski needed a breather. Over the past two full seasons he had conducted more than forty orchestras in seventeen countries.

By fall 1982 he had received offers of music directorships from orchestras on two continents. The Utah Symphony, which had approached him in 1979, still did not interest him, although he greatly admired the ensemble. An offer from the Hallé Orchestra, however, was difficult to pass up. The orchestra had a storied international reputation, and all of Skrowaczewski's guest-conducting engagements with it, beginning in 1976, had been extremely positive.

The Hallé, as it is often called, is England's oldest professional orchestra and among the oldest such organizations in the world. Pianist and conductor Charles Hallé founded the ensemble in 1858. Its prestigious history of leadership includes the Austro-Hungarian conducting giant Hans Richter, Sir Thomas Beecham, and Sir John Barbirolli, the Hallé's principal conductor from 1943 to 1970.[13]

When James Loughran's departure as the Hallé's principal conductor was announced in spring 1982, two names were on the search committee's list of possible replacements: Bernard Haitink and Stanisław Skrowaczewski. Haitink, still music director of the Concertgebouw Orchestra and of Britain's Glyndebourne Festival, was unavailable.[14] Although Skrowaczewski—the committee's first choice—was interested, he did not want to repeat his former life as a music director.

Clive Smart, then the Hallé Orchestra's secretary and general manager, recalled the courting of Skrowaczewski:

> The orchestra was just about to celebrate its 125th-anniversary season (1982–83). I had been there when Sir John Barbirolli was principal conductor. He died in 1970, and shortly after, the Scottish conductor James Loughran was appointed to replace him. James stayed with the orchestra until the end of the 125th-anniversary season. He was very popular with the Hallé audience, though toward the end of his tenure, playing standards began to slip a little. We wished to appoint as his successor a conductor who had profound musicianship with a wide repertoire. Stan had been a guest conductor [here] around this time. He was popular with the orchestra, he had some very interesting programs to present to us, and I got on quite well with him. The chairman of the Hallé and I went after Stan because we'd had a vote in the orchestra as to which of the various conductors with whom they'd been working would they be interested in as principal conductor. We decided that democracy had to play a part in the selection process, which had not been the case in the past.
>
> Stan came out [at the] top of the list, so we felt we were definitely on the right lines approaching him. Clearly I was very pleased with this decision, although Stan had made it abundantly clear to me that he'd had enough of being a principal conductor. He'd had nineteen years with Minneapolis, happy years, but having your own orchestra is a major task and very committing. And he wasn't really looking forward to embarking on a new such venture after having just relinquished the Minnesota Orchestra. Nevertheless, the chairman and I went to Brussels for a long interview with Stan, and we managed to talk him into changing his mind, albeit not on a full-time basis, but with a commitment to a minimum number of dates a year in Manchester within agreed periods. In the end we were very happy with the arrangement.

"I was very careful in accepting," Skrowaczewski said. "I was not eager to get another orchestra." He explained:

> I had had enough of all the responsibilities involved with such a position and with dealing with unions, etc. Around this same time I had yet another proposition, to become music director of the Tonhalle Orchester Zürich. Their president, a banker, took me to lunch and simply asked me. I thanked him and told him I was potentially interested because it's a wonderful orchestra with a great musical tradition, and Switzerland is fantastic. But I hadn't conducted this orchestra for a number of years, so I would have to have a week with them with rehearsals and concerts to see if there was a rapport between us. It was a very logical point to suggest. I would never blindly take an orchestra without recently working with them. Because they never gave me a concert, the proposition faded away.
>
> I did have a relationship with Hallé. It was a very fine and interesting orchestra, able to work very fast and under difficult conditions, but its devotion and attention were amazing! I was reinvited every year since 1976, and then I was reinvited for two weeks with very good results and a pleasant atmosphere.

When their principal conductor was leaving, they proposed the position to me. I was quite pleased, of course, but I didn't accept immediately. Although they wanted more, I said the maximum was twelve weeks for me, and they understood it. Now in Europe, the conductors have seven or eight weeks, and this is not enough. You cannot imprint anything special on the orchestra. I think the balance between twelve and fourteen is a proper one. Yet I still wasn't sure if I wanted to do this. But Michel Glotz and my new British manager, Stephen Lumsden, both said, "You are stupid. You must accept this wonderful orchestra! You have made your conditions, and they have accepted them." So I said to myself, "Why not?" and I did it.

"Stan always admired the Hallé Orchestra," said Krystyna Skrowaczewski. "This is why he took it. At the time it was very interesting to him musically, so he didn't mind the traveling. And actually it was a direct flight from Minneapolis to Manchester, not even through London, so it was very convenient."

On February 8, 1983, the formal press release was circulated simultaneously in Manchester and in Minneapolis announcing Skrowaczewski's appointment as principal conductor and musical advisor of the Hallé Orchestra beginning in September 1984. His official statement read in part:

> All of my guest appearances with the Hallé Orchestra have been a source of great satisfaction. I have found the musicianship, skill, and integrity of its members to be of the highest quality. Their commitment to strive for the best is a source of inspiration to me. It is this "soul" in an orchestra that is absolutely essential to great music making, and all my efforts will be dedicated to it. I have great admiration for the Hallé Orchestra as well as for British orchestras in general because of their remarkable conscientiousness and preparedness. My high opinion of the wonderful level of performance in England makes this appointment a great honor for me.[15]

The Daily Telegraph hailed Skrowaczewski's appointment as "an important event in British musical life," and the orchestra immediately nicknamed him "Stan the Man."[16] The coming years would prove to be among his most satisfying artistically, despite the difficulties he would face over the Hallé's financial problems.

TWENTY-FIVE

STAN THE MAN

I couldn't conceive of anyone more dedicated than Stan. The music is everything. The performance is everything. The details of performance and rehearsals are everything. He was 150 percent dedicated to the music, to exploring it, and to getting it right.

—Peter Worrell, Hallé Orchestra violinist

It was not long after Skrowaczewski first arrived in Minneapolis in fall 1960 that Stanley Hawks dubbed him "Stan the Man." Hawks, who died in 1971, was a former diplomat, a director and vice president of the *Minneapolis Star* and *Minneapolis Tribune*, and president of the Minneapolis Symphony Orchestra's board of directors in the 1950s. He later served the Metropolitan Opera in the Upper Midwest in the same capacity.

Skrowaczewski fondly remembered Hawks and his wife, Peggy:

> Stanley was one of the finest men we met in Minneapolis. He was impressive, like a refined English gentleman, always wearing a black hat and an elegant suit. He and his wife, Peggy, were extremely cultured and educated. They were great friends, and Peggy was especially close to Krystyna. They had a wonderful house on Lake of the Isles in Minneapolis, with a huge garden, very elegant, like a museum. They always held receptions for visiting artists after Minnesota Orchestra concerts. He began calling me "Stan the Man."

Hawks told Skrowaczewski that the nickname originated with Stan Musial, record-setting outfielder for the St. Louis Cardinals, member of the Baseball Hall of Fame, and accomplished harmonica player. Born Stanisław Franciszek Musiał, he was a second-generation Polish American whose father came from Warsaw.[1] More than two decades later, when Hallé Orchestra members dubbed Skrowaczewski "Stan the Man," the nickname was more appropriate than ever, given his vast experience and musical authority.

As a full-fledged freelancer, Skrowaczewski had a demanding 1982–83 concert schedule that was unexpectedly extended when he replaced an ailing Christoph von Dohnányi for a concert with L'Orchestre de Paris. In Toronto he also replaced Klaus Tennstedt, leading an all-Brahms program with soloist Garrick Ohlsson that commemorated the 150th anniversary of the composer's birth. Fulfilling his regular schedule, Skrowaczewski later conducted another all-Brahms program with the Cincinnati Symphony and a performance of *A German Requiem* with Kölner Rundfunk-Sinfonie-Orchester. He also helped the Minnesota Orchestra celebrate its eightieth-anniversary season with performances of Bruckner's Ninth Symphony and Chopin's Piano Concerto no. 2, with Eugene Istomin.

Skrowaczewski had met Istomin in Paris in the 1950s, and they performed together often over the years. During Istomin's last illness Skrowaczewski visited his friend whenever he was in Washington, D.C. Istomin died of liver cancer in 2003. "Artistically, he was very special to me," Skrowaczewski said. "In the Istomin-Stern-Rose Trio, he and Isaac and Leonard [Rose] continued a tradition of romantic playing. His interpretations and way of playing were quite close to my mind, feelings, and opinions on music, and having contact with him was stimulating."

His conducting highlights during the 1982–83 season involved perhaps the two greatest orchestras in their respective realms: the Juilliard Orchestra and the Berlin Philharmonic. About a year after his rousing debut with the venerated student orchestra, Skrowaczewski was back at Juilliard for a week of rehearsals and a concert. The return engagement followed the same positive pattern as before, but instead of an all-contemporary music program, the repertoire was traditional, consisting of Mozart's Piano Concerto no. 22 and Shostakovich's Symphony no. 10. George Sturm, who attended the Juilliard concert, wrote Skrowaczewski an uncharacteristically enthusiastic letter about it:

> You have known me a long time and will know that I do not indulge in gushing sentimental praise. On the other hand, it would be truant of me not to tell you once again how much I enjoyed your performance with the Juilliard kids on Friday. I went out for beer with [German composer] Manfred Trojahn after the concert, and he told me in no uncertain terms that the concert had been *the* highlight of his visit to America thus far. And, as you will affectionately have noted, our enthusiasm was shared a hundredfold by the orchestra itself. Bravo![2]

Skrowaczewski's Berlin Philharmonic engagement in spring 1983 was his first with the orchestra since 1979. The Philharmonic, now in the latter years of Karajan's tenure, was perhaps at its zenith of incomparable cohesion and artistic sensitivity. Skrowaczewski led a traditional program of Mozart's Symphony no. 34, Chopin's Piano Concerto no. 1, and both suites from Ravel's *Daphnis et Chloé*, music that he and the Philharmonic knew extremely well. Karajan was highly selective in his choice of guest conductors for his exalted orchestra. "He was very much in favor of Stan and showed it very strongly," said Michel Glotz, Karajan's closest recording collaborator.

Glotz recalled a dinner in the early 1970s that he arranged for Skrowaczewski and Karajan at the Drake Hotel in Chicago, where Glotz and Karajan were staying. Richard Cisek, who had accompanied Skrowaczewski, also attended. Glotz described the occasion:

> We had a fantastic dinner served by room service with a valet at our disposal in the dining room of the suite. Stan asked Karajan a million questions, and he in turn asked Stan a million questions on the development of the Minnesota Orchestra and the new hall. He knew very well Stan's Chopin recordings and some others because he was extremely curious about what was published on the market, particularly by artists in whom he was interested. Karajan was asking Dick Cisek about the Minnesota public, about its reactions,

about the repertoire, about the needs, the subsidies coming from sponsors, and so forth. We had a wonderful evening, which went—by the standards of Karajan—quite late, until almost midnight. After the dinner we were installed in the lounge and we had a very charming, interesting, musical, and personal talk. From then on, Karajan was always asking [for] news about Stan. Dick Cisek was deeply impressed by the way Karajan treated Stan. Karajan was a very refined person, extremely polite, exquisite socially, and so well educated. He called Stan "maestro" from the beginning of the evening to the end.

After opening the Utah Symphony's 1983–84 concert season with Verdi's Requiem, Skrowaczewski spent his sixtieth birthday on a return trip home after an engagement with the Atlanta Symphony. Then he flew to Manchester for his first concerts as principal conductor-elect of the Hallé Orchestra.

Barely off the plane after his Hallé concerts, Skrowaczewski went to Philadelphia, replacing Tennstedt in concerts with the Philadelphia Orchestra. The repertoire was a single work, Bruckner's Eighth Symphony—not the kind of piece a replacement conductor glides into, but this work was one that Skrowaczewski "owned."

Because of the breadth of his repertoire, experience, reliability, and interpretive talents, Skrowaczewski was in demand as a replacement conductor for major orchestras well into the 2000s. However, he accepted the engagements only if he were replacing a conductor he admired and respected and if he loved the programmed works.

After the concerts with the Philadelphia Orchestra, Skrowaczewski returned to Orchestra Hall in Minneapolis to lead Bruckner's Seventh Symphony. Mayo Clinic physician David Skillrud, who attended the orchestra's Rochester run-out concert of the Seventh Symphony, wrote Skrowaczewski to thank him for the "extraordinary reading" of the piece and also to express an apology: "The applause which greeted its conclusion was frightfully inadequate, and on behalf of the community, I apologize."[3] Skrowaczewski gave a thoughtful response:

> Your very kind words about our Bruckner performance in Rochester gave me a lot of pleasure and satisfaction. It is, after all, the ultimate goal of a performer to share the glory of the music which he believes is great with the listener. Even a few listeners in the audience, as you were, make the performer happy and his goal fulfilled. The reactions of an entire audience may depend upon numerous factors and can be misleading in both ways. Maybe the depth of Bruckner's music doesn't generate a loud applause? I appreciate so much your letter.[4]

After conducting Bruckner in arid Phoenix early in January 1984, Skrowaczewski moved to frigid, slushy New York City to lead the Y Chamber Symphony in music of Beethoven and Schuller. The latter's Concerto for Trumpet and Chamber Orchestra, composed in 1979, was still a relatively new piece, and Skrowaczewski balanced it with the First Symphony of Mendelssohn, written when the composer was fifteen years old.

The Y Chamber Symphony, founded in 1977 at the 92nd Street Y, was renamed the New York Chamber Symphony in 1986 and continued until 2002 under its founder Gerald Schwarz. Skrowaczewski led the twenty-six Y string players in one of his favorite Beethoven compositions, the *Grosse Fuge*. Originally conceived as the last movement of String Quartet op. 130, one of Beethoven's monumental five late quartets, the movement has been set for full string orchestra by several conductors. Skrowaczewski recorded it live with the Nippon Hōsō Kyōkai (NHK) Symphony Orchestra of Japan in 2002. He explained his fondness for the work:

> This is one of Beethoven's very special compositions. It produces a shower of feelings in me. I'm trembling when I study or play it. I've read about its history and how Beethoven's friends thought he was becoming crazy in writing such a piece, and I feel and always think about this staggering work as it was thought of in its own time. Augmented by a big string orchestra, the piece makes a shiver in me. I'm so in awe of it. I use the Weingartner arrangement simply because it is readily available. I use it as a basis because he basically has the original text with only the basses added. He put dynamics and tempo markings in that I don't follow. I do my own.

Skrowaczewski flew from New York to Philadelphia, where on a week's notice he replaced Ormandy for concerts with the Philadelphia Orchestra and violin soloist Gidon Kremer. The program was repeated in Washington, D.C., at the Kennedy Center. The next day Skrowaczewski was back home just long enough to see his family and to be a guest on Minnesota Public Radio's *Live from Landmark* program, which featured his Trio for Clarinet, Bassoon and Piano, performed by Joseph Longo, John Miller, and Paul Schoenfield. Skrowaczewski bracketed the performance with remarks about his newly revised composition. The success of the first performance of the Trio in 1982 and the aid of a McKnight Foundation Fellowship had enabled him to expand the piece to seventeen minutes in three movements.

With January behind him, the indefatigable maestro spent a week in France with L'Orchestre National de Lyon, and then he was back with the Hallé Orchestra for his second round of season concerts. A short tour included a performance in London's Barbican Centre, Skrowaczewski's first outing in the capital city with the Hallé.

Reviewers scrutinized the future leader of Britain's oldest orchestra: "As conductor-elect of the Hallé Orchestra," wrote David Fallows of *The Guardian*, "Stanisław Skrowaczewski surely has one major task ahead of him: to galvanize the musicians into a sense of discipline and responsibility so that the quality of their concerts generally reflects the sum total of the available talent."[5]

Discerning critics detected occasional problems with intonation, ensemble, and balance, but nearly all noted the commitment and passion that Skrowaczewski inspired in this orchestra.

Critics also took note of his ideas about the Hallé's future. "They should have a better hall," Skrowaczewski said. "At the moment, half of the string players are under the balconies, which creates serious problems of ensemble."[6] He also pointed out that because the Free Trade Hall is not the Hallé's property, the orchestra sometimes had to find alternative rehearsal space.

After reviewing twenty years of the orchestra's concerts, he recognized the "adventurousness of his predecessors' artistic policies, but at the same time he noticed alarming gaps" in programming (including Britten's *Sinfonia da Requiem* and Tippett's *Corelli Fantasia*, unperformed by the orchestra for two decades.)[7] "Perhaps [I] would program [more] Mozart and Haydn," Skrowaczewski said during a run-out concert to Sheffield. "[They] are like health food to an orchestra gorged on the big romantic works of Tchaikovsky, Elgar, and Richard Strauss."[8]

During summer 1984 he conducted on both U.S. coasts and in the Midwest. He was reunited with cellist János Starker in concerts with the Seattle Symphony before conducting the opening concert of the Philadelphia Orchestra's fifty-fifth season at Fairmount Park, playing in the Mann Music Center. A two-concert engagement turned into three. Once again he replaced the ailing Ormandy, who originally was scheduled to lead the opening program. A tribute to the eighty-four-year-old Ormandy and to eighty-year-old Fredric R. Mann, president of the Mann Music Center, the concert featured Isaac Stern performing the Mendelssohn Violin Concerto. Stern praised both men in his remarks to the fifteen thousand patrons who showed up for the concert on the foggy, late June night.[9] Lutosławski's Concerto for Orchestra, which Skrowaczewski led the following night, was now becoming, to some extent, regular summer fare. "The seventy-one-year-old Pole's success [in Philadelphia]," reported *The Philadelphia Inquirer* critic Daniel Webster, "is entirely due to the enthusiasm of his younger countryman, conductor Stanisław Skrowaczewski, who has led his music here on a couple of occasions."[10]

After opening the National Symphony Orchestra's Bach-Beethoven Festival, Skrowaczewski headed to Los Angeles to serve as a teacher/mentor, a role he seldom assumed; not since his 1973 Tanglewood residency had he been invited to guide young conductors in conjunction with teaching a student orchestra of young professionals. In 1982, at the end of his first season as co-principal guest conductor of the Los Angeles Philharmonic, Michael Tilson Thomas launched the Los Angeles Philharmonic Institute, an orchestra and conducting training program modeled after Tanglewood. The six-week institute engaged several conductors, who taught for a week at a time. The presence of Bernstein, who joined his protégé Tilson Thomas in co-directing the 1982 institute, immediately gave it prestige.

Skrowaczewski was a hit during his week at the institute. "The intimate rapport you built with the orchestra in only a couple of days was remarkable, but your ability to get them to play beyond their limitations was nothing short of miraculous!" wrote Jeffrey Babcock, the institute's administrator, to Skrowaczewski. "The conductors, too, found your advice to be the most valuable and clearly articulated."[11] Tilson Thomas also wrote to Skrowaczewski: "Your work with the conductors and with the orchestra was extremely meaningful to them, and they spoke highly of you all summer."[12]

After Los Angeles, Skrowaczewski had two concerts at the Meadow Brook Festival with the Detroit Symphony and then he planned to have a week off before his August engagements. However, at the Boston Symphony Orchestra's request, he replaced Edo de Waart for two Tanglewood concerts. He had not conducted the BSO since his Tanglewood residency in 1973 and has not been invited back to the festival since his 1984 concerts. His few Boston Symphony engagements in Symphony Hall have been as a replacement for other conductors on rather challenging programs.

A contributing factor to this situation may have been Skrowaczewski's support of Charles Schlueter in the trumpeter's conflict with Ozawa. The BSO had enticed Schlueter to leave the Minnesota Orchestra in 1981, but by the musician's second season with the Boston ensemble, Ozawa was displeased with his work and wanted the tenured musician to be dismissed. Great tension ensued, but in spring 1985 the trumpeter won the arbitration and kept his job.

Schlueter had been principal trumpeter in Minneapolis during Skrowaczewski's last seven years as music director. Pleased with his work, Schlueter's former maestro had no trouble writing a support letter for the trumpeter's battle with Ozawa. "When I went through the conflict with Ozawa," Schlueter said, "Stan was one of two conductors who wrote a letter on my behalf. Most of them opted for not wanting to get involved, for career reasons or something. The way things work, that might have something to do with why he's not invited here, or not."

Following concerts with the Los Angeles Philharmonic at the end of August, Skrowaczewski allowed himself one week in Wyoming with his family before beginning his position in Manchester with the Hallé Orchestra. The annual sojourn in the mountains cleared his mind so he could concentrate on his composing and the upcoming season.

His plans for a direct flight from Minneapolis to Manchester were changed to include a stopover in London, following an urgent call from the BBC. Croatian conductor Lovro von Matacic had fallen ill, whereupon Skrowaczewski saved the day by taking over the annual performance of the Beethoven Ninth by the Philharmonia Orchestra of London at the Proms in Royal Albert Hall. The concert was broadcast on Radio 3.

"The contrast between the Philharmonia's playing and the Vienna Philharmonic's Beethoven last week could hardly have been greater," wrote Stephen Pettitt of *The Times*. "Here, in addition to a superlative sound, there was imagination in place of complacency."[13] The impromptu performance en route to Manchester was a grand U.K. entry for the Hallé's new maestro. And the BBC's decision to broadcast Skrowaczewski's first Thursday series concert as principal conductor with the Hallé was, as Michael Kennedy put it, recognition that his appointment was "an important event in British, not just Mancunian, music life."[14] (Manchester natives are known as Mancunians.)

Skrowaczewski's close friends from Minnesota also recognized the importance of his new appointment. "The Yanks are coming to the Hallé" read the headline of an article about the party of seventeen Minnesotans, including Krystyna, who traveled to Manchester for Skrowaczewski's first Thursday series concert with the Hallé Orchestra (the equivalent of an American opening subscription concert).[15] Although Skrowaczewski modestly described their trip to support him as "one of the very unimportant things for them" to do during their visit, he was very touched by the gesture.[16] Judy and Ken Dayton organized the trip for the group that included former MOA past presidents and board members and other friends of the Skrowaczewskis.

This demonstration of support impressed Clive Smart, the secretary and general manager of the Hallé:

> When Stan came to do his first concert in Manchester as principal conductor, just about all the senior members of the board of the Minnesota Orchestra turned up at the concert. That impressed me to no end because I can't imagine the Hallé board doing the same going the other way! The Minneapolis people were so pro-Stan, so enthusiastic for him, and so pleased that he'd come to Manchester and the Hallé. And what impressed me was that this was five years after he'd left the Minnesota Orchestra as its music director. That spoke volumes to me about his time in Minneapolis. It was a great and moving occasion.

Skrowaczewski turned to his favorite pairing of Bruckner and Mozart—Piano Concerto no. 26 (*Coronation*), played by Alicia de Larrocha—for his auspicious opening concert. "Manchester has not lacked fine Bruckner interpretations in the past forty years (Barbirolli and James Loughran were both frequent performers of the Austrian master's works), and this was one of the finest," wrote Michael Kennedy. "Rarely has [Bruckner's Seventh] seemed so short, not because of rushed tempi but because the composer's logic, so often disguised, was presented in clear and impressive terms."[17]

Skrowaczewski's performance of the Seventh Symphony also benefited from a complete reconfiguration of the Hallé Orchestra's set-up. In an effort to combat the poor acoustics of Free Trade Hall, he used his preferred arrangement, placing the first and second violins together on his left side. This arrangement is typical in America, but in Europe the second violins often are separated from the firsts and placed on the right side.

Skrowaczewski's introductory letter to his new audience revisited themes of his writings for the Minnesota Orchestra but also presented his views on programming specifically geared toward his new public. He wrote, "A concert hall becomes a temple where music leads us gradually from the secular life into the realm of the extraordinary." He continued:

> Many people, I believe, would agree with this Schopenhauerian attitude but will say: "It depends on the program!" Certainly, there is music that holds us in enchantment and awe by its superior imagination, logic, beauty, and metaphysical ideas. And there is also music that is banal, second-hand, and flatly inspired. Fortunately, studying Hallé programs of the last fifty or more

years, I am pleased to tell you that I have found them really very good, exciting, innovative, and rich, almost making it more difficult for me to develop them in the future, adding something that is my own. Of course, I will try to do so gradually, when your response will feed my imagination.

Great music is timeless, and great composers of the past are as relevant to us as they ever were—even more so in our troubled times, when this relevance becomes an idealization of what mankind can aspire to. But this greatness of the past should not tyrannically overshadow the great composers of our time. There is also timeless music being written nowadays, only, as I said before, this music is not given to us on the golden platter of centuries of appraisals. We have to seek it individually with all our faith, doubt, and premonition.

Strangely enough, these great composers of our century, whose relevance to our times is obvious, cast a mystical light on the past, and acting retrospectively in time, bring out, underline, and enlighten the greatest values of the past music, which otherwise may happen to be forgotten or taken for granted. (Listen to a Mozart work between some Stravinsky, Britten, or Berg, and you may hear a different Mozart!)

There is one more point to my address, just to tell you how happy and excited I am to be here with this fine orchestra to play for you.[18]

To celebrate her husband's opening Hallé concert, Krystyna hosted a special dinner at the Midland Hotel in Manchester for the Minnesota visitors and some Hallé administrators. The Midland Hotel became Skrowaczewski's second home during his Hallé years.

His twelve-week commitment to the Hallé generally was divided into four periods of three weeks or four weeks with tours. Guest-conducting obligations meant that he was away from home for longer than at any point in his career. Krystyna did not accompany her husband when he was in Manchester:

I really didn't care for that area. Manchester is not a particularly attractive city. It is very industrial, and it didn't have much of anything except the wind at that time. There were some lovely women connected with the board of the orchestra that I enjoyed meeting and spending time with, but overall there was not the same kind of community of friends for me that existed with the Minnesota Orchestra. I also had trouble with their Mancunian style of English. I often couldn't understand a word they were saying. So Stan left, and I didn't go with him, which was probably a little selfish of me, but I had a job here: I had these boys. My sons were in high school, and I wanted to be here all the time. Also, whenever Stan went away I did some remodeling because he does not like to be disturbed when he is home studying and composing. All Stan does is conduct. Everything else needs to be taken care of, so that's what I did.

During one of Krystyna's rare U.K. trips, she got her husband out of the city for a weekend trip to the Lake District, Britain's largest national park, located ninety minutes from Manchester. Rain foiled their attempt to reach the park's summit, and on their drive back to their cottage on a country road, they encountered another impediment, a large flock of sheep blocking the muddy road. Skrowaczewski thought if they would just shift to one side he could get by, so he got out of his car and began directing them to move. When the shepherd's dog began barking, Krystyna quickly apologized to the man: "I'm sorry, my husband is a conductor who conducts everything, even sheep!"

Back home in Wayzata, she was busy tending to her own "sheep." Paul and Nicholas, ages sixteen and fourteen when their father undertook his Hallé position, had developed their own interests in rock and pop music. Growing up, both boys had strong reactions toward the music that was often played around the house, mostly recordings—but also occasional wisps of piano music, "very isolated, sparse events," recalled Nicholas of the sound of their father composing.

"They both took piano lessons and for one summer Suzuki violin, but we never pushed them into music," Krystyna said. "However, they loved it. They played records and conducted! I have a picture of Nicholas conducting in his yellow sleeper—he was probably five, standing on a chair and conducting Stravinsky's *The Rite of Spring*. Stan said they had good taste in music!"

The Rite of Spring fascinated both boys. Paul was obsessed with it, and the masterpiece caused a visceral reaction in Nicholas, as he related:

> When I was about age five, my dad was intrigued by my curiosity about this music, so he brought me into his studio and put on his record of *The Rite of Spring*. I had a really intense reaction to it. I was utterly charged up by the music, and I became really excited. "Louder, louder," I asked, and my parents looked at me with some concern. "Okay, that's enough for now," they said, but I was adamant that I wanted it louder. I was possessed by it. It was unlike any other experience I had had. I also enjoyed Copland; his music was cinematic to me. From age four on, I loved Ravel. When I was five, my dad promised to give me his new boxed set of Ravel records if I could ride my bike without training wheels. It worked, because I couldn't wait to get my hands on these records!

About the time the boys discovered The Beatles' *Sgt. Pepper's Lonely Hearts Club Band* and *The White Album* at ages seven and nine, they also became enamored of the "weird" records in their father's collection. "Paul and I were crazy about Jacob Druckman's piece *Animus III*, for clarinet and tape," Nicholas recalled. "And we began to connect this kind of obscure electronic music with the tape techniques used by George Martin on *Sgt. Pepper*, which was influenced by Stockhausen, whose records were also in my dad's collection. My mom was somewhat of a fan of swing music and 1950s and 1960s French *chansons*, so that was all in our listening experiences, too."

During their elementary-school years the brothers took piano lessons. Nicholas continued a few years longer than his brother but stopped in his early teens. "I put all the sheet music in a drawer," he remembered. "I wanted to just look at the keys and improvise." The brothers enjoyed making their own music. As children they used pots and pans for a makeshift drum set in their bedroom. Later they recorded impromptu songs and created imaginary bands, band logos, and plans for stage shows, activities they continued into their preteen years. "By the time we were in junior high school," said Nicholas, "we were very excited by the notion of a rock band. It was more compelling than being a violin player in an orchestra. We were taken by the whole gestalt of rock music, its presentation." Paul became enraptured with early 1980s New Wave, British pop and punk music, particular a band called Japan. Nicholas also loved that group's records, which led him to the music of Japanese pop star Ryuichi Sakamoto of the Yellow Magic Orchestra.

By the time the brothers were in high school they played instruments together. "Paul started playing guitar and keyboards, and I played drums," said Nicholas, "so we had an instant band. Instead of playing after-school sports, we were setting up gigs around the city." Joined by friends, they created their first band, Blue World.

Paul remembered, "I think in high school, with the first bands, my dad was secretly happy that we were doing something with music, playing instruments, and improving. He didn't overtly make a huge point to say, 'This is great! Go for it!' because he didn't really understand the kind of music we liked."

Skrowaczewski, however, was curious about his boys' music. Both sons recalled an instance when their father offered musical advice. Paul explained the interaction:

> We would have jam sessions at our house. One day I remember, my dad came down, and he just stood there watching. He didn't look particularly happy. He said, "Now, I have an idea about this." We followed him into his studio, and without even testing it on the piano, he played it in the right key (that's his perfect pitch coming in). He said, "OK, this is fine, but why don't you try doing it this way?" He took what was a simple IV-V chord progression and added some pretty sophisticated passing chords, introducing some unusual notes. Then with his right hand he started to play a very fast, kind of sophisticated melody on top of that. It completely changed the nature of the piece from a synthesizer-pop kind of progression to something entirely different. I think Nick and I reacted, "Great, thanks very much," but we knew it would never fly with what we were doing. It was almost like a modern-jazz moment. In hindsight, it was actually very cool, but at the time we didn't really accept it or act on it. I remember at that moment being shocked that he wanted to get involved in that way. It was great, and we totally appreciated it.

"It was one of the coolest things I'd ever heard," remembered Nicholas. "Paul and I looked at one another, and our eyes got big. We almost burst out laughing because it was so fascinating. We walked away thinking, 'Wow, he really does have some extreme imaginative power when presented with any materials, even primitive New Wave pop. I still wish I could hear that again!'"

Krystyna had her hands full dealing with two teenage rock musicians: "They went through rebellious periods. I tried to encourage them to have their parties at home. I was really a single parent during this period. Stan was in England or on tours. I had to be stern with them myself sometimes."

"My poor mom had to deal with Nick and me in our rebellious phases," Paul said. "I'm sixteen and sneaking out of my window at night and running off with my friends until the wee hours and her not knowing where I was. Dealing with that and my dad and Nick. It's unbelievable that she survived!"

Krystyna also had Anna on her mind constantly. During their preteen years, Paul and Nicholas occasionally saw their sister during visits and some meals at restaurants. Anna's trips became less frequent as she grew older; it was more difficult for her caregivers to take her outside the home where she lived. As the years passed, Paul and Nicholas became involved in their own worlds, and Krystyna often visited Anna alone.

Though Skrowaczewski's Hallé position was divided into segments, with more than forty concerts spread over eight months, he felt as if he were living in Britain. Despite his desire to escape some directorship responsibilities, he nevertheless invested the time and energy necessary to make an imprint on his new orchestra.

A few months after Skrowaczewski took the helm of the Hallé Orchestra, a piece in the *Journal of the Hallé Concerts Society* described the general impression he had made on his musicians and observers of the orchestra:

> "Skroffy," they've dubbed him in the orchestra. Or sometimes, "Stan the Stick." It is a sign of their affection and certainly not of any lack of respect for the new boss. On the contrary, Stanisław Skrowaczewski is the sort of man you cannot help but like and admire. He takes his music seriously, always doing his homework thoroughly, but with this seriousness he couples a charm, a sense of humor, and a modest politeness that makes him special. He is neither extrovert nor showman. He puts the music first, though he certainly cares about the musicians and the audience. He makes demands on both, but only because he believes in trying to achieve high standards—and wide-ranging attitudes—of playing and appreciation.[19]

The maestro was equally taken with the orchestra. The number of concerts in different locations with limited rehearsal time—to which the Hallé had been accustomed over the years—amounted to a grueling schedule at less than first-rate compensation. Skrowaczewski was "honored and enticed by the fact that the orchestra" had chosen him.[20] "They are very quick, highly intelligent, responsible, attentive to detail, and full of goodwill towards me," he said.[21]

He recalled a particularly memorable week during his second season that was emblematic of the Hallé musicians' commitment:

> Monday to Sunday, we had six concerts on consecutive days in London, and scores of other places on the way back to Manchester. We played big works, like Bruckner's Ninth, Mahler's Sixth, also Berg's Seven Early Songs, and Mozart's *Prague* Symphony. Day after day, a different program with only a one-hour warm-up rehearsal before each concert. The orchestra had played

these works earlier with me, but this schedule still put great demands on them and myself, from day-to-day travel, hotels, irregular meals, and short rehearsals. I was amazed by the concentration and the responsibility of the orchestra; even under the worst conditions they would focus and play a very good concert. There was never any slacking off. It was very rewarding to me.

During Skrowaczewski's early years with the Hallé, the artistic atmosphere and goodwill of the musicians and administration was outstanding, much like his early years in Minneapolis. To some degree the Hallé Orchestra and the Minnesota Orchestra shared similar attributes: a storied history and a problematic concert hall, a regional standing, and the hindrance of being overshadowed by other orchestras. The Hallé was one of five major orchestras outside of London; the others included the Royal Liverpool Philharmonic, Bournemouth Symphony, Scottish National Symphony, and the City of Birmingham Symphony Orchestra. Additionally, the BBC Philharmonic also toured the region and performed regularly in Manchester. Like the Hallé, these orchestras had relatively new principal conductors whose appointments began about the same time. Thanks largely to Barbirolli, the Hallé had been the leader of the pack throughout the 1950s and 1960s. Now the orchestra was poised for another Barbirolli-like era of greatness, and the musicians, audiences, and critics sensed its potential.

Skrowaczewski—who only met the celebrated British maestro once, briefly in Italy in the early 1960s—was prepared to build his new orchestra as he had his former ensemble. Given the positive atmosphere in Manchester, he hoped to exceed his Minneapolis achievements. The orchestra and Skrowaczewski found themselves quickly trying to adjust to one another's expectations:

> Some German orchestras have all week to rehearse a program. In Hamburg they have four to five hours every day. This is way too much time. In England it was very different because they are not well paid. Their whole system was to have very condensed rehearsals—and few. This was more economical financially, so generally I learned to rehearse as quickly as possible, concentrating on the most necessary elements. Musically I worked the same way as in Minneapolis, but it was all much faster in Manchester.

> One aspect I wanted to improve was the orchestra's preparation before the first rehearsals of a new program. In the beginning they didn't really do it because they often didn't have time, always running from concert to concert with their crazy schedule. But they are great readers, so they got by if they were playing a familiar work. Eventually I think I convinced several first players and leaders in the orchestra to look at their parts ahead of time, to check my bowings, etc., especially with music new to them. So this is one thing I tried to change, and it was positively taken. Otherwise, I couldn't find any other way to work.

Violinist Peter Worrell—who began with the Hallé in 1962, played during Barbirolli's last eight seasons, and remained with the ensemble until 1998—described the standards Skrowaczewski brought to the orchestra:

When Stan first came to the orchestra, he was very strict. I have a feeling that he had come with visions of George Szell, and he felt that a conductor should dominate the orchestra. In lots of ways he didn't allow us the freedom that perhaps we'd been used to under Jimmy [Loughran]. Stan imposed his own control. The details of performance and in rehearsal are everything to him. In an English orchestra, when things get difficult, everyone's inclined to laugh. That is a natural reaction for us. I don't know if in the States it is done, but if things go wrong here, to get through it, everyone ends up laughing. But Stan never understood that; he used to get annoyed with us. He would say, "I don't know how you can laugh when there is so much work to be done!"

He came with an uncompromising, rigorous approach to standards, and in many ways I think he changed the sound of the Hallé. In some respects, the actual sound had not really changed since Barbirolli's tenure. Jimmy [Loughran] brought his own gifts, but I think things went in a new direction when Stan came; it was maybe less romantic, a cleaner sound. I certainly remember I practiced like mad when he first came.

Raising artistic standards is never easy. The Hallé musicians were ready and eager for Skrowaczewski's influence, but there were challenges, as Clive Smart explains:

Stan is such a profound musician and very sincere gentleman. He understood a lot of the problems orchestral musicians face, and he got on very well with a lot of the players. One of his problems—if it was a problem—was that English orchestras are quite different from American orchestras. I think conductors in America have got to be a bit more militant against the union than in England, so it was difficult for him initially to sort of settle with the orchestra. But he knew exactly what he wanted, and he did a tremendous amount of very good work with us. He greatly increased the artistic standards of the Hallé, and the press during his time shared that opinion.

One of the maestro's early ideas—to assess the orchestra in order to make improvements—was met with surprise and some resentment from musicians, as he recalled:

Artistically they became better and better. At one point I maybe asked a little too much from them, in the sense of what is normal in England, because they have a very strong union. I wanted to hear them all separately, especially the strings, to hear how they played individually and to check their seating placement. This was a big offense to the musicians at the beginning. Some played, and some did not. This was risky from my side. They were a little surprised but not hostile, and they said, "Listen, this is not done in England. Our union would be very much against this action, and we wouldn't do it because the other players in other orchestras would be unhappy that something like this happened." This was my move to improve the orchestra, to know where the weak points were and how to treat them. You can imagine, it was an unpleasant and dangerous job and can hardly be possible today because of unions. But in spite of certain tensions and animosities during the first years, during my last years they came back with great appreciation for me. Our last tours to the States and South America were outstanding.

The Hallé musicians worked to please their new conductor, and the re-audition situation was resolved amicably—it didn't happen. Although Skrowaczewski's standards dismayed some musicians, they also enjoyed the benefits of his work, as Worrell relates:

> I remember doing a standard repertoire piece, like Beethoven Five, with Stan, and it became a different piece. The verve, the freshness, and the exhilaration in the first movement were stunning, and this experience was *after* his time as principal conductor. He did Beethoven's Third and said, "This is a 'shocking' piece!" And it was fantastic. He brought new insights, and it did become a "shocking" piece. I think [that] in his own way Stan was always searching for new things. He has a tremendous intellectual grasp of all the works that he conducts. He has both a composer's insight and a conductor's, with such a command of the form, textures, and articulations, and the color of everything. Instinctively you realize that he knows every note of the score.

Skrowaczewski's first season with the Hallé was widely hailed as an artistic triumph, but the orchestra struggled financially. Along with box office receipts, the Hallé—like most British orchestras—largely depended on the financial support of the Arts Council of Great Britain, whose funding of the orchestra was particularly weak then. Additionally, the Greater Manchester Council, which also had partly subsidized the Hallé since 1974, was abolished in 1985, leaving the financially strapped Manchester City Council to help alleviate the shortfall. Nationwide inflation greatly complicated the situation, as Skrowaczewski recalled:

> At the time, Great Britain had horrible problems with inflation, with union strikes, etc., and everything in the country was uneven until Mrs. Thatcher came and started to regulate British life. But the same Mrs. Thatcher also started a completely new conservative politics with art institutions such as orchestras. She said, "Well, we have to start the American way. They must be supported by private sponsors."

Founded in 1940 as The Committee for the Encouragement of Music and the Arts, the Arts Council of Great Britain originally provided financial assistance to cultural organizations that were struggling during World War II. The committee soon became a council funded by the government. After the war it was incorporated and named the Arts Council of Great Britain, whose goal was to "develop accessibility to and greater knowledge, understanding, and practice of the fine arts."[22] The government continued to subsidize the council. The Treasury oversaw its grant until the mid-1960s, when the Department of Education and Science assumed that responsibility. Soon afterward the council's mission was broadened educationally: it would advise the organizations it supported, opening the door for a more subjective distribution of funds.[23]

Robert Beale, author of *The Hallé: A British Orchestra in the 20th Century*—an extensive study of the history of the orchestra's musical and financial administration—titled his chapter on the Arts Council "Music's Meddlesome Friend." In it he details the council's sometimes-questionable actions towards and precarious relationships with organizations it is charged with supporting.[24]

During the 1970s, England's major regional orchestras enjoyed a strong period of council funding and excellent audience numbers. As inflation increased during the 1980s, however, these orchestras began to struggle, and the council's funding levels did not keep up with rising costs. Another thorny issue also surfaced—the parity of council funding for regional orchestras.[25] Four years before Skrowaczewski's tenure began, the Hallé Committee complained to the council that the Royal Liverpool Philharmonic and the City of Birmingham Symphony Orchestra received more funding than its orchestra, and as a result the Hallé decreased the adventuresome nature of its programming. By 1983 the British government drastically cut its support of the council, which in turn invested its more limited resources in smaller projects, contemporary music, and innovative organizations like the City of Birmingham Symphony Orchestra, which was thriving under the charismatic and widely publicized leadership of Sir Simon Rattle.[26]

In early 1985, during Skrowaczewski's first season, the Hallé hired a marketing officer for the first time in its history. Clive Smart, the person charged with this responsibility, faced the difficult challenge of reducing the orchestra's deficit. Except for the Hallé's popular series, audience attendance in Manchester and in London had fallen to below seventy percent.[27]

Although he supported Skrowaczewski's efforts to raise the orchestra's artistic standards, Smart also had to answer to its board members. They believed that audiences would be more selective in attending concerts, given the U.K.'s current economic situation, and therefore programming had to "ensure that each concert has the maximum appeal."[28] That directive, combined with a call for less rehearsal time, more concerts, and other impediments to the orchestra's progress, was not taken well by Skrowaczewski, who promptly wrote Smart about his assessment of the Hallé's situation:

> No amount of work and dedication on my part (not mentioning the financial sacrifices caused by the fall of the pound) will suffice if there will be cuts in rehearsals, restrictions in filling vacancies by top players, and less frequent competitive exposure on the London market. Also, the box office appeal can increase not only by playing (under-rehearsed) well-known "warhorses" but also by imaginative programs, and *above all*—though over a longer period of time—by the highest level of performances.
>
> Until now, I cherished the faith that intensive work with the orchestra in a favorable climate will produce artistic results not only satisfactory and exciting to me and to the orchestra musicians, but also to the audiences and to the pride of the city and the entire region. I still hope that the necessary "in-depth" discussions between you, the board of directors, and myself will reaffirm the goals we all set at the very beginning.

> I will do my utmost to meet the demands of the directors. However, I cannot totally sacrifice my beliefs, aims, and hopes that brought me to Manchester.[29]

He was willing to help the Hallé's troubled financial state by making some compromises, mainly in the area of programming, but he had his limits. He quickly dismissed the notion of reducing the orchestra's size, for example, but he agreed to cap the number of star soloists and guest conductors, albeit reluctantly.

During Skrowaczewski's first year with the Hallé, the orchestra's most famous guest soloist, Isaac Stern, played the Brahms Violin Concerto on concerts that included Honegger's Symphony no. 2 and Messiaen's *Et exspecto resurrectionem mortuorum*. Critics hailed the programming and performances as among the best and most important of the maestro's first season. Wrote Michael Kennedy, "It was a revelation at these concerts to hear music of our time interpreted by a conductor to whom its syntax and prosody are not merely an exotic vocabulary but everyday language."[30] Messiaen's music, however, was not "everyday language" for most of Manchester's conservative listeners, who merely tolerated the French composer's dense piece.

The maestro's artistic life outside of Manchester during the 1984–85 concert season remained busy and rich. During his annual Minnesota appearance, he premiered Concerto for Violin and Orchestra by Lloyd Ultan, then director of the University of Minnesota School of Music and an expert on electronic and computer music as well as early music. He composed his concerto for Young-Nam Kim, a faculty colleague who became an important advocate for new music in the Twin Cities. The Chamber Music Society of Minnesota, which Kim founded in 1992, has featured Skrowaczewski's music on several programs over the years.

Of Skrowaczewski's typical assortment of engagements in the United States and Europe, his return to Juilliard in March 1985 was the most satisfying. That visit is the subject of a chapter in Judith Kogan's book *Nothing but the Best: The Struggle for Perfection at the Juilliard School*, published in 1987. The following excerpts capture Skrowaczewski's method of working with the Juilliard Orchestra and other elite student ensembles over the years:

> "As always," he said, his Polish accent laced with traces of American and British, "I'm looking forward very much to this orchestra. So let's begin with, how do they call it, '2-0-0-1.'" This was a reference to the film *2001: A Space Odyssey*, the Hollywood extravaganza that imprinted the *Zarathustra* opening on the American public's consciousness. The orchestra cracked up. They had been ready to play, taut like a stretched elastic. The *2001* reference released some of the tension but none of the drive....
>
> And so it went. The energy never flagged, the momentum never broke. Every rehearsal was as charged as the first two.... Word about the miracle in Room 309 spread. Even students who were not in the orchestra started coming to rehearsals, standing or sitting on the bridge chairs set up across the back and sides of the room. The pieces were getting to the point where they seemed to be playing themselves. Rehearsals became more and more rewarding. A horn

player commented on how much Skrowaczewski seemed to enjoy himself on the podium. A violinist said that orchestra might even be fun if someone like Skrowaczewski conducted all the time…. [After the rehearsal] people tried to identify the quality that made them adore Skrowaczewski….

He was a gentleman. Never in the six rehearsals was there a nasty or sarcastic word, never an angry mood. He was respectful of the players. When they made mistakes, he smiled and said, "O.K., let's start again." He explained what he wanted clearly. The orchestra responded by playing well. The orchestra always wants to play well for someone who shows respect. He was efficient in his rehearsal technique. Rehearsals never felt three hours long. He lulled the players into having a good time. He didn't lecture and didn't rehearse the life out of pieces. He started rehearsals by saying what he planned to cover. At the beginning of one *Eroica* rehearsal he asked the orchestra what they thought needed work. "Fugato," came a chorus. He zeroed in on problems and criticized them in positive terms. He never dwelled on a point. Some conductors over-rehearse a troublesome portion. Skrowaczewski let trouble spots rest after he worked on them. Or he went back to them in another rehearsal. Everyone knew what needed to be cleaned up. He let the musicians play. His gestures were clear but left the players breathing room. They were aimed at the big picture, the grand architecture of Strauss and Beethoven, but were always clear and precise. The players were awed.

He seemed to be there, first and foremost, to make music. He seemed to place the music ahead of himself and ahead of the orchestra. He conducted without mannerism. At Juilliard Orchestra rehearsals, when an instrument has a solo lick in the middle of a piece, the orchestra registers approval by stamping and shuffling feet. Skrowaczewski didn't seem annoyed by the ruckus, but he ignored it, as if it wasted time. As if the point were making music, not massaging egos….

At 3:55 p.m., with five minutes left to the rehearsal, Skrowaczewski put his baton on his stand and motioned to indicate that he had some final words before the concert. "Thank you," he said. "It's wonderful for me in my professional career to get to work with people who are so passionate about their music making. Thank you." There was silence for a split second. Then the orchestra broke loose. They started clapping, whistling, stamping, and hooting as they did at the end of every rehearsal, but this time they wouldn't stop. Appreciative clapping goes on for just so long. This went far beyond that. The orchestra's feeling for Skrowaczewski had gone beyond appreciation to love.[31]

A few months after his Juilliard experience, he led twelve concertos over three nights with six different pianists. He enjoyed the challenge of conducting the finals of the Seventh Annual Van Cliburn International Piano Competition in Fort Worth, Texas. He was flexible in interpretation and met the soloists' needs. He had developed this ability over decades of working with soloists and from his experiences leading the finals of the Chopin International Competition in Poland in 1949 and 1955.

Skrowaczewski's musical workout in Fort Worth prepared him well for dealing with six soloists over two concerts at his Mostly Mozart Festival debut in Avery Fisher Hall in August. His collaborators were well-seasoned artists: Alicia de Larrocha, Richard Stoltzman, and first-chair wind players for Mozart's *Symphonie Concertante* (in a realization by Robert Levin). One concert opened with Skrowaczewski's arrangement of Rameau's *Concerts en Sextuor*, which prompted perceptive comments from *The New York Times'* Bernard Holland:

> Mr. Skrowaczewski began the evening with a suite of dances from Rameau's *Concerts en Sextuor* which the conductor himself chose and arranged for a modern string ensemble. It is the kind of adaptive updating that our new age of period instruments and performance practices regularly disowns, but with the early-music movement now so strong and pervasive, it seemed suddenly fresh and unusual—indeed rebellious in its rejection of the new status quo. One had almost the feeling that Handel-Harty, Bach-Stokowski—and Rameau-Skrowaczewski—may no longer be the anachronism they were a few years ago but in fact members of a coming avant-garde. How strange it is to watch the musical cycle take another turn.[32]

Skrowaczewski began his second season at the helm of the Hallé Orchestra with major shifts in his artistic management, which he believed no longer served him well. At the start of 1985 he terminated his nearly twenty-year collaboration with Glotz, who expressed disappointment, admiration for Skrowaczewski's talent, and protestations that he had been working hard on his behalf. He partially withdrew the termination by having Glotz continue as his representative in France for several more years. Stephen Lumsden, who studied bassoon, piano, and conducting at the Guildhall School of Music, founded Intermusica Artists' Management in London in 1981. By 1985 he was already handling Skrowaczewski's British engagements and soon became his European general manager.

Skrowaczewski also ended his relationship with Wilford and Columbia Artists. "I feel there has been a lack of communication between us for some time," he wrote Wilford, "and with all due respect and admiration for your position, I am sure you can and will understand mine."[33] More than a month later he received a response from Wilford:

> First, let me wish you good luck in all that you do. I do, however, want to make some observations. I have worked for you for a very long time; you left us once and then asked us to manage you again. I became angry at lunch one day, and since that time you and I have had very little contact; however, I have seen you on occasion.

> The one positive observation is that your career now is better than it has ever been—a lot of which is because of the activities of this office: New York Philharmonic, Philadelphia Orchestra, and San Francisco. It seems to me that you are making this move at just the wrong time.

I can tell you that perhaps you can find a different atmosphere in a different office, but you certainly will not find another office that works for you as efficiently as this one. We are all a bit older, and I would not want you in a more difficult position as the years go on.[34]

However, Skrowaczewski believed that the time for the break had arrived. He had been delegated to Wilford's assistant almost exclusively since returning to Columbia, and he was dissatisfied with the inconsistency of his American engagements. Due to changes in leadership and perhaps lack of interest, Skrowaczewski had fallen off the guest-conductor short list for some of the nation's top orchestras. Without the influential Wilford's support, this situation wasn't likely to change. Upon leaving Columbia, the maestro moved to ICM Artists, headed by Stuart Warkow, to handle his American engagements.

Skrowaczewski's programming throughout his first Hallé season had been relatively conservative, limited by works already scheduled, but his second season—the Hallé's 128th—bore his stamp. Indeed, the programs were perhaps "the most important for years," as Michael Kennedy described the season in his preview for the orchestra's 1985–86 yearbook.[35] "An attractive season, I think, with something for all tastes," Kennedy wrote. "Above all, a well-planned season, planned by a man, not a computer in Cross Street. Now it's up to you, the audience. Pack the hall and show that Manchester needs the Hallé as much as the Hallé needs Manchester!"[36] It was a clarion call only partially answered.

The thoughtfully crafted programs—only fourteen percent of which included living composers—did not attract people as much as had been hoped.[37] Audiences were particularly choosy, given inflation and ticket costs. Concerts with soloists such as Anne-Sophie Mutter, André Watts, and Nigel Kennedy, and with music by Beethoven, Brahms, and the like did well, but programs with atypical juxtapositions went half sold. On one such program Skrowaczewski included Mozart's Adagio and Fugue in C minor, Bach's *Magnificat* (a first for the Hallé), Hindemith's Music for Brass and Strings, and Ravel's *La Valse*. On another program he paired Mozart's Piano Concerto no. 25 with Bruckner's Ninth Symphony.

One of the season's most artistically substantive events proved to be the most divisive for the audience. Engaging seventy-three-year-old Witold Lutosławski to conduct a concert of his own music, which he seldom did, was a major coup for the Hallé. Lutosławski, among the artists in Poland who participated in a cultural boycott during the martial-law period of 1981 to 1985, did not resume musical activities until the free elections in 1989.

Lutosławski's concert in Manchester generated much debate among concertgoers. One audience member declared, "We were most stimulated and as the concert progressed began to wish that there might be more! It was obvious that the orchestra enjoyed playing and working with such a delightful man." Another complained, "For the only time in fifty-four years' attendance at Hallé Concerts and [as] a season-ticket holder for forty of those years, I left the hall at the interval and was not surprised to witness several other patrons doing likewise."[38]

A two-week tour of major cities in Austria and Germany gave the Hallé its first international outing with its new maestro. All twelve concerts were hits, including two programs in Vienna's Musikverein Grosser Saal, the Brucknerhaus in Linz, and in halls in Bayreuth and Munich. Adding to the tour's success was Skrowaczewski's soloist, the Austrian pianist Rudolf Buchbinder. The pair resonated musically and remained collaborators for more than twenty years. Skrowaczewski recalled the tour:

> Rudy Buchbinder played Brahms' First Piano Concerto, and I played Bruckner's Third Symphony in Munich. For publicity the Germans gave Rudy a new Mercedes sports car for his touring. I remember I traveled in his car from Munich to Cologne. This car could go up to 180 mph, and in Germany you can drive without a speed limit unless they are marked. It was an extraordinary car, so we went with the greatest speed. He was a witty and pleasant companion and a beautiful pianist.

In 2004, during an engagement with Skrowaczewski and the Minnesota Orchestra, Buchbinder reflected on their collaborations:

> At our rehearsals [Beethoven's Piano Concerto no. 3 with the Minnesota Orchestra in 2004] you could see that he doesn't need much time to rehearse. We had just one rehearsal without even any intermission. You have to breathe the music the same way, and articulate and phrase together. If you don't breathe together, it will never work. Even twenty rehearsals will not make it work. With too many rehearsals you begin to make compromises, and for me it is absolutely forbidden to make any kind of compromise in music, in any kind of art. You have to be true to your intent.

The maestro's own lack of compromise in certain artistic areas strongly characterizes his accomplishments and independence. In an article entitled "Not Completely Satisfied," published in the *Manchester Evening News* in fall 1985, John Robert-Blunn describes a scene that illustrates Skrowaczewski's determination:

> After welcoming me with a firm, warm handshake in the lounge of his hotel, Stanisław Skrowaczewski guided me to the luxurious armchairs.... When we were sitting comfortably, he began by inviting me to have anything I wanted. "Tea, coffee, a drink? Some food perhaps?" Coffee would be fine, I said, and when the waiter came I ordered it. Skrowaczewski asked him what sort of coffee. "Nescafé, sir," was the reply. "Do you have orange juice?" Yes, either those little yellow perils or a diluted cordial. "No, no, I would like freshly crushed oranges in a large glass. No ice," said Skrowaczewski. "Can you do that?" Yes they could, but it would take ten minutes. Inspired by this example, I changed my order from coffee to freshly crushed oranges, with ice. It did take ten minutes for them to arrive (both with ice, which

Skrowaczewski politely had taken away and returned without ice). But in half that time I had learned what makes him so successful. Politeness combined with quiet determination to get what he wants, whether it be fresh orange juice or excellence from the Hallé Orchestra.[39]

To his last London appearance with the Hallé Orchestra in the 1985–86 season, Skrowaczewski brought a program of Mozart's *Prague* Symphony and Mahler's towering Symphony no. 6, a work highly dependent on a conductor's sense of pacing and management of structure. "Here was an absolutely magnificent performance of Mahler's Sixth Symphony," noted *The Times*, "one which did justice to a great work and which also showed a thing or two to some London orchestras."[40]

Skrowaczewski's highest-profile engagement of the season was with the Berlin Philharmonic, which occurred immediately after he ended his Hallé season. The program featured Webern's Six Pieces for Orchestra, Prokofiev's Piano Concerto no. 2 with Mikhail Rudy, and Shostakovich's Symphony no. 1. This program was not as familiar to Karajan's Berlin as other repertory, but the ensemble played stunningly for Skrowaczewski.

He enjoyed his most accomplished season of conducting since leaving his post with the Minnesota Orchestra in 1979, but for a change his conducting did not overshadow his work as a composer. The 1985–86 season featured more performances of Skrowaczewski's compositions than any other, including two world premieres in just three weeks.

The Trio for Flute, Bassoon and Piano was released on an LP entitled *New Music from Minnesota*, on the Innova label of what was then the Minnesota Composers Forum. This album marked the first commercial recording of a Skrowaczewski chamber work. The composition also received its Philadelphia premiere by the Academy Trio (the three Philadelphia Orchestra musicians for whom it was composed). "The solidity of the construction and the luxuriance of the sound makes this work seem a recollection of romanticism rather than a vision of the future, yet nothing was nostalgic, nothing exalted the past," wrote Daniel Webster in *The Philadelphia Inquirer*.[41]

His new chamber piece, *Fantasie per Quattro* for Violin, Clarinet, Cello and Piano, received its premiere in June 1985. The Schubert Club of St. Paul commissioned the work and dedicated it to the Sewell and Hunter families. Four musicians from the two families (a father, daughter, mother, and son) gave the premiere performance.

Music at Night received its first New York performance, with Skrowaczewski conducting the Juilliard Orchestra, and a month later he led the piece with the Atlanta Symphony Orchestra. He also conducted his Rameau pieces with both the Dallas and San Francisco symphonies. Meanwhile, the maestro's orchestral arrangement of "The Star-Spangled Banner" received performances by professional and school orchestras throughout the United States.

However, the December 1985 issue of *Musical America* reported Skrowaczewski's most impressive composing achievements of the season:

> It is not often these days that a composer offers us two major premieres within a two-week span, let alone that he conducts two separate and world-renowned orchestras in these performances. But that is precisely what Stanisław Skrowaczewski did this season in introducing his Violin Concerto (with Norman Carol as soloist with the Philadelphia Orchestra) in mid-December, followed just after New Year's by the first performance of the Concerto for Orchestra by the Minnesota Orchestra. Since both performances were broadcast, the new works were heard by a much wider listenership than only those who were on hand in Philadelphia's Academy of Music and Minneapolis's Orchestra Hall.[42]

Considering Skrowaczewski's full schedule of guest conducting plus his first two seasons with Hallé, his output of chamber and orchestral compositions was remarkable. Out of necessity he had become adept at composing almost exclusively on the road, away from the sanctuary of his home studio. He exerted extraordinary self-discipline and forced himself to compose regularly, no matter where he found himself. "It's a matter of arranging your time and being willing to work as a composer in hotel rooms," he told a reporter about a month before finishing the Violin Concerto. "I find composing is refreshing and exhilarating and keeps me fresh for a concert—but it can be dangerous. Once, in Frankfurt, I was working on my Clarinet Concerto at the hotel, and I became so absorbed that I nearly missed the beginning of the concert."[43]

This method of composing is counterintuitive to Skrowaczewski's innate desire for long periods of isolation in order to create. He preferred to use his time on tour to deal with orchestration issues, although his concert activity sometimes inspired ideas for composing. He survived this intensive period simply by remaining focused on the work at hand. However, the pressure of writing two major orchestral works while meeting his heavy conducting obligations proved even too much for the tireless maestro. Both the Violin Concerto and Concerto for Orchestra had to be delayed.

After hearing Skrowaczewski's English Horn Concerto in Philadelphia in 1970, Norman Carol asked his old friend to compose something for him. Carol convinced Riccardo Muti to support the idea, and the Old York Road Committee provided the funds to commission the piece for the Philadelphia Orchestra. Originally scheduled to premiere during the 1983–84 season with Muti conducting, the Violin Concerto had a difficult birth. By summer 1983 Skrowaczewski had nearly completed the concerto, but when he met with Carol while conducting the Philadelphia Orchestra at The Robin Hood Dell, he decided that he didn't like anything about the work.

"I have good news and bad news," Skrowaczewski told Carol. "The good news is that I've finished most of the concerto. The bad news is [that] I don't like it, and I've thrown it in the garbage can." The news disappointed Carol, who had never asked a composer to write for him before and who had never premiered a violin concerto. When a new date was scheduled, Muti was unavailable. Skrowaczewski conducted the premiere, which coincidentally occurred during Carol's twentieth anniversary season as the Philadelphia Orchestra's concertmaster.

Carol jokingly referred to his piece as "an academy concerto" because Skrowaczewski composed part of it during the 1984–85 season, when he was a guest conductor with the Philadelphia Orchestra, locked up in the conductor's room with a piano at the Academy of Music. He finally finished the work at the end of July 1985, five months before its premiere.

Cast in three continuous movements, the twenty-minute concerto omits violins and trumpets from its instrumentation and bears Skrowaczewski's trademark use of wind and percussion instruments—a combined effect that contrasts wonderfully with the timbre of the solo violin. He also capitalized on the beautiful tone and romantic tendencies in his friend's playing by writing a lyrical four-note motif that presents itself in various forms throughout the piece. Playing his 1743 Guarneri del Gesù violin, Carol elegantly brought to life the concerto's qualities as described by program annotator Bernard Jacobson: "The predominant mood of the work is romantic, and the tone of its chromaticism is intimate rather than assertively expressionistic."[44] But Skrowaczewski also put technical demands on Carol. "I never practiced sevenths and ninths [intervals] when I was a kid," Carol said at the time of the premiere. "Now I'm having to practice them a lot."[45]

The use of a water gong in the Violin Concerto gave some comic relief to preparations for the world premiere. Before Skrowaczewski and the Philadelphia Orchestra headed to Carnegie Hall for the New York premiere, the percussion section added some levity to the final concert in Philadelphia. They placed goldfish in the tub of water used to create the water-gong effect. Skrowaczewski and Carol enjoyed a good laugh over the prank, although the maestro was concerned about the effect that the gong tone might have had on the defenseless little fish.

"The violin is being looked at again as a great singing instrument. It is no longer being beaten, plucked, forced, and squeezed," said Isaac Stern in *Time* magazine a few months after Skrowaczewski premiered his Violin Concerto.[46] Noting the "festival of new violin concertos" that debuted during the 1985–86 season, the article cataloged the stylistic differences among the works and their lyric commonalities, which was not the case, as Stern bemoaned, with violin works composed in the 1950s and 1960s. In addition to Skrowaczewski, four other American composers (Richard Wernick, Hugh Aitkens, Marc Neikrug, and William Bolcom) and Frenchman Henri Dutilleux had violin concerto premieres that season.

Skrowaczewski's concerto was well received by audiences, critics, and soloist Carol, although *Time* said the piece "lacks the strong stylistic profile that might have made it memorable."[47] Even the composer harbored misgivings about the work.

"I don't really like it," he admitted decades after he composed his Concerto for Violin and Orchestra (its official title). "Especially the first movement, and the second is a little too long. The third movement is quite good, effective and well written, but overall I'm not happy with the work. If I had time, I would revise a lot of things." He discarded a nearly completed version of the concerto and produced a new one on a tight deadline, a factor that contributed to his dissatisfaction. "Maybe with this haste in writing and my disappointment with my first efforts, it was hard to succeed."

He was too busy and unenthusiastic about the piece to revise it for its second and third performances, held in spring and summer 1988 with the Milwaukee Symphony and Philadelphia Orchestra, which he led with Carol as soloist. A year later Carol and Skrowaczewski also performed it with the Minnesota Orchestra. The concerto's only other performances were presented by German violinist Christiane Edinger in 1991 with the Saarbrücken Radio Symphony Orchestra and by Konstanty Andrzej Kulka with the Warsaw Philharmonic in 1992, both under Skrowaczewski's direction.

A week after the 1985 premiere of the Violin Concerto, Skrowaczewski was in rehearsals with the Minnesota Orchestra for the premiere of his Concerto for Orchestra. The genesis of the piece went back nearly as far as the Violin Concerto. In 1980 the orchestra asked Skrowaczewski to compose a commemorative piece for the tenth anniversary of the opening of Orchestra Hall. Ken and Judy Dayton, to whom the score is dedicated, funded the commission. Although Skrowaczewski had started the work by 1983, he could not finish it for the scheduled September 1984 premiere. By mid-September 1985, after working fourteen hours a day for nearly a month, he completed the piece. The next day he boarded a plane to Germany for an engagement with the Beethoven Orchester Bonn. A great weight was off his shoulders.

The world premiere fell on January 1, 1986. Cast in two movements, Concerto for Orchestra honors the musicians for whom Orchestra Hall was built, giving every section of the orchestra soloistic opportunities. The second movement, Adagio: *Anton Bruckner's Himmelfahrt* (The Ascension of Anton Bruckner), is a tribute to Skrowaczewski's most beloved composer. A few days before the premiere Skrowaczewski explained the basis for the title in an interview with the *St. Paul Pioneer Press*:

> "Himmelfahrt" is an imaginary German word coined by Skrowaczewski to suggest something of the ethereal quality he finds in Bruckner's grand finales. "First came the music, then the title," Skrowaczewski notes. "I don't know why it came to me. 'Himmelfahrt' does not exist in German, but I found it so nice I kept it."[48]

Inspired by *Siegfried's Rheinfahrt* (Siegfried's Rhein Journey), the prologue to Wagner's *Götterdämmerung*, Skrowaczewski loved the idea of honoring Bruckner in the second movement of his Concerto for Orchestra. "Wagner's *Rheinfahrt* is over ten minutes of gorgeous music in the *Ring Cycle*," he said. "*Himmel* means 'heaven' so I wanted a 'Himmelfahrt,' Heavenly Journey, for Bruckner."

In his review of the premiere, Michael Anthony summarizes views on the Concerto for Orchestra that are shared to this day by musicians and audiences familiar with the work:

> The concerto is a remarkable, striking, and surely profound composition that lingers in the memory. None of us here has heard the Violin Concerto yet. Even so, one leaps to the conclusion that the Concerto for Orchestra is Skrowaczewski's strongest work to date, certainly his most deeply felt. Perhaps, too, it is his most personal statement.
>
> At the end of the work, hearing the mighty Bruckner-like theme in the brasses poke through the busy cacophony of the entire orchestra—and the sweet tone of consolation that ensues—who can avoid seeing this as a statement from a man who has always seen music as a consoling, ennobling, transcendent force?[49]

Only Skrowaczewski's Symphony [2003] rivals the Concerto for Orchestra in emotional depth and personal expression. From the mid-1980s to the present, the Concerto for Orchestra has been his most-performed work and the one that moves musicians and audiences to recognize him as a composer of music that has lasting value.

With a reinvigorated compositional life and a thriving conducting career, the nearly sixty-five-year-old Skrowaczewski headed toward the late 1980s with the exuberance of a musician half his age. The notion of retirement never entered his mind.

TWENTY-SIX

TOURS DE FORCE

Finally, [the Hallé Orchestra] is making its first appearance in the United States…. It will be up to New Yorkers to greet a comparatively ancient English institution and decide whether they agree with the Financial Times' *judgment that Skrowaczewski has "transformed the Hallé Orchestra…. [He made it] technically surer and more alert than it has been in decades, enriched its sound, and provided "the special delight of…an orchestra which not only watches its conductor but also* listens to itself."

—Alistair Cooke

Skrowaczewski continued to instill pride in his Hallé Orchestra. The Hallé's 1986–87 season closed with Mahler's Ninth Symphony and soloist Anne-Sophie Mutter playing Mozart's last violin concerto. Among the most technically and musically challenging of all symphonies—and most transparent—the Ninth is a test on several levels for any orchestra and conductor. Karajan was seventy-four years old before he led his first performance of the mammoth symphony with the Berlin Philharmonic. Skrowaczewski had conducted the Ninth only twice before, with the Minnesota Orchestra. Although the orchestra had its technical problems here and there, this concert, according to David Murray of London's *Financial Times*, "established beyond question what has been suspected for some time: that Stanisław Skrowaczewski is leading the Hallé into a new Golden Age. They played Mozart very well; their Mahler was magnificent."[1] Noting that some listeners might find Skrowaczewski's Mahler unemotional, Michael Kennedy described the maestro's conducting of the fourth movement as a "genuinely noble and elevated account. It was moving in the best possible way, as an honest and deeply felt musical exposition of a masterpiece."[2]

Composers of new music programmed during the season included George Benjamin, Oliver Knussen, Baird, Penderecki, and Ellen Taaffe Zwilich. This repertoire complemented Skrowaczewski's signature balance of classical, romantic, postromantic, and early 20th-century masterworks. Although only sixteen percent of the programming featured works by living composers, he still faced an ultraconservative audience prone to avoid even standard 20th-century repertoire, a situation that frustrated him. When asked how he would woo the conservative public, he responded: "I ask them to open their minds, not to reject anything just because it is unfamiliar. Listen, and listen again—the man sitting next to you, he may be loving it. I believe the public will want to know what is being written now, to compare it with the past, to see how music has developed."[3] He was optimistic, but he hoped that Mancunians wouldn't take as long to accept his programming ideas as Minnesotans had.

Three important tours highlighted 1987 for Skrowaczewski. He led the Hallé Orchestra in its American debut on an eighteen-day tour covering twelve thousand miles, with concerts in Washington, D.C., New York City, Florida, and South Carolina. In the early summer he made history by leading the Juilliard Orchestra on its first Asian tour, and during the fall, with the Hallé Orchestra, he returned to Poland for the first time since 1981. The tour was only the orchestra's second visit to Poland.

Barbirolli long had dreamed of taking the Hallé to America. Tentative plans for a U.S. tour were made during the 1950s and 1960s, but without government funding it never happened. Corporate sponsorship—principally from Rolls Royce, Inc., British Airways, and American Airlines—plus Skrowaczewski's American connections and the strong will of Clive Smart and others made the Hallé's first U.S. tour a reality. "We took the decision this time that we would definitely go and then start raising the money," said Smart. "Our agent over there, ICM Artists, is also Skrowaczewski's agent, and the tour is at their risk. They have covered its costs."[4]

"Abbado is here with the Vienna Philharmonic. Rostropovich started his sixtieth-birthday celebrations with the New York Philharmonic, but the sweetest cheers I heard from Carnegie Hall were for the good old Hallé Orchestra making their New York debut," wrote Michael Owen in the *Evening Standard*.[5] The cheers for the Hallé's New York debut and first U.S. tour in its 128-year history were indeed heartfelt, given the orchestra's "scandalously late" date of finally making the journey, as Alistair Cooke wrote in a preview article in *The New York Times*.[6] Cooke was a Mancunian, longtime *Manchester Guardian* correspondent, famous author, and television personality as the host of PBS' *Masterpiece Theatre*. In a real coup for the Hallé, he wrote an expansive article about the orchestra's history to preview its American debut.

After a brilliant first concert at the Kennedy Center, the Hallé Orchestra made its New York debut in newly renovated Carnegie Hall. Bernard Holland of *The New York Times* bemoaned the standard touring program the orchestra played (Brahms' First Symphony and the Prokofiev Third Piano Concerto), but he appreciated the opening piece, Britten's *Sinfonia da Requiem*.[7] The choice of this small masterpiece paid fitting homage to Barbirolli, who conducted its world premiere with the New York Philharmonic in Carnegie Hall during his brief tenure as the Philharmonic's music director. (He had the truly unenviable task of following Toscanini as music director.)

Sinfonia da Requiem is one of Skrowaczewski's specialties; he perhaps had more success with it than with any other British composition. "He performed it better than anyone I can remember," noted Kennedy. "Stan had an affinity for that piece, which we played on our American tour," recalled Hallé violinist Peter Worrell. "It was a tremendous event to go to the U.S.A. I still have the thrill of being in Carnegie Hall and thinking about who had played there and the traditions. For Stan to take us there was completely wonderful."

Skrowaczewski was pleased with the triumphant tour, but his experience conducting in Carnegie Hall was not pleasant. The hall had been closed for nearly seven months while undergoing a $50 million renovation; it had been reopened for only three months when the Hallé Orchestra debuted there. "We played in the newly renovated Carnegie, and I was very unhappy. It had been a miracle hall," said Skrowaczewski. "It became louder, less balanced, with less crystal beauty, which had allowed the greatest *pianissimo* to the greatest *fortissimo* without distortion. It is still not like that anymore."

Complaints about the hall persisted unabated for nine years. Rumors alleged that concrete had been put under the stage and consequently affected the hall's overall resonance. Further modifications to the hall continued into the 1990s.

Finally, *The New York Times* reported in 2000 that "what was widely described as concrete was a fill material, a loose kind of mortar that existed in the original design. The loss of resonance listeners noticed…was more likely attributable to the new stage floor…"[8] Other changes made during the 1986 renovation and afterward likely affected the acoustics, such as the removal of the stage curtain, new offstage areas on both sides of the stage, a rebuilt stage extension, new fabric on the seats, and so on.

Despite Skrowaczewski's disappointment with the hall's acoustics, the Hallé's performance was well received, and the musicians were thrilled to add this milestone to their orchestra's history.

The Hallé received widespread critical acclaim in London and in other European cities. *The Times* described a concert of Tchaikovsky's Fourth Symphony as "one of the most exciting and physically and intellectually disciplined performances heard for a long time."[9] The same critic also noted the obvious lack of support for the Hallé: "It was one of those nights when it was almost painful to see the number of empty seats. The Hallé [Orchestra came] to London with no attendant hype, no part in neatly packaged series: their only heralds are the old-fashioned, ill-designed posters and, for those who have ears to hear, the name of Stanisław Skrowaczewski."[10]

The Hallé administration apparently lacked long- and short-term audience-development strategies for the orchestra's London concerts and, to some extent, even those in Manchester. Promoting Skrowaczewski presented a particular challenge. "Stan doesn't exactly sell himself to the public!" said Kennedy. "I always got the impression that he wouldn't mind much if there wasn't an audience there, as long as the music was going well. I think this is part of his character. He doesn't sell himself, and he doesn't have anyone blowing his trumpet, either."

"There was a feeling, not necessarily on my part, but a feeling generally within the organization, that Stan was difficult to market," said Stuart Robinson, deputy general manager during Skrowaczewski's tenure. "Stan's strengths are, without a shadow of a doubt, the musical integrity and real intellectual knowledge that he brings to the performances. I think integrity is the best word to describe his conducting, but it was felt he lacked charisma, to use a horrible word."

"There was some question when Stan was principal conductor about the way he communicated with an audience, that he was aloof and distant, and a lot of people did get that impression of him," said violinist Worrell. "I think you need to know Stan. Once you know him, all that disappears. He's so sensitive and courteous, and he's got such a warm personality."

The advent of a marketing-officer position during the first year of Skrowaczewski's tenure didn't help much. Marketing efforts failed to promote the orchestra's real selling point: its improved quality and artistically refined performances. This task is much harder than marketing a personality, a tactic so at odds with his artistic priorities.

"What comes through with Stan is his passion for the music," Kennedy said. "He puts it first above himself, above everything. He's too modest in a way. He has an aversion to self-promotion as well as to promotion by others if he doesn't approve of the way it's done." Smart observed that Skrowaczewski "felt that mainly the music should do the publicity. He's a very reserved gentleman, a little shy, and doesn't necessarily communicate well with a crowd."

"The British orchestras were always behind American orchestras in marketing and sponsorship deals," said Robinson. "Stan was never eager to meet sponsors after the concert and glad-hand people. He would do it, but he found it difficult."

Less than a week after the Hallé's American tour ended, Skrowaczewski was back in the United States fulfilling a two-week engagement with the New York Philharmonic. According to Tim Page in a review for *The New York Times*, "The New York Philharmonic was at its best Saturday night at Avery Fisher Hall when Stanisław Skrowaczewski conducted a program of Boccherini [Cello Concerto] and Bruckner [Symphony no. 3]."[11]

The concerts also reunited Skrowaczewski with pianist Krystian Zimerman, whose performances still created a stir. The fact that he was performing Brahms' Piano Concerto No. 2 added further interest: Deutsche Grammophon had just released new recordings of Brahms' concertos performed by Zimerman with Bernstein and the Vienna Philharmonic.

Skrowaczewski returned to New York City six weeks later to rehearse the Juilliard Orchestra in preparation for its historic Asian tour. During the first half of June, Skrowaczewski and the orchestra's 112 student musicians gave three concerts in Japan (Tokyo and Osaka), two in Hong Kong, and four in the People's Republic of China (Beijing, Shanghai, and Guangzhou). They made history as the first American conservatory orchestra to visit China after the Cultural Revolution ended.

Three months after the normalization of diplomatic relations between China and the United States in early 1979, the Boston Symphony Orchestra became the second major American orchestra to visit China since the Philadelphia Orchestra's first-ever tour there in 1973. By the time of the Juilliard Orchestra's tour in 1987, heads of state in both countries had made several reciprocal visits, and many cultural exchanges occurred. These continued until after the Tiananmen Square tragedy on June 4, 1989, when the United States abruptly ended trade relations with China and instituted sanctions in protest over the nation's human-rights violations.

Some of the Juilliard's star faculty (including renowned violin pedagogue Dorothy DeLay) joined the orchestra's tour to lead master classes at the foremost music schools in Tokyo, Beijing, and Shanghai. Juilliard's American Music Ensemble also performed.

Juilliard also featured two prominent student soloists: Wang Xiao-Dong, an extremely gifted seventeen-year-old Chinese violinist from Shanghai, and Midori, then a phenomenal fifteen-year-old Japanese violin prodigy. Less than a year before this tour Midori set the classical-music world abuzz with her 1986 Tanglewood debut with Bernstein. After breaking her E-string playing Bernstein's Serenade (after Plato's *Symposium*) for Solo Violin, Strings, Harp and Percussion, she borrowed the concertmaster's violin to proceed, as is customary in such situations. When the string broke again, she took the associate concertmaster's instrument and finished the piece with complete aplomb. Midori accomplished this astonishing feat using standard-size violins; she had been playing a child-size violin—seven-eighths the size of a normal instrument.[12]

During Juilliard's tour, Wang Xiao-Dong and Midori played Bartók's Violin Concerto no. 2 in their respective home countries. The orchestra also featured three other students in Haydn's Sinfonia Concertante in B-flat, op. 84. Strauss' *Don Juan*, Stravinsky's *The Rite of Spring*, Barber's *Medea's Meditation and Dance of Vengeance*, and Beethoven's *Eroica* Symphony rounded out the tour repertoire.

"Stan was absolutely fantastic," recalled Joseph Polisi, then in his third year as president of Juilliard. "He was always deeply committed to the music. He was very patient but also very demanding with the students." He continued:

> The tour was pretty arduous in its own way—touring China in 1987 was a little different than doing it in 2008. There were fewer joint-venture hotels, and we were the guests of the government, so we were not always in the best accommodations. I remember Stan not only conducting so extraordinarily well, but also when the orchestra started losing a little bit of tension in some of the performances, he called an extra rehearsal. He was very caring but also very professional, and the students could pick that up right away. He was just first-class, and he was also a great traveler.
>
> We were traveling internally, probably from Beijing to Shanghai on China Air, or whatever the airline was, and we were given this rather strange meal. When we looked at it, it was plastic-covered, and it included a little bird! Everybody around me, my wife and other colleagues, we're looking at this, and when we realized it was a little bird we thought, "Oh my goodness, how in the world could anyone eat this?" And then all of a sudden in front of us we hear this crunching sound, and it was Stan eating! I turned to him and said, "What do you think of the lunch?" And he said, "Very tasty, especially the little bird." So he was a real trooper. He was able to do anything, whenever or wherever we were.

"Stan mixed right in with the orchestra," said Louis Brunelli, associate dean of Juilliard. "He hung around with the kids. The rehearsals went perfectly well; the audiences were great. He's a humanitarian. He likes people. I've never seen him, in all the times he conducted at Juilliard, lose his temper for anything. He might just sit back and say, 'Now you can do that better than that,' and everyone would do better."

"The stupendous precision and clarity of the playing was uncanny," noted *The Japan Times*. "One had the impression that everyone in the orchestra really knew and understood the rhythms of his/her part—the results were enormous. Every strand of detail was clearly attended to, and throughout I could hardly detect a single case of ragged [playing]."[13]

Fresh from the high of the Juilliard Orchestra's tour, Skrowaczewski learned that he had prostate cancer. His doctors suggested that radiation treatment probably would be effective, but he wanted the cancer removed immediately. He called Stuart Warkow and canceled all his summer engagements. Although the operation was successful, Skrowaczewski endured a long, painful summer of recovery.

A bright spot during this time was the early-August premiere of his Fanfare for Orchestra, dedicated to Professor Josef Gingold. Skrowaczewski had been scheduled to lead the Pan Am Music Festival Orchestra in the gala concert, which served as a cultural prelude to the tenth Pan American Games. The orchestra was comprised of musicians from three youth orchestras from Canada, Venezuela, and the United States; principal players of the Indianapolis Symphony; and faculty from Butler University and Indiana University Bloomington. The Fanfare was composed to launch a series of concerts featuring winners of major international music competitions in North and South America.

Gingold, Skrowaczewski's longtime friend and colleague—an illustrious teacher and former concertmaster of the Detroit and Cleveland orchestras—was the ensemble's honorary concertmaster. The gesture paid tribute to Gingold's establishment of the International Violin Competition of Indianapolis.

Skrowaczewski decided to write a witty piece with a theatrical touch for Gingold:

> The concertmaster, in this case Gingold, comes out to the orchestra and signals to the oboist to give the tuning note. The orchestra takes the note, and Gingold pretends to be still tuning his violin and making little adjustments after they have finished tuning. But this is really my secret cadenza for him that starts the piece! Suddenly the orchestra—as if interrupting Gingold—bursts into the fanfare. It startled the public. I love the humor and unusualness of it.

The day after the premiere Gingold sent a telegram to Skrowaczewski, who was still home in Wayzata recuperating from surgery:

> FANFARE WONDERFULY WELL RECEIVED BY MUSIC CRITICS AND PUBLIC. CONDUCTOR AYKAL AND I THRILLED WITH MASTERFUL COMPOSITION. CONGRATULATIONS AND HEARTFELT THANKS FOR THE DEDICATION.
>
> JOSEF GINGOLD[14]

Weeks later Skrowaczewski was back in Manchester preparing the Hallé Orchestra for its tour to Poland, the first performances of its 130th-anniversary season. The only other time that the Hallé Orchestra had toured Poland was in 1958, its centenary year, during a European tour with Barbirolli.

The orchestra's tour to Poland in September 1987 was a true personal milestone for the maestro. He would be returning to Poland for the first time since his 1981 homecoming—now with his own orchestra—but also it would be his first time on the podium since his surgery.

Clive Smart recalled the tour's significance:

> On a personal, political, and musical level, the tour to Poland was highly important. The reaction of Polish audiences to Stan was incredible. It was almost like the prodigal son returning home. I've never seen anything so emotionally and musically impressive. It's difficult to put it into words, but the audiences were quite young, so I can't imagine that they would have known of Stan. But the fact that this was Stanisław Skrowaczewski returning to Poland with an English orchestra was an amazing occurrence, as far as they and we were concerned.

The first two concerts were part of the 22nd Annual International Festival Wratislavia Cantans, which was held in one of the largest churches in Wrocław, the city-site where Skrowaczewski had begun his professional conducting career forty years earlier. "It was very emotional for Stan to go back to Poland," said violinist Worrell. "I remember in Wrocław, people were so keen to come to the concert. The first half was televised, and during the intermission they cleared the platform of all the television cameras and equipment and put in more chairs because there were so many people waiting to come in from outside."

Skrowaczewski remembered the impact of the Wrocław concerts:

> We played [in] this wonderful, huge cathedral with very good acoustics. They started choral festivals there because of the fantastic sound. It was crammed with nearly five thousand people, completely full—to the point that children and young people went up high, hanging on the tiny balconies on the sides! Later, when we were back in England, the musicians told me that this was one of the concerts that they would never forget because of the silence—despite this overflow of people—all over the cathedral. You could hear a pin drop. During the *pianissimo* in the slow movement of the Shostakovich Fifth Symphony, when the oboe plays and there are long stretches of hushed sound, it was absolutely silent. It was the same for other works, too. The Hallé musicians said they had never experienced that kind of silence throughout a concert. We played two encores, mazurkas from Moniuszko operas. We practiced these before, and they are not easy because of a particular Polish rhythm. For the English, it was like non-Viennese playing a Viennese waltz. The Hallé Orchestra did them very well, and the enthusiasm of the audience was hard to believe. They kept applauding even after the orchestra left the stage. Finally, I had to make a speech in Polish saying we were tired and had to rest for the next concert.

Concerts in Kraków and Warsaw elicited similar reactions. After the tour's last concert the British Council held a reception for the orchestra that was attended by the British ambassador and the speaker of the House of Commons, who both praised the achievements of the ensemble and its conductor.

"I remember very well at the end of the tour going into Philharmonic Hall in Warsaw and seeing on the wall Stan's photograph as a young man [when he was] one of the Philharmonic's conductors," said deputy general manager Stuart Robinson. "Krystyna came with him on this tour. I think it was an emotional return for both of them."

Skrowaczewski's third Hallé season had been another artistic steppingstone. The board offered him a three-year extension to his contract, bringing it to 1990. He promptly accepted the offer.

TWENTY-SEVEN

BEING HEARD

Five different conductors will [lead] Skrowaczewski works, including the composer himself, who, by his own admission, would rather someone else conduct his [music]; he has no "definitive performance" standard.

—Ron Emery, *Times Union*, Albany, New York

Just three days after Shostakovich's dramatic Fifth Symphony concluded the Hallé's triumphant tour of Poland, Skrowaczewski brought the music of Corelli to life for the opening concert of the Saint Paul Chamber Orchestra's 1987–88 season.

With this concert Skrowaczewski made Minnesota music history. He opened the SPCO's season as its music advisor, and with his status as the Minnesota Orchestra's conductor laureate, he became the only conductor ever to hold simultaneously official titles with the state's two major orchestras.

In January 1986, celebrated violinist and conductor Pinchas Zukerman, the SPCO's music director since 1980, resigned somewhat abruptly. As his rationale for leaving he cited fatigue caused by the position's administrative aspects. But his vision of expanding the size of the chamber orchestra for romantic repertoire was at odds with the original concept of the SPCO. Under Zukerman the orchestra achieved terrific musical and commercial success. It increased audience attendance, made eight recordings on important labels, toured the United States and South America, and collaborated with stellar soloists. Zukerman was also an important force behind the building of the Ordway Theater in St. Paul, the SPCO's new performing home.

Skrowaczewski, whose appointment began in November 1986, assisted the SPCO with auditions, administrative issues, and advice on programming and guest artists. The collaboration was mutually beneficial to the orchestra and Skrowaczewski. During the search for a full-time music director, the SPCO received extraordinary short-term leadership from an artist of international standing and a major force within the Twin Cities' arts community. In return, Skrowaczewski had the opportunity to conduct three weeks of concerts with an orchestra and repertoire he loved. He had limited administrative responsibilities, but nevertheless he could influence a major orchestra during a time of transition. "It was local, artistically very satisfying, and a relatively light assignment. I knew the musicians, and they knew me. It was a warm and pleasant atmosphere with no tensions, so I took it," he said.

During his one-year tenure with the SPCO, Skrowaczewski oversaw the selection of a few string players and "an excellent timpanist, Earl Yowell," he noted. He also was an unofficial advisor to the search committee in its quest for Zukerman's successor.

Ultimately they chose a trio of artists: Christopher Hogwood as director of music, Hugh Wolff as principal conductor, and composer John Adams as creative chair. Wolff eventually became the orchestra's main conductor, but the SPCO's artistic management later reverted to a system of shared responsibility. Entering its fiftieth anniversary season in 2008, the SPCO expanded the concept of shared leadership to seven "artistic partners" (including Joshua Bell, Dawn Upshaw, and Roberto Abbado). Such broad leadership provides musicians with more input into programming and vision, but its impact on maintaining orchestral performance standards is debatable.

When Skrowaczewski's SPCO appointment was announced officially, Deborah Borda stated that he was the first choice for the position of music advisor.[1] Then in her first season as SPCO president and managing director, Borda handled the challenging situation of Zukerman's departure remarkably well by securing Skrowaczewski.

He developed a phenomenal season for the SPCO. Music of Peter Maxwell Davies, Takemitsu, Varèse, Boulez, Knussen, and Ligeti highlighted the concerts, which included fascinating pieces by traditional composers. Conductors included Yehudi Menuhin, Trevor Pinnock, Christoph Eschenbach, Catherine Comet, and Zukerman. British composer George Benjamin led a new-music series that included one of his pieces. A special Sunday Minnesota series featured compositions by students of Dominick Argento and Paul Fetler as well as works by other Minnesotans. Characteristically, Skrowaczewski did not program any of his music during the season, although Comet conducted his Rameau pieces on her programs.

Generally opposed to programming by eras, Skrowaczewski was somewhat bound by the SPCO structure already in place. For his Baroque Series program, however, he tried something different. "I have an idea," he told Minnesota Public Radio, "which I hope the public will like, of hearing the *idea* of the baroque reflected in our own time. There are contemporary composers—Alfred Schnittke, for example—writing in baroque forms, like his Concerto Grosso, or Michael Tippett's *Fantasia Concertante on a Theme of Corelli*."[2] Skrowaczewski preceded the Tippett with Corelli's Concerto Grosso in F, op. 6.

After his SPCO opening concerts he flew to Amsterdam to conduct the Concertgebouw Orchestra for the first time since 1960. His ten-day engagement with the historic ensemble included a performance that opened the spectacular new concert hall in The Hague. He presented a concert at the Flanders Festival in Brussels and opened the Concertgebouw's 1987–88 season in Amsterdam.

The season highlight for the SPCO was an all-Beethoven series with Claudio Arrau, one of the 20th century's greatest pianists. Just two weeks shy of his eighty-fifth birthday—with his deeply individualistic style and beautiful tone undiminished—the Chilean artist was making his debut with the SPCO, performing Beethoven's Fourth Piano Concerto. Arrau and Skrowaczewski, who shared artistic values, connected well in their performances over the years and in their SPCO concerts, their last collaboration. Like Skrowaczewski, Arrau had amazing performance stamina. In his eighties he was still giving up to fifty concerts a year all over the world. At the time of his death in 1991 at age eighty-eight, he was recording the complete keyboard works of Bach and was also preparing music of Haydn, Mendelssohn, and Boulez, among others.[3]

The warmth and appreciation the SPCO felt towards Skrowaczewski was evident at his final concert as music advisor, in May 1988. Michael Fleming of the *St. Paul Pioneer Press* described the chemistry between Skrowaczewski and the orchestra:

> There is something about Stanisław that inspires respect and affection, both among musicians and in the audience. It is not stick technique—at least from the back, his gestures are spasmodic, and his beat none too clear. But again and again, he pulls music from his players, as only a born conductor can. He can cajole an orchestra, plead for more, but there is no grandstanding. Coming out to take his bows, he looks almost embarrassed, and he is always ready to point out a musician who has played a larger than usual part.... The orchestra played for him as it does only for one it reveres.[4]

"In strictly musical terms," wrote Michael Anthony, "Skrowaczewski has quickly developed his own kind of voice with this orchestra: a sound bigger and weightier than other conductors elicit and a sound that's especially effective—and perhaps even necessary—in the acoustically dry Ordway."[5]

Although the SPCO appointment did not affect his commitment to the Hallé Orchestra, Skrowaczewski had to rearrange his international guest-conducting schedule to make it work, more proof of his dedication to the Twin Cities' cultural life. His loyalty extended beyond professional music organizations. When Minnesota's state legislature was reviewing a request from the University of Minnesota for funds to build a performance hall on the Minneapolis campus, Skrowaczewski wrote to the *Star Tribune* describing the recent construction of a home for the university's school of music as an "incomplete dream" without the addition of a hall. "This is akin to hiring an orchestra and then forgetting to ask them to bring their instruments," he said. "I endorse the efforts of those in the legislature and at the university who are working to finish the job of creating a significant school of music for this region."[6] (Five years later, in 1993, a fine concert hall opened at the school. It was named in honor of university alumnus Ted Mann, a noted entrepreneur in the film and entertainment industries.)

The Hallé Orchestra's 130th season (1987–88) was another critical success. It began with the triumphant tour of Poland and ended with performances of Verdi's *Requiem*, prompting John Robert-Blunn to describe the orchestra as "playing superbly, and better now than it has been in two decades."[7]

With Mstislav Rostropovich as soloist, the ensemble packed the Barbican in London. The country's greatest living composer, Sir Michael Tippett, spent an historic four-week residency with the Hallé as part of a Tippett and Debussy Festival. Three central Tippett compositions were featured: *The Mask of Time*, Symphony no. 4, and Symphony no. 3, which Tippett, age eighty-three at the time, conducted himself (something he rarely did). The season also saw the return of Michael Davis as leader of the orchestra—the British equivalent of concertmaster. (Davis began his career in the late 1960s with the Hallé under Barbirolli and worked his way up to co-leader of the orchestra before leaving to head the London Symphony Orchestra in 1979.) The completion of a recording cycle of symphonies and other orchestral works by Brahms further enhanced the Hallé's reputation.

Despite the orchestra's artistic progress, its morale declined. The promise of a new concert hall remained unfulfilled, salaries for the musicians were still poor, and they felt disconnected from the administrative and artistic leadership. Worst of all, the Hallé's 1986–87 season deficit—the largest in its history—was surpassed during the following season. Appeals to the Arts Council were in vain, and the orchestra headed into a dire situation.

After his Hallé season the maestro toured New Zealand and Australia for two weeks, leading such orchestras as the Sydney and Queensland symphonies. After the long season of heavy travel and concerts, he was looking forward to the lighter summer workload and having time for composing.

Considering his hectic conducting schedule, it is not surprising that two years had elapsed since the consecutive premieres of his Violin Concerto and the Concerto for Orchestra during the 1985–86 season. Despite this relentless pace he produced two compositions: Fanfare for Orchestra and *Fantasie per Sei*, a fifteen-minute chamber work for oboe, violin, viola, cello, bass, and piano, which premiered in spring 1989.

Although he was writing few new works, his earlier compositions were performed during the 1987–88 season more than ever before. The Concerto for Clarinet and Orchestra was heard in Europe and the United States; the Concerto for English Horn and Orchestra was performed in New Zealand (with world-renowned soloist Heinz Holliger) and in the United States; and the Concerto for Violin and Orchestra received its second round of performances after the premiere by the Philadelphia Orchestra. Skrowaczewski and Norman Carol performed the work with the Milwaukee Symphony Orchestra in spring 1988; a few months later they reprised the concerto with the Philadelphia Orchestra during Skrowaczewski's residency at Saratoga Performing Arts Center (SPAC).

In 1988 Dennis Russell Davies was in his fifth and final summer with the Philadelphia Orchestra as SPAC's principal conductor and classical-music program director. During his third year Davies initiated a composer-in-residence program, the first in SPAC's history. Philip Glass was the first composer-in-residence, followed by Lou Harrison and William Bolcom.

Less than two months before his sixty-fifth birthday, Skrowaczewski was appointed SPAC composer-in-residence, his first such position. To have this orchestra, with which he had enjoyed a long, mutually affectionate relationship, perform his music during the residency truly enhanced the honor. "It's not an ordinary matter to me," he told a reporter before the opening-night concert on August 10, which featured Concerto for Orchestra. "It's very special. The quality of the orchestra is quite important to a composer."[8]

He described his special regard for the Philadelphia Orchestra:

> We are very much a family. We enjoy working together…. They are such special people, so friendly and open. I can hardly think of any other [players] who are this open. They are not arrogant, like great musicians can be. What is remarkable about this orchestra is that they may have their personal feelings about a situation, but they always give their best. [At one of our concerts] the rain was such that all our soft passages were lost, and even in these horrible conditions they really played; they are devoted to the excellence of their profession.[9]

The Philadelphians always appreciated Skrowaczewski's signature courtesy and enjoyed playing his music. As *The Philadelphia Inquirer* reported, a number of musicians aggressively complained about performing the music of Glass and Harrison, "but they were enthusiastic about the choice of Skrowaczewski [as composer-in-residence]. Many of them find [his] scores rigorously well-crafted and meaningful, and they say they'll enjoy performing them."[10] "He has interesting ideas," observed Philadelphia Orchestra violinist Boris Balter. "His compositions are very much in the modern style. They have something to say."[11]

The Philadelphia Inquirer portrayed Davies' time at SPAC as a troubled tenure, due in part to the players' complaints about his programming.[12] To his credit, Davies tried to present a balance of American composers with a range of styles, but performing a number of pieces by minimalist-influenced composers like Glass and Harrison proved to be too much for the orchestra. Even the open-minded Skrowaczewski's tastes did not align with the popularity of minimalism during the late 1980s.

Over a two-week period SPAC audiences heard a broad range of Skrowaczewski's compositions: five orchestral works led by five different conductors. They also heard members of the Philadelphia Orchestra perform three chamber works: *Fantasie per Quattro*, Skrowaczewski's Trio for Clarinet, Bassoon and Piano, and his String Quartet, the original form of Symphony for Strings.

At the performance of *Fantasie per Quattro*, held at the Luzerne Music Center, New York, Skrowaczewski briefly introduced his piece. He quipped, "I am usually very eloquent in introducing my music, but then, I usually read the program notes!"[13]

Critics recognized the quality of Skrowaczewski's music and praised its craft, but some were lukewarm regarding the music itself. "This Violin Concerto will not draw crowds or sell tickets," noted *The Post-Star*, "but it deserves playing and deserves hearing."[14]

Of the Concerto for Orchestra another critic said, "The orchestration is extraordinarily skillful, but the musical content, the phrases and ideas themselves, are not strong enough to sustain interest."[15] Although satisfied with its musical content, Skrowaczewski made major changes in orchestration when revising the score a decade later.

Skrowaczewski was gratified to hear so many of his compositions performed with skill and verve. The performances sparked a strong desire to plumb his creative spirit ever more deeply.

TWENTY-EIGHT

THE PRICE OF INTEGRITY

In our world today, our lives are unfortunately so pervaded by the ephemera of the pop culture, not to mention the daily stresses—economic, environmental, and even global—that the meaning of our existence is lost. What remains to counter the vulgarity and desperation of our times is great art, always the reminder of our spiritual dimension. It is my hope that our concerts will stimulate our awareness of the meaning and value of music, that each concert will be our rite of initiation into an even deeper contemplation of the profound joy and rewards of opening ourselves to great art.

—Stanisław Skrowaczewski, letter to Hallé Orchestra audiences, 1989–90 season

As Skrowaczewski sat alone in his room at the Midland Hotel on his sixty-fifth birthday, he contemplated the future. He had completed his first rehearsal of the program that would open the Hallé Orchestra's 131st season, and his spirit was filled with the music of Mozart and Bruckner, two of his most beloved composers. The following week he would rehearse Haydn's Symphony no. 60 (*Il Distratto*), *The Rite of Spring,* and a Mozart piano concerto with Romanian pianist Radu Lupu. When he arrived in Manchester in late September, he recorded Bruckner's Fourth Symphony (the *Romantic*)—his first internationally released recording of a symphony by the composer with whom he is most associated.

In late fall 1988 the Hallé Orchestra was scheduled to tour Portugal and Spain, performing Mahler's Second Symphony; in winter it would tour Switzerland. For Skrowaczewski, 1989 would begin with a prominent concert leading the London Symphony Orchestra at the Barbican Centre, followed by a recording with that celebrated ensemble of *Symphonie fantastique*, one of his signature pieces. As a composer he also anticipated the premiere of *Fantasie per Sei*, the Minnesota premiere of the Violin Concerto, the New York premiere of the Concerto for Orchestra, performances of other works, and new commissions, all on his 1989-90 schedule.

Overall, Skrowaczewski's artistic life was in fine shape, but he had mixed feelings at the start of his fifth Hallé season. He had accepted the Hallé Orchestra post primarily because it was an excellent opportunity to restore and build a great institution, but the organization's fate was uncertain. Confident in his abilities and in the unanimous support from musicians and management, Skrowaczewski had expected the orchestra's artistic development to be swift, as indeed it had been.

However, he and the organization had reached a crossroads. By fall 1988 the Hallé's future was largely dependent on the whims of the Arts Council and Manchester audiences. Skrowaczewski joined the Hallé in 1983 with the understanding that a new concert hall would be built, but the project was still in the discussion phase. Serious financial shortfalls ensured a continuing struggle for resources. The Hallé's circumstances began to feel uncomfortably like the Minnesota Orchestra's situation in the late 1960s and early 1970s. Skrowaczewski nevertheless extended his contract by a year, committing himself at least until 1991.

Clive Smart summed up the situation in fall 1988:

> We feel that our fundamental musical policy and the goals we are trying to achieve are the right ones, and the only problem is a lack of public subsidy. And in that respect we are being treated less favorably than any of the comparable orchestras because we are playing to far more people than anybody else in the country, giving a much bigger service nationwide and getting a lot less money for doing it. We've done more to raise money in the private sector than any other orchestra, but we still have this very serious problem.[1]

"In my first year, because of inflation and the general economic situation, the British Arts Council was cutting support of orchestras by five to ten percent," said Skrowaczewski. "Inflation was going up in one year [by] eleven percent, so the poor musicians were badly paid. Every year Clive would say, 'Stan, I have terrible news. Next year we are getting less and less from the British Arts Council.'" Skrowaczewski also pointed out that about only forty percent of the Hallé's operating budget came from the state. "The rest," he said, "must be earned from ticket sales or from income earned from recordings. The orchestra really has to struggle for its life. They have practically no private financial support."[2]

In Britain, corporate funding of professional orchestras remained in its infancy. Orchestras were not yet skilled at obtaining it, and businesses were not accustomed to funding on a large scale. Aside from audience support—which generally could be described as complacent during this period—the Hallé really depended on Arts Council backing. Michael Kennedy described the council's funding disparity that frustrated Skrowaczewski and Smart:

> I think the unfortunate thing about Stan's tenure with the Hallé is that he was with them at a very bad time financially, and during that period the British Council for the Arts was very mean and "skinflinty." He hit the worst possible time, and the committee criticized anything adventurous that he performed because it wasn't financially successful. Yet the British Arts Council was giving loads of money to Birmingham (sometimes five times the amount) because they were terrified they'd lose Simon Rattle, and they couldn't see beyond Simon Rattle. His name and the fact that he was on TV and young, etc., made the difference. So the other orchestras suffered. The Hallé was getting one hundred thousand pounds, and the Birmingham Symphony was getting half a million. Skrowaczewski made the Hallé a fine orchestra, the performances were excellent, but he was always fighting against this sort of thing, so I think he had a rough time from that point of view.

A financial reprieve came in late fall 1988, when the Association of Greater Manchester Authorities voted to increase the Hallé's funding for the 1989–90 season if the Arts Council did the same. Both parties came through, and the "threat of possible extinction," as Kennedy described it, and the real fear of reducing the orchestra's size subsided.[3] The extra funding also gave the musicians a much-needed pay increase. For the time being, Skrowaczewski and the Hallé could continue the current season with relative confidence.

This good news arrived as the orchestra was finishing a strong fall season. Skrowaczewski's highly praised conducting of Elgar's *Enigma Variations,* both in Manchester and in London, closed out his first segment with the orchestra. Audiences, musicians, and critics lauded his performance of one of the most famous works by the composer with whom the Hallé is most associated.

Skrowaczewski had secured an outstanding group of guest conductors for the period when he conducted elsewhere in Europe and the United States during the season: renowned English conductor Sir Charles Groves and fellow "musical knight" Sir Yehudi Menuhin, Andrew Davis, Dennis Russell Davies, and James Loughran, among others. French conductor Serge Baudo, who premiered two of Messiaen's significant works in the 1960s, led an eightieth-birthday concert of the composer's *Turangalîla-Symphonie.* Continuing his tradition of engaging composer-conductors to lead the Hallé, Skrowaczewski invited Gunther Schuller, who characteristically presented diverse pieces, including his own *Dramatic Overture,* and Andrzej Panufnik, who conducted his relatively new Symphony no. 9 on a concert honoring his seventy-fifth birthday.

Before Skrowaczewski left England in fall 1988 to fulfill other engagements, he received an emergency call from the Royal Philharmonic Orchestra. Antal Doráti had died, and the orchestra needed Skrowaczewski to cover two concerts at the Barbican Centre. Mindful of their bond as former Minnesota music directors and their positive relationship, the maestro gladly agreed to the request.

The year 1989 began with Skrowaczewski the composer again in the spotlight. He led four performances of his Violin Concerto with the Minnesota Orchestra and Norman Carol, the first opportunity for his adopted hometown to hear the work.

Eighty-seven-year-old Leonard Carpenter, son of Elbert, president of the Minneapolis Symphony's board from 1905 to 1945, wrote to Skrowaczewski about the piece:

> I found your Violin Concerto most interesting. I want to hear it again and again. It was different from any other contemporary music that I have heard. A thought came into my mind which is probably too fanciful, but which I am going to mention anyway. Was the concerto in any sense a commentary on human life? Life that is at times somber, at other times determined, and inevitably at times tumultuous. Life does change so abruptly and often without any advance notice, and it does contain little sudden and unexpected statements.[4]

Skrowaczewski responded:

> This thought that came to your mind, that the concerto is a sort of commentary
> on human life, is not a fanciful but a right one. Of course, I didn't have any
> such idea while I was composing it, but most of romantic and postromantic
> music up to the present, will reflect by its development, in time, a parallel to
> human life with abrupt changes, moods, colors, surprises, etc.—all of these
> being more of a parallel than commentary (unless the composer would do it
> on purpose, i.e., Strauss in *Ein Heldenleben*).[5]

Skrowaczewski's second significant composition performance of the season occurred at Carnegie Hall in February. He led the American Composers Orchestra in his Concerto for Orchestra (its New York debut), William Schuman's Violin Concerto, and the world premiere of rising star Aaron Jay Kernis' *Invisible Mosaic III*.

Between performances of his Violin Concerto and Concerto for Orchestra, he traveled to Canada to conduct the Vancouver Symphony Orchestra, with Pinchas Zukerman as soloist, and then to the United Kingdom for the closing concert of the Images de France Festival at the Barbican Centre with the London Symphony Orchestra. While Skrowaczewski was conducting abroad, his music was being performed back in the United States. *Fantasie per Quattro* was performed in the Philadelphia area, while the Clarinet Concerto was heard for the first time in Cleveland, performed by the Cleveland Institute of Music Orchestra.

He also conducted and recorded Berlioz's dramatic *Symphonie fantastique* with the London Symphony Orchestra. The previous year he and the orchestra had recorded Brahms' Piano Concerto no. 1 with Barry Douglas, a young pianist from Northern Ireland, on the RCA label. The Brahms and Berlioz works (on Chandos) were the first recordings he had made on prominent labels since his Mercury discs of the early 1960s.

The Berlioz recording, potentially a positive career move for Skrowaczewski, displeased Smart. Although no contractual barriers prohibited the maestro from recording with another British orchestra, Smart nevertheless told Stephen Lumsden, Skrowaczewski's European manager, that he found the decision "very disappointing. Obviously, it is a record that we would have hoped to record with him in view of its historical connections with the Hallé," Smart said.[6] "I certainly have no objections to him making the record, but I think you should be aware that it will not do his relationship with the members of the Hallé Orchestra a lot of good."[7]

Smart's tart reaction to the news of the Berlioz recording also stemmed from the fact that he had been in discussions with Chandos—a decade-old label with growth in the classical-music market—about possible recording projects with the Hallé.

For his part, Lumsden was concerned that Smart was negotiating recording projects without consulting him and Skrowaczewski. Justified or not, this notion compounded Lumsden's growing disappointment with the Hallé's lackluster promotion of his client, and it also underscored the uneasy relationship between Lumsden and Smart. Thus, when the opportunity for a Chandos recording arose, Lumsden secured it for Skrowaczewski.

The other factor involved finances. Recording in London is much less expensive than in a location like Manchester or, for that matter, nearly anywhere else in the world. Most English recording companies are based in London, which boasts sixteen professional orchestras and hosts an enormous amount of commercial recording work.

Originally Skrowaczewski's recording of the Bruckner Fourth Symphony with the Hallé was intended to be the inaugural recording of the entire Bruckner symphony cycle on the RCA label, potentially a major promotional boon for him and the orchestra. The project fell through, however; the director at RCA who was enthusiastic about the idea had left, and his replacement had no interest in it. "Apparently he said, 'Bruckner? No one will listen to it,'" Skrowaczewski recalled.

Nevertheless, his recording history with the Hallé was significant. By spring 1989 his Brahms symphony cycle was released. It included the *Academic Festival* and *Tragic* overtures, along with Variations on a Theme of Haydn and *Hungarian Dances* nos. 1, 3, and 10.

Many reviewers recognized Skrowaczewski's performing ideals and generally acclaimed the Brahms series. "[He] is always attentive to interconnecting phrases and the relationships between different thematic ideas," noted *CD Review* of the Third Symphony, adding, "This performance marries warmth and logic."[8] Others singled out its virtues of balance, tone, and phrasing as well as orchestral playing ripe with character; they compared it favorably with recent high-end recordings by Karajan and Carlos Kleiber. Less enthusiastic comments tended to focus on some of Skrowaczewski's tempo choices or deficient moments in the orchestra's playing.

In his 1997 book *The Compleat Conductor*, Schuller rates Skrowaczewski's Brahms series as among the most faithful in its realization of the composer's scores (in a field of sixty-six recordings of Brahms' First and Fourth Symphonies). He describes Skrowaczewski's recording of the Fourth Symphony as "one of the finest ever."[9] A passage in the first movement (measures 130–132) is "as modern and complex as anything in Stravinsky's *Le Sacre du Printemps*," declares Schuller, who goes on to say that it is performed correctly on just one recording—Skrowaczewski's.[10]

Soon after Skrowaczewski returned to Manchester in winter 1989 for the season's second half, the Hallé concert hall was the topic of the northern British press. Representatives from the Manchester City Council, Central Manchester Development Corporation, and the Hallé Orchestra held a press conference at which they announced the choice of a site for a new performance venue to be located in the city's center, near the Midland Hotel. The planned facility would include a 2,500-seat auditorium, a rehearsal hall, and various amenities for patrons. The project had a budget of £20 million, a fund-raising plan that included support from both the public and private sectors, and a projected completion date of 1992. It was certainly welcome news for the orchestra and Skrowaczewski, who more than once had told the British press that a new concert hall was one of the conditions under which he accepted his appointment in 1983.

The Hallé's quest for a new and acoustically excellent concert hall began in the late 1800s, but that goal was never realized.[11] In 1940 the original Free Trade Hall was almost completely destroyed during the German blitz. Rebuilt by the City of Manchester with war-damage funds and reopened in 1951, it remained acoustically inadequate. Over the decades the Hallé committee tried unsuccessfully to persuade the city to improve Free Trade Hall.

Even as principal conductor-elect of the Hallé Orchestra, Skrowaczewski had criticized Free Trade Hall. By his second year with the orchestra, he began a reprise of his efforts in Minneapolis twenty-five years earlier. He reminded administrative leaders that quality acoustics had to be the top priority for a new hall. He supplied them with examples of great concert venues located around the world, information about acousticians, and other relevant advice. Skrowaczewski received letters of support from colleagues and friends in America, including a four-page missive from Ken Dayton, which the maestro released to the Manchester press.

With the promise of a better future, the Hallé Orchestra and its conductor were off to Switzerland, the seventh time the ensemble had performed in that nation since 1961. The Hallé typically performed music from its homeland that was rarely heard in Switzerland. Skrowaczewski's tour was no exception; it featured Britten's *Sinfonia da Requiem* and Elgar's Cello Concerto. But this time it offered something unique, a "world premiere" of sorts, written by its conductor.

The orchestra's concert in Basel coincided with *Basler Fasnacht*, Switzerland's biggest carnival, which starts at 4:00 a.m. the Monday after Ash Wednesday and lasts seventy-two hours. One of the attractions of this "Swiss Mardi Gras" is the steady stream of pipe-and-drum groups parading in elaborate costumes and playing incessantly throughout the city's streets. Cacophony produced by some sixty clattering bands seeped into the Basel hall during the orchestra's afternoon rehearsal, but Skrowaczewski took the interruptions in stride. During a tea break he orchestrated a melody, played audibly by one of the pipe-and-drum groups, for the Hallé's flute and percussion players. He also added a bit of an old Polish song for good measure. That evening, during the most intimate moments in the performance of Elgar's Cello Concerto, the pipers and drummers on the streets were again overheard in the hall. It was with particular delight that Skrowaczewski paid "tribute" to the sonic intruders with an encore, the "premiere" of his flute and percussion piece, much to the amusement of his Basel audience.

Back in Manchester, the Hallé's new management structure established its priorities. The Hallé administration—specifically, the Hallé committee headed by new chairman Sebastian de Ferranti—focused its efforts on artistic control. Rex Hillson, whose fine service to the orchestra began in 1948 as a committee member, stepped down at the end of January 1988. The committee no doubt hoped that Ferranti's business experience as head of a Manchester international company for nearly thirty years and as the current executive director of Britain's General Electric Company would aid efforts to obtain corporate funding.

Ferranti's influence was felt early in his tenure, as explained by a writer in an article entitled "Why I Was About to Quit—by Stanisław Skrowaczewski," published in the *Manchester Evening News* toward the end of the 1988–89 season:

> There has been a radical change in the Hallé's management structure. Industrialist Sebastian de Ferranti became chairman, and the old Hallé general committee was replaced by a much smaller board of directors, which is now well on with the hard task of rejuvenating what had become an arthritic, aging institution. Many changes are underway. In the last two months the Hallé has landed major new sponsorship from Brother International and also a pledge from the city of Manchester for a new concert hall. That pledge persuaded Skrowaczewski to stay.[12]

Relatively speaking, the 1988–89 season was a positive one financially for the orchestra. Performance income was up by twelve percent and sponsorship up by twenty percent, and the orchestra was expected to break even during the following season.[13] Nevertheless, the administration experienced increasing pressure to become less reliant upon funding from the Arts Council, which in turn had continued to treat the Hallé unfairly. By summer, when Skrowaczewski's programming again came under fire for not being "sufficiently attractive" for one concert series, a relatively short-lived battle with the board erupted.

After an exhausting Hallé season Skrowaczewski's summer engagements seemed almost like a vacation. They began with a tour of six German cities with the Bamberg Symphony and Rostropovich playing the Lutosławski Cello Concerto and Tchaikovsky's *Rococo Variations*. He then conducted three Philadelphia Orchestra concerts at the Mann Center, with repertoire including Mahler's *Songs of a Wayfarer*, with British mezzo-soprano Christine Cairns, and Janáček's *Sinfonietta*.

One program marked the reemergence of Van Cliburn on the concert stage. Still mourning the deaths of his father and his manager, and after experiencing problems with his piano technique, Cliburn had stopped performing publicly in 1978. A 1987 White House invitation to perform a recital brought him out of retirement. Cliburn's concert with Skrowaczewski was the pianist's first orchestra appearance since "retiring" and as such was widely observed.

The program, jointly chosen by the collaborators, featured sentimental pieces honoring the memories of Ormandy and Frederic R. Mann, who died in 1985 and 1987, respectively. *Don Juan* represented Ormandy's love of Strauss, and Liszt's Piano Concerto no. 1 honored Ormandy's graduation from the Liszt Academy and his Hungarian heritage. Tchaikovsky's Piano Concerto no. 1 was chosen "for reasons concerning Mann's Russian heritage," explained Daniel Webster, "but mainly because no audience could imagine Van Cliburn playing anything else."[14]

Weeks before these Philadelphia Orchestra concerts, Skrowaczewski conducted at the annual Van Cliburn International Piano Competition. Founded in 1962 by a group of Fort Worth music educators and volunteers, it has become a model for other competitions. Along with requiring competitors to perform chamber and orchestral literature, the competition specifies a contemporary-music component. To that end, each year pianists must perform a work commissioned under the auspices of the Cliburn Foundation. The impressive list of composers who have written solo piano works for the Cliburn competition include Copland, Barber, Bernstein, Schuman, Corigliano, Gould, and Bolcom.

Skrowaczewski reveled in the challenge of conducting twelve concertos with the six young finalists over three days.

Twenty-four-year-old British pianist Andrew Wilde, who competed at the 1989 Cliburn Competition and who was also a soloist with Skrowaczewski and the Hallé Orchestra, experienced the maestro's musical and professional support: "He tried to dig deeper into me and bring things out. He was certainly the greatest conductor I've worked with. He treated me as an equal."[15]

Within two weeks Skrowaczewski again performed with Wilde at another international piano competition. Since 1971 the University of Maryland has presented the William Kapell International Piano Competition and Festival, named after the American pianist who died at age thirty-one in a plane crash. In his brief twelve-year professional career, Kapell was associated with the usual great piano works as well as American contemporary pieces. He achieved his greatest recognition with the Khachaturian Piano Concerto.

Skrowaczewski collaborated with the competition's three finalists in the marathon Kapell concert with the National Symphony Orchestra, which was held at the Kennedy Center. By the time concertos of Brahms and Chopin were performed, it was already 10:30 p.m., and then the Tchaikovsky First began. Yet Skrowaczewski's mental and physical energy never diminished.

Not long after this concert he accompanied another Cliburn competition soloist, nineteen-year-old Russian Aleksei Sultanov, who won the 1989 competition with his visceral, emotional, and controversial performance of Rachmaninoff's Piano Concerto no. 2. The pair performed the same piece at the Great Woods Center for the Performing Arts in Mansfield, Massachusetts.

For his concert with Sultanov, Skrowaczewski contended with soaring temperatures and a strong-willed soloist. The intense late July heat and humidity took its toll on the Pittsburgh Symphony's intonation, and the resulting lethargy came as no surprise. Sultanov, clad in a black tuxedo, his body shedding rivulets of perspiration, gave a wayward performance of the Rachmaninoff Piano Concerto no. 2 and did not seem really engaged with his orchestral partners. "I pitied the conductor, the musicianly and disciplined Skrowaczewski," wrote Anthony Tommasini. "Trying to accompany Sultanov was like trying to rope a wild young colt."[16]

Sultanov's virtuosic technique, extreme dynamic ranges, and the wild abandonment of his playing style generated controversy among the judges and audience back in Fort Worth, but these qualities propelled him to win Cliburn's Eighth Annual International Competition.

In 1990 Teldec Classics International released *The Winners*, a double CD of performances from the 1989 Van Cliburn Competition, with Skrowaczewski conducting the Fort Worth Symphony and Sultanov playing the Rachmaninoff Piano Concerto no. 2. A PBS documentary, *Here to Make Music*, which featured competition footage, won an Emmy Award in 1989 and was aired nationally. It has been syndicated for television networks globally and was released on DVD in 2004. The brief shot of bemusement on the maestro's face after Sultanov finishes his adrenalin-driven Rachmaninoff performance is priceless.

Before his summer 1989 season concluded, Skrowaczewski interrupted his annual respite in the Rocky Mountains to replace Edo de Waart in two impromptu performances with the Los Angeles Philharmonic at the Hollywood Bowl. He caught the attention of astute listeners by opening his first concert with his orchestration of "The Star-Spangled Banner." Skrowaczewski's performance of Bartók's Concerto for Orchestra impressed Alan Rich, whose critiques are known for their acumen: "This was, simply put, one of the best performances of this glorious score I can remember, indoors or out. Skrowaczewski's splendid control over the orchestra, with the details clearly defined and neatly integrated, became a major part of the performance."[17]

Early that summer he received the final version of the thirteenth draft of the Hallé Orchestra's upcoming Sunday series, Opus One. He and Smart had worked hard to craft programs that would appeal to the orchestra's Sunday crowd yet still maintain artistic credibility. Before long, Smart informed him that the board also had difficulties with some of his programming for the 1990–91 season, including Beethoven's *Missa Solemnis*, which it deemed unsuitable for this series.[18]

After opening Hallé's 1989–90 season with Britten's *War Requiem*, Skrowaczewski met with the executive committee to defend his upcoming programs, but he also came prepared to offer some alternatives. He then learned that it was not his choice of works that concerned them; rather, "it was only the juxtaposition of the works."[19] This odd statement came from a group of largely musically uneducated people. As Skrowaczewski frequently stated publicly, his programming philosophy was grounded in the juxtaposition of works from various eras.

The committee's criticism was fueled in part by Arts Council recommendations to reduce the number of concerts expected to generate low sales. Another factor was a report from an incentive-scheme director (an accountant) that was based on a one-day "assessment" of the orchestra's situation in fall 1989. During the 1988–89 season the Hallé had applied for Incentive Funding, a program that recommends monetary awards (provided by the Arts Council) for orchestras that obtain private funding. This application was denied.[20] During the following season (1989–90), the Hallé was denied Incentive Funding for a second time, despite having recently obtained the largest sponsorship of an orchestra to date.

Moreover, a new report claimed that an unusual gulf existed between the Hallé and the Arts Council on artistic matters. It cited the council's criticism of the Hallé for lacking a "clear artistic policy or consensus" and characterized the orchestra as an "organization in artistic decline."[21] This assessment ignored all evidence to the contrary: Skrowaczewski's artistic policies and vision had always been clear. However, the lack of artistic consensus, as noted by the council, accurately depicted its ongoing conflict with Smart about its fairness to the Hallé as well as the maestro's frustration with the executive committee.

Not long after the first Incentive Funding report, the executive committee had created a music advisory committee. Skrowaczewski recognized that his control over the orchestra's programming—the most important aspect of his position, apart from his conducting responsibilities—was eroding. In reality, it already had been compromised, as Smart told the executive committee. During the previous four seasons, financial strains had forced Skrowaczewski to program more conservatively than he preferred.[22]

Adding another twist to this administrative quagmire, management also denied his request for more autonomy in selecting guest conductors. When Lumsden negotiated what was to become Skrowaczewski's final contract with the orchestra, Smart reiterated the Hallé's position that management would consult the maestro about the choice of guest conductors but "could not be under any obligation to seek his approval."[23]

During fall 1989 Skrowaczewski expressed his concerns to Ferranti, but the effort proved futile:

> He was a wealthy businessman who was supposed to help the Hallé financially with his connections in London, but it didn't happen. His interest in music was lacking. He told me once that he liked opera, the more showy works (probably by Verdi and Puccini), so he felt the public needed nice melodies and dancing music, etc. He showed no concern about music of Bach, Beethoven, Bruckner, Mahler, or Stravinsky. As such, he didn't understand my position about the importance of the artistic direction of the orchestra and what I was after. Not only did he not understand, but he also thought I was wrong. It was an impossible situation for me.

Skrowaczewski's contract stipulated that he inform the Hallé of his intent to extend his appointment no later than January 1, 1990. In early December 1989 he wrote to Ferranti, warning him that "unfortunate developments of the last twelve months and precipitated by a series of bad artistic managerial decisions" have had a "debilitating effect…on the artistic level and image of the orchestra."[24] Ferranti previously had asked him to be patient and give him more time to address the maestro's concerns. Nothing had been done, however, and Skrowaczewski informed Ferranti that unless "a clear agreement can be reached on the future artistic policy of the orchestra, and, moreover, a clear realignment of responsibility in this regard," it would be impossible for him to continue as principal conductor.[25] He explained:

> Any important cultural organization must have a clear-sighted artistic vision as the number-one priority. No amount of business plans or financial strategies can succeed in the long term unless they are underpinned by an artistic policy that aspires to the very highest level. Artistic leadership is crucial to this end, and while I have tried to provide programs and performances with this aim in mind, it has become increasingly apparent that the management's shortcomings in the choice of guest conductors/programs, not to mention image and profile building, compound and endanger my efforts.... If the ultimate artistic authority and responsibility remains in the hands of this Management, then it will be impossible for me to fulfill my responsibilities properly. In such a case, I would not seek a further contract with the orchestra. I trust you understand that I have the best interests of the orchestra at heart when making these proposals.[26]

In his letter Skrowaczewski gave the orchestra's management the option to let him remain with the Hallé, but the administration would not relinquish crucial aspects of artistic control. Ironically, in the same month during which he wrote this letter, the British government increased Arts Council funding by eleven percent; given this development, the executive committee agreed to fund the 1990–91 season largely as the maestro had conceived it.[27]

Once again Skrowaczewski maintained his musical integrity through difficult times, staying true to his artistic ideals. In doing so, he reached his breaking point with the orchestra's management.

TWENTY-NINE

AN APPRECIATION

At the end of his time as principal conductor, the Hallé are firmly back in the major league, playing as well, if not better, than most British orchestras. And he has widened a repertory which needed shaking out of a deep rut. Many of the performances which the Hallé have given under Skrowaczewski have been as fine as anything I have heard in more than forty years' Hallé-going.

—John Robert-Blunn, *Manchester Evening News*

The Boston Symphony Orchestra engaged Skrowaczewski on short notice to replace an ailing Klaus Tennstedt in January 1990. While Skrowaczewski was rehearsing the BSO, the Hallé Orchestra issued a press release announcing that its principal conductor "will not be seeking an extension to his current contract." Skrowaczewski's official statement of resignation appeared as follows:

> Speaking from the United States, where he is currently conducting the Boston Symphony Orchestra, Mr. Skrowaczewski said: "By the end of next season, I will have completed seven years as the Hallé Orchestra's Principal Conductor and Artistic Advisor during which time I have enjoyed numerous happy musical experiences with the orchestra in Manchester, London, and abroad. Although a number of my initial artistic aspirations and goals for the orchestra have still to be achieved, I do not foresee these being reached in the present financial circumstances. Consequently I do not wish to extend my current contract after 1991, but I do look forward to a continuing relationship with the Hallé Orchestra."[1]

Although its timing was completely coincidental, Skrowaczewski's engagement with the BSO may have reminded the Hallé's executive committee and the Manchester area that they soon would be losing a conductor of considerable artistic stature. At the end of the first Boston concert the musicians honored Skrowaczewski by refusing to stand when he acknowledged them.

"Skrowaczewski asked for and got a genuine *pianissimo* and a real *diminuendo*, something not heard in years from this ensemble," reported Ellen Pfeifer of the *Boston Herald*.[2] Richard Dyer, *Boston Globe* critic, wrote, "These days it's hard to make qualities like 'honesty' sound exciting, but Skrowaczewski's honest, straightforward, experienced performance of the *Eroica* was very exciting indeed."[3]

In Manchester, news of Skrowaczewski's resignation surprised no one. His concerns over the Hallé Orchestra's financial situation, the lack of a concert hall, and audiences' conservatism were well known; however, the announcement prompted analyses of Skrowaczewski's tenure and of the Hallé's new management. Within a week of Skrowaczewski's resignation, Clive Smart announced his retirement from the orchestra after thirty-three years of service, which would coincide with Skrowaczewski's departure at the end of the 1990–91 season.

There was unanimous acknowledgement that Skrowaczewski had brought the orchestra to a highly disciplined artistic level. London critics agreed. "The news that the Hallé is to lose this eloquent musician from the venerable Eastern European school is a sad blow, for London music-lovers as well as Mancunians," wrote David Murray in the *Financial Times* of London. "He and his orchestra have been setting remarkable standards, and he is not really replaceable."[4]

Gerald Larner of *The Guardian*, noting Skrowaczewski's frustration over his lack of artistic control, shared the maestro's concerns:

> What is exciting about the situation is that the Hallé now has an opportunity to make the appointments that could give it a whole new profile, a different way of life and even the artistic edge over other orchestras of the same kind. What is alarming is that most committee members who will be responsible for the appointments—though energetically and decisively chaired by Sebastian de Ferranti and generally well-endowed in business acumen—don't have the experience, the knowledge or the taste in these very specialized areas to ensure the best choices are made.[5]

Skrowaczewski's relationship with the musicians of the Hallé Orchestra was another issue. The orchestra had chosen him unanimously as its principal conductor—the first time ever that the musicians had been consulted about such an appointment—but his discipline had not endeared him to everyone in the ensemble.

His resignation triggered journalistic speculation that he had not really connected with the orchestra as people had hoped. "Like him or not," noted one 1989 article, "they play better for him than they had played for most other conductors for more than a decade. They still do."[6] Michael Kennedy, who reported rumors of unhappy relations between the players and Skrowaczewski, commented that "his disciplined rehearsal methods do not go down well in the free-and-easy, anti-authoritarian climate that prevails in Britain today."[7]

The musicians appreciated the high standards Skrowaczewski imposed on them and the resulting artistic achievement. After a certain standard had been realized, however, they expected a certain level of freedom and trust; the principal players especially believed that a loosening of the reins was necessary in order to elevate the orchestra to the next level.

"I think British orchestras respond much better when they are encouraged to do their own thing," said Smart, "whereas I think that in America, if the conductor is not in control, the players start controlling the conductor." After four or five years as principal conductor, Skrowaczewski possibly might have built a stronger personal connection with the orchestra if he had given the first-desk players a level of freedom. Then again, perhaps he derives his consistent artistry by adhering to certain principles of rehearsing and performing, a resolve that others may regard as obstinacy.

Uncompromising as he may have seemed to some Hallé musicians, Skrowaczewski projected his own brand of spontaneity, according to violinist Peter Worrell:

> I think as an artist he lives on the edge. In his own words, he's always looking for something "a little crazy." He never wants anything to settle. He wants a sense of spontaneity. We could do a standard repertoire piece, and it became a new piece with Stan. I have a feeling that if he senses anything has become too established, he'll alter a tempo just to liven everything up again. I remember most his performances of the standard repertoire. He was always "making music"—say in Mozart or Haydn—looking for the turn of the phrase.

Skrowaczewski's home life during the Hallé years typically consisted of two- or three-week periods between engagements. He missed his family but continued to be in touch, vicariously experiencing Wayzata life through daily calls to Krystyna. He was always proud of his sons' activities and their musical development.

"[Skrowaczewski] seems to have taken a real interest in his sons' music," reported the *Star Tribune* in spring 1990. "Both have played in local rock bands and compose works on tape in their home studio. 'They have high hopes,' said their father. 'What they do is very refined pop music. I cannot really judge it, but their music is pleasant and getting more sophisticated all the time. They are on the brink of getting a record contract.'"[8]

Paul and Nicholas indeed had progressed musically. During their last high school years they educated themselves about the pop-recording industry through reading, contacting independent and major labels, and studying the legal aspects of contracts and negotiations. After high school they moved to Minneapolis, where they took humanities and business courses at the University of Minnesota for two years. At the same time, their pop band, Smilehouse, performed in the Twin Cities. Its success led to Paul's joining Great Nation, a professional touring regional pop-rock band.

Ever since his senior year in high school, Paul had toured on the weekends, playing guitar and keyboards as well as singing—sometimes in front of thousands of people. He recalled his father's presence at one of his concerts:

> One night there was a local show, and I think my mom talked my dad into going. She knew I was really serious about making this my life, and she wanted to make sure he experienced what I was doing. They came with some affluent Wayzata friends to this really awful bar in St. Paul. I was petrified going up on stage. I was playing keyboards, guitar, and singing lead. I was so unbelievably nervous to do this in front of my parents. But it went fine, and afterwards he came up to me and said, "It was great. Your voice was wonderful, and I'm very happy"—but with an air of "this is fine and dandy, but what about a real

job?" He was concerned that it would lead to a limiting life. Later, when I had a successful music career and a platinum record on my wall, then it all seemed real to him, and he took it seriously.

My dad was never a narrow-scope person. Because of his education, his mind, his upbringing, and his diverse interests—science, nature, and music—I think he was fearful of us being intellectually limited in our options. So that's why whenever we see him he's always asking if we are doing anything for our minds, whether it's reading or other mind-expanding kinds of activities. At the age I am now, I appreciate this advice so much. I now see him as a role model, and I try to emulate that philosophy. But back then I sort of just said, "Yeah, yeah, I'm doing a number of things to grow," without really grasping the importance of what he was saying. [In 2006, Paul founded a website geared towards brain- and whole-body health—www.brainready.com—that clearly shows the influence of his father's "nagging."]

Around this time Paul changed his last name from Skrowaczewski to Sebastien. He wanted an identity separate from "son of the conductor," and the name "Skrowaczewski" was not exactly MTV-friendly, a concern because of the direction in which his music career was taking him. (Founded in 1981, the cable network MTV—Music Television—which aired music videos round the clock, was still in its heyday during the early 1990s.)

"I just needed something catchier," Paul said, "and I'd heard that Sebastien is a family name, so I adopted it as my stage name." When he became twenty-one he changed it legally. "I was worried about doing that because I thought my dad would kill me! But he was totally great about it. 'OK, that's fine, I understand,' he said. I still feel guilty about it, and I've contemplated changing it back or adding it on. Now I have no interest [in] whether my name is pronounced correctly on MTV."

As young adults, Paul and Nicholas entered new phases of their lives during the 1990s. Nicholas expanded his drum-set studies and explored his newfound fascination with jazz and world music. He also rediscovered the piano, exploring unusual harmonic and melodic ideas through improvisation. He took a summer course in creative composition at the University of Michigan, and soon after he enrolled in Bennington College, Vermont, where free-jazz legends Bill Dixon and Milford Graves were his mentors. These years set Nicholas on a creative path that he still pursues today.

Paul founded the electronic rock group Psykosonik, whose popularity led to the aforementioned platinum record. Psykosonik soon signed a contract with Wax Trax! Records, a major "industrial" label in the 1980s and 1990s.[9] The group's first album, *Psykosonik*, was widely distributed in the United States and abroad in 1993. Paul wrote songs and many lyrics, sang, played various instruments, and also engineered and produced the popular recording.

In late January 1990 Skrowaczewski led Mahler's Second Symphony in the first round of performances with the Hallé Orchestra after the announcement of his impending departure. The Mahler, an all-encompassing conductor's piece, reminded the orchestra that Skrowaczewski was still its foremost maestro.

When he planned the Hallé's 1989–90 season, Skrowaczewski hadn't known that it would be his penultimate as principal conductor. Ironically, his "letter" to the audience, printed in that season's opening-program booklets, cited his beliefs about programming—the core issue that led to his resignation later that season:

> I address this matter [of programming] because some of our listeners occasionally react with indifference (marked by empty seats) or even hostility against performances of contemporary works. It is my hope that this short reminder of the obvious role of a great artistic organization such as ours will increase our tolerance and promote a lively curiosity that may bear genuine rewards.
>
> Continuing my concept of featuring during a single season two or three composers from different epochs, of differing styles, although with certain hidden similarities (as in the works of Haydn and Bartók last year), this year we will focus on Mozart from the one side and on Mahler-Bruckner-Shostakovich from the other. The differences between these composers are obvious to all, but more fascinating will be our exploration of the similarities, on several levels: form, thematic building, even harmony (watch for the twelve-tone row in the finale of Mozart's G minor Symphony and his "Mahlerian" dissonances in the first movement). In several places Bruckner's harmonic beauty and purity arise directly from Mozart, and his architectural process of building huge movements reflects an Amadeus care for balance and the right proportions. It is amazing to see how much Mahler and Bruckner influenced Shostakovich in spite of all the dramatic changes in their respective times. However, what is even more important is that Mozart, while taking the classical period to its peak, was also the harbinger of romanticism. All my life I have been fascinated by the simultaneous existence of these two opposite elements within the creative horizons of the same composer. May I call them the "classical mind" (Apollo) juxtaposed with the "romantic imagination" (Dionysus)?
>
> Maybe the existence of these two different sides leads us directly into an understanding of what great art really is, or at least should be. There is no doubt in my mind that art, along with religion, reflects our need for metaphysics, for "touching the unknown." Metaphysics is not just a term invented by philosophers but is something that is intrinsic to human nature.
>
> It is my hope that our concerts will stimulate our awareness of the meaning and value of music, that each concert will be our rite of initiation into an even deeper contemplation of the profound joy and rewards of opening ourselves to great art.[10]

Britain's *Classical Music* magazine noted that Skrowaczewski's "exhortation to audiences hits the nail on the head—it deserves to be quoted fully and widely adopted." And quote it they did: "The arrival of Stanisław Skrowaczewski [to the Hallé Orchestra] offered the best chance to turn Free Trade Hall into the Free Think Hall."[11]

During the 1989–90 season Skrowaczewski typically conducted major works from the standard repertoire while guest conductors led most of the newer music. In contrast, his last season (1990–91) would be more balanced, featuring "real Skrowaczewski programming" when he conducted. Motivated perhaps by the fact that it would be the maestro's last official "hurrah" with the orchestra, the board assented to his choices, despite the "non-salability" of his programs, as some members asserted.[12] This decision made the remaining time easier for him.

Skrowaczewski's composing life was not highly productive during this period, although it was hardly dormant. Performances of his earlier works continued at a consistent pace, and his latest world premiere occurred in spring 1989, when the Atlanta Virtuosi performed *Fantasie per Sei*. The piece originated at Skrowaczewski's 1985 guest-conducting engagement with the Atlanta Symphony Orchestra, when *Music at Night* was part of the program. Juan Ramirez, an orchestra violinist and also founder and artistic director of the Atlanta Virtuosi, was so taken by that work that he asked Skrowaczewski to write something for his chamber ensemble. Composing for the group's unusual sextet instrumentation—oboe, violin, viola, cello, bass, and piano—proved to be an intriguing task.

A month after the premiere of *Fantasie per Sei*, the Chicago String Ensemble performed one of Skrowaczewski's oldest compositions, Symphony for Strings. Earlier during the 1989–90 concert season he had conducted the Rundfunk-Sinfonieorchester Berlin in a performance and radio broadcast of *Music at Night*. He conducted performances of the Concerto for English Horn by the Indianapolis Symphony Orchestra (featuring Thomas Stacy) and by the Barcelona Orchestra Nacional in Spain. During this time the Philadelphia Chamber Ensemble gave another performance of Skrowaczewski's Trio for Clarinet, Bassoon and Piano. In spring 1990, while guest conducting the Minnesota Orchestra, he sketched ideas for a string trio commissioned by Ensemble Capriccio, a Twin Cities chamber ensemble. All things considered, he was doing pretty well handling "the conflict of his lifetime: composing versus conducting."[13]

During the 1980s and into the 1990s, Skrowaczewski was practically an unofficial member of Juilliard's faculty, given the frequency of his work with its students. His continued Juilliard success led to similar engagements at the Curtis Institute of Music, New England Conservatory, and Indiana University Bloomington. In summer 1990 he was offered a position leading the Yale School of Music Orchestra and the conducting program, a full-time job that he could not imagine accepting. Short-term teaching, however, continued to interest him. He conducted and taught again at the Los Angeles

Philharmonic's Summer Institute, where Lynn Harrell was artistic director that summer, with Michael Tilson Thomas and Leonard Bernstein serving as honorary directors.

In spring 1990, Skrowaczewski took the Hallé Orchestra on a three-week tour to Germany, Austria, and Switzerland, with Rudolf Buchbinder as soloist. The Hallé reprised its previous on-the-road triumph, winning enormous critical acclaim throughout the tour.

Most meaningful to Skrowaczewski, however, was the reception the orchestra received after its performance of Bruckner's Third Symphony in the Brucknerhaus in Linz, the Austrian city located near the composer's birthplace and where he spent the formative years of his adulthood. "The big stirring event [was the] Hallé in Brucknerhaus playing Bruckner's Third Symphony," the local paper reported. "The performance left the audience almost breathless, and how Skrowaczewski dealt with changes and logic of tempos should be put into the 'Golden Book' of the Brucknerhaus."[14]

When he finished his Hallé season soon after the tour, the maestro went to Canada for engagements with the Montreal Symphony Orchestra before undertaking a summer parade of guest conducting. Entitled to a short rest after this long string of engagements, he nevertheless could not refuse a request for help from Richard Cisek, who needed someone to replace unavailable music director Edo de Waart in his last two Sommerfest concerts with the Minnesota Orchestra.

The timing and serendipity of the request could not have been better. The two Sommerfest concerts were also Cisek's last official obligations as the orchestra's president. He was retiring after thirty-two years of service to the Minnesota Orchestra, the last twelve as its president. With little rehearsal Skrowaczewski led Beethoven's First and Ninth Symphonies back-to-back on two consecutive nights.

Reviews were exceptional, lauding the orchestra and the hometown maestro who had saved the day. Although Cisek's career stretched from the Doráti years through de Waart's tenure, he had worked with Skrowaczewski longer than with any other Minnesota maestro. It seemed fitting that Skrowaczewski was the conductor to honor his leadership. "[It was] a great finish to my career here," Cisek wrote him after the concerts, "and I'm proud that you were the one to do it."[15]

Skrowaczewski's last season with the Hallé Orchestra (1990–91) was celebratory on several fronts. First and foremost, it represented the kind of programming he advocated and featured guest conductors and soloists whose artistry he admired. Second, his concerts featured a splendid mix of works: favorites that he knew extremely well and other compositions that he had never or rarely conducted. Finally, he knew that at age sixty-seven, after serving as music director for five leading orchestras—three in Poland, one in America, and now one in England—he was not likely to take another full-time position. He simply did not want to spend the next phase of his life and career attached full time to a single orchestra.

John Robert-Blunn wrote of the Hallé's start to its 1990–91 season: "By including Barber's Violin Concerto instead of one of the great warhorses which might have filled the hall, Stanisław Skrowaczewski opened the 133rd season, his last as principal conductor, as he means to go on. Boldly going where the Hallé had not been [before.]"[16] He followed his opening concert with the complete ballet music of the 1910 version of Stravinsky's *The Firebird* and Beethoven's Piano Concerto no. 4, which was to have featured Austrian pianist Walter Klien, a close colleague of Skrowaczewski. British pianist Michael Roll substituted for the ailing Klien, who died in 1991 and who sadly has been largely forgotten today. (He recorded with Skrowaczewski and the Minnesota Orchestra in 1980 and 1987 for Vox Productions.)

Just as he did during his last season with the Minnesota Orchestra, Skrowaczewski led both the Seventh and Eighth Symphonies of Bruckner during his farewell season with the Hallé. He dedicated the performance of Bruckner's Seventh Symphony to the memory of Leonard Bernstein, who died in New York City four days before this Hallé concert.

During his last season with the Hallé the maestro somewhat relaxed his self-imposed policy of not programming his own music; he included his transcription of Bach's Toccata and Fugue in D minor in one program. Manchester's Goldberg Ensemble, however, took up the matter upon hearing one of Skrowaczewski's original compositions. Founded in 1982, this diverse, internationally renowned group performs in various configurations, including a string ensemble, chamber orchestra, and a contemporary-music ensemble. The Goldberg Ensemble performed Skrowaczewski's *Fantasie per Sei* in 1990 at the Royal Northern College of Music. The concert, among the ensemble's Contemporary Europe concert series that focused on Polish composers, also featured a work by Andrzej Panufnik.

Skrowaczewski has conducted Panufnik's music sporadically throughout his career, most notably the Nocturne, which the composer wrote during the late 1940s. The maestro conducted Nocturne worldwide, especially during the late 1990s. After an exceptional performance in Buenos Aires he wrote to the composer's widow, Camilla Panufnik, about his affection for the piece and its power to transform him spiritually. She wrote back to Skrowaczewski: "The miraculous change you describe when you conduct Nocturne is partly the music, and partly your enthusiasm and love for the work and understanding of Andrzej's intentions and feelings, which takes the players with you."[17]

Panufnik's children, Roxanna and Jeremy—who are the same ages as Skrowaczewski's sons—are also composers. Skrowaczewski has supported and encouraged Roxanna's music, which has been performed internationally; her choral music in particular has won acclaim. Her younger brother has composed film scores and earned recognition in the electronic dance-music world as a producer, deejay, and record-label owner. He has also worked in graphic design and video. Jeremy Panufnik and Nicholas Skrowaczewski, who share similar musical tastes and an artistic heritage as sons of major Polish composers, have become close friends in recent years.

Skrowaczewski returned to Poland in May 1991 to conduct the Warsaw Philharmonic at a National Festival and to lead premieres of several works. The trip marked his first return to the country since his 1987 Hallé Orchestra tour. From 1991 on, he regularly guest conducted in his homeland.

The maestro's compositional achievements of the 1990–91 season included the premiere of the String Trio and the completion of his Triple Concerto for Violin, Clarinet, Piano and Orchestra. In their respective genres, each composition is a central work for Skrowaczewski. They also were the first compositions of comparable proportion (more than twenty minutes long) since the Concerto for Orchestra and Violin Concerto, written five years earlier.

For the spring 1991 premiere of the String Trio, Skrowaczewski provided the following program note:

> Formally, I am following the traditional, "classical" principle to expose horizontally and soloistically each instrument and, at the same time, to "bind" the three players by their attention to chords and harmonies (which are so important to me), and to sharp rhythmic patterns that demand perfect synchronization.

> Harmonically, each movement has one or more melodic "groups" or "themes," where patterns of certain intervals (my "obsession" of interplaying augmented fourths and perfect fourths, diminished ninths with sevenths, etc.) have a common denominator, and are repeated in all five movements. The movements are: 1. *Misterioso* (slow)—*doppio piu mosso* (fast); 2. *Adagietto*; 3. *Scherzando—capriccioso* 4. *Adagio amoroso* 5. *Furioso*.[18]

The String Trio, which was well received at its premiere, was a semifinalist for the 1991 Friedheim Kennedy Center Award. "One can only regret," noted the *Star Tribune*, "that Skrowaczewski's busy conducting career robbed him over the years of so much composing time. The Trio, organized in five movements, is less dark, less gloomy than his earlier works. It is more traditional in its harmony but without losing a certain modernist tinge."[19]

Skrowaczewski's continued advocacy for works by other composers peaked during his final Hallé season, his last opportunity to infuse the ensemble's programming with new music. The conductor achieved an artistic coup by securing two works by Luciano Berio for a fascinating and unusual concert. The program included Berio's 1988 *Concerto II (Echoing Curves)* for solo piano and two orchestral groups, and his 1989 work, *Rendering*.

The latter composition must have stunned the Hallé board, which assumed that Berio's music would be highly avant-garde and lacking in audience appeal. In essence, *Rendering* is Berio's realization of Schubert's Symphony no. 10, a work for which only sketches were left at the time of the composer's death in 1828.[20] Berio completed the symphony using music from other Schubert compositions. The concert also included music by his former colleague, Italian-born German composer-conductor Bruno Maderna, and Maderna's transcription of some of Gabrieli's music. It was not a program for the Hallé's conservative public to fear.

Skrowaczewski often paired guest conductors with contemporary music. Neville Marriner led Tippett's *A Child of Our Time*, Kent Nagano and Hiroyuki Iwaki led works by Takemitsu (marking the composer's sixtieth-birthday year), and other guests led music by Messiaen and Austrian composer Herbert Willi. Skrowaczewski presented several established 20th-century works: violin concertos by Schoenberg and Stravinsky, Hindemith's *Symphonic Metamorphosis after Themes of Carl Maria von Weber*, Shostakovich's Tenth Symphony, and even Gershwin's Piano Concerto in F. Newer music led by Skrowaczewski included Alfred Schnittke's Violin Concerto no. 4 and John Corigliano's 1986 *Fantasia on an Ostinato*.

This last season featured more music by contemporary composers than had any previous season, thus demonstrating Skrowaczewski's persuasive powers and his dedication to the cause. According to author Robert Beale, his achievements were "against the odds."[21]

Smart was another spur to this artistic achievement, according to Stuart Robinson. "Clive Smart was a big advocate of Stan," Robinson said. "We used to burn the midnight oil saying, 'Dare we go along with this idea?' We wanted to be supportive of Stan. We didn't want him to get depressed about the financial circumstances." Although there were times when Skrowaczewski and the manager disagreed, Smart believed in and tried to support the artistic integrity of the three principal conductors with whom he worked during his thirty-three-year career (Barbirolli, Loughran, and Skrowaczewski).

"[Smart] has steered the orchestra through some of the most difficult times in its long history," noted Kennedy. "His length of service is only four years shorter than Sir Charles Hallé's and is six years longer than Sir John Barbirolli's."[22] Kennedy also acknowledged Smart's role in raising the orchestra's artistic reputation by engaging top-quality conductors—Abbado, Barenboim, and Haitink, for example, made their British debuts with the Hallé—and by supporting major composers as guest conductors leading their own music.

A month after his official retirement, Smart was publicly lauded for his contributions. The occasion was one of Skrowaczewski's last concerts as principal conductor, featuring a program of Haydn's Symphony no. 49 (*La Passione*) and Bruckner's Eighth Symphony. Kennedy called the performance an "apt valediction" to Smart and asserted that "not the least of Skrowaczewski's achievements is that he has taught [the Hallé] to play Haydn and Mozart with real finesse."[23] He praised Skrowaczewski's performance of the Bruckner as "an ideal partnership" with the orchestra: "[His] tempos for Bruckner are faster than those heard from, say, Jochum, yet there is no impression of undue haste. The grandeur is there because, like Günter Wand, he has an almost infallible instinct for the work's architecture. Unlike lesser Bruckner conductors, he trusts the score."[24]

Two weeks after the Bruckner concert, Skrowaczewski led his final performances with the Hallé as its maestro. He concluded this chapter of his career with a single work—Beethoven's *Missa Solemnis*—the very piece that the board had rejected as unsuitable for the orchestra's lighter Opus One concert series in 1987.

Despite last-minute replacements of two soloists due to illness, the maestro, the orchestra, and the Hallé Choir met the formidable challenges of Beethoven's massive opus. In the program booklet Kennedy paid tribute to Skrowaczewski in *An Appreciation*. Excerpts follow:

> In his eight years he has given back to the orchestral playing a sense of discipline that had sometimes been lacking. He is, I believe, a seeker after perfection and—like the late George Szell—has probably never been fully satisfied with the performances he has achieved.
>
> Skrowaczewski has striven to widen the Hallé repertoire of contemporary music but has undoubtedly been frustrated by the management's inability to take the financial risks involved and by the public's unwillingness to submit itself to new or even different experiences. To a musician like Skrowaczewski, Berg is one of the classics, and he cannot comprehend that there are still many to whom he represents the difficult and dangerous unknown!
>
> It is clear from Skrowaczewski's demeanour on the rostrum that all that matters to him is the music. He presents it to the audience honestly and straightforwardly and believes, as Adrian Boult did, that this should be enough. But we live in an age where "hype," superstar quality, and sheer gimmickry are often prized above deep and genuine artistic quality.
>
> Time will show that his contribution to Hallé history had been a crucial one. Meanwhile, we can only offer him our thanks and express the hope that we shall hear and see him as a regular guest conductor.[25]

Manchester audiences would see him again. The quality of Skrowaczewski's relationship with the Hallé Orchestra as a guest conductor over the coming decades became almost as meaningful to him as his bond with his other professional "family," the Minnesota Orchestra.

THIRTY

ANTON'S ASCENT

When I conduct the Eighth Symphony it seems to me that it is already over in a moment. Time really stops with Bruckner. It is like a religious meditation or a dream; you lose the notion of time.

—Stanisław Skrowaczewski, 1994

As sustained applause rang throughout Free Trade Hall, Skrowaczewski earnestly attempted to pass his bouquet to his *Missa Solemnis* soloists, who refused it. Then he tried to give the flowers to Pan Hon Lee, the Hallé Orchestra's co-leader, who would have none of it. Skrowaczewski simply had to accept the fact that this moment was his: the end of the orchestra's formal season and his last time on stage as its principal conductor. He finally acquiesced, smiled, clasped his hands—slightly shaking them to acknowledge his appreciation—and bowed. He performed this ritual a few more times before leaving the stage, well before the applause began its *diminuendo*.

The orchestra and audience thanked their maestro for eight years of outstanding concerts and also for something less tangible: high-quality artistic vision and leadership. When his resignation was made public, one patron's letter expressed great disappointment that the Hallé Concerts Society management could not resolve the issues surrounding Skrowaczewski's departure. "But what is left is a tribute to you," wrote Kenneth Bayliss. "The sound of the orchestra is resplendent and breathtaking in its subtlety of dynamic and expression. Your departure will be a sad, sad loss to music in the city."[1]

Manchester's (and the U.K's) loss of Skrowaczewski's leadership at the Hallé was substantial, but his relationship with the orchestra remained strong during his post-tenure years. At the end of the 1990–91 season, he and the orchestra had recordings in the pipeline and plans for more to be made in the future. They also had a South American tour scheduled for summer 1992. By then the Hallé's new conductor, Kent Nagano, had been appointed the orchestra's music director and principal conductor-designate. The title of music director was a condition of Nagano's acceptance of the Hallé's offer. Although the title implied that Nagano and the management would have greater artistic control, ultimately the limitations they encountered would resemble problems that confronted Skrowaczewski during his years with the Hallé. These limitations would lead to complications during Nagano's tenure.

Skrowaczewski had no direct role in the appointment of his successor, although he influenced the decision, and he was pleased that Nagano was chosen. Only forty years old, the Japanese-born American conductor had enjoyed success as an assistant conductor of the Boston Symphony, as conductor of Boulez's Ensemble Intercontemporain, and as music director of L'Opéra de Lyon.

Nagano had conducted much of Messiaen's oeuvre, some of which he featured in his Hallé debut. Skrowaczewski recalled the circumstances surrounding Nagano's appointment:

> I was fighting to get Nagano as a guest conductor, and I expressed my conviction to Clive Smart that he be engaged. The board was against it because of the expense. Finally he came for the first time, which led to his appointment as music director. I was so happy about that. I thought, "Now he will make changes in the programs." It was sort of my benign vengeance on the conservative public—to have a young, charismatic conductor bringing contemporary music.

Nagano programmed a great deal of contemporary music, but the lack of audience support for innovation, among other factors, almost brought an end to the orchestra in 1998.

Along with leaving his Hallé post in spring 1991, Skrowaczewski also left ICM, a decision that filled him with mixed emotions. He had an exceptional relationship with ICM's executive vice president, Stewart Warkow, but when the maestro reviewed his past and future U.S. engagements, he was disappointed with the number. "I have always tried to give concerts in America a special time slot and priority," Skrowaczewski told Warkow. He continued:

> At this point in my life I cannot just "sit back and enjoy it," nor do I want to dedicate all my time to composition. I have three children, two of whom just started college, and family dependents in Poland, so my "golden years" have not yet begun. I feel that I am forced at this point to seek other contracts; therefore, I have to request that you release me from my contract with ICM.[2]

Warkow understood Skrowaczewski's position, and the split was amicable. The maestro continued his friendship with Warkow, even calling on him from time to time for professional advice. In many respects, Warkow was among the last of a special breed of artists' managers who had a musical background and extensive experience. His career prior to leading the conductors' division of ICM was notable. Beginning in 1968, he spent fifteen years at Carnegie Hall, first as house manager and later as executive director. Earlier he had been Stokowski's manager for all of the maestro's New York work, which included the Symphony of the Air (NBC's follow-up orchestra to the famous NBC Symphony, which ended after Toscanini retired from it) and the American Symphony Orchestra. Warkow helped Stokowski establish that orchestra in 1962. He became its general manager, and Stokowski, age eighty, was music director, a post he held for ten years. Warkow also had close relationships with other major artists for whom he worked, such as Artur Rubinstein, Marian Anderson, and Andrés Segovia.[3]

ICM was on the verge of collapse near the time of Skrowaczewski's departure. Within a few years Warkow left the organization. Considering the attention and care that Skrowaczewski had received from Stephen Lumsden and Intermusica over the past eight years, he felt confident in turning over his North American work to them. They became his sole management, and the relationship continued positively for years.

In spring 1991, at his annual Minnesota Orchestra subscription concerts, Skrowaczewski enjoyed a particularly fruitful collaboration with Berlin-born violinist Christiane Edinger. They presented the orchestra's first performances of Szymanowski's Violin Concerto no. 1. The day after his Minnesota engagement Skrowaczewski sat in the audience at Temple Israel in Minneapolis to hear Ensemble Capriccio premiere his String Trio.

During summer 1991 Skrowaczewski had more space between engagements, which gave him needed time with his family and quiet hours alone in which to compose and to plan for upcoming seasons. An invitation from the Aspen Music Festival in June allowed him to combine mountain climbing and music making. He also had the chance to socialize with his good friend Lynn Harrell, soloist for the engagement.

Skrowaczewski's September 1991 engagement with the Saarbrücken Radio Symphony Orchestra again paired him with Edinger, this time in a concert featuring the German premiere of his Violin Concerto as well as Bruckner's Seventh Symphony. Unknown to Skrowaczewski at the time, the event would launch the most important recording project of his career and the fulfillment of a cherished dream:

> It was a Sunday, 11:00 a.m. concert, and my first time back with Saarbrücken after several years absence. Christiane Edinger played wonderfully. She's a great violinist who was well known in Europe. We were fond of one another, and she wanted to play my concerto elsewhere. The concert was recorded for broadcast, as is usually done there. A few weeks afterward they sent me the tape of the concert and asked if I would mind if they did a commercial CD of Bruckner's Seventh Symphony. I listened to the tape, and the recording quality was rather poor, but the performance was quite good, especially the first two movements. My tempo in the scherzo was too fast. I didn't like it, but I thought, "So what, let them use it."

> Then the recording company mentioned that if things went well with it, and if the orchestra agreed, they would like to start a complete Bruckner symphony recording cycle. Soon they decided that we would record one symphony a year, which we began doing in 1993. Eventually we held concerts before the recordings, giving the engineers a backup recording. This was good, because the acoustics in the studio were much worse than the hall. This issue was and is my dilemma [in] recording with them. So this live and unedited performance of the Seventh in 1991 started the whole project.

The timing of the agreement also was noteworthy. A year earlier Lumsden had received a letter from Chandos Records rejecting the idea of doing a Bruckner cycle with Skrowaczewski and the Hallé Orchestra, a project Lumsden had been pursuing for some time. The managing director of Chandos wrote: "I am afraid we could only become involved if this cycle was undertaken with a major international orchestra, such as the Philadelphia, Royal Concertgebouw, Dresden, etc., and only then if we obtained substantial funding. I do not think recording with lesser orchestras around the world would have any impact, however good they turned out to be."[4]

The Skrowaczewski/Saarbrücken recordings of the Bruckner symphonies were released singly on the Arte Nova (now Oehms Classics) label and as a boxed set in 2001. During the decade in which they were released, the recordings consistently won wide international praise, despite the lack of a "star" conductor, orchestra, or label.

Recognition of Skrowaczewski as a vital force in the ever-dwindling classical-music recording market rose considerably in the early 1990s, thanks to the start of his Bruckner cycle, new recordings with the Hallé Orchestra, and CD reissues of older recordings. In fall 1991 Philips Classics announced the first ten rereleases of its Mercury Living Presence recordings of the 1960s, including discs by Skrowaczewski and the Minneapolis Symphony Orchestra. Within a few years, all of Skrowaczewski's Mercury recordings were rereleased on CD and again reviewed.

Before Skrowaczewski left his Hallé post, he recorded two Shostakovich symphonies (the Fifth and Tenth) and Mahler's Fourth, all released after his departure. Reviews of the Shostakovich recordings—works Skrowaczewski "owned" interpretatively—were filled with thoughtful praise. *Gramophone*'s review of the Fifth offers a succinct summary:

> This is a performance, in short, in which every detail has been carefully thought out in the context of an evolving structure. It is also one in which you can be quite sure that no effect has been applied by the conductor: if an event shocks or chills or moves you, it is the composer's doing; and that is a tribute to Skrowaczewski's conducting, not a depreciation of it. His refusal to exaggerate or resort to melodrama will strike some as plain, perhaps, and the orchestral sound is on the lean side. But for once, no odious comparisons. If I had to live with a single account of this great symphony, I should be very content if it were this one.[5]

Skrowaczewski's realization of Shostakovich's Tenth earned similar praise from *Gramophone*: "Here is real insight into the harmonic tensions which support symphonic drama, and which it is not given to every conductor to perceive…. For at least the first twelve-and-a-half minutes of the Tenth I was convinced that I had heard no finer performance on record or in concert."[6]

Mahler's Fourth often is described as being transparent and delicate, exposing the sections and soloists through its orchestration. Skrowaczewski programmed the symphony for his penultimate concerts as principal conductor of the Hallé, and the recording documents the state of the orchestra as he left it. *Classic CD Magazine* offered a laudatory appraisal: "Bringing a composer's sense of pace and purpose to this score, he draws a delightfully pointed performance from a top-form Hallé Orchestra, reveling in every character detail of Mahler's mock-naïf invention."[7]

In 1990 IMP Classics reissued the best of its catalog, which included Skrowaczewski's 1987 Brahms' First with the Hallé. The first reissues on CD of Skrowaczewski's later recordings with the Minnesota Orchestra also appeared in the mid-1990s; his Ravel and Bartók sets were the first to be released. *American Record Guide*, which rated Skrowaczewski's recording of Bartók's Concerto for Orchestra as "among the best available," described it as a hybrid of Bernstein's romantic interpretation with the New York Philharmonic and of Fritz Reiner's "tense and white-hot" version with the Chicago Symphony.[8]

Perhaps Skrowaczewski's most important recording rerelease on CD during this period was his Concerto for English Horn and Orchestra, out in 1991, nearly twenty years after the original LP was issued. It was the first CD of a Skrowaczewski orchestral composition and the first to reach an international audience.

Throughout the 1990s Skrowaczewski wrote more consistently than ever before. With few formal orchestral affiliations, he was free of administrative duties for the first time since departing the Hallé. As a full-time freelancer, however, he had to be his own administrative assistant, dealing with programs, shipping prepared parts, adjusting schedules, making travel arrangements, and much more. Skrowaczewski was lucky to be assisted often by Krystyna.

As always, he spent countless hours preparing his scores, even for works he had conducted dozens of times. For every hour of actual rehearsal time, a conductor may spend at least three or four hours in preparation. Besides studying the score, the process involves time for interpretive reflection, consideration, and imaginative engagement; editing articulations, bowings, and dynamics; becoming familiar with other music by the composer; and researching the score's historical context. For Skrowaczewski, preparing himself to lead foremost orchestras around the world is a never-ending artistic commitment.

Despite the long hours of his freelance career, he made composing a priority, and having commissions to fulfill was a key motivator. From 1990 to 1995 he produced five substantial works and one orchestral transcription. Some years later he mused on this period of composing:

> I am almost surprised that these compositions came, but once I started to write, other pieces came more easily. It is very hard to start from nothing, but you develop certain ideas and constantly change them. The problem is that in all these works there are similar parts, so if I had a concert of all my own music, I would have to be very careful with programming because there is so much repeated and borrowed material from myself!

His self-deprecation seems exaggerated; clearly, he was exploring new compositional aspects, particularly in his *Passacaglia Immaginaria* of 1995, which was nominated for the 1997 Pulitzer Prize.

Commissioned by the Verdehr Trio, Skrowaczewski's Triple Concerto premiered in spring 1992. As with other such projects, the composer drew his inspiration from the instrumentation.

The Verdehr Trio—comprised of violin, clarinet, and piano—has a long history of innovation, having commissioned more than two hundred works from foremost American and European composers. Yugoslavian musician and trio founder Walter Verdehr was the first violinist to receive a doctorate from The Juilliard School. Clarinetist Elsa Ludewig-Verdehr and Gary Kirkpatrick, the trio's pianist at the time, both had international careers.

An excerpt from Skrowaczewski's Triple Concerto program note sets out his philosophy of composition:

> Any concerto for solo instrument(s) I have written has at least two different aspects: one, very obvious, is the "show" of the solo instrument, a display of all possibilities of tone, technique, dynamics, lowest and highest register, etc., thus displaying the skill of the player. The other aspect is purely musical, philosophical, and tentatively metaphysical: this is a matter of content, message, self-expression, search for meaning, and beauty. This is what great masters of the past gave us, this is what music and art were and are about. I live so emotionally with the great music of the past [that] I conduct. I want to have the same feeling for every piece of contemporary music—including my own. It may sound rather presumptuous (and hopeless) to compete with the best, but for me the urge to compose consists in trying to become as emotionally moved as I am in the presence of great composers.[9]

Skrowaczewski led the Honolulu Symphony in the premiere of the twenty-five-minute, five-movement Triple Concerto. He had had no previous experience with the Honolulu Symphony, an orchestra the trio secured for the concerto's first performance, but he was impressed: "The orchestra played and responded very well," he recalled, "and all the soloists were outstanding. They took a rare ownership of the piece."

In a letter to the *Honolulu Star-Bulletin*, American composer Armand Russell wrote: "This is a work of outstanding quality, which has strong emotional content [and] colorful orchestration, and reveals an expansive human spirit. A work of this kind is certainly deserving of, and slated for, more performances around the world and, ultimately, a commercial recording."[10]

Skrowaczewski felt less sanguine about the Triple Concerto: "I was unhappy with the concerto because I thought it was written more or less secondhand. I used a lot of my own tricks in some of the same passages here and there. I wasn't pleased by my own level of invention, but I was satisfied with the performance."

The Verdehr Trio apparently was pleased, however; when the opportunity to record the piece presented itself six years later, the ensemble committed it to CD. *Trio with Orchestra: Music by Skrowaczewski and David* was released on Crystal Recordings in 1998, with Leon Gregorian conducting Solisti di Praga. There have only been two other performances of the Triple Concerto, one at the Grand Teton Music Festival in 1994 and the other a year later by the National Orchestra of Spain. Both featured the Verdehr Trio and were led by Skrowaczewski.

In 2008 Walter Verdehr contacted Skrowaczewski about the possibility of performing the work again. After listening to the recording of his Triple Concerto for the first time in years, Skrowaczewski was surprised by his own piece: "I thought I might not like it, but I actually found it interesting. There are funny things in it that would appeal even to the public. Maybe I'll play it again."

In 1993 Skrowaczewski celebrated his seventieth birthday and introduced three new works. The first, *Fantasie per Tre*, was commissioned and premiered by the Huntingdon Trio, a Philadelphia chamber ensemble comprised of Diane Gold, flute and piano; Rheta Smith, oboe and piano; and Lloyd Smith, assistant principal cellist of the Philadelphia Orchestra. Smith was familiar with Skrowaczewski's music through his engagements with the Philadelphia Orchestra, but the Huntingdon's presentation of the Trio for Clarinet, Bassoon and Piano the previous year convinced the ensemble to commission a new piece from Skrowaczewski for its twentieth-anniversary season.

He finished the piece five months before its scheduled premiere. The musicians read it immediately and Lloyd Smith wrote to him expressing their great enthusiasm for the composition:

> I could feel the hair rising on my head as I looked through it for the first time. It is a rare privilege for a trio such as ours to have such a masterful work. The fitful energy and tension it creates with the quiet *misterioso* of the first movement, the tantalizing mix of old and new in the *Pavana*, the contained whispering of the *Allucinante* that explodes with the cello's fierce triplets, the haunting—and very effective—*Lento doloroso* which seems to look inward as the *Amoroso* smiles outward, and an *inspired* Finale which left us amazed as it unfolded—the work has captured us…. You have enriched our trio, our ears, and our lives.[11]

The Huntingdon performed the piece several more times, and another Philadelphian chamber ensemble also played it, but plans for a recording of it never materialized. *Fantasie per Tre* unfortunately has become neglected among Skrowaczewski's chamber music works. It awaits new champions.

Skrowaczewski's relationship with the Saint Paul Chamber Orchestra flourished at perhaps its highest point in 1993, during which the orchestra commissioned and premiered two of his works. He had not conducted the SPCO for two seasons, but in fall 1990 he began a five-year series of annual conducting engagements with the ensemble. When the SPCO invited him to produce a new work for chamber orchestra, he chose to set madrigals by Carlo Gesualdo, among the most original composers of the 16th century and certainly one with the most notorious biography. (After becoming Prince of Venosa he married and soon discovered that his wife was cheating on him. He ordered his unfaithful spouse and her lover murdered; supposedly they were impaled by a single sword.)

Highly chromatic and prone to abrupt mood swings inspired in part by the texts, Gesualdo's madrigals were attractive to Skrowaczewski, who had known this music for decades. He explained his motivation for creating the Gesualdo pieces:

> My only reason was that I adored Gesualdo's harmonies, those drips of chords, almost *Tristan* chords. They have beauty and simplicity, but they are also refined. I experienced this music long ago, listening to choirs sing them. It was a need in me, like with the Bach Toccata and Fugue. I *had* to do it. And as with the Rameau pieces, I wanted to present the Gesualdo madrigals authentically. Like the Rameau, the pieces profit from the use of the chamber orchestra instrumentation and from some sections repeated. By repeating something, you deepen it; otherwise, it does not stay in the listener's head.

The SPCO premiered Six Madrigals for Chamber Orchestra in spring 1993. Though later it was officially titled *Gesualdo di Venosa: Six Madrigals*, the authorship was appropriately listed in the SPCO programs as Gesualdo-Skrowaczewski. His orchestral version was in fact an arrangement of music originally conceived for five voice parts. Skrowaczewski selected six madrigals from Gesualdo's familiar six books of songs. The rather melancholy themes of his choices helped to unify the set.

He created a judicious orchestration and used effects, such as an almost-Tchaikovskian string *pizzicato* in the madrigal *Al mio gioir* (When I feel happy) that contrasted with *Lo pur respiro in cosi gran dolore* (My sorrow is deep, yet I breathe). Opening with gentle woodwinds, this madrigal immediately shifts to elegiac strings, and Skrowaczewski continues this shifting throughout the work, both enhancing and magnifying these incredible vocal pieces. The twenty-two-minute set of madrigals is a fine contribution to orchestral literature—and a superb vehicle for exposing audiences to Gesualdo's unique musical language.

While Skrowaczewski was concluding his engagement with the SPCO, another chamber orchestra project was in the works. Leopold Sipe, the SPCO's first music director and its leader for twelve years, had died earlier in the season. In 1959 violinist Sipe founded the Saint Paul Philharmonic Society, which soon became the "other" orchestra on the Twin Cities scene. Originally comprised primarily of the top musicians of the Minneapolis Symphony, the Saint Paul Philharmonic specialized in chamber orchestra literature. After a decade it had earned enough support and artistic credibility to become the Saint Paul Chamber Orchestra, which today is the only full-time professional chamber orchestra in the United States.[12]

Some eighty of Sipe's friends and colleagues banded together to commission a work in his memory for the SPCO and asked Skrowaczewski to fulfill the task. In November 1993, during the SPCO's thirty-fifth-anniversary season, he led the premiere of his Chamber Concerto, *Ritornelli poi Ritornelli*. He felt a personal connection to this commission, as his program note explains:

> When the SPCO asked me to write a composition for the orchestra's thirty-fifth anniversary in memory of Leopold Sipe, I became not only excited but

also emotionally moved. I knew Leopold Sipe, admired his professional skills, and followed with great interest his concerts and work. Later I was fortunate to have a closer relationship with this unique, excellent ensemble and its wonderful musicians. My admiration for the superb qualities of all the SPCO players is expressed in my Chamber Concerto, which has exposed solos for most instruments and makes high technical demands on the entire orchestra.

Although the Chamber Concerto is in one movement, there are several changes of tempo, instrumentation, and mood. Its subtitle, *Ritornelli poi ritornelli* ["Returns after returns"], indicates my obsession in the use of a certain principle of repeats as the main building factor in the overall architecture. On a smaller scale, I use repeats in harmony to build chords and their successions. This vertical factor, the harmony, has always been to me one of the most important parameters in music, both in my composing and performing.[13]

On the Friday evening after Thanksgiving, the audience at Ordway Music Theater expressed great appreciation for the concerto.[14] "Despite its complexity," noted the *St. Paul Pioneer Press*, "this is a lovely, understated piece, almost totally lacking in brashness or bravado. Mature and contemplative, the *Ritornelli* ends on an uncommonly tranquil note of almost perfect stillness, as if ripples in a pond have just disappeared."[15]

In early 1995 the MOA commissioned a work to honor the unprecedented forty years of support that Ken and Judy Dayton had given the Minnesota Orchestra, financially and in various leadership positions. Given the Skrowaczewskis' thirty-five-year friendship with the Daytons, the MOA turned to its conductor laureate for the commission. The Minnesota Orchestra premiered the result, *Passacaglia Immaginaria*, in April 1996 but not with Skrowaczewski at the helm. Eiji Oue, then in his inaugural season as music director, led the first performance.

Composing the nearly thirty-minute-long *Passacaglia* kept Skrowaczewski busy from summer 1993 until its completion in October 1995. Nevertheless, he managed to squeeze in one more "commission": a piece for Pat Morkrid, the son of his Wayzata neighbors, in honor of their incessantly barking dog.

In tandem with his composing, Skrowaczewski's conducting thrived during his career as a freelancer. His fall 1991 season seemed like old times: several weeks with the Hallé Orchestra, performances with the Philadelphia Orchestra, and engagements with orchestras in Munich and Rome.

His Philadelphia engagement featured the world premiere of Stephen Albert's *Wind Canticle*, a clarinet concerto for David Shifrin and the Philadelphia Orchestra. These concerts featured the last orchestral premiere of his music that Albert, winner of the 1985 Pulitzer Prize, would attend. Just over a year later, the fifty-one-year-old composer was killed in a car accident in Truro, Massachusetts, on Cape Cod.[16]

Skrowaczewski eased back into his role as a Hallé Orchestra guest conductor, and his signature programming style persisted. He led pieces new to the ensemble, including Szymanowski's Violin Concerto no. 2, Nicholas Maw's *Spring Music,* and less-performed works such as Frank Martin's *Petite Symphonie Concertante* of 1945, not heard in Manchester since the late 1960s.

Mozart's music figured most prominently in Skrowaczewski's 1991–92 Hallé concerts, a season when ensembles worldwide commemorated the 200th anniversary of the Austrian master's death. Skrowaczewski led the Overture to *The Magic Flute*, the E-flat Horn Concerto with Barry Tuckwell, Mozart's arrangement of Handel's *Messiah,* and most notably, the first Hallé concert performance of *Idomeneo*. Presenting the three-hour opera in one concert was a risky undertaking, especially given a less than ideal rehearsal schedule. The novelty of the venture and the artistry of the man on the podium nevertheless convinced the Hallé to take the chance.

In spring 1992 Skrowaczewski conducted a series of programs with the Warsaw Philharmonic, the first of which was a concert of Bruckner's Symphony no. 7 and his own Violin Concerto with Konstanty Andrzej Kulka as soloist. That special event celebrated the Philharmonic's ninetieth anniversary. Born in Gdańsk, Poland, Kulka has had an international career since the late 1960s and has been a soloist with such prestigious ensembles as the Berlin Philharmonic, Chicago Symphony Orchestra, and London Symphony Orchestra. Skrowaczewski has worked with Kulka in the United States, the Netherlands, and in Tokyo with the NHK Symphony Orchestra. Another concert included Skrowaczewski's Prelude, Fugue and Postlude, a score that had not been performed for more than forty years. An additional program in the Warsaw series featured his Concerto for Orchestra and Piotr Perkowski's Nocturne. These concerts marked the first time Skrowaczewski had conducted his music in Poland since leaving there in 1960.

He also opened the ISCM (International Society of Contemporary Music) World Music Days Festival in Warsaw with the Philharmonic, presenting four new works—one of which was a premiere—all by relatively young composers from Poland, Austria, Iceland, and South Africa. The strongest of the lot was Symphony no. 2 by John Speight, an important British-born Icelandic composer.

Skrowaczewski's work with the Hallé Orchestra continued in June 1992 with a tour of South America. The trip was the orchestra's first such visit since 1968, on the occasion of Barbirolli's twenty-fifth season as principal conductor. Skrowaczewski recalled the journey:

> It was a remarkable tour, and we were very well received. We played several concerts in Buenos Aires, and then we played in Rosario, a city located almost two hundred miles from the capital. From there we performed in Santiago, Chile; Montevideo, Uruguay; São Paulo, Brazil, and two concerts in Rio de Janeiro.

One of the concerts fell on the anniversary of some British holiday. We had to play some funny, odd music as part of our encores. I had heard of these pieces, but I had no idea how they were traditionally performed. There are customs of taking repeats and doing big *accelerandos*. The concertmaster, Pan Hon Lee, was whispering to me "repeat, repeat." I was completely lost, so he took over! There was a strong British constituency in Rio, so with our concert falling on this holiday we really had to play these pieces.

The holiday Skrowaczewski recalled was the Queen's birthday parade, which has marked the official birthday of the British sovereign for more than 200 years. A military ceremony known as Trooping the Colour accompanies the parade and involves slow and quick march music. The slow music is traditionally a waltz from Meyerbeer's opera *Les Huguenots*, and the marching music is often the *British Grenadiers*, performed in slow-to-fast tempos to evoke the regiments' varying marching speeds.

In another performance tradition closer to Skrowaczewski's musical world, his execution fared much better. At the start of the Hallé season Skrowaczewski led a concert commemorating the centenary of the USDAW (Union of Shop, Distributors, and Allied Workers), a major trade union in Britain. The program, atypical for Skrowaczewski, consisted of light, popular classics, including Tchaikovsky's *1812 Overture*. Toward the end of that piece, when the cannon thunders and the strings wail their streaks of scales, the *God Save the Tsar* hymn emerges, sometimes augmented by a chorus. When the Hallé performed the piece, every available player shouted the hymn (the only way to make it heard above the cacophony), startling the audience.

This Hallé "tradition," still in practice today, originated in an Opus One concert that Skrowaczewski gave early in his tenure. Perhaps with some trepidation, Stuart Robinson had asked him to conduct the *1812 Overture* on this series. The manager may have suspected that the maestro, like most musicians, was tired of performing the overture so often, especially as an accompaniment to fireworks displays. Skrowaczewski was happy to do the favor for Robinson, but he could not resist adding a vocal "commentary" on a work he regarded as debased through overexposure. Shouting also gave the musicians a welcome opportunity to release their own pent-up frustration with it. "I learned this from Rostropovich," Skrowaczewski said. "It was a Russian tradition. I've also always believed that the *1812* is a fine and exciting overture."

For Skrowaczewski, the highlight of summer 1992 was an engagement with Orchestre Métropolitain at the Lanaudière International Festival, during which he conducted four consecutive concerts featuring all nine Beethoven symphonies. Held annually since 1977 and located in Joliette, Québec, about an hour from Montreal, the Lanaudière Festival is Canada's answer to Tanglewood, Ravinia, and the Salzburg Festival. After only a few days of preliminary rehearsals, each concert was preceded only by a dress rehearsal.

Orchestre Métropolitain was exceptionally responsive to Skrowaczewski and eager to tackle its Beethoven immersion. He had led all the Beethoven symphonies recently, but had never conducted all nine compositions consecutively over a four-day period. The experience was instructive yet deeply affecting:

> With this opportunity you perceive so clearly the greatness of Beethoven's imagination. Normally you have just one or two of his symphonies on a concert and perhaps another a week or a month later. The difference between that experience and that of performing all of these works over four days is striking. The step from the Second to the Third is, for me, always dramatic, as it is from the Fourth to the Fifth, and again from the Eighth to the Ninth. It is really incredible what this man created over a twenty-five-year span. We usually take these symphonies for granted. But when you hear the First and the Second and then come suddenly to the Third, or to the Fifth, then you can imagine how people at that time in Vienna must have felt about them. Orchestras think they have played these works a hundred times and know it all, but they forget historical perspective. When you play all nine symphonies, it opens up another world to the musicians. It is extremely moving.[17]

Skrowaczewski started his second full season as a freelancer by opening the Philadelphia Orchestra's 1992–93 concert season with violinist Joshua Bell as soloist. Two months later the orchestra turned to Skrowaczewski again to replace the ailing Klaus Tennstedt and lead concerts of Haydn's Symphony no. 100 (*The Military*), and Mahler's Symphony no. 4, with soprano Roberta Alexander as soloist.

The impromptu Philadelphia Orchestra engagement interrupted what was to have been three open weeks for Skrowaczewski, the first time in decades that he had so much free time in his fall calendar. He needed time for composing, but after a week with the New World Symphony, he was off to Europe for concerts in Spain and then in Amsterdam, where he led the Concertgebouw Orchestra. He also conducted in Australia for the first time since 1988: concerts with the Melbourne Symphony and piano soloist Richard Goode, and an all-Brahms program in Adelaide with the Australia Symphony Orchestra.

Before he departed for Australia, he attended the funeral of Charlie Bellows, one of his closest friends. Bellows and his wife, along with the Daytons, had befriended the Skrowaczewskis in 1960, when they first arrived in Minneapolis. "This meeting began our strong friendship," Skrowaczewski recalled. Until his death, Bellows also had been the Skrowaczewskis' lawyer.

Later that summer Skrowaczewski conducted concerts at the Aspen Music Festival that included his Gesualdo pieces. During the engagement he found time to attend the opening of "Warsaw-Paris-Aspen," an exhibit by Polish-American artist Witold-K (Kaczanowski). K barely survived the Nazi occupation of his native Warsaw. In the late 1950s he co-designed Auschwitz's Cultural Center, where he created one of Europe's largest fresco ceiling murals. When Witold-K encountered Picasso in France in the late

1960s, they painted each other's portraits. Later he collaborated with a Los Alamos scientist to produce a sculpture using explosives, an ongoing project.[18]

Skrowaczewski knew Witold-K from a previous visit the artist had made to Minneapolis. He and Krystyna received him in their home, and the artist gave the Skrowaczewskis one of his original paintings, which hangs near Stanisław's home studio. The maestro, who appreciates the originality of the artist's paintings, explained his personal penchant for visual art:

> I'm very sensitive to color. When I see a painting I like immediately, it is because of how its colors are blended. I like Impressionists so much because the images are delicate and beautiful, not necessarily by the shape of the images but by the amalgam of colors. Even some flower arrangements capture me when their colors are well chosen. The connection is what delights me.

Fall 1993 witnessed two significant celebrations in Skrowaczewski's life: his seventieth birthday and the ninetieth anniversary of the Minnesota Orchestra. His impromptu engagements with the London Philharmonic Orchestra, however, remain his most vivid memory of this period. The Philharmonic was scheduled to open its South Bank season at Royal Festival Hall before a quick trip to Linz, Austria, for a concert at the International Bruckner Festival with its principal conductor, Franz Welser-Möst. But appendicitis prevented Welser-Möst from doing the concerts.

Skrowaczewski had time free before his first fall engagement, so he was able to take on the London Philharmonic's concerts. After a week in London he and the Philharmonic traveled to Linz. The concert took place on October 3, his seventieth birthday. Appearing at the International Bruckner Festival seemed a perfect gift for Skrowaczewski, although the program did not include a Bruckner symphony. But Skrowaczewski came perilously close to missing the performance:

> Before the concert I went to St. Florian with the principal cellist and trumpeter and manager of the Philharmonic. St. Florian is about ten miles from Linz and is home to the St. Florian Monastery, where Bruckner sang in the renowned boys' choir and later taught and played organ there. The monastery houses the famous "Bruckner organ." His tomb is underneath this organ, as was his request. We were with a group of tourists and a guide, but we separated from them, and they eventually disappeared. It was 5:00 p.m., and we had no idea that they would close the gate. We were high up on the second floor of this huge monastery. We couldn't get out, and no one could hear us. And the concert was at 7:30 p.m. It was very dramatic. We began shouting, and after a half hour of panic, somebody heard us. They opened the door, and we made it to the concert on time.

> After the performance and the applause, the whole orchestra sang "Happy Birthday" to me. I don't know how they found out it was my seventieth birthday; I hadn't told a soul.

Back in the United States there was at least one public acknowledgement of his seventieth birthday in October. Chicago's WNIB-FM classical-music radio station presented a Skrowaczewski tribute by playing his compositions, ranging from his earliest recordings to those performed with the Hallé Orchestra. The station also rebroadcast a 1987 interview with Skrowaczewski by Brian Duffie, who produced WNIB's seventieth-birthday tribute.

A month later the maestro conducted the Minnesota Orchestra's ninetieth-anniversary concert. The programmatic re-creation of the Minneapolis Symphony Orchestra's first performance featured traditional symphonic works, light pieces, and vocal selections.[19]

During the 1993–94 concert season Skrowaczewski conducted multiple performances of seven Bruckner symphonies in seven countries over the span of eleven months. The abundance of Bruckner's music he conducted that season elicited these observations:

> People often envision Bruckner symphonies in architectural terms: as great soaring cathedrals of sound. I agree but prefer more secular surroundings. It is like the Sydney Opera House. Somehow, those disconnected shells look different. But it is all a unit, an incredible piece of art. The [challenge] of [performing Bruckner symphonies], besides learning the notes, is that you have to let it flow, let it correspond to something that doesn't have time. It is easy for those who understand.[20]

> If you understand and take pleasure in the music, then time somehow stops. It is like being in love or [being] with someone very pleasant, when you suddenly say, "Ah! So many hours just went!" The involvement comes from understanding. You cannot come to it from perceiving music like entertainment, something that has a nice melody, a refrain. You have to understand the architecture of music and the beauty of the harmonies. If you have this, you can follow the logic of the harmonic development and grasp that all repeats are really not identical. Bruckner has many changes in polyphony and structure, which makes his music fascinating.[21]

For nearly fifty years Skrowaczewski's outstanding performances of Bruckner's symphonies nurtured a growing appreciation of the composer's music throughout the world. Beginning in the mid-1990s, however, his association with the Austrian master's oeuvre—reinforced by the praise his Bruckner recordings garnered—gave him more opportunities to conduct all of the symphonies.

When Witold Lutosławski died in February 1994, Skrowaczewski lost a friend and colleague whose music he advocated and conducted nearly as often as that of Bruckner. A March engagement with the Hallé Orchestra already included Lutosławski's

Concerto for Orchestra; dedicating the performance to the composer's memory was an obvious and appropriate gesture. No one had led that work more often and in more countries—and conducted more first performances of it—than had Skrowaczewski. A *Times* review noted the connection between the two composers:

> It is not just that Skrowaczewski and Lutosławski were friends or even that, having experienced the political conditions in Stalinist Poland, the conductor is aware of the constraints his colleague was working under when he wrote the Concerto for Orchestra. They also have certain significant, professional characteristics in common, notably a well-developed sense of the dramatic and a passion for clarity. So, with the temperamental basis of a great performance already in place, it was just a matter of technical preparation and execution. The result was even better than anyone could have expected.[22]

More than a decade after Lutosławski's death Skrowaczewski spoke of his friend's character, music, and their relationship:

> Witold was a very modest man in everything, in his behavior and how he lived. He and his wife lived spartanly, and they secretly helped out numerous people financially—not only composers but also nonmusicians who simply needed money. For lots of people, and especially Poles, he was regarded as a human being and composer of the highest class. He was never an opportunist, out there promoting himself, or the kind of composer always to ask for help from the minister of culture. He was not cold, but he was somewhat restrained in his emotions. He always thanked me and appreciated that I conducted his music, but he was not lavish about it. He said it, and that was it.
>
> As a creator, he was totally dedicated to his art and his development. Even though I generally did not feel his music deeply from the Second Symphony on—and he probably would have liked for me to conduct other works more often than his Concerto for Orchestra and *Musique funèbre* (two pieces I appreciate very much)—I greatly admired his consistent evolution as a composer. His Symphony no. 4, for example, was composed two years before he died, and it is, in my opinion, his greatest work.
>
> More than any other time during our friendship, I had lots of contact with Witold during his last years. Ever since 1991, every time I conducted in Warsaw we had dinner. The last time I saw him was for dinner at his home, about eight months before he died. I congratulated and praised him for his *Interlude*, composed for chamber orchestra [premiered in 1990 by the Berlin Philharmonic with Lutosławski conducting]. I did it once in Aspen and also in Saarbrücken in 2008. He wrote the piece as a connection between his *Partita* and *Chain II*, for solo violin and orchestra, but you can play it alone. In Saarbrücken we played it twice because it's only six minutes. It's so beautiful and delicate. It doesn't start; it doesn't finish. It just floats. You could make half an hour of it. And after all his other music and its special instrumentation, new ideas, twelve-tone use, pure aleatoric use like in his Third Symphony, an almost tonal Fourth Symphony, then here comes this

non-aleatoric piece that just flows and flows. I didn't say it to him, but my idea about the piece was that it seemed like he put his aleatoric ideas into a legato, slow 4/4 tempo. However, when I did speak to him about the quality of the harmonies, the beauty of this piece that one can play forever, and praised the fact that he wrote something such as he never had before, he simply said, very shyly and timidly: "Well, after seventy years of permanent work on the matter, maybe better ideas come to a composer." He accepted that this piece was extraordinary, even for him. And it is unique. He had never written anything like *Interlude*, and it struck me.

Skrowaczewski's summer 1994 season included a Robin Hood Dell engagement with the Philadelphia Orchestra and a concert with the Interlochen World Youth Symphony Orchestra. The ensemble works with renowned international conductors and soloists each summer. His friend Henry Charles Smith, who was teaching at the Michigan summer academy for gifted international high school students, had issued the invitation.

In August the Grand Teton Music Festival held a "Skrowaczewski Salute." A chamber music concert featured his Trio for Clarinet, Bassoon and Piano, and Skrowaczewski led a concert with the Festival Orchestra of his Triple Concerto (with the Verdehr Trio) and Bruckner's Fourth Symphony. The event was the only formal concert dedicated to marking Skrowaczewski's seventieth birthday. It also was a wonderful gathering for the entire Skrowaczewski family, which now included Melissa Lundin, whom Paul married in late 1993.

The mid-1990s were significant years in the lives of both Paul and Nicholas. The latter graduated from Bennington College, majoring in improvisation and percussion with a minor in acting. He spent one semester studying at a British drama school in London. After Bennington, Nicholas moved to New York City for several years to explore various music scenes and occasionally perform. He also studied audio recording and video production. Paul wrote two Top Ten *Billboard* chart singles for his band Psykosonik, and the group's MTV videos were played worldwide. Another of Paul's songs was featured in the 1995 movie *Mortal Kombat*. Psykosonik toured extensively and performed at the Lollapalooza Music Festival.

Although Skrowaczewski did not conduct as many Bruckner symphonies during the 1994–95 concert season, they nevertheless figured prominently in his guest conducting. Near the end of the season he added Bruckner's seldom-performed First Symphony to his recording cycle with the Saarbrücken Radio Symphony Orchestra.

That fall Skrowaczewski led another work that he seldom conducted: Górecki's Symphony no. 3, *Symphony of Sorrowful Songs*, the most popular classical work of the first half of the 1990s and perhaps the most celebrated composition by a Polish composer since then. Its minimalist aesthetic did not appeal to Skrowaczewski, but when the Toronto Symphony asked him to conduct the work's Canadian premiere, he obliged.

A fifty-minute marathon for string players, Górecki's famous symphony includes many repetitive passages. At the first rehearsal Skrowaczewski described the work as a kind of meditative piece that required constant "fiddling up and down." After a single reading of the work, he announced—to the musicians' great relief—that they would only do it once more, at the dress rehearsal.

Deleting the symphony's multiple repeats to shorten the performance also would have helped the musicians, but Skrowaczewski rejected that option. Having made such cuts the first time he performed the work, he decided soon after that only on rare occasions would he impinge on music by others. He explained:

> Long ago, in the finale of Shostakovich's Eleventh Symphony, I did some cuts, and then I considered it completely wrong to do. I decided, "So what if he repeats and repeats." He obviously wanted this sort of atmosphere in the music. So I decided one cannot do it. But it does happen with a number of conductors. Cuts are done in Tchaikovsky's *Francesca da Rimini* and in some Russian symphonies, especially [those] by Rachmaninoff. I've never conducted a Rachmaninoff symphony in my life, so I don't know why some people make cuts, but apparently they can be repetitive and too long. It was popular at one time to make cuts in works. Famous conductors like Stokowski and Ormandy would do it.
>
> One of the most surprising examples I had heard of happened with Giulini. After Krystian Zimerman made his American debut with the Minnesota Orchestra, he went to the L.A. Philharmonic to record Chopin concertos with Giulini, who made cuts in the introduction to the First Concerto but didn't tell Zimerman about it. Zimerman was so paralyzed with anger he didn't even speak, and refused to play. It was strange that someone like Giulini, so religiously faithful and committed to scores, would do this. Believe it or not, cuts in Chopin piano concertos were popular in America at one time. Some people thought, "Well, there's nothing to play, it's repetitive, so we'll just play eight bars and then comes the soloist." It was musically misunderstood. But I was shocked that this would happen with Giulini.

Górecki's symphony was among a relatively large number of contemporary pieces that Skrowaczewski conducted during the 1994–95 season. At an engagement with the Toronto Symphony that reunited him with Isaac Stern, Skrowaczewski led Panufnik's Nocturne. He repeated the piece later in France and Minnesota. He also added a new Lutosławski work to his repertoire with the Berlin Symphony Orchestra. *Chain II*, a work for solo violin and orchestra from the mid-1980s, was composed originally for Anne-Sophie Mutter, who was also Skrowaczewski's soloist. Lutosławski composed three *Łańcuch* ("Chain") works, so-called because of his method of overlapping gestures like the links of a chain. In Manchester, Skrowaczewski marked Alfred Schnittke's sixtieth birthday by leading the Hallé in a performance of the Russian composer's Concerto for Piano and String Orchestra, a work from 1978.

He also had engagements that season with America's elite training orchestras. He shared his wisdom about traditional repertory pieces with the New World Symphony and others, but he also conducted new music—the New York premiere of Ellen Taaffe Zwilich's Bassoon Concerto and Joan Tower's *Fanfare for the Uncommon Woman*—with the Juilliard and Manhattan School of Music orchestras, respectively.

A Minnesota resident since 1960 and the only major international conductor residing in the state, Skrowaczewski lived less than a thirty-minute drive from the University of Minnesota. In 1995 he finally was engaged to guest conduct the university's student orchestra. Other invitations came from Gary Graffman, director of the Curtis Institute of Music, and from Richard Hoenich, former principal bassoonist and associate conductor of the Montreal Symphony, who recently had become the director of orchestral activities at New England Conservatory (NEC).

Hoenich, enamored of Skrowaczewski's musicianship since working with him as a bassoonist with the Montreal Symphony, was committed to maintaining NEC's relationship with the maestro. For his first NEC performance in 1994, Skrowaczewski led Bruckner's Eighth, a work that most likely was new to many members of the NEC Symphony Orchestra. *The Boston Globe*'s Richard Buell could not contain his excitement about the concert:

> This was a great deal more than a professional-quality performance coaxed out of [the] skilled and eager young musicians; everybody concerned seemed to be playing for their lives. The particulars—an impressive warmth and solidity to the string sound, some attractive and individual solo playing, and a transparency of texture that was at times revelatory. (So *that* is what the harps and horns have been trying to tell us in the second movement's Trio section. One felt like calling the City Room.) The veteran Skrowaczewski is clearly a painstaking conductor but—equally clearly—not a fussy one. He and his players were the medium through which Anton Bruckner was speaking to us. This, we remembered, was why people love going to concerts. For hours afterward one could think of nothing else. Bravo![23]

News of the concert's success spread across Boston. The performance was later broadcast on WGBH radio.

In February he was invited to conduct in Katowice, his first engagement there since leaving Poland. The occasion marked the sixtieth anniversary of the Silesian State Philharmonic, which Skrowaczewski had served as music director from 1949–54. It was becoming a tradition for him to start his late spring and early summer engagements in Poland.

He limited his 1995 summer engagements so he could finish his *Passacaglia Immaginaria*. Although the work's premiere was scheduled for spring 1996, he needed the summer months to complete it.

The fall season was intense, and he also had a new conducting assignment—artistic advisor of the Milwaukee Symphony Orchestra for its 1995–96 and 1996–97 seasons. The orchestra was in a state of transition. Music director Zdeněk Mácal was leaving at the end of the 1994–95 season, and the orchestra needed time to find a replacement. Although the orchestra wanted Skrowaczewski for the permanent post, he agreed only to assist the ensemble as he had helped the Saint Paul Chamber Orchestra. He was popular with the musicians, who appreciated his artistic advice and conducting. This relatively minor yet highly pleasurable commitment would evolve into a substantive relationship between Skrowaczewski and the Milwaukee ensemble.

THIRTY-ONE

SEVEN GOOD EARS

The seven kinds of ear—the seven hearings, all directed by the mind—which the compleat conductor has, are for (1) harmony; (2) pitch and intonation; (3) dynamics; (4) timbre; (5) rhythm and articulation; (6) balance and orchestrational aspects; and (7) line and continuity. I cannot think of a major conductor, working today, who possesses all seven, with the possible exceptions of Carlos Kleiber, Haitink, Skrowaczewski, and Gardiner.

—Gunther Schuller, *The Compleat Conductor*

Founded in 1959, the Milwaukee Symphony Orchestra has a remarkable record of accomplishment over its relatively short life as a major American orchestra. Although it cannot compare historically to its neighboring orchestras in Minnesota, Chicago, and Detroit, the ensemble nonetheless has made its mark on American cultural life.

Arthur Fiedler, the most famous pops conductor of all time, led the first concert of the former Milwaukee Pops Orchestra under its new name, the Milwaukee Symphony Orchestra. The orchestra later came into its own under the direction of Lukas Foss, the composer, conductor, and pianist who was its third music director. Under Foss, the ensemble made its first European tour, held American music festivals, and made recordings. His successor, Zdeněk Mácal, continued to build the orchestra's reputation through recordings and international tours. During his tenure the orchestra created expansive arts education programs, and today the Milwaukee Symphony Orchestra is a recognized national leader in those efforts.[1]

Having guest conducted the Milwaukee Symphony with distinction over the years, Skrowaczewski already enjoyed a terrific rapport with its musicians. In a preview article before his debut concert as artistic advisor, the *Milwaukee Journal Sentinel* posed the question of Skrowaczewski's popularity with the Milwaukee players: "'It's his Old World gentlemanly quality,' said Donald Haack, the orchestra's principal trombonist. 'It's a general courtesy that conveys his respect for the musicians. The music is more important to him than conducting technique. That gives us freedom to play. He allows us input.'"[2]

During this period of his career, Skrowaczewski exhibited more freedom in rehearsals and on the podium—a quality he was said to lack during his tenures in Minneapolis and Manchester. Now in his early seventies and considered a grand, "gracious master," as the *Milwaukee Journal Sentinel* described him, he was appreciated whenever and wherever he conducted.[3]

Innately modest, Skrowaczewski neither sought nor exploited this role. From his perspective, he simply was working with the musicians to approach great masterworks with respect, striving together to achieve fresh, spontaneous performances. His productivity during his seventies and eighties—in conducting, recording, and composing—matched the activity of colleagues who were decades younger.

Although Skrowaczewski's stamina and enormous capacity for work remained essentially the same as it always had been, during this next phase of his life (the mid-1990s to the present) his conducting became more authoritative yet simpler in its communication to musicians and audiences. When asked to describe the qualities of a good conductor, he offered a concise summation:

> Conducting is an enigma. It is the job of helping the musicians imagine the sound before they begin to play. The essence of it is a perfect knowledge of the score, both spiritually and technically, and a very strong interpretation of the moment, with an exceptionally robust conviction, so there is no doubt about how it is done. If the conductor is insecure or afraid, the players will feel it immediately. I always give the feeling that I have no doubt that they can play the difficult passages. It is important to keep the pride of the orchestra high.[4]

The Milwaukee Symphony Orchestra welcomed Skrowaczewski's interpretive gifts, having had few opportunities to work with a conductor of his international stature. The ensemble, which ranked among the nation's top twenty orchestras, was still a young organization, and he became the "musical father figure" it needed.

For Skrowaczewski it was an ideal short-term relationship. He enjoyed working with the orchestra in Milwaukee, only a quick flight from Minneapolis. His initial obligations consisted of four weeks of subscription concerts and a series of three concerts included in the orchestra's Russian Festival. He also assisted the ensemble in planning its 1995–96 and 1996–97 seasons, served on a committee that hires and grants musicians tenure, and advised the organization on aspects of its development.

During his two seasons with Milwaukee, Skrowaczewski led many of his favorite pieces, including several from choral literature. New to his repertoire was Bernstein's *Chichester Psalms*. He enjoyed selecting fresh or seldom-performed works, "exotic spices to a delicious meal," as he described them, such as Harbison's *Most Often Used Chords*, Revueltas' *Sensemayá,* and William Bolcom's Violin Concerto.[5] However, it was with Bruckner and the Eighth Symphony in particular that Skrowaczewski made his greatest contribution to the Milwaukee Symphony Orchestra.

By the end of Skrowaczewski's first season, the Milwaukee Symphony had secured a new music director, Andreas Delfs, a German conductor who was general music director of the Hannover Opera House and who previously had served as a resident conductor of the Pittsburgh Symphony. Delfs led the Milwaukee Symphony for twelve seasons and brought the orchestra to further national prominence. Edo de Waart became music director of the Milwaukee Symphony in 2009, and its ability to engage a conductor of such international stature underscores the orchestra's strong artistic growth.

Skrowaczewski's years in Milwaukee were greatly appreciated, according to *Journal Sentinel* music critic Tom Strini: "[Skrowaczewski] proved himself the perfect choice for the interim position of artistic advisor: a nice guy who knows his stuff, a distinguished musician with no further ambitions to be realized through a position such as this. He was there in the MSO's time of need."[6]

Twin Cities orchestras and the Hallé Orchestra continued to appreciate the maestro's experience. In 1995 he led the Saint Paul Chamber Orchestra in a program that included two first performances for the ensemble: Penderecki's Sinfonietta for Strings and Harbison's Flute Concerto, which was a joint SPCO commission with the American Composers' Orchestra and Oregon Symphony.

Skrowaczewski returned to the SPCO two years later in an all-Mozart concert that featured violinist Pamela Frank, daughter of pianists Claude Frank and Lilian Kallir. A week later the maestro and soloist repeated their Mozart Concerto no. 5 performance in Washington with the National Symphony Orchestra. Skrowaczewski and Claude Frank had collaborated several times during their careers. Frank, a longtime member of the Curtis Institute faculty, wrote to Skrowaczewski expressing his delight that Pamela would be his soloist. Frank and his wife had fond memories of "Uncle Stan" interacting with Pamela as a small child in the early 1970s when he was in town conducting the Philadelphia Orchestra. Since the 1990s Pamela Frank has had a diverse and distinguished international career as a soloist, chamber musician, and educator.

During the 1995–96 season, Skrowaczewski had a new experience with the Minnesota Orchestra—as a nonperforming conductor-composer. After his annual engagement he returned in the role of composer and attended rehearsals and the April premiere of *Passacaglia Immaginaria*. Although not performed by Skrowaczewski as often as *Music at Night* or the Concerto for Orchestra, the *Passacaglia* is one of his most important orchestral works, along with the Concerto for Orchestra and the Symphony [2003].

At the time of the Minnesota Orchestra's premiere of the *Passacaglia* under Eiji Oue, Mary Ann Feldman described the qualities that make it distinctive among Skrowaczewski's music. Excerpts from her program note follow:

> *Passacaglia Immaginaria* invites the listener into a provocative sound world of its own unique construction. Just as the passacaglia of the baroque was a [form] of continuous variation on a ground, typically proceeding in slow triple meter, Skrowaczewski's work is an expansive metamorphosis of the subject emanating in the hush of half the double basses twelve bars into the work. Their quiet statement emerges from delicate strokes of percussion, whose tints and vibrations command a significant place in this twenty-eight minute score.
>
> Out of an abstract thought in the basses emerges a symphonic movement of continuous development. Everything can be traced back to the beginning, though the listener is not expected to be aware of the changes, as the same theme, transformed and hidden, imparts unity to the music. Some of the harmonies, too, originate from the subject, but the music does not invite you to speculate about the relationship. Instead, the *Passacaglia Immaginaria*

beckons the listener into the realm of the imagination, just as its composer indulged the creative artist's prerogative of turning his imagination loose with the abundant possibilities of his originating thought.[7]

Relieved to be present only as a composer seeing his new piece meaningfully realized, Skrowaczewski nevertheless found the experience challenging. Oue devoted the majority of rehearsal time to Shostakovich's Fifth Symphony, the program's centerpiece. Ever polite and tactful, Skrowaczewski did not press Oue to work toward greater detail and clarity in the premiere of his work.

Oue considerately programmed Skrowaczewski's piece alongside a popular symphony and Barber's Concerto for Violin, performed by soloist Joshua Bell. The audience, musicians, and critics received the premiere warmly. "It sounded just like the composer himself: lean, energetic, with clarity of mind and greatness of soul," wrote Michael Fleming.[8] He offered a perspective on Skrowaczewski's achievement:

> The Skrowaczewski work, finished late last year, was much more than the usual contemporary curtain-raiser. While younger composers have fled the temple to write "Superman" symphonies and operas on Jackie O., Skrowaczewski has kept the flame burning. He offered both skill and passion in this half-hour piece, challenging both the players' technique and the audience members' ears.[9]

After hearing a recording of the work, Gunther Schuller called it Skrowaczewski's "best piece." He wrote to his colleague: "From every point of view—thematic/motivic, harmonic, timbral, textural, formal/structure—it is virtually a perfect piece."[10] Schuller was eager to conduct Skrowaczewski's *Passacaglia* and eventually did, creating a detailed performance with the New England Conservatory Honors Orchestra in 2001.

A year after the premiere of *Passacaglia Immaginaria*, Columbia University notified Skrowaczewski of its nomination for the 1997 Pulitzer Prize in Music. However, Wynton Marsalis's oratorio *Blood on the Fields* for jazz ensemble and three vocalists received the prize that year, making him the first jazz artist to win the composition award.

Seven months after the Minnesota Orchestra's premiere of *Passacaglia Immaginaria*, Skrowaczewski led concerts and recording sessions that are among his finest artistic collaborations with his former orchestra. Bruckner's Ninth Symphony was the second Bruckner symphony that he had programmed as music director in 1964; he repeated it in 1975 and again in 1983. Consequently the Ninth Symphony was not nearly as familiar to the orchestra as the more popular Fourth and Seventh symphonies. Still, Skrowaczewski was thrilled with the prospect of recording the towering work with his Minnesotans, in fall 1996.

He had not recorded with the orchestra since 1983, when he completed sessions of Prokofiev's *Scythian Suite* for Vox, his last release on the label. Marriner and de Waart both made recordings with the Minnesota Orchestra, but Oue made it a priority. He and the orchestra began a relationship with the San Francisco-based Reference Recordings, an independent classical, jazz, and vocal label whose chief engineer and technical director is Keith O. Johnson. By the time Skrowaczewski's recording of the

Bruckner Ninth was released, Oue and the Minnesota Orchestra had recorded four CDs with Johnson, and an all-Stravinsky recording had earned a Grammy nomination for Best Classical Engineered Recording.

Despite recent advancements in recording technology, the Reference engineers experienced some difficulty during the Bruckner sessions. Skrowaczewski recalled the problems:

> The orchestra was in wonderful shape with this symphony, and they played beautiful concerts. When we started to record, the special atmosphere of the performances continued, and the style was excellent. But when I heard the playback of the first movement, the balances were completely wrong. The engineers had to change the microphones, and we had to repeat the whole main section of the first movement several times. This brought down our morale, and the elevation of the atmosphere we had achieved dissipated. Unfortunately the engineers were not prepared to record this symphony. It was a blow to me. The orchestra, however, was so alert and prepared and always gave their best throughout the two days we recorded.

Whatever misgivings Skrowaczewski may have had about the results, the Bruckner Ninth CD, released in fall 1997, was a critical success. Glowing reviews described it as having surpassed many of the thirty other extant recordings of the Ninth. It won the 1998 Golden Note Award for Best Original Recording and received a 1999 Grammy nomination for Best Classical Engineered Recording (Keith Johnson).

Liner notes for the Bruckner Ninth recording incorporated Skrowaczewski's reflections on the symphony:

> Every few years I look at and study Bruckner again with more and more amazement. The Ninth is a summit of what the symphony grew to be in the course of the 18th and 19th centuries. For its content, for its emotion, this work can satisfy our metaphysical yearnings, our never-ending search for the invisible, the infinite. Unlike some composers, for whom the twilight years represent a decline, Bruckner at the end explodes with image, invention, and craftsmanship. In the Ninth Symphony, he is at his peak.[11] In fact, the last three Bruckner symphonies, especially, speak to us about everything to which mankind has idealistically aspired. They rejuvenate a spiritual healing force.

By the time of the Bruckner CD's release, recordings of three symphonies from Skrowaczewski's Saarbrücken Bruckner cycle (the Seventh, Fifth, and Sixth) were also available. In a review of the Sixth Symphony, Lawrence Hansen of the *American Record Guide* made a point echoed by critics throughout the 1990s:

> In my experience, Skrowaczewski is one of the greatest Brucknerians of our century. His talent seems to have been underrated and overshadowed by flashier, more media-friendly conductors (in this he is like Wolfgang Sawallisch). And yet, in the 1960s and 1970s, after succeeding Doráti at the Minnesota Orchestra, he gave that ensemble the polish and solid foundation that resulted in its becoming a world-class ensemble in the 1980s and '90s.

And among the high points of Philadelphia Orchestra broadcasts in the 1980s were Skrowaczewski's appearances [leading] Bruckner.[12]

An interesting old recording of Skrowaczewski's resurfaced in 1999. With the L'Orchestre de la Suisse Romande and Michel Schwalbé, he had recorded Henryk Wieniawski's Concerto for Violin and Orchestra no. 2 in January 1963. It was rereleased on the Biddulph label with Schwalbé playing other concertos led by other conductors. Born in Poland in 1919, Schwalbé was Karajan's concertmaster with the Berlin Philharmonic throughout the conductor's thirty-four-year tenure. After his retirement as concertmaster, he still attended rehearsals of the Berlin Philharmonic as an observer.

In 1999 the Minnesota Orchestra would be partner to another Skrowaczewski achievement, performing the revised version of his Concerto for Orchestra. During Christmas 1997, while enjoying some reflective time, Skrowaczewski decided to completely revise the piece. He worked on it during January and in spring and late summer 1998. "No one asked me to do this," he said. "I did it for myself."[13]

The number of corrections and revisions motivated Skrowaczewski to compose an entirely new score. He explained his rationale to Michael Anthony:

> I wasn't happy with the first movement. I found certain sections as unnecessary or not good enough. Additionally, the original idea was to use all the musicians of the orchestra for this concerto, which meant quadruple woodwinds and a large five-person percussion section. I discovered that I didn't really need these extra instruments. And without them I found that the sound didn't change; in fact, it became clearer. Also, I had had many propositions for performances of the piece, but orchestras couldn't afford the extra musicians. So the revised work has practical and musical benefits. More orchestras can play it now, and I believe I have achieved an all-around leaner character that should enable the work to register effectively beyond its original celebratory function.[14]

In November 1999 Skrowaczewski led his new Concerto for Orchestra during the Minnesota Orchestra's celebratory twenty-fifth anniversary of the opening of Orchestra Hall. The timing was serendipitous—the piece had originally been composed for the tenth anniversary of Orchestra Hall's opening. A year earlier Skrowaczewski had conducted the work's world premiere in Philadelphia with the Curtis Symphony Orchestra and soon afterward in Boston with the New England Conservatory Honors Orchestra. A few months later he gave the New York premiere of the concerto with the Manhattan School of Music Orchestra, but the Minnesota Orchestra's performances of the revised piece were the first by a professional ensemble.

Concerto for Orchestra was nominated for the 1999 Pulitzer Prize, which went to Melinda Wagner, only the third woman to win the award. Skrowaczewski was honored to have both pieces he had submitted receive nominations (the *Passacaglia Immaginaria* in 1997). He accepted the decision with a sense of perspective:

One of the jurists told me that in 1997 it was important for them to have a jazz composer, as it had never happened before. In 1999, two composers on the jury called me, but I was away. They told Krystyna that Concerto for Orchestra was among the best pieces but that the Pulitzer is now chosen not only by composers but also by a large board.[15]

Though Skrowaczewski's composing could not keep pace with his conducting and recording during the late 1990s, the recognition of his talent as a composer grew. He was less reluctant now to program his works when guest conducting, and his music was being heard more often in the United States and abroad. In Poland, however, Skrowaczewski's conducting reputation still overshadowed his renown as a composer, and he rarely was asked to lead his music in his homeland. Jan Krenz's performance of Skrowaczewski's Chamber Concerto (*Ritornelli poi Ritornelli*) with the Warsaw Philharmonic at the 1996 Warsaw Autumn Festival was the composer's second late-period work heard in Poland.

Around this time Ensemble Capriccio, with funding from the McKnight Foundation, commissioned a chamber work, Skrowaczewski's first such piece in a decade. *Musica a Quattro*, for string trio and clarinet, had its premiere by the group and Burt Hara, principal clarinetist with the Minnesota Orchestra, at Walker Art Center in 1998. The five-movement chamber work was commissioned both to honor Skrowaczewski's seventy-fifth birthday year and Hara's return to the orchestra after a year as principal clarinetist of the Philadelphia Orchestra.

The piece remains one of Skrowaczewski's most personal and expressive chamber works. Until it disbanded in 2005, Ensemble Capriccio was the chamber group that most avidly supported Skrowaczewski's music. In summer 1998 it performed the String Trio at the International Festival of Music in Costa Rica and in 2000 performed *Fantasie per Sei*. That performance found its way to the first all-Skrowaczewski chamber music CD, *Skrowaczewski's World*, released on Innova in 2002. That same year, Composers Recordings, Inc. (CRI) released a CD that included Skrowaczewski's String Trio performed by Ensemble Capriccio.

Skrowaczewski's seventy-fifth birthday—October 3, 1998—was an ideal time in which to reflect on his long career and reassess his contributions to music. No formal events marked the maestro's seventy-fifth "name day," as he calls birthdays, but the next day Minnesota Public Radio featured him and his compositions on its "The Composer's Voice" series.

In 1998 the McKnight Foundation launched its annual Distinguished Artist Award and selected Dominick Argento as its first recipient. That fall Ken Dayton submitted a comprehensive document on Skrowaczewski's career to the McKnight Foundation in nomination for the award, which the maestro ultimately received in 2004. Excerpts from Dayton's letter to the foundation reveal the perspective of a man who held Skrowaczewski and the Minnesota Orchestra in the highest regard:

> When as an old man Ormandy returned to Minneapolis as a guest conductor, he told the executive committee, "You have the last great music director.

Don't ever let him go. They just don't make us anymore." Claudio Arrau told me after a concert, in a statement so typical of numerous great guest artists during those years, "I can do things with Stan that I would never dare attempt with other conductors." I think it is fair to say that the depth of his musical interpretations has not been equaled since his retirement.

Ormandy was a young conductor learning his trade when he was here. Mitropoulos was a marvelous and exciting conductor, but a poor music director. Doráti was the opposite, a great music director and a superb recording artist but a rather pedantic conductor. Marriner, who succeeded Stan, gave his music a delightful sheen and polish, but his interpretations and repertoire lacked depth. DeWaart did a wonderful job of rebuilding the orchestra to the level Stan left it at, and Oue shows great promise for developing into both an exciting conductor and strong music director. But Skrowaczewski had it all.[16]

A longtime supporter of the Minnesota Orchestra who had been twelve years old when Skrowaczewski began his tenure as music director sent a letter thanking him for his "critical role in [the orchestra's] development." The letter is one example of similar tributes he has received over the years:

I remember the transition from Antal Doráti to yourself. You brought a new level of musical excitement and depth by programming in equal thirds the familiar with deserving unknown and contemporary works. The world premieres and new compositions were particularly memorable, such as Penderecki's *Threnody for the Victims of Hiroshima*. (Back then, the orchestra didn't seem as driven by box office considerations.) You definitely educated and challenged us through bold and daring programming.[17]

Skrowaczewski spoke to Michael Anthony about the shift in attitude toward his programming during his Minnesota career:

Let's not forget, in the early 1960s, when I conducted works by composers such as Stockhausen, Boulez, and Nono, people were outraged. Friends of mine, some on the board, some not, sent me letters saying they would cancel their contributions if I didn't stop with these kinds of programs. ...And I remember some board members, gradually from year to year saying to me, "Stan, now I'm starting to understand what you are after." After nineteen years, this public was really tremendous. I would go to Philadelphia or New York, but the public there wouldn't be nearly as alert. I was very proud of this.[18]

Anthony, in an interview with Skrowaczewski, described the next transition of programming:

Things changed in the 1980s, here and elsewhere. Music programming in the Twin Cities lost its progressive stamp.... Skrowaczewski noted two further developments: concern among orchestra boards and managements about their aging audiences, and the rise of marketing departments, which tend to push programming toward the familiar to increase ticket sales. Could Skrowaczewski hold his own today against a determined marketing department?

"I would try to convince marketing about certain things," he said firmly. "The music director, you see, is a sort of prophet. He must have reasons—deep, historical, aesthetic reasons—to make his case and to evaluate music."[19]

Skrowaczewski believes that a kind of artistic crisis developed with avant-garde and minimalism from the 1980s to the present:

> Both have gone too far. The avant-garde of the 1950s, 1960s, and 1970s was at least evolving. When it went to the extreme, composers like Jacob Druckman rightly brought a new romanticism to it. But with some minimalism, the pendulum swung so far the other way it became very dangerous. The quality was lacking. The attitude that one has to please the public in composition is terrible and tragically wrong. I'm not pessimistic. This trend is a short period of history. You don't hear this style much in other countries.[20]

Although Skrowaczewski's views on minimalism and its impact on Western classical music may be controversial, they are grounded in his knowledge of composers prolific in the genre. He has continued to keep up with what young composers are writing. For the most part he is disappointed by the compositions he hears, which he regards as too conservative and overtly populist for his taste, including the programming of even media-deemed "progressive" conductors. Younger composers he admires include British composer-conductor and pianist Thomas Adès and German composer-conductor Matthias Pintscher, both born in 1971. Of an earlier generation, he admires German Wolfgang Rihm (born in 1952), and from his own generation, Gunther Schuller and the American composer George Crumb. "He represents an incredible level in American music," Skrowaczewski said.

Musicians and concertgoers with decades of experience observing Skrowaczewski on the podium have detected a manifest transformation of his conducting style.

Michael Anthony, who reviewed Skrowaczewski's Minnesota Orchestra concerts from 1971 until 2007, called it the "greening of Skrowaczewski." Anthony described his reference to Charles Reich's bestselling book *The Greening of America* (1970):

> I have this persistent metaphor in my mind of Skrowaczewski sort of pulling the music along, holding a thick rope over his shoulder for many years. Whereas I find today he is more relaxed. There was stiffness in him before. The musicians seem to share this view. I even came to think of his transformation as the "Greening of Skrowaczewski." There's that old book *The Greening of America*, a legitimate idea and a nice metaphor, [the] coming of spring. This came to be a catchphrase of the time after the stiff 1950s. The counterculture brought this kind of earthiness, an organic connection to nature that hadn't existed before. Some of this was nonsense, but that's why I have thought of the Greening of Skrowaczewski. There is a greater warmth in his work at the podium and more relaxation.

The late Michael Steinberg, who had observed Skrowaczewski's conducting since the 1960s, also commented on the changes he witnessed:

> If I look back over the past forty years, what is striking is the fire in his best performances. I found him an enormously exciting conductor when I first encountered him. [I'm] thinking particularly of the first time with the Minneapolis Symphony and the first time with the Philadelphia Orchestra. There was a period later when I felt he was a bit stiff, a bit bottled up. I wonder if the tragedy that happened with his daughter created a bad internal havoc on him. There was something. There were barriers, and things were not coming out. I think in his older age, just about the whole fourteen years [Jorja and I] have been in Minnesota, he cut loose from that again, and the performances here have had no inhibitions. The fire that's in him has a way of being channeled through the performances into the audience.[21]

"Physically, I was active when I was young and starting out conducting," Skrowaczewski said. "Then I was all tense and excited. But later I tried to be very relaxed. It doesn't help the orchestra if a conductor is tense. Now I can do easily six hours a day of rehearsals, or more if I am recording."[22]

Although he is more relaxed on the podium, some unique characteristics of Skrowaczewski's physical conducting remain essentially unchanged. Former Minnesota Orchestra concertmaster Jorja Fleezanis explains:

> I remember the first impact of this metabolism that I have come to know and love very much. He is wired like no one else I know. He is the closest to Furtwängler of anyone I know, neurologically, in this kind of overwrought way he physically embodies the music with his entire body. It can be very tremulous or even volcanic, which is kind of the way I have seen the Furtwängler persona on videos. Working with Stan makes me nervous and excited, giving me a feeling that there is power behind what he is doing. You have to ride this wave with great certainty of yourself because his conducting is not always about straight-ahead stick technique.

> Stan always conducts a very vitaminized version of a work. If it is a Schumann symphony, it is opulent, very rich. He doesn't like fragile sonorities. Everything is very specific. He has to have conviction from the orchestra and a kind of muscular support behind it that generates both rhythmic validity and virility. He paints with a vivid brush and a sensitivity to color all the time. I have memories of all the pieces I have played with him because I never feel unsure about what is supposed to happen or the placement of gestures. It is this body language of his; it's like he's power drilling. Even if it is very quiet, there's still a feeling he is chiseling into the music.

By the time of Skrowaczewski's seventy-fifth birthday and throughout the 2000s, his annual guest-conducting engagement with the Minnesota Orchestra had become highly anticipated by the musicians. "It's an event," said vice president and general manager Robert Neu. "He's loved. Because of natural attrition there aren't many musicians in the orchestra left that were his appointments, so there are a lot of young players who didn't grow up with him. His persona is talked and whispered about. Everyone sits up and takes notice when he's on the podium. There's no question the orchestra feels they are in the presence of a master."

Giancarlo Guerrero, the Minnesota Orchestra's associate conductor from 1999–2004, related his first experience of seeing the ensemble welcome back its conductor laureate:

> The one thing that struck me when I saw him walk on the stage—and I had never seen this happen in my short career—was the orchestra started clapping and tapping their feet. That to me was a shock, and immediately I knew something special was going on, that this was a really long-term relationship and that they really love the man. They just saw him the year before, but immediately there was this rush of emotion: here comes this grandfather-type figure that we love and respect. From then on I knew that every time Skrowaczewski got up in front of this orchestra, it would be special.

Skrowaczewski's level of involvement with the music exists on a higher plane of consciousness—an intense focus and concentration sometimes produce unusual behaviors. "He's always had this dual relationship of the absolute command of the end result and also the transparency of this bizarre behavior that he has, in which he doesn't always hear what you say," Fleezanis said. "He's been like that forever; I don't think it's a hearing issue."

"On the day of the concert or right after a rehearsal," said Michael Steinberg, "it is useless to ask him anything, what day of the week it is, or anything. You can ask him any question, and he doesn't hear you because he is so 'in the sphere.'"

"He's definitely on another planet," said Minnesota Orchestra violist Michael Adams. "Every now and then the whole orchestra will laugh from something a musician said. He'll stop, look dumbstruck, and say, 'That was a joke, right?'—not knowing at all what the joke was."[23]

And yet Skrowaczewski sometimes offers his own humorous moments in rehearsals, catching the musicians completely off guard. Fleezanis relayed one example:

> He sometimes has a playfulness, a lighter agile temperament. There's this one spot, I think it is in the last movement of the Bruckner [Second Symphony]. He said, "We must play this very light, very *staccato*, very *secco*, everything extremely clean. You know like, 'Hi ho, hi ho, it's off to work we go.'" It's the last thing on the planet I expect to associate with this composer, let alone coming out of Stan's mouth. It just blows people's minds.

Guerrero admires Skrowaczewski's enduring artistry and his work ethic: "To me he is a mentor, an inspiration. When I am older, I hope I have the amount of energy in my entire body that he has in his pinky. He loves what he does, and he'll conduct and compose to the last day of his life."

"I feel absolutely the same as I felt twenty years ago," Skrowaczewski said near the time of seventy-fifth birthday. "I can't understand it."[24] He continued:

> This business keeps you young. You have to force yourself to be ready for rehearsals. You go to Europe, and you have jet lag. If you force yourself, it works. You get fired up. Then you sleep at night, and everything is okay. It all depends on what demands you put on yourself. I wouldn't like to be in front of an orchestra when I feel tired. I would rather cancel a rehearsal. I must be ready, very well prepared, and alert. This sort of need, from day to day, is probably healthy. I feel younger than I felt thirty years ago. I often have the feeling now that I had in my youth, of discovering things, this sort of amazement about beauty.[25]

Krystyna spoke of her husband's energy and work ethic:

> Stan's energy doesn't wane. He's ten years older than I am, and yet he springs out of bed in the morning, whereas it takes me hours to get going. And he has this discipline. How he can make himself exercise for an hour every day, no matter how tired he is, amazes me. I think it's that he's so enthusiastic about life and about his work. He's more relaxed now conducting, but he also has more time to study. He never stops studying. He never stops reading scores and looking for new interpretations.[26]

As Michael Anthony once noted, Skrowaczewski has "always been plugged into society" and possesses a keen awareness of the world's political and social landscape. However, his knowledge of popular culture is rather limited, due to lack of time and interest. Once, at a family holiday gathering, Oprah Winfrey's name came up. Frustrated with not knowing whom they were talking about, he finally blurted out, "Who *is* this Or-pah?"

Though not inspired to explore general pop culture, Skrowaczewski is open to new experiences, especially his sons' musical pursuits. After the success of Psykosonik, Paul helped cofound the world's first Internet audio-technology company, Headspace, Inc., with Thomas Dolby. A New Wave musician, Dolby became famous in the early 1980s with his innovative pop music, particularly with the smash hit "She Blinded Me with Science." Dolby worked closely with Paul for three years, and together they developed the revolutionary Beatnik Audio Engine technology, which was used in Microsoft's WebTV device and Nokia and Sony cell phones, among other electronic items. On one social occasion, Skrowaczewski had a long conversation with the former pop star about music, philosophy, and innovative uses of technology.

"With Thomas' erudite background and broad interests, he and my dad really hit it off," Paul remembered. "It was exciting to see them engage on such a high level."

During his seventy-fifth year Skrowaczewski had another brush with pop culture when the film *The Truman Show*, starring Jim Carrey, was released. Its soundtrack featured the second movement (Romance-Larghetto) of Chopin's Piano Concerto no. 1, recorded in 1961 by Artur Rubinstein and the New Symphony of London, and conducted by

Skrowaczewski. Nicholas and Paul got a kick out of seeing their father's name on the big screen as the credits rolled by and Chopin's music resonated in the theater.

Skrowaczewski's more relaxed demeanor may have been a new development, but another aspect of his mature years seemed more like a recapitulation, as Michael Anthony observed in 1998. Anthony reminded *Star Tribune* readers of Skrowaczewski's intense childhood reaction to hearing the Adagio movement from Bruckner's Seventh Symphony for the first time. Anthony reported that the maestro now "finds himself—almost inexplicably—recapturing that intense response to music."[27] Skrowaczewski described this sensation to Anthony:

> When I come to a work that I've done many times, I'm rethinking the interpretation from scratch. With all the experiences I've had, and not wisdom, but feeling that comes from decades of conducting, I grasp a certain perspective of the style of a work that is very special to me now. It's a great feeling, even though it may not always come to fruition. After a concert I might say, "Well, it didn't come off well for some reason. Often I'm not so inspired with certain rehearsals or concerts, but I don't blame anyone but myself.
>
> In composition, there is also now this same sort of wonderful peace. I'm trying to write music that goes beyond pleasing me. Maybe it's due to deeper introspection into the music, revealing to me things that before were covered by the technicality of how to do it. Three or four years ago I was [conducting] Shostakovich's Fourth Symphony with the Hallé Orchestra. I was crying when I reached the coda of the first movement; I couldn't see anyone. The harp player said to me afterward, "What happened to you?" I would like to write something that makes me cry. It happens so seldom.[28]

Recalled violinist Peter Worrell, "Stan talked to the orchestra about the fear Shostakovich had during the period he wrote the Fourth Symphony, how he'd sit with a suitcase waiting for someone to arrest him. Stan was in tears by the end of that performance. Anyone who heard it was moved."

The Hallé achieved some important artistic milestones under Skrowaczewski's successor, Kent Nagano, who persuaded the orchestra to accept works by such composers as Messiaen, Adams, Stockhausen, Boulez, and Dutilleux, among others. Although, as Beale has noted, Nagano's programs "were [not] any more or less successful in attracting audiences than Skrowaczewski's," performance incomes and grants from the Manchester City Council and other sources increased.[29] However, spending for expensive programming had spiraled out of control. In contrast to Skrowaczewski's tenure, the board now stayed out of programming issues, giving Nagano far greater autonomy. In an effort to balance budget deficits accrued during the 1994–95 season, the orchestra unfortunately had to draw heavily from the Hallé Trust Fund.[30]

Yet despite its financial worries the Hallé finally realized a dream whose origins are traced to the orchestra's namesake. In 1889 Sir Charles Hallé had drawn up plans for a real concert hall.[31] His dream finally came to fruition in fall 1996, when Bridgewater

Hall opened. Beale described Skrowaczewski's first concert in Bridgewater Hall as "an event of real significance." He continued:

> Ever unassuming, the Polish-American maestro made no fuss, but in reality Manchester owes him more than any other musician, I would guess, for the fact that it now has a superb concert hall of international standard. His return in the autumn of 1996, now [that] the hall is up and running, was auspicious. He galvanized the orchestra, as so often before, into playing of vigor and much distinction, and made it sound as good as I have heard it sound in these surroundings to date.[32]

"We'd been pushing for a new hall for awhile," said Clive Smart. "Stan didn't initiate this, but he put a heck of a lot of weight behind it, and whenever he had an opportunity he always said how important it was and how necessary it was to have a hall worthy of the Hallé. They're lucky now; Bridgewater is excellent, and certainly Stan played a part in encouraging the city to support it."

Although he was glad that the Hallé Orchestra had a new home, Skrowaczewski was also disappointed with its quality:

> It is a very useful and beautiful hall, but acoustically it is mediocre. Internally, I was deeply sad that all of my advice back when I was fighting for the hall was not taken. They made improvements to it later, but if they had used a designer such as Cyril Harris, as I suggested, they could have had a marvelous acoustical space.

Directly after Skrowaczewski's first concerts in Bridgewater Hall in late October 1996, he recorded Shostakovich's Symphony no. 1, the first recording made in the new hall. To complete a CD, he recorded Shostakovich's Symphony no. 6 a year later. Seldom satisfied with any of his recordings, Skrowaczewski felt this one was indeed excellent. It was due to be released immediately, and a plan called for him to record a complete Shostakovich symphony cycle.

Recording of the Fifth and Tenth symphonies had been completed and released before his tenure as principal conductor ended, but by early 1998 the Hallé Orchestra was on the verge of financial ruin. It took seven years before Skrowaczewski's Shostakovich CD was released on the Hallé's label in 2004. Two years later the Hallé rereleased his recording of Shostakovich's Fifth and Tenth symphonies. Though there were plans in 2006 to record the Second and Eighth symphonies, adding to a growing Skrowaczewski-Shostakovich symphony cycle, financial issues curtailed the project. In view of Skrowaczewski's prominent association with Shostakovich's music, this decision was regrettable.

The late 1990s found the orchestra facing bankruptcy, the loss of members, and the need for stringent measures. In an effort to help his former orchestra, Skrowaczewski reduced his fee during the Hallé's crisis. By 2000 the orchestra had a new principal conductor (British musician Sir Mark Elder), a smaller board, new administrative leadership, and a more disciplined approach to artistic planning and spending.

At his Hallé engagement in 2000, Skrowaczewski programmed his Concerto for Orchestra with Shostakovich's Fifth Symphony. Kennedy reminded concertgoers of Skrowaczewski's personal connection to the Russian master:

> [Skrowaczewski] first met [Shostakovich] in 1947 at the Prague Spring Festival where he found him a very friendly and cheerful person in spite of his naturally withdrawn character. But at their next meeting five years later, during which period Shostakovich had been savagely attacked by the Soviet hierarchy, he encountered a completely changed, brokenhearted man who would hardly speak to anybody. In the mid-1950s Shostakovich attended a performance of his Fifth Symphony conducted by Skrowaczewski in Warsaw and praised the tempi as well as his treatment of the lone *accelerandi* in the first and last movements.[33]

Like the Minnesota Orchestra, the Hallé now encountered a different Skrowaczewski when he returned to guest conduct. He was more relaxed and revealed other sides of his personality. "I think he's mellowed a lot," said Worrell, "especially since relinquishing his position. I think he has more trust now in his players." Reactions he received from audiences and the Hallé itself supported this change. The audiences' response helped Skrowaczewski excel in public speaking, something admittedly difficult for him.

"He's fantastic at communicating one-on-one," said Smart, "but give him a crowd or an audience, and there can be difficulties." Kennedy described the challenges this problem caused during Skrowaczewski's Hallé tenure:

> The general audiences were taken aback by some music like Lutosławski's. Rattle can persuade an audience that they ought to like Berio and others just by his charismatic way of putting it over. Stan wasn't that sort of conductor. He knew that they ought to hear it, but he wasn't a man who would really put it over in a proselytizing way. But today, you'd get someone like Mark Elder, who talks to the audience about it. I don't think that's Stan's thing at all. And twenty years ago, when Stan was new to the orchestra, there was a big gap in people's acquaintances with composers like Berio; he gave them too big a meal, perhaps. Maybe early on he should have fed them little snacks.

Preconcert talks had been long established at the Free Trade Hall, but the opening of Bridgewater Hall stirred renewed interest in them. Skrowaczewski participated in the talks, and to the surprise of many participants, he was a hit. "I've heard him speak at preconcert lectures, and he's funny and brilliant!" said Smart. "If only he could have done that a little more during his time as principal conductor, I think he would have come across as a person, as an individual, a lot better."

The question-and-answer format of these talks—and subsequent presentations— worked well for Skrowaczewski. The relaxed atmosphere and informality encourages the maestro to reveal his considerable charm.

In 1997 Skrowaczewski had a unique engagement with the National Youth Orchestra of Great Britain (NYO). Comprised of thirteen- to nineteen-year-old musicians, the NYO has a history of eminent guest conductors, including Adrian

Boult, Colin Davis, Rostropovich, Rattle, and Gardiner. Skrowaczewski's program gave these 154 talented teenagers the challenge of a lifetime: Beethoven's *Grosse Fugue*, Messiaen's *Et exspecto resurrectionem mortuorum*, and Strauss' *Also Sprach Zarathustra*. In addition to ten days of rehearsals, the orchestra's two-week study period included lectures on Messiaen, Nietzsche's tome on Zarathustra, chamber music experiences, and dance workshops, all under the orchestral course title "The Philosophy of Life." The young musicians absorbed it and the music with the aplomb typical of this ensemble, then celebrating its fiftieth season.

Skrowaczewski's profound connection with young musicians resonated consistently in the late 1990s and well into the next century. "He enjoys conducting young orchestras," Krystyna said in 1998. "He thinks it is one of the greatest aspects of his life at this point in his career."[34]

Skrowaczewski possibly has led more top university or conservatory orchestras during the past two decades than any other major international conductor. From 1994 through the end of 2000 alone, Skrowaczewski conducted at The Julliard School, the University of Minnesota, Manhattan School of Music (five times), Curtis Institute of Music (twice), New World Symphony, National Youth Orchestra of Britain, Interlochen World Youth Symphony, Aspen Festival, and New England Conservatory (six times).

His most consistent affiliation during this period was with the New England Conservatory of Music (NEC). From 1994 through 2002 he spent a week conducting at NEC for nine consecutive seasons—a remarkable run that added prestige and excitement to the nation's oldest independent conservatory. He reacquainted the venerable music city with his gifts as a conductor-composer. Richard Hoenich, then the conservatory's director of orchestral activities, was the force behind Skrowaczewski's annual visits. Aside from a 1990 engagement with the Boston Symphony, followed by another in 1998, Skrowaczewski's conservatory appearances were what brought him to Boston for nearly a decade. Hoenich recalled NEC's first experience with Skrowaczewski in 1994:

> His first performance here was Bruckner's Eighth, and needless to say, the students were all saying, "Who *is* this guy?" I don't know if people in my position elsewhere would be happy to see that happen. Here I am inviting a guest I greatly admired, who is in a whole different league than I am, but that's okay. I wanted these students to have the same experiences that I had with him, because they were unforgettable. I remember that at one of Stan's visits an oboist turned around in the middle of a Weber overture and said, "Wow, everything he says is so interesting! It wasn't just about 'play this shorter, play this longer.'" He was always engaged on an artistic level. All the technical issues that the orchestra was confronted with in any piece were never solved on a technical level. There were musical solutions to technical problems.

During Skrowaczewski's second NEC engagement, he conducted the students in *Music at Night*, a premiere for Boston and probably the first time anyone at the conservatory had ever heard his music. It was a hit. "Parts of it make you think of the great ballet scores of Prokofiev and Roussel," wrote Richard Dyer of *The Boston Globe*, "but the density in it, and the undertow, is Skrowaczewski's own; even as a young man of twenty-six, Skrowaczewski apparently knew everything there was to know about the orchestra and orchestration."[35]

By 1996 word was out that Skrowaczewski's annual concerts in NEC's acoustically glowing Jordan Hall were not to be missed. Tickets for the popular free concerts were allotted by reserved seating, and people frequently were turned away because the house was full. Both of Boston's major newspapers reviewed the concerts, unusual attention for a student orchestra.

The response, openness, and respect Skrowaczewski received from younger musicians gratified him. For the most part, he rehearses and performs with student ensembles as if they were a group of seasoned professionals. Skrowaczewski's respect for the young musicians and his insistence on high standards produces results that sometimes surpassed his performances with professionals.

Steinberg and Fleezanis attended Skrowaczewski's 1999 NEC concert. The experience reminded Steinberg of Skrowaczewski's work with Tanglewood students in the 1970s:

> One of the reasons why I found experiences at Tanglewood with the student conductors and student orchestra so superb was because the BSO was and is an orchestra that is often disrespectful to conductors. It can be a very badly behaved orchestra. The contrast between that and the response to Stan from both the student conductors and the Berkshire Festival Orchestra, as it was called in those days, was just extraordinary. The young players in that orchestra had no obstacles. They probably expected conductors to be a little odd, and they had no impediments to seeing what a high level of music making Stan brought to them. Jorja and I both experienced that in Boston at Stan's annual NEC concert.

Some major orchestras were interested in gaining all that Skrowaczewski had to offer while others couldn't get past his manner of rehearsing or their egos. Hoenich experienced both situations firsthand:

> Some younger members of the Montreal Symphony Orchestra, who may not have known of Stan, reacted like the NEC students. It was a "fresh-air" experience for them. He'd never let the rehearsal lose its momentum, whereas the methodical, overly technical approach taken by other conductors sometimes caused the orchestra to plod through its sessions. They would have us practice a difficult passage slowly, and the players would think, "Well, why did I practice this at home if we're going to play it like this in rehearsal?" But with Stan, it would be the opposite. If there were a problem, he would deal with it once and go on as if to say, "I know you know that's a problem that will take care of itself, right? We don't have to say a word about it." It would never be dealt with judgmentally, and by the dress rehearsal, it was ninety-eight percent there. By the concert it was one hundred percent. The

achievement was brought about because it was nurtured. It was not whipped out of the orchestra. In 1986 he did Bruckner's Third Symphony with Montreal—a revelatory experience. The points he focused on were anything but micromanaging. Everything he said instantly had relevance for the whole piece, so we knew right away how to treat such and such a phrase, etc. Five months later I was in New York City to attend Stan's rehearsals of the same piece with the New York Philharmonic. It was hell!

I could not believe how rude the Philharmonic was to Stan. My admiration— as high as it was for him at that point—shot through the roof because it was as if, from his point of view, none of this was going on. He was just working and focused. I remember him making some of the same points that he had made to the Montreal Symphony, which I think had to do with Bruckner's vertical slashes over quarter-notes and what he was hoping to achieve from that. For the Montreal Symphony such information caused reactions like "Oh, way cool!"; for the New York Philharmonic, it was, "Oh, did he say something?" It was that kind of thing. He never lost his cool, just kept working, completely professionally. But he looked so exhausted and depressed when I saw him at the break. I was so mad at that orchestra. I thought, "This is just unacceptable." I mean, he'd be talking, and the clarinet players were throwing their mouthpiece caps on the stands, "Boom!" It was as if you were in an amusement park. I thought to myself, "You couldn't pay me all the money in the world to stand up there and subject myself to an experience like this!" To see the abuse he was taking was awful. But Stan just stayed true to himself and his beliefs. His ideas are so magnificent to the people who actually want to hear them.

The Boston Symphony welcomed Skrowaczewski's ideas when he was brought in at the last minute to replace James Levine to close the ensemble's 117th season in spring 1998.

Skrowaczewski altered Levine's scheduled program, substituting Shostakovich's First Symphony for a Sibelius symphony and choosing the Second Suite from Ravel's *Daphnis et Chloé* instead of the complete ballet music. He opened with Barber's *Medea's Meditation and Dance of Vengeance*, which the BSO had not played in more than thirty years. Dyer described Skrowaczewski's body language and noted that the maestro's knowledge surprised some BSO musicians:

> His technique is sometimes jerky and spasmodic, sometimes as fluid as underwater ballet, but he is always clear, and the performances were serious, lucid, exacting, and exciting; jaws dropped when he corrected an error that has stood in the parts of the Second Suite from Ravel's *Daphnis et Chloé* which have been in constant use for fifty years and more....[36]

Though the success of this engagement did not generate another BSO invitation, it was a fitting way to conclude Skrowaczewski's thirty-two-year chronicle of guest conducting the orchestra at Symphony Hall and at Tanglewood.

During the last five years of the 1990s and into the 2000s, Skrowaczewski's engagements with elite American orchestras waned significantly. His status as conductor laureate of the Minnesota Orchestra ensured him at least an annual appearance with his former ensemble; however, engagements with other top American ensembles, such as the Baltimore, St. Louis, and Seattle orchestras, were spotty.

Beginning in the early 1990s, all U.S. orchestras again faced financial setbacks, a factor that diminished Skrowaczewski's American engagements. Stephen Lumsden worked with an assistant to improve Skrowaczewski's American presence, and Richard Cisek briefly offered his expertise on the U.S. orchestra scene via his own consulting company.

In his efforts to secure more engagements for his client, Lumsden touted Skrowaczewski's strengths as an eminent conductor, his Bruckner recordings, countless favorable reviews, and the maestro's extensive repertoire. In his contact with various major American orchestras, however, Lumsden soon discovered that they wanted to book young, up-and-coming conductors for their few available weeks each season. Although this trend was understandable, Lumsden expressed his frustration with it:

> As the culture has become more youth-oriented, Stan's level of experience and depth and value is much greater than the opportunities afforded by the marketplace. Though he's had a very distinguished career working with all the major orchestras of the world, he's not ostentatious or in any way a pushy person in terms of his own profile. I can't think of an artist less likely to "sell out." And because of that, in a world that has become more star-oriented, he didn't get the recognition that he deserved. I would have liked to have achieved much more with Stan. It has been a frustration not to deliver on a lot of things that I think he deserved. I really wish that I'd gotten him earlier in his career.

Obtaining American engagements proved to be difficult for Skrowaczewski in the 2000s, but his work flourished in Europe and particularly in Japan, where his age, experience, and international reputation were considered major assets deserving respect, even reverence.

Skrowaczewski entered the new century with the release of his complete cycle of Bruckner's symphonies and the welcome challenge of having two major compositions to complete. Both works premiered in 2003, the year of his eightieth birthday. He also continued to explore fresh interpretations of the orchestral works in the vast repertoire he conducted worldwide. He entered this next phase of his life with a renewed sense of artistic purpose, spurred in part by his growing concern about the direction in which society was heading. In his travels, in his observations of life in Minnesota, and through his interactions with people, he found humanistic and artistic values diminishing. These perceptions and subsequent events would lead to the creation of his most profound composition.

THIRTY-TWO

LIFE BELLS

The music world doesn't have an award for this, because no one would expect it to happen: A major conductor stands in front of an orchestra and conducts the premiere of his own symphony—a work of compelling depth. Then he leads the orchestra in the work of a composer of whose work he is one of the world's foremost interpreters. Here's the punch line: All this happens the night before the conductor's eightieth birthday.

—Michael Anthony

Skrowaczewski experienced a resurgence in Minnesota's regard for his work by the 2000s. *Minneapolis/St. Paul Magazine* named him Best Conductor in its Best of the Twin Cities 2000 ranking, noting that "perhaps [his critical acclaim] has at last reached even the hometown crowds in the Twin Cities, where some music watchers say this awfully good conductor has been taken for granted for decades."[1] In fall 2000 the Twin Cities expressed their appreciation of Skrowaczewski during two consecutive weeks of concerts, a rare occurrence since his days as a music director in Minnesota. He led the Saint Paul Chamber Orchestra in the Schumann Cello Concerto (with Lynn Harrell as soloist) and the Minnesota premiere of his arrangement for string orchestra of the Adagio from Bruckner's String Quintet in F major. Skrowaczewski was moved by the warm response from the audience and musicians, particularly by Harrell's solo encore piece, Schumann's *Traumerei*, the lullaby from the piano suite *Scenes from Childhood*. Before beginning the encore, Harrell spoke about his long relationship with Skrowaczewski and dedicated the performance to him.

A week later, on the day after his seventy-seventh birthday, Skrowaczewski celebrated the fortieth anniversary of his affiliation with the Minnesota Orchestra and his subscription concert debut as music director on November 4, 1960. He savored all his Minnesota performances in October 2000, which filled him with nostalgia, respect, and gratitude. "Some conductors get better and more interesting as they age," wrote Michael Anthony in a review, "and Skrowaczewski is one of them."[2]

The maestro returned to Orchestra Hall to rehearse a program of the Side-by-Side project, a massive combined ensemble consisting of the Minnesota Orchestra and 215 high school students of the 2000–01 Minnesota All-State Orchestra. Side-by-Side brought the two ensembles together for a rehearsal and concert. The collaboration marked the first time Skrowaczewski had conducted high school students in his home state, and he praised the efforts of the young musicians.

Skrowaczewski soon was off to Europe for concerts in Germany, France, and Switzerland. In Zürich he led the Tonhalle Orchester in a program that included Ligeti's Cello Concerto with Lithuanian cellist and conductor David Geringas. The maestro returned to the United States for a week at NEC, where he led Bruckner's Ninth and Schuller's *Seven Studies on Themes of Paul Klee*. Performing Schuller's most popular orchestral work was a tip of the hat to his colleague and friend (also the NEC's former president), who attended rehearsals and the performance.

While Skrowaczewski was conducting in Boston, the Dale Warland Singers premiered his *Christmas Chant* in Minneapolis. The professional chorus commissioned the work for its holiday concerts. Skrowaczewski based the piece on an old familiar Polish Christmas song remembered from his boyhood; it was his first choral piece in over forty years.

In Skrowaczewski's last engagement of 2000, he conducted the NHK Symphony Orchestra in Tokyo in its traditional year-end performances of Beethoven's Ninth. The success of his NHK debut in 1996, which produced two commercial CDs from three live concerts, earned him another invitation in 1999.

The 2001 release of *Byłem w Niebie: mówi Stanisław Skrowaczewski* (I Was in Heaven: Conversations with Stanisław Skrowaczewski) prompted the maestro to reflect on his life, albeit briefly. The book, a compilation of three days of interviews with Skrowaczewski by Kraków journalist Agnieszka Malatyńska-Stankiewicz, provided the first published accounts of some key and little-known aspects of his life. Published by Polskie Wydawnictwo Muzyczne (PWM Edition), Poland's largest classical music publisher, the book is the fourth in a PWM series entitled *People of the World of Music*, which features interviews with composers, conductors, and other musicians. Unfortunately an English (or German or Japanese) translation of the Polish-language book never appeared, thus limiting its distribution. However, publicity about the book and articles about his Bruckner cycle reminded Poles of Skrowaczewski's long, productive career, and it renewed their interest in his life.

In spring 2001 he collaborated with Leon Fleisher and the New World Symphony performing Ravel's Piano Concerto for Left Hand, which he and the soloist performed a month later at Aspen Music Festival with the Aspen Festival Orchestra. "Skrowaczewski rehearses in an ideal way," Fleisher said. "He's economical with his time, and he knows how to adjust that time. He's also totally reliable at the performance. What you agree upon at the rehearsal is what you get at the performance. It doesn't mean you don't get spontaneity, etc., but you have something to build upon."

Garrick Ohlsson elaborated on Skrowaczewski's spontaneity in performance:

> I treasure Stan's willingness to be improvisatory, to listen, and to know that at the moment here we need a little more or a little less time, or that the pace should pick up a little bit or slacken a little bit. It's not that he or I change things wildly from night to night with repeated concerts, but it's a bit different each time. Sometimes we talk about it, and sometimes we don't. Some conductors are extraordinarily consistent, even from night to night,

and that can be wonderful. Others are too consistent, and that's not so good. This is truly subjective, and it's hard to describe; Stan has just a bit more of not only the musical *rubato* but also the psychological *rubato* of the situation. I think he's so secure that he knows exactly what he's about. He's comfortable enough not to have to produce something in one particular way.

Rudolf Buchbinder described the experience of working with Skrowaczewski:

I don't want to be accompanied. With a musician like Stan it's a real partnership. We throw balls to each other. I'm able to work this way with few conductors. I think Stan and I have both changed over the years, but in the same ways. The older you get, the freer you are. There's a bit more *rubato*, which one does not tend to do as much when one is younger, when you are perhaps more narrow-minded. Now, we just make music—let it go, let it breathe, just be free—of course, still within the parameters of the style and character of the work.

Remaining faithful to the style and character of a work while bringing one's personality to its performance is a tricky balance for many artists, especially for conductors. "Stan's personality is audible in all his performances," explained Krystian Zimerman, "but it doesn't print over the composer, which means his Brahms is different from his Wagner and is different from his Chopin. This is fantastic."

Ohlsson provided further insight:

Stan's a superb interpreter of immense range and experience, and I believe his composer's mind is the key to his conducting. He looks at the deeper structure of music that is not always apparent on the surface. It incorporates the literal truth of the score but also then goes deeper than that, into what generates the symbols that become the reality of music. The decisions he makes are so firmly grounded that sometimes he'll quite easily make a small change, not only to the scoring but also to dynamics and/or phrasing. If you ask him about it, he's always quick with an explanation as to why—usually it's his idea of what was going on in the composer's head. He's not arrogant. He doesn't pretend he knows what's happening with Brahms or Mozart, but there are these compositional connections, which, if understood, can then lead to a variety of valid interpretive choices, even if they're not necessarily exactly what the composer wrote. He doesn't make a fetish out of the letter of the score, although he's a precise interpreter. Because we live in such a puritanical age musically, it's a joy for me to work with him.

In June 2001, Skrowaczewski led a program in Northrop Auditorium, a venue in which he assumed he would never again conduct. The occasion was the University of Minnesota's sesquicentennial celebration, whose finale was a concert by the Minnesota Orchestra in its former home. Despite his longstanding antagonism toward Northrop Auditorium, Skrowaczewski nevertheless was pleased to join in the festivities. The concert attracted an audience of 3,500, one of the largest single gatherings in many years for a classical music concert in the Twin Cities.

The program's first half, which reflected the historic ties between the university and the Minnesota Orchestra, also showcased the talents of university faculty. It began with a movement from Dominick Argento's *Ring of Time* and continued with Eric Stokes' *Echo's Shell*, from *Symphony(s), Book I*, a piece Stokes composed for Dennis Russell Davies. Both composers had been longtime university faculty members. Pianist Lydia Artymiw, a McKnight Distinguished University Professor, performed Schumann's Introduction and Allegro Appassionato, and Brahms' Symphony no. 2 closed out the celebration.

The Skrowaczewskis were home when the attacks of 9/11 occurred, and like millions of people around the world, they watched with horror as the tragic events unfolded on television. Two weeks later the leadership of the Minnesota Orchestra and the Saint Paul Chamber Orchestra organized a concert to commemorate the victims of 9/11. The concert soon evolved into the largest collaborative artistic effort in Minneapolis history. Nine Twin Cities arts organization came together at Orchestra Hall on October 8, 2001, for *Elegy: A Tribute Performance by the Twin Cities Arts Community*. Skrowaczewski and Andreas Delfs, who had just become music director of the Saint Paul Chamber Orchestra, shared conducting duties.

Delfs opened the program with Skrowaczewski's arrangement of "The Star-Spangled Banner" and continued with Barber's Adagio for Strings, the sixth movement from Brahms' *A German Requiem,* and Copland's *Lincoln Portrait*, narrated by longtime Guthrie Theater actor Richard Ooms. Skrowaczewski conducted the concert's second half: Copland's *Fanfare for the Common Man*, Stephen Paulus' *Pilgrim's Hymn for Mixed Chorus* (from the one-act opera *The Three Hermits*), and the finale of Mahler's Symphony no. 2.

The moving occasion marked only the second time that the Minnesota Orchestra and Saint Paul Chamber Orchestra performed as a unit. The orchestras plus the combined choirs of the Minnesota Chorale, Dale Warland Singers, and the Chorus of the Plymouth Music Series totaled nearly four hundred. Minnesota's elder statesman, Walter Mondale, was master of ceremonies.

While conducting one of the most emotional works in all of music, the finale of Mahler's Second Symphony, Skrowaczewski was deeply moved to see the hundreds of grief-stricken faces before him, seeking healing and solace. His view of the massive choir, huddled together in the comfort of unity, took in the large American flag, elegantly draped from the ceiling. For this powerful event the arts community had turned to Skrowaczewski, who was honored and proud to serve.

A few days after the *Elegy* concert, Skrowaczewski went to California for an engagement with the San Francisco Symphony and James Galway. But before he left he had time to attend a rehearsal in Minneapolis of his oldest available orchestral piece, *Overture 1947*.

He had not performed the piece since its creation, and he does not consider it a part of his active compositional output. In fact, he had basically forgotten about the work until Raymond Leppard, music director of the Indianapolis Symphony Orchestra, asked his permission to present it. Skrowaczewski happily consented to the request, but concerned about its quality, he jocularly warned Leppard to perform it "at your own risk!" Leppard and the Indianapolis Symphony gave the American premiere of the piece early in 1999.

William Schrickel, assistant principal double bass of the Minnesota Orchestra and conductor of the Metropolitan Symphony Orchestra, the state's most prominent civic orchestra, wanted his ensemble to perform a work by Skrowaczewski, who suggested that Schrickel consider *Overture 1947*. Schrickel gave the Minnesota premiere of the work at the opening of the Metropolitan Symphony's twentieth season in October 2001.

After Skrowaczewski's engagement with the San Francisco Symphony, which included warmly received performances of *Music at Night*, he went to Washington, D.C., where he conducted the National Symphony Orchestra in its first performance of Hindemith's *Kammermusik* no. 5 for Viola and Chamber Orchestra. After more concerts in Canada and Germany, he was back in Manchester with the Hallé Orchestra.

Although the program for Skrowaczewski's Hallé concerts did not include a Bruckner symphony—like most of his concerts that season—it nevertheless was among his favorites: *Cantus in Memoriam Benjamin Britten* by Arvo Pärt; Mozart's last Piano Concerto, no. 27, with Richard Goode; and Beethoven's *Eroica* Symphony. Skrowaczewski's first concert with his former orchestra occurred on Britten's birthday and honored the British master with the Pärt, but it also fêted Skrowaczewski indirectly. Critics were ecstatic about the *Eroica*'s fresh, innovative sound as well as the sublime empathy of the collaboration by Goode and Skrowaczewski. "After more than fifty years of concertgoing," wrote John Robert-Blunn of *The Manchester Charivari*, "I thought that I'd heard it all before…, [but] I heard the performance of a lifetime of Beethoven's *Eroica* symphony."[3]

Bringing out the spirit of innovation inherent in the great masterworks is a priority for Skrowaczewski, especially in Beethoven's revolutionary *Eroica*:

> A conductor has to be well read in philosophy and in history, especially about the times in which the composers lived. For instance, to know about Beethoven's Third Symphony: that nothing ever before had been created like it, nothing! And 1803–05 was a unique time in history. I always remind the musicians about that, so even if they've played the work many times, they can go back to it, and then we get the hair rising on the back of our necks, the shivers, from knowing that in those times such a work was composed.[4]

After leading his ninth annual concert with the New England Conservatory Orchestra early in 2002, Skrowaczewski spent much of the winter and spring conducting in Europe. The only music he conducted almost as frequently as Bruckner's was his own. Orchestras increasingly requested that his programs include one of his pieces, and it turned out that the Concerto for Orchestra balanced other works—particularly Bruckner symphonies—extremely well. During 2002 he led his concerto during eight engagements in four countries, including five times in the United States. In June of that year Skrowaczewski paired the concerto with Bruckner's Ninth Symphony for a concert with the National Orchestral Institute (NOI) at the University of Maryland School of Music. Most of the young musicians had never worked with Skrowaczewski; likewise, most had never played either piece. They harbored few notions about Concerto for Orchestra, but a number of them had preconceived ideas about the Bruckner, expecting it to be long and boring. Jill Werthman, a twenty-year-old violist in the orchestra, shared this notion:

> I listened to a recording and followed along with a score. I didn't like it because I didn't understand it. I didn't understand the language of it, and it was long. We met Skrowaczewski and did the read-through. I was praying that this man could guide us through the piece. And he did! I couldn't wait to go to each rehearsal because I could see how much he loved the music and understood it. When he had a section play a chord—just out of the blue—he knew exactly the pitches, he sang them, he knew the exact instrumentation, etc.—he just *knew* the music. And it was beautiful to watch him conduct. He has a gorgeous technique. It was easy to follow, and he drew a good sound from us. When I thought the NOI program couldn't get any better, it did.

The students didn't know what to make of Skrowaczewski's Concerto for Orchestra. Some found the technical challenges appealing; others were attracted to sounds from the percussion section and various effects in the work. The subtitle of the second movement, *Anton Bruckner's Himmelfahrt* (Bruckner's Heavenly Journey), intrigued them, but Skrowaczewski said nothing about his piece. He preferred that they make their own discoveries, and Werthman did:

> I've come to understand that some people are going to talk and talk and put specific pictures in your head. And you have Skrowaczewski, who really doesn't say anything [about what's behind the music]. He wants things in tune and talks a lot about balance, and he gets upset when we don't listen to one another. But there's something that is really special about a conductor who doesn't need to talk. Otherwise, it doesn't work. We don't all see the same pictures that every conductor sees.

> At first I was shocked by his Concerto for Orchestra. I decided that whatever he had in mind—and you weren't going to know unless you asked him— it's his own idea of death. The last movement is supposed to be Bruckner's ascension to heaven, but to me it doesn't sound that way. It sounds like hell, like he's going down! It is only at the end where you get, at least for me, some sort of emotional, lyrical satisfaction. I'm not sure how I feel about the piece,

or if I even like it yet, because I don't fully understand it. But I decided to take what he dealt with in the music seriously because I knew that he meant it the same way he loves Bruckner.

Praise for Skrowaczewski's Bruckner recordings had appeared for over a decade prior to the June 2001 release of the complete cycle. Few complete cycles existed: to date, three other cycles of all eleven symphonies and sixteen of partial sets by the same conductor and orchestra. Skrowaczewski's complete Bruckner cycle made news in the classical music world. The fact that the set was released on a budget label, Arte Nova Classics, and not recorded by an instantly recognizable conductor or orchestra underscored the achievement by Skrowaczewski and the Saarbrücken Radio Symphony Orchestra.

Dr. Sabine Tomek became artistic director of the RSO Saarbrücken soon after Skrowaczewski was named its first principal guest conductor in 1994, and she continued in the position until 2007. Tomek shared her perspective on the Bruckner cycle:

> The triumph of the Bruckner recordings was a phenomenon. I remember listening to Stanisław's rehearsals of Bruckner's Seventh early on, and I was amazed by what he was able to do with the orchestra. Critics had the same reaction. We are one of many orchestras in Germany. People know us, but we are not as famous as Symphonieorchester des Bayerischen Rundfunks in Munich, for example. Soon, everyone became astonished, and we could see what the future would bring with the project. People thought, "My God, what is happening in Saarbrücken? Who is this conductor?"

Dozens of articles, reviews, and interviews appeared in Europe soon after the release of the boxed set. Critics compared Skrowaczewski's recordings to Bruckner cycles by Jochum, Karajan, Haitink, and Barenboim, none of which included all eleven symphonies. Skrowaczewski's interpretations and the Saarbrücken's musicianship received unanimous critical praise. The boxed set made its way onto several "best of" lists for 2001 and 2002, including *BBC Music Magazine's* 2002 Top Ten Discs of the Decade, which noted: "What Stanisław Skrowaczewski has achieved with the Saarbrücken Radio Symphony Orchestra is little short of miraculous."[5] David Hurwitz of *Classics Today* summarized that "if forced to recommend a single Bruckner cycle at any price containing the standard versions of the symphonies, then for its surefire combination of fine playing, excellent sonics, and the deepest, most satisfyingly consistent interpretive insights, I'd gladly choose Skrowaczewski. He's that good."[6]

The Bruckner set won the 2002 Cannes Classical Award for Best Orchestral Recording of an 18th/19th Century Orchestral Work, its most meaningful honor. Established in 1995 to recognize outstanding international classical recordings, the Cannes Classical Awards encompass twenty categories, ranging from early music to contemporary compositions on CD and DVD. Hundreds of voting critics from premier music magazines from six countries select the recipients of this distinguished award.

In summer 2002 another all-Skrowaczewski recording attracted some attention, thanks to an enthusiastic campaign by its publisher, Innova Recordings, under the auspices of the American Composers Forum. The release of *Skrowaczewski's World* surprised the maestro, who simply received a copy of it in the mail. "It was such a terribly nice and thoughtful action of the American Composers Forum and Ensemble Capriccio," he said. "I did not know about their plan to do it. I was quite surprised and moved when I received it." He was also pleased with the quality of the performances on the disc. Finally there was proper documentation of his chamber music. Soon after the CD's release, Skrowaczewski told Michael Anthony that the pieces are "true chamber music, they don't cry out for a bigger ensemble."[7] He also explained the challenges for a composer using only a few instruments:

> Writing for string trio is more of a challenge than writing for the big string section of an orchestra. With an orchestra, you do ten minutes of colors, and it sounds OK, and it keeps the attention of the listener. But when you have just three instruments, it's more demanding. It needs more content. You must come up with musical ideas that keep the attention, not just rely on color.[8]

It is commonly believed that most composers reveal more of themselves—and possibly speak their truest musical language in chamber music. In his review of the String Trio CD, Paul Snook of *Fanfare* offered insights into Skrowaczewski's art:

> Skrowaczewski's idiom reflects an almost uncannily sophisticated awareness of the past century's full range of stylistic options: whenever he uses the accents of the avant-garde, he bends and blends them into a smoothly intelligible language of communicative directness…. [This recording is] highlighting probably the most talented Pole of the post-Lutosławski generation. It has to be one of the outstanding chamber music discs of the current year.[9]

Skrowaczewski lightened his summer schedule in 2002 so that he could compose. For the first time in almost twenty years he had two orchestral commissions for performances within the same year. He needed to concentrate on finishing at least one of them. The 2001–02 concert season had been among the most active of his career and left little time for composing. Skrowaczewski conducted seventeen orchestras in seven countries nonstop from September to July, with only two weeks in December and the month of January free. He devoted most of the summer to finishing *Concerto Nicolò* for Piano Left Hand and Orchestra.

The circumstances of the commission intersect with Skrowaczewski's conducting and composing, his relationship with Gary Graffman, and an outside influence. Graffman's association with Skrowaczewski began in 1960, when they met through pianist Julius Katchen. Soon after, Graffman performed with the Minneapolis Symphony Orchestra. It was the beginning of a long, sporadic collaborative relationship. By 1960 Graffman had embarked on a major career as a leading American pianist, the only one to have recorded with seven of the nation's premier orchestras (the Big Five plus the Minnesota Orchestra and San Francisco Symphony).

Upon encountering Skrowaczewski's Concerto for English Horn, Graffman was impressed. He also had heard from his former student Lydia Artymiw that Skrowaczewski's chamber music was top-notch. When Skrowaczewski was engaged to conduct the Curtis Symphony Orchestra in 1998, Graffman, then president of the Curtis Institute of Music, suggested that Skrowaczewski program one of his works. Typically he was reluctant to do so, but with Graffman's encouragement he seized the opportunity to give the first performance of his revised Concerto for Orchestra with the gifted student orchestra. Graffman now had a second chance to experience a Skrowaczewski composition, and it reaffirmed his initial assessment of his friend's music.

After injuring his right hand in the late 1970s, Graffman became a performer and advocate of left-hand literature for piano. From the mid-1990s through the mid-2000s, he premiered several left-hand concertos, most notably works by Ned Rorem and William Bolcom.

In 2002 Graffman premiered American composer Richard Danielpour's Piano Concerto no. 3, *Zodiac Variations*, commissioned for Graffman by ichthyologist Dr. Herbert R. Axelrod, who founded the world's largest publisher of animal and pet books. An important philanthropist, Axelrod donated to causes related primarily to his two loves, fish and music. An amateur violinist and Paganini fanatic, he coauthored a biography on the Italian violinist and composer. When commissioning Danielpour, Axelrod requested that the composer somehow reference Paganini's famous Caprice no. 24 for solo violin.[10] Danielpour included a citation of it in one of his work's variations.

After that work's success Axelrod asked Graffman to recommend another composer for a new commission, and the pianist suggested that he choose Skrowaczewski. Axelrod again requested that Paganini's Caprice no. 24 make its way into the piece. Skrowaczewski's approach differed from that taken by Danielpour, as Graffman relates:

> Sometimes composers don't like to be put into that kind of straitjacket. At first Stan was a little leery about the request, but then what he did, of course, was not do the obvious of having the theme and then a set of variations, which Rachmaninoff, Brahms, and others did so masterfully. Stan uses the theme as an integral part of the whole piece. He doesn't use the entire theme, however—just a snippet. It's all over the place. And it's not put in artificially; it's really part of the skeleton of the piece.

"Even though I used part of the theme," Skrowaczewski said, "it is distorted harmonically and rhythmically, giving the impression of someone who is just discovering the piece and making mistakes in reading it."

As a genre, a left-hand piano concerto normally would not have interested Skrowaczewski were it not for a commission, but ultimately the concept inspired him. "To match the tradition of especially the Ravel Left Hand Concerto, making one hand sound like four, and how to do it myself, fascinated me," Skrowaczewski said. "I didn't want to repeat the tricks of Ravel." Upon its premiere, Skrowaczewski remarked that listeners might think they are hearing two hands playing:

> I was uneasy about writing for left hand only. Compositionally I sometimes needed the right hand, too. I eventually used the entire seven octaves along with big chords jumping from down to up. In the score it looks to be extremely difficult to play, but as a pianist I checked everything with my left hand—as best I could—and I made it very playable and rich sounding. In a sense, it almost has the effect of four or more hands playing, yet technically the one hand does it all.

Graffman praised his colleague's achievement:

> Stan was a pianist. He knows what is possible and not possible. Though it's all over the keyboard, the piece really works. There are single-note gestures, which Prokofiev used a lot in his Fourth Concerto. And there are also huge chords used while playing themes: melodies on top, accompaniment on the bottom, which Ravel does all the time. But you don't think about one hand or two hands. It just works so well musically.

Skrowaczewski's decision to include Paganini's first name in the title, *Concerto Nicolò*, amused Graffman. The maestro, Graffman, and the Curtis Symphony Orchestra premiered the four-movement piece at a run-out concert in Reading, Pennsylvania, in February 2003, before their Philadelphia performance. A month after the Philadelphia premiere of *Concerto Nicolò*, Skrowaczewski and Graffman delivered performances with the Minnesota Orchestra. The concerts were a singular occasion for both Skrowaczewski and the orchestra, whose 2002–03 concert season marked the ensemble's centennial. The maestro conducted his concerto, Brahms' Symphony no. 4, and Schuller's *Seven Studies on Themes of Paul Klee*, which the orchestra had commissioned and recorded in 1959.

The celebratory season offered its share of reflections and historical assessments: a book published by the orchestra; an oral history project initiated and led by Mary Ann Feldman; a release of historical recordings; a Minnesota Public Radio documentary; and a series of articles in the *Star Tribune*. One article featured remembrances from audience members over the years:

"I liked Skrovy," said ninety-six-year-old Florence Schoff, the orchestra's oldest subscriber at the time of the centennial.[11] As a teenager, Schoff had attended and remembered concerts led by the first conductor, Emil Oberhoffer.

Terry Erkkila, a concertgoer from another generation, had a unique memory of Skrowaczewski's early years in Minneapolis. In 1963, when Erkkila was a University of Minnesota student, she composed lyrics and music for *I've This Mad Really Bad Thing for Mr. Skrowaczewski*, a torch song written for the Brave New Workshop, a Minneapolis-based satirical-revue theater. Its patrons included many fans of the Minneapolis Symphony Orchestra. (Dan Sullivan, music critic for the *Minneapolis Tribune*, helped Erkkila compose the music.) Macalester College student Mary Sweitzer-Ponthan's rendition of the torch song made quite an impression at its 1963 debut. Apparently Skrowaczewski and his wife attended a performance of the revue, but he has no memory of it. The *Star Tribune* posted a recording of the song online in 2002, with Michael Anthony on piano accompanying Sweitzer-Ponthan's singing.[12]

Minnesota Public Radio (MPR) traced the organization's history in a documentary that focused on the contributions made by each music director. Although Skrowaczewski led the orchestra through its greatest era of growth, explained narrator Brian Newhouse, "His legacy will undoubtedly be the creation of Orchestra Hall. He declared a world-class orchestra needed a world-class hall. His predecessors had all said this, too, but only Skrowaczewski made it happen."[13]

The documentary tied the increase in the orchestra's size during Skrowaczewski's tenure to his desire to perform Bruckner symphonies, which demand large orchestral forces. "Today," said Newhouse, "the orchestra numbers ninety-eight musicians. Chalk this up to Bruckner and Stanisław Skrowaczewski."[14]

The Minnesota maestro's most important performance legacy to the orchestra—and to the music world in general—will always be the symphonies of Anton Bruckner. The Minnesota Orchestra's principal cellist, Anthony Ross, told MPR why he thinks this is true:

> He kind of *is* Bruckner. He comes at the music absolutely from a composer's viewpoint because he's a brilliant composer himself. I think he totally understands the balances, the lines, and the form of Bruckner better than any other conductor I've played with. Balance and architecture are everything to Stan, and that's what Bruckner's about: hearing the correct lines, understanding the architecture of the piece and creating the depth of sound, which Stan has a knack for. If you ever watch him conduct with that kind of quivering baton, you know it really does something. It brings out a special sound. The more he starts shaking sometimes, the orchestra sound gets deeper and deeper. He really creates a unique tone.[15]

Skrowaczewski helped two other major orchestras celebrate significant birthdays. He closed out the Warsaw Philharmonic's centennial season in May 2002 in a program that included his *Music at Night*. He then began his busy 2002–03 season in September with three weeks of concerts with the Yomiuri Nippon Symphony Orchestra during its fortieth anniversary season.

After Tokyo he embarked on a whirlwind schedule of concerts over a nine-month period: six American orchestras, nine European orchestras, and a week at Aspen Music Festival. Skrowaczewski used his only free month of the season, January, to work on his new symphony.

Thanks to Krystyna, Skrowaczewski enjoyed a family vacation in spring 2003. She intended to give him a breather from his heavy conducting workload and the extra burden of composing two major works, but she also wanted to celebrate his upcoming eightieth birthday. The Skrowaczewskis spent a week in Caneel Bay, St. John, with Nicholas, Paul and his wife, Melissa, and their daughters, Madeleine and Mia. It was their first family vacation in decades. Skrowaczewski "protested" taking time away from composing his symphony—though he brought it with him and worked on it—but he in fact relished having this special time with his family. He particularly enjoyed snorkeling with his granddaughters.

A week after his short Caribbean vacation Skrowaczewski was in Saarbrücken for two intensive weeks of concerts and recordings with the RSO (Radio Symphony Orchestra) Saarbrücken. During the first week he participated in a Russian music festival, leading the orchestra in *The Rite of Spring* and symphonies by Tchaikovsky and Shostakovich. In the second week he recorded both Chopin piano concertos with Ewa Kupiec and Berlioz's *Scène d'Amour* (Love Scenes) from *Roméo et Juliette*. *Symphonie fantastique* completed the all-Berlioz disc.

The collaboration with Kupiec resulted from their performance of Chopin's Piano Concerto no. 2 with the RSO Saarbrücken earlier that season. Dieter Oehms, head of Oehms Classics, heard the concert and insisted that Skrowaczewski and Kupiec record the concertos for his label. Oehms formerly had been administrative director of Arte Nova Classics, the budget label of Sony/BMG, which released Skrowaczewski's Bruckner cycle and his other recordings with the RSO Saarbrücken. When Arte Nova stopped production, Oehms launched his own label. Retaining some of the Arte artists, he particularly wanted to work with Skrowaczewski again. Oehms breathed new life into Skrowaczewski's Bruckner cycle with its rerelease of the boxed set early in 2004.

For Polish pianist Kupiec, the opportunity to record the Chopin concertos with Skrowaczewski was a gift. She spoke about their collaboration:

> Our relationship playing these works is special. Maybe it is our history: that we have left Poland and now find ourselves "back home" playing this music. We are people for whom this music conveys something that is so deeply Polish to our nature. Even accompaniment that seems to be trivial means much more to us. Stan can transform the four minutes of introduction in the Concerto no. 2 into a small symphonic poem, exposing all these elements— some majestic, some intimate, and so personal to Chopin's music. You have to truly love the culture, his music, and the idiom of the music to do this.

Returning home in July 2003 after his last engagements of the season, Skrowaczewski learned that Ken Dayton had died a day short of his eighty-first birthday. Dayton had suffered from cancer for several years, but his death nevertheless shocked Skrowaczewski. In lieu of a public funeral service, Judy Dayton decided to honor the memory of her husband with a concert by principal musicians from the Minnesota Orchestra led by conductor-pianist Andrew Litton, then artistic director of the orchestra's Sommerfest. The program began with Skrowaczewski's *Fanfare to Ken*, composed for string quartet, which he had written a year earlier in honor of Dayton's eightieth birthday. Other works included the Adagio movement from Brahms' Piano Trio in B, the Adagietto movement from Mahler's Fifth Symphony, and the Larghetto movement from Mozart's Clarinet Quintet.

Skrowaczewski had been about to compose the Adagio, the third and final movement of his Symphony [2003], when Judy Dayton called him with the news of Ken's passing. "This compelled me to dedicate the symphony to his memory," he said.

He called Linda Hoeschler, former executive director of the American Composers Forum, whose Minnesota Commissioning Club had co-commissioned the symphony with the Minnesota Orchestra for its centennial season. The Commissioning Club was a novel idea hatched in the mid-1990s by Hoeschler and her husband, Jack. They invited other couples to contribute funds and jointly choose composers to commission.

Mary Ann Feldman's program note for Symphony [2003] continues the dedication story:

> Besides the Hoeschlers, the pairs collaborating in this Minnesota Orchestra commission include personalities familiar in the concert halls of both Minneapolis and St. Paul: David and Judy Ranheim, Hella Mears Hueg and Bill Hueg, Gloria and Fred Sewell, and Thelma and Sam Hunter. "All of us had enjoyed some kind of connection with Stan," Linda explains. "Most of us had sung under him as former members of the Bach Society." When the composer called to ask if he might dedicate "their" symphony to the memory of Ken Dayton, no one hesitated. "We were honored," Linda affirms. It was fitting: no one had done more in Minnesota to awaken the philanthropic conscience.[16]

Skrowaczewski experienced his usual struggles while composing the symphony. He told Michael Anthony that the piece had been growing in him for a while, although he had committed only a few sketches to paper. By summer 2002 he began to sense the kind of piece he wanted to write:

> I would like musically to be completely new and different. Not a continuation of the Concerto for Orchestra or the *Passacaglia*, which are more or less similar. I have certain ideas created by particular desires of an atmosphere or facing an atmosphere that influences my inspiration. These ideas are entirely in my head, nothing to do with the piano or the orchestra. I try to put them abstractly on music paper, and then I see, after a while, how they develop. I eventually go to the piano and try to get concrete tones. Then I experiment with how they may sound.
>
> So this is my process. I know certain elements that I will keep, but almost always I'm throwing out something the next day, rejecting it or bringing fresh ideas that seem to be better. Everything goes out, starting again from scratch, and this takes a lot of time. Why? Because with my experience of writing and conducting, I could easily write a symphony, sounding good, in a short time. Musically it would be something, but this is not what I want in this moment to write.

The fermentation of ideas proved fruitful. When he finally had the time to concentrate on the piece, it flowed out. Before departing for his late-spring European tour, Skrowaczewski had completed the first movement. "It has sonata form," he said, "so it was logical just to finish it. It's a movement that leads to another." He was contemplating a long adagio movement, something he had never previously composed.

More than any of his compositions, the creative spirit behind his Symphony [2003] expresses deep cultural and personal loss. For the first time he provided a subtext for a composition. On the first page of the score he added a quote from Baudelaire's *Chanson d'Automne* (Autumn Song): *"Beintôt nous plongeront dans les froides ténèbres; Adieu, vive clarté de nos étés trop courts"* (Soon we will be immersed in the cold darkness; Adieu, lively light of our all-too-short summer). Ever since his teenage years Skrowaczewski had been attracted to Baudelaire's poetry.

"The death imagery in *Chanson d'Automne*," noted Mary Ann Feldman, "has accompanied Skrowaczewski throughout his life, ever since he first encountered the poet's collection *Les Fleurs des Mal* (The Flowers of Evil, 1857)."[17] Skrowaczewski explained his decision to quote Baudelaire:

> These first two lines are so beautiful in French, not only beautiful in the language but in their gorgeous and concise content. It says everything about life. You can almost extend the words to a metaphysical conception of the universe. They are absolutely terrific to me, so I always felt that I would put them somewhere. And because of the world situation now, the lack of attention to the arts these days, disappearing slowly, I felt that using these lines was very proper.

"For the darkness of this new work, a centennial commission that does not celebrate the past one hundred years but reflects the troubled new century, embodies Skrowaczewski's concern for the latest generations, including his own two sons and granddaughters," Feldman wrote. "He worries that in the obsession with the wonders of the new technology, '[young people] have lost their connection with the humanistic arts—with poetry, painting, and especially the abstractions of music.'"[18]

Several years after the premiere of Symphony [2003], Skrowaczewski revisited his intention behind the piece: "The cultural tradition is being lost. This tragic realization is within me all the time, and it finds expression in my music. Education is lacking, especially in America. This symphony is my way of speaking out against this tendency to decay, against this tragedy of the internal impoverishment of mankind."[19]

Skrowaczewski also spoke out about other frustrations and observations to Michael Anthony in a preview article about Symphony [2003]:

> For Skrowaczewski, his symphony reflects matters both public and private. In a recent conversation at Orchestra Hall, the conductor nearly exploded on hearing the name of President George W. Bush. "Stupid! He has spoiled the position of this country for [one hundred] years," he said.[20] More wistfully, he talked about the recent deaths of friends, many of them former orchestra board members: Louis Zelle, John Myers, Charlie Bellows, and Kenneth Dayton. He sees them as symbols of a vanishing generation.
>
> He contrasted the optimism of the 1960s, when he came here from Poland to be the orchestra's music director, with today's darker mood. "It was an exciting time to be here back then," he said. "There was such interest in the arts and money donated and a care for education. All that today doesn't seem so important now, because people are struggling."[21]

Pessimism is not part of Skrowaczewski's nature, but his observations of the societal demise of intellectual curiosity and artistic sensitivity frightened and perplexed him. He couldn't understand, for example, why so many people loved George W. Bush, particularly by 2003. "He was in St. Paul and had a great reception," he remarked to Anthony. "How? This is to me terrifying."[22]

Several years later he reflected on the effect the Bush years had on him and Krystyna:

We lost confidence in the Supreme Court when they decided to ignore the Florida votes in the 2000 presidential election. From the days when Warren Burger, a Minnesotan, was chief justice, we had always believed that the Supreme Court was above politics. When Bush was chosen again for a second term, Krystyna and I were really devastated because obviously so many Americans were for him, and we couldn't understand why. It was a real blow to us. We saw America in a different light, and we lost our trust in the American system and in Americans as a body of people. Only now, in 2009, do I have a certain feeling of hope. I would like to see early success for Obama and an improvement of the overall situation in the country, at least morally.

Of Symphony [2003] Skrowaczewski said: "It is gloomy, this work, but it is not crying. The gloom is terrifying."[23] Anthony outlined Skrowaczewski's snapshot of the piece: "A church bell rings at the start and end of the three-movement symphony. The finale has a meditative quality, a 'Bruckner-like atmosphere,' as its composer describes it, while the middle movement, a *danse macabre*, is infused with 'outbursts of rage and terror,' he said."[24]

Like other 20th-century composers, Skrowaczewski sometimes expresses sonic rage with dissonance but never with noise. He discussed this point in regard to his perception of his symphony at the time of its premiere:

> Vertical-sounding harmonies are very important to me. They must be beautiful, beautiful in the sense of sound. I love wonderful dissonances. Some dissonances are ugly, but to me, mine are musical. They exist as an integral part of the composition. Composing the symphony was a purely abstract but still spiritual experience for me. As such, it may not appeal directly to the public. But eventually, to slightly more educated listeners, it may appeal as something very strong. It may be that they are moved, but they don't know why. This experience is to me like Shostakovich's Fourth Symphony. It is so abstract. But it is also moving. As you finish that symphony, you are in a different world.[25]

Feldman's program note (excerpts below) gave the first listeners of Symphony [2003] an entry into Skrowaczewski's world:

> There are three movements, the first launched by a single church bell in C-sharp; the haunting resonance of the opening bars (*Lento misterioso*) will recur some half-hour later, like the quiet closing of a door. The mood is autumnal.... The composer employs the large orchestra sparingly.

> The body of the opening movement is an Allegro whose infrastructure does not depart from tradition: two chief ideas are extended, developed, reprised. The harmonies are gritty, the textures crystalline. Skrowaczewski avoids *tuttis*, preferring to focus on sections of the orchestra, as at times does Anton Bruckner.... His thoughts are compact, and he is not given to repetition.

> The break is short—two or three seconds—before low strings launch a centerpiece that is a true symphonic scherzo, pulsing in three-quarter time, a meter that Skrowaczewski has not used for a long time. "But here

it is necessary," he says, "for this is my *danse macabre*." The heading, *Presto tenebroso*, affirms the darkness: the very word Tenebrae refers to the Matins and Lauds for the last three days of Holy Week, when the subject is death, symbolized by the gradual extinguishing of the lights.

Composed after the death of Ken Dayton on July 19, 2003, the finale is a mournful Adagio, deeply personal, and as spiritual as the music of Bruckner that this composer has absorbed, reawakening listeners to its beauty, and conducting it upon this occasion. "Now it is autumn," Baudelaire concludes his poetic song: "Echoes of departure keep resounding in the air."[26]

Skrowaczewski has always "looked to the past—to Beethoven, Brahms, and Bruckner," noted Feldman. "'The eternal qualities in their music,' he said, 'are as relevant now as they were a hundred years ago.'"[27]

Symphony [2003] is resonant with spirituality. The eternal qualities in Skrowaczewski's music have never been more present than in its last movement, where the music speaks of sadness and grief but not regret. Here is consolation but also something more: the inner wisdom of a soul that has probed the depths of art, lived its joys, and endured its sorrows.

There was unusual warmth in the applause in Orchestra Hall when Skrowaczewski left the podium after conducting his symphony's premiere on the eve of his eightieth birthday. The audience reacted not only to hearing a masterful, emotional work but also to the man himself. That night, in a sense, summarized Skrowaczewski's extraordinary life as a creative and re-creative artist, and it offered a glimpse into his future as he continues his journey seeking the infinite possibilities of music.

Skrowaczewski's entire family was present the following evening, October 3, 2003, when he celebrated his eightieth birthday by conducting the second performance of Symphony [2003] and Bruckner's Symphony no. 2. The resounding ovation after his symphony drew Skrowaczewski back to the stage twice; meanwhile, the orchestra refused to stand. He soaked in the praise briefly before insisting that the musicians rise and join him in accepting the applause.

Judy Dayton was in tears. "That third movement, the solo violin…," she murmured, her voice trailing off.

After the rousing finale of Bruckner's Second Symphony, which ended the concert, Skrowaczewski literally leapt off the podium, an impetuous Bernstein-like move that concerned family and friends. "It was a thumbing of the nose at age," quipped Feldman.

At a postconcert celebration in Orchestra Hall, the party's host, Linda Hoeschler, spoke briefly and gave Judy Dayton a framed copy of the first page of Skrowaczewski's symphony.

Backstage, the maestro warmly received dozens of people and politely deflected their praise. Somehow he looked as fresh and elegant as he had before the concert, as if he were about to go back onstage. His mind was already evaluating the concert, his heart already eager for the next spiritual journey.

THIRTY-THREE

COMMUNING WITH THE UNIVERSE

I think the ultimate goal of a creative person is to transform his whole existence into a medium that's more timeless, more spiritual.

—Karlheinz Stockhausen

Dmitri Shostakovich once said, "A creative artist works on his next composition because he is not satisfied with his previous one. When he loses a critical attitude toward his own work, he ceases to be an artist."[1]

Skrowaczewski's self-critical nature has always been a hallmark of his artistry and an indelible part of his personality. His fastidiousness is even more pronounced in composing than in conducting. "Especially when a piece of mine is first performed, I'm not even sure if I like all aspects of it," he said. "It takes time and multiple performances for me to fully evaluate my own music." To accept his music Skrowaczewski must be as emotionally moved by it as by works of master composers he admires; otherwise, he discards it.

Moments of inspiration require the right circumstances. During his Minneapolis years it sometimes happened during mountain climbing, when he was freed from the "persecution of the music" he had been conducting. In recent years, solitude in his home studio or jogging helps clear his mind. But even then, he explains, inspiration "comes very seldom and is sometimes illusory. The next day the same music sounds terrible, and I throw it in the garbage can. That happens very often." In fall 2003, during a postconcert question-and-answer session Skrowaczewski joked that he "wished more composers did the same."

Once, when Skrowaczewski discarded pages of a composition after toiling over it, Krystyna questioned her husband's decision. "Maybe you have something that you can still use," she suggested. She even retrieved some of his pages from the trash and considered showing them to one of their musician friends.

He finds it challenging to maintain his high standards for composition. As a conductor he constantly revises his approach to musical scores. Even with pieces he has conducted more than fifty times, he still reevaluates and alters his interpretations. Like Gustav Mahler and other composer-conductor perfectionists, Skrowaczewski also tinkers with his compositions after they have been performed, sometimes long afterward. Fifty years after he composed *Music at Night*, he made minor adjustments to the ending. The Concerto for Orchestra underwent a complete revision four years after its premiere, and Skrowaczewski made significant cuts in *Passacaglia Immaginaria* more than a decade after it was composed.

Trepidation always accompanies Skrowaczewski at the birth of a new work. He was almost apologetic to the Minnesota Orchestra for subjecting the players to his "gloomy monster," as he wryly described Symphony [2003]. "I don't know what this piece will really sound like," he confessed before first rehearsing the symphony. "I have no relationship with it." After the work's first reading there was a moment of silence before the musicians applauded and stomped their feet. Their acknowledgement went beyond a polite gesture. Although the musicians could process only so much of the symphony during this introduction, collectively they sensed that there was something special about their maestro's new piece. Yet despite these positive reactions from musicians and later from audiences, Skrowaczewski maintained remarkable objectivity about the work. He immediately noted its technical shortcomings while still basking in the afterglow of applause and the highly emotional response to the symphony's second performance.

Skrowaczewski's objectivity towards his music stems largely from his experiences as a conductor. The transition between the roles of conductor and composer has never been easy for him. Bernstein had similar difficulties; for him, the challenge lay in making the transition from the public adulation that his performances generated to the solitary confinement of composing. While he wrote, he also struggled to banish the music of other composers from his mind.

Skrowaczewski described his personal dilemma:

> I don't feel that I can compose when I'm in the midst of conducting. If I'm preparing rehearsals and concerts and new scores, it is more than just spending a few hours on it. My subconscious is full of problems, which I take to my dreams. I cannot compose even if I wanted to. I would feel that I was dishonest to my conducting, that I am not preparing well. Even when I'm repeating a work that I've known since my childhood, like Bruckner's Seventh, it is still completely new to me. My old interpretation doesn't count. If I have three days off I could compose, but I just cannot do it. I need more time.[2]

He was impressed by Pierre Boulez's ability to compose alongside his conducting obligations. Before undertaking a European tour in early 1975, he met with Boulez in New York to invite him to be a guest conductor in Minneapolis. The engagement didn't materialize, but he enjoyed talking with his colleague. They first became acquainted in the early 1960s, when Boulez was a principal conductor of the Sinfonieorchester Baden-Baden, which Skrowaczewski frequently guest conducted for several years.

During his tenure with the New York Philharmonic, Boulez consistently invited Skrowaczewski to conduct the orchestra. On several occasions Boulez told Skrowaczewski that he arrived daily at 7:00 a.m. to compose before his New York Philharmonic rehearsals began. "You can really do it?" Skrowaczewski asked. Boulez responded, "Why not?" Skrowaczewski envied his colleague. "The pieces I would like to write," he said when relating the Boulez exchange, "require a sort of spiritual quiescence. I need many weeks."[3]

Like Mahler, who reserved his summers for composing in a tiny lakeside cottage, Skrowaczewski requires complete isolation in order to write. Observed Dominick Argento, "The personal involvement between him and the music is almost a closed circuit until the work is finished and the audience can hear it." Argento continued:

> He's a very intellectual composer. He might not like that as a label, but he thinks a lot about music and organization. I tend to be a little bit the other way, thinking more about what kind of emotion I'm generating in the audience. Stan is probably more in touch with the music itself. With me, rather than thinking about structure and form and everything else, I'm more commonly wondering how the audience will react, or "Do I lose them here?" or "Do I have them yet?"

Neither audience nor the musicians motivate Skrowaczewski to compose:

> Only my own excitement and pleasure in finding certain beauty, or whatever you may call it, is what inspires me. It doesn't have to be beautiful to other people, but there has to be some emotional quality that makes me very happy or excited, just as the great composers make me feel. I want to be moved by my own music—at least in certain places in my compositions—as much as Mozart, Bruckner, or Beethoven move me. I must get those shivers that eventually lead to tears.

All of Skrowaczewski's compositions have strong roots in the music of past, particularly in works by Wagner and Bruckner. He cites four 20th-century composers who have influenced him: Shostakovich, Berg, Szymanowski, and Messiaen.

"Shostakovich brought into the 20th century a 19th-century depth of expression and power," said Skrowaczewski. "His great elaborate forms carry those qualities. Szymanowski's harmonic language and the way he generated colors from harmony inspired me, as did Messiaen's early music, prior to the *Turangalîla-Symphonie.*"

Schuller has described "new classicism" as a style of composing that brings "the past through renewal to the present, to translate that which is eternal in the past into our contemporary terms."[4] He cites Skrowaczewski's *Passacaglia Immaginaria* as an example:

> Few composers have written passacaglias in recent years. The most famous one is by Webern—that was composed in 1908! Stanisław's treatment of the passacaglia is very sophisticated. The piece is extraordinary in the way he uses all the previously developed techniques of using passacaglia themes with the inversions, retrogrades, and changes of rhythms and all of those methods; you speed them up, you slow them down, down to the last celesta notes, that's still the passacaglia. That is tremendous.

> The other remarkable thing is that the piece is original, which is unusual because we don't have much original music nowadays. It's not original in the Beethoven sense or in the Schoenberg or Stravinsky *The Rite of Spring* sense. It isn't some enormous breakthrough. But it is original in the way he specifically uses the accumulated 20th-century conceptions and techniques.

For example, the string clusters in the beginning: clusters have been around for one hundred years, but it is the *way* he uses them and how many notes he uses, and what harmonies they represent—because those chords happen to be the first five notes of the passacaglia, though people wouldn't necessarily hear that. Also, how the piece develops through its various phases with different tempo changes and sections is really remarkable because the timings of those sections are just right. Nothing is too long; nothing is too short. The form of the piece is outstanding.

"I've always been impressed that Stan's music has a direct language that comes out of a tradition," said Dennis Russell Davies. "From the beginning I thought, 'This is a modern Polish composer right out of Eastern Europe.' And I felt it was a very strong and honest voice. Like Mahler, here was a composer who composed like a conductor, with really [having] something to say."

John Harbison, winner of a Pulitzer Prize and a MacArthur Fellowship, also perceives the roots of the past in Skrowaczewski's music. While serving as a jurist on the Pulitzer Committee in 1999, when Skrowaczewski's Concerto for Orchestra was nominated, Harbison observed:

> Two things I noticed right away was what, for better or worse, I would call a Central European sensibility of continuity: a consciousness of wanting the ideas to follow consequentially one from another, and then an interest in instrumental virtuosity or, to some degree, the internal sense of playing the instruments, which I picked up from the Concerto for Orchestra. It definitely had a knowledgeable feel for what it was like to actually play the music, which not all music—orchestral or otherwise—has. In fact, not every conductor who writes music has that innate feeling for the actual engagement with the instrument that the player has, which I think is a very positive quality. There is a Polish music continuum that he is obviously part of. I don't know how far back you take it, but you have to broaden it to include Hungarian music of the 20th century. In general, such music has a strong feel for what I would call organic, unfolding, which we think of as very important to Bartók.

The Concerto for Orchestra also had an impact on Leon Fleisher:

> It is an extraordinarily impressive piece. There's an imaginative use of the orchestra and a seizing quality of how he used the material. It is proof that he is a most singular and unusual musician. He's a creator as well as a re-creator. It happens rarely, as with Lenny, but he was terribly American.

Lynn Harrell attributes Skrowaczewski's success as a composer, in part, to his knowledge of individual instruments:

> The general curiosity of each instrument is such that someone like Szell and Skrowaczewski would take the time to read up about string technique and also discuss [it] with players and, even more importantly, really watch and listen to wonderful string players. Their knowledge of the instruments goes way beyond the typical composer. I would say Skrowaczewski and Szell knew

more about string playing than Brahms. Of course, Brahms always contended that he knew very little about the cello, violin, and viola, yet he was able to write so well for them. Skrowaczewski and Szell would be the ones who could not only appreciate great string playing but also be able to write for string players in a more idiomatic way without musical compromise.

Jorja Fleezanis concurred with Harrell's assessment of Skrowaczewski's gift for instrumental writing:

> He has learned from the masters as a result of his clear study and brilliant analysis of knowing what a composer did to achieve an effect, and he knows how to craft it himself. That's the thing about all his fussing, even with music other than his own. He knows it will be more productive, for example, to take out the first violins and have them alternate with the second violins in a passage with those repetitions that Bruckner loves to do, building in an antiphonal manner. It is part of the way Stan sees the universe, and his music is that way, too.

Skrowaczewski's aim—to compose music that "moves him as emotionally as works by the great composers does"—has surprised some musicians. Phyllis Curtin describes the emotional qualities in Skrowaczewski's *Passacaglia Immaginaria*:

> As a conductor he was very contained much of the time, but when I heard his music, it was so uncontained. For instance, in the *Passacaglia* his imagination goes wild! There are passions and excitements that happen that I would never have imagined from singing with him. Just consider his use of solo voices that come in and out of the various works, how varied they are, how extraordinarily expressive. The vitality of his imagination is just staggering to me, and that was a great surprise.

The emotive qualities of Skrowaczewski's Concerto for Violin and Orchestra spurred Henry Kramer to write a heartfelt letter (with the four-note theme of the concerto written near the salutation) to Skrowaczewski:

> This afternoon your music has brought me across thresholds of sounds I thought I could never understand.... As you know from my previous criticism of modern music, I could not find myself liking music after Bartók. This music of yours is like the forerunner of the 21st century. You are the prototype of Mahler born one hundred years later.... I have an immediate affinity for this work beyond anything you have written before.... I feel a spirituality, a philosophy, the essence of life and reality, which I only found before in Mahler.
>
> The end of the first movement, with the violin spiraling upwards into infinity, is like a soul entering heaven.... I know you are basically a very objective person. But somehow I feel you have allowed your inner self to show through, whether you meant to or not, and it is all for the good![5]

"I can see him, I can almost feel his personality in his music," said Joseph Longo, for whom Skrowaczewski composed the Concerto for Clarinet and Orchestra in 1981. "There are moments of smooth lyricism but more often nervous, angular phrases. His soul puts its stamp on all of his music." Harrell said that Skrowaczewski's music "speaks in a new-enough musical language, but it speaks about human communication and personality and humanity—the joy and sadness of it."

Richard Hoenich described a performance he attended of "another well-known conductor" who programmed his own music: "In the end, you could detect cleverness. You can appreciate good technique, but someone who has a real message always transcends this. I get a message from Skrowaczewski's music, and it's rarely a happy one. It's often a really string-heavy, emotionally wrought effect."

A few months before Skrowaczewski completed Symphony [2003], he explained to a Polish reporter the origins of much of his music:

> Since childhood, the most beautiful music to me was always in minor keys. Haydn, Mozart, even earlier composers such as Gesualdo di Venosa, all have masterful works that are unusually sorrowful and tragic. They wounded me at a young age. To me, this tragic character reflects the interior of human life. The reason why music moves me is because through music I commune with the metaphysics of the world, with the universe. Music replaces religion or faith for me. It carries me into otherworldly regions, invariably sad and tragic. All of my music possesses this quality. Symphony [2003] in a sense is even more tragic and contemplative than the Concerto for Orchestra.[6]

Many people value the timeless spiritual messages of Skrowaczewski's music. Randall Meyers, American composer, film-music scholar, and astronomer, addressed Skrowaczewski after hearing a recording of Symphony [2003] several times:

> On one level I felt that your Symphony [2003] spoke of a musical history—a story about the almost lost traditions of depth and emotional meaning in music that the main body of Western classical music of the past represents. On another level, it sings of your own inner struggle to give a meaningful musical message to the world, which I can only imagine has changed a lot since you first began composing and conducting, and which you do not want to see fall into the darkness of nonthinking and nonmeaning, which it seems to be doing at a rapid pace. A wake-up call, if you will, from an artistic soul who has spent a lifetime passing on the musical flame to the few remaining "starved" spirits in need of truth.[7]

THIRTY-FOUR

WHERE THE WORD ENDS

When we run out of words—even when poets run out of words—we turn to the arts. And then we can express things in this sort of infinite abstract way that the arts can do.

—Gunther Schuller

Two weeks before Skrowaczewski's eightieth birthday, October 3, 2003, Michael Anthony asked him how it felt to reach the milestone. "What does it mean?" he replied. "Nothing, whether you are seventy-nine or eighty or sixteen. You live, and if you feel OK, you work."[1]

Nevertheless, the fact that he had conducted the premiere of perhaps his finest orchestral work—a symphony, no less—and then led a definitive performance of a Bruckner symphony on his eightieth birthday was indeed significant.

The occasion of a renowned conductor leading a major orchestra in the premiere of his own composition is a rare event. During the 20th century only a handful of artists could claim that achievement, notably Mahler, Strauss, Rachmaninoff, Stravinsky, Hindemith, Copland, Bernstein, and Boulez. After Bernstein's death in 1990, no other eminent conductor-composers were still active who could match the breadth and longevity of Skrowaczewski's dual career, except perhaps for Boulez (born in 1925) and André Previn (born in 1930).

Boulez, of course, earned his place in music history for developing his own post-serial language and for founding the Institut de Recherche et Coordination Acoustiquel/Musique (IRCAM). Since 1981, however, he has written most of his compositions for chamber ensembles, and several are revisions of earlier works. The extent of Boulez's conducting career has limited his compositional output even more than Skrowaczewski's has been curtailed.

Previn's output has been far more consistent and well rounded than that of Boulez in terms of genre and quantity. A highly gifted jazz and classical pianist, Previn began his composing career writing film scores in Hollywood. He has composed six concertos, several orchestral works, over a dozen chamber works, song cycles, and two operas.

The other figure of that generation who has made a major mark as a conductor-composer is Gunther Schuller (born in 1925). Regrettably, he has been engaged too rarely on the international conducting circuit. Nevertheless, his achievements and contributions to the art of conducting—his writings, teaching, and advocacy for new and forgotten composers and recordings—are stellar.

Of a younger generation, German-born Matthias Pintscher (born in 1971) has maintained a substantial career as a conductor-composer, as have Oliver Knussen (born in 1952) and Esa-Pekka Salonen (born in 1958). Salonen's career most closely mirrors Skrowaczewski's. The conductor-composer led the foremost orchestras of his native Finland and of Sweden before becoming music director of the Los Angeles Philharmonic, a post he held for seventeen years. Like Skrowaczewski, he has had long periods during which he did not compose. As of this writing, his music is being performed frequently and recorded on key labels, and he maintains a busy international conducting career. Salonen seems to stand alone as a conductor-composer of his generation, much like Skrowaczewski.

Beyond Skrowaczewski's unique achievement of premiering his Symphony [2003] with his former orchestra at age eighty, something less tangible made the occasion significant. He had reached this artistic milestone on his own terms and against all odds. He never compromised the musical values he nurtured throughout his life, even when they sometimes limited his career opportunities or led to disappointments.

The seven-year-old boy whose profound sensitivity to Bruckner's music caused an intense reaction was now an internationally acclaimed master of that composer's symphonies. The toddler who wanted to create his own music had grown up to craft and conduct a symphony that reflected his anxieties about the new century.

The triumphal Minnesota Orchestra concerts of his eightieth-birthday weekend launched a celebratory, dynamic season of guest conducting. From Minnesota he headed to France to lead L'Orchestre de Paris with Krystian Zimerman performing Brahms' Piano Concerto no. 1. In the maestro's experience it was atypical for French orchestras to exhibit strong discipline and attentiveness in rehearsals, but the Paris ensemble was keenly receptive to Skrowaczewski's conducting. The audience reaction surprised him as well; all the works on the program received lavish ovations.

For Skrowaczewski, rehearsing and performing with Zimerman was sheer pleasure: "Krystian was fantastic, especially in all lyrical places in the concerto. In the first movement, with those great *fortissimos* in octaves, he was utterly incredible. I had never heard anything like it."

Skrowaczewski's previous contact with Zimerman had been in 1999 at the Kennedy Center. Zimerman had concluded a thirty-nine-city international tour with a unique project commemorating the 150th anniversary of Chopin's death. The pianist auditioned and handpicked young Polish musicians to form the Polish Festival Orchestra, a one-time ensemble created solely to perform and record Chopin's two piano concertos. Zimerman served as both soloist and conductor. Skrowaczewski, a member of the Polish Honorary Committee for Zimerman's orchestra, was in Washington, D.C., for concerts with the National Symphony Orchestra. He attended Zimerman's rehearsal and concert and was stunned by what he heard: "His *rubatos* with the orchestra were unbelievable. Maybe if someone tried to imitate them they might come out completely exaggerated, but with his performance it worked. Then the concert—believe me, I was crying, and people next to me were crying. It was so beautiful."

Zimerman cited his 1978 American debut with Skrowaczewski and the Minnesota Orchestra playing Chopin's Piano Concerto no. 1 as one of the strongest influences on his Chopin project. "At that time Stan was undoubtedly one of the best conductors in the world with whom to collaborate in Chopin concertos," Zimerman said.

In 2009 Zimerman reflected on his fellow Pole:

> I respected Stan so much after my American debut with him in Minneapolis. Getting older and older, he seems to be getting better and better. He's a very humble and incredibly beautiful soul. With each performance I saw new aspects and respected him more. He is not regarded as a Bernstein or Karajan, in this super-league of conductors, and yet he is one. But it takes a long time to understand this point, until you learn to respect all of his features, because he doesn't impose anything on you.

Among Zimerman's goals for his Chopin project was the development of performances with great distinction and personality. He expressed his frustration with worldwide uniformity in orchestral performance: "Relying on one's ears alone, it is impossible to tell if one is listening to a London orchestra, one that is Parisian, New York-based, or from Tokyo. The recording industry has succeeded in 'globalizing' interpretation."[2]

Skrowaczewski shares his colleague's dismay over what he calls "the United Nations" approach to performance style:

> I am against this development because it diminishes character in music performance. It's like eating the same food all over the world. For example, the bassoons in Russia have always had a distinctive sound, colored, perhaps, by the *basso profundo* of Russian singing, but that is disappearing. French horns in France sometimes have sounded like saxophones, with a big vibrato. Now that is going away too. There are good reasons for these sonic accommodations; the mainstream repertoire profits from the blend. But certain nationalistic qualities in music performance are lost when colors are muted.[3]

After his second Paris concert with Zimerman in fall 2003, Skrowaczewski boarded an early-morning train to Saarbrücken to begin preparations for a two-week tour of Japan with the RSO Saarbrücken. The great success of their Bruckner-cycle collaboration prompted the invitation to tour Japan. Within six days Skrowaczewski prepared the tour repertoire of Bruckner's three longest symphonies (the Fifth, Seventh, and Eighth), and symphonies by Brahms and Mozart.

Skrowaczewski and his Saarbrücken musicians were overwhelmed by the reactions their concerts generated in Tokyo, especially at the final concert, which featured Bruckner's titanic Eighth Symphony.

"I can hardly remember any place where I had such enthusiasm from the public," Skrowaczewski recalled. "The orchestra couldn't understand that an audience could exhibit such behavior at a concert. They had never seen anything like it in their lives. They were so moved."

Saarbrücken concertmaster Dora Bratchkova described the performance as a high point in Skrowaczewski's long relationship with the Saarbrückens. "He and the musicians had tears in their eyes during the performance," she remembered. "During rehearsals Maestro Skrowaczewski is obsessed by the achievement of his vision," explained Bratchkova. "Performing, he is obsessed by the vision itself."

After coming on and off the stage ten times, Skrowaczewski finally grabbed Bratchkova by the hand, signaling for the entire orchestra to leave. But the audience remained standing, continuing the ovation. Then Skrowaczewski tried taking every principal player offstage one by one, but still the audience applauded for a half hour.

The RSO Saarbrücken's Japanese tour was a landmark in its relationship with Skrowaczewski. Since 1994 he has conducted and recorded with that orchestra more often than any other. Their bond, forged during the decade-long Bruckner project, has grown even stronger over the years. They share a mutual affection, respect, and understanding, and the Saarbrückens have become the maestro's most treasured professional relationship in the twilight of his career.

Since its formation in 1937, the ensemble has been heard throughout Europe on Saarländischer Rundfunk, the regional broadcasting corporation, and it has issued numerous recordings. (Saarbrücken is the capital of Saarland, a German state bordering Lorraine, France, and Luxembourg.) The orchestra performs regularly in Germany's top concert halls and tours internationally.

In fall 2007 the RSO Saarbrücken merged with the Radio Orchestra Kaiserslautern, based in the city of the same name and located in the nearby German state of Rhineland-Palatinate. The combined ensemble, renamed the Deutsche Radio Philharmonie Saarbrücken Kaiserslautern, is the first such ensemble created from two main radio orchestras. Based in both of its home cities, it is currently led by German conductor Christoph Poppen.[4]

After Skrowaczewski's Japan tour with the RSO Saarbrücken, the Chamber Music Society of Minnesota honored him with a post-birthday performance. The concert, held at Ted Mann Concert Hall on the University of Minnesota campus, featured Skrowaczewski's *Musica a Quattro* and Leon Fleisher performing Bach and Brahms. *Musica a Quattro* received a warm, thoughtful performance by violinist Young-Nam Kim, architect of the program and artistic director of the Chamber Society, and by clarinetist Burt Hara, violist Kenneth Freed, and cellist Jean Michel Fonteneau.

During the first five months of 2004 Skrowaczewski went from one engagement to the next with almost no break. Bruckner symphonies figured in most of his programs, along with a healthy dose of Chopin piano concertos. He traveled from Lisbon to Stockholm, back to the United States, and then to Italy, Spain, and the Netherlands before heading to Japan for three weeks of all-Beethoven concerts with the NHK Symphony Orchestra.

Beethoven symphonies had consumed Skrowaczewski for the past several years. Since 2000, after the release of the Bärenreiter Urtext Edition of the complete Beethoven symphonies, he had been using the new scores to review his interpretations.

When asked by a Japanese writer about the "secret" to achieving the proper orchestral sound in 18th- and 19th-century music, Skrowaczewski responded:

> In one word, balance. When composers wrote two hundred years ago they had different instruments that produced various timbres and dynamic possibilities. The number of string instruments used was smaller. Over the years the orchestra became larger, with more strings, but the larger bore-size of mouthpieces and overall structural development of brass instruments gave them more power. These often have to be brought down dynamically to achieve balance with the strings. And the balance between all sections is also affected by the conditions of the concert hall. Additionally, we have to keep in mind that when this music was originally performed, there were very few halls such as we have now. So we have to bring the score to life appropriately with today's conditions.[5]

Krystyna joined her husband in Japan for a week during the middle of his engagement. From a musical standpoint the tour was remarkable, but its demanding schedule fatigued Skrowaczewski. Having Krystyna with him gave him a welcome boost. After the tour he had only a week in which to recuperate before beginning another three-week stint in Europe.

The last leg of his eightieth-birthday season had a sense of homecoming not unlike what he experienced months earlier in Saarbrücken and in Minnesota. He began with the Hallé Orchestra and then traveled to Poland to prepare the National Polish Radio Symphony Orchestra of Katowice (NPRSO) in a weighty, all-Polish program for a concert at the Théâtre du Châtelet in Paris.

The NPRSO gave its best to a difficult program, comprised of pieces new to Skrowaczewski's repertoire: Lutosławski's Symphony no. 4, Pedenderecki's Symphony no. 5 (both premiered in 1992), and *Three Fragments of Poems of Kasprowicz* by Szymanowski, with renowned Polish contralto Ewa Podleś.

A month later Skrowaczewski was named the McKnight Foundation's 2004 Distinguished Artist. One of Minnesota's most prestigious awards, it was established in 1998 "to recognize a generation of artists who had dedicated their careers to enlivening and enriching Minnesota's cultural life." The award previously had been bestowed on two other prominent Minnesota musicians: composer Dominick Argento and choral conductor Dale Warland.[6] When asked for a quote about Skrowaczewski's music for the McKnight publication that highlights the recipient's career, Harbison offered the following: "The eminent conductor Stanisław Skrowaczewski is one of the finest composers now writing. Any encounter with his vibrant, adventurous, gripping music stays in the mind long after."[7]

An official McKnight event marking Skrowaczewski's receipt of the award drew more than one hundred people. Key figures from the Twin Cities' arts community, current and retired musicians from the Minnesota Orchestra, colleagues, and old friends gathered to celebrate the maestro's life and achievements. The Skrowaczewskis reveled in a singular night that honored their more than forty years of dedication to Minnesota's cultural life.

During summer 2004 Skrowaczewski divided his time between a new composing project—a flute concerto—and preparing scores for a career-long dream of recording the complete Beethoven symphonies.

Dozens of eminent conductors over the past seventy years have recorded complete cycles of Beethoven's symphonies. Skrowaczewski had studied and performed all nine masterpieces throughout his entire professional career. At age eighty-three, he at last completed his own recording cycle.

In January 2005 he began the recording project with the RSO Saarbrücken and completed it by March 2006. This pace was remarkably quick compared to the decade-long span for his Bruckner symphony cycle. Nevertheless, Skrowaczewski found recording the Beethoven works to be more challenging: "I've always thought that Beethoven is one of the most difficult composers to play," he said, "especially to record and particularly with all my subtle requests that come with old age!" His Saarbrücken colleagues initially had difficulty fulfilling Skrowaczewski's vision of the symphonies, which involved very specific bowings and balancing of orchestra sections. The technical and musical demands of the works also required more coaching from Skrowaczewski than the Bruckner symphonies did. The intense effort produced another significant artistic and critical achievement.

The recordings, released separately beginning in 2005 and as a boxed set in 2007, included an essay by Skrowaczewski in which he explained his approach to the process. Excerpts follow:

> Probably for every orchestra and conductor, recording Beethoven symphonies represents a special challenge, both from a technical and stylistic point of view as well as in terms of pure sound. The great richness and complexity of a Beethoven score with its secondary and tertiary inner voices require a perfect balance—not only between the main orchestral groups but within chords as well. This must be clearly presented in a recording.

> There has been controversy regarding Beethoven's metronome markings for a number of years. In the last thirty or more years, some conductors have almost blindly followed these markings, often, in my opinion, to the detriment of the music, its content, message, majesty, and power.... We know that Beethoven added metronome markings to his first six symphonies many years after he wrote them. But the precision of his metronomes is questionable.... [and] within a time span of several years, he put different metronome markings on the same piece.

> .... We composers and conductors well know how much our feeling for the "right" tempo can change with time, especially if the composer happens to

be of a compulsive, passionate character, as Beethoven was…. Thus, with full respect for Beethoven's metronome markings, I still take them sometimes *cum grano salis*, letting the music itself, its character, content, and message be in the tempo of prime importance, and a sort of guide for me.[8]

As with Skrowaczewski's Bruckner recordings, his Beethoven cycle received wide and nearly unanimous praise. The recording of the Ninth Symphony drew the most ardent admiration. Jerry Fox of *American Record Guide* described it as "among the best ever—and the one I would turn to first among all my Beethoven Ninths."[9] *Fanfare's* Jerry Dubin's enthusiasm for the recording gave Skrowaczewski and the Saarbrückens a rousing endorsement:

> Every so often a new recording comes along of one of music's seminal masterworks that cannot be ignored. Skrowaczewski's Ninth is such a recording. Whether you are a champion of Furtwängler or Toscanini, or whether you have one recording in your collection or twenty, Skrowaczewski's is a compelling performance—vibrant, vigorous, tensile, and authoritative. Its forward momentum never flags or sags, and Skrowaczewski galvanizes his Saarbrücken forces into playing as if they were the greatest orchestra in the world, which, for seventy minutes of magical music making, they are.[10]

In *Classics Today*, David Hurwitz's observation that "Skrowaczewski is one of those conductors who seems to operate under the radar in the public relations-dominated world of classical music performance" rang true with the release of his Beethoven cycle, despite many positive reviews.[11] The release of a new Beethoven cycle still garners attention, but in this instance the timing was not in Skrowaczewski's favor.

About the same time that his Beethoven cycle was released, Bernard Haitink's cycle with the London Symphony Orchestra on *LSO Live*, the orchestra's own label, also came out. The set received outstanding coverage, thanks to the instant name recognition of the London Symphony and Haitink, the allure of live recordings, and the superior quality of the discs—not to mention a Grammy nomination.

Ironically, Skrowaczewski's other "competitor" was his hometown orchestra. Osmo Vänskä, the Finnish conductor who took the helm of the Minnesota Orchestra in fall 2003, began recording his Beethoven symphony cycle in 2005 with BIS, his Swedish-based label. Vänskä had the luxury of recording all the symphonies over a five-year period with an orchestra that was hungry to add this achievement—a first for the ensemble—to its history. The recordings received wide acclaim, and the Ninth Symphony disc earned a Grammy nomination.

Skrowaczewski enjoyed listening to Vänskä's cycle as each disc was released. The Minnesota Orchestra's conductor laureate had been pleased with the appointment of Vänskä as music director and with all of his accomplishments. "I was so happy when Osmo accepted the position because I believe this will provide very fine years for the orchestra, which has always been so dear to me," Skrowaczewski told Michael Anthony at the end of Vänskä's first season in Minnesota.[12] Vänskä represented a work ethic and level of musical integrity that Skrowaczewski appreciated.

Skrowaczewski's new season would be nearly as hectic as the previous one. "It's funny," he mused, "it feels like thirty years ago! I had proposals for twice as much guest conducting, but I couldn't take them. I enjoy this, and it keeps me going."

Fall began with a two-week residency in Los Angeles. The Polish Music Center at the University of Southern California invited Skrowaczewski to deliver the 2004 Paderewski Lecture, lead a concert with the USC Thornton School of Music Orchestra, and give master classes in conducting and composition. The lecture, which took the form of a conversation with Larry Livingston, USC professor of conducting, was part of a chamber music concert featuring two movements of Skrowaczewski's String Trio and a Paderewski composition performed by pianist Marek Zebrowski, the center's director.

Skrowaczewski donated the original scores of his Prelude, Fugue and Postlude and *Music at Night* to the PMC's manuscript collection. In 1984 he became the first composer to donate scores to the future PMC, which today preserves more than a thousand manuscripts by most of Poland's important composers. Skrowaczewski's initial donation consisted of his Symphony for Strings and two works that have long been inactive, the Violin Concerto, op. 18 (1940) and Overture for Orchestra (1954).

Skrowaczewski spent the rest of fall and early winter mostly in Europe, conducting a string of back-to-back engagements in Saarbrücken, Hamburg, Wrocław, Bergen, Berlin, and the Netherlands.

An invitation from Poland to lead the Wrocław Philharmonic (also known as the Witold Lutosławski Philharmonic since 1994) involved dual honors. The first was leading the initial concert of the Philharmonic's fiftieth-anniversary season. The Philharmonic's origins go back to the Breslau Opera, where Skrowaczewski held his first professional appointment back in 1946, so this performance was especially poignant for him and the Philharmonic.

The day before the anniversary concert the University of Wrocław awarded Skrowaczewski an honorary doctorate, as it had honored Brahms 125 years earlier. The ceremony was included in the university's opening exercises for the academic year, which it postponed for two weeks to coordinate with Skrowaczewski's Philharmonic engagement. More than three-dozen faculty attended the event. "There were speeches about my life," Skrowaczewski said, "and they went on for a while. I was listening to them like a victim! But it was all very nice and proper from an aesthetic point of view."

On Christmas Day 2004, while Skrowaczewski scurried around his Wayzata home tending the fire and assisting with preparations for a family dinner, his concert of music of Bach, Mozart, Beethoven, and Schumann with the RSO Saarbrücken was telecast all over Germany. He had recorded the program earlier in December, taking a break from the formidable task of recording the first three movements of Beethoven's Ninth Symphony with the orchestra.

He had felt rushed trying to accomplish so much in a relatively short period, and the results did not please him. He rerecorded the Ninth several months later and convinced the orchestra and Oehms Classics to slow the pace of recording. (They had intended to record the first five symphonies over a two-week period in January 2005.) Only the *Eroica* was recorded by the start of 2005; the other symphonies were scheduled during the spring and into the next fall. Still intense, the pace was somewhat more realistic.

He spent the remaining six months of the 2004–05 season shuttling between the United States, Japan, and Europe. His relationship with the Cincinnati Symphony Orchestra was renewed partially by a performance of *Music at Night*, which was a hit with the audience and particularly with the Cincinnati musicians. His most recent engagement with the orchestra had occurred in 1982. By the mid-2000s many major American orchestras had forgotten Skrowaczewski's performance history with them. His rare returns were almost like second debuts.

In Japan, Skrowaczewski was in no danger of being forgotten. The admiration for his previous Yomiuri Nippon Symphony Orchestra concerts brought another invitation for three weeks. This engagement produced the first commercial DVD of a Skrowaczewski performance. The disc captures outstanding performances of Beethoven's Symphony no. 1 and Bruckner's Symphony no. 7. The engagement was memorable for personal reasons as well. For the first time both his sons visited him simultaneously in Japan. The trio had great fun frequenting the finest sushi restaurants after his concerts.

From Japan, Skrowaczewski went to Poland for two weeks to lead the National Polish Radio Symphony Orchestra in Katowice. The engagement culminated in an all-Polish concert of Penderecki's *Threnody to the Victims of Hiroshima*, Szymanowski's Symphony no. 4, and the European premiere of Symphony [2003].

Next he went to Zürich, where he led an all-Bruckner program. Skrowaczewski joined colleagues Bernard Haitink, Herbert Blomstedt, Philippe Herreweghe, and Riccardo Chailly in a monthlong survey of ten Bruckner Symphonies as part of the Zürich Arts Festival. Four orchestras participated, including the Tonhalle Orchester Zürich, which Skrowaczewski led in a program comprised of Symphony no. 0 (*Die Nullte*) and Symphonies nos. 1 and 2.

In August, John Harbison, director of Tanglewood's Festival of Contemporary Music, included *Musica a Quattro* in a chamber music program performed by the New Fromm Players. The concert also included a string-duo piece by George Benjamin and Harbison's String Quartet no. 4.

In a busy festival of twenty-six works over a five-day period, Skrowaczewski's piece was cited as a standout. "There was a time a century and more ago, when composers and conductors came in the same person," wrote Andrew Pincus in the *Berkshire Eagle*. "Our age of specialization made it a surprise to encounter Stanisław Skrowaczewski... on the program."[13] In his overview review of the festival, Allan Kozinn of *The New York Times* singled out *Musica a Quattro* as among the "real finds in the chamber music programs," and "a plangent, dark-hued work for clarinet and strings." He noted that "listeners who know Mr. Skrowaczewski only as a conductor are missing an important part of the picture."[14]

"I loved your *Musica a Quattro*," Elliott Carter wrote to Skrowaczewski after his colleague's Tanglewood composition debut. "I was so sorry you could not come to Tanglewood so that we could once again renew our old friendship."[15] Less than a year later, in spring 2006, at a University of Minnesota event honoring Carter, Skrowaczewski and the composer were reunited after more than twenty-five years. The ninety-seven-year-old Carter and the eighty-two-year-old Skrowaczewski relived many memories together.

Medical issues had made it impossible for Skrowaczewski to be at Tanglewood the previous summer. Vision in his functioning eye, the left, had worsened, and on his doctor's advice he underwent corrective surgery. The results initially appeared successful, and soon he was back composing his flute concerto and preparing for a new season.

But by the beginning of September his vision in that eye became foggy as a result of complications during the healing process. His composing ceased, and although laser surgery could possibly accelerate the healing, it could not be attempted for two months. The news worried and depressed him, but within a week the maestro—practically blind—headed to Salt Lake City to open the Utah Symphony's season with Beethoven's Ninth Symphony and *Grosse Fuge*. He needed a wheelchair and a guide to navigate the Salt Lake City airport.

"When I came to the orchestra I could not even make out the placement of the players," Skrowaczewski recalled. "They had to lead me between the violins to get to the podium." He also conducted all rehearsals and concerts without scores. Despite these hurdles, the performances were a huge victory.

Between his Utah Symphony rehearsals, Skrowaczewski visited the University of Utah's Moran Eye Center, whose specialists offered advice for his Minneapolis ophthalmologist and put Skrowaczewski's mind somewhat at ease. Within a few weeks his vision improved, just in time for his Minnesota Orchestra concerts.

He received effusive receptions before and after those concerts. "The performances this week [of Bruckner's Eighth], forged over a lifetime, will rank among his finest achievements," raved the *Star Tribune*.[16] "Would that we all could spend the autumn of our years leading a life as vibrant and vigorous as that of Stanisław Skrowaczewski," noted the *St. Paul Pioneer Press*.[17]

Indeed, his stamina in his eighties was remarkable. But the wear and tear of being on the road for more than sixty years finally gave Skrowaczewski some trouble. In addition to his chronic vision problem, he had popped a tendon in his foot the previous spring while jogging in his hotel room in the Netherlands. After returning home he experienced a persistent pain in his leg, so intense that there was talk of canceling his tours. He didn't, but he yielded to using a wheelchair at Poland's Katowice airport.

By winter he had bounced back, and by spring he finished his Beethoven symphony cycle, led concerts throughout Europe, and for the first time in more than fifteen years signed a contract for a professional appointment.

THIRTY-FIVE

NATURAL PHENOMENON

Stanisław Skrowaczewski, eighty-four, has graduated from being an institution to being a phenomenon. It's hard to think of another living musician who has trod a comparable path: from prodigy—he wrote his first orchestral composition at age seven—to elder statesman.

–Larry Fuchsberg, *Minneapolis Tribune*

When *Musical America* announced in winter 2005 that Skrowaczewski would become principal conductor of the Yomiuri Nippon Symphony Orchestra beginning in 2007, George Sturm wrote to his friend that he hardly knew "whether to sympathize or congratulate you. Seriously," he continued, "it's just marvelous that you still have the courage, spirit of adventure, and strength to undertake so weighty a responsibility. To me, you have always been, and continue to be, not only a model musician but also a model man. Bravo!"[1]

Indeed, it was impressive that Skrowaczewski could take on a major post at age eighty-three. Given his expressed desire to compose more and to travel less, his motivation for accepting the offer seemed puzzling. His rationale had as much to do with practical matters as it did with artistic considerations. The short-term appointment would be concentrated in two three-week segments each season, roughly half as much time required by a typical music directorship in the United States. He would have little administrative work, essentially that of choosing his programs. Longer residencies meant that he could decline other engagements. The orchestra—an outstanding ensemble— revered him, and from both an artistic and personal standpoint, the atmosphere would be positive.

Motivated by the uncertainties of his and Krystyna's health, Skrowaczewski had been carefully monitoring their personal financial situation. His worries about her health were prescient. Just over a year after Skrowaczewski accepted the Yomiuri position, Krystyna was diagnosed with Progressive Supranuclear Palsy (PSP). For several years she had experienced some symptoms of the rare disease, but it took time for doctors to pinpoint her diagnosis. PSP, a neurodegenerative brain disease that was only identified in 1964, somewhat resembles Parkinson's disease. PSP hinders mobility, balance, vision, speech, and swallowing. Unlike Parkinson's, tremors generally are not associated with PSP, and physical mobility is not affected as dramatically.

However, PSP progresses more rapidly than Parkinson's, and eye problems and difficulty in swallowing are other clear distinctions. Complications brought on by PSP, primarily infections and breathing problems, are life-threatening. Currently, no effective treatment for the disease exists other than medications often prescribed for Parkinson's patients, but these drugs usually provide only short-term relief. Approximately twenty thousand Americans over the age of sixty are afflicted with PSP (one per one hundred thousand people).[2]

Krystyna confronted the distressing news heroically. She continued her usual routines, believing that it would be about a year before the effects of PSP would limit her activities. Devastated, Skrowaczewski began to realign his professional life and pushed his management to seek more U.S. engagements in order to limit his prolonged absences. Although he wanted to be home more often, he knew that the cost of future care for Krystyna would be high.

Krystyna's diagnosis weighed heavily on Skrowaczewski throughout 2006, but events in his professional life eased his state of mind somewhat. He started the new year in Saarbrücken with more Beethoven recordings and his Symphony [2003] before heading to Manchester for another reunion with the Hallé Orchestra. His performance of Shostakovich's rarely heard Eleventh Symphony elicited one of the strongest responses he had experienced in Manchester since completing his tenure.

In spring 2006 Skrowaczewski had one last opportunity for an engagement with the NHK Symphony Orchestra before he began his exclusive principal conductorship of the Yomiuri Nippon Symphony Orchestra in 2007. (The new post prohibited him from conducting another Japanese orchestra.) The highlight for the maestro was his moving reunion with Canadian pianist Jon Kimura Parker, who performed Prokofiev's Piano Concerto no. 3 during the final week of the maestro's engagement. Parker hadn't teamed with Skrowaczewski in more than fifteen years. In the 1980s and into the 1990s, they had been frequent concert partners, presenting over twenty-five concerts together. Parker was Skrowaczewski's soloist with the Hallé Orchestra on its 1987 American tour.

In September 2006 the Skrowaczewskis celebrated their fiftieth wedding anniversary quietly, sharing a fine dinner and an outstanding bottle of cabernet sauvignon. They reflected on their life together, but the mood was dampened somewhat by the uncertain future of Krystyna's health. The couple had shared many exhilarating moments as well as deeply sad ones. The pain they had experienced as a result of Anna's condition never diminished.

Mutual respect, deep affection, and consideration for one another had helped their marriage—and Skrowaczewski's career—endure for so many years. "We really do like one another," Krystyna said. Their shared Polish origin is their most significant bond. When alone, they often speak in Polish, their language of intimacy (Krystyna's longtime nickname for her husband is "Misiu," or "Bear").

A strong and acutely perceptive person, Krystyna accepted that music was the main thrust of her husband's life. She did everything possible to support him while raising Paul and Nicholas, tending to Anna, and managing the household. Her influence helped to soften him over the years. "He's more accepting now, more open, and not quite as stubborn," she said.

Even after fifty years she still found joy and great humor in her husband's malapropisms: "foot trembler" (foot massager), "free-flying chicken" (free-range chicken), and "affiliated woodpecker" (pileated woodpecker). Observing other people's reactions to her husband's particular dietary habits and predilections also amused her.

"The threshold of perception starts with the smallest things," Skrowaczewski once said in a discussion about food.[3] His penchant for the freshest, finest foods has been a constant in his life. For decades Krystyna maintained a full garden of herbs, vegetables, and fruits where her husband foraged when he was home. "Corn that I pick from the garden and boil a few minutes later tastes better than corn picked a day or even a few hours earlier," he said. "Strawberries also change after a few hours."[4]

Skrowaczewski's views predated the whole-foods movement by forty years. "The most important thing in cooking is that the quality of the food must be first rate. Unfortunately, bad refrigeration, packing, and preservatives spoil it," he said in 1969. "Food from health stores that doesn't have preservatives tastes different. It is this small degree of difference that really makes a person a gourmet or not, a person who cares or not."[5]

He adhered to a consistent daily routine as music director of the Minnesota Orchestra (he continues it today). After awakening at 5:00 or 6:00 a.m., he devoted a solid hour to exercise involving stretches, weightlifting, and yoga. Breakfast was light, consisting of tea, bread, and honey. He arrived early for rehearsals to continue studying his scores and complete administrative work. After rehearsal he went home and had an early dinner at 3:00 p.m. "That way, when I do a concert I'm a little hungry, which is a pleasant feeling. I like not being completely full," he explained. A light supper, a snack, or a small cheese plate with a robust red wine, followed a concert.

The pace of Skrowaczewski's 2006–07 season was as intense as ever. After conducting the Jacobs School of Music Orchestra at Indiana University Bloomington, he went to New York City for the first time in five years. On his eighty-third birthday he led a rehearsal of Brahms' Symphony no. 1, Saint-Saëns' Piano Concerto no. 4, and *Music at Night* with the Juilliard Orchestra. The concert that opened the orchestra's season was Skrowaczewski's first appearance at Juilliard since 1991. His work with the students still inspired intense chemistry and an electric performance.

A few weeks later Skrowaczewski embarked on a month of rehearsals and performances with the RSO Saarbrücken, including a two-week tour of Japan with a repertoire of Beethoven's nine symphonies. Now that its CDs of the Beethoven symphony cycle had been released, Saarbrücken wanted to display its artistic achievements with its beloved principal guest conductor.

For the third time in his career he conducted all nine symphonies in a compact series of concerts, but the coming engagement would mark the first time he had done so on tour. The experience exhilarated Skrowaczewski and audiences, but it also presented artistic challenges, as he explained:

Any repertoire that uses a bigger mass of the orchestra in terms of sound, Bruckner or Mahler, for example, is, in a sense, easier. I'm not speaking about moments in Mahler that are difficult, passages for strings, trumpets, or horns, but I speak generally of *tutti* playing, when the players come together as an entire orchestra. Beethoven symphonies are magnified chamber music.

After sixty years of performing and recording Beethoven's symphonies—and other masterworks—his understanding of them had changed:

With my own growth and experience or thinking, Beethoven became even more incredible. Now, for me, his music is really full of modernist subtleties and such richness of ideas and form. Mozart became to me more vital, more bloody, more meaty. Why not? He wrote this way. And certain pieces, the symphonies—even the early symphonies—and the operas—what astounding facets are there! And of course, the concertos, especially [for] piano. The violin concertos are more benign, very beautiful, but the ideas in the piano concertos are just amazing. And the challenge is to interpret Mozart with these thoughts in mind and at the same time create clarity and a particular lightness of sound. Yet with this lightness there also must be a robust quality.

The richness in Shostakovich's music is well discerned by the instrumentation and the dynamics given by the composer, so with a good orchestra they come relatively obviously. But with Mozart, Beethoven, or Schumann, in numerous instances the richness has to be illuminated through the work of the conductor and by experienced players.

An unexpected discovery became the highlight of Skrowaczewski's Japan tour. After arriving in the city of Nishinomiya, located in Hyōgo, he went to the Hyōgo Performing Arts Center, where he performed his ritual of bellowing and clapping his hands to test the acoustics. What he heard and saw astonished him:

When I entered this hall, I was struck by its positive atmosphere. Two musicians eventually came in and started to play a bit. I couldn't believe the sonority. I thought they were somehow amplified with speakers because it was such a live and resonant sound. When the full orchestra rehearsed and we started the opening of the *Pastoral* Symphony, I saw the eyes of the musicians looking at me and smiling. They felt such joy over the quality of the sound of their instruments in this space. We all couldn't believe our ears!

This hall was only a year old and built for opera and symphonic concerts. It seats two thousand and has the shape of an old Italian opera house. It's an absolute acoustical marvel, definitely the best in all of Japan. It was such a big surprise to find this hall in a small city. It really proves, again, how much these days the Japanese are interested in symphonic music and opera.

Japan's commitment to the development and sustainability of Western music is impressive. "I believe Japan is having a bloom of interest in classical and romantic music," Skrowaczewski observed. "For them, this music is fresh, and they react spontaneously to it. It's similar to the spirit we read about in cities like Vienna, Munich, Cologne, and Leipzig during the 19th century."

Symphonic music was not heard in Japan until 1887, and the country's first professional orchestra, precursor to the NHK Symphony Orchestra, was not organized until 1926. Most of the country's nearly 2,500 theaters and concert halls were built over the past twenty-five years; a thousand halls have opened since 1990 alone.[6] The government and private businesses support the activities that fill these performing spaces in a country about the size of California. Music education programs focused on Western classical music are compulsory for Japanese children throughout their schooling. Having an orchestra and a proper venue is regarded as a matter of pride for dozens of Japanese cities and towns. Currently Japan boasts twenty-eight professional orchestras and more than 580 amateur ensembles. Tokyo and its surrounding communities have more orchestras than any other urban area in the world.[7]

The year 2007 brought Skrowaczewski a singular gift: a first-rate performance of his Concerto for English Horn and Orchestra by the Tonhalle Orchester Zürich. The orchestra's new English horn player, Martin Frutiger, performed the piece from memory—a first—and with a "superb tone," Skrowaczewski said, "close to Tom Stacy."

In Saarbrücken, Skrowaczewski recorded Schumann's First and Fourth Symphonies, launching a new project that committed all four symphonies to two CDs. Later, when he reviewed the recording sessions for balances and edits, he told recording engineer Thomas Raisig—with whom he also worked on the Bruckner and Beethoven CDs— that "here and there" he was pleased with his interpretations, finding them not "academic but quite personal," albeit "crazy" every now and then. Raisig, who has been the recording producer for more of Skrowaczewski's recordings than anyone else, believed that Skrowaczewski came the closest to "doing justice to the high standards he sets himself" with the Schumann Symphony no. 4 recording. "No other musician has taught me more about the architecture of great symphonic literature and its musical content than Stanisław has," Raisig said.

Skrowaczewski turned to Bruckner and Beethoven to inaugurate his first season as principal conductor of the Yomiuri Nippon Symphony Orchestra (YNSO). Founded in 1962 by the Yomiuri Group, a massive media conglomerate, the YNSO has since emerged as a world-class orchestra. It presents five separate concert series annually and has toured internationally since the late 1960s. Credit for developing the YNSO goes to conductor Hiroshi Wakasugi, who began a long association with the orchestra in 1965 and served as its principal conductor from 1972–75.

According to Skrowaczewski's contract with the YNSO, he would lead three series of programs at the start of the orchestra's season in April and another three programs in September, near the season's end. In his program book greeting, the maestro wrote that he hoped presenting a "wide variety of the greatest composers of different epochs and styles will please our public."[8] His first six programs featured symphonies by Bruckner, Brahms, Schumann, Shostakovich, Dvořák, Lutosławski, and Honegger; works by

Beethoven, Mozart, Stravinsky, Messiaen, and Chopin; and his Bach Toccata and Fugue in D minor plus *Music at Night*.

With the first half of his Yomiuri season behind him, Skrowaczewski went on to fulfill his spring guest-conducting assignments. In July he finished his flute concerto, the first piece he had completed since Symphony [2003].

In early August he again underwent laser surgery on his "good" eye, the left. The effects of macular degeneration, retinal deterioration, and glaucoma over the years caused increasing difficulties with his vision. The treatment proved effective for a time. Less than a month after the surgery—he still had difficulty seeing letters—Skrowaczewski returned to Japan for three weeks with the YNSO. Two weeks at home after the Japan trip provided a small break and more healing time to prepare for the world premiere of his flute concerto.

Although the twenty-minute work is structured in the typical concerto form of three movements, Skrowaczewski realized upon its completion that the music's character—its multiple cadenzas, interludes, and quick shifts in tempo and mood—was more fantasy than concerto. He titled it *Fantasie per Flauto ed Orchestra, Il Piffero della Notte* (The Piper in the Night). The subtitle was a tribute to Severino Gazzelloni, his longtime friend and colleague. The two had met in the 1950s when Gazzelloni was principal flute with the RAI National Symphony Orchestra in Rome (a position he held for thirty years) and Skrowaczewski was a guest conductor.

He had been searching for an Italian title for his flute piece and consulted his friend John Tartaglia, former Minnesota Orchestra violist and composer. Tartaglia suggested "Il Piffero" and reminded Skrowaczewski that Gazzelloni once jokingly referred to himself as a "piffero."[9]

Gazzelloni was described as the dean of Italian flutists by *The New York Times* at the time of his death in 1992.[10] A baroque-music specialist, he was even better known for his performances and advocacy of contemporary flute literature. (Stravinsky, Messiaen, Berio, Boulez, and Bruno Maderna, among others, all composed music for or involving Gazzelloni.) "He was a fantastic flutist," remembered Skrowaczewski, "one of the most celebrated in Europe. He had incredible tone, technique, and a wild musical temperament."

A flutist of another generation inspired Skrowaczewski's *Fantasie per Flauto*. Since undertaking his position as principal guest conductor of RSO Saarbrücken (now Deutsche Radio Philharmonie Saarbrücken Kaiserslautern), Skrowaczewski had admired the playing of Roswitha Staege, the orchestra's principal flutist at the time. Over the years Staege and her husband, Richard Armbruster, a percussionist in the orchestra, invited Skrowaczewski to elaborate dinners held at their home. "I began the flute piece with great innocence, just for the sheer pleasure of it," Skrowaczewski said.[11] He told *Showcase* magazine: "At these dinners I was treated royally. They served extraordinary wines, and their hospitality was so generous that once, on the spot, I spontaneously said to Roswitha, 'I will write a flute concerto for you.' And then I realized that I had to actually write it!"[12]

In fall 2007 the concerto's world premiere in the United States and its European premiere both occurred within a month's time. Skrowaczewski, who wanted the piece to feature multiple instruments, settled on the pairing of flute and alto flute. The latter instrument offered wonderful color opportunities, and Skrowaczewski featured it prominently along with the regular C flute.

The piece was written for Staege and the Deutsche Radio Philharmonie Saarbrücken Kaiserslautern, but it was not a formal commission from that ensemble. Skrowaczewski therefore had the option of presenting it first as part of his annual Minnesota Orchestra engagement, giving principal flutist Adam Kuenzel the responsibility of bringing the piece to life. Kuenzel spoke about the freedom afforded him by the concerto's multiple cadenzas:

> [The alto flute cadenza] concludes with instructions for the performer to realize: "Twenty to thirty seconds of a wild extravaganza, exploring the limits of the technical and sonic possibilities of the alto flute." And that may be something that I compose early on or something that I just have an idea about. In the concert it could go in another direction.[13]

This level of freedom for a soloist was unique to Skrowaczewski's compositions, but the work again displayed his trademark nuanced, transparent orchestration, subtle gestures balanced with surprising, virtuosic ones, and formal craftsmanship. He contributed a short paragraph directed at the first-time listener for inclusion in the orchestra's program magazine:

> Just listen for the variety of sounds and timbres, many of which will be unexpected. And listen for the alto flute, which adds new sounds and colors and elements to this music. But most important: try to discover—especially in slow-moving places—certain moments, chords, intervals, etc., that give you a feeling of beauty, that suddenly make your artistic sensitivity vibrate. Also try to discover the harmonic unity of the entire piece. I am very far from any twelve-tone, or other strict methods; however, the very first bars of the beginning contain the harmonic and melodic base on which the entire work is built.[14]

By all accounts, audiences and critics admired what he crafted for "night piper" and orchestra. The *Star Tribune* hailed the new piece as "a marvel," noting that "Skrowaczewski's music typically feels open-ended. His scores aren't self-contained, neatly wrapped musical objects; they are a means for conversing with their maker—especially when he's on the podium."[15]

As always, Skrowaczewski was too close to his piece to assess it objectively after the first three performances. He wanted to make some small changes, but he sensed a certain freshness in this piece that set it apart from his other works, and that notion pleased him. Larry Fuchsberg of the *Star Tribune* extolled the maestro's achievement:

> Stanisław Skrowaczewski, eighty-four, has graduated from being an institution to being a phenomenon. It's hard to think of another living musician who

has trod a comparable path: from prodigy—he wrote his first orchestral composition at age seven—to elder statesman. Both facets of the Polish-born composer-conductor, who has conducted the Minnesota Orchestra in each of the past forty-seven seasons, are on striking display this week in Orchestra Hall (an edifice he helped build).[16]

An unofficial "Skrowaczewski Festival" took place in the Twin Cities during the last two weeks of October 2007. The week after Skrowaczewski led three performances of his flute concerto with the Minnesota Orchestra, the Saint Paul Chamber Orchestra programmed his Symphony for Strings, led by guest conductor Yuri Bashmet. The day after the SPCO concerts, the Chamber Music Society of Minnesota performed three of his chamber music compositions (Trio for Clarinet, Bassoon and Piano, *Fantasie per Sei,* and *Fanfare to Ken*) and featured him in a master class at the MacPhail Center for the Performing Arts in downtown Minneapolis.

Twin Cities audiences heard five Skrowaczewski compositions, each written for a different type of ensemble; collectively they spanned sixty years. Not since 1988, when Skrowaczewski was composer-in-residence with the Philadelphia Orchestra at SPAC, had this number of his works been performed during such a short span. This two-week period also was the first time that so many Skrowaczewski compositions had been heard in the Twin Cities.

With his Chamber Music Society of Minnesota, Young-Nam Kim crafted a bountiful tribute concert for Skrowaczewski with music of Rameau, Bach, and Bruckner to balance the works by the program's honoree. "I find his music refreshingly honest—so rare these days—with sonority that is so attractive and expressive," said Kim. "Skrowaczewski's music and conducting truly represents the continuum of great art that is slowly disappearing. I am still puzzled as to why his stature as a composer is not recognized more widely."

Judy Dayton was deeply touched to hear *Fanfare to Ken,* Skrowaczewski's homage to her late husband, performed again at this concert.

Fresh from his Twin Cities celebrations, Skrowaczewski departed for Saarbrücken to give the European premiere of *Fantasie per Flauto.* He was delighted with the performance by the composition's dedicatee, Staege. The Saarbrücken public, generally conservative in its musical tastes, was taken by the piece and by its soloist.

Skrowaczewski began 2008 with an orchestral debut. Although he had conducted nearly all of the U.K.'s major orchestras, somehow the BBC Scottish Symphony Orchestra had not yet invited him to be a guest conductor. Orchestra, public, and press fell in love with Skrowaczewski's mastery of Bruckner's Symphony no. 4.

After a week at home, Skrowaczewski was back in Europe leading concerts in Austria and Manchester. His regular visits to conduct the Bruckner Orchester Linz (BOL) had become highlights among his engagements.

"The orchestra was taken with him and his methods of working," said Dennis Russell Davies, music director of the BOL. He continued:

> It's all about the music with Stan. That's why musicians respect him. He simply goes about the business of achieving the best performance he can. He's extremely courteous but very direct. He doesn't mince words, and he gets the results he wants. The musicians have a challenging workout, and they like it. I find that his manner of working physically, especially with excellent musicians, creates a sound that is uniquely his. It is similar to his composing. He knows how to achieve balances between the different choirs of instruments, and it changes as the repertory changes. His style of conducting and rehearsing works particularly well in central Europe.

Immediately after the engagement, Davies told Skrowaczewski that he wanted to conduct one of his works the next season and also asked him to lead a Bruckner symphony on the same program. His requests were fulfilled the next season (Davies conducted *Passacaglia Immaginaria*).

Following his Austrian success, Skrowaczewski returned to Manchester for a celebratory engagement with the Hallé Orchestra. The year 2008 marked the orchestra's 150th season, the twenty-fifth anniversary of Skrowaczewski's 1983 appointment as its principal conductor, and the maestro's eighty-fifth birthday.

The nostalgia that enveloped Skrowaczewski's Hallé concerts spilled over into his second season with the Yomiuri Nippon Symphony Orchestra in April 2008. His first set of concerts reunited him with Gary Graffman in a performance of *Concerto Nicolò*. The other repertoire during the three weeks included Bruckner's Second and Fifth Symphonies, Tchaikovsky's Symphony no. 6, and Stravinsky's *The Rite of Spring*. During the last week of his residency, the management announced that Skrowaczewski had agreed to change his original two-year contract to three years, extending his principal conductorship through March 2010.

The maestro's longstanding relationships with the Minnesota Orchestra and Deutsche Radio Philharmonie Saarbrücken Kaiserslautern, deepened during the 2000s, but his affiliation with the YNSO stood apart. Practically the entire orchestra felt a reverence towards him that bordered on awe. Respect for elders is part of Japanese culture, but certain qualities of Skrowaczewski's character and musicianship resonate deeply with Yomiuri musicians.

Co-principal clarinetist Youko Fuji explained: "Part of the Japanese character is that we are introverted, so it is important for us to express more in our music to really communicate it. Maestro Skrowaczewski's requests are sometimes very deep and difficult, but later I realize they are necessary to develop a wide range of musical expression." Solo cellist Hakuro Mori offered his thoughts:

> Sometimes a conductor tries to give feeling, expression to the orchestra by using the face or special gestures, etc. But maestro never does that. His musical spirit and structural knowledge is so solid that his expression comes

out automatically, naturally. When you see real art, a real painting, not an imitation, you get an extraordinary feeling. I can't really describe what it is, but I know I am having a great musical experience when the maestro is in front of me.

"Maestro Skrowaczewski has taught us that we must never compromise regarding music," noted Shinzo Yoshida, managing director of the YNSO from 2004 to 2009. "His rehearsals are tough, perhaps some of the hardest we ever have. But nothing makes us happier than performing with him."

Co-principal bassoonist Masaru Yoshida described a key lesson he has taken from working with Skrowaczewski:

> I've learned about life and how limited time is. During one rehearsal he got really upset with us, saying, "We rehearsed yesterday, yet we are not improving. Every day, every moment, you must be improving and going forward." He projects this feeling of moving forward. It is a great attitude towards life. You must always push and always use that life energy. This approach is different from our way of thinking about time, which is more relaxed and casual.

Skrowaczewski returned home from Japan feeling a bit worn, but he had only a week in which to recuperate before making his fourth trip to Europe that season. Even he began to wonder how long he could maintain his nonstop pace.

His worries over Krystyna's health added more stress to his life. The effects of PSP had progressed since her diagnosis in 2006. For half of that year she functioned fairly normally but frequently experienced early effects of PSP and severe pain from an unrelated back problem. Appointments at the famed Mayo Clinic and at the University of Minnesota's medical research center provided at least some hope with promising research studies. During the spring Krystyna began a medication treatment known to help some patients with Parkinson's disease. Initially the drugs helped, but ultimately it proved better for her health and spirit to stop taking them.

By 2007 she experienced more bouts of dizziness and depression. She regularly used a walker and wheelchair for mobility, and when speaking became more difficult, she began speech therapy. She bravely endured each setback and maintained a sense of humor as best she could. Skrowaczewski and his sons considered the possibility of an assisted-living situation, but ultimately they decided to postpone such a move until absolutely necessary. They opted instead to employ caretakers to work in their home.

Skrowaczewski was deeply saddened by Krystyna's worsening condition. When he was home, he did his best to be her caretaker and to assume her household responsibilities. The extra load was taxing, however; he still had many administrative tasks related to guest conducting and composing. Nicholas, who lived with them during this time, was an enormous help to his parents.

The maestro pressed Intermusica to book engagements in the United States so that he could avoid long trips overseas (his Yomiuri commitment was an exception). He tried to make contacts himself, sometimes with the assistance of friends, but the efforts were minimally effective. Europe and Japan remained the locations that most valued what he had to offer.

By the time he returned from Japan in late April 2008, Krystyna's health had stabilized somewhat, but her memory occasionally faltered and her moods sometimes changed. Through his Polish composer-conductor colleague Jan Krenz—who had recently survived cancer—Skrowaczewski learned of the Peruvian Institute of Andean Phytotherapeutical Research, headed by Father Edmund Szeliga, a Polish Salesian priest and missionary. Located in Lima, Peru, this nonprofit, private scientific association promotes and assists with the use of Peruvian plants for medicinal purposes. He wrote to Szeliga in an effort to help Krystyna:

> My wife, Krystyna, now seventy-five, has been ill for three years with PSP. In America and probably the world, the studies and research to find an antidote for PSP seems to be secondary to those for Parkinson's and Alzheimer's. I am open to believing in miracles, but first I'd like to explore all natural [possibilities]. Hence my question to you: is there any herbal, mineral concoction that would be worth trying with this disease? I would be so grateful for your kind opinion and answer.[17]

Unfortunately Father Szeliga died before Skrowaczewski could mail his letter.

The maestro also received discouraging news about his vision problems—the success of his eye surgery the previous summer proved to be temporary. He tried various drops and even new glasses, but his eye specialist was somewhat resigned to the inability to prevent further deterioration of his left eye. "The eye is simply tired," Skrowaczewski explained, acknowledging that the rate of all of his activities, particularly composing, would have to decrease.

Despite his worries over Krystyna and his own health, Skrowaczewski once again packed his bags for a trip to Europe. Then, after ten days at home, he would make his fifth and final trip to the continent that season, leading concerts in Budapest and Warsaw. During this tour he would make a special side trip with Nicholas: after an interval of almost fifty years, he would return to the city of his birth.

THIRTY-SIX

THE ESSENCE WITHIN

Skrowaczewski had not conducted in Hungary since the 1950s. His last engagement took place a year before he left Poland to become music director of the Minneapolis Symphony Orchestra. Arriving in Budapest in May 2008, he was pleased to find the city as lovely as he remembered, with its architecture untouched by World War II and the rolling hills framing the mysterious Danube River.

He recalled the sounds of the excellent Hungarian orchestras of fifty years ago, including the Hungarian National Philharmonic Orchestra, which he now would lead again. The Philharmonic had a long history with Skrowaczewski's Minneapolis predecessor Antal Doráti and with other foremost maestros, including Janos Ferencsik, Klemperer, Ansermet, Barbirolli, and Stokowski. When Skrowaczewski gave the Philharmonic a downbeat for the start of Bruckner's Seventh Symphony, he was pleased to hear his recollections confirmed.

Unfortunately, the Hungarians' refined sound was marred by the wretched, loud rehearsal hall in which they were playing. Skrowaczewski had anticipated rehearsing and performing in the concert hall of Franz Liszt Academy of Music, as he had decades before. However, all rehearsals save the last took place in a rehearsal room of a huge multipurpose arts center that had been built in the city a few years before his visit. He hoped that the center's concert hall would sound better, but the musicians warned him that it would not be so; nevertheless, the excellence of the Philharmonic, and his fine hotel tempered his disappointment.

From Hungary Skrowaczewski went to Poland to conduct the *Missa Solemnis* with the Warsaw Philharmonic. He had been looking forward to the engagement all season. Seventeen years had passed since he last conducted the Beethoven masterwork, in his last concert as principal conductor of the Hallé Orchestra.

Although he had spent a long time away from the score, he still knew it well and remembered his last interpretation, but as he said, "After so many years, you feel a little different here and there with such a work." Skrowaczewski's central concern about the piece was finding the right tempos for all five movements:

> I was interested in the past, so I listened to recordings of Toscanini, Szell, Karajan, and Klemperer. I really couldn't use any of them as a model. I have a live recording of Szell's from the last months of his life. His first movement is excellent, but other movements are too fast. He starts the *Credo*, for example, normally but suddenly during the fugues and especially at the end of the *Credo*, his tempo is unbelievable and unplayable for the orchestra and especially the

choir. But believe it or not, they do it! It is as though he knew that this was his last *Missa Solemnis,* and he wanted to show what his orchestra and choir could do. It was unusual, however, for him to take unplayable tempos for ensembles.

On the other hand, some of Karajan's movements were extremely slow, to the point of almost physical impossibility. Some of Toscanini's tempos were also very slow and sounded heavy, particularly in the fugues of the *Gloria,* while other tempos were completely too fast, like Szell's. So, in revisiting this masterpiece, I tried to find overall tempos that were really good for the music *and* for all the performers.

Skrowaczewski had a forty-nine-year history with the Warsaw Philharmonic, one of Poland's best orchestras, and its professional choir, the Warsaw Philharmonic Choir. Members of the solo quartet had varying degrees of experience, however, and their performances were uneven. Although that situation presented challenges in rehearsals and performance, it didn't bother the maestro; what really mattered most to him was the opportunity to try his new approach to the piece. By the end of the second performance, he felt uncommonly pleased with the results of his revised interpretation.

He also was relieved to have made it through the entire concert with no physical problems. A few hours before the previous night's sold-out concert, he developed a severe allergic reaction to some flowers in his dressing room. People at the Philharmonic gave him an allergy pill, but minutes before he had to go onstage, he still didn't feel well. While conducting the epic *Missa* he was tempted to put down his baton and leave the stage, but he fought off his weakness and finished the performance.

"They were well meaning," said Nicholas Skrowaczewski, who had traveled to Warsaw for the second concert. "They thought they could just give him a Benadryl or something, and he would be fine, but my dad's physiology is just not like the rest of us. The pill caused a negative reaction. He became woozy and almost passed out. Yet somehow he got through the *Missa Solemnis* that night."

A decade had passed since Nicholas had last seen his father conduct in Poland. His primary motivation for making this trip was to accompany his father on a visit to Lwów. Before arriving in Warsaw, Nicholas visited Kraków to see his Uncle Rajmund (Krystyna's brother) and cousins Justyna Polaczek and Bartek Jarosz.

A fan of cinema like his father, Nicholas was thrilled to meet famed Polish director Andrzej Wajda backstage after the concert. Among Poland's most revered 20th-century figures, Wajda has received numerous international prizes and honors, including an honorary Oscar in 2000. His 2007 Oscar-nominated film, *Katyń,* depicted the Soviets' horrific 1940 massacre of more than fourteen thousand Polish POWs. Wajda's father was among the victims, as was one of Krystyna Skrowaczewski's uncles. Wajda (born in 1926) and Skrowaczewski did not know each other well, but they had mutual friends from the maestro's days as a film composer during the 1950s. Wajda regularly attended Skrowaczewski's Warsaw concerts, as did other distinguished Poles, including Krzysztof Penderecki, who composed the music for Wajda's *Katyń.*

Soon after arriving in Warsaw, Skrowaczewski met Penderecki by chance in the lobby of the Sofitel Victoria Hotel, where both were staying. The colleagues discussed music and life over two breakfasts at the hotel. Penderecki unsuccessfully encouraged his friend to order an elaborate Polish scrambled-egg dish. Eggs seemed to be on Penderecki's mind as well as on his plate, as Skrowaczewski recounted:

> Penderecki mentioned his concerns over the increasing expense for the upkeep of his country estate in Kraków and said that in order to properly fertilize all his particular trees, he bought two thousand eggs. He explained that burying eggs under the soil made it incredibly rich—great for plants and much better (and healthier) than using any chemical fertilizer. I thought this organic method was wonderful, but the image of Penderecki receiving two thousand eggs and burying them was hilarious to me.

During their short time together in Warsaw, Skrowaczewski and Nicholas enjoyed authentic Polish cuisine in a charming cellar restaurant near their hotel. While customers around them dined on brandy-based venison, red cabbage, beets, and extraordinary honeys, father and son savored dinners of smoked eel. Prepared with a dill sauce, smoked freshwater eel is a classic Polish dish from the country's Lake District—a century-old culinary favorite with which the Skrowaczewskis satisfied their penchant for exotic Old World food.

Their flight the next day to Lwów (L'viv) lasted only an hour, but upon their arrival Nicholas felt as if they had gone back in time to another world. Leaving Warsaw—a metropolis of 1.7 million residents, with a modern skyline and pervasive signs of development—they entered a city with a million fewer people, an historic Old Town section still largely intact, and a mysterious charm reminiscent of the city's 13th-century origins.

The last time Skrowaczewski had set foot in Lwów was 1959, not long before he left Poland to start his life with Krystyna in America:

> I had a five-week tour in the Soviet Union. I remember it started in Minsk with pianist Alicia de Larrocha and then to St. Petersburg, which was Leningrad at the time. I conducted its superb Philharmonic Orchestra, then under Evgeny Mravinsky, who premiered eight of Shostakovich's symphonies. Then I was in Moscow and Kiev and finally Lwów. I remember that in Lwów I went to the grave of my sister. It was beautifully kept, clean, and with flowers. I had no relatives in Lwów at that time, so I had no idea who was maintaining it.

Skrowaczewski knew that coming back to his childhood home after forty-nine years would be jarring: "I was prepared mentally to experience the visit unemotionally. I did the trip only to reconfirm certain feelings that I knew would exist and, of course, for Nicholas." However, he had not anticipated the power that Lwów still held for him.

"Ah yes, I remember this air," Skrowaczewski remarked after walking off the plane onto the tarmac. "There's nothing quite like the quality of this air, slightly arid, soft somehow, and this warm breeze coming from the south, very dry and continental." Only in this open space at the airport could he savor this unforgettable aroma of grass, woods, and fruit. He explained to Nicholas that the air's quality was due to the elevation and Lwów's proximity to the mountains and the vast open prairies to its east. "The air felt silky, and I was immediately charmed," Nicholas recalled.

In Lwów they were met by Roman Rewakowicz, director of the Pro Musica Viva Foundation, which promotes Polish and Ukrainian musical culture through festivals and similar events. Skrowaczewski had met him a decade earlier when he tried to engage the maestro to record all the Beethoven symphonies with Symphonia Varsovia, one of Europe's finest chamber orchestras. Sponsorship for the fledgling project never developed, but Rewakowicz stayed in contact with the maestro whenever he conducted in Warsaw. He helped the American visitors get around the city.

When Skrowaczewski stepped out on the veranda of his third-floor suite in the L'viv Grand Hotel, he scrutinized the panoramic view of the city center and tried to distinguish the new from the old: "The city had been such a jewel, with the most elegant downtown, surrounded by ornate churches from the 13th century, late Renaissance, and the baroque epoch. But the Soviets closed them and turned them into warehouses, storing cars and big trucks inside, completely ruining them. They were later repaired. From this vista I saw that much had changed, but here and there you could still see the beauty of the city as it once existed."

Shortly after they checked into their hotel, a staff member of the Lutosławski Society arrived to take them to sites important to Skrowaczewski. Fluent in English, Polish, and Ukrainian, the man was the ideal guide.

Walking the streets triggered Skrowaczewski's memories. "Here there was a fantastic delicatessen with rare, individual meats and exotic dishes," he enthused to Nicholas. "It was amusing but sad," Nicholas recalled. "The building he gestured to was now a McDonald's."

As Skrowaczewski explored the sites of his childhood, he became increasingly fascinated and curious. Some areas were completely destroyed, languishing in disrepair; potholes made walking difficult. The sight of buildings with new façades in Ukrainian and Russian styles angered him. "Look what they did to these buildings! They were wonderful gray stone, [and] now they are vulgar pink, blue, and yellow colors!" He was surprised to find holes in some buildings, scars of bomb damage from World War II. "In 1959 the condition of Lwów was a little poor, but in my opinion, it is worse in 2008," he noted.

A stop at the city's conservatory tempered Skrowaczewski's pessimism. The site of his first experience conducting a full orchestra, the building had remained essentially as he remembered it. Walking into a dimly lit rehearsal hall, he watched a woman conducting a student orchestra. Nicholas savored the image of his father inside this busy institution and the continuum of music education in Lwów that it represented.

Their next stop was the apartment where Skrowaczewski was born. Although he was content simply to see the building, their affable guide rang the bell. "You've come all this way," he said. "You must go in." Speaking in Ukrainian, he told the mildly annoyed man who answered the door who they were and why they wanted to visit the apartment. "It was mind-blowing," recalled Nicholas. "Within a half hour of putting our bags down at the hotel, we were about to go into the apartment where my father was born."

As they walked upstairs to the third floor, Skrowaczewski remembered the original steps built of beautiful gray stone, now badly deteriorated. He also recognized the main door to his family's former apartment and another door to its left, the entrance to the room where his father treated patients after hours. Both were the original doors.

Inside, however, the original floor plan had vanished. Skrowaczewski described the changes:

> It had been a beautiful flat with six huge rooms, corridors in between and a balcony. That was completely gone. There was a crumbled wall right where we walked in. Those six rooms had been divided into at least three apartments. This probably happened decades ago when the Soviets imported thousands of people from the East and Far East and needed more space.

Apparently the occupant of Skrowaczewski's childhood home was using part of it as a photography studio. Upon seeing its condition, the maestro felt no desire to explore the space further. He shrugged off the experience of seeing the apartment as "interesting" and was eager to explore other parts of the city. "He's somewhat inscrutable," Nicholas observed, "but internally he certainly was experiencing intense feelings."

Back on the streets of Lwów, Skrowaczewski pointed out locations where relatives and friends had lived and worked, and he related details of their lives. Every block jogged his memory: the military hospital where his father worked, the area where the first German bombs struck, the cathedral where his parents hid him during a German raid, the apartment where Soviet troops shot one of his second cousins.

Present-day Lwów on a sunny, mild Sunday afternoon offered a welcome contrast to these distressing memories. Nicholas described the atmosphere:

> There were lots of people—teenagers, younger and older folks—walking around, talking, and socializing. There was a true sense of culture, and I didn't sense a crazy juxtaposition of wealth and poverty that you find in most big cities. People looked healthy and optimistic, [with] a great civic life perhaps still as yet untarnished. I didn't see people storming down the streets with headphones on and avoiding eye contact. There seemed to be a gentle sense of community, as opposed to what you might find in Warsaw or New York. Lwów seemed still to be in a bit of a time warp where people value the simplicity of standing around in a park drinking lemonade or wine and talking to one another. In the evening, before we went back to the hotel, a group of middle-aged people sang some traditional Ukrainian and Polish choral songs in the main square—so pleasant to observe.
>
> Of course, young Ukrainians are trying to find their own identity, and that will no doubt mean their own ultimate embrace of Western development. This is already happening.

Skrowaczewski showed Nicholas the routes he used via the electric tram to get to school and to the conservatory. These charming tramcars that had existed in Lwów since 1880 were still running, though most of the lines are now dilapidated and the cars in need of repair.

The travelers located Skrowaczewski's elementary school, which was still in operation and only slightly reconstructed. A small boy was chatting to himself while playing with a ball out front. He noticed Skrowaczewski and stopped for moment, inquisitively looking at this man who might have been playing in the same spot eighty years earlier. At home Nicholas had seen a class photograph of his father dressed in an Eaglet uniform for a pageant. The photo had been taken in front of this school.

The pair visited some of Lwów's churches, but the Bernardine church held the strongest memories for the maestro. He had to slip a "bribe" to the attendant to get inside the 17th-century Catholic Polish church, now the Ukrainian Catholic Church of St. Thomas. Sixty-four years earlier he had hidden in the church's cloister at the start of the second Soviet occupation of the city. While inside the church, Skrowaczewski remembered the time when two German soldiers discovered him playing Wagner and, thankfully, approved his musical selection.

Before father and son concluded their short trip to Lwów, they visited two of the city's important landmarks, both of personal significance to Skrowaczewski. Rewakowicz had arranged for the director of the L'viv Theatre of Opera and Ballet to give them a tour of the opera house, known as the Lwów Opera during Skrowaczewski's childhood. "They refurbished the opera house, but it was as beautiful as it had been, both outside and inside," Skrowaczewski noted.

Construction of the theater began in 1897 and was completed three years later. The most important Polish artists of the day painted original works for the house's ornate interior.[1] Designed in the opulent "Viennese pseudo-Renaissance style," the theater has a stunning main hall and an ornate side-salon replete with high ceilings, mirrors, and ubiquitous gold leaf. Nicholas was impressed to learn that the first public performance of a Skrowaczewski chamber work, a string quartet, occurred in this luxurious venue. The maestro showed his son the place in the first balcony where he used to sit with his parents and his sister, Krystyna.

Forty-nine years earlier Skrowaczewski had visited his sister's grave at Łyczakowski Cemetery. "It's one of the greatest cemeteries in Europe," he observed, "and it's gorgeous, spread across several hills, and huge, going for at least two miles in one direction and a mile in another." The resting place for more than four hundred thousand people, Łyczakowski is one of the oldest Polish cemeteries in the world.[2]

Situated on the outskirts of Lwów, the sprawling cemetery has intricate patterns of pathways, often within forest-like terrain. Skrowaczewski thought he remembered the general area where Krystyna was buried but checked with the house of records to find the exact location. They found no record of her burial site, no doubt the result of the cemetery's various administrative changes over the decades. Skrowaczewski retained a vivid mental image of his sister's unblemished marble headstone with its engraving intact.

Aided only by this memory, father and son embarked on a long search. Łyczakowski Cemetery had been designated a historical preservation site in 1975, and much of it had been beautifully restored.[3] Nevertheless, some areas were difficult to navigate. In certain places the graves of Poles, Jews, Germans, Ukrainians, Russians, and other groups existed side by side, evidence of Lwów's complex history of occupations and changing populations.

"Parts of it were not well organized," remarked Nicholas. "We walked all over and often found unkempt tombstones. Climbing around overgrown vegetation was treacherous, and a lot of areas were inaccessible."

World War II had taken its toll. Many sites within the historic cemetery had been neglected, removed, or destroyed. One of the most sacrilegious degradations was the destruction of the Cemetery of the Defenders of Lwów (Cemetery of Eaglets). The site contained nearly three thousand tombs honoring soldiers—three hundred of whom were children known as the "Eaglets"—who defended Lwów during the Polish-Ukrainian and Polish-Soviet wars between 1918 and 1920. After World War II, when Lwów became part of Soviet Ukraine, numerous Polish graves and monuments at Łyczakowski were destroyed. At one point the Soviets turned the Cemetery of Eaglets into a truck depot. Recently, the Eaglets' burial site was restored; it reopened as a mausoleum in 2005, thirty years after the cemetery's designation as a historical site.[4]

After more than three hours in the hot sun the two abandoned their search for Krystyna's gravesite. Skrowaczewski simply couldn't remember where it was. "She didn't tell us where to find her," he said wryly to his son.

"In a way, I think he really thought we might be led to it somehow," said Nicholas. "Supernatural occurrences had happened at other points in his life. His metaphysical side was coming out." The younger man vowed to come back one day and find his aunt's grave.

While driving them to the hotel, their young cab driver, perhaps sensing Skrowaczewski's melancholy mood, played a CD of old Lwowian drinking songs performed by his own folk group. He sang along in a Lwowian dialect, tapping Skrowaczewski on the shoulder in rhythm to the music. The maestro hadn't heard these songs since he was a teenager and roared with laughter at the off-color jokes sung in Lwowian slang. Within minutes he was transported back in time, cheered by an instantaneous shared identity with the driver.

That evening, over an authentic Lwowian meal complete with fine, rare Georgian wine, father and son reflected on what they had experienced during the past two days. For years Nicholas and Paul had been drawn to their father's stories about growing up in Lwów in the 1920s and 1930s and living there through the war. Now Nicholas began to understand the fascination the city held for his father:

> When he talked about his home city, there was a sense of wonder about it, a
> city so refined and cultured that it fed his soul. I know he's horrified by the
> contrast of the Lwów of his youth with the city it is today, especially with all

the layers of commercialism and "progress" since he had last visited. But since I don't know *his* Lwów, I experienced a remarkably distinctive city, still with evidence of the refinement my father knew. Even from a short visit, I felt its ineffable qualities. There is a timeless spirit in Lwów that has nothing to do with contemporary society.

Lwów still evoked intense feelings in Skrowaczewski, and his emotional response to the city's essence surprised him. His years in Lwów, especially during the war, profoundly shaped and filtered his innate talent. Experiences that nurtured his sensitivity to sound, sight, and taste gave him resolve, informed his imagination, shaped his intellect and integrity, and heralded his destiny as a great conductor and composer.

Before boarding the plane for the long trip back home, Skrowaczewski paused for one more glimpse of Lwów. Gray clouds forming in the sky diverted his gaze. As he turned his face towards a patch of sunlight, a gentle rain began. He wiped the drops of water from his face, turned around, and entered the plane. From his window seat, he saw that the sunny Lwów he and Nicholas had experienced for two and a half days had been transformed. Pressing his face to the small oval window, Skrowaczewski smiled. His mysterious, veiled, and vaporous city had been restored to him.

CODA

In summer 2008 Skrowaczewski's heart stopped after he drank a combination of nutritional supplements. Medics revived him, but the severe reaction had caused heart damage and atrial fibrillation. Although a pacemaker improved his condition, he was left weakened. He experiences shortness of breath and fatigue during physical activity—except while conducting. "I reduced the size of my gestures and try to make them more expressive," he explained. "I'm also trying to increase my concentration, and this is felt by orchestras. It gives the best results in performance." Despite his heart condition and continued vision difficulties, Skrowaczewski maintains a vigorous schedule of conducting and composing.

The effects of PSP forced Krystyna's move to an assisted-living home. She is doing well in this environment, and Stanisław visits her daily, but the disease has changed their lives dramatically. Anna, her condition unchanged for decades, remains in a long-term care facility.

Skrowaczewski's sons have continued to excel in their respective pursuits. Working in various facets of audio-video postproduction since 2000, Nicholas also is periodically involved in recording and performing as a percussionist in the free-jazz genre. In 2003, with bassist Mark Leonard and saxophonist Stanley Jason Zappa (nephew of Frank Zappa), he released *Visions*, a CD of original trio improvisations. He and Zappa performed in 2008 at the annual international Zappanale festival devoted to Frank Zappa's music. Since his mother's PSP diagnosis in 2006, Nicholas has helped provide caregiving support for his parents.

Since the 2000s Paul has held senior managerial positions with Sony Computer Entertainment (PlayStation games development), Microsoft (Xbox Live development), and George Lucas' LucasArts Entertainment. In 2010 Paul moved into the world of mobile entertainment when he joined Walt Disney Company's newly created Disney Mobile division as vice president of mobile music gaming. He combined his product leadership, music experience, and games-development expertise to help make Disney's "Tap Tap Revenge 4" the most popular music game on the Apple iPhone platform in thirty-seven countries. He also revived his music career in 2005 with a new band called Basic Pleasure Model, which produces new music and video releases.

To honor Skrowaczewski's 85th birthday in 2008, Oehms Classics released *Stanisław Skrowaczewski the Composer: Music at Night*, a CD of first recordings of the title work, *Fantasie per Flauto ed Orchestra*, *Il Piffero della Notte*, and Symphony [2003], with the maestro conducting the Deutsche Radio Philharmonie Saarbrücken Kaiserslautern.

In 2009 he led the premiere of *Music for Winds* in Saarbrücken, with subsequent performances in Munich, Minneapolis, Tokyo, and Wrocław. An international consortium of nine orchestras and wind ensembles commissioned the four-movement composition. Dissatisfied with his *Passacaglia Immaginaria*, he fully revised the work for performances in the United States and abroad during the 2010–11 season.

When Skrowaczewski completed his tenure as principal conductor of the Yomiuri Nippon Symphony Orchestra in 2010, the ensemble named him its honorary conductor laureate. Currently he has scheduled guest-conducting engagements around the globe through 2013.

As he nears his ninth decade, Skrowaczewski's spirit and tenacity remain steadfast.

In spring 2010 a concert he was to conduct in Poznań, Poland, was canceled. The country was mourning the tragic loss of its president and ninety-five other passengers who perished in a plane crash in Smolensk, Russia. All flights from Poznań were grounded because of volcanic ash from Iceland, but Skrowaczewski was determined to make his next engagement with the Hallé Orchestra. He hired a car and two drivers to take him across the continent. Reaching the ferry docks in Vallee Calle, France, at 7:00 a.m., he crossed the English Channel, making it to Manchester in time for one short rehearsal before the concert. Although he was exhausted after the 800-mile, 24-hour journey, he conducted with aplomb.

By the close of the 2009–10 season he had achieved a remarkable personal record. He had conducted 4,441 professional concerts since the start of his career sixty years earlier, an average of sixty-eight concerts annually—essentially a performance every five days. "It doesn't mean anything really," he said when the figure was brought to his attention. Nevertheless, the fact that he's kept a tally of his concerts over the course of seven decades is emblematic, to some degree, of his pride in the longevity of his conducting career.

In 2011 Skrowaczewski begins work on a concerto for cello and orchestra. He has conducting engagements in Denmark, Poland, Japan, and Germany, including a return to the Berlin Philharmonic. He also will record the complete Brahms symphonies with the Deutsche Radio Philharmonie Saarbrücken Kaiserslautern.

Sto Lat!

POSTSCRIPT

MINNESOTA ORCHESTRA: 1979 TO THE PRESENT

In his essay for the book *Minnesota Orchestra at One Hundred*, Twin Cities music critic Roy Close dubbed the period immediately following Skrowaczewski's tenure as "The Corporate Era."[1] By the late 1970s the Minnesota Orchestra—like its peers—was employing its musicians and administrative staff year-round, providing them with long-awaited health and retirement benefits, and managing a budget of almost seven million dollars. Like any corporation, it needed to focus on profits, deficits, and marketing issues. As it had for many years, the orchestra targeted a broad audience by presenting light classical or pops-oriented concert series alongside its formal subscription season and the musically diverse summer season.[2] The opening of Orchestra Hall in 1974 gave the Minnesota Orchestral Association the opportunity to offer other events, such as recitals and performances by major visiting orchestras and concerts by popular entertainers.

After Skrowaczewski's tenure, the orchestra's artistic leadership assumed a corporate-like structure. A team of five conductors divided up the season, each overseeing a specific repertoire—a departure from Skrowaczewski's early years as music director, when he led almost all of the concerts and had one assistant conductor.

Securing Neville Marriner as Skrowaczewski's successor was a coup for the orchestra, the first time the organization hired a music director who already had a longstanding international reputation. His initial commitment to the Minnesota Orchestra was only ten weeks (although it increased in later seasons). Marriner was not interested in relinquishing his existing commitments: his twenty-year leadership of the famed Academy of St. Martin in the Fields Chamber Ensemble; his posts with Detroit Symphony's summer season and the Stuttgart Symphony, beginning in 1980; and the two months he spent annually with the Sudfestfunk Orchestra in Baden-Baden. The orchestra filled Marriner's absences by naming Klaus Tennstedt as principal guest conductor and Leonard Slatkin as artistic director of the summer season. Associate conductor Henry Charles Smith covered Young People's Concerts and lighter programs (in addition to subscription concerts), and Skrowaczewski led a few programs each season as conductor laureate.

Clearly there were musical and marketing benefits to having different personalities on the podium. Marriner brought his much-recognized interpretive gifts to the baroque, classical, and British repertoire. Tennstedt was a force of nature with large-scale music by Beethoven, Bruckner, and Mahler. Slatkin was skilled at conducting contemporary music and much of the general repertoire. Skrowaczewski's vast repertoire added yet another dimension to the programming, while Smith covered a diverse range of concerts.

Recalled Ken Dayton, "I always thought that was an incredible period, because we had three levels of music making: Neville, who had all surface sheen and polish, delight, and bubbly music; Klaus, who threw blood and guts all over the stage; and then Stan, down there gnawing on the bones of the music."

However, this arrangement presented challenges to the orchestra's day-to-day artistic leadership, vision, and development. Marriner did not live in Minnesota during his tenure. "[He was] a commuting music director, and that took a toll," said Cisek. "He would fly in on a Sunday and rehearse on Monday.... It was a punishing schedule; he had no light weeks."[3] Likewise, it was difficult for everyone to cram all of the administrative tasks into the pockets of time when Marriner was on site. With the management's strong leadership and cooperative spirit, the system worked well for a while. As Marriner's tenure continued, however, so did certain problems within the orchestra, principally the issue of replacing members whose time had come to retire, and Marriner could not stomach the task.

His successor, Edo de Waart, had no difficulty making personnel changes when he began leading the orchestra in 1986. The Dutch maestro had earned a reputation as an orchestra builder in his positions with the Rotterdam Philharmonic and San Francisco Symphony, but some musicians disliked his blunt, sometimes dour leadership style. Others admired his ability to raise the level of the orchestra substantially within a relatively short period of time. De Waart conveyed his first impressions of the orchestra:

> I found the Minnesota Orchestra to be a bit nondescript. It was a bit in disarray, asking, "What are we doing? Where are we going?"—and with a public that was dying to be able to say, "We have a world-class orchestra." This is very normal in America—a syndrome where we need to talk something up more than it is. In every town and every city that has an orchestra, the title "world-class" is thrown around. It's hard to get people to move when they are sort of satisfied and are content with—I wouldn't say mediocrity—but not a really first-rate quality. There are standards that need to be set by institutions, not to be ridiculously anal about them, but to be always reaching for the unreachable. I didn't feel that that was the normal state of affairs for the Minnesota Orchestra. I didn't [detect] much pride. It was the first thing I felt that I had to try and improve, so that at 10:00 p.m., when the concert was over, the lights went up, and the applause ended, people could say, "We played very well tonight. We played our best," and be proud of it. I think to a certain extent I succeeded in [instilling] that feeling. But I'm not one to judge such things when I'm in the process of trying to make them happen.

If a malaise affected the orchestra at times during the tenures of Marriner and de Waart, it subsided for a period during the leadership of its next music director, Eiji Oue.

During the past forty years there never has been an appointment to a major American symphony orchestra quite like the one the Minnesota Orchestra made in 1993. When Oue assumed directorship in fall 1995 at age thirty-seven, his previous professional experience consisted of conducting a Boston youth orchestra, four years as an associate conductor of the Buffalo Philharmonic, and another four as music director of the Erie Philharmonic in Pennsylvania. Despite his limited experience with major orchestras, Oue possessed a future maestro's resume: studies with Hideo Saito (Seiji Ozawa's distinguished conducting teacher) and receipt of the Koussevitzky Prize at Tanglewood, where he met Bernstein, his future mentor and advocate. He assisted the legendary maestro in concert performances and in his last educational effort—founding the Pacific Music Festival in Sapporo, Japan, just months before Bernstein's death in 1990. Oue also had won a Gold Medal from the Salzburg Mozarteum conducting competition.

Oue was a public-relations manager's dream come true. Equipped with an impressive musical memory, he often conducted without a score, and like Bernstein, he had a gift for connecting with the general public. The young maestro enthusiastically participated in more outreach, educational, and marketing events than perhaps any other conductor of a major orchestra in recent times. In contrast to his predecessor's approach, he lavished praise upon the orchestra.

Oue benefited greatly from de Waart's accomplishments. The orchestra was raring to spring free and perform unencumbered, and Oue let the reins go. Initially it was just what the ensemble needed, but eventually concerns arose when the important work of maintaining the orchestra through detailed rehearsals became necessary. "It was like he loved driving a first-rate sports car," said one musician, "but he never wanted to change the oil." Oue's musical leadership received pointed criticism, internally and externally. When the time came for his contract renewal, there was not enough support for him to continue.

To Oue's credit, the orchestra made major strides over his seven-year tenure: tours of Europe and Japan (both first ever), three Grammy Award nominations, eighteen CD recordings, and substantial personnel changes that resulted in thirty-one new musicians. He was also the first conductor whose image graced the front of a Wheaties cereal box.

In fall 2003, after ushering in its centennial season, the orchestra appointed fifty-year-old Finnish conductor Osmo Vänskä as its music director. He came to the organization with a proven background as a skillful orchestra builder. Vänskä took a regional orchestra from Lahti, a city of 100,000 located sixty miles north of Helsinki, and over the course of eighteen years created a small miracle. By the time he left the Lahti Symphony in 2003, the ensemble had become Finland's premier orchestra, winning international prizes and acclaim for its Sibelius recordings. In recognition of its accomplishments, Sibelius Hall was built for the Lahti Symphony in 2000. Vänskä also had served as music director of other European orchestras, including the BBC Scottish Symphony.

His artistic gravitas garnered national and international praise for his leadership of the Minnesota Orchestra and for his guest-conducting engagements with top American and European orchestras. *Musical America* named him Conductor of the Year in 2005. By the end of his sixth season as music director, Vänskä and the orchestra had made three acclaimed European tours and completed a recording project of the complete Beethoven symphonies. The Beethoven cycle, on the BIS label, earned wide international recognition, and the recording of the Ninth Symphony received a 2008 Grammy Award nomination for Best Orchestral Performance.

With a contract recently renewed through 2015, Vänskä seems destined for a long, fruitful tenure with the Minnesota Orchestra. A gifted clarinetist who continues to perform, he spent many years as a professional orchestra player, and consequently he has a special rapport with his Minneapolis musicians, who admire his work ethic and musicianship. The Minnesota Orchestra of 2011 is experiencing renewed vigor with the promise of future artistic growth and recognition much like the achievements of Skrowaczewski's era.

In 2009 the Minnesota Orchestral Association announced a $40 million project to renovate and expand Orchestra Hall. The plan includes an expansion of the lobby, new spaces for educational work, updated backstage facilities, and state-of-the art audio and lighting systems in the hall. Though the renovation does not involve altering the acoustics, efforts are being made to improve the hall's onstage sound for the musicians. The reopening of the enhanced Orchestra Hall is scheduled for 2013.

ACKNOWLEDGEMENTS

Many gracious people helped and supported my efforts in researching and writing this book during the past nine years. My warmest thanks to:

Stanisław Skrowaczewski, who entrusted me with his life story. He gave me complete access to his home archives and unlimited time to discuss any topic openly. He has enriched my life in countless ways.

Krystyna Skrowaczewski, whose honesty, humor, charm, and warmth were a joy throughout the project. She not only shared her personal history but also provided valuable insights through her reading of chapters.

Nicholas Skrowaczewski, for friendship and support, audiovisual technical help, logistical aid, editorial assistance, and fellowship.

Paul Sebastien, for friendship and support, website creation, and enthusiasm for this book in all its stages.

My parents, Fred Harris, Sr., and Ginny Harris, for always supporting my musical endeavors. They are a constant source of inspiration.

Becky Harris, my incredible wife and greatest support system. She logged many hours transcribing interviews and editing this book at various stages.

Abbie Harris, my daughter, for giving me the gift of perspective.

A devoted reader, Carolyn Bishop brought inspiring zeal and discernment to her transcribing and editorial work. I am grateful for her outstanding efforts and support throughout the final years of this project. Woody Bishop also contributed his editorial skills to the book along the way.

Mary Ann Feldman has been a key participant in the research and composition of this book from its infancy to its conclusion. Her vast knowledge of the Minnesota Orchestra's history and her talents as a writer, editor, musicologist, and commentator added greatly to this work. She also served brilliantly as my penultimate editor. I am grateful for her friendship and support during the past decade.

Carolyn Wavrin, my final editor, brought a sharp and creative eye to her stellar efforts. She lifted this book to a new level of readability and deserves much credit for its final form. I am very grateful for her friendship, patience, support, and willingness to assist with and influence all aspects of this text.

All the people interviewed for this book listed in the appendices. They gave me the gift of their time, honesty, and memories.

Gunther Schuller, one of my greatest sources of inspiration. He defines what it means to be a complete musician. Along with being one of music's most distinguished composers and conductors, he is one of its finest advocates.

Richard Cisek, for providing important and discerning editorial comments. His expertise was invaluable.

Stuart Robinson, my connection "across the pond," who graciously assisted me with my Hallé Orchestra research and with thoughtful editorial comments.

Young-Nam Kim, one of the strongest advocates of Skrowaczewski's music. He is a shining light of musical integrity in the Twin Cities. He and his wife, Ellen, have been wonderful friends and hosts on my many trips to Minnesota.

Mark Olson, a close friend and colleague for more than a decade. He assisted me with audio and visual documentation and offered keen editorial comments.

Maciej Ołtarzewski, for translating Polish texts and conversations and also for providing key editorial comments on Polish history, particularly on events related to World War II.

Wacław Szybalski, for important information related to Skrowaczewski's early life in Lwów and for editorial comments on Polish history.

John Harbison, MIT colleague and friend, for his strong support of my work and that of Stanisław Skrowaczewski. He is a constant source of inspiration.

My MIT colleagues, who supported my work on this book: Music and Theater Arts Section Head Janet Sonenberg, Adam Boyles, Peter Child, William Cutter, Priscilla Cobb, Elizabeth Connors, David Deveau, Vanessa Gardner, Ellen Harris, Mark Harvey, Lowell Lindgren, John Lyons, Martin Marks, Michael Ouellette, Charles Shadle, Clarise Snyder, Evan Ziporyn, MIT Associate Provost Philip Khoury, MIT Dean of Humanities, Arts and Social Sciences Deborah Fitzgerald, and all my MIT students, who inspire and challenge me. I am most grateful for support from the Dean's Faculty Development and Research Fund.

Barbara Bezat of the Performing Arts Archives, University of Minnesota Libraries' Manuscripts Division, and Leslie Czechowski, former staff member of the Performing Arts Archives.

Friends who read portions of the manuscript and offered suggestions: Michael Adams, Kenneth Amis, Frank Battisti, Judy Dayton, Anita DiLullo, Jorja Fleezanis, Lea Foli, Heather Goddard, Paul Kile, Craig Kirchhoff, George Sturm, Sue-Ellen Hershman-Tcherepnin, Lior Navok, Daniel Schröter, and Peter Worrell.

Musicians and staff of the Minnesota Orchestra, particularly Sandi Brown, Paul Gunther, Kari Marshall, Robert Neu, Michael Pelton, Gwen Pappas, Eric Sjostrom, John Swanson, and Mele Willis.

Daniel Schröter, for his assistance with the Deutsche Radio Philharmonie Saarbrücken Kaiserslautern and my trip to Saarbrücken, Germany.

Yoshida Shinzo, Susumu Nakano, and Seiichiro Sakata, for their assistance with the Yomiuri Nippon Symphony Orchestra and my trip to Tokyo.

Michael Anthony, for giving me access to his notes from his many interviews with Skrowaczewski.

Marek Zebrowski, director of the Polish Music Center, University of Southern California, and Dorothy Ditmer, director of personnel at the Thornton School of Music, USC, for their interest in and enthusiasm for Maestro Skrowaczewski and this book.

The reviews of music critics from the 1950s to the present were valuable to my research. I quoted from the following writers frequently:

Peter Altman (*Minneapolis Star, Minneapolis Star and Tribune*); Michael Anthony (*Minneapolis Star, Minneapolis Tribune, Star Tribune*); Martin Bernheimer (*Los Angeles Times*); Edwin Bolton (*Minneapolis Tribune, Musical Courier*); Richard Buell (*The Boston Globe*); Roy Close (*Minneapolis Star, Minneapolis Tribune, St. Paul Pioneer Press, St. Paul Dispatch*); Richard Dyer (*The Boston Globe*); Herbert Elwell (*The Plain Dealer* [Cleveland]); Bob Epstein (*Minnesota Daily, Minneapolis Tribune*); Mary Ann Feldman (Minnesota Orchestra publications, CD liners, and program notes); James Felton (*The Evening Bulletin* [Philadelphia], *Philadelphia Bulletin*); Michael Fleming (*St. Paul Pioneer Press, St. Paul Dispatch*); Richard Freed (Minnesota Orchestra publications, CD liners, and program notes); Larry Fuchsberg (*Star Tribune*); John Harvey (*St. Paul Pioneer Press*); Donal Henahan (*The New York Times*); Allan Holbert (*Minneapolis Tribune*); Sandra Hyslop (Minnesota Orchestra publications); Harriett Johnson (*New*

York Post); Michael Kennedy (*The Daily Telegraph,* Hallé Orchestra publications); Allan Kozinn (*The New York Times*); Gerald Larner (*The Manchester Guardian*); Bain Murray (*Cleveland Sun Press, Cleveland Sun Messenger*); David Murray (*Financial Times,* London); Alan Rich (*Newsweek, Los Angeles Herald-Examiner*); John Robert-Blunn (*Manchester Evening News, The Manchester Charivari*); Winthrop Sargeant (*The New Yorker*); John Sherman (*Minneapolis Tribune, Minneapolis Star*); Harold Schonberg (*The New York Times*); Michael Steinberg (*The Boston Globe,* Minnesota Orchestra publications); Dan Sullivan (*Minneapolis Tribune*); Daniel Webster (*The Philadelphia Inquirer, Musical America*).

Frederick E. Harris, Jr.
Yarmouth Port, Mass.
June 29, 2011

Seeking the Infinite

Vistas of
music, nature
time
Probing worlds
unknown to most
mystical sunbeams
on glaciers
Catacombs of Bruckner
Jubilance of Beethoven
Darkness, loss

Sculpting time
Precise gestures reflecting
life
Soulful bells of
eloquence, grace,
profundity

Guardian of art
weaving
seamless tones amid
fractured worlds

A leap off
the podium
Beaming
Enraptured
A promise for
the future.

–F.H.

APPENDICES
Appendix A
Complete List of Compositions, Transcriptions, and Arrangements
by Stanisław Skrowaczewski

Publishers:
Boelke-Bomart, Inc.
MANY/Jerona Music, Inc.
European American Music (EAM)

Unpublished compositions are withdrawn by the composer and unavailable.

1929	Six Piano Sonatas
1930	*Overture in the Classical Style*
1931	Piano Sonata in A-flat major Piano Sonata in E-flat major
1933	Symphony for Orchestra in D minor Violin and Piano Sonata in E-flat major String Quartet no. 1 in B major
1936	Trio for Violin, Cello and Piano
1937	*Salve Regina,* Oratorio for Chorus Piano Sonata in F minor
1939	Piano Sextet for Strings and Wind Instrument in F minor Symphony no. 2 in C minor Variations for Piano
1940	Concerto for Violin and Orchestra Violin and Piano Sonata in G minor Three Songs for Alto Voice and Piano with text by Heine (also set for Alto Voice and Orchestra)
1943	Piano Sonata in B-flat major Piano Sonata in E-flat major String Quartet no. 2 in B-flat major String Quartet no. 3 in C minor Sinfonietta for String Orchestra in C-sharp minor

1944   *Anczar* for *a cappella* chorus

1945   Three Songs for Soprano Voice and Piano with text by Pushkin (also set for Soprano Voice and Orchestra)

1946   Prelude, Fugue and Postlude for Orchestra, :46
String Quartet no. 4 (Awarded second prize, 1953 Liège International Competition for String Quartets. Later arranged as Symphony for Strings.)
Mazurka for Piano
Overture 1947 (Awarded second prize, 1947 Szymanowski International Competition, Warsaw.), :09

1947-49   Symphony for Strings (MANY/Jerona Music), :22

1949   *Cantique de Cantiques* for Soprano Voice and Orchestra.
Music at Night, :17

1951   Cantata for Orchestra and Chorus
Ugo et Parisina, ballet

1952   Tone Poem on *Snow White and the Seven Dwarfs*
Piano Sonata no. 6

1954   *Opowiesc Atlantycka* (The Atlantic Tale), film score
Kariera (Career), film score
Autobus Odjezdza 6.20 (The Bus Leaves at 6:20), film score
Pod Gwiazda Frygijska (Under the Phrygian Star), film score
Symphony no. 4
Tavern under Eagle and Lion, opera
Suite Symphonique for Chamber Orchestra (Awarded 1956 Moscow Golden Prize in Composition.)
Overture for Orchestra

1955   *Tajemnica Dzikiego Szybu* (Mystery of a Mining Shaft), film score
Ballalyna, theater score
Turandot, theater score

1956   *Pozegnanie z Diablem* (Farewell to the Devil), film score

1957-58   *New Don Quixote,* theater score
Król Macius I (King Matthew I), film score

1959   *Spotkania w Ciemności* (Encounters in the Dark), film score

1968   Toccata and Fugue in D minor by J.S. Bach, transcription for orchestra (EAM), :10

1969   Concerto for English Horn and Orchestra (EAM), :17

1972   Suite from *Six Concerts en Sextuor* by Rameau, arranged for chamber orchestra (EAM), :24

1977   *Music at Night*, revised version (Boelke-Bomart), :17
Ricercari Notturni for Saxophone (or Clarinet) and Orchestra. Commissioned by the College of St. Benedict, St. Joseph, Minn. (Received 1977 Kennedy Center Friedheim Award.) (EAM), :25

1981   Concerto for Clarinet in A and Orchestra. Commissioned by the Minnesota Composers Forum (American Composers Forum). (EAM), :23

1982-84   Trio for Clarinet, Bassoon and Piano. Composed for the Philadelphia Orchestra Chamber Players. (Boelke-Bomart), :17

1983   "The Star-Spangled Banner" by Francis Scott Key; arranged for orchestra in A-flat. (MANY/Jerona Music), :03

1984   *Fantasie per Quattro* for Clarinet, Violin, Cello and Piano. Commissioned by the Schubert Club of St. Paul. (Boelke-Bomart), :12

1985   Concerto for Violin and Orchestra. Commissioned by the Philadelphia Orchestra. (Boelke-Bomart), :20

Concerto for Orchestra. Commissioned by the Minnesota Orchestra. Dedicated to Kenneth and Judy Dayton and the Minnesota Orchestra, commemorating the first decade of Orchestra Hall. Original version unavailable. (Boelke-Bomart), :32

1987   Fanfare for Orchestra. Commissioned by the Olympic Games. Dedicated to Josef Gingold. (Boelke-Bomart), :05

1988   *Fantasie per Sei* for Oboe, Violin, Viola, Cello, Bass and Piano. Commissioned by Atlanta Virtuosi. (Boelke-Bomart), :15

1990   String Trio. Commissioned by Ensemble Capriccio. (Boelke-Bomart), :25

1991   Triple Concerto for Violin, Clarinet, Piano and Orchestra. Commissioned by Michigan State University for the Verdehr Trio. (Boelke-Bomart), :26

1992   *Fantasie per Tre* for Flute, Oboe and Cello. Commissioned by the Huntingdon Trio of Philadelphia. (Boelke-Bomart), :20

Gesualdo di Venosa: Six Madrigals, arranged for chamber orchestra. Commissioned by The Saint Paul Chamber Orchestra. (Boelke-Bomart), :22

1993   Chamber Concerto (*Ritornelli poi Ritornelli*) for orchestra. Commissioned by The Saint Paul Chamber Orchestra. (Boelke-Bomart), :24

1995 *Passacaglia Immaginaria* for orchestra. Commissioned by the Minnesota Orchestra Association to honor the exceptional support of Kenneth and Judy Dayton for the Minnesota Orchestra. (Nominated for the 1997 Pulitzer Prize.) Original version unavailable. (Boelke-Bomart), :28

1998 Concerto for Orchestra, revised version. (Nominated for the 1999 Pulitzer Prize.) (Boelke-Bomart), :32
  Musica a Quattro for Clarinet, Violin, Viola and Cello. Commissioned by Ensemble Capriccio. (Boelke-Bomart), :26
  Adagio from String Quintet in F major by Bruckner, transcription for string orchestra. (Boelke-Bomart), :15

2000 *Christmas Chant.* Commissioned by Dale Warland Singers. (Music Associates of America), :04.

2002 *Fanfare to Ken* for string quartet or string orchestra. Composed in honor of Kenneth N. Dayton's 80th birthday. (Boelke-Bomart), :01

2003 *Concerto Nicolò* for Piano Left Hand and Orchestra. Commissioned by Dr. Herbert Axelrod for Gary Graffman. (Boelke-Bomart), :27

  Symphony [2003]. Commissioned by the Minnesota Orchestra and the Minnesota Commissioning Club on the occasion of the orchestra's centennial. Dedicated to the memory of Kenneth N. Dayton. (Boelke-Bomart), :36

2007 *Fantasie per Flauto ed Orchestra, Il Piffero della Notte* (The Piper in the Night), (Boelke-Bomart), :22

2009 *Music for Winds.* Commissioned by a consortium initiated and administered by Dr. Frederick E. Harris, Jr., and consisting of nine orchestras and wind ensembles. The American Composers Forum served as fiscal agent for the consortium. Consortium members: Massachusetts Institute of Technology (MIT) Wind Ensemble; New England Conservatory Wind Ensemble; Deutsche Radio Philharmonie Saarbrücken Kaiserslautern; Minnesota Orchestra; University of Minnesota-Twin Cities Symphonic Wind Ensemble; Yomiuri Nippon Symphony Orchestra (Japan); Orchestra of Indian Hill (Littleton, Massachusetts); University of Southern California Thornton School of Music Wind Ensemble; Bruckner Orchester Linz (Austria). (Boelke-Bomart), :23

2010 *Passacaglia Immaginaria* for orchestra, revised version. (Boelke-Bomart), :23

Appendix B
Complete Discography Of
Stanisław Skrowaczewski 1961–2011

BACH

Toccata and Fugue in D minor, transcription by Skrowaczewski. Yomiuri Nippon Symphony Orchestra. Denon COGQ-34, 2007.

Toccata and Fugue in D minor, transcription by Skrowaczewski. BBC Symphony Orchestra (Leonard Slatkin, conductor). Chandos, 2004.

Toccata and Fugue in D minor, transcription by Skrowaczewski. Minnesota Orchestra Centennial Set, 1997.

BARBER

Medea's Meditation and Dance of Vengeance. NHK Symphony Orchestra. King KICC3022, 1996.

Medea's Meditation and Dance of Vengeance. Cleveland Orchestra. Telarc Records, 1973.

BARTÓK

Concerto for Orchestra. Saarbrücken Radio Symphony Orchestra. Oehms Classics OC 306, 2002.

Concerto for Orchestra. Minnesota Orchestra. VoxBox 3015, 1977.

Dance Suite. Minnesota Orchestra. VoxBox 3015, 1977.

Divertimento for String Orchestra. Saarbrücken Radio Symphony Orchestra. Oehms Classics OC 306, 2002.

Divertimento for String Orchestra. Minnesota Orchestra. VoxBox 3015, 1977.

Music for Strings, Percussion and Celesta. Minnesota Orchestra. VoxBox 3015, 1982.

Suite from *The Miraculous Mandarin.* Minnesota Orchestra. VoxBox 3015, 1976.

Suite from *The Wooden Prince.* Minnesota Orchestra. VoxBox 3015, 1976.

BEETHOVEN

Symphony no. 1. Saarbrücken Radio Symphony Orchestra. Oehms Classics OC 521, 2005.

Symphony no. 2. Saarbrücken Radio Symphony Orchestra. Oehms Classics OC 522, 2005.

Symphony no. 3. Saarbrücken Radio Symphony Orchestra. Oehms Classics OC 522, 2005.

Symphony no. 3. Yomiuri Nippon Symphony Orchestra. RCA/BMG BVCC-34055, 2002.

Symphony no. 4. Saarbrücken Radio Symphony Orchestra. Oehms Classics OC 521, 2005.

Symphony no. 5. Saarbrücken Radio Symphony Orchestra. Oehms Classics OC 523, 2005.

Symphony no. 5. NHK Symphony Orchestra. Altus ALT032, 1999.

Symphony no. 6. Saarbrücken Radio Symphony Orchestra. Oehms Classics OC 523, 2005.

Symphony no. 7. Saarbrücken Radio Symphony Orchestra. Oehms Classics OC 524, 2006.

Symphony no. 8. Saarbrücken Radio Symphony Orchestra. Oehms Classics OC 524, 2006.

Symphony no. 9. Saarbrücken Radio Symphony Orchestra. Oehms Classics OC 525, 2005.

Complete Beethoven symphonies. Saarbrücken Radio Symphony Orchestra. Oehms Classics OC 526, 2005/2006/2007.

Violin Concerto in D major. Minneapolis Symphony Orchestra, David Oistrakh, violin. Minnesota Orchestra Centennial Set, 1965.

Piano Concerto no. 5. London Symphony Orchestra, Gina Bachauer, piano. Mercury-Philips 432018-2, 1962.

Calm Sea and Prosperous Voyage. Minnesota Orchestra, Phyllis Bryn-Julson, soprano, Bach Society of Minnesota. Vox 3604, 1978.

Consecration of the House Overture. Minnesota Orchestra. Vox 3604, 1978.

Coriolan Overture. Minnesota Orchestra. Vox 3604, 1978.

Creatures of Prometheus Overture. Minnesota Orchestra. Vox 5099, 1978.

Egmont Overture. Minnesota Orchestra. Vox 3604, 1978.

Fidelio Overture. Minnesota Orchestra. Vox 3604, 1978.

Grosse Fuge. NHK Symphony Orchestra. Altus ALTO31, 1999.

King Stephen Overture. Minnesota Orchestra. Vox 3604, 1979.

Leonore Overture no. 1. Minnesota Orchestra. Vox 3604, 1978.

Leonore Overture no. 2. NHK Symphony Orchestra. Altus ALT028, 1996.

Leonore Overture no. 2. Minnesota Orchestra. Vox 3604, 1978.

Leonore Overture no. 3. Minnesota Orchestra. Vox 3604, 1978.

Leonore Prohaska no. 4, Funeral March. Minnesota Orchestra, Phyllis Bryn-Julson, soprano, Bach Society of Minnesota. Vox 3604, 1978.

Minuet of Congratulations. Minnesota Orchestra. Vox 3604, 1979.

Tarpeja: Triumphal March. Minnesota Orchestra. Vox 3604, 1979.

Ruins of Athens. Minnesota Orchestra, Phyllis Bryn-Julson, soprano, Bach Society of Minnesota. Vox 3604, 1979.

Zur Namensfeier Overture. Minnesota Orchestra. Vox 3604, 1979.

BERLIOZ

Symphonie fantastique. Saarbrücken Radio Symphony Orchestra. Oehms Classics OC 319, 2002.

Symphonie fantastique. London Symphony Orchestra. Chandos CHAN 8727, 1989.

Love Scene from *Roméo et Juliette, Symphonie dramatique.* Saarbrücken Radio Symphony Orchestra. Oehms Classics OC 31, 2003.

BRAHMS

Symphony no. 1. Yomiuri Nippon Symphony Orchestra. Denon COGQ-34, 2007.

Symphony no. 1. Hallé Orchestra. IMP/Pickwick/Carlton PCD 2014, 1987.

Symphony no. 2. Yomiuri Nippon Symphony Orchestra. Denon COGQ-29, 2007.

Symphony no. 2. Hallé Orchestra. IMP/Pickwick/Carlton PCD 857, 1986.

Symphony no. 3. Yomiuri Nippon Symphony Orchestra. Denon COGQ-39, 2008.

Symphony no. 3. Hallé Orchestra. IMP/Pickwick/Carlton PCD 2039, 1987.

Symphony no. 4. Hallé Orchestra. IMP/Pickwick/Carlton PCD 897, 1987.

Symphony no. 4. National Polish Radio Symphony Orchestra of Katowice. Polskie Radio SA, Warszawa PRCD 198, 2003.

Piano Concerto no. 1. London Symphony Orchestra, Barry Douglas, piano. RCA/BMG CD 7780, 1988.

Piano Concerto no. 2. London Symphony Orchestra, Gina Bachauer, piano. Mercury-Philips 434340-2, 1962.

Academic Festival Overture. Hallé Orchestra. IMP/Pickwick/Carlton PCD 2014, 1987.

Hungarian Dances nos. 1, 3, 10. Hallé Orchestra. IMP/Pickwick/Carlton PCD 897, 1987.

Tragic Overture. Hallé Orchestra. IMP/Pickwick/Carlton PCD 857, 1987.

Variations on a Theme of Haydn. Hallé Orchestra. IMP/Pickwick/Carlton PCD 2039, 1987.

BRITTEN
Concerto for Piano and Orchestra. Saarbrücken Radio Symphony Orchestra, Robert Leonardy, piano. Arte Nova Classics 74321-27769-2, 1994.

BRUCKNER
Symphony in F minor. Saarbrücken Radio Symphony Orchestra. Oehms Classics OC 208, 2001.

Symphony no. 0 (*Die Nullte*). Saarbrücken Radio Symphony Orchestra. Oehms Classics OC 209, 1999.

Symphony no. 1. Saarbrücken Radio Symphony Orchestra. Oehms Classics OC 210, 1995.

Symphony no. 2. Saarbrücken Radio Symphony Orchestra. Oehms Classics OC 211, 1999.

Symphony no. 3. Minnesota Orchestra. Minnesota Orchestra Centennial Set, 2001.

Symphony no. 3. Saarbrücken Radio Symphony Orchestra. Oehms Classics OC 212, 1996.

Symphony no. 3. Warsaw National Philharmonic Orchestra. Muza SX 2093, 1981.

Symphony no. 4. Saarbrücken Radio Symphony Orchestra. Oehms Classics OC 213, 1998.

Symphony no. 4. Hallé Orchestra. Pickwick/Carlton 30367-00282, 1993.

Symphony no. 5. Saarbrücken Radio Symphony Orchestra. Oehms Classics OC 214, 1996.

Symphony no. 6. Saarbrücken Radio Symphony Orchestra. Oehms Classics OC 215, 1997.

Symphony no. 7. Yomiuri Nippon Symphony Orchestra. Denon COGQ, 2011.

Symphony no. 7. NHK Symphony Orchestra. Altus ALT030, 1999.

Symphony no. 7. Saarbrücken Radio Symphony Orchestra. Oehms Classics OC 216, 1991.

Symphony no. 8. Yomiuri Nippon Symphony Orchestra. Denon COGQ-47-8, 2010.

Symphony no. 8. Saarbrücken Radio Symphony Orchestra. Oehms Classics OC 217, 1993.

Symphony no. 9. Yomiuri Nippon Symphony Orchestra. Denon COGQ-41, 2009.

Symphony no. 9. Saarbrücken Radio Symphony Orchestra. Oehms Classics OC 218, 2001.

Symphony no. 9. Minnesota Orchestra. Reference Recordings RR-81, 1996.

Complete Bruckner symphonies. Saarbrücken Radio Symphony Orchestra. Arte Nova 74321-85290-2/Oehms Classics 207-218, 2001/2004.

Overture in G minor. Saarbrücken Radio Symphony Orchestra. Oehms Classics OC 208, 2001.

Adagio from String Quintet in F major, arrangement by Skrowaczewski. Saarbrücken Radio Symphony Orchestra. Oehms Classics OC 209, 1999.

CHOPIN
Piano Concerto no. 1. Saarbrücken Radio Symphony Orchestra, Ewa Kupiec, piano. Oehms Classics OC 326, 2003.

Piano Concerto no. 1. Orchestre de la Société des Concerts du Conservatoire, Alexis Weissenberg, piano. Angel/EMI Classics 7243-5-73317-22, 1967.

Piano Concerto no. 1. New Symphony Orchestra of London, Artur Rubinstein, piano. RCA/BMG Classics LSC 2575, 1961.

Piano Concerto no. 2. Saarbrücken Radio Symphony Orchestra, Ewa Kupiec, piano. Oehms Classics OC 326, 2003.

Piano Concerto no. 2. Orchestre de la Société des Concerts du Conservatoire, Alexis Weissenberg, piano. Angel/EMI Classics 7243-5-73317-22, 1967.

Variations on *Là ci darem la mano* (from *Don Giovanni*). Orchestre de la Société des Concerts du Conservatoire, Alexis Weissenberg, piano. Angel/EMI Classics 7243-5-73317-22, 1967.

Andante spianato et grande polonaise. Orchestre de la Société des Concerts du Conservatoire, Alexis Weissenberg, piano. Angel/EMI Classics 7243-5-73317-22, 1967.

Fantaisie sur des airs nationaux polonais. Orchestre de la Société des Concerts du Conservatoire, Alexis Weissenberg, piano. Angel/EMI Classics 7243-5-73317-22, 1967.

Grand Rondeau de Concert *Rondo á la Krakowiak.* Orchestre de la Société des Concerts du Conservatoire, Alexis Weissenberg, piano. Angel/EMI Classics 7243-5-73317-22, 1967.

ELGAR
Enigma Variations. Saarbrücken Radio Symphony Orchestra. Arte Nova Classics 74321-27769-2, 1994.

HANDEL
Music for the Royal Fireworks. Minnesota Orchestra. Vox QTV S34362, 1976.

Water Music Suite. Minnesota Orchestra. Vox QTV S34362, 1976.

HENZE

Ode to the West Wind. Saarbrücken Radio Symphony Orchestra, Gustav Rivinius, cello. Arte Nova Classics 74321 89404 2, 1999.

LALO

Cello Concerto. London Symphony Orchestra, János Starker, cello. Mercury-Philips 432010-2, 1962.

LISZT

Piano Concerto no. 2. Berlin Philharmonic, Krystian Zimerman, piano. Coup d'Etat CO 505, 1979.

LUTOSŁAWSKI

Concerto for Orchestra. NHK Symphony Orchestra. Altus ALT031, 1999.

MAHLER

Symphony no. 4. Hallé Orchestra. IMP Classics/Pickwick PCD 972, 1991.

MAYER

Two Pastels. Minnesota Orchestra. Phoenix PHCD 120, 1971.

Andante for Strings. Minnesota Orchestra. Phoenix PHCD 120, 1971.

MENDELSSOHN

Symphony no. 4. Minneapolis Symphony Orchestra. Mercury-Philips 434363-2, 1961.

MESSIAEN

Et exspecto resurrectionem mortuorum. Yomiuri Nippon Symphony Orchestra. Denon COGQ-29, 2007.

MOZART

Symphony no. 29. NHK Symphony Orchestra. Altus ALT029, 1996.

Symphony no. 41. Yomiuri Nippon Symphony Orchestra. RCA/BMG BVCC-34055, 2002.

Piano Concerto no. 17. Minnesota Orchestra, Walter Klien, piano. Vox VU 9037, 1978.

Piano Concerto no. 27. Minnesota Orchestra, Walter Klien, piano. Vox VU 9037, 1978.

OHANA

Livre des Prodiges. Orchestre National De France. Erato STU 71548, 1983.

Chiffres de Clavecin. Nouvel Orchestre Philharmonique, Elisabeth Chojnacka, harpsichord. Erato STU 71548, 1983.

PENDERECKI

Concerto for Violin and Orchestra. Minnesota Orchestra, Isaac Stern, violin. Sony Classical SMK 64507, 1978.

PROKOFIEV

Romeo and Juliet Suite no. 1. Kölner Rundfunk-Sinfonie-Orchester. Denon CO-78840, 1994/1995.

Romeo and Juliet Suite no. 1. Minneapolis Symphony Orchestra. Mercury-Philips 432004-2, 1962.

Romeo and Juliet Suite no. 2. NHK Symphony Orchestra. King KICC3022, 1996.

Romeo and Juliet Suite no. 2. Kölner Rundfunk-Sinfonie-Orchester. Denon CO-78840, 1994/1995.

Romeo and Juliet Suite no. 2. Minnesota Orchestra. Vox 3016, 1977.

Romeo and Juliet Suite no. 2. Minneapolis Symphony Orchestra. Mercury-Philips 432004-2, 1962.

Romeo and Juliet Suite no. 3. Kölner Rundfunk-Sinfonie-Orchester. Denon CO-78840, 1994/1995.

Suite from *The Love for Three Oranges*. Minnesota Orchestra. Vox 3016, 1977.

Scythian Suite. Minnesota Orchestra. Vox 3016, 1983.

RAVEL

Alborada del gracioso. Minnesota Orchestra. VoxBox 5031, 1974.

Boléro. Minnesota Orchestra. VoxBox 5031, 1974.

Daphnis et Chloé Suite no. 1. Minnesota Orchestra. VoxBox 5032, 1974.

Daphnis et Chloé Suite no. 2. Minnesota Orchestra. VoxBox 5032, 1974.

Fanfare for the ballet *L'Eventail de Jeanne*. Minnesota Orchestra. VoxBox 5032, 1974.

La Valse. Minnesota Orchestra. VoxBox 5032, 1974.

Le tombeau de Couperin. Minnesota Orchestra. VoxBox 5032, 1974.

Ma mère l'oye, complete ballet. Minnesota Orchestra. VoxBox 5032, 1974.

Menuet antique. Minnesota Orchestra, Ferald B. Capps, English horn. VoxBox 5031, 1974.

Pavane pour une infante defunte. Minnesota Orchestra. VoxBox 5031, 1974.

Rhapsodie espagnole. Minnesota Orchestra. VoxBox 5031, 1974.

Une barque sur l'océan. Minnesota Orchestra. VoxBox 5032, 1974.

Valses nobles et sentimentales. Minnesota Orchestra. VoxBox 5031, 1974.

SCHUBERT

Symphony no. 5. Minneapolis Symphony Orchestra. Mercury-Philips 289 462 954-2, 1962.

Symphony no. 8. Minneapolis Symphony Orchestra. Mercury-Philips 289 462 954-2, 1961.

Symphony no. 9. Minneapolis Symphony Orchestra. Mercury-Philips 434 354-2, 1961.

Rosamunde, Incidental Music. Minneapolis Symphony Orchestra. Mercury-Philips 289 462 954-2, 1961.

SCHUMANN

Symphony no. 1. Deutsche Radio Philharmonie. Oehms Classics OC 707, 2007.

Symphony no. 2. Deutsche Radio Philharmonie. Oehms Classics OC BVCO-37455, 2007.

Symphony no. 3. Deutsche Radio Philharmonie. Oehms Classics OC BVCO-37455, 2007.

Symphony no. 4. Deutsche Radio Philharmonie. Oehms Classics OC 707, 2007.

Symphony no. 4. Yomiuri Nippon Symphony Orchestra. PCM Digital, Columbia Music GES-13954, 2007.

Symphony no. 4. NHK Symphony Orchestra. Altus ALT029, 1996.

Complete Schumann symphonies. Deutsche Radio Philharmonie. Oehms Classics OC 741, 2007.

Cello Concerto. London Symphony Orchestra, János Starker, cello. Mercury-Philips 432-010-2, 1962.

Piano Concerto. Minneapolis Symphony Orchestra, Byron Janis, piano. Mercury-Philips 432-011-2, 1962.

SHOSTAKOVICH

Symphony no. 1. Yomiuri Nippon Symphony Orchestra. Denon COCQ-84575, 2008.

Symphony no. 1. Hallé Orchestra. Hallé Concerts Society HLL 7506, 1996.

Symphony no. 5. Hallé Orchestra. IMP Classics/ Hallé Concerts Society HLD 7511, 1990.

Symphony no. 5. Minneapolis Symphony Orchestra. Mercury-Philips 434 323-2, 1961.

Symphony no. 6. Hallé Orchestra. Hallé Concerts Society HLL 7506, 1997.

Symphony no. 10. Deutsches Symphonie-Orchester Berlin. Weitblick SSS0076-2, 2003.

Symphony no. 10. Hallé Orchestra. IMP Classics/ Hallé Concerts Society HLD 7511, 1990.

SKROWACZEWSKI

Chamber Concerto (*Ritornelli poi Ritornelli*). Saarbrücken Radio Symphony Orchestra. Albany Records TROY 481, 2000.

Concerto for Clarinet in A and Orchestra. Saarbrücken Radio Symphony Orchestra, Richard Stoltzman, clarinet. Albany Records TROY 481, 2001.

Concerto for English Horn and Orchestra. Tokyo Metropolitan Symphony Orchestra (Jean Fournet, conductor), Miriam Jakes, English horn. Fontec FOCD9355, 1994.

Concerto for English Horn and Orchestra. Minnesota Orchestra, Thomas Stacy, English horn. Desto 7126/Phoenix PH 120, 1971.

Concerto Nicoló for Piano Left Hand and Orchestra. Minnesota Orchestra, Gary Graffman, piano. Reference Recordings RR-103, 2003.

Concerto for Orchestra. Minnesota Orchestra. Reference Recordings RR-103, 2003.

Concerto for Orchestra. National Polish Radio Symphony Orchestra of Katowice. Polskie Radio SA, Warszawa PRCD 198, 2003.

Fantasie per Flauto ed Orchestra (*Il Piffero della Notte*). Deutsche Radio Philharmonie, Roswitha Staege, flute. Oehms Classics OC 712, 2008.

Fantasie per Sei. Ensemble Capriccio and Friends. Innova 568, 2000.

Music at Night. Deutsche Radio Philharmonie. Oehms Classics OC 712, 2005.

Music at Night. Louisville Orchestra (John Nelson, conductor). First Edition LS778, 1983.

Musica a Quattro. Ensemble Capriccio and Friends. Innova 568, 1997.

Passacaglia Immaginaria. Saarbrücken Radio Symphony Orchestra. Albany Records TROY 481, 2000.

String Trio. Ensemble Capriccio. CRI 853, 1997.

String Trio. Ensemble Capriccio. Innova 568, 1997.

Symphony [2003]. Deutsche Radio Philharmonie. Oehms Classics OC 712, 2006.

Trio for Clarinet, Bassoon and Piano. Joseph Longo, clarinet, John Miller, bassoon, Paul Schoenfield, piano. Innova LP MN 102, 1982.

Triple Concerto. Solisti di Praga (Leon Gregorian, conductor). The Verdehr Trio: Walter Verdehr, violin; Elsa Ludewig-Verdehr, clarinet; Gary Kirkpatrick, piano. Crystal Records 749, 1998.

STRAUSS

Also Sprach Zarathustra. Yomiuri Nippon Symphony Orchestra, Hamao Fujiwara, violin. Denon COCQ-84575, 2008.

Also Sprach Zarathustra. National Youth Orchestra of Great Britain. Carlton Classics 30366-00932, 1997.

STRAVINSKY

Firebird Suite (1919). Minnesota Orchestra. Vox Box 3016, 1983.

Petrushka (1947). Minnesota Orchestra. Vox Box 3016, 1977.

The Rite of Spring. NHK Symphony Orchestra. King KICC3022, 1996.

The Rite of Spring. Minnesota Orchestra. Vox Box 3016, 1977.

TCHAIKOVSKY

Symphony no. 5. NHK Symphony Orchestra. Altus ALT028, 1996.

Serenade for Strings. Yomiuri Nippon Symphony Orchestra. Denon COGQ-39, 2009.

WAGNER

Tannhäuser: Overture and *Venusberg* Music. Minnesota Orchestra. Vox QTV-S34642, 1976.

Tannhäuser: Arrival of the Guests. Minnesota Orchestra. Vox QTV-S34642, 1976.

Tristan und Isolde: Prelude to Act III. Minnesota Orchestra. Vox QTV-S34642, 1976.

Tristan und Isolde: Prelude and *Liebestod*. Minnesota Orchestra. Vox QTV-S34642, 1976.

WIENIAWSKI

Concerto no. 2 for Violin and Orchestra. L'Orchestre de la Suisse Romande, Michel Schwalbe, violin. BID 164, 1963.

WEBER

Euryanthe Overture. Hallé Orchestra. RCA/IMP Classics PCD 1105, 1989.

Der Freischütz Overture. Hallé Orchestra. RCA/IMP Classics PCD 1105, 1989.

Oberon Overture. Hallé Orchestra. RCA/IMP Classics PCD 1105, 1989.

The Ruler of the Spirits Overture. Hallé Orchestra. RCA/IMP Classics PCD 1105, 1989.

Abu Hassan Overture. Hallé Orchestra. RCA/IMP Classics PCD 1105, 1989.

Preciosa Overture. Hallé Orchestra. RCA/IMP Classics PCD 1105, 1989.

Peter Schmoll Uns Seine Nachburn Overture. Hallé Orchestra. RCA/IMP Classics PCD 1105, 1989.

Jubel Overture. Hallé Orchestra. RCA/IMP Classics PCD 1105, 1989.

DVD

Bruckner: Symphonies nos. 8, 9. Yomiuri Nippon Symphony Orchestra. Live at Suntory Hall. [Blu-ray] COXO-1024, 2009, 2010.

Beethoven: Symphony no. 1, Bruckner: Symphony No. 7. Yomiuri Nippon Symphony Orchestra. Live at Suntory Hall. VPBR-12470, 2005.

Appendix C
Stanisław Skrowaczewski
Awards and Honors

2011	Joseph Kilenyi Medal of Honor, The Bruckner Society of America Medal of Merit, City of Wrocław, Poland
2009	Honorary Doctorate, New England Conservatory of Music
2005	Honorary Doctorate, University of Wrocław, Poland
2004	The McKnight Distinguished Artist Award, The McKnight Foundation
2004	Paderewski Lecture at the Polish Music Center, University of Southern California
2002	Cannes Classical Award, Best Recording of Eighteenth/Nineteenth Century Orchestral Work (for *Bruckner: Complete Symphonies*, Arte Nova)
2000	Best Conductor, Best of the Twin Cities, *Star Tribune* [Minneapolis]
1999	Poland's Commander of "Polanda Restituta" with "White Star" Pulitzer Prize Nomination, for Concerto for Orchestra Grammy Nomination, Best Classical Engineered Recording, for Bruckner's Ninth Symphony with Minnesota Orchestra
1998	Golden Note Award for Best Original Recording, for Bruckner's Ninth Symphony with Minnesota Orchestra
1997	Pulitzer Prize Nomination, for *Passacaglia Immaginaria*
1982	Karol Szymanowski Medal (Poland) City of Philadelphia Medal of Appreciation City of Detroit Medal of Appreciation
1979	Minnesota Medal of Appreciation Honorary Doctorate, University of Minnesota Gold Medal, Mahler-Bruckner Society
1962–1979	Five ASCAP (American Society of Composers, Authors and Publishers) Awards, for "presenting music of our time in a major concert format"

1978   Minnesota Heritage Award

1977   Kennedy Center Friedheim Award, for *Ricercari Notturni*
City of Minneapolis Distinguished Service Award
City of Philadelphia Distinguished Service Award

1974   President's Medal, College of Saint Benedict [Minnesota]

1973   Ditson Conductor's Award, Columbia University, New York
Honorary Doctorate, Macalester College, St. Paul

1970   Minnesota Maestro Award
Man of the Year Award, American Council of Polish Cultural
Clubs

1963   Honorary Doctorate, Hamline University, St. Paul

1962   KUXL Twin Cities Radio Award for Excellence

1956   First Prize, International Competition for Conductors,
Rome
Gold Medal, Moscow, for *Suite Symphonique*

1953   Polish National Award for Composition
Second Prize, International Competition, Belgium, for String
Quartet

1949   Radio Award, Paris, for *Cantique des Cantiques*

1947   Second Prize, Szymanowski Competition, Warsaw, for
Overture 1947

Appendix D
Interviews
Conducted by Frederick E. Harris, Jr.

Michael Anthony (1/26/05)
Writer; former *Star Tribune* (Minneapolis) music critic; biographer of Osmo Vänskä

Dominick Argento (12/18/06)
Composer; composer laureate, Minnesota Orchestra

Emanuel Ax (9/8/05)
Concert pianist

Julie Ayer (2/27/07)
Assistant principal second violinist, Minnesota Orchestra

Andrew Barnhart (6/22/02)
Cellist; member of 2002 National Orchestral Institute; principal cello, Orchestra of the Southern Finger Lakes

Mark Berger (8/4/2005)
Violist; member of 2005 New Fromm Players, Tanglewood; resident composer-violist, Worcester (Mass.) Chamber Music Society

Zofia Bieniewska (*née* Sieradzka) (1/8/04)
Friend of Stanisław Skrowaczewski from his early years in Katowice

Louis Brunelli (10/6/2006)
Arranger; former associate dean and director of performance activities, The Juilliard School

Rudolf Buchbinder (10/2/04)
Concert pianist

Norman Carol (2/13/03)
Former concertmaster, Philadelphia Orchestra and Minneapolis Symphony Orchestra

Elliott Carter (11/17/04)
Composer

Richard Cisek (10/27/01)
Associate, Management Consultants for the Arts; former president, Minnesota Orchestra

James Clute (6/28/01)
Former associate principal bassist, Minnesota Orchestra

Phyllis Curtin (6/15/07)
Soprano vocalist and educator

Semiramis Costa (8/4/05)
Cellist; member of 2005 New Fromm Players, Tanglewood

Dennis Russell Davies (10/1/09)
Conductor, music director, Bruckner Orchester Linz and Sinfonieorchester Basel; former music director, The Saint Paul Chamber Orchestra

Michael Davis (5/24/05)
Violinist; former concertmaster, London Symphony Orchestra and Hallé Orchestra

Judy Dayton (6/11/04)
Philanthropist, wife of Kenneth N. Dayton

Kenneth N. Dayton (11/1/01)
Former CEO, Dayton Hudson Corporation; philanthropist; board member, vice president, president, and emeritus director, Minnesota Orchestral Association

Edo de Waart (6/24/03)
Conductor, music director, Milwaukee Symphony Orchestra and Hong Kong Philharmonic Orchestra; former music director, Minnesota Orchestra and San Francisco Symphony

James Dixon (6/18/03)
Conductor, former music director, University of Iowa Symphony Orchestra; former assistant conductor, Minneapolis Symphony Orchestra

Mary Ann Feldman (2/3/03, 10/20/07)
Writer, editor, lecturer, historian, former staff and program annotator, Minnesota Orchestra, 1960-2003

Frederick Fennell (6/22/01)
Conductor, founder and former music director, Eastman Wind Ensemble; professor, Eastman School of Music; former conductor, Tokyo Kosei Wind Orchestra; former associate music director, Minneapolis Symphony Orchestra

Jorja Fleezanis (10/1/03)
Violinist; professor of music, Jacobs School of Music, Indiana University Bloomington; former concertmaster, Minnesota Orchestra

Leon Fleisher (11/16/03)
Concert pianist

Anthony Fogg (7/16/03)
Artistic administrator, Boston Symphony Orchestra

Lea Foli (6/29/01)
Former concertmaster, Minnesota Orchestra

Richard Freed (3/24/06)
Music critic; program annotator, National Symphony Orchestra

Mira Frisch (6/22/02)
Cellist; member of 2002 National Orchestral Institute; assistant professor, University of North Carolina at Charlotte

Youko Fuji (9/11/09)
Co-principal clarinetist, Yomiuri Nippon Symphony Orchestra

Hamao Fujiwara (9/12/09)
Concertmaster, Yomiuri Nippon Symphony Orchestra

Charles Fullmer (7/28/05)
Former assistant manager, Minnesota Orchestra

Michel Glotz (12/6/03)
Artists' impresario-recording producer

Gary Graffman (3/29/03)
Concert pianist; former president, Curtis Institute of Music

Giancarlo Guerrero (9/30/03)
Conductor, music director, Nashville Symphony Orchestra; former associate conductor, Minnesota Orchestra

Bruce Hangen (3/24/06)
Conductor, music director, Indian Hill Symphony; director of orchestral activities, Boston Conservatory

Burt Hara (11/21/03)
Principal clarinetist, Minnesota Orchestra

John Harbison (10/28/05)
Composer-conductor; Institute Professor, Massachusetts Institute of Technology

Lynn Harrell (12/20/04)
Solo cellist; founder, board officer, and artist ambassador, HEARTbeats Foundation; former professor of music, The Shepherd School of Music, Rice University

Richard Hoenich (2/15/02)
Conductor-bassoonist; former director of orchestras, New England Conservatory

Karel Husa (6/17/03)
Composer-conductor; Kappa Alpha Professor of Music Emeritus, Cornell University

David Hyslop (2/10/06)
Owner and CEO, Hyslop and Associates; former president, Minnesota Orchestra, St. Louis Symphony, and Oregon Symphony

Sir Michael Kennedy (8/17/06)
Music critic, writer, historian; former music critic and editor, *The Daily Telegraph*; former chief music critic, *The Sunday Telegraph* (U.K.)

Ewa Kupiec (11/1/08)
Concert pianist

Libby Larsen (5/6/04, 11/18/04)
Composer; cofounder, Minnesota Composers Forum (now American Composers Forum)

Joseph Longo (5/10/05)
Former co-principal clarinetist, Minnesota Orchestra

Jan Łopuszański (1/8/04)
Physicist; former professor, University of Wrocław

Stephen Lumsden (10/7/09)
Founder and managing director, Intermusica

Sir Neville Marriner (5/2/03)
Conductor, founder, and life conductor, Academy of St. Martin in the Fields; former music director, Minnesota Orchestra

Agnieszka Mazur (6/25/03)
Programming and publishing manager, Warsaw National Philharmonic Orchestra

John Miller (3/26/07)
Principal bassoonist, Minnesota Orchestra

Chester Milosovitch (11/17/03)
Former clarinetist, Minnesota Orchestra

Hakuro Mori (9/12/09)
Solo cellist, Yomiuri Nippon Symphony Orchestra

Robert Neu (10/28/05)
Vice president and general manager, Minnesota Orchestra

Marilyn Carlson Nelson (7/12/10)
Former CEO and current chair, Carlson Companies, USA; philanthropist, former officer and vice president, Minnesota Orchestral Association

David Nolan (9/12/09)
Concertmaster, Yomiuri Nippon Symphony Orchestra

Toru Nose (9/14/09)
Hornist, Yomiuri Nippon Symphony Orchestra

Garrick Ohlsson (1/26/02, 6/16/05)
Concert pianist

Maciej Ołtarzewski (6/25/03)
Lawyer, translator; former Solidarity leader, jailed during martial law period in
Poland; translator for Lech Wałęsa at Harvard University

Joel Pargman (8/4/05)
Violinist; member of 2005 New Fromm Players, Tanglewood; Los Angeles Chamber
Orchestra

Krzysztof Penderecki (1/30/06)
Composer-conductor

Joseph Polisi (3/17/04)
President, The Juilliard School

Stuart Robinson (8/9/03, 5/24/05)
Former deputy chief executive, Hallé Orchestra

Dennis Rooney (4/1/06)
Audio producer, audio archivist, and writer; former producer and host of Minnesota
Public Radio's Minnesota Orchestra concert broadcasts

Charles Schlueter (4/4/02)
Former principal trumpet, Boston Symphony Orchestra and Minnesota Orchestra

Gunther Schuller (1/30/02)
Composer-conductor, author, historian, educator, and record producer

Paul Sebastien (6/27/05)
Elder son of Stanisław and Krystyna Skrowaczewski

Eric Sjostrom (10/3/03)
Associate principal librarian, Minnesota Orchestra

Krystyna Skrowaczewski (10/28/01, 9/30/03, 5/10/05, 3/30/06)
Wife of Stanisław Skrowaczewski

Nicholas Skrowaczewski (12/17/03, 5/29/08, 8/23/08, 12/21/08)
Younger son of Stanisław and Krystyna Skrowaczewski

Roman Skrowaczewski (6/25/03)
Cousin of Stanisław Skrowaczewski

Stanisław Skrowaczewski (5/31/01 to 10/3/09, 128 interviews)
Conductor-composer

Leonard Slatkin (2/2/06)
Conductor, music director, Detroit Symphony Orchestra and Orchestre National de Lyon; former music director, St. Louis Symphony, National Symphony Orchestra; former principal guest conductor and founder of Sommerfest, Minnesota Orchestra

Clive Smart (7/13/05)
Former general manager, Hallé Orchestra

Henry Charles Smith (10/4/03)
Conductor-trombonist; former music director, South Dakota Symphony; former associate and resident conductor, Minnesota Orchestra

Thomas Stacy (4/28/06)
Former English hornist, New York Philharmonic and Minnesota Orchestra

Michael Steinberg (10/1/03)
Writer, former music critic, *The Boston Globe*; former program annotator, Boston Symphony Orchestra, San Francisco Symphony, Minnesota Orchestra, and New York Philharmonic

Richard Stoltzman (3/8/05)
Solo clarinetist

Herman Straka (6/27/01)
Former first violinist, Minnesota Orchestra

George Sturm (12/1/03)
Executive director, Music Associates of America

Erin Svoboda (8/4/05)
Clarinetist; member of 2005 New Fromm Players, Tanglewood; neoLIT ensemble

Wacław Szybalski (1/19/05, 2/5/05)
Professor emeritus, University of Wisconsin

Sabine Tomek (9/22/03)
Musicologist; former artistic director, Saarbrücken Radio Symphony Orchestra

Jill Werthman (6/22/02)
Violist; member of 2002 National Orchestral Institute

Ronald Wilford (8/10/05)
Chairman, CEO and former president, Columbia Artists Management, Inc.

Peter Worrell (8/10/05)
Former violinist, Hallé Orchestra

R. Douglas Wright (10/1/03)
Principal trombonist, Minnesota Orchestra

Masaru Yoshida (9/14/09)
Co-principal bassoonist, Yomiuri Nippon Symphony Orchestra

Krystian Zimerman (8/28/09)
Concert pianist

David Zinman (12/18/06)
Conductor, music director, Tonhalle Orchester Zürich; former music director,
Baltimore Symphony Orchestra; former artistic director, Aspen Music Festival;
former artistic director, Sommerfest, Minnesota Orchestra

Interviews via e-mail correspondence:

Dora Bratchkova (10/9/09)
Concertmaster, Deutsche Radio Philharmonie Saarbrücken

Michael Colgrass (2/21/07)
Composer, educator

Young-Nam Kim (1/7/11)
Violinist; professor, University of Minnesota; founder and artistic director, Chamber
Music Society of Minnesota

Zohar Lerner (1/16/05)
Violinist; substitute musician, Deutsches Symphonie-Orchester Berlin

Jerry Luedders (12/30/07, 1/23/08)
Saxophonist; professor, California State University, Northridge

William Mayer (6/2/07, 6/12/07)
Composer

Thomas Raisig (10/29/09)
Recording engineer, Deutsche Radio Philharmonie Saarbrücken

George Trautwein (4/14/06)
Conductor; former professor, Wake Forest University; former associate conductor,
Minnesota Orchestra

Shinzo Yoshida (8/25/09)
Former managing director, Yomiuri Nippon Symphony Orchestra

STANISŁAW SKROWACZEWSKI
LIFE CHRONOLOGY

1923
Stanisław Paweł Stefan Jan Sebastian Skrowaczewski born October 3 in Lwów, Poland (now L'viv, Ukraine), to Zofia, a concert pianist, and Paweł, a laryngologist. Older sister, Krystyna, was born in 1918.

1927
At age four begins piano lessons with Flora Listowska. Studies Bach, Haydn, and Mozart. Begins composing small piano pieces, and collecting and learning full orchestral scores.

1930
At age seven composes first orchestral work, *Overture in the Classical Style*, for a Mozart-size orchestral instrumentation. Begins informal violin lessons with a colleague of his father's.

1934
Gives his first public piano recital at age eleven in a Lwów radio studio. The thirty-minute program of Haydn and Bach is broadcast throughout Poland.

1936
At age thirteen plays and conducts Beethoven's Third Piano Concerto with a professional orchestra. It is his conducting debut.

1940
Lwów Philharmonic performs *Overture in the Classical Style* and Three Songs for Alto Voice and Orchestra, set to poems by Heine.

1941–45
Hands are damaged during a German bombing attack. Performs in a "string quartet in hiding" during the German occupation. Attends underground classes of Polish philosopher and aesthetician Roman Ingarden.

1945
Receives composition and conducting degrees from the Lwów Conservatory. Earns same degrees a year later from the State Conservatory of Music in Kraków.

1946–47

Appointed associate conductor of the Wrocław (Breslau) Opera Orchestra. Wins second prize at the Szymanowski Competition for *Overture 1947*. Obtains a French government grant to study in Paris.

1947–49

Lives in Paris and is mentored by Nadia Boulanger in composition and Paul Kletzki in conducting. Joins Groupe Zodiaque, wins the Paris Radio Award for *Cantique des Cantiques*, conducts L'Orchestre Philharmonique de Radio France in the premiere of *Overture 1947*, and composes *Music at Night*.

1949–54

Appointed music director of the Silesian State Philharmonic of Katowice. Wins second prize at the Belgium International Competition for his String Quartet and the Polish National Award for compositions.

1955–59

Appointed music director of the Kraków Philharmonic. Wins first prize at the 1956 International Competition for Conductors, held in Rome. Marries Krystyna Jarosz in 1956. Appointed permanent conductor of the Warsaw National Philharmonic Orchestra. Wins the Moscow Gold Medal for Symphonic Suite. Makes American debut with the Cleveland Orchestra in 1958.

1960

Appointed music director of the Minneapolis Symphony Orchestra (later the Minnesota Orchestra). Serves in this position for nineteen years; introduces 250 works to the orchestra's repertoire. Instrumental in the creation of Orchestra Hall in Minneapolis.

1961–63

Makes professional recording debut on the Mercury Living Presence label. Symphony for Strings is performed by the Cleveland Orchestra, New York Philharmonic, and Chicago Symphony Orchestra.

1964–69

Debut at the Vienna State Opera with *Fidelio*. Birth of daughter, Anna, in 1966. Salzburg Festival debut with the Vienna Philharmonic. Conducts the Minnesota Orchestra at the Human Rights Day concert at the United Nations in 1968. Birth of son Paul in 1968. Composes Concerto for English Horn and Orchestra in 1969.

1970–77

Debut at the Metropolitan Opera with *The Magic Flute*. Birth of son Nicholas in 1970. Leads the Minnesota Orchestra on its 70th-anniversary tour to Mexico City in

1973. Conducts the Minnesota Orchestra at the 1974 dedication concert of Orchestra Hall, Minneapolis. Receives the 1977 Kennedy Center Friedheim Award for *Ricercari Notturni*, a saxophone concerto.

1979

Leaves post as music director of the Minnesota Orchestra. Becomes the first music director in the orchestra's history bestowed with the title "conductor laureate."

1984–91

Serves for seven seasons as principal conductor of the Hallé Orchestra in Manchester, England. Leads critically acclaimed tours in the United States and Europe. Records works by Brahms (complete symphonies), Bruckner, Mahler, Shostakovich, and Weber. Philadelphia Orchestra commissions and premieres Concerto for Violin and Orchestra. Serves as music advisor for The Saint Paul Chamber Orchestra during its 1987–88 season.

1994–99

Appointed first principal guest conductor of the Saarbrücken Radio Symphony Orchestra. Serves as artistic advisor of the Milwaukee Symphony Orchestra, 1995-97. Receives Poland's Commander of "Polonia Restituta" with "White Star."

2001–02

First CDs of all-Skrowaczewski chamber music, and orchestral compositions released. Finishes a ten-year recording project of the complete Bruckner symphonies with the Saarbrücken Radio Symphony Orchestra. The CDs receive the 2002 Cannes Classical Award for Best Recording of 18th/19th Century Orchestral Work. Release of the book *Byłem w Niebie: mówi Stanisław Skrowaczew*ski (I Was in Heaven: Conversations with Stanisław Skrowaczewski).

2003

Conducts premiere of *Concerto Nicolò* for Piano Left Hand and Orchestra with Gary Graffman and the Curtis Symphony Orchestra. Conducts the Minnesota Orchestra in premiere of Symphony [2003] on the eve of his 80th birthday. CD of *Concerto Nicolò* and Concerto for Orchestra with the Minnesota Orchestra released. Appointed first principal guest conductor of the National Polish Radio Symphony Orchestra of Katowice. Leads the Saarbrücken Radio Symphony Orchestra on a two-week tour of Japan with a program featuring three Bruckner symphonies.

2004

Leads three-week tour of Japan with the NHK Symphony Orchestra. Oehms Classics releases Chopin's Piano Concertos nos. 1 and 2, with Ewa Kupiec and the Saarbrücken Radio Symphony Orchestra.

2005–07

First Skrowaczewski DVD released: Beethoven's Symphony no. 1 and Bruckner's Symphony no. 7, with Yomiuri Nippon Symphony Orchestra. Performance of *Musica a Quattro* at Tanglewood Festival of Contemporary Music. Tours Japan for a month with the NHK Symphony Orchestra and for two weeks with the Saarbrücken Radio Symphony Orchestra (conducts all of Beethoven's symphonies). Oehms Classics releases complete Beethoven symphonies with that ensemble. Celebrates fiftieth wedding anniversary, 2006. Conducts premiere of *Fantasie per Flauto ed Orchestra, Il Piffero della Notte* with the Minnesota Orchestra. Begins three-year appointment in 2007 as principal conductor of the Yomiuri Nippon Symphony Orchestra.

2008–09

Oehms Classics releases *Stanisław Skrowaczewski the Composer: Music at Night*, all-Skrowaczewski orchestral compositions (in honor of his eighty-fifth birthday), and complete Schumann symphonies. Both recordings with Deutsche Radio Philharmonie Saarbrücken Kaiserslautern. Conducts premiere of *Music for Winds* in Saarbrücken.

2010–11

Named honorary conductor laureate of Yomiuri Nippon Symphony Orchestra. Conducts premiere of *Passacaglia Immaginaria* for orchestra (revised version) with Minnesota Orchestra. Denon releases DVD of Bruckner Symphonies nos. 8 and 9, with Yomiuri Nippon Symphony Orchestra. Continues to lead concerts in Europe, Japan, and the United States. Returns as guest conductor of Berlin Philharmonic. Begins work on a cello concerto. Records the complete Brahms symphonies with the Deutsche Radio Philharmonie Saarbrücken Kaiserslautern for release by Oehms Classics.

For more information and special features about Stanisław Skrowaczewski go to:

www.seekingtheinfinite.com

ENDNOTES

All quotations not cited in the following endnotes are excerpted from interviews by the author. A complete list of these interviews is located in Appendix D.

Chapter 1

1   Agnieszka Malatyńska-Stankiewicz, *I Was in Heaven: Conversations with Stanisław Skrowaczewski* (Kraków: Polskie Wydawnictwo Muzyczne SA, 2000), 11.
2   Ibid., 11.
3   Mary Ann Feldman, program note, *Showcase*, January 1986, 12.
4   Norman Davies, *Heart of Europe: The Past in Poland's Present* (Oxford: Oxford University Press, 2001), 99.
5   Malatyńska-Stankiewicz, 26.
6   Ibid., 24.
7   Ibid., 28.

Chapter 2

1   Norman Davies, *Heart of Europe: The Past in Poland's Present* (Oxford: Oxford University Press, 2001), 105.
2   Ibid., 104.
3   Agnieszka Malatyńska-Stankiewicz, *I Was in Heaven: Conversations with Stanisław Skrowaczewski* (Kraków: Polskie Wydawnictwo Muzyczne SA, 2000), 19.
4   Ibid., 22.
5   Ibid., 21.
6   Ibid., 26.
7   Towarzystwo Miłośników Lwowa i Kresów Południowo – Wschodnich. Radio w Grodzie Orląt (z 1939), 1998. http://www.lwow.home.pl/semper/rad.html (accessed Dec. 10, 2005).
8   Maurycy Bryx, "Stacja Radiowa we Lwowie," (2009, updated), http://www.historiaradia.neostrada.pl/stacja%20nadawcza%20Lwow.html (accessed Oct. 15, 2009).
9   Steven Ledbetter, "Ludwig van Beethoven: The Piano Concertos," in *The Beethoven Piano Concertos Live at Monadnock*, perf. Russell Sherman, Monadnock Music Festival Orchestra, dir. James Bolle, liner notes, compact disc (GM Recordings, 2001).
10 Malatyńska-Stankiewicz, 18.
11 Ibid., 20.
12 Ibid., 19.
13 Ibid.

Chapter 3

1   Martin Gilbert, *A History of the Twentieth Century, Volume Two: 1933-1951* (New York: Avon Books, Inc., 1998), 265.
2   Norman Davies, *Heart of Europe: The Past in Poland's Present* (Oxford: Oxford University Press, 2001), 57.
3   Gilbert, 277.

4   Gilbert, 276–277.

5   Wacław Szybalski, phone interview by author, Madison, Wisconsin, February 4, 2005.

6   Geoffrey Norris and David Nice, s.v. "Shostakovich, Dmitry," *The Oxford Companion to Music*, ed. Alison Latham. *Oxford Music Online*, http://www.oxfordmusiconline.com/subscriber /article/opr/t114/e6164 (accessed Jan. 15, 2005).

7   Gilbert, 335.

8   Ibid., 345.

9   Ibid., 370.

Chapter 4

1   Martin Gilbert, *A History of the Twentieth Century, Volume Two: 1933-1951* (New York: Avon Books, Inc., 1998), 383.

2   Norman Davies, *Heart of Europe: The Past in Poland's Present* (Oxford: Oxford University Press, 2001), 39.

3   Zygmunt Albert, *Kaźń Profesorów Lwowskich - Lipiec 1941/studia oraz relacje i dokumenty zebrane i oprac. przez Zygmunta Alberta* (Wrocław: Wydawnictwo Uniwersytetu Wrocławskiego, 1989). Fragment trans. Wacław Szybalski, http://www.lwow.home.pl/Lwow_profs.html (accessed February 19, 2005).

4   Roy Close, "Skrowaczewski: Behind the Public Baton Lives a Very Private Man," *Minneapolis Star*, October 18, 1974.

5   Agnieszka Malatyńska-Stankiewicz, *I Was in Heaven: Conversations with Stanisław Skrowaczewski* (Kraków: Polskie Wydawnictwo Muzyczne SA, 2000), 28.

6   Ibid., 32.

7   Gilbert, 379.

8   Ibid., 405.

9   Ibid., 415.

10   Ibid., 380.

11   Ibid., 391.

12   Wacław Szybalski, "The Genius of Rudolf Stefan Weigl (1883-1957), a Lvovian Microbe Hunter and Breeder: In Memoriam," in *International Weigl Conference, Microorganisms in Pathogenesis and Their Drug Resistance Programme and Abstracts*, ed. R. Stoika et al. (Sept 11–14, 1998).

13   Ibid.

14   Ibid.

15   Arnie Thomasson, *Stanford Encyclopedia of Philosophy*, http://plato.stanford.edu/entries /ingarden/ (accessed Feb. 21, 2005).

16   Gilbert, 426.

17   Warsaw Uprising 1944: August 1–October 2, http://www.warsawuprising.com/faq.htm (accessed May 16, 2010).

18   Ibid.

19   Polish Ministry of Internal Affairs, *Ukrainian Clues Regarding Katyń* (1995), 9-10.

20   Gilbert, 426.

21   Davies, 66.

22   Gilbert, 584.

23   Davies, 66.

Chapter 5

1   Martin Gilbert, *A History of the Twentieth Century, Volume Two: 1933-1951* (New York: Avon Books, Inc., 1998), 593.

2   Norman Davies, *Rising '44: The Battle for Warsaw* (New York: Viking, Penguin Group, 2004), 249.

3   _____, *Heart of Europe: The Past in Poland's Present* (Oxford: Oxford University Press, 2001), 68.

4   Gilbert, 602.

5   Ibid.

6   Ian C.B. Dear and Michael Richard Daniel Foot, "Warsaw Risings," *The Oxford Companion to World War II* (Oxford University Press, 2001). *Encyclopedia.com*, http://www.encyclopedia.com (accessed November 26, 2004).

7   Lesya Lantsuta, s.v. "Kolessa, Nikolai Filaretovich," *Grove Music Online. Oxford Music Online*, http://www.oxfordmusiconline.com/subscriber/article/grove/music/45596 (accessed November 11, 2004).

8   David Fanning and Laurel Fay, s.v. "Shostakovich, Dmitry," *Grove Music Online. Oxford Music Online*, http://www.oxfordmusiconline.com/subscriber/article/grove/music/52560pg6 (accessed November 15, 2004).

9   Gilbert, 637.

10   Davies, *Rising '44*, 69.

11   Davies, *Heart of Europe*, 55.

12   Ibid.

13   "Potsdam," *The Columbia Encyclopedia*, 6th ed., 2008. *Encyclopedia.com*, http://www.encyclopedia.com (accessed November 12, 2004).

14   Davies, *Heart of Europe*, 69.

15   "The Potsdam Proclamation," July 26, 1945. Pamphlet No. 4, Pillars of Peace (Pennsylvania: Book Department, Army Information School, May 1946), http://www.ibiblio.org/pha/policy/1945/450726a.html (accessed September 8, 2005).

16   Davies, *Heart of Europe*, 70.

17   Davies, *Rising '44*, 511.

18   Zygmunt M. Szweykowski et al, "Kraków," *Grove Music Online. Oxford Music Online*, http://www.oxfordmusiconline.com/subscriber/article/grove/music/40067 (accessed June 20, 2004).

19   Adrian Thomas, s.v. "Panufnik, Sir Andrzej," *Grove Music Online. Oxford Music Online*, http://www.oxfordmusiconline.com/subscriber/article/grove/music/20837 (accessed May 16, 2004).

20   Szweykowski et al, "Kraków."

21   Teresa Chylińska, "Polskie Wydawnictwo Muzyczne," *Grove Music Online. Oxford Music Online*, http://www.oxfordmusiconline.com/subscriber/article/grove/music/22039 (accessed May 10, 2004).

22   Szweykowski et al, "Kraków."

23   Mieczysława Hanuszewska, s.v. "Bierdiajew, Walerian," *Grove Music Online. Oxford Music Online*, http://www.oxfordmusiconline.com/subscriber/article/grove/music/03059 (accessed June 20, 2004).

24   Warsaw Philharmonic Orchestra, http://www.filharmonia.pl/start.en.html (accessed June 20, 2004).

Chapter 6

1   Gordon A. Anderson et al, "Paris," *Grove Music Online. Oxford Music Online*, http://www.oxfordmusiconline.com/subscriber/article/grove/music/40089 (accessed December 11, 2004).

2   Jonathan Griffin and Richard Langham Smith, s.v. "Barraud, Henry," *Grove Music Online. Oxford Music Online*, http://www.oxfordmusiconline.com/subscriber/article/grove/music/02106 (accessed December 11, 2004).

3   Polish Music Information Center, Polish Composers' Union, May 2002, http://www.culture.pl/en/culture/artykuly/os_palester_roman (accessed Dec. 15, 2004).

[4] Léonie Rosenstiel, *Nadia Boulanger: A Life in Music* (New York: Norton & Company, Inc., 1982), 159-160.

[5] Ibid., 163.

[6] Jerôme Spycket, *Nadia Boulanger* (Paris: Payot Paris, 1987), 68.

[7] Caroline Potter, s.v. "Boulanger, Nadia," *Grove Music Online. Oxford Music Online*, http://www.oxfordmusiconline.com/subscriber/article/grove/music/03705 (accessed December 17, 2004).

[8] Ibid.

[9] Spycket, 120.

[10] Rosenstiel, 337.

[11] Humphrey Burton, *Leonard Bernstein* (New York: Doubleday, 1994), 336.

[12] Bryce Morrison, s.v. "Katchen, Julius," *Grove Music Online. Oxford Music Online*, http://www.oxfordmusiconline.com/subscriber/article/grove/music/14758 (accessed December 11, 2004).

[13] Pariserve Sightseeing: Montparnasse, http://www.pariserve.tm.fr/English/paris/montparnasse.htm (accessed Dec. 12, 2004).

[14] Nigel Simeone, "La Jeune France," *Grove Music Online. Oxford Music Online*, http://www.oxfordmusiconline.com/subscriber/article/grove/music/51331 (accessed December 11, 2004).

[15] Caroline Rae, s.v. "Ohana, Maurice," *Grove Music Online. Oxford Music Online*, http://www.oxfordmusiconline.com/subscriber/article/grove/music/20292 (accessed December 11, 2004).

[16] Agnieszka Malatyńska-Stankiewicz, *I Was in Heaven: Conversations with Stanisław Skrowaczewski* (Kraków: Polskie Wydawnictwo Muzyczne SA, 2000), 33.

[17] Ibid., 34.

[18] Eric Walter White, *Stravinsky: The Composer and His Works*, 2nd ed. (Berkeley: University of California Press, 1985), 441.

[19] Malatyńska-Stankiewicz, *I Was in Heaven*, 51.

[20] Martin Anderson, "Paul Kletzki," *International Record Review* (August 2004).

[21] Ibid.

[22] Rosenstiel, 340.

[23] Martin Cooper, s.v. "Münch, Charles," *Grove Music Online. Oxford Music Online*, http://www.oxfordmusiconline.com/subscriber/article/grove/music/19347 (accessed December 15, 2004).

[24] Charles Bodman Rae, s.v. "Lutosławski, Witold," *Grove Music Online. Oxford Music Online*, http://www.oxfordmusiconline.com/subscriber/article/grove/music/17226 (accessed December 5, 2004).

Chapter 7

[1] Silesian Philharmonic, *Culture.pl*, http://www.culture.pl/en/culture/artykuly/in_mk_filharmonia_katowice (accessed March 10, 2005).

[2] Biography of PNRSO, Polish National Radio Symphony, http://www.nospr.org.pl/english/about_us/nospr_biograqphy.xml (accessed March 10, 2005).

[3] Teresa Chylińska, s.v. "Fitelberg, Grzegorz," *Grove Music Online. Oxford Music Online*, http://www.oxfordmusiconline.com/subscriber/article/grove/music/09757 (accessed March 14, 2005).

[4] Adrian Thomas, s.v. "Górecki, Henryk Mikołaj," *Grove Music Online. Oxford Music Online*, http://www.oxfordmusiconline.com/subscriber/article/grove/music/11478 (accessed March 14, 2005).

[5] Jolanta Guzy-Pasiakowa, "Katowice," *Grove Music Online. Oxford Music Online*, http://www.oxfordmusiconline.com/subscriber/article/grove/music/40407 (accessed March 14, 2005).

6   Simon Emmerson and Denis Smalley, "Electro-acoustic music," *Grove Music Online. Oxford Music Online*, http://www.oxfordmusiconline.com/subscriber/article/grove/music/08695 (accessed March 20, 2005).

7   http://www.polishculturenyc.org/printIndex.cfm?itemcategory=30817&personDetailId=198 (accessed March 13, 2005).

8   Tadeusz Miczka, "Cinema Under Political Pressure: A Brief Outline of Authorial Roles in Polish Post-War Feature Films 1945-1995," *Kinema, Journal for Film and Audiovisual Media* (spring 2008), http://www.kinema.uwaterloo.ca/article.php?id=336&feature (accessed March 10, 2008).

9   Stowarzyszenie Willa Decjusza, "Tadeusz Konwicki," *Culture.pl*, http://www.culture.pl/en/culture/artykuly/os_konwicki_tadeusz (accessed March 13, 2005).

10   Ewa Mazierska, "Wanda Jakubowska's Cinema of Commitment," *European Journal of Women's Studies* 8:2 (2001), http://ejw.sagepub.com/cgi/content/abstract/8/2/221 (accessed March 2005).

11   Andrzej Panufnik, *Composing Myself* (London: Methuen London Ltd, 1987), 187.

12   "Roman Palester," *Culture.pl*, http://www.culture.pl/en/culture/artykuly/os_palester_roman (accessed March 13, 2005).

13   Alistair Wightman, s.v. "Baird, Tadeusz," *Grove Music Online. Oxford Music Online*, http://www.oxfordmusiconline.com/subscriber/article/grove/music/01810 (accessed March 20, 2005).

14   "The Third Tadeusz Wronski Solo Violin Competition," *Culture.pl*, http://www.culture.pl/en/culture/artykuly/wy_km_wronskiego_skrzypce_solo_2004 (accessed March 15, 2005).

15   Prohelvetia, http://www.prohelvetia.ch/Home.20.0.html?&L=4 (accessed March 14, 2005).

16   Geoffrey K. Spratt, s.v. "Honegger, Arthur," *Grove Music Online. Oxford Music Online*, http://www.oxfordmusiconline.com/subscriber/article/grove/music/13298 (accessed March 21, 2005).

Chapter 8

1   "The Legend of the Wawel's Dragon," http://culture.polishsite.us/articles/art292fr.htm (accessed June 14, 2005).

2   Zygmunt M. Szweykowski et al, "Kraków," *Grove Music Online. Oxford Music Online*, http://www.oxfordmusiconline.com/subscriber/article/grove/music/40067 (accessed June 14, 2005).

3   "Kraków," *Holocaust Encyclopedia*, United States Holocaust Memorial Museum, http://www.ushmm.org/wlc/article.php?ModuleId=10005169 (accessed June 15, 2005).

4   "History," Kraków Philharmonic, http://www.filharmonia.krakow.pl/index.html (accessed June 15, 2005).

5   Mary Ann Feldman, "Musical Citizen of the World," in *Stanisław Skrowaczewski: 2004 Distinguished Artist* (Minneapolis: The McKnight Foundation, 2004), 19.

6   Halina Rodziński, *Our Two Lives: The Story of an Extraordinary Marriage and a Brilliant Career in Music* (New York: Charles Scribner's Sons, 1976), 347-348.

Chapter 9

1   Barbara Przybyszewska-Jarminska and Zofia Chechlińska, "Warsaw," *Grove Music Online. Oxford Music Online*, http://www.oxfordmusiconline.com/subscriber/article/grove/music/40487 (accessed June 8, 2005).

2   Warsaw Philharmonic Orchestra, http://www.filharmonia.pl/start.en.html (accessed June12, 2005).

3   "'Warsaw Autumn,' International Festival of Contemporary Music," *Culture.pl*, http://www.culture.pl/en/culture/artykuly/im_fm_warszawska_jesien (accessed June 12, 2005).

4   Harold Schoenberg, "Szell, the Greatest Since Toscanini, Achieved Glamour with No Tricks," *New York Times*, July 31, 1970, online (accessed June 15, 2005).

5   Michael Charry, s.v. "Szell, George," *Grove Music Online. Oxford Music Online*, http://www .oxfordmusiconline.com/subscriber/article/grove/music/27305 (accessed June 16, 2005).

6   Ibid.

7   Donald Rosenberg, *The Cleveland Orchestra Story: Second to None* (Cleveland: Gray & Company, 2000), 244.

8   Ibid., 362.

9   Christian Labrande and Donald Sturrock, *The Art of Piano: Great Pianists of the 20th Century*, DVD (Warner Music Vision, 1999).

10   Ibid.

11   Expo 58: The Exhibition, http://users.skynet.be/rentfarm/expo58/exhibition/index.htm (accessed June 20, 2005).

12   Paul Griffiths, s.v. "Varèse, Edgard," *Grove Music Online. Oxford Music Online*, http://www .oxfordmusiconline.com/subscriber/article/grove/music/29042 (accessed June 20, 2005).

13   Martin Bernheimer, s.v. "Totenberg, Roman," *Grove Music Online. Oxford Music Online*, http://www.oxfordmusiconline.com/subscriber/article/grove/music/28204 (accessed June 20, 2005).

14   Janusz Korczak, http://korczak.com/Biography/kap-0.htm (accessed June 20, 2005).

15   Ran Blake, email communication with the author, July 18, 2006.

16   Bain Murray, "Conductor from Poland Brings Cheer," *Plain Dealer* (Cleveland), December 5, 1958.

17   George Szell, interview by Paul H. Lang, as quoted in Harold Schonberg, *The Great Conductors* (New York: Simon and Schuster, 1967), 337.

18   Norman Lebrecht, *Who Killed Classical Music?* (New York: Carol Publishing Group, Secaucus, 1997), 95-98.

19   Ibid., 99, 130.

20   Ibid., 104.

21   Ibid., 104-107.

22   http://www.geocities.com/laosw/Classical_Html/stokowskiBio.htm (accessed June 19, 2005).

23   http://www.stokowskisociety.net/transcriptions.html (accessed June 19, 2005).

24   Herbert Elwell, "Polish Conductor Electrifies Severance Hall," *Plain Dealer*, December 18, 1959.

25   Ibid.

26   Klaus George Roy, "Second Skrowaczewski Visit," *The Christian Science Monitor*, February 6, 1960.

27   Herbert Elwell, "Pole's Baton Brings Best from Orchestra," *Plain Dealer*, December 26, 1959.

28   Roy, "Second Skrowaczewski Visit."

Chapter 10

1   John Sherman, *Music and Maestros: The Story of the Minneapolis Symphony Orchestra* (Minneapolis: Lund Press, 1952), 18-19.

2   Barbara Flanagan, *Ovation: A Partnership Between a Great Orchestra and a Great Audience* (Minneapolis: The Minnesota Orchestra, 1977), 15.

3   Sherman, 20.

4   Ibid., 27-29.

5   Ibid.

6   Sherman, 22.

7   Ibid., 27.

8   Ibid., 27-29.

9   Ibid., 39.

10   Ibid., 44-48.

11   Ibid., 49.

12   Ibid., 51.

13   Ibid., 51-53.

14   Ibid., 53.

15   Roy Close, "One Hundred by Nine—The Music Directors," in *Minnesota Orchestra at One Hundred* (Minneapolis: Minnesota Orchestra, 2002), 4.

16   Sherman, 78.

17   Ibid., 80.

18   Ibid., 156.

19   D.C. Parker, s.v. "Verbrugghen, Henri," *Grove Music Online. Oxford Music Online*, http://www.oxfordmusiconline.com/subscriber/article/grove/music/29183 (accessed November 16, 2006).

20   Sherman, 154-156.

21   Richard Freed, "Recording and Broadcast—Paths to the World," in *Minnesota Orchestra at One Hundred* (Minneapolis: Minnesota Orchestra, 2002), 94.

22   "History of Radio," *Wikipedia*, http://en.wikipedia.org/wiki/History_of_radio (accessed November 7, 2006).

23   Freed, 96.

24   Sherman, 167.

25   Close, 6.

26   Sherman, 194, 212-213.

27   Ibid., 201.

28   Ibid., 200.

29   Ibid., 202.

30   Ibid., 225.

31   Michael Steinberg, "This Evening's Program…," in *Minnesota Orchestra at One Hundred* (Minneapolis: Minnesota Orchestra, 2002), 120.

32   Freed, 98.

33   Ibid.

34   Freed, 100.

35   Ibid.

36   William R. Trotter, s.v. "Mitropoulos, Dimitri," *Grove Music Online. Oxford Music Online*, http://www.oxfordmusiconline.com/subscriber/article/grove/music/18799 (accessed November 16, 2006).

37   _____, *Priest of Music: The Life of Dimitri Mitropoulos* (Portland, Oregon: Amadeus Press, 1995), 65-66.

38   Ibid.

39   Trotter, 78.

40   Ibid., 82.

41   Sherman, 228.

42   Henry Kramer, *Following the Beat* (n.p., 1996), 7.

43   Freed, 116.

44   Trotter, 142.

45   Sherman, 275.

46   Trotter, 135.

47   Mary Ann Feldman, "On the Road to Fame—Our Touring Orchestra," in *Minnesota Orchestra at One Hundred* (Minneapolis: Minnesota Orchestra, 2002), 36.

48   Freed, 113.

49   Pamela Hill Nettleton, "Musical Values—A Community's Pride," in *Minnesota Orchestra at One Hundred* (Minneapolis: Minnesota Orchestra, 2002), 61.

50   Sherman, 270.

51   Ibid., 271.

52   Noël Goodwin, s.v. *"Dorati, Antal,"* *Grove Music Online. Oxford Music Online*, http://www.oxfordmusiconline.com/subscriber/article/grove/music/08025 (accessed November 11, 2006).

53   Flanagan, 7.

54   Close, 14.

55   Goodwin, s.v. "Dorati, Antal."

56   Ibid.

57   Kramer, 6.

58   Flanagan, 55.

59   Dennis Rooney, "The Early Years," in *Minnesota Orchestra at One Hundred: A Collection of Recordings and Broadcasts*, compact disc booklet (Minneapolis: Minnesota Orchestra, 2003), 32.

60   Freed, 102.

61   Ibid., 104.

62   Sherman, 298.

63   Sandra Hyslop, "Burton Paulu: Broadcast Pioneer," in *Showcase*, October 2002, 17.

64   Ibid.

65   Feldman, 37.

66   Ibid.

67   Julie Ayer, *More Than Meets The Ear: How Symphony Musicians Made Labor History* (Minneapolis: Syren Book Company, 2005), 160.

68   Close, 14.

69   Flanagan, 56.

Chapter 11

1   John Sherman, "Skrowaczewski, Wife Welcomed in City," *Minneapolis Tribune*, September 6, 1960.

2   Sherman, "For New Maestro, Gypsy Life Is Over," *Minneapolis Star*, September 7, 1960.

3   Sherman, "Skrowaczewski, Wife Welcomed in City."

4   John Harvey, "Skrowaczewski? The Name's Stan," *St. Paul Dispatch*, September 6, 1960.

5   Ibid.

6   Ibid.

7   Henry Kramer, *Following the Beat* (n.p., 1996), 1.

8   Carl T. Rowan, "Maestro, Musicians Make Beautiful Music Together," *Minneapolis Tribune*, September 29, 1960.

9   Micha Namenwirth, "Rehearsal Reveals Qualities of New Symphony Conductor," *Minnesota Daily*, September 30, 1960.

10   Kramer, 3.

11   George Grimm, "Skrowaczewski, Symphony Score Win in Brainerd Gym," *Minneapolis Tribune*, October 2, 1960.

12   Bill Zickrick, "Symphony Quickly Captures Audience," *Brainerd Daily Dispatch* (Brainerd, MN), October 3, 1960.

13   "Skrowaczewski Applauded in Premiere Symphony Event," *Little Falls Daily* (Brainerd, MN), October 3, 1960.

14   Paul S. Ivory, "Symphony Gets Exciting Start," *St. Paul Pioneer Press*, October 2, 1960.

15   Advertisement, Dayton's Department Stores, *Minneapolis Tribune*, November 4, 1960.

16   Daniel J. Hafrey, "Stanisław Skrowaczewski—Man of Modest Confidence," *Minneapolis Tribune*, October 20, 1960.

17   Roger Anderson, "Opening Triumph for Skrowaczewski and Minneapolis Symphony," *Wanderer*, November 10, 1960.

18   Ibid.

19   Harvey, "Minneapolis Symphony Opens," *St. Paul Pioneer Press,* November 5, 1960.

20   Sherman, *Minneapolis Tribune*, November 5, 1960.

21   "About Northrop," Northrop Auditorium, http://northrop.umn.edu/about/history (accessed June 11, 2005).

22   Ibid.

23   Ibid.

24   Sherman, "Symphony Opens Friday in New Northrop Shell," *Minneapolis Tribune,* October 8, 1961.

25   Lester Trimble and Severine Neff, s.v. "Luening, Otto," *Grove Music Online. Oxford Music Online,* http://www.oxfordmusiconline.com/subscriber/article/grove/music/17140 (accessed January 16, 2010).

26   Debby Charnley, "New Sounds to Fill Northrop," *Minnesota Daily,* February 17, 1961.

27   Kramer, 38.

28   Ibid.

29   Sherman, "Defender of Modern Music Likes the Spur of Challenge," *Minneapolis Tribune*, March 19, 1961.

30   Kramer, 43.

31   *Minneapolis Symphony Orchestra Young Peoples Concert View Book,* November 29, 1960.

32   Stanisław Skrowaczewski, personal script, Young People's Concert (n.d.).

33   Ibid.

34   Kramer, 4.

35   Stanisław Skrowaczewski, "Should Composers Conduct?" *Music Journal* (November/ December 1960), 12, 65.

36   "Skrowaczewski Gets Mixed Reviews from N.Y. Critics," *Minneapolis Sunday Tribune*, January 1, 1961.

37   Ibid.

38   Ibid.

39   Ibid.

40   "Critic Praises Skrowaczewski for His Drive," *Minneapolis Sunday Tribune*, February 26, 1961.

41   George Szell, letter to U.S. Immigration and Naturalization Service, December 21, 1960.

42   Ibid.

43   Ibid.

44   "Mr. S Wins Acclaim of Critics from San Francisco to Israel," *Minneapolis Tribune*, June 4, 1961.

45   Ibid.

46   Edmund Bolton, "Minneapolis," *Musical Courier*, May 1961.

Chapter 12

1   John Sherman, "Symphony Opens Friday in New Northrop Shell," *Minneapolis Tribune*, October 8, 1961.

2   John P.L. Roberts and Ghyslaine Guertin, eds. *Glenn Gould: Selected Letters* (Toronto: Oxford University Press, 1992), 57.

3   Stanisław Skrowaczewski, "Maestro Dips Baton for Women–Open Letter to WAMSO Members," *Minneapolis Tribune*, November 9, 1961.

4   E. Eugene Helm, *Musical America,* April 1962.

5   Arthur Judson, letter to Stanisław Skrowaczewski, March 28, 1961.

6   Norman Lebrecht, *Who Killed Classical Music? Maestros, Managers, and Corporate Politics* (Secaucus, New Jersey: Birch Lane Press, 1997), 139-140.

7   Lebrecht, 152.

8   Howard Shanet, *Philharmonic: A History of New York's Orchestra* (Garden City, New York: Doubleday & Company, 1975), 346.

9 Henry Kramer, *Following the Beat* (n.p., 1996), 5.

10 Stanisław Skrowaczewski, letter to Spryers, May 13, 1962.

11 John Myers, letter to Stanisław Skrowaczewski, July 9, 1963.

12 Stanisław Skrowaczewski, statement in Minneapolis Symphony Orchestra 1962-1963 season flyer.

13 Herbert Fiegl, letter to Stanisław Skrowaczewski, April 1963.

14 Ibid.

15 Stanisław Skrowaczewski, letter to Herbert Fiegl, April 1963.

16 John Sherman, "He Demolishes Classical Music: Symphony Will Perform Pole's Avant-Garde Work," *Minneapolis Tribune,* September 16, 1962.

17 Ibid.

18 John Harvey, *St. Paul Pioneer Press,* December 14, 1963.

19 Ibid.

Chapter 13

1 *Minneapolis Tribune,* January 7, 1962.

2 "Maestro Has Place to Reflect and Work," *Minneapolis Tribune,* (n.d., Winter 1962).

3 Ibid.

4 Ibid.

5 John Sherman, "Skrowaczewski Finds Vienna a Surprise," *Minneapolis Star,* June 16, 1963.

6 Ibid.

7 Stanisław Skrowaczewski, speech at Hamline University, June 1963.

8 Eric Stokes, *Minnesota Daily,* April 4, 1963.

9 John Sherman, "Jack Benny's Sour Notes Sweet Music to Audience," *Minneapolis Star,* November 8, 1963.

10 Richard Evidon, "Guests of Honor," in *Minnesota Orchestra at One Hundred* (Minneapolis: The Minnesota Orchestra, 2002), 155.

11 Barbara Flanagan, *Ovation: A Partnership Between a Great Orchestra and a Great Audience* (Minneapolis: The Minnesota Orchestra, 1977), 63.

12 John Sherman, "Concert Reflects Shock, Grief of Both Audience, Orchestra," *Minneapolis Star,* November 23, 1963.

13 Arthur M. Schlesinger, Jr., *A Thousand Days: John F. Kennedy in the White House* (London: Mayflower-Dell, 1965), 926.

14 Dan Sullivan, "As Fourth Year Begins, Skrowaczewski Looks at Music, Musicians and a Fresh Season," *Minneapolis Sunday Tribune,* October 11, 1963.

15 ———, "Comments on Skrowaczewski in Cleveland," *Minneapolis Tribune,* December 22, 1963.

16 William Westbrook Burton, *Conversations about Bernstein* (New York: Oxford University Press, 1995), 59.

17 Philadelphia Orchestra promotional flyer, 1964.

18 Winthrop Sargeant, *New Yorker,* April 1964.

19 Albert Goldberg, "Orchestra Back in Top Form with Skrowaczewski on Podium," *Los Angeles Times,* July 23, 1964.

20 In *Confidential Outline of Action Program,* Minnesota Orchestral Association Executive Committee's special meeting (Stillwater, Minn.), June 27–29, 1964.

Chapter 14

1 Bruce Bawer, "The Other Sixties," *The Wilson Quarterly,* Spring 2004.

2 Burton Hersh, "The New Twin Cities," (n.p., possibly *Twin Citian,* June 1966).

3 Ibid.

4 Ibid.

5   Al McConagha, "In Twin Cities Culture Outdraws Big Leagues," *Minneapolis Tribune,* May 30, 1965.

6   Associated Press, "Skrowaczewski Wows Viennans," *Minneapolis Tribune,* quoting Vienna paper *Volksblatt,* September 9, 1964.

7   Louis Baincolli, "Gluck Scores at Carnegie," *New York World Telegram and Sun,* March 24, 1965.

8   Miles Kastendick, "Iphigenia: A Glowing Premiere," *Journal American,* March 24, 1965.

9   "Minneapolis Symphony Signs 5-year Contract," *New York Times,* August 5, 1965.

10 "Mpls. Symphony Adds Concerts," *Minnesota Daily,* August 6, 1965.

11 Harold Schonberg, "Accent on Polish," Music, *New York Times,* February 13, 1965.

12 Henryk Szeryng: 1918–1988, http://www.henrykszeryng.net/en/main.php (accessed October 15, 2006). UNESCO (United Nations Educational, Scientific and Cultural Organization).

13 William Bender, "Poland Tribute Via Minneapolis," *New York Herald Tribune,* February 12, 1965.

14 Allan Holbert, "New Symphony Manager Seeks Answers," *Minneapolis Tribune,* August 29, 1965.

15 "Orchestras: The Elite Eleven," *Time,* April 8, 1966.

16 John Sherman, "Minneapolis: City of Lakes and Music," *International Musician,* April 1965.

17 H.D. Webster, "Is Musical Hotline Hot Again?" Special to *Minneapolis Tribune* from *The Philadelphia Inquirer,* September 25, 1965.

18 Pauline Walle, "Towards Becoming a Regional Orchestra," *Rochester Bulletin* (Rochester, Minn.), September 28, 1965.

19 Ibid.

20 Allan Holbert, *Minneapolis Tribune,* October 10, 1965.

21 Ibid.

22 Harold Schonberg, "In Modern Mode," Music, *New York Times,* February 10, 1966.

23 Ibid.

24 *Time,* "Orchestras: The Elite Eleven," April 8, 1966.

25 Allan Holbert, "Rx Double Dose of Schoenberg," *Minneapolis Tribune,* April 16, 1966.

26 Stanisław Skrowaczewski, speech for All-Request Concert, April 15, 1966.

27 Patrick J. Smith and Maureen Buja, s.v. "Craft, Robert," *Grove Music Online. Oxford Music Online,* http://www.oxfordmusiconline.com/subscriber/article/grove/music/06771 (accessed January 17, 2010).

28 Julie Ayer, *More Than Meets The Ear: How Symphony Musicians Made Labor History* (Minneapolis: Syren Book Company, 2005), 188.

29 Robert Craft, email communication with the author, November 12, 2009.

30 Ibid.

31 John Harvey, "Stravinsky Given Thunderous Salute," *St. Paul Pioneer Press,* January 22, 1966.

32 Gerhard Brunner, s.v. "Scherchen, Hermann," *Grove Music Online. Oxford Music Online,* http://www.oxfordmusiconline.com/subscriber/article/grove/music/24807 (accessed March 15, 2006).

33 Wendell Borgium, letter to Paul Christopher, December 21, 1969.

34 Ibid.

35 Eugene Ormandy, letter to Stanisław Skrowaczewski, June 18, 1966.

36 John Sherman, "Analysis by Composer Dulls Concert by Symphony," *Minneapolis Star,* July 2, 1966.

37 R.C. Hammerich, "Personalized 'Eroica' Conducted Sunday by Skrowaczewski," *Boston Herald,* August 8, 1966.

38 Geoffrey P. Hellman, "Tanglewood Soloist Projects Minimal Sensitivity," *Boston Globe,* August 8, 1966.

39　Stanisław Skrowaczewski, "U.S. May Now Lead Europe in Culture," *Minneapolis Tribune,* October 9, 1966.

40　"America's Cultural Boom," New York Philharmonic, program book (1965-1966), citing "MBI Concert Music in 1966" pamphlet.

41　Mary Ann Feldman, letter to Stanisław Skrowaczewski, October 5, 1966.

42　Mieczysław Tomaszewski, *Symphony No. 3/Threnody for the Victims of Hiroshima for 52 Strings,* perf. Polish National Radio Symphony Orchestra, dir. Antoni Wit, liner notes on Penderecki, compact disc (Naxos, 2000).

43　Artur Rubinstein, letter to Kenneth Dayton, February 3, 1967.

44　Allan Holbert, "Symphony Turnover—Coincidence or Discord?" *Minneapolis Tribune,* May 7, 1967.

45　Ibid.

46　Ibid.

47　Ibid.

48　*Minneapolis Star,* "Some Dissatisfied 15 City Symphony Members Leaving," May 8, 1967.

49　Ibid.

50　Ivan Hlebarov, s.v. "Vladigerov, Pancho," *Grove Music Online. Oxford Music Online,* http://www.oxfordmusiconline.com/subscriber/article/grove/music/29559 (accessed March 2006).

51　Holbert, "Symphony Begins 65th Year: Cyclic Programs Make Musical News," *Minneapolis Tribune,* October 7, 1967.

52　Ibid.

53　Ibid.

54　Allan Holbert, "Polish Composer Arrives for Oratorio Premiere," *Minneapolis Tribune,* October 29, 1967.

55　Bernard Jacobson, "Passion by St. Luke Has Its U.S. Premiere," *Chicago Daily News,* November 3, 1967.

56　Holbert, "Polish Composer Arrives for Oratorio Premiere."

57　Peter Altman, "'Saint Luke Passion' Stuns Audience at 'U' Premiere," *Minneapolis Star,* November 3, 1967.

58　Ibid.

59　Holbert, "Polish Composer Arrives for Oratorio Premiere."

60　Altman, "'Saint Luke Passion' Stuns Audience at 'U' Premiere."

61　McCannel Eye Clinic, http://www.ophpa.com/ThePractice.cfm (accessed March 13, 2006).

62　Sherman, "'Passion' Called New Musical Language," *Minneapolis Tribune,* November 4, 1967.

63　*Time,* "Orchestras: Big Five Plus One?" November 10, 1967.

Chapter 15

1　"Salzburg Festival," *The Oxford Dictionary of Music,* 2nd ed. rev., ed. Michael Kennedy. *Oxford Music Online,* http://www.oxfordmusiconline.com/subscriber/article/opr/t237/e8911 (accessed June 16, 2006).

2　Official program, Salzburg Festival (1968).

3　Ibid.

4　George Szell, letter to Stanisław Skrowaczewski, September 28, 1968.

5　Nachrichten, review quote reprinted in *Minneapolis Tribune,* ca. August 1968.

6　Richard Wang, s.v. "Goodman, Benny," *Grove Music Online. Oxford Music Online,* http://www.oxfordmusiconline.com/subscriber/article/grove/music/11459 (accessed June 19, 2006).

7　*Confidential Outline of Action Program,* Minnesota Orchestral Association Executive Committee's special meeting, (Stillwater, Minn.), June 27–29, 1964.

8　Meeting agenda, memorandum, "From Stillwater to Thunderbird", October 19, 1966.

9　Meeting agenda, annual symphony retreat, November 12, 1967.

[10] Meeting agenda, president's report from minutes, annual symphony retreat, November 12, 1967.

[11] Ibid.

[12] Eugene Ormandy, letter to Judson Bemis, September 14, 1968.

[13] Allan Holbert, "Skrowaczewski Is Opposed to Name Change," *Minneapolis Tribune*, September 24, 1968.

[14] Ibid.

[15] Minnesota Orchestra members, letter of petition to Judson Bemis, September 23, 1968.

[16] Judson Bemis, letter to board of directors, Minnesota Orchestral Association, September 25, 1968.

[17] Press release, Minnesota Orchestral Association, September 25, 1968.

[18] Letter to Bemis, September 23, 1968.

[19] Judson Bemis, letter to MOA board of directors, September 25, 1968.

[20] Bemis, September 25, 1968.

[21] Allan Holbert, "Petition Fails; Symphony Changes Name," *Minneapolis Tribune*, September 25, 1968.

[22] Holbert, "Skrowaczewski Is Opposed to Name Change."

[23] Mr. and Mrs. S.L. Markoff, telegram to Judson Bemis, September 25, 1968.

[24] Holbert, "Skrowaczewski Is Opposed to Name Change."

[25] Letters to editor, *Minneapolis Tribune*, September 24, 1968.

[26] Judson Bemis, letter to Eugene Ormandy, October 2, 1968.

[27] Eugene Ormandy, letter to Bemis, October 8, 1968.

[28] Gertrude Hill Ffolliott, letter to Richard Cisek, n.d.

[29] Editorial, *St. Paul Dispatch*, September 26, 1968.

[30] John Harvey, *St. Paul Pioneer Press*, September 29, 1968.

[31] "Symphony Is Now Minnesota Orchestra," *St. Paul Dispatch*, September 24, 1968.

[32] Barbara Flanagan, *Ovation: A Partnership Between a Great Orchestra and a Great Audience* (Minneapolis: The Minnesota Orchestra, 1977), 95.

[33] Thomas Gifford, "Orchestra Hall: How Business Made It Happen," *Greater Minneapolis, Magazine of the Greater Minneapolis Chamber of Commerce* 26, no. 9 (1974): 12.

[34] Artistic Advisory Committee of the Minnesota Orchestra, memorandum to executive committee, board of directors, Minnesota Orchestral Association, March 18, 1974.

[35] Ibid.

[36] Ibid.

[37] Musicians, Minnesota Orchestra, "What's in a Name?" petition, March 18, 1974.

[38] Don Engle, letter to Name Change Committee, May 29, 1974.

[39] Final report, board of directors, Minnesota Orchestral Association, June 19, 1974.

[40] Annual report, Minnesota Orchestral Association, 1973-74.

[41] "Minnesota Orchestral Association in Perspective: A Comparison of Three Seasons," document, Name Change file, Touring, and 1966-85 Folder.

[42] Don Engle, notes, Operating and Maintaining the Minnesota Orchestra and Orchestra Hall, Minnesota Orchestral Association, January 1, 1977.

[43] Ibid.

[44] Musicians, "What's in a Name?"

[45] Bob Jones, letter to Richard Cisek, September 14, 1981.

[46] Final report, Name Change Committee, September 1981.

[47] Ibid.

[48] Ibid.

[49] David Hyslop, letter to Rollin Ronalds, July 21, 1992.

[50] Kenneth Dayton, remarks to Minnesota Orchestral Association, December 14, 1976.

51   Pamela Hill Nettleton, "Musical Values—A Community's Pride," in *Minnesota Orchestra at One Hundred* (Minneapolis: Minnesota Orchestra, 2002), 71.

52   Julie Ayer, *More Than Meets The Ear: How Symphony Musicians Made Labor History* (Minneapolis: Syren Book Company 2005), 80.

53   Dayton, remarks to Minnesota Orchestral Association, December 14, 1976.

54   Stanisław Skrowaczewski, remarks to New Dimensions Fund meeting, October 1968.

55   Ibid.

56   Gifford, 69.

Chapter 16

1   Mike Zerby, "Stanisław Skrowaczewski 'Relaxing' in Wyoming's Grand Teton Mountains," *Minneapolis Tribune Picture Magazine*, October 6, 1968.

2   Ibid.

3   Stanisław Skrowaczewski, "The Light of Our Eye," *Symphony*, October 1968.

4   "Symphony Conductor Back after Busy Tour," *Minneapolis Star*, September 24, 1968.

5   "Conductor Bears Up Under Challenge," *St. Paul Dispatch,* September 13, 1968.

6   Allan Holbert, "Minnesota Symphony Opens New Season under New Name," *Minneapolis Tribune*, October 12, 1968.

7   John Sherman, "Orchestra Shines in Opening," *Minneapolis Tribune*, October 12, 1968.

8   N. Sparrow, "Maestro Views Opening," *The Minnesota Daily*, October 11, 1968.

9   Harold Schonberg, "Skrowaczewski Conducts Bach," Music, *New York Times,* December 6, 1968.

10   Elliott Carter, letter to the editor, *New York Times*, October 20, 1968.

11   Ibid.

12   Winthrop Sargeant, "Musical Events—To Take the Fifth," *New Yorker*, December 14, 1968.

13   Patrick J. Smith, s.v. "Sargeant, Winthrop," *Grove Music Online. Oxford Music Online*, http://www.oxfordmusiconline.com/subscriber/article/grove/music/47676 (accessed May 24, 2006).

14   "Norman Corwin, http://www.normancorwin.com/ (accessed July 2, 2010).

15   John Sherman, "It's Minneapolis Week on New York Stages," *Star Tribune*, December 11, 1968.

16   Mary Ann Feldman, "On the Road to Fame—Our Touring Orchestra," in *Minnesota Orchestra at One Hundred* (Minneapolis: Minnesota Orchestra, 2002), 42.

17   Norman Corwin, email communication with the author, August 8, 2006.

18   Howard Zinn, *A People's History of the United States* (New York: HarperCollins, 2003), 483.

19   National Educational Television, Human Rights Day Broadcast, 1968 (video).

20   Ibid.

21   "Berlin Philharmonic Orchestra," *The Oxford Dictionary of Music*, 2nd ed., rev., ed. Michael Kennedy. *Oxford Music Online*, http://www.oxfordmusiconline.com/subscriber/article/opr/t237/e1143 (accessed October 15, 2009).

22   "Elliott Carter: Concerto for Piano," G. Schirmer, Inc., http://www.schirmer.com/default.aspx?TabId=2420&State_2874=2&workId_2874=26717 (July 29, 2006).

23   Music, *Time*, January 30, 1969.

24   Ibid.

25   Tully Potter, s.v. "Du Pré, Jacqueline," *Grove Music Online. Oxford Music Online*, http://www.oxfordmusiconline.com/subscriber/article/grove/music/08362 (accessed August 1, 2006).

26   Donal Henahan, "Minnesotans Give Carnegie Concert," *New York Times*, March 6, 1969.

27   Henahan, "Religiously, a Free Spirit. Politically?" *New York Times*, February 23, 1969.

28   Ibid.

29   M.S., "The Sound of Poland," *Newsweek*, March 17, 1969.

30   Harold Schonberg, "*St. Luke Passion*," Music, *New York Times*, March 7, 1969.

31   Bain Murray, "Penderecki 'Passion and Death' Hailed as Masterpiece," *Cleveland Sun Press*, March 16, 1969.

32   Alan Rich, "The Music Critic as Sex Symbol," Music, *Newsweek*, March 17, 1969.

33   Schonberg, "*St. Luke Passion.*"

34   Murray, "Penderecki 'Passion and Death' Hailed As Masterpiece."

35   Schonberg, "*St. Luke Passion.*"

36   _____, "Romanticism Coming Up?" Music, *New York Times*, March 17, 1969.

37   Ibid.

38   Ibid.

39   Edwin Bolton, "Skrowaczewski's Concerto Represents Renewed Effort," *Minneapolis Tribune*, November 17, 1969.

40   Ibid.

41   Ibid.

42   Ibid.

43   Stanisław Skrowaczewski, "Concerto for English Horn and Orchestra," in *Two Pastels, Andante for Strings and Concerto for English Horn and Orchestra*, perf. Minnesota Orchestra, dir. Skrowaczewski, liner notes, compact disc (Phoenix Recordings, 1991).

44   Bolton, "Skrowaczewski's Concerto Represents Renewed Effort."

45   Ibid.

46   Skrowaczewski, *Two Pastels*, 1991.

47   Bolton, "Skrowaczewski's Concerto Represents Renewed Effort."

Chapter 17

1   James Felton, "Cliburn Turns On 30,000, Half-Hour Encore," *Evening Bulletin* (Philadelphia), July 1, 1969.

2   Ibid.

3   James Felton, "First Radical Music Since 1948," *Evening Bulletin*, July 2, 1969.

4   _____, "Rugged Performance, Mahler's Second Symphony Given By Orchestra, Choir," *Evening Bulletin*, July 5, 1969.

5   "Demons in Santa Fe," Music, *Newsweek*, August 25, 1969.

6   Harold Schonberg, "U.S. Debut in Santa Fe: 'The Devils of Loudon,'" *New York Times*, August 16, 1969.

7   Adrian Thomas, s.v. "Devils of Loudun," *The New Grove Dictionary of Opera*, ed. Stanley Sadie, 2004. *Grove Music Online. Oxford Music Online*, http://www.oxfordmusiconline.com /subscriber/article/grove/music/O004356 (accessed August 18, 2006).

8   Frank Hruby, "New Opera Has Problems," *Cleveland Press*, August 16, 1969.

9   "Demons in Santa Fe," *Newsweek*.

10   "Opera—The Devils and Reardon," Music, *Time*, August 25, 1969.

11   Martin Bernheimer, "'Devils of Loudun' Given U.S. Premiere by Santa Fe Opera," *Los Angeles Times,* August 16, 1969.

12   Stanisław Skrowaczewski, letter to Andrew March, September 3, 1969.

13   Thomas, "Devils of Loudun."

14   "American Orchestras: The Sound of Trouble," *Time*, June 13, 1969.

15   Ibid.

16   Howard Taubman, "For Orchestras, A Ray of Hope," *New York Times*, March 11, 1970.

17   Schonberg, "Bernstein Lists Season's Music; Conductor Thinks Symphony Is Out of Date," *New York Times*, April 28, 1965.

18   Ibid.

19   "The Symphonic Form Is Dead," Music, *Time*, August 30, 1968.

20   Shirley Fleming, "Skrowaczewski Named Musician of the Month," *Musical America*, September 1969.

21 John Harvey, "An Interview with Skrowaczewski," *Showcase,* October 1970.

22 Ibid.

23 John Harvey, "Conductors on the Move: Orchestra Musical Chairs," *St. Paul Pioneer Press,* January 26, 1969.

24 Harlold Schonberg, "After Leonard Bernstein, Who?" *The New York Times,* December 10, 1967.

25 Ibid.

26 Martin Bernheimer, "A Game of Musical Chairs Around Symphony Circuit," *New York Post,* December 12, 1967.

27 Schonberg, "After Leonard Bernstein, Who?"

28 P. Witter, "How to Say Skrowaczewski," *International Herald Tribune,* February 13, 1969.

29 John Sherman, "Maestro's Horizon Continues to Grow," *Minneapolis Star,* March 5, 1969.

30 John Harvey, "New Concerto Highlights Concert," *St. Paul Pioneer Press,* November 13, 1969.

31 Edwin Bolton, "Isaac Stern, Skrowaczewski, Schumann: Orchestra Delights," *Minneapolis Tribune,* November 22, 1969.

32 Allan Holbert, "Isaac Stern Performs with Orchestra," *Minneapolis Tribune,* November 22, 1969.

33 Harold Schonberg, "Skrowaczewski Conducts His Own Horn Concerto," *New York Times,* April 16, 1970.

34 Ibid.

35 Ibid.

36 Mary Ann Feldman, program notes, Minnesota Orchestra (Nov. 2, 1969), 10.

37 Jack Hiemenz, "The Metropolitan Opera, *Die Zauberflöte* (January 10)," *High Fidelity/Musical America,* April 1970.

38 Arthur Satz, *High Fidelity, Musical America,* January 19, 1970.

39 Stanisław Skrowaczewski, interview by Sharon Eisenhour, Eugene Ormandy Memorial Oral History Project, October 18, 1991.

40 James Felton, "When Szeryng Was Unsurpassed," *Evening Bulletin,* July 22, 1970.

41 Ibid.

42 Ibid.

43 Richard Vincent, "George Szell 1897-1970," *Plain Dealer,* August 1, 1970.

44 Theodore Price, "Conductor, Pianist Shine with Mozart," *Akron Beacon Journal,* August 16, 1970.

Chapter 18

1 Harold Schonberg, "After Leonard Bernstein, Who?" Music, *New York Times,* December 10, 1967.

2 Helena Matheopoulos, *Maestro: Encounters with Conductors of Today* (New York: Harper & Row, 1982), 8.

3 Michael Anthony, "The Maestro Is Ready for a New Season," *Minneapolis Tribune,* October 10, 1971.

4 "Music Figures in Tribute," *New York Times,* April 7, 1971.

5 Winthrop Sargeant, "Musical Events: Good-Conduct Medals," *New Yorker,* December 1970.

6 Anthony, "The Maestro Is Ready for a New Season."

7 Ibid.

8 Luciano Berio, *Sinfonia, Eindrücke,* perf. Orchestre National De France, New Swingle Singers, dir. Pierre Boulez, liner notes, compact disc (France: Erato Records, 1992).

9 "The Swingle Singers," http://www.swinglesingers.com/media/programmes/orchestral.html (accessed May 5, 2007).

10   U Tank, U. *Haydn Cello Concertos*, Mstislav Rostropovich, perf. Academy of St. Martin in the Fields, dir. Iona Brown, liner notes, trans. Clive Williams, compact disc (Hayes Middlesex, England: EMI Records, 1987).

11   Artur Rubinstein, 1968 interview in *The Art of Piano*, DVD (NVC Arts, Warner Music Vision, 1999).

12   Barbara Flanagan, *Ovation: A Partnership Between a Great Orchestra and a Great Audience* (Minneapolis: The Minnesota Orchestra, 1977), 114.

13   Flanagan, 63.

14   Peter Franklin, s.v. "Mahler, Gustav," *Grove Music Online. Oxford Music Online*, http://www.oxfordmusiconline.com/subscriber/article/grove/music/40696 (accessed May 10, 2007).

15   Ibid.

16   Harriett Johnson, "Minnesotans Score in Mahler," *New York Post*, April 18, 1972.

17   Irving Kolodin, "A Week of Mahler and Visiting Maestros," *Stereo Review*, May 6, 1972.

18   Ibid.

19   Mary Ann Feldman, "On the Road to Fame—Our Touring Orchestra," in *Minnesota Orchestra at One Hundred* (Minneapolis: Minnesota Orchestra, 2002), 43.

20   Steven Dornfeld, "State Orchestra Is Acclaimed at Kennedy Center," *Minneapolis Tribune*, April 22, 1972.

21   Frederick E. Harris, Jr., *Conducting with Feeling* (Galesville, Maryland: Meredith Music Publications, 2001), 89-90.

22   Stephen Rubin, "Ronald Wilford: Muscle Man Behind the Maestros," *New York Times*, July 25, 1971.

23   Stanisław Skrowaczewski, letter to Ronald Wilford, February 25, 1972.

24   Ibid.

25   Louis Calta, "Hurok Concerts Ousts Sheldon Gold as Its President," *New York Times*, May 5, 1976.

26   Charles Bellows, letter to Stanisław Skrowaczewski, August 20, 1976.

Chapter 19

1   William Westbrook Burton, *Conversations about Bernstein* (New York: Oxford University Press, 1995), 73.

2   Barbara Flanagan, "If Conductor Has His Way, Concerts Won't Be Relaxing," *Minneapolis Star*, September 1, 1972.

3   Jeff Holman, "Skrowaczewski: Somehow I Don't Feel the Orchestra Means Too Much to the University," *Minnesota Daily*, January 26, 1973.

4   Ibid.

5   Lyn Farmer, "Skrowaczewski," *Minnesota Daily*, January 21, 1972.

6   Ibid.

7   Flanagan, "If Conductor Has His Way, Concerts Won't Be Relaxing."

8   N. Hoffman, "Skrowaczewski," *Minnesota Daily*, February 1969.

9   Ibid.

10   Flanagan, "If Conductor Has His Way, Concerts Won't Be Relaxing."

11   Stanisław Skrowaczewski, memo to John S. Pillsbury, Jr., Donald Engle, Richard Cisek, May 18, 1972.

12   Ibid.

13   Ibid.

14   Harold Schonberg, "Starker's Cello Debut with Philharmonic," Music, *New York Times*, October 21, 1972.

15   Harriett Johnson, "Words & Music, Skrowaczewski at Philharmonic," *New York Post*, October 20, 1972.

16   John Harvey, "Szeryng Proffers Paganini 'Prize,'" *St. Paul Pioneer Press*, November 10, 1973.

17   Raymond Ericson, "Two Novelties by Philharmonic," Music, *New York Times*, November 25, 1972.

18   Donal Henahan, "Conductor's Turn," Music, *New York Times*, April 21, 1973.

19   Lyn Farmer, Reviews, *Classic Currents*, ca. April 1973.

20   *Buffalo News*, ca. April 1973.

21   Alfred Frankenstein, "Skrowaczewski: Concerto for English Horn and Orchestra. Mayer: *Two Pastels*, Andante for Strings," *High Fidelity*, August 1972.

22   Eugene Ormandy, letter to Stanisław Skrowaczewski, February 18, 1973.

23   Ibid.

24   Henry Kramer, *Following the Beat* (n.p., 1996), 110.

25   Julie Ayer, *More Than Meets The Ear: How Symphony Musicians Made Labor History*, (Minneapolis: Syren Book Company, 2005), 174.

26   "Persistent Bioaccumulative and Toxic (PBT) Program: DDT," United States Environmental Protection Agency, http://www.epa.gov/pbt/pubs/ddt.htm (accessed May 25, 2007).

27   Kramer, 15-16.

28   William J. Nazzaro, "Stanisław Speaking...," *Sunday Bulletin* (Philadelphia), April 22, 1973.

29   Ibid.

30   Ibid.

31   Karel Husa, letter to Stanisław Skrowaczewski, May 11, 1973.

32   David Fullmer, "Karel Husa," in *A Composer's Insight*, ed. Timothy Salzman (Galesville, Maryland: Meredith Music Publications, n.d.), 72-74.

33   Ditson Award press release, Office of Public Information, Columbia University, May 3, 1973.

34   Daniel Webster, "Tucker, Merrill Share Stage at Dell," *Philadelphia Inquirer*, June 26, 1973.

35   Laurie Modell, "Conducting Sparks Mozart Program at Tanglewood," *Berkshire Eagle*, July 9, 1973.

36   Raymond Morin, "Thousands Attend Tanglewood Festival," *Worcester Telegram*, July 23, 1973.

37   Ibid.

38   R.C. Hammerich, "14,307 Beethoven Lovers Get an Earful of 'Eroica,'" *Union* (Springfield, MA), July 23, 1973.

39   Robert Finn, "Maestro Beats Rehearsal Pinch," *Cleveland Sun Messenger*, July 30, 1973.

40   Bain Murray, "Music by Bain Murray," *Cleveland Sun Messenger*, August 2, 1973.

41   Ibid.

42   *NOTES from the Cleveland Orchestra*, Special Edition, New Zealand/Australia, 1973.

43   Frederic Rogers, *Brisbane Sunday Mail*, September 22, 1973.

44   Ibid.

45   John Sinclair, *Melbourne Herald*, September 28, 1973.

Chapter 20

1   "Minnesota: A State That Works," *Time*, August 13, 1973.

2   Ibid.

3   Stanisław Skrowaczewski, letter to Peter Chrisafides, May 30, 1973.

4   Peter Chrisafides, letter to Skrowaczewski, April 20, 1973

5   "Gary Karr," http://www.garykarr.com/purchase/fr_main.html (accessed June 15, 2007).

6   Stanisław Skrowaczewski, letter to Gary Karr, January 29, 1973.

7   Gary Karr, letter to Stanisław Skrowaczewski, February 26, 1973.

8   Stanisław Skrowaczewski, letter to Larry Singer, May 30, 1973.

9   Daniel Webster, "Conductor's Door Open to Original Music," *Philadelphia Inquirer*, April 8, 1973.

10   Richard Cisek, in *Thank You Maestro*, documentary, Twin Cities Public Television, May 1979.

11   Stanisław Skrowaczewski, notes from a talk given to American music journalists, 1961.

12   Julie Ayer, *More Than Meets The Ear: How Symphony Musicians Made Labor History* (Minneapolis: Syren Book Company, 2005), 1996.

13   Harold Schonberg, "How the Philharmonic Survived the Flood; The Philharmonic," *New York Times*, May 19, 1974.

14   Stanisław Skrowaczewski, memorandum to musicians' union, ca. spring 1972.

15   Stanisław Skrowaczewski, memorandum to John S. Pillsbury, Jr., Donald Engle, Richard Cisek, January 18, 1974.

16   Ibid.

17   Stanisław Skrowaczewski, memorandum to Minnesota Orchestral Association board chairman John S. Pillsbury, Jr., and members of executive committee, February 14, 1974.

18   Roy Close, "One Hundred by Nine—The Music Directors," in *Minnesota Orchestra at One Hundred* (Minneapolis: Minnesota Orchestra, 2002), 17.

19   Stanisław Skrowaczewski, memo to Richard Cisek and Donald Engle, January 30, 1973.

20   Comments from Minnesota Orchestra audience survey, spring 1973.

21   Stanisław Skrowaczewski, letter to Mrs. F. Lindsay Power, January 28, 1974.

22   Stanisław Skrowaczewski, letter to Mr. Perry M. Wilson, Jr., January 29, 1974.

23   Audience survey, spring 1973.

24   Audience survey, 1973.

25   Austin Clarkson, s.v. "Druckman, Jacob Raphael," *Grove Music Online. Oxford Music Online*, http://www.oxfordmusiconline.com/subscriber/article/grove/music/08200 (accessed June 2007).

26   Ibid.

27   Roy Close, "Skrowaczewski Series Fills Long Need," *Minneapolis Star*, February 8, 1974.

28   Michael Anthony, "Music Review, Minnesota Orchestra," *Minneapolis Tribune*, February 9, 1974.

29   Stanisław Skrowaczewski, handwritten notes, first Exploration Concert, February 7, 1974.

30   Stanisław Skrowaczewski, handwritten notes, Exploration Concert, March 15–16, 1975.

31   Ibid.

32   Stephanie Miller, "When in Rome, Skrowaczewski Copes," *Minneapolis Tribune*, March 17, 1974.

33   Jonathan D. Kramer, program note, Cincinnati Symphony Orchestra, January 26-27, 2007.

34   Ibid.

35   M. De Schauensee, "Skrowaczewski Makes Philadelphia Opera Debut with *Magic Flute*, Philly Lyric Opera," *Evening Bulletin*, May 1, 1974.

36   Stanisław Skrowaczewski, letter to Michel Glotz, May 9, 1974.

37   Michael Anthony, Music, *Minneapolis Tribune*, May 10, 1974.

38   Stanisław Skrowaczewski, letter to Ken and Judy Dayton, May 15, 1974.

39   George Trautwein, "A Musician's Musician," in *Stanisław Skrowaczewski: 2004 Distinguished Artist* (Minneapolis: The McKnight Foundation, 2004), 28.

40   Stanisław Skrowaczewski, letter to Gianna Guggenbuhl, December 28, 1973.

41   Miller, "When in Rome, Skrowaczewski Copes."

42   David Markle, "Skrowaczewski: An Interview with David Markle, Classical Music Columnist for *Twin Citian* Magazine." *Symphony*, October 10-31, 1969.

43   Peter Altman, "Nation's Top Music Halls," *Minneapolis Star*, May 19, 1969.

44   Ibid.

45   Ibid.

46   Stanisław Skrowaczewski, memorandum to Minnesota Orchestral Association executive committee, December 29, 1972.

47   Dayton Design Philosophy on Hall, August 1973.

48   Ibid.

49   Ibid.

50   Donald L. Engle, letter to Wayne C. Johnson, April 1, 1974.

51   Peter Altman, "Hall's Opening Climaxes Decades of Hopes, Labors," *Minneapolis Star*, October 18, 1974.

52   Ibid.

53   Richard Cisek, letter to Stanisław Skrowaczewski, July 16, 1973.

54   Pamela Hill Nettleton, "Musical Values—A Community's Pride," in *Minnesota Orchestra at One Hundred* (Minneapolis: Minnesota Orchestra, 2002), 65.

55   Program book, Orchestra Hall dedication concert, October 21, 1974.

56   Harold Schonberg, "In Minneapolis, the Acoustics Are Almost Too Good to Be True," Music View, *New York Times*, November 3, 1974.

57   Michael Steinberg, "The World's Worst Concert Hall Gives Way to One of the Best," *Boston Sunday Globe*, October 27, 1974.

58   "Minneapolis Opening," Music, *Time*, November 4, 1974.

59   Harold Schonberg, "Minnesota Hall Acoustically Sound," *New York Times*, October 23, 1974.

60   Ibid.

61   Robert Commanday, *San Francisco Sunday Examiner & Chronicle,* October 1974.

62   Ken Dayton, letter to Stanisław Skrowaczewski, November 7, 1974.

63   Judson Bemis, in *Thank You Maestro*, documentary, Twin Cities Public Television, May 1979.

64   Mary Ann Feldman, "A Walk through Orchestra Hall with Cyril M. Harris," in program book, Orchestra Hall dedication concert, October 21, 1974, 9.

65   Robert Finn, "Orchestra Hall," *Plain Dealer*, October 23, 1974.

66   Feldman, 11.

67   William Littler, "Toronto's Search for a Perfect Concert Hall," *Toronto Star*, February 22, 1974.

68   Finn, "Orchestra Hall. "

69   Ibid.

70   Paul Goldberger, "Orchestra Hall's Design: A Rebuke to Red Velvet," *New York Times*, October 22, 1974.

71   John Harvey, "Superb Acoustics, Visually Exciting," *St. Paul Sunday Pioneer Press*, October 27, 1974.

72   Ibid.

73   Barbara Flanagan and Stanisław Skrowaczewski, in *Thank You Maestro*, documentary, Twin Cities Public Television, May 1979.

74   Ibid.

75   "Minneapolis Opening," Music, *Time*, November 4, 1974.

76   Steinberg, "The World's Worst Concert Hall Gives Way to One of the Best."

Chapter 21

1   Robert M. Eich, "Skrowaczewski at Ease: A Candid Interview with the Conductor of the Minnesota Orchestra," *Minnesotan,* Spring 1974.

2   Ibid.

3   Roy Close, "Behind the Public Baton Lives a Very Private Man," *Minneapolis Star*, October 18, 1974.

4   Henry Kramer, *Following the Beat* (n.p., 1996), 9.

5   Ibid.

6   Stanisław Skrowaczewski, notes for speech to Minnesota Orchestra, September 1965.

7   J.W.N. Sullivan, *Beethoven: His Spiritual Development* (London: George Allen & Unwin, 1964), 38.

8   Sullivan, 125.

9   Close, "Behind the Public Baton."

10   Kramer, 62.

11   Kramer, 63.

12   Ibid.

13   Artur Rubinstein, letter to Stanisław Skrowaczewski, February 15, 1974.

14   Max Loppert, s.v. "Rubinstein, Artur," *Grove Music Online. Oxford Music Online.* http://www
      .oxfordmusiconline.com/subscriber/article/grove/music/24054 (accessed May 9, 2007).

15   Richard Freed, "Ravel and the Orchestra," in *Ravel Complete Works for Orchestra*, Vol. II, perf.
      Minnesota Orchestra, dir. Stanisław Skrowaczewski, liner notes, compact disc (Hackensack,
      New Jersey: VoxBox, 1975, and The Moss Music Group, 1991), 4.

16   Roy Close, "Orchestra, Hall Receive High Marks at Recording," *Minneapolis Star*, November
      2, 1974.

17   Royal S. Brown, "Ravel in Minnesota: The Real Thing," *High Fidelity*, July 1975.

18   Paul Meunier, *"Ravel: All the Works for Orchestra*, perf. Minnesota Orchestra, dir. Stanisław
      Skrowaczewski (Paris: *Classiques* Télérama), July 19-25, 1975.

19   Gunther Schuller, *The Compleat Conductor* (New York: Oxford University Press, 1997), 459.

20   _____, letter to Ken Dayton (including Schuller's letter to Skrowaczewski), August 27,
      1975.

21   Bob Epstein, "Ravel," *Minnesota Daily*, April 2, 1975.

22   Enos E. Shupp, "*Handel: Water Music Suite, Royal Fireworks Music*," *The New Records,* October
      1976.

23   Christopher Morehouse, "Ivesian Borrowing, Imagery, and Place in Eric Stokes' 'The
      Continental Harp and Band Report: An American Miscellany' (1975)," Ph.D. dissertation
      (University of Cincinnati, 2005), 31.

24   Morehouse, 32.

25   Ibid.

26   Barbara Flanagan, *Ovation: A Partnership Between a Great Orchestra and a Great Audience*
      (Minneapolis: The Minnesota Orchestra, 1977), 115.

27   Ibid.

28   Stanisław Skrowaczewski, letter to George Trautwein, September 26, 1974.

29   Brian Newhouse, "Sounds of Summer," in *Minnesota Orchestra at One Hundred* (Minneapolis:
      Minnesota Orchestra, 2002), 137.

30   Stanisław Skrowaczewski, in *Thank You Maestro*, documentary, Twin Cities Public Television,
      May 1979.

31   Michael Anthony, unpublished interview with Stanisław Skrowaczewski, August 1975.

32   Ibid.

33   Stanisław Skrowaczewski, letter to John S. Pillsbury, Jr., December 9, 1974.

34   John S. Pillsbury, Jr., letter to Stanisław Skrowaczewski, December 13, 1974.

35   Yehudi Menuhin, letter to Skrowaczewski, February 26, 1975.

36   Flanagan, *Ovation,* 117.

37   Minnesota Orchestral Association, letter from Stanisław Skrowaczewski to subscribers, April
      4, 1975.

38   Ibid.

39   Feldman, note to Minnesota Orchestra musicians, September 27, 1975.

40   Michael Anthony, "Orchestra Performs World Premiere," *Minneapolis Tribune*, March 11,
      1976.

41   Ibid.

42   Michael Colgrass, email correspondence with author, February 20, 2007.

43   Vivien Schweitzer, "Once-Shy Pianist Tells, Um, Not Quite All," *New York Times,* August 3,
      2008.

44   Katherine Kolb, *Berlioz Society Bulletin* 89 (October 1975).

45   Irving Lowens, "Classical: Minnesota's Moving Mahler," *Washington Star*, April 25, 1977.

46   Stanisław Skrowaczewski, resignation letter to George T. Pennock, June 24, 1977.

Chapter 22

[1]   William Schuman, letter to Stanisław Skrowaczewski, July 25, 1977.

[2]   James Felton, *Bulletin* (Philadelphia), July 28, 1977.

[3]   Ross Tolbert, letter to Stanisław Skrowaczewski, June 27, 1977.

[4]   Basil Reeve, letter to Stanisław Skrowaczewski, July 3, 1977.

[5]   Ibid.

[6]   John W. Miller, Jr., letter to Stanisław Skrowaczewski, June 27, 1977.

[7]   Mary Ann Feldman, letter to Stanisław Skrowaczewski, June 29, 1977.

[8]   Stanisław Skrowaczewski, letter to Ross Tolbert, June 29, 1977.

[9]   Roy Close, "Minnesota Orchestra Turns 75," *High Fidelity, Musical America*, March 1978.

[10]   Bob Epstein, "An Interview with Stanisław Skrowaczewski," in *Showcase* (September 8–October 8, 1977), 1.

[11]   Ibid.

[12]   Roy Close, "One Hundred by Nine—The Music Directors," in *Minnesota Orchestra at One Hundred* (Minneapolis: Minnesota Orchestra, 2002), 18.

[13]   Cabrillo Festival of Contemporary Music, http://www.cabrillomusic.org/about/history.html (accessed November 30, 2007).

[14]   Dale Pollack, "Santa Cruz Cabrillo Music Fest Rivals European Events; Attendance Hits All-Time High," *Variety*, September 6, 1977.

[15]   Bill Akers, "Music Festival Orchestra Fashions 'Another Gem of the First Quality,'" *Register-Pajaronian* (Watsonville, CA), August 27, 1977.

[16]   Dominick Argento, letter to Stanisław Skrowaczewski, September 27, 1977.

[17]   Les Percussions de Strasbourg, http://www.percussionsdestrasbourg.com/ (accessed December 1, 2007).

[18]   Bob Epstein, "Minnesota Orchestra Offers Daring Program," *Minneapolis Tribune*, October 14, 1977.

[19]   Ibid.

[20]   Gottfried von Einem Foundation, http://www.einem.org/en/komp_ll.htm (accessed December 1, 2007).

[21]   According to Richard Cisek, Ormandy was known for his exaggerations. Ormandy's remark must be tempered by the fact that the Philadelphia Orchestra then had a marketing department. Additionally, the orchestra performed at The Robin Hood Dell and Saratoga Performing Arts Center, and was not responsible for promoting or selling tickets or raising funds for these venues. It is not accurate to compare the two orchestras in terms of administrative size; as it grew into having a year-round season, the Minnesota Orchestra had to generate more income on its own.

[22]   Eugene Ormandy, letter to Stanisław Skrowaczewski, November 12, 1977.

[23]   Doris Evans McGinty, s.v. "Fountain, Primous, III," *Grove Music Online. Oxford Music Online*, http://www.oxfordmusiconline.com/subscriber/article/grove/music/42699 (accessed November 26, 2007).

[24]   Mary Ann Feldman, "Concerto for Violin and Orchestra by K. Penderecki," program note, *Showcase*, January 7–29, 1978, 5.

[25]   Ibid.

[26]   Roy Close, "Penderecki's Work Has Worthy Premiere," *Minneapolis Star*, January 5, 1978.

[27]   Ruth Leon, letter to Stanisław Skrowaczewski, March 29, 1978.

[28]   Isaac Stern, Krzysztof Penderecki, and Stanisław Skrowaczewski, in *Tonight at Carnegie Hall*, WETA-TV, March 11, 1978.

[29]   Mary Ann Feldman, "*Ricercari Notturni* for Saxophone and Orchestra," program note, *Showcase*, January 7–29, 1978, 5.

[30]   Jerry D. Luedders, email communication with the author, December 31, 2007.

31 Feldman, "*Ricercari Notturni* for Saxophone and Orchestra."

32 Bob Epstein, "Minnesota Orchestra's Main Dish Includes Work by Skrowaczewski," *Minneapolis Tribune*, January 19, 1978.

33 Roy Close, "Write on, Stanisław, Write on," *Minneapolis Star*, November 9, 1978.

34 Ibid.

35 Michael Anthony, unpublished interview notes, April 1979.

36 Erich Leinsdorf, letter to Stanisław Skrowaczewski, November 15, 1977.

37 W.R. Sinclair, "Hallé Concert, Free Trade Hall, Skrowaczewski," *Daily Telegraph*, February 17, 1978.

38 John Robert-Blunn, "Hallé Triumph," *Manchester Evening News* (England), February 17, 1978.

39 Bob Epstein, "An Interview with Stanisław Skrowaczewski," *Showcase*, September 8-October 8, 1977, 1.

40 Martin Mayer, "Elliott Carter: Out of the Desert and into the Concert Hall," *New York Times*, December 10, 1978.

41 Ibid.

42 William Schuman, letter to Stanisław Skrowaczewski, May 4, 1979.

43 Stanisław Skrowaczewski, letter to William Schuman, May 10, 1979.

44 "Backgrounder on the Three Mile Island Accident," United States Nuclear Regulatory Commission, http://www.nrc.gov/reading-rm/doc-collections/fact-sheets/3mile-isle.html (accessed December 3, 2007).

45 Ibid.

46 Julie Ayer, *More Than Meets The Ear: How Symphony Musicians Made Labor History* (Minneapolis: Syren Book Company, 2005), 164.

47 Ibid, 165.

48 "Study Links Three Mile Island Radiation Releases to Higher Cancer Rates," *Washington Post*, February 24, 1997, A6. Online. http://www.washingtonpost.com/wp-srv/national/longterm/tmi/stories/study022497.htm (accessed December 15, 2007).

49 Michael Anthony, "Skrowaczewski Era Nears Low-Key Finale as Conductor Plans Future of 'Purely Music,'" *Minneapolis Tribune*, April 29, 1979.

50 Ibid.

51 Ibid.

52 Roy Close, "Skrowaczewski Conductor Leaving Rich Legacy," *Minneapolis Star*, May 9, 1979.

53 Ibid.

54 Feldman, "Symphony no. 8 in C minor," program note, *Showcase*, April 26–May 19, 1979, 9.

55 Richard Cisek, "Stanisław Skrowaczewski: A Tribute," program note, *Showcase*, April 26–May 19, 1979, 9.

56 Stanisław Skrowaczewski, letter to David Kamminga, May 18, 1979.

Chapter 23

1 Stanisław Skrowaczewski, letter to George T. Pennock, June 24, 1977.

2 "Debut Concert Thrills Abravanel, Patrons," *Salt Lake Tribune*, September 15, 1979.

3 Michael Anthony, "Skrowaczewski Leads St. Paul Chamber," *Minneapolis Tribune*, October 8, 1979.

4 Stanisław Skrowaczewski, letter to Saint Paul Chamber Orchestra, March 25, 1980.

5 Stanisław Skrowaczewski, speech for University of Minnesota honorary doctorate presentation, October 8, 1979.

6 Stanisław Skrowaczewski, letter to Michel Glotz, December 26, 1979.

7 Michael Anthony, "Skrowaczewski Conducts under New Title," *Minneapolis Tribune*, November 8, 1979.

8 "Mount St. Helens, *Wikipedia*, http://en.wikipedia.org/wiki/Mount_St._Helens (accessed December 12, 2007).

9 Walter Simmons, *Fanfare* 4:4 (March/April 1981).

10 Bruce Surtees, *FM Guide*, April 1981.

11 Stanisław Skrowaczewski, letter to Ira Moss, August 31, 1979.

12 Michael Kennedy, "Hallé Concert," *Daily Telegraph*, November 24, 1980.

13 Norman Davies, *Heart of Europe: The Past in Poland's Present* (Oxford: Oxford University Press, 2001), 9.

14 Piotr Wandycz, speech for the exhibit opening, *Emblem of Good Will*, Library of Congress, May 2, 1997. Online, http://www.electronicmuseum.ca/Poland-USA/usa_and_poland_2 .html (accessed December 18, 2007).

15 Davies, *Heart of Europe*, 15.

16 Wandycz, speech for the exhibit opening, *Emblem of Good Will*.

17 Dave Durenberger, letter to William E. Schaufele, Jr., February 4, 1981.

18 Dave Durenberger, letter to Charles Bellows, February 4, 1981.

19 Davies, *Heart of Europe*, 18.

20 Ibid., 16.

21 "Background Note: Poland," U.S. Department of State, http://www.state.gov/r/pa/ei /bgn/2875.htm (accessed December 18, 2007).

22 "Wojciech Jaruzelski," *Wikipedia*, http://en.wikipedia.org/wiki/Wojciech_Jaruzelski (accessed December 18, 2007).

23 Davies, *Heart of Europe*, 19.

Chapter 24

1 Michael Anthony, "Debuts and Reappearances," *High Fidelity/Musical America,* September 1981.

2 Leonard Duck, "Skrowaczewski Concerto for Clarinet in A & Orchestra," in Hallé Orchestra program book, March 27, 1983.

3 Roy Close, "New Clarinet Concerto 'Shimmers Like Moon,'" *St. Paul Pioneer Press*, April 18, 1981.

4 Edward Rothstein, "Contemporary Music: Juilliard Concerts," *New York Times*, January 25, 1983.

5 Mary Ann Feldman, "Concerto for Clarinet and Orchestra," in *Passacaglia Immaginaria, Chamber Concerto, Concerto for Clarinet in A & Orchestra*, perf. Saarbrücken Radio Symphony Orchestra, dir. Stanisław Skrowaczewski, liner notes, compact disc (Albany, NY: Albany Records, 2001), 4.

6 George Sturm, letter to Stanisław Skrowaczewski, August 18, 1980.

7 Thomas Putnam, "Conducting His Own Work Is 'No Fun' for Skrowaczewski," *Buffalo Courier-Express*, April 3, 1982.

8 Garry Spector, "Philadelphia Concert Truly Unforgettable," *Times-Union*, August 24, 1981.

9 Valerie Scher, "Orchestra Strains to Overcome Setbacks," *Philadelphia Inquirer*, January 7, 1983.

10 Jacob Siskind, "NACO Mozart Program a Sheer Delight," *Citizen Ottawa*, July 30, 1981.

11 Stanisław Skrowaczewski, letter to Emy Erede Moresco, May 7, 1979.

12 Roger Covell, "Orchestra Shines under Polish Conductor's Hand," *Sydney Morning Herald*, November 9, 1981.

13 Michael Kennedy, *The Hallé 1858–1983: A History of the Orchestra* (Manchester, England: Manchester University Press, 1982), 7.

14 Robert Beale, *Music, Money, Maestros & Management: The Hallé, A British Orchestra in the 20th Century* (Manchester, England: Forsyth Brothers Limited, 2000), 78.

15 Debbie Blakeley, press release, Minnesota Orchestra, February 8, 1983.

16   Michael Kennedy, "Hallé Concert/Bruckner's 7th," *Daily Telegraph*, September 28, 1984.

Chapter 25

1   "Stan Musial," *Wikipedia*, http://en.wikipedia.org/wiki/Stan_Musial (accessed February 19, 2008).
2   George Sturm, letter to Stanisław Skrowaczewski, February 28, 1983.
3   David Skillrud, letter to Stanisław Skrowaczewski, November 15, 1983.
4   Stanisław Skrowaczewski, letter to David Skillrud, November 17, 1983.
5   David Fallows, "Hallé," *Guardian*, February 17, 1984.
6   Hugh Canning, "Nurturing a Close Relationship with the Public: Hugh Canning Meets the Hallé's New Principal Conductor Stanisław Skrowaczewski," *Classical Music*, July 1984.
7   Ibid.
8   Stephen McClarence, "Bringing Dash to the Hallé," *Doncaster Star*, International Press-Cutting Bureau, *Sheffielder*, February 27, 1984.
9   Daniel Webster, "Orchestra Opens Its Summer Series at the Mann," Music, *Philadelphia Inquirer*, June 19, 1984.
10   _____, "Skrowaczewski Conducts Lutosławski Concerto," Music, *Philadelphia Inquirer*, June 20, 1984.
11   Jeffrey Babcock, letter to Stanisław Skrowaczewski, July 30, 1984.
12   Michael Tilson Thomas, letter to Stanisław Skrowaczewski, August 21, 1984.
13   Stephen Pettitt, "Concert Take Note: Celebrate Philharmonica/Skrowaczewski at Albert Hall," *Times*, Radio 3 Announcement, September 15, 1984.
14   Michael Kennedy, "Hallé Concert/Bruckner's Seventh," *Daily Telegraph*, September 28, 1984.
15   "Yanks Coming to the Hallé," *Manchester Evening News*, September 19, 1984.
16   Ibid.
17   Michael Kennedy, "Hallé Concert/Bruckner's Seventh," *Daily Telegraph*, September 28, 1984.
18   Stanisław Skrowaczewski, notes for Hallé Orchestra program book, September 1984.
19   Paula Radcliffe, "An Interview with Skrowaczewski," *Hallé News: The Journal of the Hallé Concerts Society*, December 1984.
20   Ibid.
21   Ibid.
22   "Arts Council of Great Britain: Records, 1928–1997," Victoria and Albert Museum, http://www.vam.ac.uk/vastatic/wid/ead/acgb/acgbb.html (accessed March 20, 2008).
23   Robert Beale, *Music, Money, Maestros & Management: The Hallé, A British Orchestra in the 20th Century* (Manchester, England: Forsyth Brothers Limited, 2000), 147.
24   Beale, 152.
25   Beale, 153.
26   Beale, 79.
27   Ibid.
28   Clive Smart, letter to Stanisław Skrowaczewski, January 24, 1985.
29   Stanisław Skrowaczewski, letter to Clive Smart, January 31, 1985.
30   Michael Kennedy, "Hallé Concert/Messiaen, Brahms," *Daily Telegraph*, April 26, 1985.
31   Judith Kogan, *Nothing but the Best: The Struggle for Perfection at the Juilliard School* (New York: Random House, 1987), 186, 190-193.
32   Bernard Holland, "Concert: Mozart Pieces For Clarinet and Piano," *New York Times*, August 4, 1985.
33   Stanisław Skrowaczewski, letter to Ronald Wilford, February 1, 1985.
34   Ronald Wilford, letter to Stanisław Skrowaczewski, March 11, 1985.
35   Michael Kennedy, "Michael Kennedy Previews the 128th Season: The Most Important for Years," *Hallé Orchestra 1985–86 Yearbook*.
36   Ibid.

37   Beale, 196.

38   Lutosławski—the Great Debate," letters in *Hallé News, The Journal of the Hallé Concerts Society,* May 1986.

39   John Robert-Blunn, "Not Completely Satisfied," *Manchester Evening News,* October 9, 1985.

40   "Hallé/Skrowaczewski Festival Hall," Concerts, *Times,* May 2, 1986.

41   Daniel Webster, "Second Chamber Concert," Music, *Philadelphia Inquirer,* December 12, 1985.

42   *Musical America,* December 1985

43   "Limelight, Casually Classical," *Washington Post,* June 2, 1985.

44   Bernard Jacobson, "Concerto for Violin and Orchestra," program note, Philadelphia Orchestra program book, December 5, 1985.

45   Daniel Webster, "Violinist Gets a Custom-made Concert: For Norman Carol, a Very Special Twentieth Anniversary," Music, *Philadelphia Inquirer,* December 8, 1985.

46   Michael Walsh and N. Newman, "Making the Strings Sing Again, Six New Concertos Offer a Lively Survey of Modern Styles," Music, *Time,* May 19, 1986.

47   Ibid.

48   Roy Close, "Skrowaczewski Concerto Debuts," *St. Paul Pioneer Press and Dispatch,* December 29, 1985.

49   Michael Anthony, "Skrowaczewski Unveils Orchestra Concerto," *Star Tribune,* January 3, 1986.

Chapter 26

1   David Murray, "Hallé Orchestra/Festival Hall," *Financial Times,* May 13, 1987.

2   Michael Kennedy, "Mahler and Mozart," *Daily Telegraph,* May 8, 1987.

3   Jane Fickling, "Stan's New Hallé Hoops," *Cheshire Life* (Manchester, England), October 1986.

4   Michael Kennedy, "The Hallé Is the Talk of Charleston," *Daily Telegraph,* March 20, 1987.

5   Michael Owen, "Friday People in New York," *Evening Standard,* March 13, 1987.

6   Alistair Cooke, "A Fond Look at an English Orchestra," *New York Times,* March 8, 1987.

7   Bernard Holland, "Britain's Hallé Orchestra at Carnegie Hall," Music, *New York Times,* March 10, 1987.

8   David Dunlap, "Carnegie Hall Grows the Only Way It Can; Burrowing into Bedrock, Crews Carve Out a New Auditorium," *New York Times,* January 30, 2000.

9   Hilary Finch, "Hallé/Skrowaczewski, Barbican," *Times* (London), February 17, 1987.

10   Ibid.

11   Tim Page, "Concert: Bruckner by Philharmonic," *New York Times,* March 30, 1987.

12   John Rockwell, "Girl, Fourteen, Conquers Tanglewood with Three Violins," *New York Times,* July 28, 1986.

13   Marcel Grilli, "Symphony Orchestra and an Unusual Performance," *Japan Times,* June 14, 1987.

14   Josef Gingold, telegram to Stanisław Skrowaczewski, August 6, 1987.

Chapter 27

1   Roy Close, "Skrowaczewski Gets Encore from SPCO," *St. Paul Pioneer Press and Dispatch,* November 6, 1986.

2   John Michel, "After Pinky: An Interview with Stanisław Skrowaczewski," broadcast, Minnesota Public Radio, February 1987.

3   "Claudio Arrau," *Wikipedia,* http://en.wikipedia.org/wiki/Claudio_Arrau (accessed June 12, 2008).

4   Michael Fleming, "Orchestra Plays for Conductor It Reveres," *St. Paul Pioneer Press and Dispatch,* May 14, 1988.

5   Michael Anthony, "Skrowaczewski Conducts Farewell Concert with St. Paul Orchestra," *Star Tribune,* May 16, 1988.

6   Stanisław Skrowaczewski, letter to *Star Tribune,* ca. 1988.

7   John Robert-Blunn, "Hallé Concert," *Manchester Evening News,* May 3, 1988.

8   Lesley Valdes, "An Old Friend Soothes the Orchestra's Psyche: Enthusiasm for Skrowaczewski Rules," *Philadelphia Inquirer,* August 10, 1988.

9   Ibid.

10   Ibid.

11   Ibid.

12   Ibid.

13   Ibid.

14   Don Metivier, "Maestro Introduces Song in Lake Luzerne," *Post-Star* (Glens Falls, NY), August 17, 1988.

15   Ron Emery, "Rousing Opening by Philly," *Times Union* (Albany, NY), August 12, 1988.

Chapter 28

1   Terry Grimley, "Beyond the Free Trade Hall," *Classical Music* 3, September 1988.

2   Ibid.

3   Michael Kennedy, "The Band Is Back in Business," *Daily Telegraph,* December 13, 1988.

4   Leonard G. Carpenter, letter to Stanisław Skrowaczewski, January 16, 1989.

5   Stanisław Skrowaczewski, letter to Leonard G. Carpenter, January 18, 1989.

6   The Hallé had historical ties to Berlioz's innovative score. In 1879 the Hallé, led by its founder, Sir Charles Hallé, a friend of the composer, presented the first performances of *Symphonie fantastique* in Britain.

7   Clive Smart, letter to Stephen Lumsden, July 27, 1988.

8   *CD Review* (London), April 1989.

9   Gunther Schuller, *The Compleat Conductor* (New York: Oxford University Press, 1997), 401.

10   Schuller, 288.

11   Michael Kennedy, *The Hallé 1858–1983: A History of the Orchestra* (Manchester, England: Manchester University Press, 1982), 6.

12   John Robert-Blunn, "My Hallé Dream: Why I Was About to Quit, by Conductor Stanisław Skrowaczewski," *Manchester Evening News,* May 2, 1989.

13   Robert Beale, *Music, Money, Maestros & Management: The Hallé, A British Orchestra in the 20th Century* (Manchester, England: Forsyth Brothers Limited, 2000), 87.

14   Daniel Webster, "Van Cliburn, Philadelphia Orchestra," *Musical America,* September 1989.

15   W.L. Gay, "The Conductor," *Fort Worth Star-Telegram,* June 7, 1989.

16   Anthony Tommasini, "Van Cliburn Winner Lets Loose at Great Woods," *Boston Globe,* July 28, 1989.

17   Alan Rich, "A Splendid Soirée at the Hollywood Bowl," *Los Angeles Herald Examiner,* August 31, 1989.

18   Beale, 90.

19   Beale, 91.

20   Beale, 88.

21   Beale, 158.

22   Beale, 90.

23   Clive Smart, letter to Stephen Lumsden, January 4, 1989.

24   Stanisław Skrowaczewski, letter to Sebastian de Ferranti, December 6, 1989.

25   Ibid.

26   Ibid.

27   Beale, 91.

Chapter 29

1   Sebastien de Ferranti and Clive Smart, "Hallé Orchestra Announces That Stanisław Skrowaczewski Will Not Be Seeking an Extension of His Current Contract After 31st July 1991," press release, Hallé Orchestra, January 18, 1990.

2   Ellen Pfeifer, "BSO Conductor Comes Through," *Boston Herald*, January 13, 1990.

3   Richard Dyer, "Skrowaczewski's Honest Work with BSO," *Boston Globe*, January 12, 1990.

4   David Murray, "Hallé Orchestra, Barbican Hall," *Financial Times* (London), February 13, 1990.

5   Gerald Larner, "Baton Change," *Guardian* (Manchester, England), February 1, 1990.

6   John Robert-Blunn, "My Hallé Dream: Why I Was About to Quit, by Conductor Stanisław Skrowaczewski," *Manchester Evening News*, May 2, 1989.

7   Michael Kennedy, "Hallé's Troubled Maestro Makes Decision to Quit," *Daily Telegraph* (London), January 19, 1990.

8   Michael Anthony, "No Time for Nostalgia: World Podiums Lure Skrowaczewski, Who's Leaving Hallé Job," *Star Tribune*, April 6, 1990.

9   Industrial music, a broad term that originated during the mid-1970s, refers to various experimental music: electronic, noise, or ambient, and production techniques that manipulate or create various sounds. "Industrial" also may include performance art, installations, and other alternative-art productions.

10 Stanisław Skrowaczewski, "Letter from Principal Conductor," program book, Hallé Orchestra, September 1989.

11 G. Kay, "First Desk," *Classical Music,* November 18, 1989.

12 Robert Beale, *Music, Money, Maestros & Management: The Hallé, A British Orchestra in the 20th Century* (Manchester, England: Forsyth Brothers Limited, 2000), 131.

13 Anthony, "No Time for Nostalgia."

14 *Kronenzeitung Linz*, May 5, 1990.

15 Richard Cisek, letter to Stanisław Skrowaczewski, July 30, 1990.

16 John Robert-Blunn, "Hallé, Free Trade Hall," *Manchester Evening News*, October 5, 1990.

17 Camilla Panufnik, letter to Stanisław Skrowaczewski, ca. 1997.

18 Stanisław Skrowaczewski, letter to Judith McElhatton, May 1991.

19 Michael Anthony, "Minnesota Orchestra Ex-Director Has Gem in New Composition," *Star Tribune*, May 26, 1991.

20 "Luciano Berio, *Rendering*," in *Classical Music, The Rough Guide,* ed. J. Staines and J. Buckley (London: Penguin Books, 1998).

21 Beale, 78.

22 Michael Kennedy, "Tribute to Clive Smart," program book, Hallé Orchestra, April 18, 1991.

23 _____, "An Ideal Partnership," *Daily Telegraph* (London), April 24, 1991.

24 Ibid.

25 Michael Kennedy, "An Appreciation," program book, Hallé Orchestra, May 2, 1991.

Chapter 30

1   Kenneth Bayliss, letter to Stanisław Skrowaczewski, February 9, 1990.

2   Stanisław Skrowaczewski, letter to Stewart Warkow, May 24, 1991.

3   "Encounters by George Sturm: Stuart Warkow," Music Associates of America, http://www.musicassociatesofamerica.com/madamina/encounters/warkow.html (accessed 16 Aug. 2008).

4   Brian Couzens, letter to Stephen Lumsden, October 12, 1990.

5   M.E.O., "Shostakovich Symphony 5," *Gramophone,* August 1991.

6   D.J.F., "Shostakovich Symphony Ten," *Gramophone,* October 1991.

7   Ian MacDonald, "Mahler's Worlds," *Classic CD,* March 1992.

8   Jerry Fox, "Bartók Concerto for Orchestra," *American Record Guide,* March/April 1993.

9   Stanisław Skrowaczewski, "Triple Concerto," program note, Honolulu Symphony, April 19, 1992.

10   Armand Russell, "Letters to the Editor," *Honolulu Star-Bulletin,* April 25, 1992.

11   Lloyd Smith, Rheta Smith and Diane Gold, letter to Stanisław Skrowaczewski, September 16, 1992.

12   Henry Kramer, 1996. *Following the Beat,* (n.p., 1996), 29-30.

13   Stanisław Skrowaczewski, "Chamber Concerto (*Ritornelli poi ritornelli*)," program note, Saint Paul Chamber Orchestra, November 26, 1993.

14   The Ordway Music Theatre was renamed the Ordway Center for the Performing Arts in 2000.

15   Tad Simons, "Skrowaczewski Leads SPCO on a Pleasant Trip Backward in Time," *St. Paul Pioneer Press*, November 27, 1993.

16   Allan Kozinn, "Stephen J. Albert, 51, Composer; Won a Pulitzer for His 'Riverrun,'" *New York Times*, December 29, 1992.

17   Ilse Zadrozny, "Skrowaczewski's Direction Is an Inspiration," *Montréal Gazette*, August 3, 1992.

18   "Curriculum Vitae," Witold-K, http://www.witoldk.com/about.htm (accessed August 20, 2008).

19   Michael Anthony, "Orchestra Will Play an Encore of 1903," *Star Tribune*, November 7, 1993.

20   Michael Smith, "Heaven, Hell, and Bruckner," *Age* (Melbourne), June 1, 1994.

21   Nancy Raabe, "MSO Program Breaks Some Barriers," *Milwaukee Journal Sentinel*, April 10, 1994.

22   Gerald Larner, "Concerts: Witold Lutosławski Remembered; Fitting Polish Tribute," *Times*, March 23, 1994.

23   Richard Buell, "Emboldened Bruckner, Savvy Strings," *Boston Globe*, December 13, 1994.

Chapter 31

1   Milwaukee Symphony Orchestra, http://www.mso.org/main.taf?p=2,1,4 (accessed December 12, 2008).

2   Tom Strini, "A Gracious Master," *Milwaukee Journal Sentinel*, September 10, 1995.

3   Ibid.

4   Ibid.

5   "Every Program Is a Highlight," in Milwaukee Symphony Orchestra program book, September 1995.

6   Strini, "Skrowaczewski a Key to MSO's Strength," *Milwaukee Journal Sentinel,* June 12, 1997.

7   Mary Ann Feldman, "Passacaglia Immaginaria," program note, *Showcase*, April 1996.

8   Michael Fleming, "Variety, Passion Mark Program," *St. Paul Pioneer Press*, April 11, 1996.

9   Ibid.

10   Gunther Schuller, letter to Stanisław Skrowaczewski, March 3, 1997.

11   Mary Ann Feldman, "Bruckner Symphony 9" in *Bruckner Symphony 9*, perf. Minnesota Orchestra, dir. Skrowaczewski, liner notes, compact disc (San Francisco: Reference Recordings, 1997).

12   Lawrence Hansen, "Bruckner Ninth Symphony," *American Record Guide,* July/August 1998.

13   Stanisław Skrowaczewski, unpublished interview by Michael Anthony, November 4, 1998.

14   Skrowaczewski, unpublished interview by Michael Anthony, November 5, 1999.

15   Ibid.

16   Kenneth N. Dayton, letter to Michael O'Keefe, September 7, 1998.

17   George "Jake" Jaquith, letter to Stanisław Skrowaczewski, November 11, 1998.

18   Skrowaczewski, unpublished interview with Michael Anthony, November 4, 1998.

19   Michael Anthony, "Grand Stan," *Star Tribune*, November 22, 1998.

20   Skrowaczewski, unpublished interview with Anthony, November 4, 1998.

21   Steinberg, husband of former Minnesota Orchestra concertmaster Jorja Fleezanis, died July 26, 2009.

22   Skrowaczewski, unpublished interview with Anthony, November 4, 1998.

23   Anthony, "Grand Stan."

24   Skrowaczewski, unpublished interview with Anthony, November 4, 1998.

25   Ibid.

26   Anthony, "Grand Stan."

27   Ibid.

28   Skrowaczewski, unpublished interview with Anthony, November 4, 1998.

29   Robert Beale, *Music, Money, Maestros & Management: The Hallé, A British Orchestra in the 20th Century* (Manchester, England: Forsyth Brothers Limited, 2000), 103, 133, 166.

30   Beale, 103.

31   Michael Kennedy, *The Hallé 1858-1983: A History of the Orchestra* (Manchester, England: Manchester University Press, 1982), 6.

32   Beale, "Abraham Moss Memorial Concert, Bridgewater Hall," *Manchester Evening News*, November 1, 1996.

33   Kennedy, program note, Hallé Orchestra booklet, January 20, 2000.

34   Anthony, unpublished, April 1998.

35   Richard Dyer, "Skrowaczewski Excels as Conductor, Composer," *Boston Globe*, January 25, 1996.

36   _____, "Inspiring Season Finale," *Boston Globe*, May 1, 1998.

Chapter 32

1   "Arts & Entertainment: Best of the Twin Cities," *Minneapolis/St. Paul Magazine*, May 3, 2000.

2   Michael Anthony, "Skrowaczewski Proves He's One for the Ages," *Star Tribune*, October 6, 2000.

3   John Robert-Blunn, "Music at Bridgewater Hall: Hallé, Skrowaczewski, Goode," *Manchester Charivari* (England), December 2001.

4   Frederick E. Harris, Jr., "The Communication of Musical Feeling and Its Implications for Teaching Conductors," Ph.D. dissertation (University of Minnesota, 1999), 264.

5   Howard Smith, "Top Ten Discs of the Decade," *BBC Magazine*, November 2002.

6   David Hurwitz, "Complete Bruckner Symphonies," *Classics Today*, June 2001.

7   Stanisław Skrowaczewski, unpublished interview by Michael Anthony, September 17, 2002.

8   Ibid.

9   Paul Snook, "Skrowaczewski's World: Chamber Music of Stanisław Skrowaczewski," *Fanfare*, January/February 2003.

10   "About Dr. H.R. Axelrod," Axelrod Institute of Icthyology, http://www.axelfish.uoguelph.ca /about_axel.html (accessed January 17, 2009).

11   Michael Anthony, "Wednesday Nights at 7:30," *Star Tribune*, September 8, 2002.

12   _____, "Satirical Lover Once Sang Mr. Skrowaczewski's Praises," *Star Tribune*, October 20, 2002.

13   Brian Newhouse, "Minnesota Orchestra at 100," Minnesota Public Radio broadcast, November 2003.

14   Ibid.

15   Anthony Ross, on "Minnesota Orchestra at 100," hosted by Brian Newhouse, Minnesota Public Radio broadcast, November 2003.

16   Mary Ann Feldman, "Symphony [2003] Stanisław Skrowaczewski," program note, *Showcase*, October 2–3, 2003.

17   Ibid.

18   Ibid.

19   Christoph Schlüren, "Symphony [2003]" in *Stanisław Skrowaczewski, The Composer, Music at Night*, perf. Deutsche Radio Philharmonie, dir. Skrowaczewski, liner notes, compact disc (Munich: Oehms Classics, 2008), 15.

20   The original published quote said fifty years, but Skrowaczewski requested it be augmented to 100.

21   Michael Anthony, "Gloomy, Not Crying," *Star Tribune*, September 28, 2003.

22   Skrowaczewski, unpublished interview by Michael Anthony, September 16, 2003.

23   Anthony, "Gloomy, Not Crying."

24   Ibid.

25   Skrowaczewski, unpublished interview, September 16, 2003.

26   Feldman, "Symphony [2003] Stanisław Skrowaczewski."

27   Ibid.

Chapter 33

1   Associated Press, "Amity Is Voiced by Shostakovich," *New York Times*, October 25, 1959.

2   Stanisław Skrowaczewski, interview by Brian Duffie, produced for WNIB (Chicago), October 3, 1987.

3   Stanisław Skrowaczewski, unpublished interview notes by Michael Anthony, April 1979.

4   Gunther Schuller, *Musings: The Musical Worlds of Gunther Schuller* (New York: Oxford University Press, 1986), 174.

5   Henry Kramer, letter to Stanisław Skrowaczewski, February 6, 1989.

6   Stanisław Skrowaczewski, interview by Waldemarem Miksa for "Through Music, I Commune with the Universe," in *Stanisław Skrowaczewski, Concerto for Orchestra, Brahms Symphony No. 4*, perf. National Polish Radio Symphony Orchestra in Katowice, dir. Skrowaczewski, CD liner notes (Warsaw: Polskie Radio SA, 2003), 21–22.

7   Randall Meyers, letter to Stanisław Skrowaczewski, August 26, 2004.

Chapter 34

1   Michael Anthony, "Gloomy, Not Crying," *Star Tribune*, September 28, 2003.

2   Polish Music Reference Center, University of Southern California, newsletter, March 1999. http://www.usc.edu/dept/polish_music/news/mar99.html (accessed May 12, 2009).

3   Kenneth LaFave, "Conductor Laments Lack of National Styles," *Arizona Republic*, April 19, 1998.

4   Markus Waldura, "Deutsche Radio Philharmonie Saarbrücken Kaiserslautern," in *Schumann Symphonies One & Four*, perf. Deutsche Radio Philharmonie, dir. Skrowaczewski, liner notes, compact disc (Munich: Oehms Classics, 2007)

5   "Tokyo Bunka Kaikan," *Onmyako Magazine*, Summer 2004.

6   Neal Cuthbert, "About the Award," *Stanisław Skrowaczewski: 2004 Distinguished Artist* (Minneapolis: The McKnight Foundation, 2004), 46.

7   John Harbison, in *Stanisław Skrowaczewski: 2004 Distinguished Artist* (Minneapolis: The McKnight Foundation, 2004), 35.

8   Stanisław Skrowaczewski, "Stanisław Skrowaczewski on This Recording," in *Beethoven Symphonies Nos. 1-9*, perf. Saarbrücken Radio Symphony Orchestra, dir. Skrowaczewski, liner notes, compact disc (Munich: Oehms Classics, 2007), 9-10.

9   Jerry Fox, "Beethoven Symphony No. 9," *American Record Guide*, September/October 2006.

10   Jerry Dubins, "Beethoven Ninth, Skrowaczewski," *Fanfare*, November/December 2006.

11   David Hurwitz, "Beethoven First and Fourth Symphonies," *Classics Today*, July 2007, http://www.classicstoday.com/review.asp?ReviewNum=11078 (accessed July 23, 2007).

12   Stanisław Skrowaczewski, unpublished interview by Michael Anthony, June 29, 2004.

13   Andrew Pincus, "Of Beauty and War," *Berkshire Eagle*, August 7, 2005.

14   Allan Kozinn, "Composers in a Five-Day Berkshires Jamboree," *New York Times*, August 10, 2005.

15   Elliott Carter, letter to Skrowaczewski, August 9, 2005.

16   Larry Fuchsberg, "Skrowaczewski Conducts Bruckner with Grace, Finesse," *Star Tribune*, Oct 7, 2005.

17   Rob Hubbard, "Orchestra Delivers a Brilliant Bruckner with Power and Pathos," *St. Paul Pioneer Press*, October 7, 2005.

Chapter 35

1   George Sturm, letter to Stanisław Skrowaczewski, December 16, 2005.

2   "Progressive Supranuclear Palsy Fact Sheet," National Institute of Neurological Disorders and Stroke, National Institutes of Health, http://www.ninds.nih.gov/disorders/psp/detail_psp.htm (accessed May 24, 2009).

3   Beverly Kees, "Italian Salad Plant Thrives in Conductor's Wayzata Garden," *Minneapolis Star*, November 19, 1969.

4   Ibid.

5   Ibid.

6   "A Look at Classical Music in Japan," FanFaire webzine, http://www.fanfaire.com/japan/japanmusicmain.html (accessed June 10, 2009).

7   Ibid.

8   Stanisław Skrowaczewski, letter to Shinzo Yoshida, September 3, 2007.

9   Eric Bromberger, "Stanisław Skrowaczewski, *Fantasie per Flauto ed Orchestra, Il Piffero della Notte* (The Piper in the Night)," program note, *Showcase*, October 2007.

10   "Severino Gazzelloni; Flutist, 73," *New York Times*, November 24, 1992.

11   Christoph Schlüren, "*Fantasie per Flauto ed Orchestra* (2007)," trans. Janet and Michael Berridge, in *Stanisław Skrowaczewski, The Composer, Music at Night*, perf. Deutsche Radio Philharmonie, dir. Stanisław Skrowaczewski, liner notes, compact disc (Munich: Oehms Classics, 2008), 16-17.

12   Bromberger, "Stanisław Skrowaczewski, *Fantasie per Flauto ed Orchestra.*"

13   Adam Kuenzel, video interview. Online, http://www.minnesotaorchestra.org/ (accessed October 15, 2007).

14   Bromberger, "Stanisław Skrowaczewski, *Fantasie per Flauto ed Orchestra.*"

15   Larry Fuchsberg, "New Skrowaczewski Flute Concerto a Marvel," *Star Tribune*, October 19, 2007.

16   Ibid.

17   Stanisław Skrowaczewski, letter to Edmund Szeliga, July 15, 2008.

Chapter 36

1   The L'viv Theatre of Opera and Ballet, http://www.lvivopera.org/ (accessed June 2, 2009).

2   "Lychakiv Cemetery," http://www.lvivtourist.com/pamyatky-en/26-lychakovske-kladovishhe-en.htm (accessed June 2, 2009).

3   Ibid.

4   Ibid.

Postscript

1   Roy Close, "One Hundred by Nine—The Music Directors," in *Minnesota Orchestra at One Hundred* (Minneapolis: Minnesota Orchestra, 2002), 18.

2   Ibid.

3   Close, "One Hundred by Nine—The Music Directors."

EPIGRAPH SOURCES

Chapter 1 Metaphysical Shivers
Stanisław Skrowaczewski, "The Resurrection of the Invisible," *Showcase*, October 1974, 7.

Chapter 2 Entering the Temple
Stanisław Skrowaczewski, "The Light of Our Eye," *Symphony*, October 1968.

Chapter 3 State of Occupation
Robert Rhodes James, "War Speech, September 3, 1939, House of Commons," *Winston S. Churchill: His Complete Speeches 1897-1963*, vol. 6 (New York: Bowker, 1974).

Chapter 4 The Underground
Quote from author interview.

Chapter 5 Formal Education
Quote from author interview.

Chapter 6 Paris
Léonie Rosenstiel, *Nadia Boulanger: A Life in Music* (New York: Norton & Company, Inc., 1982), 350.

Chapter 7 Maturation
Quote from author interview.

Chapter 8 Open Doors
Quote from author interview.

Chapter 9 Electrifying the States
Herbert Elwell, "Polish Conductor Electrifies Severance Hall," *The Plain Dealer* [Cleveland], December 18, 1959.

Chapter 10 We Build Instead of Merely Dwell
Chapter title: Stanisław Skrowaczewski, in *Ovation: A Partnership between a Great Orchestra and a Great Audience,* by Barbara Flanagan (Minneapolis: The Minnesota Orchestra, 1977), 11.

Chapter quotation: Mary Ann Feldman, "The Spirit of Enterprise," in *Minnesota Orchestra at One Hundred: A Collection of Recordings and Broadcasts*, CD booklet (Minneapolis: Minnesota Orchestra, 2003), 10.

Chapter 11 **Oasis of the North**
Barbara Flanagan, *Ovation: A Partnership between a Great Orchestra and a Great Audience* (Minneapolis: The Minnesota Orchestra, 1977), 55.

Chapter 12 **Settling In**
Stanisław Skrowaczewski, "Maestro Dips Baton for Women–Open Letter to WAMSO Members," *Minneapolis Tribune*, November 9, 1961.

Chapter 13 **Minneapolis Maestro**
Arthur M. Schlesinger, Jr., *A Thousand Days: John F. Kennedy in the White House* (London: Mayflower-Dell, 1965), 926.

Chapter 14 **Big Five Plus One?**
Stanisław Skrowaczewski, letter to Dr. Mohammed H. Siddiqui, September 16, 1964.

Chapter 15 **What's in a Name?**
John Sherman, *Music and Maestros: The Story of the Minneapolis Symphony Orchestra* (Minneapolis: Lund Press, 1952), 299.

Chapter 16 **Reemergence**
Quote from author interview.

Chapter 17 **Beating the Drum**
David Markle, "Skrowaczewski: An Interview with David Markle, Classical Music Columnist for *Twin Citian* Magazine," *Symphony*, October 10-31, 1969.

Chapter 18 **Modulations**
Roy Close, "Skrowaczewski: Behind the Public Baton Lives a Very Private Man," *Minneapolis Star*, October 18, 1974.

Chapter 19 *Allegro energico, ma non troppo*
Barbara Flanagan, "If Conductor Has His Way, Concerts Won't Be Relaxing," *Minneapolis Star*, September 1, 1972.

Chapter 20 **Resurrection of the Invisible**
Stanisław Skrowaczewski, "The Resurrection of the Invisible," program booklet, Orchestra Hall dedication concert, October 21, 1974.

Chapter 21 **Ending with a Beginning**
T.S. Eliot, *Four Quartets* (Orlando: Houghton Mifflin Harcourt, 1968).

Chapter 22 **Toward New Vistas**
"Skrowaczewski's Contributions Not Ending," *Minneapolis Tribune*, May 9, 1979.

Chapter 23 **Homecoming**
Quote from author interview.

Chapter 24 **Call from Across the Pond**
David Fanning, "Hallé/Skrowaczewski," *The Guardian* (Manchester), October 25, 1983.

Chapter 25 **Stan the Man**
Quote from author interview.

Chapter 26 **Tours de Force**
Alistair Cooke, "A Fond Look at an English Orchestra," *The New York Times*, March 8, 1987.

Chapter 27 **Being Heard**
Ron Emery, "Pray for Cool as Orchestra Enters SPAC," *Sunday Times Union* (Albany, N.Y.), July 8, 1988.

Chapter 28 **The Price of Integrity**
Stanisław Skrowaczewski, "Letter from the Principal Conductor," in program book, Hallé Orchestra, September 1988.

Chapter 29 **An Appreciation**
John Robert-Blunn, "Grand Finale," *Manchester Evening News,* May 2, 1991.

Chapter 30 **Anton's Ascent**
Michael Smith, "Heaven, Hell, and Bruckner," *The Age* (Melbourne), June 1, 1994.

Chapter 31 **Seven Good Ears**
Gunther Schuller, *The Compleat Conductor* (New York: Oxford University Press, 1997), 17-18.

Chapter 32 **Life Bells**
Michael Anthony, "Skrowaczewski's New Work Resonates," *Star Tribune,* October 3, 2003.

Chapter 33 **Communing with the Universe**
Jonathan Cott, *Stockhausen: Conversations with the Composer* (New York: Simon & Schuster, 1973), 53.

Chapter 34 **Where the Word Ends**
Gunther Schuller, interviewed by Brian Bell, WGBH Radio, broadcast of *Where the Word Ends*, February 6, 2009.

Chapter 35 **Natural Phenomenon**

Larry Fuchsberg, "New Skrowaczewski Flute Concerto a Marvel," *Star Tribune*, October 19, 2007.

SELECTED BIBLIOGRAPHY

Books

Ayer, Julie. *More Than Meets The Ear: How Symphony Musicians Made Labor History* (Minneapolis: Syren Book Company, 2005).

Beale, Robert. *Music, Money, Maestros & Management: The Hallé, a British Orchestra in the 20th Century* (Manchester, England: Forsyth Brothers Limited, 2000).

Burton, Humphrey. *Leonard Bernstein* (New York: Doubleday, 1994).

Burton, William Westbrook. *Conversations about Bernstein* (New York: Oxford University Press, 1995).

Cott, Jonathan. *Stockhausen: Conversations with the Composer* (New York: Simon & Schuster, 1973).

Davies, Norman. *Heart of Europe: The Past in Poland's Present* (Oxford: Oxford University Press, 2001).

————. *Rising '44: The Battle for Warsaw* (New York: Viking, Penguin Group, 2004).

Eliot, T.S. *Four Quartets* (Orlando: Houghton Mifflin Harcourt, 1968).

Flanagan, Barbara. *Ovation: A Partnership Between a Great Orchestra and a Great Audience* (Minneapolis: The Minnesota Orchestra, 1977).

Fullmer, David. "Karel Husa." In *A Composer's Insight*, edited by Timothy Salzman. Galesville, Maryland: Meredith Music Publications, n.d.

Gilbert, Martin. *A History of the Twentieth Century, Volume Two: 1933-1951* (New York: Avon Books, Inc., 1998).

Harris, Frederick E., Jr. *Conducting with Feeling* (Galesville, Maryland: Meredith Music Publications, 2001).

Hyslop, Sandra, and Gwen Pappas, eds. *Minnesota Orchestra at One Hundred* (Minneapolis: Minnesota Orchestra, 2002).

Kennedy, Michael. *The Hallé 1858–1983: A History of the Orchestra* (Manchester, England: Manchester University Press, 1982).

Kogan, Judith. *Nothing but the Best: The Struggle for Perfection at the Juilliard School* (New York: Random House, 1987).

Kramer, Henry. *Following the Beat* (Publisher s.n., 1996).

Lebrecht, Norman. *Who Killed Classical Music?* (New York: Carol Publishing Group, Secaucus, 1997).

Malatyńska-Stankiewicz, Agnieszka. *I Was in Heaven: Conversations with Stanisław Skrowaczewski* (Kraków: Polskie Wydawnictwo Muzyczne SA, 2000).

Matheopoulos, Helena. *Maestro: Encounters with Conductors of Today* (New York: Harper & Row, 1982).

Nelson, Lynn Ingrid and Gayle Thorsen, eds. *Stanisław Skrowaczewski: 2004 Distinguished Artist* (Minneapolis: The McKnight Foundation, 2004).

Panufnik, Andrzej. *Composing Myself* (London: Methuen London Ltd., 1987).

Pincus, Andrew. *Scenes from Tanglewood* (Boston: Northeastern Press, 1989).

Roberts, John P.L., and Ghyslaine Guertin, eds. *Glenn Gould: Selected Letters* (Toronto: Oxford University Press, 1992).

Rodziński, Halina. *Our Two Lives: The Story of an Extraordinary Marriage and a Brilliant Career in Music* (New York: Charles Scribner's Sons, 1976).

Rosenberg, Donald. *The Cleveland Orchestra Story: Second to None* (Cleveland: Gray & Company, 2000).

Rosenstiel, Léonie. *Nadia Boulanger: A Life in Music* (New York: Norton & Company, Inc., 1982).

Schlesinger, Arthur M., Jr. *A Thousand Days: John F. Kennedy in the White House* (London: Mayflower-Dell, 1965).

Schuller, Gunther. *The Compleat Conductor* (New York: Oxford University Press, 1997).

————. *Musings: The Musical Worlds of Gunther Schuller* (New York: Oxford University Press, 1986).

Shanet, Howard. *Philharmonic: A History of New York's Orchestra* (Garden City, New York: Doubleday & Company, 1975).

Sherman, John. *Music and Maestros: The Story of the Minneapolis Symphony Orchestra* (Minneapolis: Lund Press, 1952).

Spycket, Jerôme. *Nadia Boulanger* (Paris: Payot Paris, 1987).

Sullivan, J.W.N. *Beethoven: His Spiritual Development* (London: George Allen & Unwin, 1964).

Trotter, William R. *Priest of Music: The Life of Dimitri Mitropoulos* (Portland, Oregon: Amadeus Press, 1995).

Wagar, Jeannine. *Conductors in Conversation: Fifteen Contemporary Conductors Discuss Their Lives and Profession* (Boston: G.K. Hall, 1991).

White, Eric Walter. *Stravinsky: The Composer and His Works*, 2nd ed. (Berkeley: University of California Press, 1985).

Zinn, Howard. *A People's History of the United States* (New York: HarperCollins, 2003).

Articles

Anthony, Michael. "Debuts and Reappearances." *High Fidelity/Musical America*, September 1981.

Bawer, Bruce. "The Other Sixties." *The Wilson Quarterly*, Spring 2004.

Canning, Hugh. "Nurturing a Close Relationship with the Public: Hugh Canning Meets the Hallé's New Principal Conductor Stanisław Skrowaczewski." *Classical Music*, July 1984.

Cisek, Richard. "Respected Worldwide, He Calls Minnesota Home." In *Stanisław Skrowaczewski: 2004 Distinguished Artist*, edited by Lynn Ingrid Nelson and Gayle Thorsen. Minneapolis: The McKnight Foundation, 2004.

———. "Stanisław Skrowaczewski: A Tribute." *Showcase*, April 26–May 19, 1979.

Close, Roy. "One Hundred by Nine—The Music Directors." In *Minnesota Orchestra at One Hundred*, edited by Sandra Hyslop and Gwen Pappas. Minneapolis: Minnesota Orchestra, 2002.

———. "Minnesota Orchestra Turns 75." *High Fidelity, Musical America*, March 1978.

Eich, Robert M. "Skrowaczewski at Ease: A Candid Interview with the Conductor of the Minnesota Orchestra." *Minnesotan*, Spring 1974.

Epstein, Bob. "An Interview with Stanisław Skrowaczewski." *Showcase*, September 8–October 8, 1977.

Evidon, Richard. "Guests of Honor." In *Minnesota Orchestra at One Hundred*, edited by Sandra Hyslop and Gwen Pappas. Minneapolis: Minnesota Orchestra, 2002.

Feldman, Mary Ann. "Musical Citizen of the World." In *Stanisław Skrowaczewski: 2004 Distinguished Artist*, edited by Lynn Ingrid Nelson and Gayle Thorsen. Minneapolis: The McKnight Foundation, 2004.

———. "On the Road to Fame—Our Touring Orchestra." In *Minnesota Orchestra at One Hundred*, edited by Sandra Hyslop and Gwen Pappas. Minneapolis: Minnesota Orchestra, 2002.

———. "A Walk through Orchestra Hall with Cyril M. Harris." In program book, Orchestra Hall dedication concert, October 21, 1974.

Freed, Richard. "Recording and Broadcast—Paths to the World." In *Minnesota Orchestra at One Hundred*, edited by Sandra Hyslop and Gwen Pappas. Minneapolis: Minnesota Orchestra, 2002.

Gifford, Thomas. "Orchestra Hall: How Business Made It Happen." *Greater Minneapolis, Magazine of the Greater Minneapolis Chamber of Commerce* 26, no. 9 (1974).

Harris, Frederick, E., Jr. "A Lifelong Love Affair with Music." In *Stanisław Skrowaczewski: 2004 Distinguished Artist*, edited by Lynn Ingrid Nelson and Gayle Thorsen. Minneapolis: The McKnight Foundation, 2004.

Hersh, Burton. "The New Twin Cities," *Twin Citian*, June 1966.

Nettleton, Pamela Hill. "Musical Values—A Community's Pride." In *Minnesota Orchestra at One Hundred*, edited by Sandra Hyslop and Gwen Pappas. Minneapolis: Minnesota Orchestra, 2002.

———. "Balancing the Scales, Stanisław Skrowaczewski Conductor/Composer." *Showcase*, October 2000.

Kennedy, Michael. "Michael Kennedy Previews the 128th Season: The Most Important for Years." *Hallé Orchestra 1985–86 Yearbook*.

Markle, David. "Skrowaczewski: An Interview with David Markle, Classical Music Columnist for *Twin Citian* Magazine." *Symphony*, October 10-31, 1969.

Radcliffe, Paula. "An Interview with Skrowaczewski." *Hallé News: The Journal of the Hallé Concerts Society*, December 1984.

Steinberg, Michael. "This Evening's Program…." In *Minnesota Orchestra at One Hundred*, edited by Sandra Hyslop and Gwen Pappas. Minneapolis: Minnesota Orchestra, 2002.

Skrowaczewski, Stanisław. "The Resurrection of the Invisible." In program book, Orchestra Hall dedication concert, October 21, 1974.

———. "The Light of Our Eye." *Symphony*, October 1968.

———. "Should Composers Conduct?" *Music Journal* (November/December 1960): 12, 65.

Szybalski, Wacław. "The Genius of Rudolf Stefan Weigl (1883–1957), a Lvovian Microbe Hunter and Breeder: In Memoriam." In *International Weigl Conference, Microorganisms in Pathogenesis and Their Drug Resistance Programme and Abstracts*. Edited by R. Stoika et al. Sept 11–14, 1998.

Trautwein, George. "A Musician's Musician." In *Stanisław Skrowaczewski: 2004 Distinguished Artist*, edited by Lynn Ingrid Nelson and Gayle Thorsen. Minneapolis: The McKnight Foundation, 2004.

Walsh, Michael, and N. Newman. "Music: Making the Strings Sing Again, Six New Concertos Offer a Lively Survey of Modern Styles." *Time*, May 19, 1986.

Program Notes

Bromberger, Eric. "Skrowaczewski, *Fantasie per Flauto ed Orchestra, Il Piffero della Notte* (The Piper in the Night)." *Showcase,* October 2007.

Feldman, Mary Ann. "Skrowaczewski, Symphony [2003]." *Showcase*, October 2–3, 2003.

———. "Skrowaczewski, *Passacaglia Immaginaria*." *Showcase*, April 1996.

———. "Skrowaczewski, Concerto for Orchestra." *Showcase*, January 1986.

———. "Skrowaczewski, *Ricercari Notturni* for Saxophone and Orchestra." *Showcase,* January 7–29, 1978.

———. "Penderecki, Concerto for Violin and Orchestra." *Showcase*, January 7–29, 1978.

Freed, Richard. "Britten, *Sinfonia da Requiem*, op. 20." In program book, National Symphony Orchestra, November 2003.

———. "Bruckner, Symphony no. 8 in C Minor." In program book, Philadelphia Orchestra, November 1, 1983.

Jacobson, Bernard. "Skrowaczewski, Concerto for Violin and Orchestra." In program book, Philadelphia Orchestra, December 5, 1985.

Kennedy, Michael. "An Appreciation." In program book, Hallé Orchestra, May 2, 1991.

———. "Tribute to Clive Smart." In program book, Hallé Orchestra, April 18, 1991.

Skrowaczewski, Stanisław. "Chamber Concerto (*Ritornelli poi ritornelli*)." In program book, Saint Paul Chamber Orchestra, November 26, 1993.

———. "Triple Concerto." In program book, Honolulu Symphony, April 19, 1992.

———. "Letter from Principal Conductor." In program book, Hallé Orchestra, September 1989.

———. Notes for program book, Hallé Orchestra, September 1984.

CD Liner Notes

Feldman, Mary Ann. "Concerto for Clarinet and Orchestra." In *Passacaglia Immaginaria, Chamber Concerto, Concerto for Clarinet in A and Orchestra*, perf. Saarbrücken Radio Symphony Orchestra, dir. Skrowaczewski (Albany, New York: Albany Records, 2001).

———. "Bruckner Symphony 9." In *Bruckner Symphony 9*, perf. Minnesota Orchestra, dir. Skrowaczewski (San Francisco: Reference Recordings, 1997).

Rooney, Dennis. "The Early Years." In *Minnesota Orchestra at One Hundred: A Collection of Recordings and Broadcasts, 1924-2003*, perf. Minneapolis Symphony, Minnesota Orchestra, dir. various conductors (Minneapolis: Minnesota Orchestra, 2003).

Miksa, Waldemarem. "Through Music, I Commune with the Universe." In *Stanisław Skrowaczewski, Concerto for Orchestra, Brahms Symphony no. 4*, perf. National Polish Radio Symphony Orchestra in Katowice, dir. Skrowaczewski (Warsaw: Polskie Radio SA, 2003).

Skrowaczewski, Stanisław. "Concerto for English Horn and Orchestra." In *Two Pastels, Andante for Strings and Concerto for English Horn and Orchestra*, perf. Minnesota Orchestra, dir. Skrowaczewski (Phoenix Recordings, 1991).

————. "Stanisław Skrowaczewski on This Recording." In *Beethoven Symphonies Nos. 1-9*, perf. Saarbrücken Radio Symphony Orchestra, dir. Skrowaczewski (Munich: Oehms Classics, 2007).

Schlüren, Christoph, "Symphony [2003]." Trans. Janet and Michael Berridge. In *Stanisław Skrowaczewski the Composer: Music at Night*, perf. Deutsche Radio Philharmonie, dir. Skrowaczewski (Munich: Oehms Classics, 2008).

————. "Fantasie per Flauto ed Orchestra." Translated by Janet and Michael Berridge. In *Stanisław Skrowaczewski, The Composer: Music at Night*, perf. Deutsche Radio Philharmonie, dir. Skrowaczewski (Munich: Oehms Classics, 2008).

Audio

Gunther Schuller, interview by Brian Bell. During WGBH (Boston) broadcast of *Where the Word Ends* by Schuller, perf. Boston Symphony Orchestra, February 6, 2009.

Stanisław Skrowaczewski, interview by Brian Duffie, WNIB (Chicago) broadcast, October 3, 1987.

————, interview by John Michel. "After Pinky, An Interview with Stanisław Skrowaczewski." Minnesota Public Radio broadcast, February 1987.

Newhouse, Brian. "Minnesota Orchestra at 100." Minnesota Public Radio broadcast, November 2003.

Video

Thank You Maestro. Documentary. Twin Cities Public Television, broadcast May 1979.

1968 Human Rights Day Concert. WNET-TV (New York City), broadcast 1968.

Dr. Frederick E. Harris, Jr., is music director of the Massachusetts Institute of Technology (MIT) Wind Ensemble and Festival Jazz Ensemble. He also has served as acting music director of the MIT Symphony Orchestra, as assistant conductor of the Boston University Tanglewood Institute Young Artists Wind Ensemble, and as a guest conductor in Minnesota and throughout New England. Dr. Harris is a strong advocate for the creation and performance of new music, having commissioned and/or premiered more than sixty-five works for wind, jazz, and mixed ensembles. He has recorded for the Innova, Albany, and Half Note labels. Dr. Harris' first book, *Conducting with Feeling*, was published by Meredith Music in 2001. He lives on Cape Cod with his ornithologist wife, Becky, and their daughter, Abbie.

INDEX

Made in the USA
Charleston, SC
06 April 2013